M000287033

STONES OF ARAN

LABYRINTH

STONES OF ARAN

LABYRINTH

TIM ROBINSON

THE LILLIPUT PRESS

First published 1995 by
THE LILLIPUT PRESS LTD
4 Rosemount Terrace, Arbour Hill,
Dublin 7, Ireland.

Reprinted, with emendations, 1995.

A CIP record for this
title is available from
The British Library.

ISBN 1874675 50 3

*The Lilliput Press receives financial assistance from
An Chomhairle Ealaíon/The Arts Council of Ireland.*

Many islanders are named with affection and respect in this book. As
for the few treated less positively, I've involved the island in a magic
mist, and anyone who claims to have identified them is mistaken.

Set in 11.5 on 13.5 Adobe Garamond
by Verbatim Typesetting & Design Ltd, Dublin
Printed in England
by Hartnolls Ltd of Bodmin, Cornwall

CONTENTS

However, it will already be clear that Aran, of the world's countless facets one of the most finely carved by nature, closely structured by labour and minutely commented by tradition, is *the* exemplary terrain upon which to dream of that work, the guidebook to the adequate step. *Stones of Aran* is all made up of steps, which lead in many directions but perpetually return to, loiter near, take short-cuts by, stumble over or impatiently kick aside that ideal. (Otherwise, it explores and takes its form from a single island, Árainn itself; the present work makes a circuit of the coast, whose features present themselves as the stations of a *Pilgrimage*, while the sequel will work its way through the interior, tracing out the *Labyrinth*.)

(from 'Timescape with Signpost', *Stones of Aran*, Vol. 1, *Pilgrimage*)

From this point ... I see once again the ruined watch tower perched high above the Sound, marking the resting-place of St Gregory of the Golden Mouth. It suggests the possibility of going round the island once again, looking at everything in more detail, or in others of the infinity of ways of looking. Perhaps another circuit would be more rewarding now that my pace has been chastened by so many miles, my breath deepened by so many words. But for a book to stand like an island out of the sea of the unwritten it must acknowledge its own bounds, and turn inward from them, and look into the labyrinth.

(conclusion of *Pilgrimage*)

I
EAST

Unquestionable answer to unanswerable question, this volume must close what the first opened, so that I can store them away safely, like two mirrors face to face. Therefore I must begin now at the place where my circuit of the coast of Árainn ended, and from which I am to broach the interior. That place, determined long ago by the structure of the whole book, is at the eastern tip of the island, where a hillside of rock and weather-beaten grass rises from the arc of sand and shingle about a little bay to a small ruined tower. At what era Túr Mháirtín watched over the safety or the subservience of Aran is unknown; but for some years now, in my mind, its function has been to keep my place in the book, marking a promise to return from long wanderings in Connemara and see my way through this island. Old maps call the tower St Gregory's Monument. The saint of the golden mouth, even after years of prayer and fasting, felt himself unworthy of a grave in Aran of the Saints, and on the approach of death commanded that his body be consigned to the sea in a barrel. Port Daibhche, the port of the barrel, is where the corpse was brought ashore by a miraculous current, in sign of his worthiness of the holy ground. I have now to write myself back onto that ground, and without benefit of miracle.

But finding the entrance to the labyrinth is not the simplest of steps, for I find myself separated from it by another labyrinth. I no longer live in Aran; I cannot jump on my bicycle and go and have another look at that harsh grey hillside. My sight-lines and thought-lines to it are interrupted by the thick boggy hills and dazzling waters of Connemara. I am too far for touch, too near for Proustian telescopy. There is also a dense forest of signposts in the way, the huge amount of material I have assembled to help me. Here to my hand are a shelf of books, thirteen piled volumes of diary, boxes bursting with record cards, a filing-cabinet of notes, letters, offprints from specialist journals, maps and newspaper cuttings. Also, three ring-binders of writing accumulated over a dozen years towards this work, some of it outdated, misinformed, unintelligibly sketchy, some so highly polished it will have to be cracked open again in order to fuse with what is still to be written. What tense must I use to comprehend memories, memories of memories of what is forgotten, words that once held memories but are now just words? What period am I to set myself in, acknowledging the changes in the island noted in my brief revisitings over the years, the births and deaths I hear of in telephone calls? In what voice am I to embody the person who wrote that first volume with little thought of publisher or readership during a cryptic, enisled time, I who live nearer the main and have had public definitions attached to me, including some I would like to shake off – environmentalist, cartographer – and whose readers will open this volume looking for more of the same and will be disappointed if they get it? How am I to lose myself once again among the stones of Aran?

Looking around for inspiration in this quandary I remember that from the saint's monument one can just make out a mark, a greyish dot, on the brink of the highest cliff of Inis Meáin, a mile away across the sound. This is Cathaoir Synge, Synge's Seat, a low structure of massive stones like a roofless hut open to the west, of unknown date and purpose. Here the writer used to sit and brood upon the abyss:

The black edge of the north island is in front of me, Galway Bay, too blue almost to look at, on my right, the Atlantic on my left, a perpendicular cliff under my ankles, and over me innumerable gulls that chase each other in a white cirrus of wings ... As I lie here hour after hour, I seem to enter into the wild pastimes of the cliff, and to become a companion of the cormorants and crows.

I would like to use Synge's vision of it to situate myself on that black edge, the beginning of my work, but at this crucial moment he is alienated from me. In an essay on his book *The Aran Islands* that grew out of his intense meditations on the cliff-top, I wrote that Synge was mistaken in thinking that the Irish name for the maidenhair fern is *dúchosach* (black-footed), and that as he knew so little about it he was wise not to treat of the Aran flora. Since then I have heard Aran people call that fern the *dúchosach;* my earlier source was wrong, and I am caught out in a petty rivalrousness. As if Synge, with his deep, intuitive eyes, cares whether or not I have more facts on Aran than he! The sage turns from me, listening to those clamorous gulls, whose language, he says, 'is easier than Gaelic'. I shrink back to my filing-cabinet.

My efficient record cards remind me, however, that that hillside I would like to refind myself on is called An Teannaire, the pump, from a recess in the cliffs below it where waves rush in and compress themselves into waterspouts, and that it has already been appropriated, if not by literature, then by the oral tradition.

Thug sé an Teannaire mar spré dhó ...

He gave him the Pump as dowry ...

This is from *Amhrán an 'Chéipir'*, the song of the 'Caper', composed in his head by Taimín Ó Briain, of the poetical O'Brians of Cill Éinne, near the beginning of this century. The 'Caper' was a young fisherman from Cape Clear in Cork, who came with a boat called the *Lucky Star* to work out of Cill Rónáin, and married a girl from Iaráirne, the easternmost village of the island. My translation is a rough piece of work – but so is Taimín's original:

> Molaimid thú a Chéipir
> Ar thús na bhfear in Éirinn,
> Mar is tú a fuair an bhean ba géimiúla
> Dár rugadh riamh san áit
> San oíche a dtáinig tú dá hiarradh
> Bhí an baile trína chéile,
> Is gurbh fhearr leat bheith i gCill Éinne
> Ná i do chléireach sa chaisleán.

> Oh Caper, we praise you
> Above all men in Ireland,
> For it's you that won the liveliest girl
> That ever was born in this place.
> The night you came to ask for her
> The village was upside-down,
> And you'd rather be in Cill Éinne
> Than be a clerk in Dublin Castle.

But although she was fine-looking girl (and I am told the Caper 'wiped the eye of the local lads'), her family was desperately poor, and all her father could provide as dowry was this salt-blasted hillside and the dunes just north of it, plus the gear for scratching a living off the shore:

> Thug sé an Teannaire mar spré dhó,
> Poll an Ghamhna agus Port Daibhche dhó,
> Sin agus beart cléibhe,
> Agus máilín na mbaoití,
> An gliomach a bheadh faoin áfach,
> An portán rua agus an cráifisc,
> Agus na duáin a bhí fágtha
> A bheadh aige lena shaol.

> He gave him the Pump as dowry,
> The Pool of the Calf and Barrelport too,
> Sally-rods to make a basket,
> And the little bag for bait,
> The lobster down in its hole,
> The red crab and the crayfish,
> And the fishing-hooks left over
> Would last him all his life.

Can I imagine myself taking the island into my possession like this, in her penniless beauty? The welcome was generous enough:

Bhí arán is jam is feoil ann,
Is bhí ceathrar ag seinm ceoil ann,
Bhí fuisce is lemonade,
Fíon is punch dá réir ann ...

Bread and jam and meat was there,
And four musicians playing,
There was lemonade and whiskey
And wine and punch as needed ...

But while the girl's father sat with his back to a creel of turf politely ignoring the goings-on and her mother started keening, the whiskey somehow disappeared into the night, the guests, *ag déanamh 'joy' den oíche*, making 'joy' of the evening, broke up the bridal bed, and nobody got a wink of sleep. Fortunately the weather was too bad for the steamer to bring out the fifty policemen who were to search the place or the Justice and Crown Attorney to try the cases arising from that night.

Nothing suits me in this precedent. The island is no longer the village maiden of ninety years ago. The identification of a territory with a woman, a theme of great significance in Celtic mythology and one which tempted Synge too, is nowadays fraught with tensions. And, although I trust prayer no more than whiskey, I would rather drift ashore in a barrel than accede to a holding of this island through such ructions.

However, through all this frowning over my scrawled difficulties and disorderly data, I find that I have now arrived, unbeholden to saint or sage or father-in-law, and by my preferred literary transition, a slinking behind my own back. Nothing could be better adapted to this broken ground, riven by quantum jumps and contradictions. Now, all those problems of tense and person can be left to piecemeal solution. In the glow and hum of my word-processor I am already mooching about below the half-abolished tower, as tenebrous as ever, trying to understand what it is I am to understand, peering into the crevices of the crag like the wise old women of Aran, in search of a simple for a complex.

MAIDENHAIR

In shadow, a recessive shade. Greyish-green flakes floating in an elaborate and slightly dishevelled pattern. The eye slowly sorts it out into perhaps five or six triangular fronds. On a closer look an individual frond breaks up into a small number of triangular sprays of five or six leaflets the size of a little fingernail. Each leaflet is fan-shaped, with straight sides and a scalloped outer margin, and is attached at the apex to a fine stalk, which in its turn branches off the slightly thicker axis of the spray, and so is connected back to the stem of the frond. Even these stems are so slender that the fronds bend outwards under their own weight, so that each leaflet offers its upper surface to the eye and the whole array canopies a curved darkness below. The articulations are so delicate that a breath is enough to start a flickering fan-language of display and concealment, chaste provocation, coquetry – or so one reads it, prompted by the fern's English name. The Irish goes bluntly to the root: *dúchosach*, black-footed. Part the foliage and see how the wire-thin stalks emerge in a dense bundle like a jet of earth-force from a crack in the rock, glossy brownish-black, grading into green as they diverge into their parabolic trajectories. The peasant, sturdily rooted in the compost of its ancestors.

Adiantum capillus-veneris (to take up its Linnaean binomial as one would a magnifying glass for scientific objectification) is the Aran plant *par excellence*. It is extremely rare in Britain and in Ireland except on the Burren and Aran limestone, and the earliest Irish record of it commemorates the first visit of a scientist to the island. Edward Lhuyd, writing from 'Pensans in Cornwall, Aug. 25, 1700', says:

In the Isle of Aran (near Galloway) we found great plenty of the *Adianthum verum*, and a sort of matted campion with a white flower, which I bewail the loss of, for an imperfect sprig of it was only brought to me; and I waited afterwards in rain almost a whole week for fair weather to have gone in quest of it.

The campion would merely have been the common sea campion; *Adianthum verum* was the old name for the maidenhair fern; and without the rain there would be no such fern here. Lhuyd was Keeper of the Ashmolean Museum in Oxford, and catalogued its collection of fossils; he was at the same time establishing himself as a Celticist, and his visit to Aran was in connection with the preparation of his great work *Archaeologia Britannica*, described on its title-page as 'giving some account Additional to what has been hitherto Publifh'd, of the LANGUAGES, HISTORIES AND CUSTOMS OF THE ORIGINAL INHABITANTS OF GREAT BRITAIN: From Collections and Observations in Travels through *Wales, Cornwal, Bas-Bretagne, Ireland* and *Scotland*'. In his second chapter, 'A Comparative Vocabulary of the Original Languages of Britain and Ireland', I notice:

Adiantum ... *The Herb Maydenhair*; Ir. Dúv-xofax... Black-fhank

which perhaps records the rusty voice of some Araner of nearly three hundred years ago. Another name for the fern I have heard, *tae scailpreach* (*scailpreach* meaning a place of rocky clefts), probably dates only from the last century when tea became such a comforter of the poor. Dinneen gives it in his Irish dictionary, with the remark that the fern was used as a substitute for tea; this seems unlikely, and I imagine it was the appearance of its sere and shrivelled fronds in winter that made people think of the craved-for drug.

But why does a plant of the warm south grow on these bleak islands, whose other botanical stars are the limestone bugle, from northern and mountainous areas of Europe, and the spring gentian, best known from the Alps? In an old encyclopedia I read that the maidenhair fern is 'abundant in the south of Europe, where it covers the inside of wells and the basins of fountains (as at Vaucluse) with a tapestry of the most delicate green'. Fontaine de Vaucluse is where Petrarch retired to in a vain effort to forget his Laura. What brings the delicate Provençale to Penultima Thule? The answer begins to open up the labyrinth of Aran.

On a hillside like that leading up to St Gregory's tower (through which I am feeling my way into the matter of Aran) one sees the geometry of limestone exposed in black and white. Because this rock originated over a period of millions of years as the layered sediments of a sea that changed in depth, turbidity, temperature and living contents, its strata vary in their chemical and physical constitution. Hence such a slope, carved out of a succession of almost horizontal strata of different resistances to erosion, consists of a number of more or less well-defined terraces separated by vertical 'risers' of anything from a few inches to twenty or more feet. As one climbs, the rim of each step or cliff running across the hillside ahead shows up against the sky. Here, because of the particular direction one takes in coming up from the beach, these successive horizons have an extraordinary appearance that reveals another, vertical, set of divisions in the rock. Each rim, seen from below, has the profile of a row of blocks with gaps of a few inches between them; where the gaps are very close together the blocks are reduced to mere blades an inch or two thick, and the hillside looks as if it were built out of arrays of knives set on edge. These fissures are the surface expression of a system of cracks or 'joints' cutting vertically through the limestone, the result of tensions in these strata caused by movements in the earth's crust at some period after the Carboniferous. Rainwater has eroded out these hairline cracks into fissures of various widths and depths on exposed surfaces of the limestone; once opened up, the fissures receive all the run-off from the level rock-sheets and channel it underground. In the curious international jargon of geology such a fissure is a 'gryke' and the flat rock-sheet is a 'clint' – Yorkshire dialect-words, adopted because such formations are best known from limestone areas like Malham in Airedale. A limestone terrain with subterranean drainage, as here and at Malham, is called a 'karst', a term equally expressive of stony barrenness, borrowed from the name of such a region in the former Yugoslavia. In this particular corner of Aran the grykes are generally only a few inches wide and a few feet deep, but in other parts they are sometimes over two feet wide and ten or more feet deep. The principal set of grykes runs with amazing parallelism across the islands from a few degrees east of north to a few degrees west of south. This happens to be the direction in which one climbs towards the tower, so here the hillside is sliced before one's eyes by the brightness of the sky.

This dissection of the rock not only underlies the detailed accidentation of the coastline, as I have shown in my first volume, but it orders many aspects of life, including that of humans, in the interior. Because of the general nakedness of the terrain, it immediately provides two contrasted environments for lime-loving plants. The differences between the 'microclimates' of the flagstone-like ground-surface and the grykes are as sharp as those between two climatic zones hundreds of miles apart. In the shady water-gardens of the clefts the maidenhair fern can enjoy a mild, moisture-laden, Gulf-Stream ambience without the concomitant gales; a few inches above, the merest skim of soil provides for plants adapted to extreme exposure, good drainage, heavy grazing and high light-levels. Because of this rare conjuncture of oceanic climate and karst topography, the maidenhair can survive so far north as to consort with plants that are equally far from their headquarters on mountain and tundra, here at sea-level in the ultimate west.

Thus the block of stone allots its frugal abstractions of horizontal and vertical to separate plant-communities, neither of which would prosper in fatter conditions. And each contributes to the support of a scavenging fauna. When Synge first stayed in Cill Rónáin in 1898 he walked out to the east end of the island, and on his way back two little girls followed him for a while:

They spoke with a delicate exotic intonation that was full of charm, and told me with a sort of chant how they guide 'ladies and gintlemins' in the summer to all that is worth seeing in their neighbourhood, and sell them pampooties and maidenhair ferns, which are common among the rocks. As we parted they showed me the holes in their own pampooties, or cowskin sandals, and asked me the price of new ones. I told them my purse was empty, and with a few quaint words of blessing they turned away from me and went down to the pier.

Similar accounts by other visitors make one wonder how the maidenhair survived the Victorian passion for fern-collecting. Fortunately Aran's human children no longer need to exploit this particular ecological niche, and one can still find its delicate, exotic charm enfolded in the rocks.

SERMONS IN STONES

In climbing past the ruined tower and onwards to the crest of the hillside one has to clamber over a few loosely built dry-stone walls, or diverge from one's goal to find gaps in them. But when the summit is attained (a mere hundred and forty feet or so above the shoreline) the eye is totally beset by walls. The plateau that comes into view here, slightly tilted southwards towards the Atlantic cliff-tops, and stretching, with just two interrupting lowlands, for eight miles along the island, is a walled landscape, uniting the monotonous grandeur of the desert with the petty territorialism of suburbia. This uninhabited back or dip-slope of the island escarpment is referred to as Na Craga, the crags, although most of it is less craggy and more grassy than the areas of bare limestone pavement on the terraces along the northern coast. The first section of it stretches away to the west-north-west for over two miles; then, beyond a valley invisible from here, the higher, central section of the plateau forms a long, straight horizon declining very gently from north to south, blocking off the farther half of the island.

Balancing on top of the nearest sound-looking wall to scan the disconcerting vista, one makes out that the pattern, for all its countless haphazard irregularities, is dominated by walls roughly parallel to that north-south horizon, and since the controlling direction of this volume is westwards, it is clear that progress is going to be problematic. The waist-high or head-high walls are so close-set that from this low viewpoint they hide the ground between them as if the better to conceal their purposes; they constitute an obstacle not merely to the body but to the understanding. The network seems too vast and repetitious to be the product of human intentions; the decisions of an individual brain in this transcendental structure are as the gropings of a coral blob immured in its reef. Usually nobody is to be seen in this desolation; if anything is being done or suffered here the act is hidden in the obliquity of the grille. If labour reveals its presence at all it is by sound, and almost solely by the clank of stone on stone. One hears how, over centuries, this landscape was created by the placing of stone on stone, how it is nowadays barely maintained by replacement of the fallen stone, and how it will lapse into rubble, stone by stone.

I have tried to reduce this inordinate perspective to arithmetic and geometry. The Ordnance Survey map at six inches to the mile shows the field-boundaries as an eye-tormenting tangle of fine lines. By superimposing a square-inch grid on the map and counting squares and bits of squares, I find that the thickly walled areas of Árainn total ten and a half square miles. (Another one and a half square miles, comprising commonage and big unenclosed crags, may be omitted from the following calculation as they contribute comparatively little to the results.) The number of fields in thirty randomly selected squares averaged thirty-seven. (In several squares that fell near villages there were over seventy fields, giving an average area of field of only 1240 square yards, *i.e.* typically thirty-one yards by forty.) Hence there are about 14,000 small fields, of average area 2300 square yards or just under half an acre. A random sample of twenty individual fields measured on the map suggests that their average perimeter is 233 yards. (NB: Sampling by such methods as dropping a pencil onto the map will produce a misleadingly large proportion of the comparatively big fields, and it is not easy to avoid this effect.) Since nearly all walls separate two fields, the total length of wall is 928 miles. Adding a bit to allow for irregularities that do not show up on the six-inch scale, and for some nests of small fields in the generally open areas omitted, and rounding off, I think it is not wildly inaccurate to say that there are a thousand miles of wall in Árainn. Inis Meáin and Inis Oírr would add about 300 and 200 miles respectively, giving a total of 1500 miles. So the islanders exaggerate when they say that the walls of Aran, put end to end, would stretch all the way to Boston – but that is understandable, since it is to Boston that so many of them have fled, rather than be sucked dry as dead flies by the economics of this stone web.

As to the general pattern of this field-system, it is clear that something so regular over such large areas, even if riddled with inconsistency and wilfulness, is structured by overpowering natural phenomena. In fact two elemental strengths have laid the foundations for this labour of generations. First, the cracking of the limestone by earth-forces acting on a continental scale. There are two principal sets of vertical fissure-planes or joints, the more fully developed one being oriented roughly north-south. (The bearing is about fifteen degrees east of north, but I will say simply 'north' rather than 'approximately north-north-east'. In fact, since the bearing is much more fundamental to Aran geography than true north or magnetic north, I could call it Aran north.) The other set is at right-angles to the first, and on certain levels of the islands a third, oblique set appears, confusing the pattern.

The second elemental force is erosion, which has been guided by the joint system. The small-scale effect of rainwater, widening the cracks into little canyons and dividing the surface into rectangular flags or long strips, has already been mentioned. Vastly greater was that of the huge thicknesses of ice pushing across this region of Ireland for a period of perhaps ten thousand years, ending about fifteen thousand years ago. The glaciers ripped out strips of blocks to create valleys of all sizes, from the sea-ways between the islands and the wide depressions that almost divide the big island in three, to narrow ravines and little glens, all oriented to Aran north. It is difficult even today to override this impressed topography, and in the past the currents of life had to flow with it. An oblique walk across an area of open crag is a continuous struggle with little cliffs and ridges and gullies, with no two successive steps on the same level, whereas if one follows the direction of the jointing, smooth flagged paths seem to unroll like carpets before one. Inevitably, walls accept these natural ways, and many of them spring from the natural pedestals provided by long unbroken ridges of rock. East-west walls often have to clamber down into narrow glens and then clamber out again, and tend to do this by the shortest way, confirmed in this labour-saving intention by the bearing of the minor set of fissures. Hence the fields tend to be rectangular and elongated north-south, especially on the plateau where the schema has room to spread itself. It is as if the walls make explicit the nature of the rock; the geometry that could be stepped over and disregarded underfoot is erected into barriers before one's face.

Of course almost the only visitors who do stray from the boreens, the walled paths between the fields, are those with some botanical, archaeological or geological drive, and in the scientific literature there are many complaints about these walls. H.C. Hart, who made the first careful botanical survey of the islands in 1869, writes feelingly on the subject:

These barricades are erected with no consideration for the shins of scientific explorers. It seems unfair to kick them down, as the natives do in the most reckless manner, whether crossing their own or their neighbours' lands. If you adopt the alternative of climbing, which is often an operation of considerable difficulty, it is most probable that your descent will be followed by an avalanche of loose stones – still, as the wall falls from you, this is safer than to kick it down in front, where there is a great risk of the stones falling towards and laming you. I found the safest plan was to climb up the wall with the utmost delicacy, balance yourself on the top, and then jump. It will be seen, however, that the frequent recurrence of such jumps for a long day's work is a mode of progression that may prove both wearisome and slow.

A few years later the botanist Nathaniel Colgan took a bolder line:

My first day's work among these stone dikes was so tedious and disheartening that on the following days I engaged a stout native boy who proved very useful, rather as a dilapidator than as a guide and porter. He carried my camera and vasculum, and cheerfully threw down with a push of his shoulder any uncommonly difficult or dangerous wall that happened to lie in our path. I should have hesitated to do this for myself; but the young islander, with an adroit touch of flattery, gave me to understand that though the natives would be loath to take such a short method with the walls for their own convenience, they would never dream of objecting to its use on behalf of a distinguished stranger.

These imperial modes reveal a blindness to the 'native' and his ways. To cross a wall without bruising one's shins or jolting one's spine, one should look for stones that run right through the wall and stick out on either side, and step up and over on these as on a stile, refraining from leaning out from the wall or clutching at the topmost stones to lever oneself upright, but keeping one's centre of gravity as close to the wall and as low over its top as possible. Araners learn this as part of learning to walk. I have seen an Aran father stand back, watchful but not interfering, as a toddler heads up a six-foot wall. If that child does not leave the island he or she will grow up able to cross walls with such fluency one cannot see how it is done. I remember an old man leading me across his land; before my eyes he repeatedly made the transition from being on the near side of a wall to being on the far side with no noticeable intermediate stages, complaining all the while of his rheumatism. A ghost's proficiency in passing through walls would seem to be only the natural result of such a lifetime's apprenticeship. But I suspect that that child will leave Na Craga to the old men, and the old men are already leaving it to its ghosts.

The range of rectangularity held up for inspection by the facets of individual stones in these walls, from dog-eared squares to thin bony oblongs, images the variability of the field-shapes; one could imagine that each wall is a map of the terrain it hides. The flaw in this fantasy is that whereas the partitioning of the land into fields is virtually complete and every square yard is appropriated with what comes to seem like a miserly and obsessive clutch or a scholarly fussiness over definitions, the stones in a wall are usually not tightly packed and admit a modicum of empty space, slippage and instability. An individual wall's degree of compaction depends on its function, the sort of stone to hand, and the skill and taste of the builder. On exposed terrain like Na Craga an open-work wall will dilute the gale more effectively than a solid one which would merely provoke the wind to hammer down onto the ground a few yards to its lee side. Sunset skies often show up a wall like a lace trim to a horizon, a filigree of light and dark. In certain areas, for instance to the south-west of Túr Mháirtín, the loose stone on offer consists of shaggy crusts or scales two or three feet across like battle-hacked shields, and the field-boundaries there are scrawled in leap-frogging triangles made by leaning these shards together at capricious angles. Elsewhere, and especially along waysides, the walls are sober and solid uncoursed masonry-work of well-adjusted blocks; the more substantial 'double wall' has two faces of carefully set blocks, bound together here and there by through-pieces of longer stones, and with a filling of small stones between them. To enclose a vegetable plot with some hope of excluding rabbits a *claí fidín* (which one could translate as 'fragment fence') is used; this consists of a row of pillar-like uprights (*clocha mháthar*, mother-stones) set two or three feet apart, the spaces between them built up with small stones carefully packed, and the whole finished off with a row or two of weighty blocks. A visiting preacher once took this type of wall as a metaphor for slipshod construction on inadequate foundations, thinking that the word *fidín* sounded disparaging; let ye not be a *claí fidín* of the faith, he urged the congregation, but rather a soundly built wall. However, since the *claí fidín* is a highly regarded wall that demands care and patience in the building, his rhetoric fell flat. Some goatish spirits among his hearers might even have wondered if faith is better represented by those walls I mentioned south-west of the tower, which incorporate a lot of nothing by artful adjustment of non-sequiturs, the more economically to hem in the flock.

Some of the purposes of this vast communal construction will have emerged from what I have said about its structure. Since grass is scarce, especially on the crags used as winterage, cattle have to be confined to small areas so that they will eat up the less tasty herbage as well as the choicer stuff before being allowed into other fields. The walls give shelter to stock and crop, and loose stones littering the ground are piled along the tops of them – although excess stone is more easily stacked into ricks, and in many fields one sees a little ziggurat of stones standing on a rock outcrop. Virtually all the appurtenances of the field-system are of stone. Occasionally one comes across a small stone-built barn, usually roofless; though near Iaráirne two or three of them still have a decrepit thatch held down by ropes or bits of fishing net to pegs under the eaves. There are little stone hutches too, for goat-kids, and many walls have lintelled openings at ground level, about two feet high, easily closed with a few stones, for letting sheep through. A more developed-looking item of field-furniture is the water-trough fed by the run-off from a slanting surface of stone or concrete. Springs are very few on the plateau, and in the old days there was a constant coming and going of women and children carrying water in small wooden stave-barrels to the cattle, until, it is said, these troughs were invented by a Cill Éinne man about a hundred years ago. While it may be true that this individual – a Roger Dirrane, whose dramatic contribution to island history I shall be recounting later on – brought the troughs to a standard form and propagated the idea, one finds on the open crags and in the fields examples from every stage of what looks like a long evolution, from natural basins improved with a dab of cement and filled by rainwater trickling down a shelving rock-face, to the roughly rectangular Dirranean trough of mortared stonework with a tilted surface like a draining-board of smooth and carefully pointed flagstones built along one side of it, or modern versions of this in concrete, grant-aided by the Department of Agriculture, with precisely squared and rimmed catchment-surfaces several yards long. These are the only signs of innovation on Na Craga, where no implements are of use other than the spade, the sickle and the scythe, and a granite boulder to sharpen them on.

Coming across such structures in rambling across this rather inscrutable terrain, one feels reassured that the field-system has or at least had its uses. But after an hour or two of struggling in its toils, the endless proliferation of walls seems inordinate to any practical requirements; one is forced to read it as the expression of an urge to control space for its own sake, to hug and hoard and hide away the land in minute parcels. In fact these walls are the fossilized land-hunger of the 'Congested Districts', of the Land War, of the Great Famine and above all of the century of population growth that preceded it. As such, they do not necessarily express bitter competition. A farmer in an equally subdivided tract of the Burren once told me about two brothers who inherited a few tiny fields there some time in the famine century. One of them was married, and it seemed the only future for the other was emigration. But on the eve of his departure the married brother said suddenly 'Don't go!'; and they took the wooden yard-stick the wife used for measuring her homespun, and divided each plot equally, marking a line down the middle with small stones. The mearing-stones of brotherly love must have divided Aran's fields as well and have been built up into walls between later generations grown apart. Down to the present day, the nuisance of holdings in scattered lots and acrimony over rights of way to them are part of the island's patrimony. Having produced a map of Aran, I came to be regarded as a semi-official cartographer, and as I was almost the sole guardian of such occult lore as:

$$30\tfrac{1}{4} \text{ square yards} = 1 \text{ square rod, pole or perch}$$
$$40 \text{ square poles} = 1 \text{ rood}$$
$$4 \text{ roods} = 1 \text{ acre}$$

which I found in an old pocket-diary, I was often called upon to measure and divide land. Once I calculated the areas of no fewer than twenty-six patches broadcast over the hillsides of Cill Éinne for a man who was sharing the inheritance of them with his cousin in America, and found myself drawn into conniving with him in dividing them so that access to the absentee's portions would be across my client's land, putting him in a strong position to persuade the other to sell out. I took no money for it, I was paid as usual in place-names, in which these subdivisions are most prolific; nevertheless, I am implicated in the peasant cunning of these crooked walls, and the devil has me in their net.

DISCREPANCIES

If there are only fourteen thousand fields in Árainn, it would not take a lifetime to explore them, devoting a day to each. I have probably looked into the majority of them in my obsessive coursing about the island. On the lower levels many fields are so overgrown they defy inspection, but on Na Craga they exhibit their little economies of grass as resignedly as nineteenth-century objects of charity. In one field there may be nothing but a grey, taut-looking sheet of rock crossed by a few shaggy lines of tufted, wiry stuff rooted in fissures; in the next, a hollow filled like a pool with feathery grasses and meadow flowers, with the stones that have been dredged out of it piled in cairns around its brink. The walls are all shifts and accomodations too; swerving from their rectilinear principals to incorporate a boulder too big to be removed or a heap of masonry that some residual use-value or superstitious regard has preserved from centuries ago. In spring and summer and autumn each field is a sample garden of flowers and butterflies so specific to the season that one could tell the date to within a week or two by them; in winter they are as cryptic as a jigsaw puzzle all made up of missing bits.

In exploring this terrain it is best to let oneself be led by its inbuilt directionality. A few fields in the possession of a single household will be linked into a sequence, nearly always running north-south, by gaps closed with stones if there are cattle to be confined and otherwise left open. It is often stated that the Aran farmer lets his cows into a field by knocking down a length of the wall and rebuilding it after them. This misconception arises from the fact that when the gap is closed with stones it looks superficially like the rest of the wall. However, this is an illusion, as was revealed to me by a rain-shower that briefly wiped across the island one day when I was wandering on Na Craga. The limestone, both of the ground and in the walls, was left black with wet, and took some time to evaporate back to pale gray when the sun came out again. But dotted all over the landscape around me were what looked like brightly glinting doors in the dark walls – the gaps, all filled with granite boulders. This focused my mind on the question of gaps, and after some research I wrote the following little treatise:

The Aran *bearna* or gap is no mere hole blocked with a loose assemblage of stones, but a specialized and adaptive structure. It is usually two or three feet wide, with an upright stone on either side, and often these jambs slant apart slightly so that the stones piled between them are held in the wedge-shaped space. The granite erratics brought over from Connemara by the last Ice Age and strewn here and there on Aran's crags are preferred to limestone for filling the gaps, because they are naturally ovoid and very tough, so that the gap is easily 'knocked' by tumbling the stones aside, and they do not crack up after repeated use. The Aran farmer and even his child can 'raise up' such a gap in the time it would take an outsider to bruise his or her fingers arranging the first few stones of it. This temporary fence is unstable, and often a short length of briar or a blackthorn branch is wedged among its topmost stones to discourage cattle or horses from nosing it down. Clearly, the gap is not the place to climb the wall since it is built for collapsibility, but somewhere close to it will be a stile, or at least a through-stone or two adequate to the practised foot of the landowner.

Having thus formulated the Aran gap, I wandered out to have another look, eyes sharpened by theory. And behold! Every conceivable *ad hoc* concoction of concrete blocks, thorn bushes, driftwood, worm-eaten oars, carcases of oil drums, iron bed-heads, complicated pipework looted from wrecks, bicycle-frames – anything and everything redundant and outworn will serve to stop a gap just as well as the granite boulder. So it is at least around the fallen world of houses and roadsides, but up on Na Craga, closer to the Platonic ideal of Aran, the classic gap exists, as theory prescribes.

But I see these things all wrong. It is the world of Na Craga that is out-worn and redundant. I remember coming across an elderly man harvesting a rye-field in a sheltery glen up there. In fact I heard him long before I saw him, for when the straw is wanted for thatching, the rye is pulled up by the roots and the harvester slaps each *dornán* or fistful against his boot or the wall to knock the soil off it, and the spacious, lazy rhythm of this sound is characteristic of hot July and August days in the fields. It is sweaty and tiring work, and men hate it; the endlessly repeated, quietly vicious slaps sound out against themselves, against the walls that bind their lives. And yet every stage of the harvest is visually charming – the area of stubble or bare ground, decorated with the lines of fistfuls, slowly widening through the day as the standing crop dwindles, the sheaves each belted with a twist of straw, the plump stacks of sheaves topped off with an upside-down sheaf like a huge sun-hat, the donkey waiting to carry the stacks one by one to the outhouse. On Na Craga that day I learned the arithmetic of straw:

> *Cúig cinn de dhornáin a dhéanas punnán*
> *Punnán 'is fiche a dhéanas beart*
> *Ceithre bheart a dhéanas teach*

– five fistfuls make a sheaf, twenty sheaves and one make a load (*i.e.* what can be carried roped together on one's back), four loads make (that is, thatch) a house. My instructor, who had learned the hard way, added a footnote, that fifty fistfuls make a half-load. So the extra sheaf, the extra five fistfuls in the full load of a hundred and five fistfuls, is like the extra twelve pounds in the so-called 'hundredweight' of a hundred and twelve pounds, and whether it is to be regarded as generosity or extortion depends on the perspective of power relations. For once, this man, who had no doubt always been at the thin end of that perspective, found that he had something of value to impart, his multiplication table, and extorted a little money from me. He was uneasy about it, simultaneously ingratiating and brazen; his earthworm-sad features told me he needed the money for drink. I imagine his daughter is one of the smart young women I see driving into Cill Rónáin as if they were on a freeway to a shopping mall, slamming themselves through the island's spaces, trading them in for time; she runs a chilly, hygienic, tourist-board-approved b&b, and hardly tolerates her father in the back kitchen. He is a discrepancy, the old reprobate of Na Craga; he whines like a dog left behind as our world drives off into the future. I am, I know, less interested in the concerns of the forward-looking generations than I should be (perhaps because they are so tediously univer-sal); my sympathies hang around with those trapped in or fascinated by the fading mazes of the past. Not all of these are old and despairing; they

include, in Aran, some joyously creative souls. But all I can do for my man
of straw is to reveal him in his predicament, while hiding away his identity
in my cryptographic reconstruction of his island.

DWELLING

When the mind begins to weary of the intricacies of Na Craga and the
body to balk at walls, one naturally welcomes any sequence of gaps that
tends in the general direction of the inhabited, northern side of the island.
And usually this homing instinct is rewarded, for it is the daily coming and
going of farmers between house and field that have written those ways into
the palimpsest of walls. There are two or three such escape-routes from the
terrain west of Túr Mháirtín; they lead up the gentle rise of the back of the
island to the ridge-line and connect with narrow, walled paths on the
steeper, north-facing escarpment, which in turn are gathered up by a wider
track running across the slope, and so crookedly down to Iaráirne.

Pausing at the crest of the escarpment, it takes a few moments to ascertain one's relationship to the suddenly opened vista. The cluster of a dozen
cottages and bungalows is a few hundred yards down to the left, the north-
west. Its background is an oval expanse, of sea or of sand depending on the
state of the tide, almost enclosed by long levels of dune-fringed grassland.
A congregation of grey, standing forms is gathered on a knoll on the nearer
rim of this bay, the gravestones of St Enda's ancient cemetery; from here
they appear to float above the roofs of the village. Above them again, out
beyond the western rim of the bay, a child has left a toy aeroplane; as one
watches it teeters forward a little, turns and sniffs the wind, gives a puny
growl, and takes itself off – one identifies it as the Aer Árann ten-seater –
into a tremendous sky that has a tiny dark blue panoramic replica of Connemara's mountains all along its foot. The road that passes just below the
village goes by the graveyard and the airstrip and disappears into the crumpled patchwork of Cill Éinne's walls and roofs nearly a mile away, among
which the old castle ruin shows as a dark stain. In Cill Rónáin harbour,
another mile away and on the far side of a further bay, breadcrumb boats
manoeuvre at a matchstick pier. The town itself is a spill of lozenges, some
of them scattered up the treads of the hillside beyond.

In this perspective the terracing of Árainn's northern flank is very clear;
the island is visibly carved out of a small number of enormous beds of limestone laid one upon another. The geology is so simple in its nakedness that

the lacy ribbon of habitation laid along it appears as a passing fancy, a frivolity, a plaything. And yet the pattern of settlement also has an impersonal structure to it; the two abstractions twine together in some paradoxical geometry of tenderness. One aspect of this relationship is obvious as soon as one begins to descend from the ridge-line and drops out of the prevailing south-westerly wind; the scarp-slope of the island offers a degree of shelter. Almost every one of the villages has its heart, its original core, snuggled into a concavity of the escarpment. At Iaráirne the ridge is quite low, but it rises close behind the village, and to the west a slight but distinct swelling of the slope tempers the wind to the old cottages and the modern bungalows occupying old sites; the newer houses off to the right and left forego this advantage, for the sake of privacy or the view. In other parts of the island houses have recently been built on heights not previously settled, and not only do they look uncomfortable and irremediably bleak, but unmannerly towards the landscape, disdainful of its hospitality. Admittedly, the degree of shelter to be enjoyed anywhere in Aran is small; in Iaráirne, for instance, it is obviously difficult to grow trees, and its two bent mountain ashes perpetually mime a westerly gale. But the traditional sites of settlement were determined by the coincidence of various small amenities of the rock, as I shall show, and while modern building technology may liberate us from this determinism, it can deafen us to old harmonies between house and land.

If the cardinal directions of the Aran field-system are given by the joints criss-crossing the limestone, to understand the situation of the villages one has to descend into the third dimension of the rock and consider its natural horizontal partings. This dimension is time-wise; it arises from the succession of deposits on the Carboniferous sea floor. Sundry geographies came and went during that era, untrodden, unwritten-up, and were reduced to distinctive layers of sediment. In the sequence of Aran's strata, the nearly horizontal beds of limestone are interleaved with thinner layers of shale. Where a hillside now cross-sections one of these it is visible as a dark band, usually two or three feet thick, with the limestone rising above it in a steep scarp or a cliff ten to twenty feet high. In places the shale seems to have been eaten back so that the impending limestone overhangs and shadows it. For instance that track leading down into Iaráirne – it is called Róidín Mháirtín, Martin's little road, no doubt from the same shadowy figure whose name is attached to the broken-down tower further east – runs along the top of a north-facing grassy bank. At one point a few trodden footholds lead down from it to a recess almost under the *róidín* itself, from which the hart's-tongue fern sticks out its long pointed fronds, and cool water lies in a small stone-lined basin below a thick ledge of limestone.

A few flattish stones lie at the rim of the basin like uncomfortable kneelers before a shrine; if you stoop and peer under the great limestone altarpiece you see the shale at the back of the recess. It glistens with moisture, and it comes away in horizontal flakes when you pick at it. It looks like the edge of a huge mouldering book, shut forever by the weight of rock above it, and in fact it is the history of one of those fleeting lands whose hills were weathered away and carried off as mud by rivers, and piled in layers on the sea-floor during the gestation of Aran. There are about eight such shale-beds running right through the body of the island, very nearly level but with the same slight dip to the south-south-west as the limestone. On the Atlantic cliffs they show as slots and ledges etched back into the rock-face by the waves. The very highest cliffs are divided into four stories by these recessed string-courses. On the northern side of the island the land steps up from shore to ridge-line in abrupt slopes or cliffs separating broad levels, and the same shale-bands crop out along the feet of these risers.

These north-facing scarps are hospitable to human settlement as well as to fern growth. The spring well by Róidín Mháirtín is Tobar Iaráirne, and it is the proximate reason for the siting of the village nearby. There are good green pastures all along the foot of the scarp here; a skim of soil weathered out from the shale-band has added to the attractions of the locality. The correlation of shelter, water and soil along particular levels of the island suggests the thought that all possibilities of life derive from material differences, just as electric currents are powered by potential differences. In Aran the difference is that between limestone – rigid, susceptible to fracture, soluble in water – and shale – plastic, foliated, impermeable. The joints of the limestone, enlarged by erosion down to a certain depth, do not penetrate the shale-bands. Therefore the rainwater they swallow off the surface is channeled laterally through the web of fissures until it seeps out of a scarp-face, trickling down the shale exposure and filling any natural or artificial basin at its foot, before overflowing and disappearing into the grykes of the next terrace, reappearing as another line of springs below the next scarp, and so on until it reaches the sea.

But why are there these scarps? Their formation obviously has to do with the different resistances to erosion of the alternating layers of limestone and shale, but the processes by which a hillside is sculpted into steps are not known beyond argument. Limestone exposed to weathering on a hillside will tend to degenerate into loose blocks, which further erosion (and perhaps glaciation) would eventually annihilate, whereas the limestone protected by a shale-layer will stand firm; one can imagine the terraces being roughed out in this way. On the other hand the shale itself is vulnerable to attack along its exposures, and just as on the sea-cliffs it is gouged out by the waves to leave grooves along the cliff-faces, so in many places it is being worn back under the inland cliffs, by weathering and perhaps by the spring-water perpetually washing out over it. The overhang of fractured limestone will eventually collapse, and in fact along many of the scarps there are huge fallen blocks of limestone. This rubble no doubt protects the shale for a bit but breaks down in the end, allowing the process to recommence. Thus once a scarp is formed it will slowly recede; in fact the whole sequence of terraces and steps will gradually bite its way back and consume the hillside. Something similar is happening on the Atlantic coast, where the cliffs, pounded by winter gales, are an ongoing catastrophe. On the northern slopes, however, sapping and ruination proceeds on a time-scale that human beings can live under; indeed it is the ground of their existence.

Because Cill Éinne bay takes a huge bite out of the eastern third of the island, reducing it to less than a mile across, the sequence of scarps and terraces is not fully developed here. Most of the other villages have terraces below them as well as above, but Iaráirne is unique in that immediately to the north of it is a wide tract of sandy land just above sea-level. Na Muirbhigh Móra, the big sea-plains, it is called; ecologists would describe it as 'machair', from a Scots-Gaelic synonym of *muirbheach* that has been adopted into their terminology. Its smooth ground-hugging sward is a closely-woven web of plant-species resistant to salty winds and heavy grazing. Together with its long north-easterly extension, Barr na Coise, it is commonage, shared in proportion to their other land-holdings between about a dozen households of Iaráirne, and used for grazing dry cattle in summer. Milk-giving and calf-bearing cattle are kept in the meadows of lush grass watered by the springs under the scarp, handy to the village. Sometimes one sees the beasts galloping madly around these little fields, tormented by warble flies that puncture their skin to lay eggs in their flesh, edible housing for the grubs. This is another reason for not keeping the cattle on the crags in summer, where they would be more likely to break their legs in the grykes. But in winter the crags have the advantage of being well drained and comparatively dry underfoot, and as in this mild oceanic climate cattle do not have to be brought indoors, they are wintered on Na Craga, and get by on its sparse grass and the occasional sackful of mangolds. (I am told, however, that the poor *slóchtaí*, the cattle brought in from Connemara for the winter, whose keep was paid for in turf, would spend it on the open commonage – though their Connemara owners may not have been aware of this frugal arrangement.)

Thus the economy rotates around the village like a year-hand on a clock, turning the land to best advantage with the turning seasons. Wells like Tobar Iaráirne are crucial to the mechanism, though since the village is now piped up to the mains coming from the big reservoirs behind Cill Rónáin, they are only used for watering the cattle. (When I revisited the well to refresh my memory recently, I found its water full of what looked like handfuls of chopped lettuce. I brought a bit of this stuff home to identify: *Aneura pinguis*, a liverwort. Liverworts, obscure denizens of wet and shady places, absorb their nutriment directly through their leaves, and, having no roots or interior canals, rank below flowering plants in the Whig view of evolution. They are not a life-form that had much caught my attention previously, so I note here that Tobar Iaráirne not only supports *Homo sapiens* but also houses this other creature, and no doubt a thousand others to whose life-cycles I am oblivious.)

The *róidín* by the well long predates the main road, which was extended to Iaráirne only in this century. West of the well it winds down the scarp and enters the village without much changing its half-grassy half-stony nature; indeed the terrain hardly alters either, as there are little hay-fields and tillage-plots between the houses, and overgrown empty sites where long-gone cottages have mouldered into craggy mounds. Coming from above in this way, one takes in the village by its roof-tops. The nearest is a dishevelled straw thatch sprouting thistles, nettles and yellow rag-wort flowers; beyond it are old grey cement tiles, modern curved red tiles, thunder-blue slates, and – the very newest – a pin-sharp reed thatch that curves over an upstairs dormer window and has a decorative trim along the roof-ridge. The boreen branches within the village; each way leads down to the main road, and the little circuit knots together most of the houses, except for two recent bungalows that have strayed along the road to the east, the reed-thatched house isolated in the fields to the west and, a hundred yards beyond it, a guest-house that has recently expanded almost into a hotel, called Árd Éinne, Enda's height, on the hillside above the old cemetery. One cottage has a little garden with eight-foot-high tree mallows brought over from the cliffs, a red rambling rose, nasturtiums, and by the doorstep a big clump of bloody cranesbill on which the baby's bibs are spread out to take the sun. In the lee of one of the taller gables two *Pittosporum*, an evergreen shrub that does well on the western seaboard, have attained to tree-height. The long thatched cottage at the top of the village turns out to be disused except as an outhouse, and all the surviving cottages have had their thatches replaced with something less laborious in the upkeep. The smart reed thatch of the isolated house is of a style promulgated by government-funded craft training schemes, and this is its first appearance in the island; it makes one think of prosperous English villages, and has nothing in common with the shaggy Aran thatch roped down to pegs beneath the eaves like a woolly cap pulled well down over the ears in the face of the storm.

Iaráirne – the name is rather puzzling since at first hearing it seems to mean the western or back part (*iar*) of Aran, or of a ridge (*ára*). There is a similar puzzle about the name of the easternmost of the Aran Islands, Inis Oírr, pronounced very much as if the last element were *iar*. In the latter case the solution is clear. In some early sources the island is called Ára Airthir, the Aran of the east, or Inis Airthir, the island of the east. (For instance the *Annals of the Four Masters* record that in 856 the High King of Tara burned and plundered Munster and carried off hostages from every corner of it. One of these corners is specified as Ára Airthir; presumably the other two Aran Islands were considered to be in Connacht.) The more modern spelling, Inis Oirthir, first appears in the seventeenth century in Roderic O'Flaherty's *West or H-Iar Connaught.* Since the word *oirthear* (*oirthir* is the genitive case) is not in use in Aran speech, it has been corrupted and simplified until hardly distinguishable from a word meaning the exact opposite. The same has happened in the name Iaráirne, which presumably started out as Oirthear Áirne, meaning the eastern portion of Aran. It is curiously easy to slip from east to west in the phonology of several European languages, in which north and south are kept poles apart. Perhaps the distinction between north and south, between shade and sun, winter and summer, demands so much commonsense from us, that the practical outweighs the symbolic; the other, the east-west journey travelled so quickly by each of our days, resonates with concerns we prefer not to articulate too clearly. From Aran, evening after evening, we see how the glorious career of the sun only serves to paint it into a corner, so that it has to escape down a mouse-hole into some cellar of the world in which, whatever its state, it is no longer the sun. Perhaps east and west are the names of buried hopes and fears that betray themselves in this slip of the Indo-European tongue.

All but one of the houses of Iaráirne have their longer axes east-west, and this orientation is dominant throughout the island. In my early years in Aran I took it that this pattern represented the alignment of the houses with the main road, which on the whole runs east-west, and was probably due to some bureaucratic ideal of neatness imposed by the planning authorities, so when a family in Cill Mhuirbhigh consulted my aesthetic sense in the siting of their bungalow I had them put it at an angle to the road; the result is disconcerting now that I understand that the pattern long predates the road. The island itself provides the level terraces running along its northern flank on which the villages have developed, and these have origins vastly senior to all human custom, as I have shown. However, the alignment of individual houses answers not only to the topography and to mete-orology, but to a complex mystique of westernness. Occidentation, rather than orientation, would be the best word for this simultaneously domestic and otherworldly compass bearing.

The houses of Iaráirne nearly all derive either by multiple extensions or by replacement from thatched cottages of the nineteenth century or earlier, and inherit their orientation from a tradition common to most of the west of Ireland. Several of these cottages were joined together end to end in twos or even threes, to save the building of a gable, and in such cases one could be sure that the westernmost cottage was the oldest. Dara Ó Conaola, a writer born in Inis Meáin and now living in Inis Oírr, explains this in his account of the richly meaningful simplicities of Aran's domestic architecture:

Nothing was built onto the west of a house because *'Fear níos fearr ná Dia a chuireadh fad as an teach siar'* ('Only a man better than God would lengthen his house to the west'). It was thought that anyone who did that was showing he had no respect for God, and that no luck would come to him out of it. I never heard what the reason for this belief was. I suppose that it was because in the old days people thought God was in the west. In the pagan times they worshipped the set-ting sun, and the idea stuck in their minds long afterwards. That's only what I think myself, but it stands to reason.

Front and back of these cottages were the same; the two doors were opposite one another, and which was in use depended on the way the wind was blowing.

These houses were no wonderful palaces but they were comfortable enough. They were thought-out and suited to the times and the surroundings. Their design was simple enough – an oblong, with two walls and two gables. There was a door in either wall. There weren't many windows because at that time even sunlight was taxed! One of the doors would be left open to do the work of a window as well as that of a door. It was called the sheltered door (*doras an fhascaidh*), or the open door, and the other was called the wind door (*doras na gaoithe*) or the closed door.

In Aran, keeping the driven rain out of the house during a gale is not easy, and the wind door often has old sacks stuffed under it, with a length of plank or something similar to hold them in place, and opening it is not just a matter of turning a key. Again before I knew about these things, when calling on an islander I would knock at what I took to be the front door because it was the one facing the road, and sometimes there would be an obscure shout from within, which I gradually came to understand as *'Doras eile!'* ('Other door!'). But the next time, if I went round to the back, I was just as likely to get the same response, the wind having changed.

If in the layout of the cottage the distinction between north side and south depends on the wind, east and west are sharply differentiated:

Our house had two rooms when it was built, but later on it was altered, and it had three rooms in my own time. When you came in at the door you would be in the kitchen. The kitchen was in the middle of the house, with the 'big room' (*seomra mór*) on its west, behind the chimney, and the 'little room' on the east. There were two beds in the little room, and not much room for anything else. The kitchen was about twelve feet square once the little room had been cut off it. That left it cramped enough, I suppose, but as the old man who lived with us used to say to anyone who came to the door, 'Come in, if we're cramped we're not unwelcoming.'

There was a door by the chimney, the door of the big room. Above this door, next to the chimney and under the scraws of the thatch, was a way into the 'small loft', which was over the big room. It was a dark hole with no light but what leaked in from the kitchen past the chimney. It was a place for storing things, or of course for hiding them.

On the east of the kitchen above the small room was the loft, which compared to the small loft was spacious and well-lit. It was open to the rafters. It stuck out a couple of feet over the wall of the little room to make it deeper. There was a beam running across the house under this edge of the loft. Many a pig or beef carcase was hung from 'the beam of the loft' in its day. Fishing gear, baskets of salted fish and so on were kept in the loft. People would put turf up there. Often when something couldn't be found, they would say 'I don't know where it is, if it isn't at the back of the loft.'

The kitchen was the main room, and the hearth was the heart of the kitchen, but the big room had its own importance. In our house two generations came into the world in it. Two generations died in it. Many a person breathed his last in it. There was a fireplace in it; we called it the little chimney, and it was at the back of the main fireplace in the kitchen wall. It had a wooden mantelpiece, plain but well finished. There was a press or cupboard set into the wall near the fireplace; *muifíd* we called it. Any ornaments in the house would be kept there, and medicines, and perhaps a drop of the hard stuff. There was a big feather bed, and a coffer or chest which was their bank.

> *Dóite brúite suas amach*
> *Bhfuil aon duine ag dul an bóthar*
> *A chuirfeadh an chóra mhór amach?*

(Broken up burnt out, is anyone going the road who would put the coffer out?) That's what the old man said when he thought the house was on fire.

Thus the hearth is central, what is to the east is merely functional, and the west is heavy-laden with consequential matters. The uncanny sometimes taps on the western gable. When I happened to learn that a fairy path runs just west of a certain house, I was asked not to tell the young wife who was moving into it, lest she become anxious and start imagining things. (I only mention it now because I know she has long since bravely faced down what seemed indeed to be an initial spitefulness of the place.)

The bygone Iaráirne one can sense beneath the present layout dates, it seems, from the early nineteenth century, for the census of 1812 names all the fourteen villages of the island except this one, implying that there was not enough of it to be worth discriminating from Cill Éinne, whereas the census of 1821 lists eight households and sixty-one inhabitants here. (The population-figures for the island as a whole were 1785 in 1812 and 2285 in 1821; the first census may have been inadequate, but in any case this was a period of very rapid growth, for by 1841, shortly before the Famine, the figure was 2592.) Seven of the heads of Iaráirne households in 1821 were farmers with holdings of a quarter to one and a half cartrons (a cartron being a nominal sixty-four acres), and one was a labourer; two of the farmers and a few others of the menfolk also made kelp or were 'boatmen', probably employed in carrying kelp and seaweed to the mainland. Among the womenfolk three were wool-spinners, two flax-spinners, and one a stocking-knitter. Nobody is listed as 'fisherman' (in contrast to Cill Éinne, a village of fishermen, net-makers and so on with no land), but no doubt most of the men fished for breams and rockfish from the shore. This was a self-sufficient community – self-insufficient, perhaps, for the famine known as the Famine was not the first – and not even a track linked the settlement to Cill Éinne until some time after the turn of the century; the wide open spaces of Na Muirbhigh Móra and Máirtín's rambling *róidín* took it wherever it wanted to go: to the well, the crags, the shore.

In that census of 1821 a seven-year-old schoolboy, Edmund, is listed among the sons of a John Flaherty of Cill Rónáin. Ned Sheáin, as the child was called, later settled in Iaráirne, and from him are descended Muintir Neide, the Neds. Some generations later, probably in the 1930s when landholdings were being rationalized, a Land Commission official came out to arrange for Muintir Neide to exchange their bit of land in Barr an Phointe near Cill Rónáin for a share of Iaráirne territory. He and Beartla, the Ned of that era, ascended to Carn Buí, the rocky knoll on the ridge-line behind the village, and surveyed the dreary plateau foundering seawards beyond it. 'What's out there?' he asked, waving his arm to the south-east. 'Rock,' replied Beartla Neide. 'Then you might as well have the lot!' said the official. So it comes about that today my friend Pádraicín Neide farms over eighty acres, much of it indeed rock, but with enough grassy little glens hidden among the crags for him to be able to sell off four two-year-old cattle each year. His farming is done before and after his day's work as a builder, and so when I arranged to meet him, to hear how it is with the Iaráirne of 1993, it had to be late in the evening.

It was the end of June; the days were at their longest. At half past nine when I knocked at his door he was not yet home; his young daughter Cathy led me across the village, hopping over low walls and cutting through enclosures I don't know whether to call fields or back-gardens, and pointed out his bent back showing like a boulder above the dense green foliage in the further corner of a big potato-plot. Pádraicín is a blocky, vigorous man in his early forties; he climbed out over the field-wall, slightly glistening in the last of the sunshine, all ready to fill me up with facts and opinions. As we strolled back to the house he told me what the other Iaráirneans do for a living nowadays. There are four fishermen, one working out of Cill Éinne harbour and the others out of Ros a' Mhíl and Cill Rónáin. (The more recent, eighty-foot, trawlers of the developing Aran fleet cannot berth at Cill Rónáin, and in any case Ros a' Mhíl, the designated fishery port of the area, has the ice-plants, auction halls and processing factories the industry depends on, which unfortunately leads to fishermen's families leaving the island either temporarily or permanently for houses on the mainland.) The huge growth in tourism of the last few years is transforming even Iaráirne. A sparklingly white bungalow with its coign stones painted blue and scalloped beige blinds showing in its big windows belongs to the owner of some of the eleven minibuses that carry visitors up and down the island. Another villager hires out bicycles in Cill Rónáin; there are a thousand bicycles on the island now. However, apart from Ard Éinne, which is technically over the border in Cill Éinne territory, Pádraicín's is the only Iarairne house to keep guests in the summer. There are also one or two old-age pensioners, a teacher, a 'retired Yank' (that is, an islander returned from the States), and a Dubliner whose wife stands in for the island doctor now and again.

Back in the big kitchen built onto the rear of his house, Pádraicín's wife Nora broke off from cajoling the children into bed to make us sandwiches and tea. An eight-year-old daughter, Caoimhe, appeared in her nightdress and twisted up her foot to show him the progress of a white lump on her sole. While he filed away at the verruca and dabbed some medicament from a tube onto it, he talked about children. Four households here have clutches of three to five, whereas other villages have few or none coming forward to the primary schools. But fifteen of the nineteen children from Iaráirne and Cill Éinne starting school next year are girls. ('The nights weren't cold enough!' said a Cill Rónáin man to whom I mentioned this odd fact the next day – which seems to imply that only great hardship drives Aran couples to the comfort of sex with the extra application necessary to create the male.) And since, on finishing school, girls leave the island more readily than boys, taking jobs in shops and offices, this is not a reassuring statistic. Every year the Vocational School organizes a survey of population that is less subject to chance distortions than the official census, and in 1992 for the first time the number of people living in the big island dropped below eight hundred.

Pádraicín is keen on sports and coaching the island children. There used to be a football field or at least a pair of goalposts on the *muirbheach* below the village, but when the thin sward was worn through the wind quickly excavated a sandpit there and exposed bare rock. What he had done to stop further erosion was, he told me, 'unsightly but effective'. His youngest son Aodhán had silently added himself to our conversation, so Pádraicín scooped him into his arms and we went down to look at these works. The piles of old fridges and other rubbish he had brought with his tractor from the dump behind Cill Rónáin a year or two ago to plug breaches in the fringe of dunes around the beach still showed in one place, but in others they seemed to be trapping and stabilizing the blown sand and were already covered. We discussed coastal defences, a topic forced upon the community by the storm of January 1991 which, in near con-junction with a spring tide, ripped away the shore road or heaped it with boulders in various places, so that at Port Chorrúch and Cill Mhuirbhigh big concrete sea-walls are now in building. Was that storm a fluke? Are we squandering money on defences which will never be tested or which are quite inadequate to what is in store for us? Is global warming angering the earth against us, are we outstaying our welcome here? On this calm mid-summer evening still redolent of disseminated sunlight, it was difficult to feel so. We walked eastwards towards Port Daibhche to see how the marram grass was doing, where during that storm the waves almost broke across the neck of the peninsula. It was too dark underfoot for me to be able to point out the purple milk-vetch, the great rarity among the many unusual plants making up this smooth flower-spangled sward. I remembered uneasily almost stepping on a lark's nest here once, a cupful of life. A few years ago it was proposed to make Na Muirbhigh and part of Barr na Coise into a golf-course; when I heard of it I had hastened to inform the main propo-nent of the scheme, a Connemara-based politician, of the existence of the purple milk-vetch, and he was less than delighted to hear of it. The pro-posal was not pressed forward at that time, partly because it seemed no grants would be forthcoming for such a development in the habitat of a legally-protected species and an officially-designated 'Area of Scientific Interest', and also perhaps because some of the twelve commonage holders were unpersuaded that either they or the island in general would much benefit. But the idea is still in the air, and there are powerful arguments for it: the prospect of increased 'quality' tourism, more jobs, more amenities to keep the young at home. When I talk to some of the islanders who are in favour, and try to explain why I think that area should be preserved inviolate, I find myself using wooden language: that 'machair' is a rare landform, vulnerable to touristic developments such as caravan parks and golf-courses; that we must conserve biotic diversity not just in the rain forests but at home too; and so on. But if I suggest they read 'Sand in the Wind', *Stones of Aran*, Vol. I, for my deeper feelings about this little wilderness, I am in difficulties, for those pages seem to show that I was lonely and mournful out there, and that nothing would have taken me out of myself better than a game of golf.

By the time we reached the eastern shore, stumbling in the rabbit-holes – though the rabbits are gone; someone introduced myxomatosis, it seems – Aodhán was fast asleep in his father's arms. We sat among the tussocks of marram above the empty curve of the beach, and Pádraicín told me about the days of his own father, when Port Daibhche was home to eight or nine currachs belonging to Cill Éinne and Iaráirne men. They used to row twice a day out to Na Carracháin off the southern cliffs after bream, and when they were seen coming back up the channel the children would rush down from the village on donkeys with pannier-baskets to carry up the catch. The bream were gutted, filleted, salted and laid out flat in the sun on the walls of the fields to cure. When they were hard as boards they were tied up in threes – an undersized fish could be passed off sandwiched between two big ones – and a 'hundred' threes, that is three hundred and sixty fish, would buy a boatload of turf from Connemara. Hard-working times – those fishermen were also farmers with cattle and potato fields to tend, and they kept their children busy every hour they were not at school.

What changes in the island since Pádraicín's childhood! His worries about his own children in these strange times, he told me as we made our way through the twilight back to the village, are those of a city parent. Drugs are coming into the island; young men coming in for the summer season are sniffing something – he doesn't know if it's cocaine or crack or what, but it's not snuff! – and sharing it with local lads; the gardaí are said to be 'watching the situation'. Children might be visiting certain homes where they are allowed to watch who knows what sort of rubbish on videos. Pádraicín often supervises the Hall in Cill Rónáin when there is a dance, and afterwards has found teenagers hanging around in the street at two or three in the morning. With thousands of tourists pouring in during the short season, some islanders are so busy they have no idea what their kids are up to; they throw them the most expensive presents to be bought in

Galway – but what those children are not getting is love.

Pádraicín, hunched over his burden, was breathing heavily as we climbed the path to his house. Love! It was as if at the very threshold of home he had stumbled on the word we had been searching for through the gathering dark. I could have founded this chapter on it, had I known it was going to turn up.

THE FITZPATRICKS

As one walks the road from Iaráirne towards Cill Éinne, the old farmhouse known as Killeany Lodge comes into view on the hillside above the harbour. A pair of tall monuments on a rocky terrace below it attracts the attention, obviously with the intention of making a public statement. But it is not easy to get close enough even to gather the nature of this statement, for they do not stand by the present way up to the Lodge, nor indeed by the older way shown on nineteenth-century maps, and when one has scrambled across field-walls to reach them one finds that they are sited so close to the brink of a scarp that viewing the inscriptions on their northern, and clearly frontal, faces, is awkward. They stand a few yards apart like huge gateposts, but there is no easy access to the past through them. However, the name 'Fitzpatrick', repeated in the inscriptions, catches the eye; clearly these are cenotaphs to people of consequence, who presumably lived in the Lodge or some predecessor of it.

The two monuments are rectangular masonry pillars with pyramidal caps surmounted by stone crosses, about twenty feet in overall height and eight by five in plan. Each has four plaques lettered in bas-relief, one set into each face. A few yards to the east is a much smaller monument not noticeable from the distance, with just one plaque.

> PRAY FOR THE SO
> VL OF IOHN FFITZP
> ATRICK WHO DYE
> D THE 3 DAY OF
> FEBRUARY   ANN
> OD   1709

So one is bidden by the front of the tall cenotaph on the east. Its back says:

> PRAY FOR THE SO
> VL OF SARAMSW

EINY WIFE TO IO
HN   FITZPATRIC
K WHO DIED THE 5
DAY OF NOVEMB ER
1   7   0   9

The left and right sides ask one to pray for the souls of a Florence Fitzpatrick who died in 'Iannary' of that same year, and a Rickard Fitzpatrick
who died in 1701. Two of the letters 'Z' are back to front.

The western cenotaph has rather more elegant lettering, in which the
uprights of the letter 'H' in the words 'THE' and 'THEIR' also serve as
uprights for the T and E, and the spaces between the words are marked
with a small diamond-shaped point. The front and sides commemorate
three Fitzpatrick men who died young: Dennis died in 'Disember' 1753
aged twenty-three, John died in 'Ianvary' 1754 aged 25, and Peter died in
March 1754 aged seventeen. And on the back:

PRAY · FOR · PATR
ICK · FITZ · PATR
ICK · & · HIS · WIF
E · MARGRETT
FITZ · PATRICK
WHO · ERRECT
ED ·THIS · MONNV
MENT · IN · THE · YE
ARE · OF · OUR · LOR
D · 1754 · & · THEIR · P
O S T E R E T Y

Surely it must have been the loss of three young men over the winter of
1753/4 that prompted Patrick and Margrett to build this memorial. (A
local tradition, that is perhaps no more than an old speculation, is that the
three died of typhus.) And perhaps the opportunity was taken of commemorating the loss of an earlier generation at the same time, for the two
pillars are so nearly identical, apart from the lettering of the plaques, as to
suggest that they were built as a pair.

Having puzzled out this much, one turns to the smaller monument,
which has just one plaque. Above the inscription is an incised motif like a
downward-pointing arrow, which I take to represent the three nails of the
Crucifixion with their points together below. The inscription itself is illeg-
ibly worn, and only by taking a rubbing does one find, disappointingly,
that it duplicates the inscription to 'SARAMSWEINY' on the taller monument beside it. (Uncrabbed, her name must have been Sara MacSweeney.)

But how can one pray for a soul of whom one knows so little? Only a believer in a vast essentialist bureaucracy of the hereafter can send up a prayer labelled with a name and a date of decease, and be confident that it will be credited to the right account. The secular equivalent is more difficult. These people, Sara, John, Patrick and the rest, have gone beyond hearing; they will not answer to our historical echo-soundings, and the pious best we can do – for ourselves, not for them – is to inform ourselves enough to understand something of them and their times, and so, by reflection, of ours.

Of course all biography is potentially interminable, and our brief lives demand brief pieties. Fortunately, without going beyond the first few chambers of the archival labyrinth, we can know something of these Fitzpatricks, thanks to the nineteenth-century Galway historian James Hardiman. Among the generous stuffing of miscellaneous information in the appendices to his 1846 edition of Roderic O'Flaherty's *West or H-Iar Connaught* is this:

In the early part of the last century the family of 'Fitzpatrick, of Aran' was one of the most opulent families of this part of Ireland; but the name is now extinct, or sunk in poverty. It may, however, be curious to trace it a little, in consequence of its having been, with some probability, supposed to be a branch of the ancient and noble stock of Upper Ossory. It appears ... that in A.D. 1642, Richard Fitzpatrick was seneschal of Ibrickan, in the County of Clare, and receiver there for the Earl of Thomond; also, that Teige (Thady) Fitz-Patrick resided there at the time. Ibrickan lies next to Aran. In A.D. 1686, John Fitzpatrick, gent., resided at Loughmore ... in the south island. His son Richard, in the same year, married Joan French, of Spiddle ... Richard died A.D. 1701, leaving four sons, Scander, Denis, Peter, Patrick. John, the father, died A.D. 1709, at the house of his son-in-law, George Morris, in the west suburb of Galway ... leaving chattels to the amount of £6000, and £1500 in silver and gold, which he kept in a cellar of his in that town. John had a second son, Edmond, who married Annable Martin, of Dangan, and died about A.D. 1717, leaving a son, Rickard. Annable his relict intermarried with Michael O'Flaherty, the son of our author [*i.e.* Roderic O'Flaherty]. Rickard represented Galway in the Irish Parliament for several years, and died A.D. 1761, without issue. Edmond Fitzpatrick, his nephew, sheriff of Galway, A.D. 1769 and 1797, left an only son James, who died without issue. Whether any of the name now exist the Editor has not ascertained.

In the reign of Charles I, Sir Stephen Fox granted leases of the islands of Aran to John and Richard Fitzpatrick, at £500 per annum; and afterwards made them abatements in the rent, for losses sustained on account of the frequent landing of the enemy's privateers on those islands, and committing depredations there. In A.D. 1713, Sir Stephen, in consideration of £8200, conveyed the islands to Patrick French of Monivea and Edmund Fitzpatrick, of Aran, one moiety to the former, and the other to the latter, their heirs and assigns, for ever. Patrick French was trustee for Simon Digby, Lord Bishop of Elphin, whose moiety was granted, by lease for ever, to Edmond Fitzpatrick, at £280 per annum. On 15th February, 1744, Rickard Fitzpatrick , in consideration of £2050, released his moiety of the three islands to Robert French, in trust for Robert Digby of Landenstown, his heirs and assigns, for ever.

Identification of the various places, persons and times mentioned in this skeletal history will add some flesh and much blood to it, even if the resonant title 'Seneschal of Ibrickan' may lose some of its spectral glamour. First, the surname Fitzpatrick: this is a pseudo-Norman anglicization of the Irish Mac Giolla Phádraic, son of the devotee of Patrick, and the ancient sept of that name was particularly associated with Ossory, in what is now County Laois. Fitzpatricks were prominent in Galway in the seventeenth century, and Hardiman's *History of Galway* lists several of that name among the sheriffs and mayors of the city. Nevertheless, the above implies that the Aran Fitzpatricks derive not from Galway but from Clare, where in 1642 it appears that a Richard Fitzpatrick was seneschal of Ibrickan and receiver for the Earl of Thomond. (Thomond, from Tuadh-Mhumhain, north Munster, included County Clare, of which Ibrickan was a barony situated on the coast a little south of Inis Oírr. The Earl of Thomond would have owned most of Ibrickan, and the intermediary between him and his tenants would have been his seneschal or steward and receiver of rents.) And this fact 'appears' out of the fog of slaughter, for in 1642 there was civil war in England, and Ireland was in rebellion. The Catholic gentlemen who had taken up arms against the King's Dublin government in 1641 had claimed to be protecting him and themselves against the ferociously anti-Catholic Parliament he was struggling with in England. By October 1642 Parliament had gone to war with Charles I, and had decided upon the final subjection of Ireland; the 'Confederate Catholics' had met in Kilkenny to concert the rebellion, but were themselves divided between those who were ready to treat with the King's forces in Ireland and those who cared nothing for King or Parliament but only for the Catholic cause. Barnaby, the Sixth Earl of Thomond, was a descendant of the O'Briens who had ruled Munster for centuries before the imposition of the English feudal system from which his title derived its legitimacy. But in the native hierarchy of the O'Briens he was not the mightiest, and in the rip-tides of rebellion he had to handle the ship of his own state very carefully, for, according to a contemporary account,

... the Brians in the county of Clare (not withstandinge the crubbing of the earle of Tomond to the contrary) observing the cause of comotion in the whole Kingdome to be one, and the oathe sworn by the Irish now in armies to be just and lawfull, thought it a blemish in their honors not to be conformable therto in defence of religion, Kinge and Kingdome joining hands together, whither Tomond would or not, took all the forts and castles that belonged to Protestants or puritans in all the countie ...

It was Barnaby's ancestor the Fourth Earl, loyal to his upbringing in Elizabeth's court, who had brought in English settlers to his estates, creating a lasting fear among his Catholic neighbours of a Protestant plantation, at their expense, on the Ulster model. Some of these settlers were small yeoman farmers, others middlemen leasing large areas of land and subletting in smaller lots, and there were thirty or more small castles or towerhouses owned by such Englishmen in the county. The Sixth Earl had refused them permission to form themselves into a force against the rebels, and had warranted the captains of his own Irish army to disarm those of the English who did not dwell in castles. At the outbreak of fighting and pillaging the English inhabitants of unprotected farms fled to the shelter of the English-owned castles. When these strongholds were picked off one by one, the survivors in many cases fled to the Earl's great castle of Bunratty, for he was trying to keep on terms with England – no easy task when its King and Parliament were at war – and at the same time with his powerful O'Brien cousins who had sided with the Catholic Confederation.

What might have been the role of the seneschal of Ibrickan – remembering his Old Irish family connections, and his long-established daily dealings with his Lord's English tenants – in such events? As it happens, the only reason Hardiman (representing History, for our purposes here) notices the existence of Richard the seneschal is that he is named in a deposition given in the following year by a John Ward about the sack of his father's castle of Tromra in Ibrickan. It was Colonel Edmund O'Flaherty of Connemara (as recounted in *Pilgrimage*) who led the assault, sailing via Aran from Galway where he had been engaged in the siege of the English fort. Ten years later, the rebellion having been crushed by Cromwell's army, the fate of Tromra was recalled during O'Flaherty's trial. The Colonel confessed as follows:

... that deponent and his company went in their boats to the countie of Clare, to a castle called Trennrowe, which was possessed by one Mr. Ward, whom he heard was an honest gentleman, and never heard of him before, and neither doth know of what religion or nation he was of; and came to said castle in the beginning of the night ... they made some shotts from the castle at him, and continued suteing all night, with which shotts some of his men were wounded. And saith, they could not find the doore nor window of the said casle that night, but eleven of his men went to the hale which was joyning of the castle , thinking to get in, whereupon they threw stones from the topp of the castle, by which one of his men was wounded and bruised in his arm, and another in his back, and also they let falle a bundle of straw upon said halle by which it was burned, and the next morning they sett on to storm the castle, in which storm one of his men was killed, and three wounded. And saith he continued seige to the said castle, from Sunday night to Wednesday morning, at which time conditions were made by John Ward for his own life, which said John this examinent employed as a messenger to his father in the castle, desiring him to take quarter several times, but the answer of Peeter Ward was, that he would nott take the quarter of Belleek or Sruell.

Being further examined, he saith, that ... the sonne and heire of the said Peeter came oute on tuesdaye, and was slained in the way. ... And saith, that Peeter Warde did keep his chamber in the castle, from Tuesday night until Wednesday morning, and that the said Peeter Ward's wife was slaine by a shott through the window of the said chamber, but who made the shott he knoweth not. And further saith that he ordered his men to keepe the said Peeter Warde awake, with intention to give him quarter, and the said Peeter Warde making a thrust out of the dorre with some weapon, was taken by the arme and drawen foorth, and there slained. And further said that he defended himself in his chamber, for foure and twenty hours after the rest went foorth. And saith, that he and his companie plundered the said house, and divided it, havinge first carried the said plunder to Straw island.

Peter Ward's badger-like desperation in defence dominates this scene of war – war on a horribly intimate and domestic scale, up and down stairs, in and out of chambers – and it is only through his son John, who made conditions for his own life, and survived to make his deposition of 1643, that we glimpse our quarry:

The said Edmond continued siege to the said castle for three daies and three nights ... murthered the said Alson and George ... caused the castle to be fired ... the said Peter Ward was then traytorously murthered, who together with the said Alson and George was stripped and they three buried in or neere the castle walls, from whence... they were removed and enterred in the parish church. Yeet notwith-standing the Mass-preist caused their corps to be digged up againe and buried without in the churchyard, for noe other cause but that they saide no unsanctified or hereticall corps of protestants (as they tearme them) must remaine within their churches. This deponent likewise saith, that the said Edmond O'Fflahertie was abetted, councilled, and assisted in the said rebellious and traytorous designe, by [among others] Richd. Fizpatrick (seneschall of Ibrackane aforesaid, and then and now receaver to the Earle of Thomond within the said Barony). That he saw and observed the said parties in armes at the seidge of the said castle, and divers times consulting and advising howe to surprise the same.

By the end of the Parliamentarians' vengeful campaign of 1651/2 most of Clare had been left 'totally ruinated and deserted by the inhabitants thereof', and we do not know how Rickard the seneschal came through, or whether he suffered any penalty for his part (if he was actually involved) in the massacre of his neighbours and clients at Tromra. The next generation of Fitzpatricks was located, not in Clare, but in Aran. The earliest of them to be commemorated on the Cill Éinne monuments are the John Fitz-patrick who Hardiman says died possessed of a cellarful of riches, his wife Sara and son Rickard. One assumes, without proof, that John is the son of Rickard the seneschal, and therefore, cynically, that the latter had done well out of the war.

Aran, of course passed into Protestant hands after the Cromwellians' victory. By 1686 John and his son Rickard were leasing the islands from a Sir Stephen Fox, former Paymaster of the Forces under Charles II. John was living in 'Loughmore', which is Ceathrú na Locha, the quarter of the lake, the nearest part of Inis Oírr to the Clare coast. Nowadays this would be regarded as an eccentrically reclusive address for a rich man, but at that period seaways were still more passable than land routes, and Inis Oírr, commanding a principal opening of Galway Bay, probably saw much traf-fic. Infestations of French privateers, though, were grounds for abatement of rent. John died in February and Sara in November of 1709 – but the year began in March until the calendar reform of 1754, so it was John, not Sara, who was widowed. Hence no doubt, Sara's separate little monument, made redundant by Patrick and Margrett's later and grander retrospective memorializing but for some reason left standing.

In the next generation the family fortunes were assured by intermar-riage with three of the fourteen great merchant families known as the Tribes of Galway. Rickard married Joan French of Spiddle (An Spidéal, a village nine miles west of Galway), a sister married George Morris (one of whose descendants, Lord Killanin, takes his title from the Parish of Cill Ainthín, west of Spiddle), and the second son Edmund married Annable, daughter of Richard Martin, the famous 'Nimble Dick' who had obtained much of the vast territories confiscated from the O'Flahertys in Connemara and, although a Catholic, had been confirmed in possession of the largest directly owned estate in the Three Kingdoms.

In 1713 Fox sold Aran to Edmund Fitzpatrick and Simon Digby, the Protestant bishop of Elphin, and Bishop Digby leased his moiety to Edmond, who thus became effectively the landlord. Edmund died in about 1717, leaving a son, another Rickard or Richard. Edmund's widow soon married the historian Roderic O'Flaherty's son Michael. This must have been a troubled alliance, for her father Nimble Dick Martin had swindled Roderic out of five hundred acres, the only portion of the former O'Fla-herty lands remaining to him after the post-Cromwellian settlement, and Michael was pursuing the matter through the courts at the time. In the event, her husband won his case against her father, and in 1736 assigned the estate to his stepson, Rickard Fitzpatrick.

This Rickard (or Richard, again) became sheriff of Galway in 1730, so he was probably the first of the family to become, at least in form, a Protestant. The trade of the city had been savagely curtailed by penal legislation against its Catholic merchants, and by the Wool Acts passed by the English Parliament in 1689 and 1698, prohibiting the exportation of woollen goods from Ireland. While Rickard was sheriff an attempt was made by the Galway council to persuade Parliament to designate the city as a port for the exportation of wool; this failed, but no doubt the council, which included several people sympathetic to the oppressed Catholic interest, turned a blind eye to certain moonlight activities, and in 1737 an informer reported to the authorities as follows:

Richard Fitzpatrick of Aran Esq. has so much a year from the King and he sees all this wool transported and he gives the runners no hindrance, for he has done well by the runners; he gets good bribes from them.

The accusation of corruption did him no harm, it seems, for in 1738 he was elected Mayor and later became one of Galway's two representatives in the Irish Parliament. In 1744 he sold his moiety of the islands to the Digbys, and died in 1767 without issue.

According to Hardiman, Edmond Fitzpatrick, sheriff of Galway in 1769 and 1797, was the nephew of Rickard, but this conflicts with accounts implying that Rickard was an only son; perhaps this Edmond was a son of Rickard's cousin Patrick (of the monument). Edmond himself had one son, James, who died without issue, and since Hardiman (who was born in 1790 and was the librarian of Queen's College, Galway) did not know of the existence of any of the family in his own times, it must, as he says, have sunk into obscurity.

But it seems that it was not extinct. There are Fitzpatricks in Aran today – one family in Gort na gCapall and another in Cill Rónáin – and the evidence for a link between the former, at least, and the old 'Fitzpatricks of Aran' is tenuous, but somehow convincing. I quote from an unpublished history of Aran written by the parish priest, Fr Thomas Killeen, at the behest of his archbishop in 1948:

There is an Aran tradition that the Fitzpatricks lived in Aran till 1798 in the house later occupied by Martin O'Malley. ... Páidín Ó Confhaola of Inishmaan, now nearly 80, told me that one day he was in Clare with his father a *fuireacht caladh* [storm-bound]. They met a very old man, who asked if any of the Fitzpatricks were still there. Páidín said there was a family of that name in Gort na gCapall. 'Yes,' said the old man, 'the family had to fly in the year of the Fleet Franncach, and one of them went to Gort na gCapall.' This meeting must have been in 1880-90 and the old man's birth 1800-10. ... What they did in 1798 is unknown.'

One might guess that what they did in that 'Year of the French' was to harbour rebels, for after the French fleet landed at Killala in Mayo and unleashed an unsuccessful Irish rebellion, many of the 'United Irishmen' fled into the mountains of Connemara from the yeomanry's revenge on Mayo, and some even crossed to Aran. It is said that a French officer was hidden by the O'Flahertys of Cill Mhuirbhigh, and if the Fitzpatricks were implicated in something of that sort they may well have had to leave the neighbourhood of the Cill Éinne garrison and bury themselves among the peasantry.

By what narrow paths between the gulfs of oblivion does even the basis of this speculation come down to us! An archbishop has the happy idea of asking his clergy to write up the history of their parishes; most of them never get down to the uncongenial task, but the Aran priest finds his vocation in it. An old islander recalls for him a tale heard in his youth while waiting for the wind to drop, in Fisherstreet, which he would have known as Sráid na nIascairí, near Doolin in County Clare. The tale is one an old Clareman remembers being discussed over his head when he was a child, not long after the Year of the French. And the hearsay that has been handed down in this way could well be mistaken, just as the accusation concerning the seneschal at the sack of Tromra could well be false.

As to the rest of the people named on the monuments, by juggling dates and ages I arrive at this: of Patrick, that he was, most likely, one of the four sons of Richard the son of John; of the three youths who died in one winter, that they were probably the sons of Patrick and Margrett (two of their names occur in Hardiman's account among those of Patrick's brothers, and whether this means he had evidence unavailable to me, or merely got as confused as I did in this maggoty-headed antiquarian pursuit of the lost generations, I cannot tell); and finally of Florence, died 1709, nothing.

What then do I recover of the Fitzpatricks of Aran, by bringing my books and arithmetic to bear on the two grey pillars on the hillside? At the best, lacunary personages, short of perhaps a birth-date or a definite relationship to another family member, or of any other of the properties as necessary to full existence as a definite weight or height, or a shadow. A life's story is completed at or by death, but then begins its career of disintegration. The intangibility of ghosts is our ignorance of the dead; to pray for a soul is to wish it a life whole enough to be recognized. Recognized, at least, as one of ourselves, with our meaningless titles and void relationships and self-forgotten histories.

TALES FROM THE HILL

Killeany Lodge stands only a hundred and fifty yards from the Fitzpatricks'
cenotaphs, and according to the tradition preserved by Fr Killeen was their
home until 1798. However, a tale taken down in the 1930s from a Connemara storyteller asserts that it was built by a smuggler called O'Malley
from An Caorán on the Ceathrú Rua headland of south Connemara, just
opposite Aran. Certainly by the 1820s the O'Malleys had succeeded the
Fitzpatricks as tenants of the Hill Farm, as the four hundred acres that went
with the house were called. There is probably truth in both versions, and
perhaps a core of older masonry is to be found in the fabric of the present
Georgian farmhouse. This is a plain one-storied building with a small fan-
lit porch facing east, and ramshackle outhouses and gapped orchard walls
to the rear. High on the north gable wall, eyeing one's approach from the
village, is a little diamond-shaped loft window that twinkles with a racon-
teur's anticipation of a new audience for old anecdotes; it suggests a voice,
a tone, that might tempt the past to show itself:

Smugglers and rebels, all those Connemara O'Malleys, descended from Grace
O'Malley's piratical crew, the O'Malleys of Mayo. Odd corners of Connemara –
Ballynakill, Streamstown, Bunowen – were thriving in those days; wool going out,
wine and brandy and tobacco and silk coming in, common boatmen pluming
themselves in *éadach uasal*, upper-class clothes, tailcoats, knee breeches, silk cra-
vats from Guernsey, the funny old high hats they called carolines. Máirtín Mór,
the great O'Malley of An Caorán, was famous for old-style hospitality – always a
cask of wine in his house, the lid off and permission for all to fill their cup, and
when he killed a cow or a sheep the whole beast would be eaten before he needed
to salt it. He was only a *ceithearnach*, a middleman, though; his landlord was
Colonel Martin, great-grandson of that Nimble Dick who grabbed all Connemara. The Colonel was a great man in Dublin and in London – it was the
Prince Regent nicknamed him Humanity Dick for his kindness to animals – but
for the Connemara folk his highest honour was to have O'Malley as his tenant.
Tom Moore mentions the Colonel –

> Oh! place me 'midst O'Rourkes, O'Tooles,
> The ragged royal blood of Tara;
> Or place me where DICK M-RT-N rules
> The houseless wilds of CONNEMARA –

– but it was Blind Raftery himself put O'Malley in a poem, and that's real fame.

'Fiach Sheáin Bhradaigh', the hunting of scoundrely Seán, another wandering ragged balladeer and a rival of Raftery's. Raftery has him run out by the hunting gentry, tallyhoing him all round Mayo, up Croagh Patrick, down to the butt end of Connemara. Then Seán takes a boat to Aran, O'Malley drives him off to Kinvara, and in the end he's torn to bits by the hounds of the Galway Blazers.

This O'Malley died in a duel. He had the Bishop of Kilmacduach to dinner one day – a day of abstinence, so it was fish for the Bishop, but without thinking O'Malley poured meat gravy on it. The bishop just put his plate aside without remark – but his nephew Lord French heard of it and took it as an insult; he challenged O'Malley and killed him with his first shot. Colonel Martin was a great duellist himself – his other nickname was Hairtrigger Dick – but he was sad about this duel. 'O'Malley preferred a hole in his guts to one in his honour,' he said, 'but there wouldn't have been a hole in either if I'd been told of it.'

Martin O'Malley, O'Malley of the Hill as they called him, was Máirtín Mór's nephew. His brother Pat was an excise man, travelling round Connemara collecting taxes, married a low-born Cill Éinne woman Martin disapproved of and sent his children to the hedge-school in Cill Rónáin. Pat's daughter Mary must have been born in 1840 because she was 68 when the Old Age Pension came in in 1908. Martin O'Malley died some time before the Famine; they say he's buried somewhere on the Hill. Then his wife – he'd married a Miss D'Arcy of the Dublin Distillery family – had the farm. When she was old and doddery the O'Flaherty of Kilmurvey made her an offer for the lease of it, a hundred pounds a year for the rest of her life. He reckoned she wouldn't last long, but she hung on for sixteen years, and he was so disgusted with his bargain he never did much with the land.

Then the O'Flaherty died, and his son James died, and James's son-in-law was drinking the estate. He tried to sell the lease of the Hill Farm to the Congested Districts Board but nothing came of that because the rent was too high and the Digbys wouldn't reduce it. But the idea that the land should be bought out for the islanders was in the air, and the priest set up a branch of the United Irish League to press for it. They started refusing to pay their rents, and Roger Dirrane the bailiff – the fellow who invented those rain-tanks – was frightened to try and collect in case they boycotted the pub he had in Cill Éinne. Roger was in charge of letting out the grass of the Hill Farm. When Fr Farragher finally persuaded the CDB to buy it out for the poor fishermen, Dirrane felt he should have got the land himself, and he started a quarrel with the priest. That was the Time of the Saucepans, June 1908. A terrible bang in the middle of the night – they'd bombed the priest's house! Unfortunately Farragher was away, but his sister and the servant-girl got such a fright they didn't put their heads out till morning. Sittingroom window blown in, plaster dust everywhere – and bits of a saucepan on the windowsill. The RIC searched Dirrane's shed on the quayside and found the tin cans they'd mixed the gunpowder in. They arrested him and a relative, Fitzmartin. Dirrane had an alibi – a woman swore she'd seen him in his pub – but he got three years anyway, and the other man got three months. That wasn't enough revenge for the PP though. He named them from the altar, refused confession to anyone who had anything to do with them or their families. So all the 'Saucepans' – the Dirrane faction, *'Lucht na Tincans'*, the tincan lot – stopped paying their dues. Great ructions! It gave Liam O'Flaherty the idea for a book. The PP of course was President of the League, and he used it to get the Tinnies boycotted. One of the Galway newspapers said he was as big an autocrat as the Tzar of Russia!

There were some rebels, though. Costelloe's donkey needed shoeing, but Costelloe was boycotted and the Cill Rónáin blacksmith wouldn't do it. Costelloe had hopes of the Oatquarter smith, King. He saw him on the pier one day and tested him out tactfully – walked up and down past him saying he'd have to send his donkey to Galway on the steamer with a label round its neck. 'I'll put shoes on it for you,' said King, 'and I won't do it before dawn either, or after the sun has set, but in broad daylight!'

The boycott divided the island, engagements were broken off and so on; there were lots of old bachelors and maids among the Saucepans in the end. And suicide attempts. Mrs Macdonagh found her son trying to hang himself, had to get the police to cut him down. He'd lost his job on the hulk the CDB stored ice in because he spoke to a Saucepan, and he was replaced by two members of the League. So politics came into it, and the Unionists took it up. Questions asked in Parliament, even! 'Is my honorable friend the Chief Secretary for Ireland aware...?' The Saucepans made Westminster aware of this ridiculous little island! Some of the islanders still respect them for their defiance – I heard someone saying not long ago the bomber was 'before his time'!

Fair play to the Saucepans, though, they stood up to the priests! After he came out of prison Roger Dirrane was walking up the Carcair one day, and one of the clergy went by, squeezed himself into the wall to keep as far off him as he could. Roger looked round at him, and the priest turned on him and said 'Only for I don't like, I'd put horns on you!' – people still believed the priests could do that, in those days, maybe some of the priests half believed it too. But Roger wasn't afraid. 'And if you did,' he said, 'I'd ram them up your backside!' – And once a cow of his died, and a lad from Cill Éinne helped him bury it. Farragher cornered the lad later on – in Bóithrín an Bhabhúin, that little dead-end by the castle – and told him off for helping with the cow. The lad's father came along, and he said to the priest, 'If there'd been an 'altar' on it, you'd have been there yourself!' – the altar is money collected at funerals for the priest.

So that's the history of the Hill for you. I suppose we'll never know if it was really Dirrane that served up the gunpowder sauce to the priest! The fishermen got the stripes of land in the end, the boycott faded out, Farragher was moved to Athenry. The old lodge used to be let out now and again to summer visitors. In the Twenties the 'Lá Breás' came and went – teachers doing Irish language courses; all the Irish they had was *'Lá breá!'*, 'fine day!', so they said it to everybody whatever the weather. Then for the most part the place was empty and falling to bits. Now it's all spick and span, thanks to Celtic Spirituality – but that's another story.

Those are the tales from the Hill I have picked up here and there –

from a book of Connemara folklore, from an old, bedridden lady in Cill Rónáin, from the Aran postman met on the road – and strung together as a dinner-table amusement. But such anecdotes handle their subjects so uncaringly, dismissing them with holes in their honour, reducing them to single utterances of the sort that acquire a polish through retelling, that even the amateur enquirer into little local histories owes them better treatment. On professional historians, ambassadors of the past to present times, devolves the solemn duty of representing it in its integrity, but the humblest attaché in the Embassy of the Dead is also sent to lie abroad for his country, and must do his best with scrappy briefings.

While I was mapping the south Connemara coast I looked for traces of the smuggler O'Malley in the townland of An Caorán Beag (which means 'the small moorland hill'), a mile or so south of the modern town of An Cheathrú Rua. A side-road serves the few houses of a village still called An Diméin, the demesne, and then becomes a grassy track between granite knolls and boggy hollows criss-crossed by dry-stone walls, going down towards the sea and the three grey silhouettes of the Aran Islands on the horizon. Within sight of the head of an inlet are traces of old walls, the remains of the O'Malley home, which the Ordnance Survey map of 1898 names as 'Keeraun House'. I had been told about a chair-like rock called Suístín Uí Mháille, O'Malley's little seat, from which he used to watch his sloop unloading in the creek below, but I failed to locate it and perhaps it has been removed to straighten the track. Presumably he was elderly when he sat there, no longer relishing the seas, happier dispensing the rough hospitality of scoops from the winecask and cuts from the freshly killed beast to his admiring followers, or looking forward to a meal intended to be more elegant, with the Bishop of Kilmacduach. How did he view his trade? His landlord Richard Martin was a Member of Parliament, first in Dublin and then at Westminster, having voted for the Act of Union in 1800. No doubt a proportion of O'Malley's silks and brandy went to Martin's house twenty miles away in the wilds of Ballynahinch; in 1796 the Chief Secretary for Ireland was informed that 'Mr Martin's command of smugglers and fishermen cannot be less than a thousand', and that the chief under him was 'one O'Mealy, an old venerable man'. Such feudal prerogatives merely added the spice of the illicit to the Colonel's urbanity in the ballrooms of London and Paris, but perhaps for O'Malley, on his bare Connemara foreland, smuggling had a deeper meaning, and the sloops nosing into the familiar muddy creeks of his black economy had in their sails winds from the age of the unconquered O'Malleys of old. '*Terra marique potens*', a power by land and sea, was the motto of his seafaring ancestors; I hear him mumbling it to himself as I stroll down the green track by his little throne in the rock.

O'Malley of the Hill Farm is less recoverable to the imagination. The census of 1821 shows him in place: 'Martin O Maley, 32, Gentleman Farmer'; also Mary Anne, his wife, his brother Pat, a 'gentleman' called Pat Taylor, two servants, and living close by is his herdsman. It is noted that O'Malley holds a large tract of land in the Parish of Kilcummin (this would have been the demesne in An Caorán Beag) plus a large parcel of land in the Parish of Ballindoon (and this would have been the O'Malley territory near Slyne Head in the south-western tip of Connemara). Pat, the déclassé brother who married locally, I see as loitering between the Lodge and the village, neither one thing nor the other, ready to latch onto any chance comer. I owe this picture, probably quite false, to George Petrie, who met him in 1821:

The proprietor of the islands is of course an absentee. The aristocracy may be said to consist of two gentlemen, who claim the title more from ancient family rank than from wealth or landed possessions. We had no opportunity of becoming acquainted with Mr. O'Mally. His brother, a worthy Araner, met us on the shore at our landing, and conducted us to the house of Mr. O'Flaherty, to whom we had previously signified, through a friend, our intention of becoming his guests, and in the free spirit of the place, stayed with us for some days to add to our hilarity and comforts.

By 1857, according to Griffith's Valuation, Hill Quarter was occupied by a Maryanne O'Malley; presumably this is the Mary Anne of the census, now a widow. I have no image of this dowager, long withering out O'Flaherty's bargain; perhaps she retired to Dublin on the strength of his hundred pounds per annum and enjoyed her uncalled-for longevity there.

Other protagonists in the later anecdotes of the Hill Farm, such as the Kilmurvey O'Flahertys and Fr Farragher, will figure in various contexts further on in this book. The Saucepan episode was filled out with a bitter realism about island mentalities by Liam O'Flaherty, in his novel *Skerrett*, and Roger Dirrane, deservedly or not, will have to live with the character O'Flaherty gave him in this *roman-à-clef* (the key to which is simple enough: Moclair is Farragher, Ardcaol is Cill Éinne and Griffin is Dirrane):

This young man was very ambitious and greedy, quite of the priest's own kidney; so that, at first, they got on very well together. ... Now Griffin, becoming bailiff of the Ardcaol estate through Father Moclair's influence, suffered his ambition to develop into a mania, like the frog that tried to swell into an ox. He wanted the estate for himself.

Liam's childhood coincided with the period in which Fr Farragher was beating the island like a recalcitrant donkey along the road to modernity; he served as altar-boy to the priest, while his schoolmaster, David Callaghan, was the original of Skerret, the progressively unhinged champion of 'Republican nationalism, anarchism, and the cause of the Irish Language'. According to Fr Killeen, Liam's family, the O'Flahertys of Gort na gCapall, supported the Saucepan faction, and 'as a result developed a bitter anticlerical attitude. Liam's filthy novels illustrate the fact. Possibly there was unnecessary antagonism on the side of the angels.' But there are no angels in Liam O'Flaherty's world; it is the violent and overbearing who are the carriers of history. In his version of the Saucepan events, which he uses to precipitate the culminating struggle between priest and schoolmaster, the origin of Griffin's swelling ambition is clear:

[Moclair's] avarice made life unpleasant and set an evil example to these simple islanders, who were quick to imitate their pastor's character. Indeed, great though the beauty of a march towards civilisation may be, whether on a gigantic scale like that of the Greeks and of the Elizabethan English, or on a small scale, like that of this handful of islanders, the beauty is always stained by the demons which the advance lets loose. It seems a people cannot progress without losing their innocence in the cunning necessary for ambitious commerce; and that avarice brings in its train dissention, strife and manifold corruption.

So it was the demons of progress that puffed up the simple frog to its pathetic little explosion.

When the land was subdivided the Lodge was sold off by the Land Commission to a Mr Smith, the representative of a British trawler company resident in Cill Rónáin, and later sold on by him to the McDonaghs of the pub by Cill Rónáin harbour. It was briefly the home of Coláiste Gaeilge Mhic Phiarais, which had been founded in Galway in 1919, and after a few years in Cill Éinne moved to Na Forbacha six miles west of Galway. In more recent years, left to the damp in the winter and subjected to raucous holiday lettings in the summer, it became more and more delapidated. Then, suddenly, in 1986, these deleterious atmospheres were replaced by the holy and the ecologically sound. The Lodge became the headquarters of an interdenominational community called Aisling Árann (roughly, Aran vision), led by Fr Dara Molloy and inspired by the early Celtic Christianity whose memorials are all around one in Cill Éinne. Now it has been beautifully restored, and offers its hospitality to anyone ready to share its frugal and spiritual lifestyle.

But that took place after I had left the island, and for this and other reasons I do not feel competent to assess the transformation. Therefore, to end with, I go back to another vision of Aran, from the Lodge's dozy middle years. In May 1895 two ladies in their thirties took it for a fortnight's holiday: Edith Oenone Somerville and her cousin Violet Martin. Each was the daughter of a Big House, Edith of Drishane in Castle Townshend, Cork, and Violet of Ross House on the Galway side of Connemara. (The Martins of Ross were the senior line, from which that of Ballynahinch had diverged in the time of Nimble Dick.) The literary partnership of 'Somerville and Ross', which through the medium of Edith's 'automatic writing' was mysteriously to outlive Violet herself, had then been in existence some six years. Their equally longer-than-life love, which perhaps only revealed itself in the automatisms which haunt all writing, breathes in their account of this vernal fortnight, when 'land and sea lay in rapt accord, and the breast of the brimming tide was laid to the breast of the cliff, with a low and broken voice of joy.'

If the Aran landscape proved worthy of their sensitive natures, most of its human aspects only awoke their patrician and sometimes overwrought sense of humour. Life at the Lodge on the hill, they wrote, had 'aspects that were wholly ideal, and aspects that were unreservedly scullion.' Among the latter were the pampootied and beshawled creature that began the 'strange, arduous, trifling day' by coming in with a bucket and the monosyllabic announcement: 'bath', and a glance of saturnine amusement at 'the weakling of a later civilization still in bed'; the lack of saucepans, obliging them to boil their eggs in a portly black pot and fish them out with the tongs; the 'tall, brindled dogs that gnawed sapless bones in the porch, as in an accustomed sanctuary'; the tactless cuckoo sending its hoarse and hollow cry down the chimney – 'Not thus does the spirit voice poise the twin notes in tireless mystery, among the wooded shores of Connemara's lakes.' Ideal, though, was the outlook from the chief windows across a plain of sea to that beloved homeland:

When, at some ten of the clock the rooms in the lonely house had passed from gloaming to darkness, and the paraffin lamp glared smokily at the semi-grand piano and the horsehair sofa, the wild and noble outline of Connemara was still sharp, the gleam behind it still a harbourage for the day.

A fitting hour for the séances it is said they held in the Lodge, but of which they left no record. Perhaps on such evenings they called up Florence Fitzpatrick, so uninformatively memorialized by her relatives, and had her tell her story, or materialized O'Malley of the Hill, to find what manner of man he was. For the Lodge is full of ghosts unamenable to the séances of history.

THE INVISIBLE TOWER

Tangible and intangible, the remains of St Enda's monastery are all around one, along the track between the Lodge and the village. Three miscellaneous vertical objects form a line leading the eye up the hill to the west: nearest the track, in a hayfield, the shaft of a high cross; on a terrace of the hillside beyond that, the drum-like stump of a round tower; and perched on the crest of the slope, a little oratory, roofless, its two gables sharp against the sky. On the other side of the track, to the east, hummocks and ridges in the grass sketch vague plans of sizeable buildings. A thousand yards beyond them the cemetery by the sea is visible, in which is the church known as Teaghlach Éinne, Enda's household, half buried in the sand. Ecclesiastical stones are secreted here and there in the village. The sill of a musket-loop in Cromwell's castle wears a Latin cross as the badge of its previous career; an octagonal wayside pillar lies in the tide below; another cross-inscribed block retrieved by an antiquary schoolmaster decorates the garden of the one-time teacher's residence, together with a few 'bullaun stones', small granite boulders with bowl-shaped hollows, thought to have been used by the monks as mortars. The walls of one or two little haggarts over the road from the castle ruins are draped in clambering hops which may have rambled on since the days when the Franciscan brothers brewed their own beer. Until recent years these leafy vines proved useful to the villager gathering seaweed for his potato patch, who would lay wads of them on his horse's back under the wooden straddle to protect its hide from the trickling salt water. Like this relict plant, once the bearer of modest religious indulgence, and the crumbs of fallen churches that serve as doorstops, even the miracle tales which once magnified the saints and through them the Lord are nowadays dedicated to lesser ends, and furnish a couple of lines for a holiday brochure or a joke for tourists in the bar. These fragments – of architecture, life's modes, ultimate meanings – appeal to the renovating mind. A vast vacant axis, the absence of the round tower from which St Enda's bell was rung, centres his scattered patrimony. Reconstruction is as impossible as climbing its spiral stairs of empty air. I begin the task on the eastern rim of the broken circuit, at the chapel foundering in the dunes of the graveyard.

This outlier of monastic Cill Éinne is a simple rectangular building measuring about nineteen feet by ten inside. All of it is present save the roof, and perhaps it survived the Cromwellians' depradations because of its distance from Arkin Castle. In the eastern gable wall is a narrow little window of Early Christian style, its round head formed in a single stone. Clearly this end of the church dates from a time when stone churches were so new an idea, at least in Aran, that their builders were still constrained by the forms of wooden structures, for the side-walls are continued six inches or so beyond the gable-wall to form a pillar running up either side of it like the corner-post of a wooden chapel. These 'antae', as they are called, may not have been totally superfluous features, though, as they could have supported the barge-boards or end-timbers of a wooden roof projecting over the gables and giving them some shelter from rain. This east gable and part of the north wall are of very large slabs set on edge (one of them is a good ten feet long), and in general appear to be very early. Professor Waddell of Galway suggests the ninth century, whereas Peter Harbison thinks there is little evidence that any of the Aran churches are earlier than the twelfth century, and mortar from the masonry of the old part of Teaghlach Éinne has recently been radio-carbon-dated to the eleventh or twelfth century. There is a small round-headed window near the eastern end of this wall, and the big squarish slab in the wall under it under it carries an Old Irish inscription: OROIT AR SCANDLAN, a prayer for Scandlan. The window looks later than the one in the gable, and perhaps there was some reconstruction of the chapel even in this early phase, for the inscribed slab has evidently been moved and is set on its side so that the inscription runs vertically, with scant regard for Scandlan. The present ground level outside the church lies above this slab, but in recent times the sand has been dug out from in front of it so that the inscription can be read.

The rest of the church is of the more easily handled blocks indicative of a later period, when perhaps common sense had prevailed over the zeal that drove the early monks to megalithic excesses. The door, at the west end of the north wall, belongs to this later westward expansion of the church and has a slightly pointed arch of late medieval style, each side of which is a single curved stone. Two square-topped window openings also belong to the same period, one in the south wall and another in the west gable. The date of this enlargement of the church could well be 1666, when the last of the great chieftains of Connemara was buried here. He was Sir Morough O'Flaherty of Bunowen Castle, known in Irish as Murchadh na Mart, Morough of the 'beeves' or fatted cattle. For his part in the rebellion of 1641 Sir Morough had been dispossessed of his vast estates, and he retired to Aran where he died in poverty. He must have been witness of the final desolation of St Enda's monastery, the long-deserted buildings of which had recently been quarried for stone to rebuild the castle at Cill Éinne. Perhaps the already ancient church in the graveyard was also disused by that time, and he thought to save it by having it reconstructed as his mortuary chapel.

Since then both the Early Christian and late medieval portions of Teaghlach Éinne have been progressively overwhelmed by blowing sand. Nowadays the door is largely below ground-level, and until recent years one had to scramble down a steep hollow to enter, inevitably followed by avalanching sand-grains. Left to itself the interior would fill like an hour-glass in a decade or two. During an archaeological investigation of the church in 1984, the Office of Public Works took a commonsensical stand against this process and had a trench dug all round the church, robbing it of a most evocative feature, the timescape seen through its little south window of the layered depths of sand blocking it on the outside.

If the light is right as one enters the church, certain shallow markings in a block at head-height just west of the door may catch the eye. This block is a little pillar-like cross-slab which as recently as 1952 was standing inside the church and has been recycled to fill the place of a missing quoin-stone, without respect for the sacred symbol on it, which now lies hori-zontally. The grooves forming its linear cross and the two concentric circles around the junction of the arms and shaft are as simple as fingertip tracings on sea-washed sand. Another small slab like this one, but with a single-ringed cross on either face, was found partly underlying a modern grave-surround near the church in the course of the 1984 investigations. Despite their great age, such Early Christian cross-inscribed slabs, of which there are about twenty to be seen in and around Aran's churches, have the fresh-ness of works from the first decade of modern abstract art, and in one or two of them Kandinsky would have recognized a spiritual fervour behind the ingenuous charm of their oddly balanced crosses and circles.

Other figured stones rescued from the village have been assembled in the church. Some are cemented into the simple altar under the east window, and one of these has a spiral motif incised in it which is dark from the touch of hands lifted to it in prayer. Another has a rudimentary Latin cross and, in the four quarters into which this divides most of its surface, these cryptic syllables (reading clockwise): BENT, DIE, FAN, and SCAN. Expanded according to the customary rules of such time-saving messages to eternity, this says 'Bendacht die for ainm Sanctan', God's blessing on the soul of Sanctan. This stone was found face-down in the church in 1936 by Cill Éinne's national school-teacher, James Donnellan. (I mention such facts, if I happen to know them, not out of pedantry but in recognition of the way in which the patina of history is built up of individual finger-prints.)

Just inside the door the same schoolmaster assembled three fragments of a high cross, cemented together one above the other to make a little pillar. Two of these were rescued by the Aran doctor, O'Brien, when they were on site for use in the building of cottages in Cill Éinne, where they had long been lying in the ruins of the castle – and so this is at least their fourth phase of existence. The other was found, heavily whitewashed, built into a cottage garden-wall. They have been shown to belong to the cross-shaft in the field below the round tower, which itself is not in its original (and unknown) location. One of these fragments has the figure of a horse and rider in relief on it, blackened like the spiral in the altar by the hands of people kneeling in prayer beside it. It would be interesting to know what meanings have been seen or felt in this motif over the centuries, for it has been suggested that it bore a very definite ideological charge when the cross was carved. According to a study by Liam de Paor this fragmentary cross shares a number of characteristics with the high crosses in two ecclesiastical centres of north Clare, Kilfenora and Dysart O'Dea. The styles of the abstract and animal ornamentation on it are close enough to those of the Kilfenora crosses to suggest that they are by the same hand or at least from the same workshop; for instance a particular square labyrinth-pattern on the part of the cross-shaft near the round tower also occurs on what is called the West Cross at Kilfenora, but is unknown outside this group. Below this square fret on the Cill Éinne shaft is a panel filled by four scrolls, which on close examination one can make out to be coiled-up animals with little ears and large jaws; and below this again is a purely abstract panel of shell-like spirals; these motifs are Scandinavian in origin, and may indicate that the mason had connections with the Scandinavian-influenced areas of northern Britain. Earlier high crosses such as those at Kells and Clonmacnois usually had their surfaces divided into a number of panels illustrating scriptural incidents, but this local group of limestone crosses are of a late eleventh- or twelfth-century type in which one face carries a large figure of the crucified Christ, and in a number of cases the other side figures an equally large clerical figure, as in the famous Doorty cross at Kilfenora. (And since Dr de Paor's article, Françoise Henry has published a tentative reconstruction of the Cill Éinne cross, in which the missing central portion has a crucified Christ on one side and an ecclesiastic with a crozier on the other; most of this portion is missing, but hints towards it remain on the other fragments.) Whether the cleric represents a bishop or a pope (the experts disagree) his authoritarian stance may reflect the reforms in church administration initiated by Pope Gregory VII, under which the abbots of the ancient monastic foundations lost their power over church affairs to the bishops in their sees. The figure of the mounted horseman is also known from east Scotland, and recurrs on the Doorty cross, where it seems to be riding over a church-like building. Given the apocalyptic terms in which the Gregorian reformers fulminated against monkish laxity, this may represent the terrible rider of the Apocalypse of St John, who will tread out 'the wine-press whose wine is the avenging anger of Almighty God'.

A fragment of another high cross was found under about two feet of sand just east of the church by Conleth Manning, director of the 1984 investigations. It consists of the central and upper portion of the cross plus one arm, with part of the ring that linked the arms and shaft. On one side is an abstract, interlace ornament and on the other a crucifixion, both carved in relief. A naive Christ with a big doll-like head occupies the hub of the cross, and on the surviving arm of the cross is a peculiar little manikin crouched under Christ's outstretched hand, holding a pole with a cup on it: Stephaton, the Roman soldier who offered Christ the sponge. Only the head and arm survive of his traditionally opposite number, Longinus, who is thrusting his spear into Christ's side. This is the only known example of a high cross in which these two attendant figures are placed on the arms so that the crucifixion scene spans the full width of the crosspiece. The prominence of the crucifixion again suggests the twelfth century. Most probably there were several such high crosses around the monastery. Originally they would have been painted, and in the severe Aran light they must have been very dominating presences. But to my mind, and even disregarding the tentative interpretation of the late crosses of Clare and Aran in terms of the imposition of diocesan structures, high crosses in general are unlovely assertions of authority. What is most worth saving from the sands of time of the spirit of Cill Éinne is the metaphysical wit of the earlier cross-inscribed slabs.

Four churches have totally vanished from the core of the Cill Éinne settlement; their exact sites are unknown but, thanks to the devotion of two churchmen and the intervention of pure chance, their names have been preserved. During the early years of the 1640s John Colgan, a Franciscan teacher in the University of Louvain, was labouring to fulfil a command to collect the lives of the Irish saints. Fr Colgan wrote up all the saints with feast-days in January, February and March, but never took this systematic attack further. Fortunately St Enda's day is the 21st of March. At about the same time the Archbishop of Tuam and Confederate leader, Dr Malachy O'Cadhla, made a list of the churches of his archdiocese, as if he foresaw his own defeat and death in battle in 1645 and the great levelling of churches that was to follow the Cromwellian victory. The diligent Colgan had obtained from Dr O'Cadhla the relevant part of his list of churches, which he appended to the *Life of St Enda* and which is the only part of the list to have survived. So, in *Acta Sanctorum Hiberniae* (Louvain, 1645) we

have the following, from 'a tabular description of the churches of the diocese of Tuam, lately transmitted to us, and faithfully written by the most
illustrious lord Malachias Quaelaeus, archbishop of Tuam, a man distinguished for his zeal in religion, and endowed with every virtue; extracted as
they lie':

1. The parish church (to wit of the first island) commonly called *Kill-Enda*, lies in
the county of Galway and the half barony of Aran; and in it St. Endeus, or Enna,
is venerated as patron, on the 21st of March.

2. The church called Teglach-Enda, to which is annexed a cemetery, wherein is the
sepulchre of St. Endeus; with one hundred and twenty-seven other sepulchres,
wherein none but saints were ever buried.

3. The church called *Tempull mac Longa*, dedicated to St. Mac Longius, is situated
near the parish church, which is called sometimes *Kill-enda*, that is the cella or cell
of St. Endeus, and sometimes *Tempull mor Enda*, or the great church of Endeus.

4. The church called *Tempull mic Canonn*, near the aforesaid parish church.

5. The church called of St. Mary, not far from the same parish church.

6. The church which is named Tempull Benain, or the Temple of St. Benignus.

... and the list continues with seven other churches farther east in the island, two in Inis Meáin, and three churches and a former monastery in Inis
Oírr.

   The second of the Cill Éinne churches on this list is (in modern Irish)
Teaghlach Éinne, and the sixth is Teampall Bheannáin, the little oratory on
the skyline to the west. Of the missing churches, three would have belonged to the ancient monastery: the parish church, Cill Éinne, from which
the village takes its name, and two presumably smaller chapels close to it.
The 'Mac Longius' to whom one of these was dedicated might be the same
as the St Mac Luagna, mentioned by Colgan as a brother of St Ciaráin and
the successor of St Enda as abbot. Equally dubiously, the 'Mac Canonn' of
the other chapel might have some connection with St Gregory of Inis
Meáin, who is known in Connemara as St Ceannan or Ceannanach.

   The fourth missing church, St Mary's, must have been the chapel of the
Franciscans' monastery, for the old annals of the order state that it was *sub
vocatione Sanctae Mariae Virginis et omnium Sanctorum*. Very little has been
recorded of the history of the Franciscans in Aran, except that they came in
1485, probably under the patronage of the O'Briens, and that they were of
the Third Order. Perhaps they took over the buildings of St Enda's foundation, which may have been deserted by that date. O'Flaherty supposes
that the line of St Enda's successors in Aran continued unbroken to 'the

time of the suppression of abbeys', *i.e.* the reign of Henry VIII (who was declared King of Ireland in 1541), but the last of these successors he found mentioned in his sources (lost, it seems, to us) was 'Donatus O'Leyn, abbot of Aran, Anno Domini 1400'. Long before Henry's time, though, the abbeys of the old Gaelic church, torn between the English colony and the resurgent Gaelic chiefdoms, were in decline, and by the early sixteenth century both Clonmacnois and Armagh were almost deserted and open to the sky, and the word of God had been largely abandoned to the vigorous hands of the friars of the European orders. When the Franciscans came to Aran they may have found St Enda's sunk in weeds and torpor; in 1506 their report was that 'in the islands of Aran of the Saints ... things of the church are neglected and there is ignorance of Christian doctrines.' Nothing seems to be known about their monastery thereafter until 1629, when it was recorded as being deserted. In 1645 there were monks here again, under the rule of a Fr Gaspar Fonte. He was among the priests held prisoner in Aran by the Cromwellians after their triumph in 1652, and probably saw the quarrying of his monastery for stone to rebuild the castle. After the Restoration in 1660 the Franciscans returned, using what buildings we do not know, and their abbots are recorded down to a Fr Proinsias Bodkin in 1697. The Penal Laws must have driven them out after that, for although abbots were appointed down to 1717 none of them took up the office.

The only physical trace of the Franciscan monastery, Tobar na mBráthar, the well of the friars, is reached by a little dog-leg track running westwards past the hayfield with the fragmentary high cross in it, behind Cill Éinne village. It is a round, stone-lined hollow with the remains of steps down into it, waterless, full of the long pointed fronds of hart's-tongue fern. O'Donovan said that the Franciscan monastery was to the south of it and that the older monastery's churches were to the north, but on what evidence he based this one does not know.

Leaving these dry speculations and the Franciscans' dry well, by following the crooked boreen for a few more yards to the west and climbing with it up the first scarp, one attains to a more heaven-inspired level. To the right, the terrace above the scarp continues around the curve of the hillside like a broad grassy promenade overlooking the back gardens of the village; this is Cosán na nAingeal, the path of the angels, where it is said that St Colm Cille used to stroll every day with celestial acquaintances. To the left is the stub of the round tower, and straight ahead, against the next little rise, is St Enda's holy well, with a roughly built stone altar beside it. The 'well' is only a dry hole in the ground, but an old lady of the village told me it was a spring, until someone stepped into it wearing his boots, whereupon it dried up. (Holy wells are touchy things and stories of their with-drawing themselves when insulted are widespread.) Its name is Dabhach Éinne, a *dabhach* being either a deep pool or a barrel, and former genera-tions regarded it as that very barrel in which the seed-corn came sailing to Aran from Corcomroe, leaving a wake of perpetually calm waters, by the ministry of angels and to the consternation of the pagan Corban, who was persuaded by this miracle to make over the island to St Enda. Barren women used to sleep by this well, in hope that the saint might ease their condition.

The tower was known as Cloghas Éinne, Enda's belfry (but in today's Cill Éinne Irish it is simply *an Rountower*), and there is a tradition that the saint's 'sweet-toned bell' is buried somewhere near his holy well. O'Dono-van in 1839 'made every cautious enquiry about the tradition preserved amongst the oldest inhabitants', and learned that the tower was once five stories high; my own enquiries, less cautious, in Fitzpatrick's bar, tell me that its top was level with St Benan's chapel on the hillside above. Like most of the extant towers of Ireland, this one was no doubt slightly tapered, with a slit window on each storey, a door fifteen feet or more above ground level, and topped by a conical roof of corbelled stonework. But before investi-gating the tower further, which is a matter of sounding the great well-shaft its absence sinks into the sky, it would be wise to finish with the material remains of the monastic complex, by ascending to this little ruined chapel, a hundred feet or so higher up.

Teampaill Bheanáin is its proper name, the church of Benan, which the lazy centuries have reduced to 'An Mionnán', and since one sense of *mion-nán* is 'a goat-kid' some locals will tell you it is 'the kid's chapel'. Indeed there is something goatish in its horned and shaggy outline and its sure-footed stance on the very edge of the skyline, looking down into the green crescent of monastic fertility around the base of the hill, alert and frisky, as if at any moment it might take itself off into the stony hinterland of the plateau behind it. O'Donovan found that it was also called The Hermitage, 'from some modern Maniac who took up his residence in it.' Nothing is remembered of this man – perhaps a scapegoat from the village below or from that outer world whose hilltops, visible from here, stand around a vast three-quarter-circle arc of the horizon. Perhaps it was this 'maniac' who left a clay pipe found here recently, with a cock stamped on its bowl and the legend WHILE I LIVE I'LL CROW.

Watchfulness must always have been the keynote of life on this perch. Sixty yards to the north-north-west, on a small, crudely revetted terrace on the verge of the steep drop to the village, are the confused remains of a stone hut known nowadays as The Watchman, from which I am told

would-be pilots used to look out for sailing ships that might be persuaded
they needed guidance into Galway harbour. The archaeologists who studied Teampall Bheanáin in 1984 also ferreted into this 'subrectangular dry-
stone structure of indeterminate plan', which it turned out was originally a
little square hut with a window to the north, later enlarged to the east and
wrapped around with another wall against the weather; all had long collapsed, and odd corners of it been resurrected as goat-pens. As well as
shards of nineteenth-century crockery, residue of merry picnics perhaps,
two lead musket-balls were found on its rock floor, suggesting that it
started life as a lookout-post connected with the Cromwellian citadel
below. Another ruined hut just a few paces north of the chapel itself, of
which two walls are the living rock of a right-angled nook of the hillside,
looks as if it must have been the ideal anchorite's troglodytic nest, half
burrow, half eyrie; however, the rubbish found under its fallen-in stones
was all seventeenth-century or later.

Teampall Bheanáin stands only a couple of yards from the edge of a
natural shelf of the hillside, which has been supplemented by a bit of dry-
stone terracing to the east, to make up a little walled enclosure, scraps of
which can be traced around the south and west of the chapel. The building is tiny, just ten foot nine inches long by seven feet wide inside. Its long
axis runs almost north-south, parallel to the major fissuring of the bare rock
it stands on. If this basic structure of the site helped to determine this very
unusual orientation, the prevalence of south-western and western winds
must have supplied stronger arguments; the little building confronts the
worst of the weather with solid masonry, the door being in the north gable-
wall, while the one little window, unexpectedly but logically, is in the eastern side-wall. This window is a round-headed slit twenty inches high and
only four inches wide on the outside, slightly narrower at the top than at
the bottom, and splaying generously inside; there was no doubt originally
an altar below it. The side-walls are over two feet thick, and they lean
inwards slightly as if hunched against the elements. Some of the blocks of
the western wall look like the work of giants, one of them being over four
and a half feet square, but they are in fact rather thin slabs set on edge and
do not make up the full thickness of the wall. The roof is missing; it was
presumably of timber, and it must have been very steep, for the gables rise
to fifteen feet even though they have lost their finials, making the little
building about as tall as it is long. There may well have been corbels projecting at the bases of each gable, as in a similarly primitive chapel in Inis
Meáin, but some masonry is missing or has been replaced at each of these
points. The door is only five foot six high and tapers upwards in harmony
with the side-walls and the slit window, from one foot nine wide at the

bottom to six inches less than that at the top, so that it seems to crouch under the five-foot-long block above it. Such flat-lintelled doors with inclined jambs are characteristic of early stone churches, as are those putative corbels and the masonry of slabs set on edge.

As to dates, the only firm evidence is from radio-carbon dating of charcoal in its mortar to about the eleventh century. The only inscription is the word CARI running down a quoin-stone at the south-east corner, which it seems is uninformative even to epigraphists. Dates and names recently scratched by brats from the village do not fall under the notice of archaeologists, and nor does the huge footprint in the bare limestone a few paces west of the chapel, which an old islander tells me was made by the saint himself. Neither can the name of the church help, for St Benan or Benignus is supposed to have been St Patrick's disciple and successor at Armagh, where, if there is any reality in the chronologies of the medieval annals and the Lives of the early saints, he died in 467, at which date Enda perhaps had yet to set eyes on Aran; and so it was not he who founded this church.

For some unknown number of centuries, then, an unrecorded succession of anchorites stood at the altar in the vertical blade of dawn from the east window, and by craning their necks this way and that could have squinted at the round tower, perhaps co-eval with this hilltop oratory, and the populous confusion of buildings around its base, until first St Enda's churches and then the Franciscan abbey were left unpeopled and finally demolished in favour of Caisleán Aircín. 'Soe all-devouring time "Diruit, aedificat, mutat quadrata rotundis",' sighs Roderic O'Flaherty, recounting this matter thirty years after the Cromwellian catastrophe by which he too had been pauperized. But for long after that, the headless trunk of the tower would have still dominated the scene of desolation, for according to Petrie it stood eighty feet high, having lost only two storeys to the Cromwellian delapidators, until it was struck by lightning and collapsed early in the nineteenth century. O'Flaherty's Horatian tag about Time which destroys, builds and makes what is square round, reminds one to ask what became of those hundreds of splendid blocks cut to the curve of the tower's wall? According to the invaluable Fr Killeen, whose manuscript history shows that he was one of those who hearken to such reminders, these stones went into the foundations of the quay in Cill Éinne, the quay called Céibh an Rice because it was built by men working for payment in rice, during the famine of 1822.

What stands today of the tower is a stone drum about fifty feet in circumference and twelve feet high, on a plinth that forms a little kerb around its base. The masonry, of large, closely fitted and mortared blocks, is time-scarred enough for one to be able to scramble up and lean across its four-foot thickness, and look down into the interior – empty, and pungently carpeted with the white flowers of garlic mustard. The circle of stone is uninterrupted, for the threshold of the doorway would have been higher up the shaft and reached by a ladder that could be pulled up in times of danger. Most round towers date from the late eleventh and the twelfth centuries, and it has been suggested that they were a response to the pilgrimage frenzy of that period, that as well as being belfries and symbols of heavenly aspirations, they served as beacons to guide the distant traveller, and that the monasteries' greatest attractions, their sacred relics, were displayed to the multitudes from their high doorways.

But the round towers were also refuges, invulnerable to anything less than prolonged siege or the fire that could turn them into crematorial chimneys. The Cill Éinne tower could have seen the unheralded horizoning of sails in 1334, when Aran was one of the places plundered and burned by Sir John D'Arcy, the Viceroy, working round the coast of Ireland with fifty-six ships. This was perhaps in response to the revolt of the de Burgos, the Anglo-Norman lords of Connacht who in the previous year had renounced their allegiance to the Crown and adopted Irish dress, language and titles, so that he who had been Sir William de Burgo now was the Mac William Eighter (lower), and pronounced himself Lord of Galway. The town soon disengaged itself from this rebellion, but the O'Briens of the Clann Thaidhg, who held Aran at the time, may well have been supporters of the Mac Williams, and the abbey of Cill Éinne suffered for it.

Thinking now of how this invisible tower sings in the winds of history, in a spacious antiphony with those other towers – on the limestone plain of Kilmacduagh, reflected in the Shannon at Clonmacnois, floating above the rooftops of Kells – of the monasteries founded by alumni of St Enda's foundation, I do in imagination what I never did while living in Aran – climb down into that stone drum, lie there among the herbs, looking up at swallows darting through the vanished rooms piled above me, and try to remount the cloudy centuries, from the last known abbot of Aran back to the coming of St Enda himself.

No names of the coarbs or successors of St Enda, as the abbots were called, are known from a period of over two centuries before 1400, the date Roderic O'Flaherty gives for Donat ua Laigin (he latinizes the name as Donatus O'Leyn), the last of them of whom he could find record. The silence of history may convey the somnolence or exhaustion of the religious impulse of Aran, which was only briefly to be reawakened by the Franciscans for a few decades before the suppression of the monasteries. The great years of Cill Éinne were much earlier. From 1167 (two years before the Norman invasion of Ireland) back to 654, the obits of the successors of

Enda stand in the *Annals of the Four Masters*. Solemn bell-strokes, recurring
with long intervals, their names:

Giollagóri hUa Dubacán (†1167)
Maolcolaim Ua Corbmacáin (†1114)
Flann hUa hAoda (†1110)
Macc Maras Ua Caomáin (†1095)
Fland Ua Donncada (†1011)
Eccnech, Bishop and Anchorite (†916)
Maoltuile mac an gobann, Abbot of Ára Airtir (†865)
Gaimdibla (†755)
Saint Nem Mac Ua Birn (†June 14, 654)

The most recent of these, Giollagóri or Gildegorius, would have heard
of, perhaps even witnessed, the assembly of kings and bishops at the con-
secration of Mellifont, the first Cistercian monastery in Ireland, in 1157,
and the synod of Kells in 1152, at which Ireland was divided up into episcopal sees grouped into four archbishoprics – events that signalled the end
of the old order in which his own title of *Comharba Éinne*, successor of
Enda, carried such weight. The Diocese of Kilfenora, corresponding to the
old territorial unit of Corcu Modruad (Corcomroe, in Clare), was amongst
those brought into existence by the synod of Kells, and later documents
indicate that it included Aran. Maolcolaim, the predecessor of Giollagóri,
had become abbot on the death of Flann, just before another great synod
presided over by the High King and the bishop of Armagh, at Ráith Bre-
sail near Cashel in 1111, at which the first division of Ireland into bish-
oprics had been undertaken. These three abbots, then, would have been
able to read the message of the horseman on the new-style high crosses
being carved in their own monastery workshops, which perhaps forebode
the decline of their authority.

Macc Maras is the only abbot of Cill Éinne the manner of whose death
we know; the Four Masters' entry for 1095 reads:

There was a great pestilence over all Europe in general this year, and some say that
the fourth part of the men of Ireland died of the malady. The following were some
of the distinguished persons, ecclesiastic and lay, who died of it ...

and Macc Maras Ua Caomáin is in the death-list.

Macc Maras probably saw the last Viking raid on Aran, in 1081 according to the *Annals of Inishfallen*. The long gap from his entry back to that
for his predecessor Fland in 1011 (the Annals say 1010 but O'Donovan
identifies this as an error) represents some loss of information, pages torn
out of manuscripts, perhaps, or minds knocked out of skulls, for the Four

Masters tell us of Viking raids in 1020:

Ard-Macha was burned, with all the fort – and the old preaching chair and the chariot of the abbots, and their books in the houses of the students, with much gold, silver and other precious things. Cill-dara, with its oratory, was burned. The burning of Cluain-Iraird, Ara, Sord, and Cluain-mic-Nois.

while the *Annals of Inishfallen* record plague in Aran in 1019 and another Viking attack in 1015 – one year after the Battle of Clontarf, popularly supposed to mark the end of Viking power in Ireland. The stone oratories such as Teampall Bheannáin and the oldest part of Teaghlach Éinne, and the round tower itself, may well have been raised during this violent century.

Almost another century is unrepresented in the Annals, from Fland back to the death of Eccnech, Bishop and Anchorite, in 916; what desolations, what rebuildings and replantings, what forbodings and forgettings, filled those blank decades is a field for guesswork. And it is unlikely that Aran was not raided by the Vikings in Eccnech's time, for the ninth century saw the repeated plundering of the sea-monasteries from Iona to the Skelligs in Kerry, the bishop driven out of Armagh, a Viking king's fleet on the Shannon, and, it is said, that king's wife uttering pagan oracles from the high altar of Clonmacnois. Ireland was at that period a chaos of petty kingdoms warring among each other and ready on occasion to ally themselves with the Norse settlers. The dominant sept in the south were the Eoghanacht of Cashel, whose circle of influence covered Aran, while the most powerful northern line was the Uí Néill of Tara. In 908 the High King of Tara, Flann Sinna, defeated the Eoghanacht in battle, and the King-Bishop of Cashel was among the slain. Eccnech would have mourned this scholarly churchman, Cormac mac Cuilennáin, who loved Aran and had written of it:

There are four harbours between Heaven and Earth where souls are cleansed, the Paradise of Adam from which came the human race, Rome, Aran, Jerusalem. No angel who ever came to Ireland to help Gael or Gall returned to Heaven without first visiting Aran, and if people understood how greatly the Lord loves Aran they would all come there to partake of its blessings.

There must have been substance to this vision of Aran, despite the Annals' catalogue of disasters. Each winter, armouring the islands with breakers, must have offered months of security from marauders, and in any case the storms of swordsmen probably swept through Aran only once or twice in each abbatial reign. There were occasional summers of angels' breath playing around the islands, as there are still, and long uninterrupted sequences of the annual cycle of the liturgy. But anything that was easily portable, precious, or fragile of the material product of those pious and laborious times in Aran is gone, and lies unfound in Viking graves or unidentified in museum cases, or was smashed or burned or lost at sea. The elusive playful mystery of crosses and circles on a few grave-slabs alone remains. Of all the millions of words spoken or written out of the passionate meditations of generations of monks, almost none but that mysterious one, cut into stone on Teampall Bheanáin: CARI, to the beloved.

But perhaps King-Bishop Cormac was warming his hands at a residual fervour from earlier centuries, for to these men the church in Ireland was already immensely old, and even before the Viking invasions it had been in decline for a slothful, greedy, contentious, century. Maoltuile, the abbot of Inis Oírr who died in 865, having seen a previous high king of Tara taking hostages from the island in a campaign against the Eoghanacht in 856, had perhaps been brought up in the reforming generation of the Céli Dé, the servants of God, who looked back to and sought to emulate the exorbitant spirituality and asceticism of the founder saints. In a famous manuscript called the *Martyrology of Tallaght*, written in the Céli Dé monastery of Tallaght in about 800 (before the Dublin that now includes Tallaght had been founded by the Norsemen), Maoltuile could have read what for us is the first and remarkably early mention of St Enda, and which to him would have been a rehearsal of things deep in the past.

The names of just two abbots of Aran, Gaimdibla and St Nem, have to cover the eighth and the seventh century, and that originary radiance behind them is as full of darkness as the empty summer sky when one stares up into it. If Nem died in 654, and if, as the medieval *Vita St Eindii* states, Enda got permission to settle in Aran from a king of Cashel who died in 491, then there were 'successors of Enda' before Nem, who are today unknown and likely to remain so for ever. The majestic tower of history tapers into nothingness, leaving the earliest lifetimes of the monastery lost like stars in the day sky somewhere above the vertex of its roof. Was there in fact a St Enda? In what space of the mind are we to site his miraculous life?

ORIGIN AND VANISHING-POINT

Let us first listen to the story, calling like a matins bell in a dawn of astringent simplicity, before reconsidering it in this complicated age, so long after Cill Éinne has had its day.

Aureo illo saeculo quinto. ... In that golden century, the fifth, in which the saints of Ireland almost equalled in number the stars of the heavens, began the wonderful conversion and wonder-working acts of St Enda, abbot, a man illustrious by the nobility of his race and more so by the splendour of his heavenly virtues.

So begins the Latin *Life of St Enda,* compiled by John Colgan from much earlier manuscripts and published at Louvain in 1645. It goes on to detail the saint's ancestry: his father was Conall Dearg (red) the son of Daimen, Lord of Oriel (a territory comprising the present counties of Louth, Armagh and Monaghan, in Ulster), and his mother was Briga, the daughter of Anmir the chief of Ard Ciannachta (now called Ferrard, in Louth). Of his four sisters, three were saints – Fanchea, Lochein and Cairech – and the fourth, Darenia, married a king, Oengus mac Nadfroích of Cashel. On the death of his father Enda became leader of his people; he was still very young, and, having grown 'like a rose among thorns', was ignorant of the ways of the flesh.

One time, when he was importuned by his comrades to go with them to take revenge on some enemies, he, as one knowing nothing of wrong or evil-doing, agreed. They killed one of their enemies there and were returning home when they came to the hermitage where the holy virgin Fanchea lived, and they were singing a song asserting their victory over the enemy. When Christ's virgin heard their voices she said to her sisters, 'Be sure, my sisters in Christ, that this frightful din is not pleasing to Christ.' In the spirit, she recognized the voice of the leader, Enda, and spoke in prophecy to the other sisters. 'He whose voice that is is the son of the kingdom of heaven.' The holy virgin Fanchea and another holy virgin went out to meet him, and standing at the door of the monastery, Saint Fanchea said to him, 'Come no closer, because you are defiled by the blood of a slaughtered man.' Enda replied, 'I am innocent of the blood of this slaughtered man. Not only am I free from the sin of murder, but I am, so far, free from the other vices of the flesh.' And again the virgin said to him, 'Why, wretched man, do you thus provoke the Lord God to anger? Why, by diverse crimes, do you plunge your soul into the depths of evil?' Enda replied, 'I am keeping my father's inheritance and therefore I have a duty to fight against my enemies.' Then his sister said to him, 'Your father is in hell, and your inheritance from him is sin and crime. The punishment for these is hell.'

Enda, mistaking the holy virgin's words, said, 'Give me for my wife the royal maiden whom you are fostering and I will do what you urge.' The holy virgin replied, 'I will soon give you a reply to your request.' And at once she came to the place where the aforementioned maiden was and said to her, 'You are now given a choice, whether you wish to love the bridegroom I love or a fleshly one.' The maiden replied, 'I will love the bridegroom you love.' The holy virgin said to her, 'Come with me into this chamber so that you may rest there awhile.' The maiden came, and lying on the bed there she breathed her last, and gave her soul to God, the bridegroom she had chosen. Then the holy virgin covered the face of the dead maiden with a veil, and returning to Enda said to him, 'Young man, do you wish to see the maiden whom you desire?' Then Enda went with the virgin into the chamber where the dead maiden was. Uncovering the dead girl's face the virgin said to him, 'See now the face of her whom you desired.' Enda said, 'She is not fair now, but deathly pale.' 'So also will your face be,' said the holy virgin. Then Saint Fanchea preached to him about the punishments of hell and the joys of heaven until the young man wept. O wonderful mercy of God, in the conversion of this man to the true faith! ... Therefore, having listened to the discourse of the holy virgin, he rejected the vanities of the world and took the habit and tonsure of a monk.

The immediate task of this 'new athlete of Christ' was to raise defences around his sister's nunnery, digging the earth with his bare hands. Then he turned to the first of his many future foundations, a monastery called 'Kill-aine' (which is perhaps Killanny in Monaghan). While he was at work on it he nearly fell from grace; some robbers attacked the place, and he seized a timber from the construction to help his people defend it. Fanchea rebuked him severely for this and ordered him to leave his country and become a humble disciple in the monastery of Rosnat (probably the famous Whithorn or 'Candida Casa' in Galloway, Scotland). Enda asked how long he should remain there, and she answered, 'Until your good fame shall have reached us.' So Enda left Ireland, and after a time at Rosnat went to Rome to be ordained, and founded a monastery called Latium some-where in Italy. Eventually Fanchea heard an account of her brother from pilgrims coming from Rome, and she set out with three of her virgins to see him, sailing on her mantle spread on the sea. And she said to him, 'When you come to Ireland, do not first enter your native land but seek an island in Ireland's western sea, the name of which is Aran. There you will serve your God faithfully.' (The *Life* here gives an interpretation of the name 'Aran' that has become traditional: The island is called Aran, that is 'kidney', because it is like the kidney in an animal, being narrow in the middle and wide at the ends.)

In fact on his return Enda landed in Meath at the mouth of the Boyne, with a hundred and fifty disciples, and founded a number of churches on either bank of the river. Then he went to Cashel in Munster, where his brother-in-law Oengus mac Nadfroích was king:

St Enda asked the king for the aforesaid island, which is called Aran. The king replied, 'Saint Patrick ordered me to offer to the Lord my God only good and fer-tile land, near me. I grant you therefore, to choose for yourself a place for build-ing a monastery near my royal town, Cashel, and I will give you the surrounding lands for your monastery.' Enda replied, 'Grant me the island I spoke of, and that is enough, since it has been granted to me by the Lord as my inheritance on earth, for my resurrection will be there.' The king replied, 'How can I offer an island which I have not seen?' Enda replied, 'Follow me south from your town.' The king did so, and they stood in a place called Ysel. Enda said to the king, 'Bend your knees, O king, and put your face over my feet.' The king thought that St Enda wanted to rebaptize him, since St Patrick had baptized him before. But this was not St Enda's intention. Therefore, as the saint had commanded, the king, bending down on his knees, put his face over the feet of St Enda. Then a marvellous and utterly astonishing thing happened. The ground rose up high beneath them until it nearly touched the sky. And then they saw easily the often-mentioned island, called Aran. The king said, 'This is a good land which I see.' And St Enda said, 'Offer it then, as a sacrifice, to God and to me.' Then the king offered the island to God and St Enda.

After this, the king asked and received St Enda's blessing, and returned to his town. The saint returned to his holy company, and took them with him to a suitable harbour, where they could conveniently get onto the island. Then, because they had no other boat for getting onto the island, the saint ordered eight of his brothers to carry down to the sea a great stone which was on the shore. What more? Through the virtue of him who walked with dry feet over the waves of the sea, the saint climbed onto that rock, and soon, from his storehouse, Christ produced a favourable wind, and thus, with all good success, brought his saint to the island. How great is the power of this, our God, whom the winds and the sea and even the rocks obey, so that, setting aside their own natures, they offer wonderful obedience to his saints!

There were some pagans in the island at that time, of the race of Corcu Modruad (Corcomroe, in the east of the Burren); they fled from Enda 'like darkness when daylight appears'. But their leader Corban, 'a second Pharoah hardened in evil', remained and set a trap for Enda, whom he took to be a magician until he saw the saint shut himself in the cleft of a rock, and said to himself, 'That magician is no human being with a body, but has a body made of air.' When Enda asked Corban to grant him the island, the pagan agreed to retire to Corcomroe for forty days. After he had gone, the saint saw Corban's horses grazing in a place called Ard na gCaorach, the height of the sheep, and drove them into the sea; they swam to the middle island and landed at the place called Trá na nEach (nowadays called Trácht Each), the strand of the horses; and then they swam on to the place of the same name in the third island. Meanwhile Corban, on the mainland, ordered a barrel to be made and filled with seed-corn, and said, 'If that God whom Enda preaches wishes him to possess that island, let him send this barrel to him.' And by the ministry of angels that barrel sailed to Aran (as I have already told in my first volume), leaving in its wake a path of perpetual calm.

Then St Enda established ten monasteries in the island, each with its superior, his own monastery being at what is now called Cill Éinne, the church of Enda. Half the island he gave to his own monastery, and the rest was divided among the others. The other superiors thought this arrangement was unjust, and they fasted for six days, that the Lord might show them what to do in the matter. Their prayer was heard, and on the conclusion of the fast an angel appeared to St Enda bearing two gifts from God, a book of the four Gospels, and a '*casula* of priestly ministry' – perhaps a chasuble is meant – implying that he was worthy above the others of the double honour of teaching and governing.

There is another version of this last story, which Colgan gives although he remarks that it appears to be apocryphal. In this version, three Irish monks, Helueus, Pupeus and Enda, went to Rome after a period in Rosnat, and while they were there the Pope died, and a wonderful white dove alighted on Pupeus as a sign that he would be a worthy successor. But Pupeus declined the honour and a St Hilarius was chosen in his place. When the three Irishmen set off for home, Hilarius blessed them and gave them a gift of vestments. But they had not gone far when, to test their obedience, he sent a messenger after them demanding the return of the vestments. Helueus and Pupeus were angry at this, but Enda said, 'Let us thank God for the time they were given to us, and likewise we should thank God when they are taken back from us' – which example of saintliness persuaded the others to accept him as their superior. They then proceeded to the island granted to Enda by heaven. On their arrival, Enda and his one hundred and fifty monks fasted for three days, until God sent a fish big enough to feed them all into 'the spring of Leamhchoill' (Roderic O'Flaherty argues that this is an error for Eochaill, Leamhchoill being on the mainland), and a wonderful cow, the legend of which I gave in *Pilgrimage*. Seeing these miracles, the people together with all the saints gathered together to choose a chieftain over the island. Enda proposed Pupeus, but he said that he was old and feeble and had only come there on pilgrimage, and that if, having spurned the headship of the universal Church he should now hold sway over the worldly, he would only make a fool of himself. So three monks, Jarlath, Maccrethe and Finnian the younger, were sent off to Rome to get a decision on the question. The Pope sent them back again with instructions to gather all the people together to receive God's judgment. And when all were gathered, three white birds came flying from the east; one of them carried in its beak the Gospel of Christ and laid it in Enda's lap; the others brought a most precious casula and placed it at his feet. Then, flying three times round the island, they disappeared. And all accepted Enda as their abbot.

The next miracle is that of the angel who cleft the channel into the harbour at Cill Éinne, as told in *Pilgrimage*. There follows an account of St Ciarán's seven years of service under St Enda, which I will retail when we come to Mainistir, the site of his labours, and of an excursion with Ciarán to places around Loch Corrib, where various miracles were performed. Finally, Ciarán leaves Aran for his great work of the founding of Clonmacnois. They all go down to the shore to see him off, and return weeping bitterly.

But St Enda went a little way back from the shore and burst into tears again, saying, 'Not without reason, my brothers, do I now shed tears, because, as it has been revealed to me, today rigour of learning and vigour of religion have begun to depart from this island.' When they heard this, the brothers who were present likewise wept. Going a little from there, he wept again. When asked by the brothers why he wept so much, he replied, saying, 'Now I weep because, as my God has revealed to me, the day will come when no pious monks will dwell in these neighbouring islands, but laymen and men of no religion, who serve the desires of the flesh.' When they heard these words of the true prophet, the followers of the man of God were exceedingly sorrowful. After this, the saint, coming to another place, was inspired with sudden joy and said, 'We must give thanks to our God. For before the consummation of the world, when wrongdoing will abound and the charity of many will grow cold, many will come to these islands in flight, that they may not themselves perish with the unbelievers.' After prophesying this and other things of this kind about the end of the world, he returned to his monastery, and commending his soul into the hands of Almighty God, he breathed his last.

A word on the context and transmission of this strange document. Medieval Ireland was prolific in the writing of saints' Lives, both in Latin and Irish. Over a hundred Latin Lives, treating of about sixty saints, are still extant, and there are about fifty in Irish, of about forty saints; some saints are celebrated in both languages. Other sources include nearly a hundred and twenty short tracts and anecdotes, and a number of martyrologies, lists of saints' names and genealogies. Local oral traditions celebrate many hundreds of saints unrecognized by the written word. Of St Enda, there is no Irish Life, and one Latin Life. This is preserved in two manuscript collections of saints' Lives in the Bodleian Library at Oxford, one of which is a copy of the other, and the printed version edited by John Colgan, who worked from a transcript made on his behalf of the second of the two manuscripts now in Oxford; that transcript is also still extant, in the hands of the Franciscan House of Studies in Killiney. Thus it seems that the story of St Enda comes down to us through a single channel and might very easily have been irrecoverably lost, for not a single medieval Irish library has been preserved as a whole, and the survival of such fragments as we still have of the corpus of Irish hagiography is due to a few scholars whose hands remained steady through dangerous times.

What item should one snatch to safety, as an ancient house collapses in flames? For some, it would be its archive, the memorial of its honoured founders. When Irish Catholicism was under seige by England and the Reformation, with its schools suppressed, monasteries going under grass and priests on the run, a group of exiles on the Continent dedicated themselves to the task of collecting, copying and printing the Lives of the Irish saints. One of the initiators of the project was Fr Hugh Ward, of the Mac an Bhaird (son of the bard) family, hereditary scholars of Ulster. Like many sons of important Gaelic families he had left Ireland secretly to study abroad, first at Salamanca and then at the Franciscan college in Louvain in Belgium. Here he met Patrick Fleming, who similarly had fled the suppression of his faith in Ireland and had studied at Douai. Another recruit was Brother Michael O'Clery from Donegal, best remembered today as one of the four compilers of that stupendous synthesis of earlier records to which Colgan gave the name of the *Annals of the Four Masters*. During his travels in Ireland O'Clery collected several hundred Lives of saints, though only a small proportion of these survive in any form. The continental libraries yielded many more to Ward and his network of correspondents; at Clairvaux, Bobbio, Rome, St Gallen and many other foundations with Irish connections, manuscripts were patiently copied and sent off to Louvain. Fr Francis Matthews, the Franciscan Minister Provincial in Ireland, arranged for a copy to be made of a manuscript from Saints' Island, a monastery in Lough Ree on the Shannon; this contained, among thirty-nine Lives, that of St Enda. Strangely enough, Fr Matthews also had access to a most important collection of manuscripts in the library of the Protestant Primate of Ireland, Archbishop James Ussher. This man is remembered with a smile for his calculation of the date of the Creation (in 4004 BC, as mentioned in the very beginning of my book), but he also played an important though two-faced role in the history of Gaelic culture. While he supported the strict enforcement of the law against Catholic clergy, and opposed Bedell's translation of the Bible into Irish and the use of Irish in the Protestant Church, he carried on a dangerous correspondence, using pseudonyms, with the lurking Catholic hierarchy in Ireland on ecclesiastical history, and assembled the largest of the three surviving collections of manuscript Lives, now in Trinity College Library.

In 1631 Fr Fleming was murdered by Protestant fanatics in Bohemia; Fr Ward died a few years later, and the great work of publication was passed on to Fr John Colgan. He was from Inishowen near Derry, had left the country as a youth and been ordained somewhere on the Continent, entered the Franciscan order at Louvain in 1620, and became Professor of Theology there soon after Fr Ward's death. The first massive tome of his *Acta Sanctorum Hiberniae*, the Lives of the Irish Saints, appeared in 1645. It covers, in date-order, those saints whose holy days fall in January, February and March; Enda appears near the end, at the 21st of March. A second volume dealt with just three pre-eminent saints, Patrick, Colm Cille and Brigid; after that, money ran out, Colgan fell ill, and the remaining five or six projected volumes never appeared.

Both the original manuscripts containing the Life of St Enda later came into the hands of the Protestant James Ware, Auditor-General of Ireland, who, encouraged by Ussher and advised by the Gaelic scholar Duald Mac Firbhisigh, had interested himself in Irish antiquities. The one from which a transcript was made for Louvain in 1627, according to a note written on it, belonged at that time to a nobleman 'G.E.', otherwise unidentified. It had already passed through many hands (one of its marginalia reads: 'Jhon Monny his booke. God make him an old blinde thiefe as hee is.') The other ms had belonged to the Franciscans of Dublin in late medieval times, but since then had been roughly treated and had collected in its margins a scribbled mass of contradictory evidence as to its successive owners. By the time of the Catholic rebellion of 1641 Colgan's assistant Brendan O'Connor was urging that such manuscripts be gathered into the comparative safety of collections like Ware's, and indeed much of what was not in Protestant keeping must have perished in the succeeding years of the Cromwellian holocaust. After Ware's death, his library was sold to the Earl of Clarendon and went to London. It was acquired by the Duke of Chandos in 1707, and Dean Swift appealed in vain for it to be returned to Ireland; instead much of it was sold to an important antiquarian and collector of manuscripts, Dr Richard Rawlinson, who bequeathed his library to the Bodleian in 1756. And that is the current resting-place of the two manuscripts known to scholars as Rawlinson B. 485 and 505.

But what is it that has been, through such effort, excepted from oblivion? Both manuscripts are in a Gothic script that experts date to the early fourteenth century. Colgan states that the one from which he drew the Life of St Enda was written by a well-known scribe, Aughuistin Magraidhin, Canon of Saint's Island, who was born in 1350. A recent study suggests that both manuscripts originated in the Lough Ree area rather earlier than Maghraidin's time, but that the one Colgan refers to was indeed associated with Saint's Island and may perhaps have been borrowed by Maghraidhin from elsewhere and not returned, for he was a great translator of Latin lives into Irish – not that an Irish version of St Enda's is known of – and many manuscripts must have passed through his hands.

So the number of centuries intervening between the saint, in the fifth, and the scribe, in the fourteenth, is greater than that between the scribe and ourselves. The Life we have may be based on earlier written sources, but the great era of this genre was several centuries later than the Age of the Saints it celebrates, and very nearly all Irish saints' Lives were dealing with the distant past even when they were first put on paper. Historical truth was not the prime concern of the hagiographers; nevertheless, historians try to elicit truth from them. The old-fashioned way of doing this was to ignore all the obviously fabulous and miraculous stuff, and take the residue seriously; thus the various clerics who wrote on the saints fifty and a hundred years ago, took care to distance themselves from 'monkish credulity' and 'medieval superstition' (while feeling no difficulties, one supposes, with the equally surprising events reported from Cana and Galilee). The late Hubert Butler satirized this method as equivalent to saying, 'While the cow certainly did not jump over the moon, we have no grounds for denying that Miss Muffet sat on a tuffet and Jack Horner in a corner.' This is a sharp stroke; but when one thinks of all the indubitably historical figures around whom absurd legends have accrued – Aristotle is one I will bump into most unexpectedly in my explorations of Aran – it is not totally convincing. So it still seems worth while trying to apply the old-fashioned method to St Enda.

Jettisoning the obviously counter-factual in his Life, we are left with these skeletal assertions: that Enda was the son of Conall Dearg, ruler of Oriol, that one of his four sisters married Oengus mac Nadfroích, king of Cashel, that he studied probably at Whithorn, was ordained in Rome, was granted Aran by Oengus and founded a monastery there. And since (according to the *Annals of the Four Masters*) Oengus died in 489, we have some indication of the date of that foundation.

However, in the calendar of saints known as the *Martyrology of Tallaght*, St Enda is mentioned as follows:

Ennae Áirni mac Ainmire maic Ronain de Cremhthannaib,

that is, 'Enda of Aran, son of Ainmire son of Rónán of the Cremthanna', who were a people associated with Meath rather than Oriel. This text dates from about AD 800, and according to Zimmer the genealogy it records is the correct one; the other was first given in a later martyrology which confused our St Enda with another Enda, one of three sinful brothers who repented and undertook a sea-pilgrimage, as told in the fabulous tale, the *Voyage of the Currach of the Uí Corra*; it is because of this confusion of the saint with the navigator that medieval narratives about St Brendan of Clonfert have him visiting St Enda to obtain his blessing before departing on his own equally fabulous voyages. But if this is so, the family connection with Oengus of Cashel falls away (it is in any case inconsistent with other old material relating to this king), and with it the only evidence for the date of Enda's arrival in Aran. (It is fair to say, however, that Zimmer does piece together from the thicket of references to the two Endas' ancestors in the Martyrology, the Voyage, the Life, and various commentaries on them, a coherent-looking family tree that brings Enda into contemporaneity with Oengus – but it seems to me that he does so by picking and choosing what to accept and what to dismiss, guided mainly by the result he wants to achieve; in this he was probably acting in the spirit of the medieval compilers of these 'facts'.) If sources so ancient disagree, there is no probability of the question being settled today. St Enda and his family reduce to mere names, none of which mean anything outside the contradictory genealogies and histories in which they are inscribed. The very question of the existence of St Enda seems empty of content.

But the stones of Cill Éinne – solid evidence of some act of origination, surely? There was a monastery here; therefore there must have been a first monk here, one would suppose. But is even so much knowable? The ruins extant today are probably of twelfth-century buildings; these probably replaced earlier structures of which no evidence as to their date survives. The christianization of Ireland was a gradual process; there must have been stages in which it would have been hard to say whether or not the people of a certain locality understood and accepted the Christian message to the exclusion of their native polytheism. The interpretation of acts of worship in Aran may have fluctuated for centuries; a community that eventually came to regard itself as a community of Christian monks may have been consolidated out of intermittences and ambivalencies over generations, and having recognized its own stability called for a history of its origins. Foundation is often a retrospective, not a prospective, act. Enda, like nearly all the other saints, is a projection if not of the imagination then of *post-facto* rationalization of ill-remembered gossip.

If this is so in the typical case of St Enda, then the Lives of the Saints, preserved with such diligence and bravery by those seventeenth-century clerics, are valuable only as illustrating the beliefs and customs of the times of their composition many centuries after the so-called Age of the Saints, and the misappropriation of tradition by rivalrous monasteries and petty kingdoms. But, just as their pages seem to be crumbling to dry dust, comes a bold and passionate attempt to rejuvenate them, to assert the importance of their testimony – and from a surprising quarter, the liberal and Protestant essayist Hubert Butler, whose sarcasm at the expense of modern hagiographers I have quoted above. The thesis of his book *Ten Thousand*

Saints (which, whether it is right or wrong, does not seem to have been given the attention it deserves from the experts) is that the thousands of saints mentioned in ancient sources – the twenty-seven St Fintans, the fifty-eight St Mochuas, the forty-three St Molaises, the saints with bizarre epithets to their name like 'dirty-fist' or 'badger-faced', or whose vomit turns to gold, who slay enemies with a blow from an eyelash, and who are, collectively considered, incredible – never existed as individuals; instead:

... the saints were the fabulous pre-Christian ancestors of pre-Celtic and proto-Celtic tribes and amalgamations of tribes and, in their pilgrimages and pedigrees and in the multiplicity of their names, nicknames, cult-centres, we can read the true story of the wandering of tribes. But since on this early pattern of history writing later patterns have been superimposed, we have a palimpsest that is very hard to decipher.

Also, since the names of many of these population groups would have been in some non-Celtic language, they were interpreted by the Celts of a later time through word-play; the names and epithets of the saints and the weird biographies concocted to explain these names are, Butler suggests, elaborate puns on the underlying tribal names.

Although two or three saints, most notably St Brigid, are generally admitted to have originated in Celtic mythology rather than in Christian history, Butler is the first to cast such a disillusioned eye on the whole lot of them – though for him the obscure picture that emerges of Ireland's prehistoric politics is intrinsically more exciting than the traditional tale of fifth and sixth-century fanatics thrashing their way through the forests of paganism. He is even brave enough to apply his pun-craft to such eminent figures as St Fursey, well known in Ireland, England and Gaul, and whose Life was written by one of his disciples only a decade or two after his death, according to the traditional view; Fursey, he asserts, was Forseti, the ancestor-god of the Frisians. He does not undertake to repaganize St Colm Cille, though. In a later essay, Butler pursued the saints of Aran in particular, and on St Gregory or Grigóir he is very convincing. This saint, celebrated in the islands on either side of Gregory's Sound, is said to be a native of Kerry, where the strait between the Blasket Islands and the Dingle Peninsula is another Gregory's Sound:

Opposite Aran on the Clare coast were the Grecraige or Crecraige [an early population group], with one ancestor called Grecus and another called Grec mac Arod. There are Grecraige on Lough Gara in Co. Sligo, and their territory is called the Gregories, so obviously Grecraige turns easily into Gregory and makes St. Grigoir-Gregory look like a Christian incarnation of the pagan ancestor Grecus. At the base of the Dingle Peninsula is Castle Gregory and inevitably I would claim it for St. Gregory, but an Anglo-Norman famiy called Hoare once lived nearby and it is alleged that one of their number was called Gregory. Yet St. Gregory's claim is stronger because he was patron of a church at Glenbeigh in the next barony of Iveragh. But even here, like mocking spirits from pre-Celtic and pre-Christian past, the Grecraige are recorded in Inis Crecraige or Beare Island, a few miles off in Bantry Bay.

But of course Gregory has no imposing *Vita Sancti Gregorii* to back his claim to existence, and everything we read or hear of him is fabulous. What of St Enda himself, then?

I have noted nine or ten saints called Enna or Eanda, but no doubt there are many more; the most illustrious of them is St. Enda of Aran ... Many famous saints were his pupils. He was vigorous and wordly and even brutal and dissipated, before he became a saint; at the moment he enjoys considerable favour, and jet-planes have been named after him. In spite of all this there is no denying that he is very odd. There is no mention of him in the Annals, though many impossible people have been chronicled there. I think his early wickedness derived from the fact that his monastic biographers failed to distinguish him from a secular Enna, who must have been his prototype and bequeathed to him his pedigree. ... Plummer and Kenny try to persuade us that, owing to the misreading of a pedigree, a real and saintly Enda has got confused with a wicked and fictitious one. Yet everything we know of both is equally fictitious, and St. Enda's former wickedness is an obsession with all his biographers. ...

No modern scholar has questioned the existence of St. Enda, and Fr. Ryan attributes to him a certain originality of method. 'He followed a rule of astonishing severity.' This is to be inferred from the story that on Aran he used to send out his monks in curraghs without any hide covering and that they all came back bone dry, except one, who had stolen some food. Thought on such lines is 'corrupting to the mind'. Enda did not exist. ... I suggest that Enda's travels by sea might be echoes of the voyages of the Veneti of Brittany, who were the most famous sea-travellers in Gaul. And there may be more distant echoes from the Eneti of Venice and Paphlagonia, from whom the Veneti were supposed to be descended, and whose travels were celebrated in Homeric legend. Some say that Aeneas was the ancestor of their tribe.

Julius Caesar claimed to have put to death all the 'senate' of the Veneti and sold the rest for slaves after defeating their fleet of two hundred ships at Bordeaux, but as Hubert Butler points out it is possible that many of them escaped to Britain and Ireland, and some Irish placenames such as Fanad in Donegal and Fenit in Kerry have been said to reflect their presence here. However, Enda as an ancestor figure of the Veneti seems a shadowy hypothesis to me, much as I would like an excuse to welcome Aeneas to Aran.

Perhaps a vaguely syncretic agnosticism is the only rational attitude to the truth-value of the Lives of the Saints; they may contain reminiscences of the adventures and rivalries of the monks and hermits who founded Ireland's thousands of churches, but they have been so hopelessly entangled with stories of many other sorts, including the origin-myths of hundreds of early tribal groups, and then exaggerated to magnify the prestige of much later civil and religious potentates, moralized to edify the credulous and fantasticated to entertain the simple, that all their assertions must be taken as unfounded.

However, I am reluctant to reduce the miraculous history of St Enda to such tepidity. As cosmologists now sense through their radio-telescopes a faint radiancy that has been batting about an expanding universe for so long that it has cooled almost, but not quite, to absolute zero, so, when I pore over these strange pages – photocopied from the 1947 facsimile of Colgan's 1645 printing of a transcript of a manuscript copied from another compiled in a fourteenth-century scriptorium from writings already then venerated as ancient records of extinct oral traditions – I feel some warmth of truth still emanating from them. The crackling of the unimaginable fire out of which our galaxies, suns and planet were born is itself only a rumour of the single point from which all things sprang; from his tower the inexistent saint's bell recalls that dawn of terrible perfection. I need this chapter of Aran's foundation-myth as reassurance that something more can always be founded on these stones. But absolute beginnings are too aflame with potentiality to contemplate with the naked eye, and only lapse of time and corruption of report make them bearable. The abyssal upward perspective to the point of origin has to be clouded with fables and tales of false miracles, to celebrate and obscure the fact that there is only one true miracle, which itself is all-inclusive.

DARK ANGEL

Against the dazzle of its foundation myth and the pale ardour of monastic days, the Cill Éinne of the last century, huddled around the abandoned fort, has in my mind a broken and blackish silhouette. The relative nearness, the existence of documentation, of that darkening time lets us hear the sounds of those smoke-filled hovels, the hawking, coughing and sighing, enchained with laughter and the cries of new-born life. The angel Sarial who (according to Colm Cille) came to pour out God's benificence on the bare flagstones of Aran each Thursday had long abandoned the task, Thursday as dole-day was yet to come, and the islanders were left to their own resources. The fateful cross-multiplication between potato and human being was mounting up towards the Great Famine. Large families could live off the bounty of a few small plots, and save all other income for the rent; the potato thrived on the plenteous labour of those families, the carting of sand and seaweed that created the plots out of rock, the spadework that doubled up the shallow soil into ridges, the weeding and watering that could be done by children. Fecundity led to overcrowding: the ridges full of low-quality potatoes vulnerable to drought, pests, diseases and prolonged salty winds that scorched their stems; the cottages crammed with young and old forcibly habituated to this monotonous diet, and with no money to invest in any alternatives.

The first season of 'distress' – this was the term used for the state of near-famine that recurred throughout the next hundred years – was in 1822, when the ending of the Napoleonic wars had already led to a widespread agricultural depression, and kelp prices had fallen away as European sources of alkali were opened up. In the years of distress small charitable donations from British voluntary organizations were distributed through the clergy and resident gentry, or the government organized public works on which men and women laboured for a portion of oatmeal. In 1822 many were employed quarrying the huge ashlar blocks used to edge various piers which the engineer Alexander Nimmo was building in Connemara, and a beginning was made on a pier, to Nimmo's design, to replace Cill Éinne's aboriginal quay. In 1831 another pier was built, on the south of the harbour at Cill Rónáin. Despite these interventions, life in Aran became impossible for many islanders, caught between the fixity of rents imposed in more prosperous times at the beginning of the century, and the decline in all sources of income. A large group left for America in 1822, and in the three years before 1836 five hundred more went, while others would have gone had they not been disappointed in their arrangements with the ship that was to carry them from Galway. Many exiled Cill Éinne men were employed in fishing between New York and Boston.

By the middle of the nineteenth century whatever prestige Cill Éinne had acquired from the garrison in the fort or the barracks that succeeded to it, or from the residence of the Fitzpatricks and the O'Malleys, was lost, and the Cill Éinne villagers found themselves in a worse situation than the other islanders. Even in the early decades of that century Cill Éinne's economics were precarious. Its land was on a barren arc of terraces called An Screigín (which means merely the small stony place), west of the Hill Farm's ample tracts, but many villagers had no land and were totally dependent on fishing, apart from periodic employment in cutting blackweed and shipping it to Kinvara as manure, or carrying the islanders' cattle to Casla Bay in Connemara, whence they would be driven fifteen miles along the coast road to the September fair in Galway.

In the 1820s the Aran fleet consisted of about forty sail-boats – small hookers of five to ten tons burthen, only five of them half-decked and the rest open, and two hundred currachs. The majority of the sail-boats worked out of Cill Éinne. In January, February and March they pursued the herring shoals; the village must have been festooned with the 120-fathom nets made (from locally grown flax), barked, dried and mended by their families. Through the summer until September cod, ling, pollock, bream and mackerel were caught with spillards (long lines with about three hundred hooks) or hand-lines, and the roofs of Cill Éinne were golden-tiled with split-open fish curing in the sun. But bad weather would keep the Aran fleet at home, and the herring could desert Galway Bay for years at a time. When the fishery was good, it was dominated by boats from the Claddagh, the fishing village on the outskirts of Galway; sometimes there were two thousand boats in the bay, and the Aran men complained of the Claddagh men taking away their nets and fish, and beating them if they protested. Salt was in short supply, and often herring could not be got to market in good condition. Buyers were rapacious, insisting on buying the herring in 'thousands', each of eleven 'long hundreds' of 123 fish. Long-line fishing was inefficient, but the Claddagh men forbade trawling, which they feared would disturb the fish and destroy the spawn – sheer prejudice, in the opinion of Alexander Nimmo. In the spring the sunfish or basking sharks were to be harpooned on the banks forty or fifty miles to the north-west beyond Slyne Head, but the little Aran boats were unfit for such expeditions.

When famine and the cholera came to the islands in 1822, and the winter fishing failed, the Cill Éinne people were unable to buy potatoes, and went hungry the following year too. Similarly in 1825 there were reports of Cill Éinne people stealing potatoes. In 1832 a severe outbreak of cholera spread from Cill Rónáin to Cill Éinne; the O'Malleys fled to Cill Mhuirbhigh, the villagers deserted their cottages to live in little caves and huts among the crags, and it was reported that their womenfolk were making coffins out of bed-heads. The Great Famine of the 1840s, strangely enough, was not so severe in Aran as elsewhere; it seems that the fishing was so good during those years that islanders still speak of it as miraculous; nevertheless, there was hunger and fever, and a desperate shortage of fuel, for Connemara was too weak to provide turf and Aran had no money or goods to exchange for it. Throughout the rest of the century bad years recurred in every decade, and the Aran fleet dwindled almost out of existence; foreign steam-trawlers appeared on the fishing grounds, guano imports to Galway meant the end of the seaweed-carrying trade, the Cill Éinne boatmen shipping cattle to the fairs found that they could not compete with the new paddle-steamer. Cill Éinne declined into a slum, until the Congested Districts Board brought some tentative relief to the fishing industry, striped the Hill Farm, and built a row of cottages to replace the knot of hovels sheltering in the ruined fort.

Newspaper accounts of these specific years of 'distress' are voluminous and pitiful, and the condition of the Aran poor gave rise to many denunciations of the landlords, their agent, and the government. Even during the unreported in-between years, it is clear that either stormy or rainy or dry or still weather meant less than usual to eat. Malnutrition and overcrowding made the community helplessly vulnerable to disease. There was no doctor until 1845, after which there was intermittently a medical officer serving the three islands from Cill Rónáin, and until the turn of the century the two smaller islands had not even a resident nurse. The ill-lit, smoke-filled, earth-floored cottages were ideal homes for the tuberculosis bacillus, and there was no possibility of isolating the infected, who just had to carry on working as long as they could and then sit in the sun or by the fire until they died. The islanders were fatalistic about *an cailín*, the girl, as they evasively called it; they thought it was 'in the blood' of certain families, with the consequence that people often tried to hide away its occurrence in their own family. As Ruairí Ó hEithir writes, in his study of Aran folk medicine:

In these surroundings the disease took a terrible toll, especially where an adult first contracted it: whereas a child or young person often died quickly, an adult would hold out for much longer, spreading the disease among others and, in the process, almost insuring their own re-infection if they succeeded in overcoming the original attack. No wonder that whole families were wiped out and tuberculosis was regarded as an inevitable part of every island family's life.

Folk medicine was largely a cruel delusion; it was not a matter of the herbal remedies we buy in charming bottles for our modern insomnias and hypochondrias. An infusion of mullein leaves was supposed to cure 'the girl', but as an islander remarked bitterly to me – for TB is still not just a memory – 'There was a lot of them it didn't cure.' Other treatments were based on misunderstandings of the nature of the disease, and must have caused unnecessary suffering. Pains in the chest, which might have been the result of anything from heartburn to cancer, were ascribed to a mysterious ailment called *cleithín* or *cleithín do thitim* (literally, 'fallen chest or breastbone') in which one of the floating ribs was supposed to have become bent in. The cure was to turn it out again with the fingers. Alternatively a lighted candle-end was placed on the breastbone with a tumbler inverted over it; as the air in the tumbler was consumed the flesh would be dragged into the resulting vacuum, and (in theory) the rib pulled into its right position again.

Midwives and bone-setters were probably the only genuinely effective practitioners in this murk of ignorance. Every village had its wise woman ready with capable if not clean hands at the doors of life, though an especially renowned midwife might be sent for from village to village or even from island to island, bringing comfort and sometimes deadly infection; it is recorded that the famous Róisí Mhór, from Fearann an Choirce, was drowned going to Inis Meáin by currach some time in the 1840s. Bone-setting also demanded deft manipulation, but, being concerned with the dry mechanics of the human frame, it was a male vocation. Several islanders could deal with dislocations, a very few could fix up fractures. Synge met an old bonesetter in Inis Meáin in 1898 who was well known throughout the islands and on the mainland; and long after the coming of conventional medicine to the islands people would visit certain famous bone-setters in Connemara. Local accounts of these men show them besting the official experts, in a way that is delightful to those who have suffered the condescension of learned doctors. Thus the blacksmith of Fearann an Choirce tells me of a Dublin surgeon who decided to test the skills of a Connemara bone-setter (probably the well-known Micil Pheaitsín Mhocháin of Leitir Mealláin). The surgeon called at his cottage with a sack containing all the bones of a human skeleton plus one small extra bone, emptied them onto the floor, and challenged him to put them together. This was soon done, and when the surgeon picked up the extra bone and asked, 'What about this?' the countryman replied, 'You may throw that away.'

Most island medicine was magic, of some shade from white to black. Certain people claimed knowledge of *arthaí* or charms for stopping bleeding or choking, for curing erysipelas, toothache or the stitch. Migraine ('the little fever') was thought to be due to a condition that was diagnosed by measuring the head with a tape in various directions; if the measurements did not tally, the skull was open at the top. The cure then was the recitation of an *artha* in the form of a little sacred narrative:

Saint Peter and Saint Paul were walking the road one day and they sat down on a heap of stones. 'What's wrong with you?' said St Peter to St Paul. 'Headache and the little fever.' 'Three persons I will put to taking it from you,' said St Peter, 'Brigit and her cloak, Michael and his shield, the two bright pure hands of the Virgin Mary.'

There were also one or two women who had the power to transfer a disease from one person to another. The botanist Nathaniel Colgan accidentally learned about this practice during his visit to Aran in 1892:

I was on hands and knees one morning, in search of the rare Milk Vetch, when I was startled by this remark, which came from one of a knot of puzzled Killeany men who had gathered round me to watch my doings with embarrassing patience: 'That's a very dangerous thing you're about; I've known a man killed that way.' At first I thought the speaker, a grave, middle-aged man, meant to warn me against injury from some poisonous plant, but on close cross-questioning it became evident that he was a firm believer in disease-transference by witchcraft.

His story was shortly this. Some years ago a friend of his, a man named Flanagan, living in the neighbourhood of Oghil, in Aranmore, lay sick of an incurable disease. He had been 'given over' by the doctors, and, face to face with death, his fears, after a long struggle, got the better of his religion, and he made up his mind to call in the services of a *cailleach*, who lived away in Onacht, at the other end of the island. This hag was known to have the power of transfering mortal sickness from the patient, wicked enough to employ her, to some healthy subject, who would sicken and die, as an unconscious substitute. This was her method, evidently a combination of a plant-spell with the *gettatura* or evil eye. When fully empowered by her patient, whose honest intent to profit by the unholy remedy was indispensible to its successful working, the *cailleach* would go out into some field close by a public road, and setting herself on her knees, just as I was kneeling then, she would pluck an herb from the ground, looking out on the road as she did so. The first passer-by she might cast her eye on, while in the act of plucking the herb, no matter who it was, even her own father or mother, would take the sick man's disease, and die of it in twenty-four hours, the patient mending as the victim sickened and died. My informant had known the *cailleach* well, but had only heard for certain of one case, the case of his friend Flanagan, where she had worked a cure in this way. Unfortunately he could not tell me what the mystic plant was, though he was sure it was not the Milk Vetch, which I had the good fortune to find before we parted. More unfortunate still, the *cailleach* and Flanagan, as he told me, were both dead.

Another way of passing a disease on to a randomly chosen victim was to deck a cockerel in coloured ribbons and let it loose on the crags, far enough away for it not to return home; the first person to see it would die of the disease, or else his cattle would die, while the patient recovered. A herb-woman called Nellóg, who lived in Corrúch in the last century, was known to practise this method.

The 'evil eye' was a constant threat to mental and physical health. A person could put the evil eye quite unintentionally, for instance by praising someone and omitting to add the customary *Bail ó Dhia*, the blessing of God. The remedy then was to spit on the victim, and if it was not known who had put the evil eye, everyone would have to contribute their saliva. District Nurse Hedderman railed against the custom in her account of her years of duty in Inis Oírr:

I have seen lives ruined and lost that might have been saved, if only means could be found for dispelling this black ignorance when sudden illness attacks the young and healthy. The first resort is the saliva cure, and should the person accused of casting the spell resent the insinuation and not be friendly disposed in that special direction, the patient's progress and relief from suffering are supposed to be hindered until he enters the sickroom and saturates the bedclothes with this filthy secretion.

Many illnesses, especially of children, were blamed on the fairies, and medical help, even if available, was disregarded in these cases. It was thought that the fairies stole human children, especially boys, and left changelings in their place which soon faded away and died. To prevent this, boys were dressed as girls, in petticoats, up to a certain age. A retarded or deformed baby was likely to be regarded as a changeling, and might be left outside overnight on the blade of a spade for the fairies to take away, or be burned in the mouth with the heated tongs to make it go away of its own accord. The virtue of iron as a prophylactic against enchantment played some part in these horrific practices.

Shortly before the beginning of the sequence of distressful years, a woman came to live in Cill Éinne who was to personify the community's dealings with birth, sickness and death; Nell an Tower is still vividly present to the islanders, and her legend has already flitted across a page of my first volume. The census of 1821 lists her and her household:

> John McDonough, 41, fisherman
> Nelly McDonough, 34, woolspinner
> Pat McDonough, 6
> Ann McDonough, 3

They lived in a cottage built against a small round tower forming a sort of bastion at the south-west corner of the old castle, which has long since vanished, and from which she got her name, Nell of the Tower. Island tradition is uncertain of her origins, but its best opinion is that she was of the Greelish family of Ros Muc in south Connemara, and that she was already married with a son when she came to Aran. Perhaps her husband soon died, for it is as a widow that she is remembered. She may have brought a certain reputation with her, for she was related to a *bean feasa* or wise woman in Connemara who came into conflict with the parish priest, a dangerous state in those days when priests had magic powers, and who was found naked and dying in a field in which the crop had been levelled as if by a gale.

The older Aran people have no doubts about Nell's supernatural powers; one man said to me 'She could fly, though there was no talk of jet planes or scooters in those days!' However the various stories in which a husband comes from a distant village on horseback to bring her to attend upon his wife in childbirth, and Nell refuses a seat on the rump of his horse, saying she will follow him on foot, but still reaches the house before him, do not make it clear how she is thought to have travelled so quickly. She was highly regarded as a herbalist, and no doubt she employed the usual Aran pharmacopoeia of ferns, mosses, flowering plants and seaweeds, some of which, such as comfrey, had genuine curative properties; but it was the ceremonies with which she gathered her ingredients and applied her potions that gave them their effectiveness, and here she was understood to be doing her best with powers that were not totally in her control. Once, when she was picking a certain herb, she looked out to sea, to avoid trans-fering the disease she was treating to anyone who might be passing by, but her eye fell on a man rowing a currach, and he died; she was very upset about it, I was told, but she could not help it. Another story confirms her stance on disease transference:

There was a man in Creig an Chéirín who got a sort of stroke – but a very light one, his mouth twisted, as if the sinews had shrunk. The priest and the doctor were coming to him but I think he didn't get much out of them as he wasn't very twisted. But he was bad enough for his wife to think he wouldn't live at all. And she was horrified because he was a good man, and he had three sons. And Nell was sent for. But when she came, she didn't go to look at him. And the wife was so wild with fear he might die that she started to bargain with her in advance. She was suggesting that she would would rather send off one of the sons and keep the father – that was what the Creig an Chéirín woman had in mind.

'Ah' said Nell, 'Isn't that murder? I couldn't do that.' Probably she thought she would go to hell! 'But' she said, 'If you have a sheep or a goat for me to put to death, I wouldn't think twice about it.' 'Well' said the wife, 'there's a heifer that was in calf, that's all.'

But they say that there never was a night as bad as that with rain, and it was as black as the pot, at twelve o'clock or later, when she had to be on her way.

'Well, I'll go now,' said Nell, 'and I'll get that beast, and when you shut the door after me,' she said, 'on the skin of your ears, don't any of you open the door whoever knocks, until I knock on it myself.'

Off she went. I think two of the sons were at the fireside, whether the third was there or not, and a long time later in the evening she came to the door and she ordered them to shut it firmly behind her. And she went to the fireside, and her two feet were nothing but blood, cut by briars when she was walking in the dark. After a bit she said 'Well now, when dawn comes, be looking out, and you will find that beast in the back corner of the Crogán. And in the other place there is a hollow' she said, 'and there is enough earth in it to cover a good bit of the crag. And drag it to that spot, and bury it there. It is dead.'

And indeed it was. They went back there in the morning and they found the heifer dead, and they dragged it across, and they had never known of such a hollow in that little craggy field. And they dug out the earth from it and threw the beast in and covered it over.

And they say that that land never had a good day ever after. The man who lived there had no luck with cattle or anything, but beasts dying on him, dying in strange ways.

There are several stories of Nell's ability to foresee the hour of birth or death; when a man came from one of the western villages to tell her his wife was in labour, she sent him away, saying 'I know the time to go west.' In Mainistir once she saw some men making a coffin, and asked who it was for. The men told her that an old man of the village was nearing death, but Nell replied, 'He will live. The one who will go into that coffin is still alive and running around.' And indeed the old man survived, while a young lad who was out hunting rabbits on the cliff-tops at the time fell into the sea and drowned, and was buried in that coffin.

It is said that Nell knew of a death-curse, but there is no memory of her having used it. However, in the following tale there is a hint that it was wise not to cross her:

A man in Eochaill was very ill and his family sent for Nell. She looked after him for a bit, until he was thought to be well again. Then the family were not willing to pay the amount of money Nell asked them for, and after an argument she took whatever they gave her.

Not long afterwards the man fell ill again and the wife told the son to go and tell Nell. 'Do you think she'll come?' he said. 'Well, try her anyway,' said his mother. The son went east on his horse, and she said she would come. He told her to ride pillion, but she told him to go on and she would be able to come by her- self. He rode off west. When he was nearing the house he saw her sitting by the road, and he asked her how she had got there before him. 'Don't mind that,' she said, 'I'm going back east.' 'Were you down at the house already?' he asked. 'I was not,' she said. 'He's passed on already, and there is no need for me to go down.' And away she went.

As it happens, we have a precise date for the most famous illustration of her powers of second sight:

A man from Bun Gabhla, one of the Ó Tuathail family, was out on the crags one day. He came across a flagstone and he turned it over. Whatever was under it, a horrible smell came up from it. A weakness came over the man and he went home. He got dizzy then and he had to go to bed. He was ill, and Nell an Tower was sent for. She came, and spent a long time working on him. In the end she cured him, with some herb, probably. She went to bed herself then, exhausted.

In the morning the family were up when Nell an Tower suddenly opened the door and shrieked 'My son is killed! What shall I do without him?', and started to weep and wail. The people of the house tried to find out what was wrong or what had happened to her, but she ran out of the house and eastwards towards Cill Éinne. It was on that same morning that her son was drowned at Aill na nGlasóg, and fourteen others with him, on the fifteenth of August, 1852.

Most islanders today, if asked about the truth of such stories, would reply, 'You wouldn't know!' – an answer at three subtle grammatical removes from either asseveration or denial. The stories I have recounted here are often told, but rarely nowadays in the detail of these versions, which I have translated from the Irish given in Ruairí Ó hEithir's treatise. He recorded them in about 1980 from his grandfather Pádraic Ó hEithir, who had come to Aran as a schoolteacher in the 1920s and married a daughter of the most genial of Aran families, the O'Flahertys of Gort na gCapall. For Pádraic, the zest of Aran life was its speech, the oblique sayings, the bizarrely comic anecdotes, in which Araners are so profuse. He would have relished the juxtaposition of the weird and the homely in these stories, picked up in those days when the long evenings took their moods and rhythms from the blazing or smouldering of the turf fire. But however much he appreciated their native savour, the literate and sophisticated teacher would not have wasted much time on their truth-value, any more than would his grandson the Dublin University College graduate, forty years later. For a less sophisticated, older contemporary of the teacher's, Pat Mullen, it was important explicitly to discount the reality of such incidents. Nell of the Tower is an important character in his novel *Hero Breed*, published in 1936, in which the hero himself comes to live in Cill Éinne and falls in love with Nell's beautiful daughter. Here he questions his future mother-in-law about her powers:

'Nella, why is it that you pull your herbs at night? Wouldn't the daylight do just as well or better?'

'It is this way, Avic: half the power of my medicines is the belief by the person who takes them that they *will* cure. It is in daytime that I pull them really, but if people saw the herbs I pull they would soon lose faith in my powers of healing, because some of those herbs are weeds and are considered good for nothing by the islanders. On the other hand, by making the people believe that I pull them at night I bring an air of mystery over my work. ... Of course there *are* herbs that must be pulled before sunrise because their medicinal properties are much better when they are gathered in the freshness of the early morning dew. What knowledge I have of herbs and medicine has been handed down in our family for more than a thousand years. Lots of witchcraft stories have also been told about me, but

the one Orla and I laugh at the most at is the one about the Iararna man who galloped his horse five miles to Kilmurvy to bring me to his house when his wife was
nearing her confinement. ...'

– and she continues with an unquotably lengthy account of how this man
left her to make her own way to his house while he went off for a sup of
poitín, and then pretended to be amazed that she had arrived before him,
and said that she must have crossed the Black Crag by witchcraft. For the
purposes of his plot Pat Mullen brings Nell fifty or sixty years nearer our
own time, so that she is still flourishing during the modernising of the fishing fleet in the 1890s. But there is a deeper anachronism in this collusion
between character and author in turning out the dark side of her work to
the light of common sense. Mullen's Cill Éinne is brimming with life – the
novel is hardly more than a succession of vividly physical episodes, stick-
fights, feats of sailing, rowing, horse-riding and weight-lifting, interspersed
with the materials of a manual of nineteenth-century fishing techniques –
but it has no shadows, it is all lit by the solar vigour of his protagonists. The
real Nell an Tower picked her herbs beneath the moon because, like the
society she was born into, she was groping among the ultimate mysteries;
scepticism, like sanitation, was still a hundred years away. She shared the
common belief in the powers of her own charms, in those times that
offered no other recourse apart from the priest's equally incomprehensible
rites, because they seemed to work often enough to offer a fingerhold to
hope. At the very least they had that sometimes curative ingredient: care,
the human touch. As for her moving through the island as swiftly as
rumour, as disease, as death itself, there are in fact certain short cuts, only
known to those who have reason to use them, by which it was possible to
go from village to village with surprising speed even at night, as I shall
reveal in the right place; there is even one across An Chreig Dhubh, the
'Black Crag' of Mullen's novel. But for the moment I leave Nell an Tower
her mystery, which was necessary to the only angel serving those benighted
dwellers among stones hallowed by saints, cursed by Cromwell, and bled
dry by landlords.

MEMENTOS OF MORTALITY

Most of Nell's contemporaries are buried in the old cemetery by the sea
with St Enda and his hundred and twenty companions, where the rain is

washing the names off the limestone slabs lying on their graves. Some of them, however, are also commemorated by vertical inscriptions, and therefore more lastingly, on monuments standing in rows along the road northwest of the village. The lettering on these is still legible, especially when a westering sun cuts its shadows deeper, and I have screwed my eyes up into an antiquarian mode and puzzled out all the inscriptions, and published them in a book, so that the names of Patrick Flaherty, Peter Wiggins, and three dozen others, together with their meagre life-data, will last as long as such books do.

These cenotaphs are stout squarish pillars rather higher than a man (islanders like to cod visitors that people are entombed upright inside them), about four feet broad across the sides parallel to the road and a little less the other way, flat-topped, and surmounted by a stubby cross carved out of a single piece of stone. They are built of natural limestone blocks carefully fitted together with a little mortaring, and nearly all have two plaques with incised inscriptions, set one above the other in the side facing the road and framed by dressed stones; one inscription names the person commemorated and the other the person who raised the monument. The first such monument one meets as one walks out of Cill Éinne stands in a field on the left-hand side; one can lean over the roadside wall in front of it, and let the tall stony presence address one directly:

> This   monume^t.
> erect^d.   by   his
> Wife   Ann   Fla
> herty   -   Al^s.
> Wiggins   -
>
> Lord   have   Mer
> cy on the Soul of
> Patr^k.   Flaherty
> who   died   in   th^e
> 33   yr   of   his   age
> 1830

The little letters above the lines are hard to decipher among the blotches of lichen. The cross on top is no longer standing but lies propped against a small stone. As one moves on from monument to monument – there are eight in a row here, a few yards apart – one becomes aware of more regularities in their structure and repetitive oddities in their orthography, and of the haphazard effects on them of time. The top half of the next has collapsed, and its upper plaque lies in the grass at its foot:

This   Monu
ment erect. by
his Wife Cathe
rin   Wigginns

O Lord   have
Mercy on the soul
of   Pet.   Wig
gins who Dept.
this life in the 68
y. of his age 1826

Then comes one crowned with a rather fine cross leaning askew, with rounded arms and head, and a shallow square recess in its shaft – a feature an archaeologist tells me derives from the form of glass-fronted shrines for the display of relics. A coping on the top of the monument projects a few inches all round immediately above the upper plaque, and the base is a little wider and thicker than the rest of the pier, giving a narrow ledge around the sides and back just below the lower plaque. Ivy obscures one side of the monument but on the other one can see how the stones framing the plaques are dressed, reamed with inch-wide chisel strokes all round their margins and the central areas lightly pocked with a punch. The plaques themselves have neoclassical sunburst motifs in each corner and margins of a lozenge pattern. The inscriptions are more elaborate than the norm too:

This Monument
Erect. by order of their
son & his wife Pat. &
Cather. Dirrane to perpu
ate their Memory ~

The Lord
have Mercy on y. soul
Mich. Dirrane ~
died in y. 119 y. of
his age 1817 ~
& his wife Cathern
Dirrane Al. Coneely
died in y. 97.th y.
of her age 1817 ~

And so the mournful litany goes on. After these eight, and a gap of a few hundred yards, comes a group of five, one of them reduced to a mere stub a foot high, close together by a cottage on the right of the road; then an isolated one on the right, and another on the left which serves a house as a gatepost. This last has an extra plaque lettered in block capitals in memory of a Peter Gill, died 1892; this is the latest inscription in the series, and is clearly an insertion into a monument which the main plaques show to date from 1840. Not far beyond this point the road descends a steep scarp to shore-level by An Charcair Mhór, the big slope, and so leaves Cill Éinne territory. There are no such monuments in Cill Rónáin, but ten more are scattered along the road through the western villages from Eochaill to Eoghanacht; there are none in the other Aran islands.

These rather forbidding structures address one with questions both historical and mortal, and even the former, easier, sort, cannot be answered with much conviction. Counting one which has totally vanished but is mentioned in a late nineteenth-century source, and two of which only the plaques survive, set in a wall, there are twenty-eight in all, with dates ranging from 1811 to 1876. Individually they are not very different from sundry eighteenth-century memorials, mainly to individuals of the landlord class, to be seen, for instance, near Cong and in other places north and east of Galway city, but as a series the Aran roadside monuments are unique, in their number, in their late date, and in the fact that they concern ordinary members of the tenantry. There is nothing like them in Connemara or the parts of County Clare the islanders might have visited. What suggested the building of such elaborate memorials, in a time of such want? Their only local forerunners are the Fitzpatrick cenotaphs of 1754, looking down on Cill Éinne from the Lodge; but why should the tenants start to 'trot after the gentry' two generations later?

There was in Aran a humbler funerary custom that both predated and outlasted the era of these monuments. At certain traditional points along the route of a funeral procession, the coffin would be set down while a few of the relatives put together a little cairn from the loose stones of a crag by the road. Dozens of these survive in the west of the island, and I believe there used to be some at the top of An Charcair Mhór. Some consist merely of three or four long stones leaned together, while others are neat conical piles several feet high. Also, in the fields below An Charcair Mhór there is a cairn rather nearer the inscribed monuments in bulk and form; it even has a stone set vertically on it which with a little imagination can be seen as almost cross-shaped. It stands by an overgrown boreen running below the scarp, north-east of the road, that I am told was a long time ago the main way to Cill Éinne. If the anonymous stone-heaps evolved into the highly formalized inscribed monuments, with promptings from the Fitzpatrick cenotaphs, the process included a sudden leap of invention. This characteristic assertion of human creativity (characteristic also in that it was then followed slavishly) was perhaps taken by a relative of one of the two people whose plaques bear the earliest date, 1811. Unfortunately this cannot be ascertained, for neither of these plaques (one in Eochaill and the other in Eoghanacht) is in its original position and we do not know what shape their setting took.

That English should be used in these inscriptions is less surprising than would at first appear. The very possibility of writing in Irish was little known outside of scholarly circles until the spread of the language revival movement in the 1890s. Also, limestone Aran, being largely composed of potential tombstones, used to export them to granite Connemara, and these slabs were inscribed and decorated by island craftsmen; so the island had the set phrases of funerary English off by heart – or, as some of the plaques on the roadside memorials seem to show, copied them, mistakes and all, from example to example. Mortality and error being two related universals of the human predicament, the latter acquires prestige from the former; the curious abbreviations and corrections by means of superscripts became part of the rite of inscription, arcane but reassuring, to be reproduced as carefully as the architecture of the whole. In fact the dignified parade of these monuments along that outer reach of communal survival represented by Aran in the mid-nineteenth century, asserts a companionship between the living and the dead. But who is escorting whom, in this petrified funeral procession?

'These monuments of the dead have by moonlight a ghastly appearance,' wrote one of the first visitors to describe them, Oliver J. Burke, in 1887. This is still true despite the increasing suburbanization of their setting; not night alone but fog and rain and wind, in making it impossible to connect them with imaginable individuals, turn them into looming frights. On a fine day, however, one lingers and notices their individual quirks and stances; they have the air of men breaking off from work in the field for a chat with the passer-by. In the west when you pass someone at work you say *'Bail ó Dhia ar an obair!'* – 'God bless the work!' What work is being done by these monuments, that concerns us? I gave my little monograph on them a seductively lugubrious epigraph from Sir Thomas Browne, who in his *Urn Burial* explains that it was the Roman practice 'to bury by highways, whereby their monuments were under eye; – memorials of themselves, and mementos of mortality unto living passengers; whom the epitaphs of great ones were fain to beg to stay and look upon them.' The commerce between those of us still on the road and those who have gone before is two-way; the departed remind us of death, the inexorable general condemnation to oblivion, and at the same time demand from us an attention to the particulars of their epitaphs, as if hopeful of their own case for exemption.

Synge saw the roadside monuments on his first day in Aran, and in his book merely mentions them as part of the grey waste of stone and rain he depicts, to throw into relief the vitality of the girls who hurried past him 'with eager laughter and great talking in Gaelic, leaving the wet masses of rock more desolate than before.' But in his pocket-book he scribbled a thought about them:

The idea is that passers by seeing the inscription should offer a prayer for the soul of the deceased and thus alleviate his portion of purifying flames. A similar notion is seen in most of the old Celtic inscriptions which run usually thus 'a prayer for the soul of —' with the name given in full.

This idea of assistance between souls is profound and fertile quite other than it is read naively in the churches.

But there he breaks off, and leaves us in the lurch. This idea of assistance between souls: was it merely some theosophical fancy brought with him from Paris, or was it consonant with the realistic humour he learned from Aran? In fact the roadside monuments, unlike those of the Fitzpatricks, do not ask for our prayer, but offer up their own. Nevertheless, they call upon us for witness, for a response, even in this unbelieving or indifferently agnostic age, in which true Catholic Aran is letting them fall into ruin. Or is the call we hear from them merely an echo of our own thoughts?

One wearisome damp day when I was studying the monuments of Cill Éinne, I broke off to explore a side-road running up to the crags west of the village. I will try and relive that excursion as a train of thought, to advance me through the labyrinth, and because I think better with my feet than my head. The side-road is called Róidín Docherty after the Limerick family whose holiday-home is the former teacher's residence at its foot, next to the disused Killeany National School. It is also called Róidín Donnellan after a teacher who lived there about fifty years ago, and Róidín Seoirse after someone who flourished no one knows when. It is a narrow, grassy, walled track that angles its way between the fields and up the hillside for half a mile, then pauses by a wet hollow before scrambling around it and up the scarp behind it. The hollow is Turlach na mBráthar, the turlough of the friars; nobody knows why, but it might have belonged to the Franciscans of Cill Éinne. It is fed by the run-off from a long narrow ravine crossing the plateau south of it called Gleann Ruairí Óg, the glen of young Ruairí (and again nobody knows who he was), the significance of which is that it divides Ceathrú an Chnoic, on the east, from Ceathrú na gCat, the quarter of the cats, on the west. The former was the land of the Hill Farm, the latter the quarter in which the villagers had their land; the cats were probably pine martens, which are no longer seen in the islands. The path then follows the brink of the scarp for a few hundred yards to the west, and on its left is an antique-looking hut of large stone slabs. One of the stony little fields opposite this hut, just below the scarp, is called something that sounds like Creig hÍobairt, which an islander translated for me as 'sacrifice crag'. There is said to be a bullaun stone set in one of its walls, which is why I had come. The owner of the field had told me its story. Long ago, a man went up to the field one Sunday to fetch his horse, intending to collect some seaweed from the shore. On entering the field he saw a priest saying the Mass, with two candles burning, and he knelt down. Afterwards the priest vanished. That made him think that there must have been a church there whose priest had been killed, and he looked around the field and found the bullaun stone, a granite boulder with a hollow in it. The owner of the field also told me that once when he was troubled by a painful stye, he dipped his finger into the water in the stone and put a drop on the stye, and the pain stopped immediately.

The bullaun stone does suggest an ecclesiastical connection, and I suspect that some half-forgotten scrap of oral history suggested the ghost story. But although I searched along every wall, and trampled to and fro in the long grass, I could not find the stone. In fact there was nothing at all in the field. Nothingness was palpable and oppressive, as it often is in these tiny enclosures, where a thousand or two thousand blocks in the walls present blank faces, and a few harebells stand up out of millions of grass-blades. Why might the ghost of a priest be seen here? Perhaps some lonely friar lurked for a while here after the Cromwellians had plundered the monastery and imprisoned its abbot; his legend might have attached itself to the common folktale of a priest whose soul has to wait in a ruined church for a living witness to hear him perform some rite neglected or interrupted. Once when I was helping two Aran men to pull down the loose stones of a double wall that needed rebuilding, around the garden of the old teacher's residence in Fearann an Choirce, I noticed them flicking at something, as if they had disturbed a moth in the core of the stonework and were sending it flitting off across the crags. Their mime was half joking, and they laughed as they told me about old Moloney, the schoolmaster who had had the wall built, and of how people used to believe that the dead lingered around the scenes of their life for a while before their final release. In fact Aran's walls with their endlessly varied grey facets and dark crevices look as if they had absorbed all the faces and gestures of the generations of shadows cast upon them. But I saw nothing in that field; or perhaps I should say, as an Araner would in such circumstances, I saw nothing worse than myself. Perhaps I was in the wrong field, for the directions I had been given to it were not perfectly clear, or perhaps it was my resolute scepticism that held at bay the faded figure of the priest appearing like a lichen stain on the wall. It is our own shadows we are frightened of, I reason, the fears of our own extinction shadowing us, and we lend our shadows to the departed who have none of their own, colluding with them in a delusion of survival, for ghosts frighten us less than our own future inexistence.

On my way back I paused to look at the turlough again. A meaningless marshy spot with a few spires of purple loosestrife, between a tumbled, overgrown wall and the path climbing the scarp like a little staircase of worn treads. Watching it, watching nothing happen there, I had an intense premonition that I would never see this place again. I, who do not believe in ghosts even for an instant, heard the footfalls of my own ghost in my tired heart that afternoon. Time has told the falsity of this presentiment; I have revisited the spot and hope to do so again (if only to prove something). But I returned rather shaken from my walk and mental detour, to the task of transcribing epitaphs in order to publish them in a book, with my name on the front and my brief biography on the back asking posterity to wrap me in its shadows.

SOMETIME PLACES

An Screigín is the name of the scraggy western end of Cill Éinne territory where the villagers had their holdings, in the days when the Hill Farm monopolized the better land to the east; the name conveys nothing but stoniness. It is served by a wide, rough side-road, Bóthar an Screigín, which branches off the main road at the top of the 'big slope', An Charcair Mhór, and makes a wide turn to the west and then the south, almost to the brink of the Atlantic cliffs. In summer a few tourists walk along it or even try to cycle, following the directions of a finger-post to the promontory fort of Dún Dúchathair, which is not far from its termination. Apart from this road An Screigín is an almost trackless tangle of field-walls. I remember, before my map of the island was published, seeing a knot of bemused Japanese there, who hailed me plaintively but politely across several intervening walls: 'We would like to see something, if there is anything to be seen!' That what was to be seen was exactly this grudging parcelling-out of barrenness, was more than I could explain; I put them back on the way to the grand spectacle of the fort. In other seasons only a few farmers visiting their cattle use the road. I was leaning over the roadside wall talking to a man in a potato-field once, when a stoat which must have been interrupted in the kill by my approach scampered up the road and, when we did not move, applied itself to the neck of a rabbit I had not noticed, lying about ten yards away. Occasionally one sees a pair of goats, miserably shackled together by the necks to restrict their wanderings, dragging each other hither and thither. This is not generous land.

The road for most of its length keeps within a hundred yards or so of the top of an arc of low cliffs forming the edge of An Screigín. This rim is even barer than the rest of the quarter; it is divided by walls into a number of areas that one would call fields if they had grass in them but are in fact sheeted with rock; only in the occasional hollow or the fissures between the broad level clints are there some rough tangly herbs. In Aran-English such a barren enclosure is called a 'creig', from the Irish *creig*; I have here and there translated this in place-names as 'crag'. Immediately below the scarp are some enviably green meadows belonging to the Cill Rónáin people, and a sheet of fresh water which appears after rainy weather, five or six acres of it, and disappears again. Here the low land around the bay to the north gathers itself into a valley, and then contracts further into a ravine that almost notches through to the south coast, where the islanders prophecy the ocean will break in one day and divide the island. An open tract of bare pavement on the rim of An Screigín provides a natural esplanade for gulls to strut and preen on after splashing for eels in the turlough below; it is called Creig na bhFaoileán, the crag of the gulls. If they are particularly clamorous there in the evening, it is a sign that there will be rain within three days, I am told. (Some island forecasters provide themselves with an even more generous margin of error than these three days, by adding, '... or if it doesn't rain here, it will somewhere else.') This creig has some fine sheets of unblemished rock, and one of these blanks bears a memorial to a young Galway fisherman, T.B. Barrett, lost at sea in 1966. A fishing-instructor, Captain Woolley, punched it out, with shipshape decorations of reef-knots and of two hands holding a heart, the 'Claddagh ring' emblem of Galway's ancient fishing quarter. The inscription tells us that his dead comrade was 'a fine seaman, a better friend'. The older generation of Aran skippers, who learned their craft from Captain Woolley, remember him sitting out here for days, tapping this measured judgment into place.

An Turlach Mór, the big seasonal lake on the Cill Rónáin land, is such rich and complex terrain, and in such absolute contrast to the crags above it, that it is best approached on its own terms, as it were, after having returned to the main road and gone a little farther north around the curve of the bay towards Cill Rónáin village. Here another side-road sets off westward through fields in which a few bungalows have been built over the last few years, making the area almost a suburb of the island capital. This is Bóthar an 'Phump' – the English word being subjected to Irish grammatical rule – from the old drinking-water pump at its beginning. It is also known as the Committee Road (with the stress on the last syllable of the long word), because it was originally a famine-relief work of the 1880s carried out under the auspices of a local charitable committee (the misdeeds of which I shall be investigating later on), and I am told that the reason the walls defining it on either side are lower than the norm is that they were built by women. Much further west it becomes Bóthar na gCrag, the road of the crags, and climbs over the central heights of the island to Gort na gCapall. But the turning to the turlough is only a quarter of a mile down it from the main road. This grassy track (the third on the left), Róidín an Turlaigh, is a primrose way in early spring, and in May the scent of hawthorn blossom makes it as sweet as an old ballad. It also affords me an occasion of pedantry, that sentimental attachment to little things. The genitive form in this toponym, Róidín an Turlaigh, shows that the final syllable of *turlach* is not, as the OED states and as the anglicization 'turlough' implies, the word *loch* (genitive *locha*), a lake or lough, but is in fact a mere postfix of place; thus *turlach*, from *tur*, dry, could be explicated as 'a place that dries up'.

Turloughs (except for one example recently discovered in England) are only known from the limestone karst areas of western Ireland, which is why the Hiberno-English term has been adopted into the polyglot jargon of geology. They form in enclosed depressions and are filled and emptied not by streams but from below, through openings in their beds which act alternately as springs and swallow-holes, as the general level of ground-water held in the fissures of the limestone rises or falls. In Aran the joints in the limestone have been opened by solution only down to a depth of twenty or thirty feet, below which they are tight, with the result that the water contained in them is draped like a mantle over the island's core of unfissured rock. The thickness of this mantle varies in average with the seasons, and fluctuates with every shower of rain, and wherever and whenever it rises above ground-level in the bottom of a hollow, a marsh or pond or lake appears. In An Turlach Mór, this hydrology works like a dream: one day you see cattle grazing in a meadow; the next, when you pass, water lies there like a drawn blade.

The repeated comings and goings of a turlough make its vegetation very different, in organization if not in species-lists, from that of a normal marsh or lakeshore. Praeger's classic study of the turloughs of the Gort lowlands and the east of the Burren describes the stratified arrangement of their flora, from the rare 'turlough violet' found in the deeper parts of the basin and which spends most of the year underwater, to the bushes around the rim which can take a certain frequency of flooding, and the mosses further up that need an occasional watering but less than what would kill off the bushes. In a large bowl-shaped turlough such as the one that gives its name to the village of Turlough in the Burren, the upper and lower limits of the range of each species are visibly graspable contour lines, but An Turlach Mór has a very flat bottom and is bounded by sharply rising scarps, and so one has to discover its zonation by treading to and fro across the quaggy sward and parting the wattled stems and branches of shrubs climbing through each other up to its rocky rims.

If the turlough is at its fullest, the boreen to it runs straight into the waters; if the level is low, the path opens out into a soft water-meadow intersected by meandering channels, from which often a hundred gulls will rise on your approach. During long dry spells the water shrinks back into a few muddy hollows; I once found P.J. Mullen with his ear to one of these, listening to a peculiar snorting which, he said, was eels gasping for breath. A few mearing-stones mark the division of this lush grazing between seven Cill Rónáin farmers. The field-wall along the northern side of the turlough is clad in a blackish moss; Praeger gives me its name that sounds like falling water, *Cinclidotus fontinaloides*, and notes that it is diagnostic of turlough conditions, marking the level of a certain low frequency of flooding. Along the foot of the low cliffs forming the eastern and western rims of the turlough, are groves of purple loosestrife and meadow-sweet, a lovely pairing characteristic of the West's damp marginal places. On the valley floor, tall meadow buttercups occupy little hummocks that are slightly drier than the rest, which is densely carpeted with another buttercup, the lesser spearwort, and wet tangles of bogbean, the tiny white marsh bedstraw, lady's smock and marsh pennywort. The water speedwell roots in the muddy bottoms of little holes a foot or so below ground level.

The cliffs converge towards the south, where the valley becomes a tapering glen rising to a cleft in the skyline not far short of the south coast. Honeysuckle and dog-roses clamber among the hawthorn, buckthorn, spindletree and hazel scrub on the cliff-faces, sheltering patches of sunwarmed rock decked with bloody cranesbill, wild valerian and tufted vetch. The ground rises very slightly southwards, and about four hundred yards up the valley a field-wall across it divides the main space of the turlough from a pasture pungently scented by watermint, where marsh orchids stretch up to the light through a dense carpet of silverweed. Then come a few little fields of drier grassland curving up at either side into brambly slopes, the home of countless rabbits; on one's entry here, clouds of the every-summer's-day butterflies – meadow-browns, walls, ringlets, large heaths, common blues – rise out of the bushes and pursue each other in mad whirls without distinction of size or colour. Beyond, the narrowing glen is densely thicketed and the cliffs are taller, with herons' nests in their heavy canopies of ivy.

The difficulty of experiencing such a place, rich in vivid and fascinating detail, is that it demands a list-making, note-taking sort of consciousness (and I have mentioned only a few names of the more striking plants, leaving out the sedges, horsetails, waterweeds and dozens of flowers of more covert beauty and obscure individuation that the botanist will be searching for among them), so that the crucial moment at which it becomes one place may be crowded out of recollection; in fact the clamorous, colourful, press of sense-data can be so close-packed as to stifle that moment in the seed. It has been important to me, therefore, to linger in such places until their fragments reform into a whole like a reflection in a disturbed pool: here at the turlough, to lie in the lap of one of those last fields, the sun in my lap like a warm puppy, until the anxious herons that have flown up to perch on the lip of the terrace above forget about me and drift back one by one to their nests and young. Sometimes it is then possible for the quietened mind to smooth out such scrappy notes, and fit them together into the page from which they were torn. Those butterflies, though, that a whim of the breeze takes from one field to another or away across the crags: I am not the most firmly located of humans, but that absolute place-freedom perturbs me, to a degree I find difficult to understand. And when I see butterfly-behaviour that contradicts the stereotype, I am obscurely reassured: a dappled pair of wall butterflies at rest, facing one another, antennae touching, in deep mutual communion, one of them slightly vibrating its wings; or a big dark red admiral that suns itself on a stone, then darts off in a jagged circuit of the whole turlough, and returns to exactly the same spot, again and again. Sunning myself in such a field, by degrees I locate and concentrate myself; the herons even stop raising their periscope heads out of their nests to eye me; there is such a place as 'here'. And then the 'here' blurs, and flows, and yawns: I am in An Turlach Mór, Árainn, Ireland, Europe, the World (as one used to continue, with childish profundity), the Solar System, the Galaxy, the Universe, the ...

One also has to wake out of the topographical drowse sooner or later, and its after-effect is to make the choice of direction almost impossibly arbitrary. There is a tempting little path branching south from the end of Róidín an Turlaigh. Just three feet wide between waist-high walls, and full of deep grass and arching brambles one has to lift aside individually, it has the air of leading to a secret. After about fifty paces it reaches the foot of a cliff; the steps it takes to the top are not obvious at first glance, but a little casting around finds them out. They seem to propose that, if you knew where you were going, this would be a useful short-cut. Above is a flat crag, plinth to a hillside rising like a shallow ruined ziggurat beyond. And here at my feet is written '... a good seaman, a better friend'. Repetition, circularity, error! – this is An Screigín again, from another angle.

However, having misled myself this far, I might as well cross the crag, climb the wall into Bóthar an Screigín, and follow it southwards, uphill, and then scramble across the head of the ravine south of the turlough. Here, with shocking suddenness, one is at the brink, and the vastness of the ocean rushes to one's feet. Only a crack in the ground, a long step, separates the land from the top of a hundred-foot-high rock-stack, An Aill Bhriste, the broken cliff, still leaning in arrested collapse as it was when I wrote about it ten years ago. Evidently the same major joints running across the island that guided the formation of the ravine also define this projecting buttress of the cliffs. Nearby to the west must be Poll Talún, the hole in the ground that opens like a skylight into the roof of a huge undercutting of the cliff, giving a dizzy vertical view of breakers a hundred feet below. In *Pilgrimage* I gave the legend of the fox that had its lair on a ledge of this cavern's roof, which it reached by swinging by its jaws from a fern growing in the hole. Now I would like to revisit the place and add a few details to the story. According to an old Cois Fharraige story-teller recorded in the 1920s, this fox was brought across from Connemara. Some boatmen who were loading turf at Barr Roisín in Ros an Mhíl saw the fox lying on a wall, apparently dead, and they threw it in on the turf, intending to show it to any Aran fishermen they might meet – sheer malevolence, this, for it is unlucky to see a fox when going fishing; an old curse says:

> *A fox on your line,*
> *A hare on your bait,*
> *And may you kill no fish*
> *Until St Brigid's day.*

But as soon as they made fast at the quay in Cill Rónáin, the fox jumped ashore and ran off to Gort na gCapall, where it left neither duck nor goose alive that night. When the villagers discovered the slaughter the next morning, they borrowed a pack of hounds from the O'Flaherty of Cill Mhuirbhigh and hunted the fox. The hounds pursued it so hotly that, when it ran to the cliff and swung itself down by a briar (in this version), they plunged over the brink, and were dead before they hit the water. The next day the fox raided Eochaill, and another pack of hounds was lost in the same way, but this time a man in a currach below saw how the fox escaped. Bun Gabhla lost its fowl next, and the men from that village came and cut through the briar except for a bit of its skin, and hunted the fox with hounds borrowed from Inis Meáin. And when the fox swung on the briar, it broke, the fox fell, and the hounds went down with it.

But where is the site of this disturbing little fable? Revisiting in 1991, I walked along the cliff-top looking for it, two or three hundred yards west of the rock-arch and, as I remember, about thirty feet in from the edge. Failing to find it, I walked on around the bay, and looked back. A great rim of the cliff, about a hundred and fifty yards long, had fallen, and lay piled in gigantic rubble below. The fox's hole no longer exists, and a page has been torn out of my book. The Atlantic has bitten into the island's neck like a stoat, and will in time consume it all. Aran is a dying moment.

GOLD AND WATER

The hillside gently rising westwards from the turlough is so full of the vaguely wonderful, the ghosts of stories half forgotten and half reinvented, dateless ruins foundering in blackberry bushes, crooked paths to dreams of buried treasure, that before broaching it I should establish its prosaic chief landmark. This is the old reservoir a quarter of a mile up the slope, a squat truncated pyramid of sombre masonry, infinitely preferable to the dull concrete slabbishness of the new tanks below it. Water supply has always been a problem in this leaky little island, and nowadays, what with the islanders' own appreciation of washing machines and bathrooms, and the tourists' natural expectation of showers, public toilets and well-swilled beer glasses, more and more storage tanks have had to be constructed here and there, and the lovely otherness of Aran is squandered as if it were an inexhaustible resource. The old reservoir, built in 1956, is a good-looking structure though; it gazes with Egyptian solemnity back across the valley and the centuries to Dún Dúchathair, the 'black fort', which from this height shows itself in profile against a brilliant vista of sea and the distant hills of Clare.

A boreen angles up the cliff at the north-western corner of the turlough and crosses the terrace above it, by the new reservoir, to the next scarp, where there is a spring and a small pump-house which is sometimes muttering away to itself as one passes, driving water further up to the old reservoir. This area is called An Carna (which must relate somehow to the word *carn*, a mound or cairn or height), and there is a song, 'Uisce Glan an Charna', about the bringing of 'the clean water of An Carna' from here to the cottages of Cill Éinne through 'beautiful pipes of white plastic'; its composer, old Antoine Ó Briain, used to sing it in Fitz's pub *ar an sean-nós*, in the traditional, modal, semi-tonal, nasal, 'old style' which reports all events, from the mundane to the tragic, with the same timeless dolefulness. Here he is describing work in progress on laying the pipes:

> *Nuair a thosaigh siad ar dtús air,*
> *Bhí na bóithre cumhanga,*
> *'S bhí an chontúirt go han-mhór*
> *Dul thar na trinnsí.*
> *Dá mbeadh fear ann a bheadh óltach,*
> *Le fuisce nó le pórtar,*
> *Ba mhór an chontúirt báis dó,*
> *Nó giorrú lena shaol.*
>
> *'S nuair a tháinig siad Cill Éinne,*
> *'Gus thosaigh siad a' pléascadh,*
> *Bhí claidheachaí 's geataí réabtha,*
> *'Gus binneana na dtithe;*
> *Na mná siúd a bhí pósta*
> *Tá siad scannraithe fós ann,*
> *Nuair a théadh na clocha 'n airde*
> *'S iad a' tutim ar an tslinn ...*

When they first began
The roads were very narrow
And it was very dangerous
Going by the trenches.
If a man was drunk
With whiskey or with porter
He risked a deadly danger
Or shortening of his life.

And when they reached Cill Éinne
And began the blasting
Walls and gates were shattered
And the houses' gables.
And the married women
They are frightened still
From the flying stones
That were falling on the roofslates ...

And so on.

During this great work heaps of periwinkle- and limpet-shells were turned up around the site of the pump-house, the refuse of an old settlement. The local tradition is that during a cholera epidemic (of 1832, if it is the one recorded in newspaper reports) the sick were sent off to live here in little *botháin* or huts, the stones of which can be glimpsed here and there among the roots of elder-bushes under the scarp. But at some much earlier date An Carna was an ecclesiastical settlement. In the centre of a field opposite the pump-house are the remains of two rectangular buildings, one reduced to its foundations and the other, said to be a church, collapsed except for a five-foot-high fragment of neat unmortared masonry in its east gable. There is no record of the original name of this church – its present name, Cill Charna, or Kilchorna as it appears on OS maps, derives merely from the name of the area – but there are reasons, too tenuous and tedious to rehearse here, for thinking that it might be an otherwise unknown Cill na Manach, the church of the monks, listed among the churches of Aran by Archbishop O'Cadhla in the 1650s. When O'Donovan was investigating on behalf of the Ordnance Survey in 1839, a six-foot-high cross-inscribed pillar-stone stood about forty paces south-west of the church. His artist assistant William Wakeman sketched it – a beautiful piece of work in Early Christian style, with a Latin cross drawn in outline above a circle containing the sort of X-shaped pattern one learns as a child to make with a pair of compasses. In the 1940s this stone was recorded as lying broken in the ruins of the church, but unless it is buried under fallen stone and moss it must have been carried off since then.

I met the owner of this plot once when I was mapping my way around this hillside; it was as if he had been waiting with all his lore at the ready for me to come by. He showed me around the field, which at first glance was rather bare but in which he disclosed marvels, though it was a little difficult to attend to it all with his two bullocks staging a mock bullfight with the brightly coloured shoulder-bag in which I had my camera. Most of what he knew, he had from his grandfather and father (who would have been one hundred and three if he had lived, he told me, as if proud of this posthumous longevity). Once when he was young he began to shift one of the flags lying near the church, and an old man working in a field higher up shouted to him to stop, because they were gravestones. Maybe because it is holy ground, it is the most fertile field in Aran; it can be grazed eight or nine times a year, and in summer if it is grazed bare it can be grazed again in two weeks' time. It has never been tilled, yet the white clover grows in it, 'however it got there!' He showed me a big quern-stone, a flat disc of granite, lying in the long grass, and told me that Donnellan the teacher had taken off another one to his house in Cill Éinne. There used to be a stone here that people used to visit to pray for a change in the wind, to their own advantage or to spite a neighbour, but the parish priest came and stopped this pagan practice by breaking it up. He pointed me to the holy well under the cliff two fields south of the church – afterwards I fought my way to it down a tiny *róidín* filled head-high with hazel, brambles and nettles. It is dry now and and has not been visited for decades, and the pot of gold said to be buried near it has never been found.

A fold of the hillside above the reservoir, called Fán an Uisce, the slope of the water, holds another legend of buried gold. A Cill Rónáin woman called Peggy once dreamed that there was treasure hidden there. She told her husband, and he went off one night with two other men to dig it up. They had with them torches made out of tin cans fitted with long wire handles and filled with turf ash soaked in paraffin oil. They were working away in the gully with shovels and crowbars when Peggy's husband stopped to ask how the money was to be divided. 'Equal halves!' said the others, but he held out for an extra share for his wife, and they began to fight. The noise woke the birds roosting in the bushes behind them, which rushed out into the light of the torches and gave the men such a scare they all ran home thinking the fairies were after them.

That is one version of the story, so prosaic it could be the truth. Here is another, to which a number of scraps of folklore have attached themselves, as if it were ripening and would become a well-rounded folktale in a few generations more, if grandson could still hear grandfather over the ravings of the television set. One night a man who lived at the top of the old road in Cill Rónáin was visited by the ghost of a Spaniard called Mac an Bhaird (!). He said he had been guarding a treasure in Fán an Uisce for seven hundred years, and the Aran man could have it if he went for it by himself and either at midnight or at twelve o'clock of a Sunday morning. Since twelve o'clock was the time of Sunday Mass in those days, the man was afraid to go. But the Spaniard appeared again one night, and told him he could take anything he liked with him in the way of holy water or his rosary beads, but that he must go alone, and that if he did not, a red-headed man from Eochaill would get the treasure. That decided him, but since he was frightened of going alone he told the village tailor and another man, and one night they set off. Half-way across Creig an Chosáin they had a terrible fight because the tailor demanded a share for his wife, who had nothing to do with the matter, but they made up their differences and went on to Fán an Uisce. While they were 'rooting' there, they looked round and saw that the bushes at the end of the gully were on fire, and they ran off in a fright, expecting the devil to appear at any moment.

It was Dara Mullen, the postman, who gave me this more elaborate version of the tale. I often used to meet him on his rounds when I was mapping the island; as he drove by we would exchange respectful salutes like two knights whose quests cross, and then when he was delivering the mail to our house in Fearann an Choirce he would report to M on my progress: 'He's measuring the road back in Cill Éinne!' Dara was Aran's chief channel of information, island-long, carrying as much old lore as news of the moment, and retailing all with the same sardonic grin. Sometimes he would stop beside me on the road, wind down his window and tell me tales that seemed absurd but that turned out to have something in them. Once he kept me bowed to listen so long that when I straightened up I had a twinge in the back, as if I had shouldered a too-heavy post-bag of messages from the past.

Having heard so much about this treasure hunt I got Dara to guide me to the site of the adventure. From his house, close to where the man in the story lived at the top of 'the old road' running up west from Joe Watty's pub in Cill Rónáin, we crossed nearly a mile of crag by an old right-of-way which I would never have found by myself, as some of the stiles in the field walls are blocked up and hardly identifiable. This debouched by Creig an Chosáin, the crag of the path, into Bóthar na gCrag just north of An Carna. We turned up the hill there, leaving behind us the rubbish dump with its pennant of scavenging seagulls, the furthest intrusion to date of our century into the island's core of confabulating stone. The region we entered there is likened by my memory to Dara himself, almost skeletally sombre but winking with glints of mirth.

On the left of the road where it cuts and ramps its way up the first scarp is a little nook, almost a cave, in the cliff-face, called Pluais an Ghréasaí, the den of the cobbler, and a spring, Tobar Ghréasaí na Scilleacha, the well of the cobbler of the shillings. If you succeed in catching a leprechaun he will promise you the shilling in his purse, but he is sure to find some way of tricking you into taking your eyes off him for an instant, and escaping with his shilling. Oddly enough Dara did not know these particular place-names, which I have from another islander, and whether they are in fact connected with a leprechaun tale is more than the latter is prepared to assert. For Dara, the steep rise here was Carcair na gCat, the slope of the cats, and again it is from another source that I hear that Carcair na gCat was a fairy dwelling – for I have reconstituted this hillside, this hinterland of Nod, out of many fragmentary testimonies.

The level above this first scarp is called An Coinleach, the stubble field, and it is indeed rather less uncultivable than the great crags below, though nobody has tilled any of its fields in recent years. A boreen branches to the south here, gets up onto the next step of the hillside, and twists and turns for nearly a mile, following now the warp and now the woof of the field-pattern, working south-westwards towards the great cliffs, but then stopping short as if bewildered within sound of the ocean. Fán an Uisce is a long gully beside its penultimate southwards tack. We stood on a wall and looked down into it. The spoil-heaps of the treasure hunters are still to be seen; the blazing bushes, where the path twists across the south end of the gully, are still to be imagined. It was a peerless evening. The tide was very high in the bay a mile to the east, the sea utterly motionless, the island becalmed in time.

On our way back Dara stopped for a moment where the boreen angles out of the north end of the gully. This path, he told me, used to be very narrow – it was widened in the thirties – and for a long time the key of a clock lay in it at this corner, and people would take great care to step over without treading on it. I record this because he made a point of telling me about it. If I understood it, I would understand much about this island. It is no doubt the key I have been searching for these many years, up and down the winding paths.

Though it means a long doubling-back to the bustle of Cill Rónáin, I will follow Bóthar na gCrag farther west now, and pick up a few more scattered bones of stories lying about this rumorous hillside. Fortunately the Rocks Road, as it is often called, is too rough for traffic; it usually unwinds in utter quietness apart from one's own pebbly footfalls and perhaps the wishbone-thin scream of a lapwing overhead. At the scarp above An Coinleach it leaves Cill Rónáin territory – the boundary is a wall not much stouter nor much less crooked than all the others, that comes dog-legging across the island from north to south. A few hundred yards further on is a crossroads; the right-hand turn leads eventually to the main road, the left zigzags south-westwards, and after half a mile abandons you among a ragged patchwork of *creigeanna* or crags and *creigeáin*, plots hardly to be called fields but not quite as barren as crags. Bóthar na gCrag itself climbs on ahead, eventually to traverse the entire central section of the plateau of Na Craga. It is a good deal wider than the other boreens, and is edged by double walls topped with good-sized blocks of stone, every second one of which is set on edge and stands proud of its neighbours, forming a sort of rustic crenellation that gives the road an official presence. In my early days of enquiring out the island's history I asked a lady from one of the western villages how long ago the Rocks Road had been built. She looked rather mystified, and said, with a smile at herself, that she had supposed it was there since the beginning of the world. Later on I came across a reference to it having been 'built by Balfour' in 1891. Arthur Balfour was at that time Chief Secretary for Ireland. So this remote road, emanating from Westminster via Dublin Castle, was part of the network of measures with which the government sought to placate the desperation of the West; it was a 'relief work', built by hungry men, and one could see those crenellations as marking off the hours before they got their feed of Indian meal.

The road backs to the south-west to climb the last of the hill above the crossroads, and on its right here is an area well known as a *bruíon* or fairy dwelling. An Oatquarter man of two or three generations back, Col Citte, used to say he once heard the sound of milk being churned here, and of keening or wailing for the dead; but it was on a Sunday morning and he was late for Mass, and so he hurried by without investigating. The place is called Clochán an Airgid, the stone hut of the money, and if you leave the road and struggle across four field-walls straight up from the crossroads you might stumble upon the ruins of the *clochán* in question, sunk among hazel-thickets under the brow of the hill. Enough of its basis is visible among the collapse of its roof to show that it was circular, and about twelve feet across. The idea that there is treasure buried in it has been its ruination; it is nothing but a spoil-heap of frustrated hopes. The stories about the place are so disjointed and faded, though, that collecting them is like trying to read a rain-soaked page found tattered in a thornbush.

The same is true for another ruin in the vicinity, of which the scarcely decipherable foundations lie in the second field on the left, going north from the crossroads; it is said to have been a church, and for that reason it is left perplexed by undergrowth, but it is otherwise unremarked by tradition, nameless, and unvisited. But here I found out once more how many crossroads of perception there are, in incalculable permutations with those of the physical path. I had come to find this church, of which I had been told by Dara Mullen, and as I was crossing the field to its ruins, as obscure as everything else on this occult hillside, I heard through the whispering of the still summer afternoon something that could have been Col Citte's otherworldly churning. Falling water is so rare on Na Craga that I did not identify the sound until I saw a recess under a little scarp at the back of the field, in which silvery drops were cascading through fronds of maidenhair fern and making them tremble continuously. Around this lovely spring were more wild-flowers than I had ever gathered in a single glance. On one side of it was a small hawthorn bush with honeysuckle and meadow pea climbing through it, and a lemon-yellow spire of agrimony below, while on the other a tutsan leaned forward to display its flame-coloured berries. Brooklime was growing in the shadow behind the fern leaves, and the other flowers of damp pastures – purple loosestrife, yellow pimpernel, silverweed – mingled with the meadow flowers at my feet – purple clover, kidney vetch, meadow buttercup, tormentil, bird's foot trefoil. The stonier slope above the well assembled the flora of the crags at the level of my eyes: burnet rose, bloody cranesbill, mountain everlasting, milkwort, quaking grass, the tiny squinancywort, the last of the early purple orchids and the first of the common spotted orchids, all with a minutely delicate inter-weaving of fairy flax. Along the foot of the scarp beside the well I could see wild strawberry, scarlet pimpernel, sanicle, the elegant St John's wort. There were tall mulleins flowering on the top of the slope, and twayblades in the shadow of the thickets around the ruin. The band of grey limestone above the well gave it the solemnity of an altar, around which the plants were gathered, each in the colours of its faith. What truth, distilled moment by moment from the rock, was held in perpetual reservation in the dark cup below? The church behind me, brought to its knees among penitential thorns, attended humbly upon the priestcraft of water.

I will go a little farther, though I must turn back soon. The grey, knit brow of the hill, and the level heights beyond like a huge fossil mind, with echoes of old stories and whispers of 'they say' circulating in its stony cor-rugations, are to be read in wonderment. The road slants across the last rise of the hill, then turns 'Aran west' to integrate itself with the vast perspec-tive of the plateau top, in which a few thousand little fields, each a more or less remote hearsay version of a rectangle, are jigged into a grid of awesome regularity. Straighter and more determined than any other in Aran, the rocky road looks as if it is going to Dún Aonghasa on the distant skyline, though in fact it will drop into the intervening lowland a mile or so away and hidden from here. But at this point, which commands mountains pale with distance in Kerry, Clare and Connemara, and a wide threshold of the Atlantic, my attention always goes to a wild rose rooted in the loose stones of the verge. It forms a knee-high thicket several paces around, with hun-dreds of flowers like small ivory cups stained inside with purple-red in grainy streaks, and some grains of yellow too. When I check out its char-acteristics in a botanical key it seems to be a burnet rose, but perhaps it is crossed with another, for in Aran the burnet (*Rosa spinosissima* as it used to be called, the rose that perhaps tripped you into metaphysical associations in my 'Timescape with Signpost' long ago) is a sparse ankle-clutching thing with just a few stems and creamy-white petals. I have not had the heart to go and see if this exceptional beauty has survived the attempt that was made to 'improve' the road a few years ago; I prefer to leave its ghost as sen-tinel there.

And beside it, what is this odd wisp of small white cross-shaped blos-soms? *Arabis hirsuta*, the hairy rockcress, to be ticked off in the book. And then, ranks of tall valerian, swags of honeysuckle, red carpets of bloody cranesbill ... They say there was a couple once who often walked this road to their home farther west. Whoever they were, their eyes must have been full of flowers.

DEVELOPMENT

From its enchanted hinterland back to the plain town of Cill Rónáin the shortest, but not the most certain, route is by a neglected right-of-way of an oblique and secretive sort I shall be discussing later on in this book. It begins with the path of Creig an Chosáin, which connects with a sequence of not very noticeable stiles in walls leading across Creig na gCaorach, the crag of the sheep, and finally An Chreig Mhór, the big crag – in all, a traverse of nearly a mile of the most irremediably barren rock in Aran. Arriving somewhere (probably not where one intended exactly, given the obscurity of the way) on this desert tract's farther rim, a steep scarp or in places a cliff about twenty feet high, one finds oneself on a level with the rooftops a short distance ahead. This unofficial viewpoint shows that rock as well as sea has had its say in the siting of the town. The scarp runs north from the innermost point of Cill Éinne bay, and then curves to follow the general outline of the coast westwards, and Cill Rónáin has developed along an arc around and in the shelter of this shoulder of land. Like all the major scarps it has a line of springs along its foot and a narrow band of fertile land immediately below it, both due to the stratum of shale underlying the limestone. Such areas of naturally occurring soil are too precious to have been built on, so the houses are a little farther out, on the poorer ground along the rim of the next terrace below the great crag. In fact the buildings in the foreground of the view from the scarp-top are additions from the 1950s and '60s: the health and dental clinics, and the community hall. Nearby is the Catholic church, a stolid blue-limestone building dedicated in 1905; it stands on a little road that bypasses most of the town, slipping between small green fields frisky with calves in spring, in the lee of the scarp. The buildings just mentioned are at the back of the town, and what one sees beyond them in this rear view are the generally greyish and unkempt backpremises of the shops, b&bs and bars of Iochtar an Bhaile, the 'bottom of the village', the nucleus of old Cill Rónáin, focused on the old quay.

The other essential stay of the modern community is the vocational school, Gairmscoil Éinne, where children can now study up to Leaving Certificate level without making that break with the island their parents so much fear as the first step into emigration. The large planes of its pitched, tiled roofs show over the house-tops at the other extremity of the town, a third of a mile north along the gentle rise of the terrace. That neighbourhood was once the hamlet of Baile an Dúin, named, it is supposed, from a long-gone ring-fort or some such ancient enclosure. It had its own boreen to the sea at Trá na bhFranncach, and felt little need of connection with the original Cill Rónáin; in fact the Ordnance Survey map of 1839 shows one road running north from Baile an Dúin to Port Mhuirbhigh, and another running south from Cill Rónáin to Cill Éinne, but no road at all linking the two clusters of cottages. By the time of the revised map of 1898 the Protestant establishment had filled this gap; the constabulary barracks, the coastguard station, the Episcopal church of St Thomas and the rectory, with their slate roofs and plastered façades, were the first substantial buildings in Cill Rónáin, four cornerstones of Protestant rule spanning the gap between one clump of thatch around the old quay and the other to the north. The barracks, a grey-faced two-storey house on the main road, has long been shared between a pub and the post-office, and its earlier role is witnessed only by the names that two or three of its former occupants passed a few of their boring hours inscribing on the natural limestone flag paving its little forecourt. The coastguard station is down a little side-road opposite, and still looks out across the bay with a degree of professional smartness; a corner of it is occupied by the gardaí, another by the telecommunications link with the mainland, and the rest has recently become a heritage centre, and both buildings are welded by the press of more recent developments into the lower part of the town. But the zone just beyond them has again become rather void with the extinction of the Protestant presence since Independence, for St Thomas's stands roofless and sky-windowed in a tussocky roadside field around the edges of which are a few graves, the National School has taken over half of the rectory grounds as its football field, and the rectory itself has been reduced to low ragged walls and broken outhouses, its stone gone into the Catholic curate's house nearby. The rector's untrodden drive curves down from broken iron gates into a shadowy grove of sycamores, the wind-bevelled tops of which make a huge bank to the road, buzzing like a generator with flies in the summer, turbulent and gesticulatory in winter, as opulent and alien a presence in the otherwise treeless town as was the Protestant ascendancy in its day.

Iochtaír an Bhaile ('Downtown' might translate it without too much satire) is where Aran happens, in the eyes of most visitors and many islanders. Two or three pubs, the bright and orderly supermarket which has replaced the shadowy old village shop with its chaotic shelves, the smart restaurant that has been made out of the dingy court-house and obsolete dispensary, several craft-shops and half a dozen guest-houses, cluster where the main road is linked to the water-front by a twisty alley and the triangular space – which one might almost call a place – the vertex of which is a high cross, to remind us of the parish priest who set the town on its feet a century ago. For the summer visitors, sitting on the wall outside the American Bar with their pints or their icecreams from the shop opposite, this bottle-neck of minibuses and pony-traps is something between street theatre and street party, exotic enough to hold the attention as spectacle, homely enough to make lingering there comfortable. But for misanthropes like ourselves, inhabitants by choice of the secluded western hamlets, this is the invasive fringe of the Pantown we had hoped to leave behind us; it is Development, of which the future promises more and more. Pushing our bikes laden with shopping through the social rapids we escape it as quickly as possible; we sneer at its 'pub culture' of slurred philosophy and incipient brawl, and profess only to like the place in winter, comatose under a yawning skyful of rain. The dilemma of topographical writing is this, that to omit the areas one feels alienated from is to disrupt one's mirroring of the earth's continuities, while to include them is to exhibit as blemishes what may in fact merely be dull spots of the mirror, failures of sympathy or comprehension. And the usual escape from this dilemma is into the time dimension, where even drab contingencies have their precedents and pedigrees. Perhaps the interest of the little town will emerge from my indirections, if I poke around in its history awhile.

I begin by revisiting the high cross, and looking up what I wrote in *Pilgrimage* about the man it honours :

He was Father Michael O'Donoghue, parish priest of Aran from 1881 to 1892, and he is said to have sent a telegram to Dublin Castle in 1886:

SEND US BOATS OR SEND US COFFINS

– an act which, if not so miraculously or electrically causative of the C.D. Board's intervention as oral history would have it, is the perfect emblem of his dedicated representation of his flock in the face of governmental delay and the agent's rapacity.

I detect a note of polite acquiescence in this; it reads as if I had felt that in the absence of hard facts I had better go along with the conventional pieties. Let me take a closer look at those crucial years in the fortunes of Cill Rónáin.

In fact this famous telegram, mentioned in several accounts of the islands, has proved hard to pinpoint. Antoine Powell, the author of the most thoroughly researched history of Aran, found no official record of its having been received. However, recently I came across the following, in *Memories: Wise and Otherwise*, the memoirs of Sir Henry Robinson, who was an executive of the Local Government Board at that period:

'Send relief or send coffins,' was another dramatic effort of the part of a Galway priest to waken the Government to the necessity of relief works, and the effect of this portentious telegram would have alarmed the Government very much less than it did had they seen the parish priest taking it round the town and showing it with the utmost hilarity to his friends. Among others, he took it to his old friend the late member for Galway, George Morris, the Vice-President of the Local Government Board. The official utterance of the Vice-President on this occasion was, 'Begorra, Father James, you are the boy who knows how to talk to them.' No one really took the telegram seriously except the Irish Office, who were rather upset about it, as although they referred it to the Local Government Board for observations, the Vice-President could not very well explain that he himself on the previous day had highly commended the parish priest for the humour of it.

Morris became Vice-President of the LBG in the winter of 1890, and so, if Sir Henry's memory here is one of his wise ones, the telegram was sent between that time and Fr O'Donoghue's leaving the islands in 1892. Whether this was one of the hungrier periods in Aran is doubtful. Sir Henry, a staunch Loyalist, regarded the various Catholic priests he had to deal with in the west as wily buffoons, and he has some disgracefully funny anecdotes to back his opinion. He also felt that the government's policy of funding relief-works in time of shortage led to gross exaggerations of the prevalence of 'distress':

Who indeed could be surprised at it? Conceive what weekly payments of wages must have meant to a people living on credit, who never had the handling of money and only caught a fleeting glimpse of it after the sale of their livestock as it passed from their possession to the pockets of shopkeepers, landlords, and cess collectors and other creditors. ... Small wonder, then, when relief works were hinted at, that the people were almost beside themselves in their efforts to persuade the Government that the distress was acute and overwhelming near their homes. They found willing helpers in every quarter to back them up, as the famine was a godsend to everyone. The shopkeeper saw in it a means of wiping off his bad debts, the clergy received their dues with punctuality, the police got 4s. per head per day for superintending the work, and the landlords and cess collectors had arrears of rent and rates reduced and found that they were no longer engaged in the hopeless task of trying to get blood out of a stone.

Even W.L. Micks of the CDB, who was committed to the nationalist cause, had much the same to say, in his own buttoned-up manner:

I was for many years entrusted with the supervision of Poor Law administration at different times in counties embracing congested districts, in which I was a resident inspector when failures of the potato crop and other calamities caused distress more or less serious. At such times I was painfully conscious of my serious responsibility for ascertaining the actual condition of the poor. It was my two-fold duty to give such information as would enable the Department to adopt measures for the prevention of suffering from destitution by the poor, and at the same time to submit such accurate reports as would tend to avert an unnecessary expenditure of public funds in deference to exaggerated assertions of the existence of destitution. ... There used to be a most natural desire on the part of some shopkeepers and others, including the indebted poor, to have money brought into and spent in a locality. This led to a competition in the making of grossly exaggerated statements as to the condition of the inhabitants in order to secure the starting of relief-works. If the promoters succeeeded in their efforts, almost every man in the district, whether in need or not, tried to 'get a share of what was going'.

Is there an objective truth about the degree of suffering, to be estimated by averaging out the reports of priests and officials? Both classes would have been inured to seeing the vast majority of the people around them in circumstances so different from their own as to preclude imaginative identification. Their assessments of those peoples' distress in any given year or neighbourhood would not have been relative to their own circumstances but to the indigenous community's welfare in previous recent years and similar nearby districts. In these terms, in terms of a forecasted death-count for the year in question, Fr O'Donoghue's telegram probably exaggerated. But to begin to feel what life was like for his flock, it helps to consider how it changed during his pastorship. There is also the question of how instrumental he personally was in the improvement; the 'hilarity' of Sir Henry Robinson's disturbing anecdote might throw some light on that.

When Fr O'Donoghue came to Aran in 1881 the talk must have been of the latest dirty deed – poison in a cattle-trough, a bullock blinded – in a furtive campaign against the landlord's agent, the Protestant vicar, O'Flaherty the middleman, and the bailiffs; also, of hunger and crop failures, and of the government's response, the extra police sent in to man the new barracks at Cill Mhuirbhigh, the gunboats *Bruiser* and *Merlin* nosing round the coast. Whereas in the year of his departure, 1892, all attention was on the catches being landed by the *Rover's Bride, True Light, Mystical Rose*, and the other exotically named fishing-boats from Arklow that had come to work out of Cill Rónáin; and in the next year, the year of his early death, of the Aran boats that joined them, the *St Enda, Mary and Joseph, Louisa Mary Ann, Hero, M'Laren Smith, St Patrick, Breaker*, and the *Father O'Donoghue* itself, an Arklow-built nobby bought, like two of the other boats, out of a fund raised by Fr O'Donoghue. And although after the 1894 season the Arklow crews were so poor that a collection had to be made to get them home, and only one of the Aran boats was not in debt, a fleet and a fishery had been established, which persisted with some fortune until the disturbances of the 1920s. While it was true, as a critic writing in the *New Ireland Review* a few years later pointed out, that the number of Aran boats was very small for a community of 530 families, Mr Micks was justified in the longer term in claiming that

The development of the Aran fishery improved the condition of the islanders wonderfully, as others beside fishermen were employed in icing, packing, curing and handling the boxes of fish. All classes in the islands seemed to benefit, shop-keepers included, as larger earnings caused greater expenditure.

So it was fitting that a boat of the new Aran fleet should be named in memory of the priest who had piloted Aran out of the stormy gloom of the 1880s to within sight of the shores of the new century. But undoubtedly that was the way the tide was setting, as is clear when the Aran story is read in the context of the changing policies of British government.

The widespread 'distress' of 1879, an exceptionally cold and wet year in the west of Ireland, and the wave of evictions that followed on failure to pay the rents, had been answered by the foundation of the Land League to fight for tenants' rights. By the end of 1880 most of the Aran tenants were members of the local branch, whose treasurer was the Catholic curate Fr Fahey. A famine had been averted, largely by the efforts of Dublin-based voluntary committees which collected funds world-wide. An American relief organization sent a frigate full of food and clothes, some of which were distributed by British warships around the inaccessible coasts and islands of the west; the Duke of Edinburgh's visit to Cill Éinne, mentioned in *Pilgrimage*, was in this connection. Sir Henry Robinson sailed on some of these missions, and noted the contradictions of English policy:

The multifarious functions of the gunboats on the West coast were very puzzling to the islanders. The same vessels which came with food supplies for the people and departed with bonfires blazing on the beach in their honour would return in a few days with bailiffs, process servers and police to sweep the island bare for rents or rates. Then, after a pitched battle, away would go the bailiffs with their seizures, and back again would come the gunboats after a few weeks' interval with tons of meal to help the people to tide over the further distress caused by its previous visit!

This deathly comedy was symptomatic of the government's contradictory impulses, faced simultaneously with the distress and the terrorism of the Land League, a menacing shadow behind Parnell's Home Rule campaign at Westminster. The Aran outrages, culminating in the tumbling of the O'Flaherty's cattle over the cliffs into the Atlantic, were just part of the Land War, and they happened to coincide with one aspect of the government's response, the Coercion Act of January 1881. Fr O'Donoghue's arrival in August of that year coincided with the other aspect, the Fair Rents Act, under which tenants gained the right to sell their leases and were protected against eviction except for non-payment of rent, and a Land Commission was instituted to adjudicate on fair rents.

Events in Aran answered to the polarities of these policies. Two islanders, including the secretary of the local Land League branch, were arrested on suspicion of complicity in the cliffing of the O'Flaherty cattle and were held without trial under the Coercion Act for four months; the island was so 'disturbed' that the Galway JP could not come out to hear the rent-arrears cases pending, while the bailiff was shot at and had his sheep stolen. But Aran calmed down, like the rest of the country, after the 'proclamation' of the Land League as an illegal organization, and with the growing willingness of tenants to try their luck with the Land Courts.

In fact so many cases were initiated that it was not until the summer of 1884 that a sitting was held in Cill Rónáin, at the request of Fr O'Donoghue. The court heard a hundred and seventy cases, and in most of them rents were reduced by a third or more. In July 1886 another fifty tenants had their rents decreased by 40 per cent. A Land Commission barrister present on this occasion, Oliver J. Burke, was moved to write a book, *The South Islands of Aran* (London, 1887). This is the first comprehensive account of Aran's natural features, ancient monuments, history and contemporary modes of life, but his main motive in writing it was 'to direct the attention of those in power to the long neglected islands'.

Burke describes a typical session of the Land Court, with the Araners 'squatting like Mahomedans' to hear the solicitors' arguments. On the one side are the legal representatives of Miss Digby and the Hon. Thomas Kenelm Digby St Lawrence, second son of Thomas, twenty-ninth Baron, third Earl of Howth, and on the other, 'Michael O Donel', tenant. ('My father and his father were tenants on that holding since the Deluge at all events – couldn't swear longer than that!' – 'Do you swear that?' – 'Well of coorse I couldn't swear it out and out.') The tenant's holding consists of twenty-two acres of which five are nothing but rocks and stones; his rent is £3.18s.6d, the house and barn are his own, he pays £3 a year for a boatload of turf, he grew 80 stone of potatoes last year, but no grain. His stock consists of a cow and a veal calf, a horse, five sheep, eight lambs and two pigs. He keeps the wool for his family, and the stock last year realized £12; the sheep go to Ennistymon fair in Co. Clare, the cattle and pigs to Galway on the mailboat, at a freight of 2s 6d for calves and 1s for pigs; he was sixteen days weather-bound in Galway after last February's fair. Next Mr Thompson of Clonskea Castle, Co. Dublin, is sworn in. The total rental of the three islands, he explains, is £2067, and has hardly varied since the beginning of the century. The tenants have manure and seaweed free of charge. Seaweed was very valuable in 1866 when £2577 worth of kelp was made, at £5 a ton, but now no kelp is made owing to the fall in price. The sub-commissioners then inspect the farm, and in due course the rent is reduced by 40 per cent to £2.7s. 6d.

But, asks Mr Burke, can any reduction of rent or even security of tenure really improve the islanders' condition? What is needed is schools to instruct them in deep-sea fishing, navigation, ship-building and net-making, as well as improved piers and a telegraphic link with Galway so that the steamer can come out and collect the catch. The people are too poor to buy first-class boats. He quotes a letter from the rector, Mr Kilbride, dated December 1886:

Men's wages vary. No constant work. Spring and the seaweed gathering the chief harvests for the labourer, who seldom has more than four months' work in the year, so it is a necessity for him to get gardens on hire. Until last year or the year before he got 1s to 1s 6d with his diet in the spring, at harvest about 1s with his diet, three meals in the day, bread and tea for breakfast etc. When there is a hurry at seaweeding time he used to get 2s 6d and diet, but this only lasts a week twice in the year. ... What kept the poor rate down last year and this was the amount of relief given out. Thompson laid out £140 on a road and £136 on seed potatoes. Sir John Barrington has given me upward of £100 for the object, and this year he gave me £80 or £90 for seed potatoes and £120 for relief and also money to assist emigration and to buy turf. The people will suffer terribly for want of fuel. The potato crop is all gone. No fish whatever taken. Any further information you want I will freely give.

Indeed the years between 1884 and 1887 were hard on the islands, because of failures of the potato crop. When Fr O'Donoghue's representations to the government produced nothing, he appealed to the public through the *Freeman's Journal,* and was generously answered by private donors, among them a lawyer, George Shee, of Ipswich in England.

It was from this stony-broke community, in 1886, that the Galway authorities attempted to squeeze out nearly £2000. The sum was made up of arrears of rates unpaid since 1882, plus a communal fine of £452, being the compensation that had been paid out to owners of stock and goods destroyed in the Land War, and another £622 for the cost of the extra police force sent in 1881. The rates collector was a Frank Kelly, butcher, of An Spidéal; Antoine Powell tells us how he fared:

It was not long before he was made aware that every mother's son in the islands would be out against him if he came gathering rates. So he had to ask the authorities to provide an escort before he could go to the islands. The Government gave him the defence force, but no boat owner between An Spidéal and Galway was agreeable to renting him a boat. In the end he had to put off the rate collection until the next year. In April 1887 Kelly managed to rent a boat from a servant of Sir Valentine Blake's, and the government agreed to provide a warship to bring him and his guard to the island and to tow the boat for the distrained beasts. On the 26th of May the warship Orwell sailed from Galway with Frank Kelly and his escort of fifteen RIC men under the command of a sergeant... It was evening by the time they reached Árainn Mhór, and so they decided not to start posting notices until the next day. The police escort was landed for the night, but Kelly and the sergeant stayed on board.

At six o'clock of the 27th, they both came ashore in a rowboat. While the sergeant was going up to the barracks for the defence force, the rowboat with Kelly pulled back from the quay because a noisy crowd was gathering. When he saw two constables on the quay he decided to land immediately, but as he was getting out of the boat he was hit by a stone. The man who threw the stone was arrested straight away and when the rest of the force arrived he was taken to the barracks. Then Kelly and his escort went along the road westwards from Cill Rónáin posting up bills, with about a hundred people following them. After they had gone about two miles they turned back, the crowd still following. Outside the barrack in Cill Rónáin another stone was thrown and again the man who threw it was arrested. As soon as he was under lock and key they went on towards Cill Éinne. But when they got as far as An Charcair Mhór the villagers came out to meet them, women carrying stones in the forefront. The sergeant halted the police, who were drawn up in a square around Kelly, and went forward to talk to the crowd. While he was doing so Kelly panicked, broke out of his escort, and set off at a run for Cill Rónáin. When the crowd saw him running they burst past the sergeant and those that were not able to get through the police square leaped over the walls and followed Kelly, throwing stones at him and at the police. At last the police caught up with Kelly again, a shot was fired in the air as a signal to the Orwell to launch its boats, and the sergeant threatened to fire on the crowd if any more stones were thrown. Kelly and one constable had head-wounds, another constable was wounded in the back, and the rest, though they had been hit, were uninjured.

After that Kelly resigned his post and nobody was appointed in his place. In 1890 the Council offered to waive the islands' arrears if the government was satisfied to do so. In 1891 the government agreed to wipe out the debts apart from the £452 fine imposed because of the Land War crimes.

Eventually the fine was paid, at the urging of a later parish priest, Fr Farragher, and after many visits from the sheriff and the RIC. Nevertheless, An Charcair Mhór was a famous victory, and a song was written about it. A few lines about a huge islander nicknamed 'the Wren' are still remembered:

> *Tháinig Kelly ag cur cíosa*
> *Ar mhuintir Árainn Mhór,*
> *Ach bhuail An Dreoilín mullán eibhir air*
> *Ag gabhail sios An Charcair Mhór.*

(Kelly came to put the rates / On the folk of Árainn Mhór, / But the Wren hit him with a granite boulder / Going down the Carcair Mhór.)

It was the pecks of countless wrens like this that eventually forced the British government to act on the condition of the west.

The Cill Mhuirbhigh barracks was closed in 1887 and the extra police withdrawn, and the latter years of Fr O'Donoghue's incumbency were relatively peaceful and productive. He had long been agitating for better school buildings, but though grants had been forthcoming for this purpose since 1882 no sites were made available until some years later – it is said that the agent Thompson refused to facilitate the education of 'papist brats' until the Viceroy, Lord Carnarvon, intervened, having heard of this during a visit to the islands. By 1889 the neat, slated schools had been built, and teachers' residences were in construction. In 1890 Fr O'Donoghue petitioned the Government for a regular steamer service from Galway, an idea he had been pursuing unsuccessfully since his earliest days in the islands, and in the following year the steamer *Duras* of the Galway Bay Steamboat Company began thrice-weekly sailings. This link was to be the key element in the government-assisted development of the fisheries in the next few years.

The Congested Districts Board, set up under a Land Act of 1891, was the government's instrument in its belated undertaking of responsibility for the economic welfare of the west-of-Ireland peasantry. As M.L. Micks, the CDB's first secretary, wrote in his history of the organization:

The circumstances of these tenants, including the utter impossibility of their raising themselves by their own unaided effort, were recognised by Mr. Arthur Balfour in 1891, and he has the credit of being the first British Minister who acknowledged in a practical way that the universal poverty of the West of Ireland was a disgrace to British government.

The 'congested districts' comprised those areas, mainly of the Atlantic seaboard from Donegal to Cork, whose resources were inadequate for their populations, and were initially defined as those Poor Law Electoral Divisions in which the total rateable value per head of population was less than thirty shillings. By this or any other definition of inadequate means, the Aran Islands had a call on the CDB, and since the development of fisheries was the area of expertise of some of the initial members of the Board, it was inevitable that it would soon take Aran under its wing. In fact Cill Rónáin with its steamer link now had an advantage over comparable ports in Connemara and elsewhere, for fish could be brought to the rail-head in Galway in much better condition by steamer than, for instance, by cart from Roundstone. The traditional long-line fishing for cod, ling and glassan was encouraged by the Board's guaranteed prices, loans for purchasing better equipment, and the introduction of Scottish methods of fish-curing. The Rev. W.S. Green, who was Chief Fisheries Inspector as well as a Board member, was convinced that a spring mackerel fishery by drift-netting could be established in Galway Bay, and the Board offered bounties to the Arklow boats to come and prove it. It also undertook to subsidize the steamer company to transport the catch, arranged net-mending classes, had a hulk full of Norwegian ice moored in Cill Éinne bay, instituted a telegraph link by which contact could be maintained with markets, and in 1900 opened a boat-building yard. The transformation of the seaward aspect of Cill Rónáin, described in my first volume, was the sign of these forward-looking times.

Micks, in his history of the CDB, does not mention Fr O'Donoghue and it is unlikely that the PP's representations to the government were crucial to these developments. What Sir Henry Robinson's anecdote about the telegram shows, though, is that the priest was a man of the world who thoroughly understood the opportunities afforded by the new governmental policy (often satirized as 'trying to kill Home Rule by kindness'), and was on familiar terms with the officials charged with executing it. To the islanders, for whom the government spelt gunboats and constables, his powers of leverage must have seemed heroic, if not supernatural.

So it was indeed the O'Donoghue decade that put Aran in tow to the way of the world – and only a few years after he had gone, the writers and artists and Irish-language enthusiasts who flocked to the newly accessible islands were lamenting a simplicity that was being lost even as they discovered it. Synge expresses the dilemma of 'development' concisely:

One feels ... that it is part of the misfortune of Ireland that nearly all the characteristics which give colour and attractiveness to Irish life are bound up with a social condition that is near to penury, while in countries like Brittany the best external features of the local life – the rich embroidered dresses, for instance, or the carved furniture – are connected with a decent and comfortable social condition.

Was there any other way out of the miseries of that time? Could it be that Fr O'Donoghue's memorial marks a historical juncture, from which there was another road, not taken? Given the universality of the changes then impending on the island, I doubt if any purely local way forward would have been viable. Perhaps, though, now that the whole world finds that the highway of development ends in a squalid cul-de-sac from which we will have to back out with much difficulty, Aran will live to see a re-evaluation of that quality it still holds within itself, just over the wall, as it were, from Cill Rónáin. On winter evenings in the 1970s I occasionally attended, out of a flickering sense of civic duty, public meetings in the community hall. Debate sometimes shrank away into wrangles between two personages I came to think of as the delegate from the future and the delegate from the past, the latter a talking archive of discouraging precedents, the former's visions fuddled by drink. Nevertheless, valuable work was done by a handful of islanders, and some intermittently effective structures representing the community to itself and the outside world were set up. But what I chiefly remember from those tedious sessions, is my slipping out and standing at the door of the hall to watch the moon, that fourth, aloof and elusive Aran Island, float up from the dimly gleaming rim of crag behind the town.

STATISTIC AND SENTIMENTAL TOURISTS

If the Islands of Aran had formed a portion of the Hebrides or Orkneys, or stood in view of any part of the British coast, they would, long since, have been made the theme of the statistic and sentimental tourist; but, though abounding with many particulars, valuable to the Antiquary, Historian and Philosopher, they have been hitherto neglected.

So begins John T. O'Flaherty's 'A Sketch of the History and Antiquities of the Southern Isles of Aran, lying off the West Coast of Ireland; with Observations on the Religion of the Celtic Nations, Pagan Monuments of the Early Irish, Druidic Rites, &c.', published in *Transactions of the Royal Irish Academy* in 1824. Thus we have no Aran equivalent of the solemn organtones of Dr Johnson treading Iona, 'that illustrious island, which was once the luminary of the Caledonian regions', or of Boswell's irrepressible fife-music trotting after. None of the well-known eighteenth-century travellers through Ireland, from the *spirituel* Chevalier de Latocnaye to the dry and 'statistic' Arthur Young, considered Aran worth the detour. Roderic O'Flaherty had devoted two dozen pages to Aran 'as in a sea-parenthesis' to his *West or H-Iar Connaught*, but even that remained unpublished until 1846. So it is J.T. O'Flaherty (a member of a branch of the Connemara O'Flahertys who had removed to Kerry) who inaugurates the first re-imagination of Aran since the medieval vision of it in mystic constellation with Jerusalem, Rome and the Garden of Eden. The Romantic rediscovery of Nature sets the scene for his version of Aran:

The approach to the Isles of Aran presents a view awfully sublime. Elevated above a wide tract of deep and boisterous ocean, and opposing to the beating billows an impregnable and perpendicular barrier of massy and lava-coloured rock, several hundred feet high, one may easily associate with the sublimity of the scene, and its Alpine grandeur, something of the terrors of a Vesuvian eruption, or of that violent shock, which is supposed to have torn these isles from the neighbouring continent.

Something of the history of Aran was available to J.T. O'Flaherty – the traditional account of the Fir Bolg, then believed to be factual, a few names and dates of early abbots put together from the Annals by editors of lives of the saints, a few records of transfer of ownership gleaned from the *History of Galway* Hardiman had recently published. O'Flaherty recapitulates this stuff, but more importantly, in his 'statistic' mode, he sketches the economics of the islands – an economics of modest sufficiency, not yet sapped into destitution by rack-renting and crop failure:

The prevailing crops are potatoes, rye, and a small kind of black oats, all of which ripen early, and are of good quality, and sufficiently productive. The islanders sow some small quantities of barley and wheat, and in that operation employ an increased amount of manure. They have also small quantities of flax. On the whole their harvest seldom exceeds domestic consumption; agriculture, however, is daily improving. Their pasture land is appropriated to sheep, goats, and a few small cows and horses, for which latter they reserve some meadow. The mutton is considered delicious; but their most profitable stock consists of calves, which are reputed to be the best in Ireland. The general longevity of the inhabitants proves the excellent temperature of the air. There is a late instance of an Aranite having died at, or about, the age of one hundred and fifty. ... The frugal meal of the Aranite, and his active habits, secure to him those inestimable blessings, to which the pampered and the great are strangers – security of mind, good health, and green old age.

Fish, kelp, and yearling calves, are almost the only articles of traffic; Galway, and the surrounding country, the chief mart. There are belonging to the three islands about 120 boats, 30 or 40 of which have sails, and are from five to ten tons burden; the rest are row boats. The spring and beginning of summer are employed in the Spillard [*i.e.* long-line] fishery; here are taken immense quantities of cod, ling, haddock, turbot, gurnet, mackrel, bream, &c. and, in the season, abundance of lobsters, oysters, crabs, scollops, cockles, muscles, &c. They look much to the herring fishery, which sometimes disappoints, but generally gratifies, their best expectations. In May, the pursuit of the sun-fish gives employment to many. This rich supply of sustenance seems perfectly providential, when we consider the scanty soil and dense population of the islands. ... These several islands are the estate of Mr. Digby. ... His annual rental on the islands, is £2700.

This reads like a summary of on-the-spot enquiry, but unfortunately in treating of loftier matters such as Aran's druidical marvels O'Flaherty abandons the 'statistic' for the 'sentimental'. He offers no enumeration or description of these 'open temples, altars, stone pillars, sacred mounts of fire worship, miraculous fountains, and evident vestiges of oak groves'; his antiquarianism was not of the tedious measuring kind. For him, imbued with the enthusiasm for the Celtic of such turn-of-the-century antiquarians as Charles Vallancey, not only were cairns and cashels the fire-temples of druidism, which he equates with both Zoroastrianism and the ancient Jewish religion, but the 'cromlechs', now known to be Neolithic tombs, were druidical altars, while round towers, 'if not themselves covered fire temples, were, at least, constructed, more or less, on the model of our minarets of paganism'.

It is the solidarity of the islanders with their Celtic past that most excites his faculties of sentiment:

The Aranites in their simplicity, consider these remains of Druidism still sacred and inviolable; being, they imagine, the inchanted haunts and property of aerial beings, whose powers of doing mischief they greatly dread and studiously propitiate. For entertaining this kind of religious respect, they have another powerful motive: they believe that the cairns, or circular mounts, are the sepulchures, as some of them really are, of native chiefs and warriors of antiquity, of whose military fame and wondrous achievements they have abundance of legendary stories. The well-attended winter-evening tales of the *Scealuidhe*, or story-tellers, are the only historical entertainments of this primitive, simple and sequestered people. ... In language, habits, and customs, they retain more of the primitive Celtic character than any of the contemporary tribes of that stock, at least, in this kingdom. Sequestered and almost unmixed as the Aranites have been for a long succession of generations, history has always considered them as full of that ancient spirit, which has been made elsewhere made to disappear by the force of revolutionary and colonial innovations. ... Their immemorial traditions and practices may, without stretch of imagination, be viewed as the graphic annals of 'olden' days.

However, even as the Aranites were being rediscovered in their Celtic Eden, rumours of the Fall began to circulate. The young painter and archaeologist-to-be, George Petrie, visited in 1821 (though his report on 'Aran – character of the islanders' was not published until 1868):

I had heard so much of the virtues of the Aran islanders, of their primitive simplicity, their ingenuous manners, and their singular hospitality, that I could not help doubting the truth of a picture so pleasing and romantic, and felt anxious to ascertain, by personal observation, how far it might be real. ... The introduction, a few years since, of a number of persons into Aranmore for the purpose of erecting a lighthouse, has had an injurious effect on the character of the native inhabitants of the island ... and their interesting qualities have been in some degree diminished. ... The proximity of the island of Innisheer to the Clare coast rendering an intercourse with the parent counrtry easy, has long given to the inhabitants of that island a superior shrewdness, marked with an occasional want of principle, which causes them to be dreaded in their dealings, and in some degree disliked by the other islanders. ... In the island of Innishmain alone, then, the character of the Aran islander has wholly escaped contamination, and there it still retains all its delightful pristine purity. Collectively, however, the inhabitants of the Aran islands may be said to exhibit the virtues of the Irish character with, perhaps, as little intermixture of its vices as the lot of humanity will permit. They are a brave and hardy race, industrious and intelligent, credulous, and, in matters of faith, what persons of a different creed would call superstitious; but being out of the reach of religious animosity, they are as yet strangers to bigotry and intolerance. Lying and drinking – the vices which Arthur Young considers as appertaining to the Irish character – form at least no part of it in Aran; for happily their common poverty holds out less temptation to the one or opportunity for the other. ... They are to be considered, not as a fair specimen of the wild Irish of the present day, but rather as a striking example of what that race might generally be, under circumstances equally happy.

These circumstances, one gathers from the glowing account of them that follows, consist in the patriarchal benevolence of Patrick O'Flaherty of Cill Mhuirbhigh, with whom Petrie lodged, and the sanctity of the parish priest, Fr Francis O'Flaherty, both living representatives of the Celtic chieftaincy of old. Nevertheless, shadows of emigration, fever and hunger show here and there between the lines of Petrie's sketch of this last sea-protected bastion of simplicity.

Petrie, unlike J. T. O'Flaherty, actually sought out and looked carefully at Aran's ancient monuments, and it was his first-hand studies in Aran and throughout Ireland, that rendered speculations of O'Flaherty's sort obsolete. In 1833 he wrote a paper, 'The Round Towers of Ireland', showing from both material and textual evidence that these towers were monastic appurtenances. This and his 'Military Architecture in Ireland' of 1834 mark the introduction of scientific discipline into Irish archaeology. At this period the government were undertaking the preparation of detailed maps of Ireland, primarily so that rates could be more equitably imposed. In 1835 Petrie became Director of what was called the topographical department of the Ordnance Survey, charged with compiling historical and antiquarian information, which it was hoped would be published in memoirs accompanying the maps. This department took on so vigorous a life of its own that in the end it was seen as a threat to the original purposes of the survey.

Petrie's principal colleague was John O'Donovan, the foremost expert of his age on the ancient manuscripts of Ireland, and an incredibly energetic field-worker. For a decade, from 1834, O'Donovan travelled Ireland,

recording placenames, local history and folklore, and describing antiquities; his Letters to the Ordnance Survey, written from the field to base,
amount to a hundred and three large volumes – a vast mosaic of Ireland's
past as reflected in its ruins, lore and manuscripts, all held together as if by
ivy, in a knotted and vivid account of his travels. Although the Ordnance
Survey was eventually ordered by a parsimonious government to 'revert
immediately to its original object under the Valuation Acts', and the topographical department was disbanded, so that O'Donovan's vast corpus of
work was left unpublished (as most of it is to this day), his informed enthusiasm for Aran would have fed back into the world of scholarship by
numerous channels; for instance his memoirs on Aran and Connemara
took the form of commentary on Roderic O'Flaherty, and were reproduced
with very little alteration (or indeed acknowledgment) by Hardiman in his
edition of *West or H-Iar Connaught* in 1846.

O'Donovan came to Aran in excited expectation that it would 'afford a
rich mine of ancient remains.' But his was an empirical and sardonic temperament. Had he condescended to notice J.T. O'Flaherty's ideas on cromlechs and round towers, he would have applied to them the treatment recommended in his circle for refuting the Celtomaniac fantasies of
Vallancey's followers: 'First, break into an immediate horse-laugh, and then
suddenly altering from gay to grave, from lively to severe, with one immortal and terrific frown desire them to go to the devil for drivelling twaddlers.'
Also, having been brought up on a little farm near Waterford, attended a
hedge-school and learned Irish from native speakers, O'Donovan was not
such a naive enthusiast for the Irish countryman as O'Flaherty or even
Petrie. Here is his arrival in Cill Rónáin with his colleague the artist
William Wakeman, at three in the morning after a twelve-hour voyage in a
Claddagh fishing-boat:

We climbed up the big stones of which the little quay of Kilronan is built, and
finding ourselves on the solid rocks of Aran we proceeded by the guidance of the
two Claddagh men, and one native Aranite, to the head Inn of Aranmore, in
which being now chilly and fatigued, we were anxious to get our heads in, and lay
down our heads to sleep for a few hours. ... On arriving at the house, our sailors
rapped at the door several times, but no answer was made, which made me believe
they had brought us to the wrong house, at which the youngest of them pushed
in the door! Immediately after this I observed a glimmer of light, and heard a voice
inviting us in. The man of the house was drunk, and having been very unruly the
evening before in quarrelling with his wife and all that came in his way, he was
after getting a beating from the priest, who deemed it his duty to beat him into
something like rationality. I heard a good deal about his history since, but I dis-
dain to waste my time in talking about such a being.

The low life which in hovels grovels, novels
May paint.

After a glass of 'mountain dew punch' O'Donovan went to bed hungry
and got a few hours fitful, feverish sleep; then after breakfast he set off for
Dún Aonghasa. Wakeman describes O'Donovan's ecstasy there:

A smart walk brought us in sight of the object of our day's pilgrimage; and I shall
never forget O'Donovan's burst of enthusiasm when the old palace fortress of the
days of Queen Maeve first met our view. He literally shouted with delight, and,
after launching his umbrella a marvellous height into the air, threw himself on the
ground, and shouted again and again.

They spent the day examining the fort, and walked back to the inn;
O'Donovan later wrote, 'I never felt so fatigued by any journey, having all
day walked about on the solid rock.' The next day they visited Cill Éinne,
and were disappointed to find the churches they had read about in Colgan
nearly all destroyed. O'Donovan's settled determination, during field-work,
was to keep clear of the gentry; as he said of the Connemara landlords, 'Any
information they could afford me, would not be worth a pinch of salt. All
a waste of time!' But at Cromwell's fort he bumped into Martin O'Malley
of the Hill Farm, 'who told us that this fort had been built on the site of
the castle of Arkin for the purpose of defending the Dutch fishermen to
whom the English government in the reign of William III sold the fisheries
on the western coasts of Ireland. I did not feel inclined to believe this to be
a fact'. On the other hand he was always anxious to search out the aborig-
ines, as he called them, in whatever locality he was investigating, in order
to hear their pronunciation of place-names and collect their folklore. The
name of Dún Aonghasa itself was, he found, 'now forgotten by all the
inhabitants except one old man of the name of Wiggins dwelling at Killeany. He, though not of the primitive Irish race, but of a colony planted
here by Cromwell, remembers that the old people were accustomed to call
it Dun Innees, which is the true Irish pronunciation according to the Connaught accent. All the other inhabitants style it Dun mor, and in English
the Big Fort.' Thus the crucial link with the Celtic past was preserved only
by a descendant of the English garrison, an irony that probably appealed to
O'Donovan's humour.

O'Donovan spent just six days in this whirlwind rush from site to site
throughout the three islands. Then, leaving Wakeman to sketch all the
remains they had identified, he set off in a hired boat for Galway. His
description of the voyage, during which they were blown nearly to Casla
Bay, tossed for half an hour with the sails down through a fierce squall, and

only reached Black Head by seven in the evening after countless tackings, slips in and out of colloquial Irish and even incorporates a parody of the Four Masters' account of the shipwreck of a famous *stiúrasmann* or navigator of the O'Malleys off Aran in 1560; then:

I got into the forecastle of the boat to avoid the dashing of the waves which annoyed me not being able to bear much wet, but there I got quite sick from the smoak and the water dashing down the scuttle-hole which served for a chimney. When the storm had subsided a little, the sailors reefed and hoisted the sails again and found to their great satisfaction that during the squall the wind had veered about a little to the S. west at seeing which the Stiúrasmann cried out in Irish all is right now, thank God, we shall get to Galway now in a few half hours. In this, however, he was disappointed, for we did not reach Galway till 10 o'clock.

There O'Donovan settled down in Hardiman's library to write up Aran, and over three weeks produced two hundred and forty pages, including lengthy transcriptions and translations from Roderic O'Flaherty, the *Life of St Enda*, and other sources. (We nowadays can hardly comprehend the physical labour involved in scholarship before the invention of type-writers and photocopiers.) He begins his 'lucubrations' with a line from the medieval poem in which Colm Cille bids farewell to Aran on leaving for Iona, 'Ceileabhradh uaim-se d'Árainn', and he ends them with some impromptu doggerel based on the same poem. I copy this curiosity (with an English version kindly done for me by Dr Máirín Ní Dhonnchadha), as it has not been published before. The pun on *árainn*, meaning 'kidney' (in certain sayings it is a seat of the affections, like the heart) is untranslatable. Nor can I explain the reference to '*Áine álainn*', lovely Ann; perhaps there is some tender secret here, though it is scarcely conceivable that O'Donovan's breakneck progress through the islands left time for romance.

> *Ceileabhradh uaim-se d'Árainn; –*
> *'se théidheas anun trem árainn*
> *Scaramhuin leat a ghradh mo choim,*
> *Uair duit-se námá ádhroim.*
>
> *A sherc mo chroidhe 's mo árann,*
> *A thréig mé a n-inse Arann*
> *Soraidh uaim chugat gach luan*
> *Uair duit-se námá adhroim.*
>
> *Go dtigid cach die Sathrainn*
> *De nimh chugat a n-Arainn*
> *Aingil mhóra ag cantain ceoil*
> *Ad' bhenncadh a Áine Álainn.*

A farewell from me to Aran
And to that which goes through my kidney
To bid farewell to you, oh love of my bosom,
For it is you alone I adore.

Love of my heart and my kidney,
Whom I abandoned in the isle of Aran
A blessing from me to you each Monday
For it is you alone I adore.

May they come to you each Saturday,
From Heaven to you in Aran
Great angels singing music
Bestowing blessings on you, lovely Áine.

Finally, O'Donovan made a pilgrimage to the ruins of the house at Park, a few miles west of the city, where Roderic O'Flaherty had spent his last years in studious penury, having failed to regain the lands of which his father had been robbed by the Cromwellians. O'Donovan was deeply indebted to O'Flaherty's *Chorographical Description of West or H-Iar Connaught*, which was written at Park in 1684, apparently in connection with Sir William Petty's 'Down Survey', a cartographical summation of changes in land-ownership during the Cromwellian interregnum and the Restoration. But Roderic used to be better known as the author of a chronology of Irish history, *Ogygia: seu Rerum Hibernicarum Chronologia*, published in Latin in 1685; its mysterious title alludes to the fact that

Ireland is justly called Ogygia, *i.e.*, very antient, according to Plutarch, for the Irish date their history from the first oeras of the world: so that in comparison with them, the antiquity of all other countries is modern, and almost in its infancy!

In his day the penniless O'Flaherty was regarded as inheritor of this antiquity compared to which all others are in their infancy, and it was as an awe-struck disciple that O'Donovan came to the tomb of the scholar he calls 'the Ogygian':

I never felt so much moved, as when I sat on the little hill ... a low rock covered with mossy sward, commanding a panoramic view of the sea, the three islands of Aran and of a considerable extent of the northern coast of the Co. of Clare, on which the historian is said to have spent a great part of his time in the summer season, studying and enjoying the beauty of the prospect before him. ...

How genuine O'Donovan's emotion sounds, after the vapourings of his predecessors! And he must have felt he had earned the right to share the Ogygian's view of the Aran Islands from that hillock.

A web of cultural nationalism was being spun in those middle decades of the last century; Aran was involved from the start. The career of Samuel Ferguson – a Belfast Protestant, in his early days a supporter of Young Ireland, called to the Dublin bar in 1838, a poet and re-teller of old Irish legends, author of a scholarly work on ogham inscriptions, centre of the most entertaining and cultured circle of like-myriad-minded men and women, later Sir Samuel, and President of the Royal Irish Academy – draws together many of its threads. In 1852 he visited the three Arans, and found that:

The people themselves, so fine-natured, genial, and intelligent, are more worthy of regard than all their monuments from the fifth century downwards. ... They are a handsome, courteous, and amiable people. Whatever may be said of the advantages of a mixture of races, I cannot discern anything save what makes in favour of these people of the pure ancient stock, when I compare them to the mixed populations of districts on the mainland. The most refined gentleman might live among them in familiar intercourse, and never be offended by a gross or sordid sentiment. ... To see the careful way in which the most has been made of every spot available for the growth of produce, might correct the impression so generally entertained and so studiously encouraged, that the native Irish are a thriftless people. Here, where they are left to themselves, notwithstanding the natural sterility of their islands, they are certainly a very superior population – physically, morally, and even economically – to those of many of the mixed and planted districts.

A few years later, in 1857, Ferguson and his wife were of the company on that pinnacle of antiquarian passion for Aran I described in *Pilgrimage*, the banquet in Dún Aonghasa. On that glorious occasion, it is clear from the official chronicle of the excursion, every detail of Aran was bathed in the light of enthusiasm. The seventy Members and Associates of the Ethnological Section of the British Association, led by William Wilde of the Royal Irish Academy, had sailed out from Galway on the steam yacht *Vestal* on the previous day, when 'the Excursionists were in the best spirits; and it was evident that a keen anticipation of something of more than ordinary interest had been excited in the breast of all'. Coming ashore at Cill Éinne, they found the inhabitants of the village, in their picturesque costumes, had crowded to the shore to see them.

Mr. Wilde's duties as cicerone now commenced, and piping all hands with a small whistle. ... he explained in a few words the origin and character of the old walls of Arkin; and, observing that they were only a Saxon, and comparatively modern innovation, he sprang over a neighbouring wall, and away went the whole bevy of ethnologists, old and young, learned doctors, reverend divines, eloquent men of law, profound science scholars, artists, naturalists, enthusiastic archaeologists, and all, over innumerable walls ... surmounting every obstacle, and anon clambering up the sides of the rocky hill, to the utter amazement of the poor natives, who looked like people who had passively abandoned their island to invaders.

The only shadow on this summer's day of archaeological bliss was the degenerating condition of the monuments; Dr Petrie remembered that the round tower in Cill Éinne had been much higher at the time of his earlier visit, and Mr Wilde found the stone huts in Dún Dúchathair greatly delapidated since he first saw them ten years previously. On the way from that *dún* to Cill Rónáin they paused at a square, flat-roofed *clochán* while Mr Wilde addressed them upon the structure and formation of such early buildings; an islander 'afforded the foundation of a facetious story' by saying he had built it himself as a donkey-shed a year before, but fortunately the Ordnance Survey map made in 1837 and 1838 was on hand to prove the man lied. In general it seems the natives were not treating their heritage with sufficient respect, and a principal theme of the speeches at the banquet next day was the damage being done to the ruins by lads hunting rabbits. Nevertheless, as the *Vestal* left Cill Rónáin, firing a last salute, the excursionists felt that Mr Wilde's stated objective, 'to render Aran an object of attraction, and an opposition shop to Iona', had been 'crowned with a glorious success'. Petrie and some of his eminent colleagues stayed on in Aran, in an ecstasy of enthusiasm, as he later described to a correspondent:

How happily those days were spent you may easily imagine, when I tell you that I had for my companions, my beloved friends, Dr. Stokes, and his son; Frederick Burton, the painter; Samuel Ferguson, the poet and antiquary; and lastly, Eugene Curry, the Irish Shannachee!... The weather was glorious; and we scarcely left a church, or grave, or cloghan, a Saint, or a Dun of a Firbolg, in the three islands unvisited or unexamined.

Before long the islands were in a perpetual state of being investigated. A natural-historical expedition followed a similar course in 1864; two professors, Melville and Cleland, from Queen's College, Galway, and George Kinahan of the Geological Survey, chartered the Galway Bay steamer *Pilot*, and shepherded a group of students around the island, 'shooting and studying some of the rarer wildfowl', and viewing the antiquities. Once again Dún Aonghasa was the culmination of their visit:

Prof. Melville assembled the group at the centre of the fort, and it being the anniversary of Her Majesty's birthday, called for a cheer for the Queen, which was responded to with such a good will that the very puffins forsook their native cliffs in sheer fright.

Botanists had visited the islands long before this, the pioneers being Edward Lhwyd in about 1699, and in 1806 J.T. Mackay of TCD's newly founded botanic garden. In the middle decades of the century a number of botanists, mainly Scottish and English, published accounts of their 'rambles' in Aran: J. Ball in 1839, W. Andrews and L. Ogilby both in 1845, D. Oliver in 1851 and 1852, J.H. Balfour in 1853 and D. Moore in 1854. Between them they recorded fifty-four species, but did not aim to be exhaustive. Then in 1867 Professor E.P. Wright of Dublin University published a list of 159 species from Aran, being, he claimed, 'all, or nearly all, the species to be met with in the month of August', and the discoveries made by H.C. Hart in 1869 soon doubled that number. This was hard-won knowledge; Hart complains about the interminable and disheartening obstacle-course of the field-walls, while Wright suggests that the botanist would do well to bring with him

... a few creature comforts to supplement the meagre fare of the place; and above all ... a store of good candles. The sufferings that the writer endured while trying to investigate with a half-inch objective some gatherings made near the Holy Well at Kilronan, were indeed great, the only choice of light being between a farthing dip-candle of the worst description – *i.e.* with the thickest possible wick and the smallest amount of tallow – and a slender cotton thread lying in a saucer of fish oil.

Meanwhile the islanders themselves suffered scientific identification for the first time. A Dr Beddoe came to Aran in 1861, and later wrote in his book *The Races of Britain*:

The people of the Aran Islands have their own strongly marked type, in some respects an exaggeration of the ordinary Gaelic one, the face being remarkably long, the chin long and narrow but not angular, the nose long and straight and pointed, the brows rising obliquely outwards, the eyes light with very few exceptions, the hair of various colours but usually dark brown. We might be disposed, trusting to Irish traditions respecting the islands, to accept these people as representatives of the Firbolgs, had not Cromwell, that upsetter of all things, left in Arranmore a small English garrison who subsequently apostasised to Catholicism, intermarried with the natives and so vitiated the Firbolgian pedigree.

This question of the racial purity of the islanders was to trouble many minds, as the ideological significance of the Aran Islands ramified over the next half-century, and still excites undue curiosity today. In the 1950s the conclusions of a blood-group survey of the islanders were much more widely commented on than would have been the case for a similar investigation on the mainland; there is a fear that facts might 'vitiate' the dreams that enchain us with the primeval. (This study in fact showed that the blood-group frequencies of Aran differed sharply from those of adjacent mainland areas and were more like those of the east of Ireland or even the north of England where Gaelic and English stock have mixed. Such findings prompted a Dublin magazine to tease nationalists and 'nativists' with a cartoon of Aran islanders playing cricket.)

There was a lull in the scientific investigation of Aran, perhaps due to the depressing and disturbed state of the country, during the Land War, but two legal gentlemen connected with the sittings of the Land Court in Cill Rónáin in the mid-1880s published accounts of the islands. James G. Barry's 'Aran of the Saints' was a brief paper largely devoted to the monuments recently restored by the Board of Works, but with a few interesting details of land-divisions not available elsewhere. Oliver J. Burke's *The South Isles of Aran*, published in 1887, was the first book devoted to the islands. Much of it rehashes J.T. O'Flaherty, O'Donovan's Ordnance Survey Letters and Hardiman's appendices to *West or H-Iar Connaught*, but it also contains the first critical assessment of the economic state of the islanders and suggestions for its improvement. This book must have helped to disabuse many subsequent visitors of romantic notions about the noble peasants and their even nobler masters.

Thereafter the islands continued to attract an extraordinary number of enquirers. In 1895 there were mass assaults by archaeologists and by natural historians. The Royal Society of Antiquaries of Ireland arrived on the 4th of July, most of it by the SS *Caloric* having sailed north-about from Belfast and visited Tory Island, Inishmurray and High Island *en route*, while a hundred or so more came out on the SS *Duras* from Galway. Among the excursionists were the Provincial Secretary for Connaught of the Society, Edward Martyn of Tullyra Castle in south Galway, and the leader of the party was Thomas Westropp, who had been visiting the islands since 1878 and was later to publish detailed studies of its forts and stone huts. The *Caloric* moored off Cill Mhuirbhigh, and getting ashore was not so easy:

A few corraghs at once put out from shore, and in an hour there must have been more than twenty at the ship's side. Many of the natives came on board, and some of them sang Irish songs, and danced jigs remarkably well. ... The corragh ... is very buoyant, and can be rowed with great rapidity. They contain no seats except those for the rowers. This makes them inconvenient boats for passengers, who are obliged to accommodate themselves on the bottom of the boat sometimes in not very comfortable attitudes; while many carry away on their clothes reminders that tar takes some time to dry. They are excellent seaboats, however, riding over waves which would swamp a heavier boat, and with any reasonable care are perfectly safe. One accident only occurred during our stay – an accident which might have led to very serious consequences but for the gallant conduct of the first officer of the ship. This accident was caused by an act of great carelessness on the part of a young boatman.

In fact two of the party were nearly drowned by this drunken currachman; the Society's later official reprint of the original account in the *Belfast Newsletter* glosses over some of the upsets of the expedition.

Next day the party landed in the bay of An Gleannachán, on the advice of the Rev. Mr Kilbride, who was a member of the Society, and visited most of the island's great monuments. The following day was spent in the two smaller islands, and they were outraged by the womenfolk of Inis Meáin who stretched a rope across the entrance to Dún Chonchúir and tried to levy a toll; some paid, some refused, the police were called, but came too late to be of help. However, they were well satisfied with their finds, which included bronze pins and two 'methars' or large cups. The archaeological account of the three islands that Westropp had prepared for this occasion remains a most useful summary guide.

This influx almost coincided with the visit of a hundred or so naturalists, the members and friends of members of the Belfast, Dublin, Cork and Limerick Field Clubs, brought together by a joint conference in Galway. They had already toured Connemara and the Burren, discussing and studying their numerous discoveries over dinners at the Railway Hotel, and had taken afternoon tea with the President of Queen's College, Galway. The trip to the Aran Islands on July the 16th was another day of vigorous tramping and close observation, and was 'in every way successful'. Their leader was the Secretary of the Irish Field Club Union, the indefatigable Robert Lloyd Praeger:

Punctually at 5.30 A.M. the Secretary's shrill whistle called members down for an early cup of tea. A prompt response was made, and at 6 o'clock sharp the SS 'Duras' cast off her moorings. ... A heaving tide-run off the shore of Aranmore proved disastrous to some of the naturalists, but they speedily recovered as the steamer dropped anchor at Portmurvey. ... The members who visited Dun Aengus – the larger proportion of the party – were amply repaid for their exertion. ... Floating on the Atlantic swell far below, a keen-eyed member descried a fine specimen of the Great Sun-fish, which considerately remained in full view for a length of time. On the vegetation here and elsewhere many observers noted the great abundance of the handsome rose-beetle (*Cetonia aurata*). The presence of this species – so rare on the Irish mainland – was a great surprise to the entomologists. A small flower-beetle (*Meligethes rufipes*) new to Ireland, was found, as well as a minute spider (*Micariosomia festivum*), also apparently new to the Irish list. ...

On the beach at Kilronan, Miss Gardiner had a sumptuous tea prepared, to which the members did ample justice; after which, undeterred by frequent showers which now began to fall, a numerous party started southward to visit the primitive church of St. Eany, &c., and to attempt further discoveries among the fauna and flora. The botanists were well pleased to find, at the last moment, that very rare Irish grass, the Wood Rush, in one of the two Aran stations given by Mr. H.C.

Hart in his paper on the botany of the islands, and in the fading light a hasty return was made to the steamer, which left at 8 o'clock punctually, and the hotel in Galway was once more reached at 11.0.

Praeger returned to the island a few days later with a few colleagues, and went over it with his usual thoroughness. The floristic result of this excursion was an additional twenty-three new records. (A few other botanical visits brought the total of reliably recorded species up to 408 by the end of the century, and the present known flora numbers about 450 species.)

By the 1890s hundreds of day-trippers were disembarking at Cill Rónáin in the summer months. A pleasure-boat service to the islands from Galway had been initiated as early as 1863, and the paddle-steamer *Citie of the Tribes*, so called from an old appellation of Galway, had begun its long career in 1873. Mary Banim's *Here and There through Ireland* has the first account of Aran from this new age of holiday-making, of people coming as she did, to enjoy 'a mitigated Robinson Crusoe life'. She had read much about Aran's saints, prehistoric monuments and wild-flowers, and above all about the charming innocence of the islanders. To avoid corrupting this last, she had left behind her an appendage of her travelling suit, the 'dress improver', four iron bars that gave a skirt a fashionable outline; and when she found, hanging behind the door of her room in the Atlantic Hotel, a feminine costume with the same unmistakable bulge in its skirt, she felt the shock Crusoe suffered on seeing the footprint in the sand. More seriously, she was also shocked to find that the natives of this delightful holiday-resort were hungry:

I was in Arran at a time when great distress yet prevailed after the famine of 1885 – a small, a scandalously small sum had been given by Government for relief works, and a little harbour was to be made. The sum allowed of the employment of but one out of each family proved to be in dire necessity, that one to receive one shilling a day – six shillings a week for perhaps ten in family. I saw the poor men besieging the priest, the gentleman in charge of the works – even begging us to intercede for them for work. ... It was no fit labour for women, yet one fine young girl came weeping and praying so earnestly that it was impossible to refuse her, and she joyfully toiled as hard as anyone, carrying huge stones and doing all required of a strong man, that she might get that pittance with which to support her little orphan brothers and sisters – for father and mother were dead.

What must have appeared to the islanders as the tourists' curious fetishism about certain minor aspects of Aran life was already proving a marginal economic resource:

Sitting on the edge of the pier and darting here and there amongst the men were a number of boys carrying for sale pampootys and large bunches of the beautiful maiden-hair fern which grows in the chinks of the rocks ... and they patiently waited that I might examine the relative merits of brown or white pampootys, before finally deciding on one all brown and one sweetly mottled.

The 'pampooty', a moccasin-like shoe made of a single strip of untanned cowhide, hairy side out, with a few stitches at heel and toe and shaped to the foot by draw-strings above, was simply the *bróg úrleathair*, raw leather shoe, to the islanders; the more exotic word, which has been speculatively derived from words for 'slipper' in a wide variety of languages and is seemingly a seventeenth-century introduction, has always appealed more to the tourist. Mary Banim repeats what was to become a standard trope of Aran literature, that the light and graceful carriage of the islanders is due to this footwear. Synge was later to make the pampooty, as contrasted with 'the heavy boot of Europe', the very emblem of the Araners' closeness to nature.

In that same period certain young men who would become internationally renowned Celticists and linguists visited Aran. The first of them, Heinrich Zimmer, saw the island during the Land War in 1880, and was moved to address the islanders at a Land League meeting in Cill Rónáin, urging them to stand together and protect their land. I have mentioned his unravelling of the genealogy of St Enda, which forms an aside to an extraordinarily dense study of *The Voyage of St Brendan*. He later became professor of Celtic philology at Berlin (and the father of another Heinrich Zimmer, the great Indianologist). Kuno Meyer, who was to found the School of Irish Studies in Dublin in 1903 and later to succeed Zimmer at Berlin, first visited the islands in 1889 during his lectureship in Celtic and German at Liverpool University. Both the Copenhagen linguist Holger Pedersen and his disciple Franz Nikolaus Finck came; the latter's two-volume work *Die araner Mundart* of 1899 being the first detailed study of an Irish dialect. The American Jeremiah Curtin collected material in Aran for his *Myths and Folklore of Ireland*, published in 1890. Irish-language enthusiasts of the Gaelic League, founded in 1893, who came to the islands as to a shrine of the reviving spirit of the nation, include Eoin MacNeill, Eugene O'Growney, Dr O'Hickey, Una Ní Fhaircheallaigh, Thomas MacDonagh and Pádraic Pearse. Glancing ahead to the roles these people were to play, it seems the nation itself went to school in Aran. MacNeill was the first professor of Early and Medieval Irish History at UCD, Chief of Staff of the Irish Volunteers from 1913, and the first Minister of Education under the Free State; MacDonagh (whom an old man told me used to lead the Volunteers in rifle-practice out on the crags of Inis Meáin) taught at St Enda's, Pearse's school in Dublin, and both of them were among the leaders of the Easter Rising elevated to martyrdom by the British in 1916.

O'Hickey was Professor of Irish at Maynooth from 1896, and Una Ní Fhearcheallaigh became Lecturer in Modern Irish in University College Dublin on its foundation in 1909, and Professor there in 1932. Fr O'Growney was Professor of Irish at Maynooth from 1891, and his *Simple Lessons in Irish* began to appear from 1893; his successor at Maynooth, Fr Donncha Ó Floinn, much later wrote of them:

It is difficult for people today to imagine the zeal and zest for learning that possessed every class of person in Ireland as a result of those little green books composed by Fr. Eugene. Clergy and laity, high and low, scholars and tradesmen, every one of them had the little green books in his pocket, the first book and the second book and the third book. ... 'I knew Irish once,' said Frank Fay to me long ago. 'I had done the Third Book of O'Growney.'

However, to these zealots, Cill Rónáin was already touched with linguistic corruption. O'Growney, at the time of his first visit in 1885 a seminarian at Maynooth for whom only his soul's salvation was closer to his heart than Irish, came in search of the spoken word. He was met here by his college friend, Peadar Yorke, whose father was from Aran and who visited his grandmother here every summer. Yorke has described O'Growney's thirst for uncontaminated springs of Irish:

I remember one day we exhausted our store of Irish, and our patience too, trying to get the word for 'round' out of an old woman we met on the road. Devil a word of English she had, and we drew a little circle in the dust of the road and asked her to name it, but we couldn't get anything out of her but 'roundáilte'.

The next summer O'Growney told him it was a waste of time trying to learn Irish in the big island because it was so polluted by *béarlachas* (mixed formations like *roundáilte*, an English word with an Irish suffix), and took himself off to Inis Meáin. In fact so many other scholars did the same that the one lodging-house there became known as Ollscoil na Gaeilge, the university of Irish, and the overflow of visitors sometimes had to sleep out in the Dún overlooking it.

Pearse was another of these intemperate adolescent lovers of Aran – his sister wrote of him, 'He went to Aran a boy, and came back a man!' On his first visit in 1898 he met an Inis Meáin man recently returned from Mexico, Tomás Bán Ó Concheanáinn (his brother had founded the famous Concannon vineyards in California, which supplied Ireland with communion wine). Tomás Bán was already a League member, and later became its most respected and formidable roving organizer. The two of them decided to set up a local branch, and took a currach across to Cill Rónáin to consult with the parish priest Fr Farragher, and the school-teacher David

O'Callaghan. On the next Sunday the inaugural meeting was held in the Cill Rónáin school house; Pearse described it for the League's journal in his school-essay Irish:

People came from Inis Meáin, Inis Oírr and Galway. I think there were at least seven hundred people gathered there. Father Muircheartach [Farragher] was in the chair. We had talk and chat and speeches without a single word of English. Aran of the Saints found its soul that day and it'll be a long time, with God's help, before it is lost again. ... Will the Irish language ever die in Aran? I think not. Now that they have set up a branch, people will be interested in Irish, it will be taught to the young and soon they will be able to read and write it. It will not be allowed to decline but will be supported until Aran will again be a university and a torch of knowledge for all the people of Ireland as she was in the old times.

Nevertheless, in his own speech Pearse had to refer to

... the pain with which he noticed that while Irish was the language of the grown people of Kilronan, a marked and growing tendency to use English was visible in the children.

Simultaneously the islands were being mined for themes by the English-language writers of the Irish literary revival. Previous appearances of Aran in literature, admittedly an Aran entirely concocted out of his imagination, had been as the setting of Charles Lever's *Luttrell of Aran* and of scenes in his *The Martins of Cro' Martin*. Emily Lawless's *Grania, the Story of an Island*, set in an Inis Meáin that owed something to at least one visit, and published in 1892, was evidently required reading, as both Yeats and Synge had it with them on their first trips. Yeats came in 1896, looking for local colour for a novel he never finished, *The Speckled Bird*, the action of which was to oscillate between the Paris of the mystical sects and an equally spirit-ridden Aran; as he explains in a letter to a friend, 'The book is to be among other things my first study of the Irish Fairy Kingdom and the mystical faith of that time, before I return to more earthly things.' He and the English littérateur Arthur Symons were staying at Tullyra with Edward Martyn at the time, and hired a Connemara hooker to bring them out to Aran. Symons describes their coming:

Nothing is more mysterious, more disquieting, than one's first glimpse of an island, and all I had heard of these islands, of their peace in the heart of the storm, was not a little mysterious and disquieting. ... Here one was absolutely at the mercy of the elements, which might at any moment become unfriendly, which, indeed, one seemed to have but apprehended in a pause of their eternal enmity. And we seemed to be venturing among an unknown people, who, even if they spoke our own language, were further away from us, more foreign, than people who spoke an unknown language and lived beyond other seas.

He goes on to describe their arrival at the Atlantic Hotel ('a very primitive hotel; it had last been slept in by some priests from the mainland, who
had come on their holiday with bicycles, and before that by a German
philologist who was learning Irish'), and their meeting with a man who for
two generations of enquirers had represented Aran, and who must have
been totally satisfactory to this boatload of dreamers:

... a professional story-teller, who had for three weeks been teaching Irish to the
German philologist who had preceded us on the island. He was half blind and of
wild appearance; a small and hairy man, all gesture, as if set on springs, who spoke
somewhat broken English in a roar. He lamented that we could understand no
Irish, but, even in English, he had many things to tell, most of which he gave as
but 'talk', making it very clear that we were not to suppose him to vouch for
them. His own family, he told us, was said to be descended from the roons, or
seals, but that certainly was 'talk'; and a witch had, only nine months back, been
driven out of the island by the priest; and there were many who said they had seen
fairies, but for his part he had never seen them. But with this he began to swear
on the name of God and the saints, lifting up his hands, that what he was going
to tell us was the truth; and then he told how a man had once come into his
house, and admired his young child, who was lying there in his bed, and had not
said 'God bless you!' (without which to admire is to envy and to bring under the
power of the fairies), and that night, and for many following nights, he had wak-
ened and heard a sound of fighting, and one night had lit a candle, but to no
avail, and another night had gathered up a blanket and tried to fling it over the
head of whoever might be there, but had caught no one; only in the morning,
going to a box in which fish were kept, he had found blood in the box; and at
this he rose again, and swore in the name of God and saints that he was telling
the truth, and true it was that the child had died and as for the man who had ill-
wished him, 'I could point him out any day,' he said fiercely. And with many
other stories of the doings of fairies and priests, (for he was very religious), and of
the 'Dane' who had come to the island to learn Irish ('and he knew all the languages, the Proosy, and the Roosy, and the Span, and the Grig'), he told us how
Satan, being led by pride to equal himself with God, looked into the glass in
which God only should look, and when Satan looked into the glass, 'Hell was
made in a minute.'

Two people who were later to be associated with Yeats and Martyn in
the Irish National Theatre, Synge and Lady Gregory, made their first visits
to Aran in May 1898; they were not acquainted at the time, and though
they saw each other at a distance they took care not to meet, for outside of
the summer season Aran was still unfrequented enough to afford the luxury
of solitude and the excitements of anthropological pioneering; Lady Gregory later wrote:

I first saw Synge in the north island of Aran. I was staying there, gathering folk-lore, talking to the people, and felt quite angry when I passed another outsider walking here and there, talking also to the people. I was jealous of not being alone on the island among the fishers and sea-weed gatherers.

Lady Gregory's findings eventually appeared in her *Visions and Beliefs in the West of Ireland* (1920). Synge was there for reasons so deep it is doubtful if he understood them himself at that time, and he too was to become passionately possessive, especially of Inis Meáin; in his private notebook he wrote:

With this limestone Inishmaan I am in love ... and hear with galling jealousy of the various priests and scholars who have lived here before me. They have grown to me as former lovers of one's mistress, horrible existences haunting with dreamed kisses the lips she presses to your own.

Yeats had met Synge, who was pursuing desultory studies in medieval literature, in Paris in 1896, and according to Yeats's own account of it, had said to him, 'Give up Paris, you will never create anything by reading Racine, and Arthur Symons will always be a better critic of French literature. Go to the Arran Islands. Live there as if you were one of the people themselves; express a life that has never found expression.' Perhaps then Yeats had really enjoyed a moment of second-sight and been inspired to a matchless matching of place and person, for the outcome was that modestly titled love-story, *The Aran Islands*; and the whole series of Synge's plays, which draw their themes from tales heard and incidents observed by him in Aran, their language from the Irish he learned there, and their energy (I suspect) from the initiation into the world's amoral loveliness he underwent during long lonely vigils on the cliff-tops.

On that first visit, the old man, Máirtín Ó Conaola or Martin Connolly, whom Symons had described, called on Synge in the Atlantic hotel:

He told me that he had known Petrie and Sir William Wilde, and many living antiquarians, and had taught Irish to Dr. Finck and Dr. Pedersen, and given stories to Mr Curtin of America. A little after middle age he had fallen over a cliff, and since then he had had little eyesight, and a trembling of his hands and head. As we talked he sat huddled together over the fire, shaking and blind, yet his face was indescribably pliant, lighting up with an ecstasy of humour when he told me anything that had a point of wit or malice, and growing sombre and desolate again when he spoke of religion or the fairies.

He had great confidence in his own powers and talent, and in the superiority of his stories over all other stories in the world. When we were speaking about Mr. Curtin, he told me that this gentleman had brought out a volume of his Aran stories in America, and made five hundred pounds by the sale of them.

'And what do you think he did then?' he continued; 'he wrote a book of his own stories after making that lot of money with mine, and he brought them out, and the divil a halfpenny did he get for them. Would you believe that?'

Although after a fortnight on the island Synge confided to his journal that 'the very bareness of the rock has lured from me a limpet-like attachment,' he found little worth describing in Cill Rónáin itself apart from the picturesque groupings of the womenfolk sitting on the sea-wall to watch the excitement of the arrival of the Indian meal sent as relief, and the almost Italianate sumptuousness of colour in their dress, 'the dull red of the petticoat especially if surmounted by a deep blue shawl,' which remind him of what Petrie had written about it; in fact the description in *The Aran Islands* of the effect of the red petticoats against the grey limestone closely echoes Petrie's own words. But Synge is the first writer on the islands to go a little beyond a carefully aestheticized response to the beauty of the island girls. In his private notebook he confesses that 'I cannot dare under the attention I excite to gaze as I would wish at a beautiful oval face that looks out under a brown shawl near where I stand.' In Inis Meáin he was to get to know at least one girl who made him dream of lingering there and marrying a woman who would personify what the place meant to him. And this unknown beauty on the quayside at Cill Rónáin is also spiritualized by his prose into a tutelary goddess of the territory:

The whole day I spent wandering with Martin Connolly, my blind guide, through the western wonders of the islands. As we set out among the groups of girls who smile at our incongruous fellowship – by Martin himself we are compared to a cuckoo with its attendant pipit – I saw suddenly the beautiful girl I had noticed on the pier and her face yet haunted me all day among the rocks. She is Madonna like yet has a rapt soul wrought in a jesting ... as far from easy exaltation as from the maternal comeliness of Raphael's later style that she speaks rather as an immaculate unfearing goddess than the awe weighed mother of a God. I understand for the first time as we go further and Martin tells me of a beautiful young woman who has just been taken by the fairies in her first childbed that an interposition may have seemed needful to the older poets of Ireland to lift these women – these 'averties' of Maeterlinck – by some mysterious glamour from the profane sacrilege of life and that they pressed pre-extant fairy-land to their aid.

This walk was on Synge's last day in the big island. Having decided that the Cill Rónáin of the CDB era was too banal to satisfy his thirst for the primitive and for the aboriginal purity of Gaelic, he left for Inis Meáin, and in so doing transcended the orbit of this chapter. I merely add that his book, appearing in 1907 when *The Playboy of the Western World* was provoking riots in Dublin, spread word of Aran famously, and that his memory has obliterated the name 'Ollscoil na Gaeilge', for the lodgings occupied by so many great scholars is known to countless visitors from all over the world simply as 'Synge's Cottage'.

While Synge was at least flirting with the idea of sentimental attachments, the most 'statistic' of all investigators of Aran were at work in the big island. A.C. Haddon, Professor of Zoology at the Royal College of Science in Dublin, and C. R. Browne of Trinity College Dublin had recently set up an Anthropometric Laboratory, and the paper on Aran they published in 1893, inaugurating a series of systematic studies of the communities of the western seaboard, they describe as 'the first fruits of the Anthropometric Laboratory in its peripatetic form.' Utterly different from Synge's descriptions, but perfectly confirming them, are such of their findings as these:

Height – The men are mostly of a slight but athletic build... Aran average is 1645 mm or about 5 feet 4 ³/4 inches, that of 277 Irishmen is 1740 m. or 5 feet 8 ¹/2 inches.

Head – The head is well shapen, rather long and narrow; but viewed from above the sides are not parallel, there being a slight parietal bulging. The mean Cephalic Index, when reduced to the cranial standard, is 75.1, consequently the average head is to a slight extent, mesaticephalic; although, as a matter of fact, the number measured is nearly evenly divided between mesaticephalic and dolichocephalic. The top of the head is well vaulted, so that the height above the ears is considerable.

Face – The face is long and oval, with well-marked features... In many men, the length between the nose and the chin has the appearance of being decidedly great.

The battery of instruments with which these results were obtained – The Traveller's Anthropometer, Flowers' Craniometer, a sliding rule as used in Galton's Anthropometrical Laboratory, and Chesterman's steel tape for taking the horizontal circumference of the head – must have impressed the islanders, for measuring skulls was powerful magic in the hands of their native healers. As to what was going on inside those skulls, Haddon and Browne admit that the question of psychology is very difficult and delicate, but nevertheless, advance the usual intrusive generalizations Aran has to put up with:

Naturally to the casual visitor the inhabitants show to their best advantage, and to such they appear as a kindly, courteous, and decidedly pleasing people. Though begging is becoming more prevalent than formerly, owing to the opening up of the island to tourists, a pleasant independence is often exhibited. We believe them to be 'good Catholics'. They have had the character of being exceptionally honest, straightforward, and upright. On the other hand, we have been told that the men have no unity or organisation, that they are cunning, untrustworthy, and they certainly are very boastful when in liquor. They rarely fight, but will throw stones at one another. Occasionally the old people are badly treated; and when an old man has made over his farm to his married son, the young people have been known to half starve him, and give him the small potatoes reserved for the pigs. The men do not appear to have strong sexual passions, and any irregularity of conduct is excessively rare; only five cases of illegitimacy having been registered within the past ten years. There is no courtship or love-making, marriages being suddenly arranged for, mainly for unsentimental reasons. The marriages appear to be as happy as elsewhere; and the women can quite hold their own with the men.

Among innumerable journalistic accounts of the islands from the early years of this century, one curiosity stands out, an article James Joyce placed with *Il Piccolo della Sera*, a newspaper of Trieste, where he was living at the time. Its bemusing title is (in translation), 'The mirage of the fisherman of Aran – England's safety valve in case of war', and it describes a day trip he made to 'Aranmore, the holy island that sleeps like a great shark on the grey waters of the Atlantic Ocean'. The mirage, one obscurely learns, is a project he happened to read about during the voyage, for making Galway into a transatlantic port which would reinvigorate Ireland and assure England's contact with the New World in time of war; Joyce associates this vision with one seen by an Aran fisherman said to have accompanied St Brendan on his voyages. Everything else in Joyce's brief evocation is equally adrift.

We stop in one of the steep little streets, uncertain. An islander, who speaks an English all his own, says good morning, adding that it has been a horrible summer, praise be to God. The phrase, which at first seems one of the usual Irish blunders, rather comes from the innermost depths of human resignation. ... Around the stunted shrubs which grow on the hills of the island his imagination has woven legends and tales which reveal the depth of his psyche. And under his apparent simplicity he retains a slight trace of scepticism, and of humour. He looks away when he has spoken and lets the eager enthusiast jot down in his notebook the astounding fact that yonder hawthorn tree was the little tree from which Joseph of Arimathea cut his walking stick.

Joyce did not share Synge's empathy with the West; in fact he seems to have feared it as an atavistic and deathly trait in the mentality of his times. The old man of the West is a spectre Stephen Dedalus has to face, almost on the eve of his going-forth to encounter life and to forge the conscience of his race:

I fear him. I fear his redrimmed horny eyes. It is with him I must struggle all through this night till day come, till he or I lie dead, gripping him by the sinewy throat till ... Till what? Till he yield to me? No. I mean no harm.

And the badinage in *Ulysses*, when Stephen is told, 'The tramper Synge is looking for you. He's out in pampooties to murder you', is not to be taken too lightly. To incorporate this peasant world of legends that could be jokes into his own psychic record, Joyce himself would have to invent 'an English all of his own,' full of what seem at first to be 'the usual Irish blunders'. His throw-away scrap of newspaper column-filling can therefore be read as a prospectus for *Finnegans Wake*; I claim the moment of conception of that work for Aran.

After the First World War, the Easter Rising, the War of Independence, the Civil War, after scores of those jolly excursionists to Aran had died in the trenches, and the graduates of the 'University of Irish' had been shot as rebels or acheived high office in the Free State, after the dislocation and depression of tourism by the 'economic war' with Britain, the filming of *Man of Aran* in 1932 set the Aran mirage industry on its feet again. Robert Flaherty, his family and film-crew and visiting admirers, spent money freely, and laughed away the inhibitions of the islanders about the miraculous new medium that would present them in their ragged nobility on the silver screen of the world. When the film appeared, the 'man of Aran' himself was hailed as a star, and Flaherty as a benefactor to the cause of popular entertainment:

> *Tiger, Tiger burning bright*
> *In the cinema at night*
> *Two and six and one and three*
> *Good old Robert Flaherty.*

Thus Aran was launched on a career of mass appeal.

The film itself, despite its innocency, is deep enough to sustain numerous reinterpretations of its own reinterpretation of Aran. It is interesting that in the Venice Film Festival of 1934 it won the Grand Prix or Mussolini Cup, and was well received in Hitler's Germany, where its theme of man striving against the forces of nature aligned it with the cultish mountaineering films of the time. Even its title is subject to all the inflexions 'man' is heir to. As a portrait of a community rooted through the family in the land, or in labour, it needs only the slightest of changes in emphasis, a few words added to its subtitles, to swing this epic of struggle to the left or to the right. And if, as he has been pronounced, Man is dead, the nihilistic magnificence of Aran's storm-beaten cliffs would add grandeur to his drowning.

It may well have been *Man of Aran* that brought Aran its strangest visitor. A middle-aged Frenchman who stayed for a few days in August 1937 and left without settling his bill, he is still dimly remembered as 'Franncach Sheáinín Bhile', from the name of the man he lodged with in Eoghanacht village. It is also remembered that the children used to tease him by pretending to steal his walking-stick. The bright, cruel eyes of children are drawn by signs of psychic trouble, and perhaps they sensed that a wind from hell was blowing this man through Aran, that his stick was a lightning-conductor for the storms of war soon to overwhelm the world. He was Antonin Artaud, the dramatist and theoretician of 'the theatre of cruelty'. He had recently left the clinic in which he had undergone courses of 'detoxification' for his opium addiction, and had been living rough and begging in Montparnasse. As he wrote to a friend just before leaving for Ireland:

I do not know what I am but I know that for 22 years I have never ceased to burn, and they have made a pyre of me. ... I greatly fear that from October and November the fire will be everywhere in Paris. Those whom I love will be sheltered and warned.

For he had lost the power to keep symbols in their own domain, and all the monstrous inventions of his literary genius had become for him painful realities about to break out of his mind into the world: 'My life fulfils Prophecy', he wrote to a friend from Galway. A few months earlier he had received certain illuminations, and deduced others by 'cabbalistic reduction' – arithmetical hocus-pocus – of the digits of certain dates, which he expressed in a work called *New Revelations of Being*:

The absolute male of nature has begun to move in the sky. ... Because a Cycle of the World is finished which was under the supremacy of the Woman: Left, Republic and Democracy. ... That means that the Masses will go under the yoke, and it is just that they should be under the yoke. Because the Masses are by nature Women and it is Man who rules Woman, and not the contrary.

This event was due to take place in five months from June 1937, because:

... on the 3 June 1937 the five serpents appeared which were already in the sword of which the power of decision is represented by a cane! – What does that mean? – That means that I who speak have a Sword and a Cane. A cane with 13 knots and that this cane carries on the ninth knot the magic sign of thunder; that 9 is the numeral of destruction by fire and – THAT I FORESEE A DESTRUCTION BY FIRE. ... *I see this Cane in the middle of the Fire and provoking the destruction by Fire.*

Some years later he explained the significance of his cane, in a note written on a copy of *New Revelations of Being*:

The cane discussed here and which was that of St. Patrick in Ireland is in reality essentially and before all that of Jesus Christ himself. ... From June to September 1937 it was in the hands of the signatory of these lines, and did its work. I have not had it for now for six years and it is now in a safe place. And CHRIST alone will reappear with it or one of the persons of the most holy Trinity.

This copy of his book was dedicated by him (in December 1943, and from the asylum of Rodez) to Adolf Hitler. He had come to Ireland with the idea of returning the cane to its rightful home; but what was it that brought him to Aran in particular, while in the grip of an apocalyptic and Fascistic fantasy, in which it is clear that he himself was to play the role of Führer? In a letter to his family he said that he was looking for the last true descendants of the druids, who would understand that humanity must disappear by water and fire. While J.T. O'Flaherty's druidical fire-temples and sacrificial altars would have appealed to the author of *Heliogabalus*, it is unlikely he would have heard more than the faint echoes of this theme in later writers on Aran. Synge's vision of Aran as the last stronghold in Europe of the primitive could have been the magnet, or, as I have hinted, the politically ambiguous storms of *Man of Aran*.

The impending catastrophe did not relieve Artaud of mundane troubles while in Aran. As he wrote to André Breton:

Life in Ireland seems to me horribly expensive. I doubt if you could get by in the towns on less than a pound a day. Here where I am it's a pound a week, there are 9 houses, 3 bushes in the graveyard, and it takes over 2 hours walking to get to the village of Kilronan, where there is a post office, four hotels, 2 bars and about sixty houses. The boat from Ireland calls twice a week. So much for practical details.

But practical details became so pressing after a few days that he left his lodgings, leaving a reassuring note in English for his hosts: 'I go to Galway with the priest to take money in Post Office.' Since the money he had implored his publisher Jean Paulhan to send him had not arrived, he fled from Galway too, leaving his bill at the Imperial Hotel unpaid. In Dublin he got into street-fights, lost the cane, was arrested and deported as an 'undesirable'. On arrival at Le Havre, after some trouble with the crew of the ferry, he was taken in a strait-jacket to hospital. There followed over eight years of incarceration, and the fifty-one electro-shock treatments, administered without anaesthetic, that failed to torture him back into normality. There also followed the destruction of much of Europe by fire.

In the decades since Artaud's fire-storms, tourists have become more a matter of statistical interest to the islanders than vice versa; each season is 'up' or 'down' on the last by so many per cent. Correspondingly, new treatments of Aran in old and new media have to be reckoned in batches. Of the many books now available a favourite is *Aran, Islands of Legend*, by P. A. Ó Síocháin (published in 1962 and doing well in the New Age), according to which the islands are but the tiny fragments of a great Atlantis, of which the Aran forts were the defence-line until it subsided into the ocean without geological fuss 'about 2,200 years ago', halving Dún Aonghasa in the process and leaving behind the ancestors of today's Araners. In contrast, *Oileáin Árann, stair na n-oileáin anuas go dti 1922,* a well researched history, particularly good on nineteenth-century politics (it has saved me weeks in old newspaper files), by an island-born teacher, Antoine Powell, has been unjustly neglected; one elderly shopkeeper of Cill Rónáin said to me, 'I suppose because he's one of our own we think it can't be any good.' Almost too late for me to mention it here appears a competent multidisciplinary study with the comic title, *The Book of Aran.* Seamus Heaney has written on these 'three stepping-stones out of Europe', as have his contemporaries, Michael Longley and Derek Mahon; there are dozens of television films in various languages, an opera (*Opéra d'Aran*, by Gilbert Bécaud, first performed in Paris in 1962), pamphlets, pop-songs, pocket-guides, maps. ... The islands are perpetually stormbound in interpretations.

Finally, Aran has evinced a sentimental interest in tourists too. For some time it has been offering its own temperate version of the sun-sand-&-sex culture of more torrid shores. A few of 'the lads' took to hanging around on the beaches hoping to pick up 'women'; one of them, I remember, was so assiduous his mates used to say, 'Pity he can't swim, he'd make a great life-guard.' And then, one summer in the 'seventies, a scattering of girls of a new breed arrived, like rare butterflies from some exceptional hatching far away. They knew enough about sex to intimidate the local experts, but they wanted something more – total mystical identification with the island through love. One of these girls, a Californian, somehow drifted into our home and settled there for a bit, sustaining herself on a little jar of tofu she had with her and an occasional lettuce leaf from the garden. Her project was simple: to have an affair with a man called George or the local equivalent, on as many famous islands as possible. We heard a good deal about her adventures in this parodic quest. She soon picked out and got to know one Seoirse, a handsome young fisherman devoted to the quiet pint. She suggested a stroll through the fragrant, twilight boreens; he was agreeable, and they met by appointment. When he went stumping off ahead of her, shoulders bowed as if he were carrying a sack of feed-beet to the cattle, she scampered after him crying 'Seoirse! You might at least hold my hand!'; and then, running ahead to ambush him, 'Seoirse! I'm the best thing that ever happened to you – why don't you recognize that?' But Seoirse was slow to recognize that, and she became impatient. The affair reached its climax when her island love was due back from a few days away skippering his trawler. She put on a floaty cotton dress and highlighted her hair, and waited for him in the American Bar, in company with the wife of one of the boat's crew. When at last the trawler appeared in the mouth of the harbour, the Californian suggested that they should both run down onto the quay to welcome their menfolk home from the sea; but the Aran woman was amazed at the idea and hastily said that she had to go home and put on the spuds. So California teased up her hair into a storm of sparks and went skipping down the harbour road alone. Seoirse, peering out of the dingy window of the deck-house, saw this maenad approaching, and dived into the hold, where he busied himself gutting fish for an hour or so, until she had given up and gone away disconsolate. Later that evening she sat under a wall in a field, wondering if she should leave the island, and waiting for Nature to send her a sign. As dusk gathered about her, a strange rippling mystic music drifted to her on the breeze; she looked over the wall and found it was a cow copiously urinating. And so she decided to leave Aran. We used to get postcards from her now and again; she was screeching around Capri on the pillion of Giorgio's Vespa, or sweeping up broken glass in Giorgos's taverna on Mykonos. As a mistress of ironies she will forgive me for having merged her story with that of one of her sister visionaries.

And so Aran, and especially Cill Rónáin, continues through the years to disappoint, to be a little discrepant to the visitors' dreams. Nowadays something like 150,000 people visit the islands each summer. Long after midnight the roar of the pubs spewing out their clientele can be heard as far as where St Enda's bones rest on the farther side of the bay, and at the end of the season it takes a fortnight of autumn gales to hose the town into sobriety again. A line of Yeats suggests we should tread softly upon dreams, but in truth dreams themselves are heavy-footed, whether they wear pampooties or jackboots. Sometimes I tremble for the stone that has to bear all their trampling.

AN EAR TO THE COFFIN

The closely built-up Cill Rónáin that measures itself by the bed-nights and coffee-spoons of tourism, Iochtaír an Bhaile, fades out only a couple of hundred yards north of the harbour, and beyond it Lár an Bhaile, the 'middle of town', is made spacious by the disused grounds and empty shells of the Protestant church and rectory. That faith, in its complicity with economic and social power, is extinct in Aran, and its practice restricted to private observation. Only a few elderly islanders still feel resentful of the stony

contempt with which the select little community stared down its neighbours, and what they remember of its history is reduced to a few grotesque
motifs that could furnish the beginnings of a ghost story. Some years ago,
before the bright clean waves of electricity and tourism had swept out the
old pub of the area, a descendant of a member of that Cill Rónáin ascendancy – a rather aberrant member in the eyes of his co-religionists – came
back to Aran looking for his roots:

The last of the daylight, sodden with porter, eased itself out of the door, but the
creature of sticks and crumpled brown paper behind the bar showed no inclination to replace it with the cheer of a lantern. Three or four elderly islanders on a
wooden bench along one wall looked down as if observing the occasional involuntary shiftings of their boots on the concrete floor, glanced from under their
brows at the stranger on the bench opposite, looked down again, left the silence
to thicken, broke it with a brief sardonic interchange about the old sack that had
been thrown over the vomit left in the corner from the previous night, let their
eyes stray across the stranger again. George Stoney, professor of Film and Television at New York University, noted with an eye trained by his medium the symptoms of their reluctance to answer his queries. That afternoon he had located the
grave of his grandfather in the farthest corner of the Protestant churchyard; it was
marked, not by a proper tombstone like those of the coastguards but by two small
boulders, like an unbaptized child's grave, one of which bore the name 'Dr.
Stoney', and no date. As a doctor, Stoney would have been one of the élite. What
then was the reason for this ignominy? So far all he had prised out of the taciturn
natives was some gossip about Dr Stoney's wife, a drunkard. Stoney used to lock
her in her bedroom to keep her away from the public house, and still he would
find her roaring drunk when he came home, for the old crone from the shebeen
would come round with a sup of *poitín* for her, which Mrs Stoney would suck up
with a straw through the keyhole. The professor sighed, and nodded to the
lugubrious publican, and waited while another round of pints materialized like
fungus on the damp counter. The natives were all leaning together in whispering
consultation. Apparently one of them was seeking the authority of the rest to tell
the tale of Dr Stoney's burial, for he eventually leaned a little forward of the others,
and a slow hesitant muttering emerged from between the peak of his cap and the
great knot of fingers before his face. With difficulty the American disengaged a
narrative from the repetitious web of obscurities. Dr Stoney, he gathered, had been
a drunkard too, and also used to take laudanum from the dispensary he ran. One
day he had been found dead, or apparently so. Mr Kilbride, the minister, didn't
like the doctor because once when some poor people were in arrears and their cases
were due to be heard, he had got into the land-agent's office – it shared a building
with the dispensary – and forged the agent's signature on the dockets saying the
rent had been paid, and the agent hadn't noticed the signatures, so that when he
produced the dockets in court everyone laughed and the judge threw out the case,
and the poor people couldn't be evicted. All the same, Dr Stoney was a Protestant,

so Mr Kilbride had to let him be buried in the Protestant graveyard. Four men carried the coffin on their shoulders, and each one of them thought he heard the body shift in it, but didn't like to say so for fear of making a fool of himself. And some say that Mr Kilbride heard Dr Stoney stirring too, but 'he got him buried while he had him ill, because there was a rumour out that Stoney was going to turn Catholic'. ...

Professor Stoney is not a horror film-director – he had come to Aran, not just to look up his grandfather's grave, but to make a documentary on the filming of *Man of Aran* – and so I will develop this promising scenario no further. Instead I will consider this incredible allegation, that the Protestant rector allowed one of his flock to be buried alive rather than risk losing him to the Catholic faith. How could such a thing come to be believed? Sadly, the whole history of Protestantism in Aran answers that question.

In the far background of Irish folk attitudes to Protestantism stands Cromwell, synonymous with massacre and sacrilege, and in Aran there are ruined churches and the battlements of Arkin Castle to keep his memory alive. But by the early nineteenth century the garrison had so long departed and the abandoned fort had been so thoroughly recolonized by the village that his long shadow would have been greatly attenuated. Protestantism then was a handful of government officials and the twice-yearly visits of the landlord's agent; it was in the long-settled nature of things that the alien faith went with a secular authority emanating from so far away as to be almost abstract, and whose representatives on the ground of Aran were not too pressing, not too hard to outwit. In practice the islanders were ruled by their priest and by the Catholic middleman, Patrick O'Flaherty. A Protestant school had been opened in 1826, funded by the London Hibernian Society and later taken over by the Irish Island Society, a charity founded expressly to service the Protestant communities of such remote areas as this. There was also, briefly, a Protestant minister in Aran in 1835, whose congregation was composed of a few coastguards, and there were schools in Kilmurvey and Kilronan at which both the Protestant and the Catholic catechisms were used. Such a state of affairs was to become unthinkable within twenty years.

However, even in that relatively ecumenical pre-Famine period Protestantism was held in strict quarantine by the Catholic priest. In 1841, when a Presbyterian missioner, the Rev. Henry M'Manus, asked an Aran boatman in Galway docks to bring him over, he was told 'Sure we're ordered not to take any Jumpers into the islands.' (The OED states that the word 'jumper', meaning a Protestant, originated from the leapings of a Welsh sect.) The offensive term was new to M'Manus, but he ignored the insult and jumped into the boat, saying in Irish 'I'll go in, in the name of God.' This half-convinced the Aranmen that he was a priest, and they carried him to Cill Rónáin for nothing and were kind to him in his seasickness during a stormy crossing that took thirteen hours. Once on the island, however, he found he could do nothing to bring the Bible to the people. A coastguard told him that the priest allowed no communication, not even a common salutation, between his flock and the Protestants, while a Methodist missionary who was lodging with the coastguard was 'barely permitted to exist on the island' and was denied all access to the people. M'Manus wanted to preach a sermon in Irish, but he was told that 'even if the people were willing to come, they durst not, so great was the persecution that would ensue.' Taking his Irish Testament he went from door to door, but was everywhere politely refused permission to read from it, and eventually he retired to a lonely place among the rocks and spent a solitary Sabbath reading comforting words in view of the great Atlantic. Then, having found no 'door of usefulness' open to him, he decided to return to Galway; but no boat would carry him, and it was only after eight days of detention that he was rescued by some Galway gentlemen who happened to land on the island. The experience showed him 'the utter inexcusableness of that system of intolerance to which they [the islanders] were subjected by their clergyman', for that clergyman was not putting into their hands the means of enlightenment, the Scriptures, in the Irish language. In fact M'Manus claims that in twenty years of travelling in the Irish-speaking west and south he never once found an Irish school set up by the Catholic clergy, or an Irish Bible circulated; whatever had been done in that way was exclusively the work of Protestant Churches. And as for the Catholic idea that the means of salvation could be taught without Scripture books, it was in his opinion totally discredited by the instances of gross superstition and blind credulity he had come across in Aran, such as an attempt he had witnessed to calm a storm by immersing a bag containing two temperance medals and a scapular in the sea.

Nevertheless, the Island and Coast Society (as the Irish Island Society had renamed itself) could report some progress in that decade before the Famine. In 1833 their officers had found not a single native who would listen to the Gospel, but ten years later their school in Cill Rónáin had twenty-five scholars on its rolls despite that fact that 'the most unworthy means have been used to induce the parents to withdraw their children'. In 1845 it was supporting a minister in Aran, the Rev. Mr Cather, who joined with the Catholic clergy, Patrick O'Flaherty and other members of the local relief-committee in gathering money and distributing meal to the starving. By 1846 the church had been built, and 'though as yet silent and unconsecrated, the erection of this beautiful edifice, sacred to the worship on which they have hitherto looked with contempt, seems already to have produced an effect on the minds of the natives, who now treat with respect those persons they had been taught to despise – formerly a walk around the largest Island, nineteen miles in circuit, without food, was the penance for communication with any of the Protestants or converts – this is entirely done away with'. The boiler brought in by the Society was providing two hundred quarts of soup a day to the Aran poor – and in this charitable act, here as throughout Ireland, were the poisonous seeds of 'souperism', the use of food to bribe the hungry to quit their native faith.

It was not until 1851 that Aran got a permanent and resident minister. The Rev. Alexander Hamilton Synge spent four complaintful years in the island, which was not for him the adored if difficult mistress it was to be for his nephew J.M. Synge nearly thirty years later. The minister's letters to his brothers show him cringing away from the place in disgust. At first he lodged in the inn, where

... the bad cooking & dirty things & sour milk etc are some of the little inconveniences of my present abode the screaming of the women and children sometimes is dreadful it quite addels my head & it is too hot & close to shut the window – shd you happen to come to Dunmore that week w you bring some small *cookery* book for me for I must learn to make up some mess of some sort – meat is not to be had & their bacon poisons me & the fish is not always to be had either.

He saw himself as a castaway from all comforts:

Here I am Lord of all I survey – surrounded with dirt + ignorance ... it is a very wretched Island. The soile very scanty almost all a barren rock – we have a little church – 20 & 25 make our congregation mostly of the families of the coastguard ... I shall have one dirty little chap for my man Friday – who I expect will always be where I don't want him to be + never to be had when he is wanted however we must not be nice – it is very hard to make off a living here ... I am a regular prisoner – I get on with the people so far very well but how will it be when we begin to attack their bad ways & religion etc. I don't know.

In fact his letters report only one such attack:

I have succeeded in putting a stop to a ball match that used to go on here every Sunday. I attacked them very sharply the other Sunday & the next Monday the *priest* was the first to begin pulling down their wall tho' the rascal had seen them playing there 100 times before.

As for his ministry to the Protestants, 'the sermon writing is the most difficult of all & takes up a great deal of time – then preaching it to a very small number makes it some thing harder I think'. The newly built rectory he moved into in December of the next year was 'a wet and windy concern – it leaks like a sieve & rocks in the wind'. From all this his refuge was the open sea and the deck of his fishing smack, the *Georgiana*, which he bought within months of arriving in Aran, and the fortunes of which fill most of his letters. At that period the fishermen of the Claddagh, the Irish-speaking and semi-autonomous village outside the walls of Galway, claimed exclusive rights in the whole of Galway Bay, and the 'Jumper's boat' aroused their resentment. Unable to market his catch in Galway, Synge had to have it basketted and sent by the recently established railway to Dublin, and even to Liverpool. The Claddagh men then became dangerously threatening. The *Galway Vindicator* of 2nd June 1853 reported the confrontation:

The Rev. Gentleman with a crew of one boy and three Arran men, had been trawling in his yacht off Costello Bay, when a fleet of Claddagh boats bore down upon him, with the view of boarding his little craft. The crews of the attacking boats were armed with sunfish spears instead of boarding pikes, and stones instead of hand grenades, which missiles they discharged to some effect. Mr Singe was struck on the arm with a large stone, and severely hurt; some of his men were also more or less injured; and one of the hookers came under the boom of the yacht and prepared to board, but was beaten off by Mr. Singe, who presented a loaded musket at the formost assailant, and threatened to shoot him if he advanced further. ...

Two similar incidents took place the next year, after which:

With the view of bringing the perpetrators of the outrage to justice, the Rev. Mr. Synge proceeded last night to the Claddagh Quay, for the purpose of identifying the owners of several boats whose register numbers he had noted on the former occasions. But, being recognised by the Claddagh women, he was immediately assailed with stones and every available missile. Attempting to make his escape through the Fish Market, he was met by the denizens of that fragrant locality and was thus literally hemmed in by his assailants. No other means of escape being left he jumped into the river with the intention of fording it, but even there his pursuers continued the attack and it is difficult to say what might have been the result had not the Police immediately come to his assistance.

As a result the authorities stationed a paddle-steamer in the bay to protect the fishery, several Claddagh boats were seized, and twenty-five of their crew members taken prisoner. However, it was clear that only desperate poverty had driven the men to attack boats better equipped than their own, and the Harbour Committee suggested a collection be taken up to assist them in acquiring the gear for trawling. Synge himself spoke in favour of this, and a fortnight later the newspaper was able to state,

It is gratifying to see these men, instead of committing acts of lawless violence, and unsuccessfully endeavouring to prevent others from availing of the natural resources that Providence has bountifully bestowed, abandoning those unfounded prejudices, and peacefully entering upon a career of industrial occupation.

At the assizes a month later, the prisoners all expressed their regrets, the Crown did not press for prosecution, and the Claddaghmen walked free, 'loudly protesting their gratitude to the judge', while Synge had the riot charges against their womenfolk dropped.

It seems probable that Synge's disinclination to strenuous evangelism, the dangers he shared with his Aran crew, and the magnanimous resolution of the Claddagh cases, made his term in the islands one of relative interdenominational warmth. If so, the arrival of the young Rev. William Kilbride, who replaced him in 1855, must have been felt like a squall of hailstones. Kilbride's previous posting had been at Salrock in the north of Connemara, on the estate of a retired Peninsular War veteran, General Thomson. At that period Connemara was infected by a much more virulent strain of proselytism than Aran had suffered from. An English high-church evangelical rector, the Rev. Alexander Dallas of Wonston in Hampshire, had convinced himself and a number of rich and influential supporters that he was to be the tool of Providence in the liberation of Ireland's peasants from 'the anti-Christ of Rome'. The task was one that the established Church of Ireland was too well-dressed to plunge into:

I know what miserable, grovelling, ignorant, superstitious creatures they are. ... If their filth, and folly and superstition and passion repel your love you are not fit to go amongst them. You must be able to see the jewel of God in the midst of that dunghill, and condescend to be the scavenger to get it.

Fortunately the Famine, 'a direct judgment from God on account of the tolerance of idolatry', had softened that dunghill for his digging:

The state of Ireland during the whole of this year [1848] was most appalling: disease, in the shape of fever and cholera, had followed upon starvation. Many hearts were thus being prepared to receive those consolations which the glorious Gospel of God can alone impart. The oil of this joy was to be poured in by His missionary servant, and his tours there were full of encouragement, speaking as he did beside the dying and the dead with the full realisation of eternal truths.

In Connemara, where untold thousands had died and the enfeebled survivors were for years to be dependent on the charity of their betters, Dallas obtained the backing of several Protestant landlords, and most crucially of the Rev. Hyacinth D'Arcy of the Clifden union of parishes (which in fact included Aran until Synge's arrival). By 1849, when Dallas formally founded his Society for Irish Church Missions to the Roman Catholics, he already had a number of mission schools in operation around Lough

Corrib and Clifden. Substantial churches and rectories followed, around which little communities of converts, shunned by their former neighbours and cursed by their priests, huddled for protection. A contemptuous rhyme is still remembered in Connemara about the congregation of a church built under the patronage of General Thomson:

> Dá bhfeicfeá Jumpers Dhumhaigh Ithir
> Agus iad cruinnithe ar chrocán amháin
> Pota den 'soup' a' dul timpeall
> Agus freangach ag snámh ar a bharr ...

(If you should see the Jumpers of Dooyeher / All gathered on one little knoll / A pot of the soup going round / With a dogfish floating on top ...)

It was from this background of degradation and bigotry that Kilbride came to Aran in 1855. Soon he was joined by a Protestant schoolteacher, Thomas Charde, who had been involved in proselytism in Inishbofin, and in fact was thrown out of that island for it, according to accusations made against him by the Aran priest some years later.

Dr James Johnston Stoney arrived soon after Kilbride, in 1858. The younger son of a moderately well-off Anglo-Irish family from Tipperary, he had graduated from Trinity and acquired his Fellowship of the Royal College of Surgeons at Edinburgh. As he must have been married and had children at this time (he was to die in 1869, having had fourteen children by two wives), the move to Aran in itself calls for explanation, but nothing in the meagre records suggests whether it was an ideal of service that moved him so to seclude himself, or an addiction to the laudanum that killed him in the end. By the time of Stoney's arrival Thomas Thompson had succeeded his father George as landlords' agent, and so all the characters of the next few years little tragi-comedies were assembled on the bare stage of Aran.

At that time Thompson was already feeling it necessary to post notices ordering the Catholic clergy to desist from speaking against the Protestants from the altar. Nevertheless, when the potato crop failed in 1861 and another famine threatened, Thompson and Kilbride joined with Patrick O'Flaherty and his son James to form a relief committee, and Thompson supplied eighteen tons of meal and fifteen tons of coal for distribution. Stoney declined to join the committee, alleging that priority for relief was being given to those who sent their children to the Protestant school. By the next year the Catholic clergy, who did not join the relief committee, were forbidding any of their flock to supply the Protestants with food, and so Thomas Charde opened a shop himself, which was so successful it forced its only rival out of business. Some relief-work was started, for which the wages were potatoes to the value of 6d a day, the potatoes being supplied by Patrick O'Flaherty and the scheme funded by the Digbys, the Protestant Bishop of Tuam and others. Kilbride oversaw the work, and it was alleged that he was forcing religious instruction on his captive congregation of labourers. In January 1863 fever broke out, and a doctor sent by the Galway Board of Poor Law Guardians to look into the state of affairs reported that he had never seen such poverty, that Cill Rónáin and Cill Éinne were filthy and unwholesome, with manure heaps and pools of stagnant water at the doors of almost every cabin, that there were thirty-five fever cases in the island, including the Medical Officer's daughter, and that he had found Dr Stoney himself in bed, leaving the sick unvisited. Stoney had explained that he was 'utterly prostrated by fatigue and stimulants', which he later glossed as meaning that he had 'been obliged to resort to small quantities of stimulants to keep him on his legs on account of the work, and the usual effect of such stimulants was to add to the subsequent prostration'.

Other inspectors in April of that year found that there had been thirty-nine fever cases, with two deaths; however, the filthy state of the villages had been exaggerated, and in Cill Éinne there were only three offensive accumulations of dirt, at the backs of the houses. Evidence about Dr Stoney's intemperance was conflicting: both the Catholic priest and the Protestant minister said they had never seen him drunk, but the proprietor of the Atlantic Hotel claimed that on two occasions he had had to help him home the worse for liquor. On the whole it was felt that the doctor had 'left himself open to the charge'. The situation of the poor was found to be unsatisfactory. Kilbride was the only active member of the relief committee, and the poor regarded the relief as being given by him personally, while the Rev. Mr O'Malley accused him of 'tampering with the faith of the Catholic poor' and had challenged him to a controversy in the presence of the people at the relief-works. Kilbride agreed that he had read the Scriptures to the relief-workers, but that none had objected or left the works. The inspectors commented that 'such a course must have been irritating to the feelings of the poor whose circumstances of distress left them no alternative, their poverty obliging them to accept the relief though accompanied by transparent attempts to undermine the religious conceptions in which they had been reared'. Their recommendation was that a Relieving Officer be appointed, to preclude religious discrimination. Thomas Thompson opposed this on the grounds that it would increase the rates (which, because nearly all the tenants' holdings in the islands were very small, fell almost exclusively on the landlords), and he threatened that the proprietors would 'ease the islands of the cause of the increased taxation'. The Board of Guardians debated what he meant by this, and took it to be 'a gentle phrase for extermination ... in other words send the poor people adrift.' Nevertheless, an officer was appointed, whereupon Kilbride's committee refused to employ anyone receiving aid from him.

The case of a Thomas O'Brien came before the Guardians in the next Spring. The relieving officer had seen O'Brien digging a field over again after the potatoes had been lifted, 'to pick up a stray potato that might have escaped the diggers.' In his cabin there was 'no food, no fuel, nothing that could be called furniture, hardly the rudest utensil; no appearance of a bed, except a little straw packed up into a corner.' His wife Bridget said that her family was starving since she withdrew her children from the Rev. Kilbride's school, but that she would prefer to endure any amount of privation rather than have the priest speaking of her family at the chapel. The officer then gave her meal to the value of 3s 9d, and told her that further relief could only be had by going into the Galway workhouse. For this, O'Brien claimed, he had been refused work by Kilbride, and other people rejected by Kilbride because they had been relieved by the officer were now begging through the islands. Also, Kilbride had opened a school in Cill Éinne in charge of a Scripture reader, and was giving relief to those who sent their children to it. Kilbride denied that he was doing any more than relieving the children themselves. It seems from this officer's report that Kilbride's schools in Cill Éinne and Cill Rónáin had been forced to close, probably because the priest had made parents withdraw their children. The *Galway Vindicator* thought that the officer's report on the state of society in Aran made it clear that souperism was the greatest persecution affecting the Irish peasantry; however, there had been only one 'pervert' and he had now been received back into the Church.

In October 1864 Patrick O'Flaherty died, and whatever affection and respect the Aran folk had for this representative of the old patriarchal order was not inherited by his son. James O'Flaherty JP soon became hated as a land-grabber and as an associate of Thompson's in his extortionate schemes. One of these was the Irish Iodine and Marine Salts Co., whose story I told in *Pilgrimage*. Having by threat of eviction forced the islanders to sell their kelp to him, at his prices, paid in credit at Charde's shop, Thompson forbade them to transport the kelp to Galway in any boat except O'Flaherty's. Similarly, when the main road through the island was to be widened, all tenants except O'Flaherty had to work unpaid on it; and to compensate O'Flaherty for the land he gave up for the road, a tax of one shilling a household was levied on the island. As Antoine Powell puts it in his history of these episodes, the islanders were '*i ngreim ag siondacait*', in the grip of a syndicate. Dr Stoney wrote to the newspapers about the kelp racket, and when an increase in his salary was proposed (from £80 to £100 a year) the dispensary committee, which was dominated by O'Flaherty, protested that this would again increase the rates. The Board of Guardians gave in, and Stoney did not get his rise.

In 1868 arose another cause of offense to the Catholic faction. A young widow had emigrated to America, leaving her four children in the charge of her father, who had returned from Galway to live with his relatives in Aran. The father soon died, and the widow's mother and uncles felt the pinch and wanted the children adopted. The Catholic priest refused to have them put in an orphanage, so they turned to Mr Kilbride, who had Mr Charde take them to a Dublin 'Bird's Nest' (as the institutions in which Catholic orphans were brought up as Protestants were called). The uncles started attending the Protestant church, with the result that no one would employ them except Mr Charde. The Catholic clergy called for a boycott of his newly opened bakery, until the 'kidnapped' children should be returned and placed in Galway Workhouse, where they would be brought up in the Catholic religion. Thompson and O'Flaherty, joint owners of the *Arran Yacht*, which brought in goods to the islands, retaliated by refusing to carry either bread or flour for any other outlet. Just before Christmas 1868 the *Galway Vindicator* published:

THE SONG OF THE ARRANMAN
The island in beauty lay sleeping,
Far out on the waves as of yore,
But a feeling of hunger came creeping
O'er us as we sailed for the shore. ...
We looked for the light which they bade us
Expect in the breadshops of each,
But tho' darkness was chasing the shadows
No gleam could be seen from the beach.

We flew into one, it was empty,
As if the gaunt famine were there.
A vanithee*, haggard, unkempt she
Thus muttered in tones of despair:
'A parson and justice in council
To free trade in bread put a stop.
They decree that we'll ne'er get an ounce till
We deal in their own little shop.'

Early in the New Year the Rev. Corbett wrote to the owners of the islands, Lady Howth and Miss Digby: 'Mesdames – Is it by your wish that the islanders are refused bread unless they buy from a proselytising schoolmaster, who was obliged to fly from Inishboffin for the same reason?'

Shortly afterwards Thompson called off the bread blockade, and towards the end of the year the orphans were retrieved from the Bird's Nest and handed over to the priest, for their mother was to come back from America to collect them. That round seems to have gone to the Catholics, though Thompson's kelp monopoly continued until 1872, and even after that he extorted a royalty from the islanders on the kelp they sold elsewhere, until his company went out of business a few years later.

Dr Stoney died in 1869, of an overdose of laudanum according to his death certificate. (The last of his children, who had been born the year before, was to emigrate to America and there father the future professor, George Stoney.) An old lady of the island told George Stoney that his grandfather the doctor had visited a family in Oatquarter 'at the time of the black flu', had found every member of it suffering from this illness, and soon after returning home had come down with it himself. He dosed himself with the same medicine he gave his patients, and died; he was found dead (if he was dead) by a young lad, Peter Gill, who acted as his assistant and pony-trap driver. At the time there were so many people needing funerals (as the old lady put it), that there was no time for a proper laying-out. There followed the hasty burial, and the rumour spreading like another black infection.

I will trudge on to the end of this squalid sectarian history to show how hospitable the holy soil of Aran was to such germs. A few years later in 1877 there was some talk of 'distress' in the islands after a droughty season had caused the potatoes to fail and stormy weather was stopping the islanders from fishing. According to the *Vindicator*, because the tenants were so hard hit, the landless labourers could get no work and would starve unless relieved. The Digbys contributed £50 to Kilbride's relief fund, and Thompson claimed that a famine had been averted by the minister's timely actions, but the parish priest, Fr Concannon, and the relieving officer denied that there was any distress.

In that year another complex row began, which soon became linked to the national agitation against 'land-grabbing' that culminated in the Land League crisis. It started with the eviction of a Pat Ganly and his mother from their farm. Pat was the son of the engineer Thomas Ganly who came to the island in 1853 to build the pier and married a Mainistir woman. After being evicted Pat Ganly was readmitted to half of his farm, and the rest of it was given to the Rev. Kilbride (whose acquisition of 'a nice farm of land' near Cill Rónáin was recounted in *Pilgrimage*). Some months later a stone was thrown through Kilbride's window, and on another occasion when Ganly saw Kilbride's man working on what had been his farm, he produced a gun and ordered him off the land. The police searched his house as a result but found nothing. Then a bullet was fired through Kilbride's window. Kilbride about this time handed his half of the Mainistir farm over to Richard Charde, son of the schoolteacher and shopkeeper. The Chardes' shop window was then broken, and Fr Concannon threatened to curse anyone who dealt there until the farm was given up. Thompson put out a notice asking people to ignore the priest, saying that if Charde was forced out of business no one else would be allowed to open a shop in his place, and that if the agitation did not cease he would evict the Ganlys from the rest of their farm. Ganly was soon in prison for attacking Kilbride's workman on the disputed farm again, and while he was there an attempt was made to kill Richard Charde's cattle by poisoning a watertank. In June 1879 the authorities announced that if there was any further interference with Kilbride or Charde extra police would be sent to the island, at the islanders' expense. Despite this, two of Charde's cattle were found dead on the Ganly farm in December. The Land League came into existence in August of that year, and it seems that an Aran branch was founded soon afterwards by a new Catholic curate, Fr Fahey. The Land War in Aran was given a particularly vicious twist by the conjunction between the nationwide anti-landlord agitation and the local interdenominational feuding (which was an anachronism by then, with the general moderating of evangelical zeal, except in the parishes of Kilbride's former colleagues in Connemara).

That winter, after two generally cold and wet years, there was a threat of famine throughout the land. In Aran the people lacked not only food but fuel, as they were dependent on the turf which was still lying in soaking stacks out on the bogs of Connemara. Frs Concannon and Fahey set up a relief committee with the Medical Officer, Dr Bodkin, and in January of 1880 wrote to the voluntary relief-organizations recently inaugurated in Dublin:

Sir, Behind the fragments of the last fortress beseiged by Cromwell in Ireland stands the village of Killanny with its hundred huts. It is the fishing centre of Aran, and every hut there is a fisherman's home. Though its inhabitants, poor fellows, point to a stone in those battlements against which Cromwell's nose was rubbed in a brief defeat, and boast of his final repulse from their walls, still worse than all, Cromwell's curse, we fear, remains. Nothing else could bring on the people such cold and nakedness as we witnessed. No later than today we walked through the village and saw children entirely – this is true – entirely, absolutely naked, gathering themselves around their poor old granny in the corner where the fire used to be ... Returning to the house where we left the old woman and the naked children depending, Berkeley-like, on their imagination for heat at the quenched hearth, we found a strong man, idle and careworn, leaning against the black side-wall ...

'There are thirty men like myself in Killanny; we are too poor to get anyone to bail us for the fishery money. The people who want money most in those bad times won't get any from the Government Offices, but if we had one pound, each of us, to buy a Spilliard, we'd try to put a fagot of clothes on the children, a spark in the hearth, and a bit in our mouths, with the help of God.' Thinking as we came away on the best mode of seeking succour for this deserving man, we said we will venture to write to the three great Relief Funds, and we are sure they will not grudge to spend £10 each on a charity of this kind. These £30 would place the thirty wasting Killanny men in reproductive works. It will give them a chance of gathering, as they say, the riches that are waiting for them at the bottom of the deep.

The policy of the Mansion House Fund, headed by the Lord Mayor of Dublin, was to distribute relief through local committees on which clergymen of both denominations would sit, together with the medical officer and the 'prominent laymen' of the neighbourhood. According to the Mansion House Committee's later report on this period:

In only three instances throughout Ireland, was there found the slightest difficulty in combining the Catholic and Protestant clergy in hearty brotherhood, on the Committees. The exceptions were parishes in Connemara where the Protestant clergymen happened to be also members of the Irish Church Mission Society.

But since these parishes were 'literally threatened to be devoured by famine', it was resolved to make grants to separate local committees there:

It was the only occasion on which, during six trying months, any shadow of religious division vexed the plain course of charity. It served simply to throw into stronger light the heartiness with which, upon more than eight hundred Local Committees in every corner of the country, Catholic, Protestant and Presbyterian were found working side by side with the same unity, loyalty and breadth of sympathy which were the foundation-stones of the Central Committee.

However, things were hardly better in Aran, and the Central Committee soon received complaints from Thompson, that he had been kept off the Aran committee, and from Kilbride, that the Aran committee was 'utterly unfit, from its composition, mode of management, and general conduct, to carry on such a work'. A lawyer, Mr John Adye Curran, was sent down in June to investigate matters on the spot. His report is like a window of intelligence and humanity flung open in the murk of those times; one reads it with a feeling that an emissary from an enlightened age has visited the past, and is telling us the truth of controversies that we could not otherwise have disentangled. I will lay myself open to the risk of delusion, in following Curran.

At first Kilbride and Thompson, who had demanded the investigation, refused to participate in it, claiming that intimidation would make it impossible for them to bring forth their witnesses; however, Curran in a brisk exchange of letters made it plain he thought that they were shirking the investigation, and on a Monday morning all parties assembled in a large room of the Atlantic Hotel, and the hearing of the charges against the committee began. In the initial skirmishings Thompson stated that the committee was improperly constituted because the Protestant clergyman was not on it, and Curran informed him of the resolution of the Central Committee allowing the formation of religiously exclusive committees, and that Aran was one of the few cases in which they had had to allow the formation of a committee without the participation of the Protestant rector; it had been open to Mr Kilbride to form a committee of his own, but he had stated that he was able himself to provide for the only two Protestants needing relief. Then Curran disposed of Thompson's complaint that he had been studiously kept off the committee; in fact the correspondence of the committee showed that he had been invited to join and had refused. Mr Kilbride then alleged that none of the committee's business had been given to Mr Charde's shop; Mr Curran replied that that was a matter within the discretion of the committee, unless Mr Kilbride could show that the poor had in any way suffered from it.

The next charge was one Thompson had preferred in a letter: '... that ten heads of families were put on one list. This was called the "Soupers' List", all these were refused relief. The reason assigned was that some worked for Mr Kilbride, others for Mr Chard, and others again went to his shop.' In evidence Kilbride produced written statements that he said had been made by parties now too intimidated to come forward. The committee denied the existence of intimidation, and, Curran reports:

Dr. Bodkin requested Mr. Kilbride to give him the names of these parties he said were so intimidated, and whose attendance he was unable to procure. This was done, and in less than five minutes, the Doctor having picked them out of a large crowd waiting outside the hotel, paraded all the parties named before us in the room, apparently, to my mind, much to the Reverend Gentleman's surprise, if not disgust.

One of these was then called, a Mary Flaherty who worked at the barracks and whose husband worked both for Kilbride and for Charde; she said that she had not had any difficulty in getting her rights from the committee. Mr Kilbride reminded her of a statement, at variance with her present evidence, to which she had put her mark in his presence and in that of Mr Thompson. She became very much excited, and Kilbride and Thompson said it was quite clear she had been intimidated from telling the investigator the truth. Curran's report is unambiguous:

I could not help believing there had been a species of intimidation practised in this case, but not by the parties suggested. One can well imagine a scene enacted during a period of deep distress, in a room in the house of the Rev. William Kilbride, in which this nervous, excitable, poor, ignorant, uneducated woman, in the presence of her husband's employer, standing face to face with the agent to whom her husband had to pay his rent, might easily be induced, if not coerced, by that husband, himself unscrupulous, to make or sign with her mark a statement which, he considered, might be palatable to those two gentlemen, and which they no doubt believed at the time to be true.

Later on in the proceedings the husband, Patrick Flaherty, was examined by Kilbride, and stated that on one occasion when relief was being given out he had heard Fr Fahey say to another man, 'Go down to Mr. Chard, he knows what side to put the spoon before you;' also that Fr Fahey said, 'Come on now, let us read out the Soupers' List', and read out ten names including Flaherty's, who got no relief that day. But it emerged that Flaherty was in employment at that time, and not with Charde or Kilbride, and that he and his family had been relieved on other occasions. However, a most theatrical interruption then took place:

Just as the witness had given the last answer, there was a commotion at the door and Mrs Flaherty sprang in, caught hold of her husband in a manner less polite than determined, and calling out that she would allow him tell no more lies, disappeared with him in her grasp. The entire incident occupied less time than it has taken me to narrate the circumstances. After the disturbance had subsided, Mr. Kilbride informed me, that after such an exhibition of intimidation, he could not possibly proceed further with that branch of the inquiry. I saw no evidence of intimidation in the act of Mrs. Flaherty, but I did see evident signs of deep anger on her part against her husband for telling, what she believed to be, a false story, and against those who, she thought, were backing up her husband in his acts.

Having considered this case and several others in which witnesses did not confirm the written complaints against the committee to which, Kilbride alleged, they had previously put their marks, Curran found as follows:

I believe that a list of names was made out from week to week by the Committee, not of 'Soupers,' for, with one exception, they were all Catholics, but of men and women who were at the time earning money: these parties were refused, and properly refused, relief. The Rev. Kilbride and Mr. Chard were two of the principal, if not the principal, employers on the Island, and it followed as a necessary result that many persons must have been refused relief from time to time as a consequence of their working for either of these two gentlemen. ...but recollecting the ill-feeling between the clergy of both denominations, and the evident anxiety of the Catholic Clergy to prevent as much as possible members of their flock being brought into contact with either the Rev. W. Kilbride or Mr. Chard, I have no doubt but that the list made out from time to time of those who were working for those two gentlemen, became to be known commonly among the Islanders as the 'Soupers' List'.

Curran finally concluded that some islanders who had quite properly been refused relief, took advantage of the ill-will between the Catholic and Protestant clergy to impose upon Mr Kilbride; that their written statements had been exaggerated by anger and disappointment, and that Kilbride should not have been surprised that in calmer moments they had reverted to the truth, which was harmless; finally, that the Aran Committee had thoroughly cleared themselves of all charges.

A new barracks was opened in Cill Mhuirbhigh in that year of 1880, and six extra policemen were brought in, but the Land War continued to skulk up and down the twisty boreens. The Chardes, or their animals, were the principal sufferers of the Land Leaguers' twilight deeds; their mare was backed over a cliff at Mainistir in April, and in June their sheep and lambs went the same way. In September, when Thompson had imposed fines on certain villages for taking stones from the disused lighthouse buildings in Eochaill, the Catholic clergy called a public meeting outside his office; it was, according to the new curate, the Rev. McLoughlin, the first time in seven hundred years that the people had come together in their hundreds to call their agent 'a public, infamous and scandalous liar'. As Thompson had rejected their demand for reductions in rent in consideration of recent bad fishing seasons and the failure of the kelp and pig markets, they would appeal over his head to Miss Digby and the government. A young German visitor addressed the crowd too, and told them they were honest, hard-working and over-rented people; he was the philologist Heinrich Zimmer. An islander reminded the crowd of how they had been forced to make roads and buy Charde's bread, and had had their parcels searched for Galway bread, and exhorted them to stand shoulder to shoulder against tyranny and proselytism, for now they were awakening from their slumber at last.

About this time it was found that the rent-books had been stolen out of the Cill Rónáin courthouse, making it difficult to prosecute for arrears of rent. Dr Bodkin suggested that perhaps they had not been stolen by the tenants but by Thompson himself, to cover up his crooked dealings over kelp; however the doctor may have been trying to divert suspicion from himself, for oral history says that Pat Ganly got him drunk, borrowed the dispensary keys from him, and broke into the rent office next door through the common roof-space to steal the documents. Soon afterwards a house used as a courthouse in Cill Éinne was burned down, and Kilbride's boat was damaged. Then, just after the New Year of 1881, the famous cliffing of James O'Flaherty's cattle took place, and in April more sheep and lambs of Charde's were driven off the Mainistir farm and drowned. Pat Ganly's brother Thomas, secretary of the local Land League branch, was arrested with another man on suspicion of their part in the killing of O'Flaherty's cattle, and taken off to Galway Gaol. The bailiff Ó hIarnáin was shot at, and a Gort na gCapall man was arrested and imprisoned for it; the alleged motive was that his father was in arrears, and that since the rent-books had been stolen the bailiff was the only person who could swear to this. Minor acts of vengeance against the 'land-grabbers' continued, and a calf of Charde's was found stabbed in the belly. The last deed of the Land War in Aran was at harvest time in 1882, when a field of rye on Charde's half of the Mainistir farm was cut and the rye removed to Ganly's half. After that, as economic stress was moderated by the Land Courts' reduction of rents, and then by the development of the fisheries, sectarianism lost its fire. Personal antagonisms were outlived, or were carried off to the respective graveyards of their faiths.

Curiously enough, the most lasting memorial of Protestant evangelism in Aran is a stirring profession of Catholicism, written by an Aran poet and still occasionally to be heard as a song. The story goes that one day Kilbride met the poet, Séamas Ó Conchúir, going to collect his pension, and promised him both land and money if he would write a poem against Catholicism. According to another version of this incident, it was Thompson who demanded the poem, and when he received this spirited answer, evicted the poet, who had to go to America with his nine small children! Here is the first verse of Ó Conchúir's lengthy reply, with a translation:

Dá bhfaighfinnse culaith éadaigh a mbeadh ór ag sileadh léithi
As ucht dán a dhéanamh do thaobh chreidimh Gall,
Ní thiocfadh le mo chlaonta sliocht Liútair a moladh ar aon chor,
A d'iompaigh ar an lámh chlé agus a thréig Máthair na nGrást.
Nár dhona an cara domhsa, tráth m'anam a bheith á scrúdadh,
Cnagaire den dúiche seo ar chuntar dá bhfaighinn
Mo chreideamh féin a phlúchadh, ar nós an mhadaidh dúchais,
Agus mé a bheith go brónach, tráth mbeadh cúntas le tabhairt ann.

If I got a suit of clothes with gold dripping from them
As payment for a poem in support of the foreign faith,
It wouldn't suit my inclinations to praise the breed of Luther
Who took the evil turning and forswore the Mother of Grace.
What a worthless friend when my soul is to be tried,
A cnagaire of this land, if I'd been given it
For smothering my faith like a dog gone mad,
And me to be in sorrow when called to judgment for it.

Kilbride seems to have played little part in the belated end of the islands' dark ages; he probably concerned himself with his farm. His wife died in 1891, and it is ironic that her tombstone, the nearest thing we have to a memorial to Kilbride, names him in a rather strange Irish, as *'Uilliam Mac Giolla Bhrighde, bhiocar Aránna'*. The perception of the one or two old-timers who remember him is that he had learned Irish only to accomplish his evil purposes of perverting the people's faith. (His Irish versions of the Psalms had been published by the Society for Irish Church Missions back in 1863, at the height of his proselytising activities.) Kilbride himself died in the winter of 1898/9; J.M. Synge received a letter from one of his Inis Meáin friends telling him that the minister's boat had been on anchor in the harbour and that the wind blew her to Black Head and broke her up after his death. In 1907 Peter Gill, Dr Stoney's driver of long ago, returned from years in America, and discovered to his distress that the doctor's grave was unmarked. He carved a tombstone himself, and set it up in its obscure position. His nephew, then a boy, remembers sitting on the churchyard wall that day; it was snowing – a rarity in Aran – and when his uncle removed his black felt hat in reverence to his long dead master, the youngster shied a snowball and hit him on his bald head.

Little is remembered of later Protestant pastors; as their congregation dwindled they evidently had less and less of an influence on island affairs. By the time the last minister left in 1921 the only Protestants in Aran were two of the Charde family, for an elderly islander tells me that most of the later coastguards were English Catholics, and he remembers going to school with their sons. Later on, the roof of the disused church was removed so that rates would not have to be paid on it, an act which is still resented by those old natives who remember its last days, for they fear that visitors suppose the Aran people had wrecked the church out of bigotry, whereas 'we never touched a window of it'. The empty shell of St Thomas's stands to this day, a stark reminder of seventy years of barren ministry.

BACKWATERS

Heading out of Cill Rónáin with our shopping, we have to make up our minds whether to take the coast road, which is level but rough, or to face the steep hills of the main road. The point of choice comes just beyond the rectory grounds, opposite a pub called Joe Watty's, where a turning to the right dips into the shade of the Protestant sycamores, and within a few dozen yards swings left again into a sheltery backwater of the town, separated from the main road by a scarp, with a row of cottages and a few little barns and stores and roofless walls representing an earlier, more stunted generation of cottages. This is, or was, the hamlet of Baile an Dúin; so called either from a *dún* or cashel, or, according to other equally unverifiable sources, from a chapel or *domhnach*, perhaps Cill Rónáin or Rónán's church itself. Both cashel and chapel are untraceable today (the OS map of 1898 marks the site of a church about 150 yards north of the turning, which was probably a mass house or some relatively recent precursor of the present Catholic chapel), but Baile an Dúin (nicknamed Sleepy Hollow) seems to harbour a number of abolished histories, so I will look around it before heading for the west.

The turning down to Baile an Dúin is Carcair an Atharla, the slope of the burial ground, because St Rónán is said to be buried at its foot. Leaba Rónáin, Rónán's 'bed' or grave, is a plot about four yards square, delimited by a low wall, where the road turns right. There is a small altar in it, on which stands a stone inscribed with a cross and the name 'St. Ronane', very like another in Teampall Macduach in Cill Mhuirbhigh which is the work of a local stonecutter of the last century, John Burke. Up to perhaps fifty years ago it was the custom for people to sleep in the *leaba* on the eve of the saint's day, the 15th of August, and one or two old folk remember seeing crutches left there after the lame had been cured by such vigils. They tell me too that an Englishman once uprooted an elderberry bush there, saying it was a limb of St Rónán, and was smitten with a stroke.

In 1947 the parish priest, Fr Killeen, decided to have the *leaba* cleared out so that one of the outdoor benedictions of the Whit Sunday procession of the Blessed Sacrament could be held there. Fr Killeen was devoted to processions; in fact Dara the postman tells me that he was always making the route longer, 'going up and down narrow boreens with the people banging themselves on the walls, so that everyone was jaded by the time we reached the church; if he had stayed on the island any longer we would have ended up walking to Bun Gabhla!' At that time there was a small forest growing in the enclosure in place of the one alder tree O'Donovan had noted there during his 1839 researches. Fr Killeen describes the felling:

The people talked. It was not right to cut the trees down. Alders grew wherever the saints were. It was no use telling them that the use of the Leaba for Benediction would give more honour to St. Rónán than any old tree could. I gave the hatchet to Fr. Patrick Delaney and told him to go himself and do the work. He set to it with a will. A crowd stood on the road about thirty yards away looking at the priest whaling away with his axe, and apparently waiting for something to happen to him. They were thinking of the last man who tried to cut the trees down. He was a Scotch Presbyterian and a first class bigot. His clearly expressed reason for interfering with the Leaba was to show contempt for the holy place. But it fared ill with him. He had no sooner begun to use his hatchet than he broke his leg. That settled him. (This story appears to be quite true.) As the priest continued to remain unharmed, first one young man and then another broke away from the crowd and came down to help. Then they all came and made a first rate job of the clearance. That year too the custom of saying the Rosary at the Leaba on the eve of the Assumption was revived.

This passage is from the history of Aran Fr Killeen put together at the behest of his archbishop, a work of a hundred folio pages in typescript, particularly copious on all the saints ever mentioned in connection with Aran in the most obscure of ancient sources, a topic he poured his scholarly heart into. But even Fr Killeen cannot tell us anything about St Rónán. I need not quote the lengthy reasons he gives as to why our St Rónán is not to be identified with Rónán of Locronan in France, Rónán of Kilronan in Roscommon, Rónán Finn of Laind, Rónán Finn of Uí Eachach or Rónán mac Beraigh of Dromiskin. Perhaps his name was really Crónán, perhaps he is not buried here at all (O'Donovan thought he was not), perhaps he never existed – but one thing is certain, he was a mighty saint.

Just west of the *leaba*, according to early nineteenth-century maps, stood another monument to a most obscure facet of the island's history: Digby House, of which I believe not a trace remains. The Digbys are the great absence in Aran's history, not only as being for the most part absentee landlords of the classic sort, syphoning off the islands' tiny capital resources to be spent as the small change of a metropolitan, high-society lifestyle, but as blanks in the island record. What history of them I can offer here has been pieced together out of widely scattered references, and as to the islanders' own knowledge of them, that is and was virtually nil. When Synge in the late 1890s asked who owned the islands, the answer he got was, 'Bedad, we've always heard it belonged to Miss Digby, and she is dead.'

The Digbys, as I have mentioned, acquired Aran in the first half of the eighteenth century. In 1713 the Cromwellian Sir Stephen Fox sold the islands for £8200, in two 'moeities'; one to Edmund Fitzpatrick of Aran, and the other to the Rev. Simon Digby, Lord Bishop of Elphin, in Roscommon. The bishop leased his moeity to the Fitzpatricks for £280 per annum, but in 1744 the next generation of Fitzpatricks sold their own moeity for £2050 to the Digbys, then represented by a Robert Digby of Landenstown in Kildare. Perhaps this name Robert is an error in the source, for the bishop's son was called John, and it is recorded that John Digby was the proprietor in 1745, and that in 1754 he demised Inis Oírr to a William

McNamara of Doolin (on the Clare coast opposite the island), for thirty-one years at £90 per annum.

The 1745 reference to John Digby is in connection with a curious legal dispute between himself and the Mayor of Galway, concerning a whale stranded on the island of Muínis in south Connemara. Digby had harpooned this whale and extracted from it blubber and whalebone to the value of £160. The oil from this blubber was seized by the Galway authorities, and then somehow repossessed by Mr Digby. Galway took him to court, claiming that these products were a royal franchise, and that the Crown at some distant period had made a gift of that franchise away from the O'Briens of Aran to the Mayor, he being Admiral of Galway Bay. Digby's lawyer on the other hand argued, successfully, that a whale is not the King's property to grant, as the tail half belongs to the Queen, to keep her boudoir in whalebone.

The incident shows that at least part of the Digby family were in the west at the time, and they may even have lived in Aran for a while. Local tradition is that a Digby removed from An Spidéal to Cill Rónáin, bringing with him his tenants, the Gills and the Folans, whose surnames are still frequent in the island, and built the three-storey dwelling known as Digby House. However, by the time of the earliest documentary reference to Digby House I have come across, in the census for 1821, it was leased to a John Brown Moyne, and was occupied by a caretaker, James Connor, and his family (the future poet Séamas Ó Conchúir was his son, aged one at the time), and twenty-five years or so later it was in ruins. I am told that its stones were used in the building of the Rev. Synge's rectory, and that when the rectory in its turn was abandoned it was quarried for stone for the Catholic curate's house.

To continue with the history of the absentees. In 1822 there was some 'distress' in the islands due to potato blight, and the then landlord, Mr John William Digby of Landenstown, contributed to a relief fund. He was, according to J.T. O'Flaherty's paper of 1824,

a Gentleman of popular character, much esteemed by his tenantry, and considered one of the best of landlords. He allows annually 20 guineas to school houses, for the instruction of orphans; and £20 annually for clothing the poor, with other pecuniary donations. His annual rent, on the three islands, is £2700. Mr. Thomson, his agent, visits them twice a year, not only to receive rents, but to adjust all differences.

However, the popular character of the Digbys did not survive for long in the miserable years that followed. The potato harvest failed in 1825, and the consequent distress was said to be worse than in 1822. By March of the next year the *Connaught Journal* was attacking the landlord, now the Rev. John Digby, for neglecting his tenants. The land-agent George Thompson (father of the Thomas Thompson who succeeded him in this post) wrote to the newspaper in his master's defence:

You state that people are Dying of Starvation with no help from the landlord. The landlord in the past gave meal and potatoes to the people and empowered a gentleman living in Arran to do likewise at his expense. Enquire of Patrick O'Flaherty if you believe this to be false.

The newspaper refused to apologize to either Digby or Thompson, saying that the parish priest, the Rev. Gibbons, had asked them before Christmas to publish the plight of the people and that the resident gentleman (*i.e.* Patrick O'Flaherty of Cill Mhuirbhigh) had asked them to press on the government and the landlord the need for aid:

On Christmas Day we saw several people with starving children asking for some of the oatmeal he had got the previous day. We later truthfully published what we saw and within the last fortnight heard of three deaths from starvation. Only one ton of oatmeal was distributed by Mr. O'Flaherty from the landlord, only enough to whet the appetite and not to appease hunger.

By April, however, the paper could report that the Rev. Digby had purchased meal and potatoes for his tenantry, and added 'If we spoke harshly the reader will appreciate the circumstances.' In 1831, though, conditions in Aran were again 'as bad as in 1822', and Digby distributed a free cargo of potatoes. Cholera spread from Galway to Cill Rónáin in the next spring and claimed two lives; there was neither doctor nor dispensary in the islands, and the *Connaught Journal* urged the landlord to do something for his tenants. In August the coastguards in Aran reported that there had been twenty-five deaths, people had deserted Cill Rónáin and Cill Éinne to live among the rocks, and the O'Malleys had fled from the Lodge to Cill Mhuirbhigh. A messenger had come to Galway for medicine, but it was felt that in the absence of a doctor medicines could do more harm than good. By September there had been fifty-seven deaths. Mr O'Malley and Mr O'Flaherty contributed £5 each to a relief fund, but according to the *Journal* nothing had come from the landlord or the agent. The epidemic was over by the spring of 1833. The parish priest was then building the chapel at Eochaill, and the *Journal* 'joyfully' announced that the Rev. Digby had contributed £21.

At the time of the Great Famine that started with the blighting of the potato crop in 1845, the owner of the islands was Miss Elizabeth Francis Digby of Landenstown. By the next spring a local relief committee had been instituted and there was a dispensary in Cill Rónain; unfortunately the doctor, Surgeon Richardson, was dangerously ill himself, and a Dr Stephens was enquiring into the extent of an outbreak of fever. The *Connaught Journal* in November had a rather indefinite report of deaths from starvation, but since none such are mentioned in a letter they published from the parish priest, the Rev. Harley, in the January of 1846 it seems likely that the strong Aran belief about the Famine, that the islands were spared the worst of the blight and that only one person died, is soundly based. However there was immense distress, as the priest's appeal makes clear – poor crops of potatoes, a shortage of turf due to the stormy weather interrupting supplies from Connemara, a failure of the herring fishery for some years previously, no government relief or public works, no resident gentry or local institution to look after the people's interests. According to his figures, about two thirds of the population was without food and dependent on the others, who he claimed would soon be reduced to the same state. Only two tons of meal had been received from Miss Digby. The Rev. Harley's appeals for government aid were finally answered, and in the next February he received a second contribution of £100 from the Central Relief Committee. That spring the potatoes were sound, though not many had been planted.

The divergence of fortunes between the Digbys and their tenants thereafter became more and more glaring. Miss Digby's niece, Henrietta Barfoot of Landenstown, married Sir Thomas St Lawrence, the third Earl and twenty-ninth Baron of Howth, KP, Vice Admiral of Leinster. It was his second marriage, the first having been to a daughter of the thirteenth Earl of Clanricarde. He died in 1874 and Henrietta in 1884; thereafter the owners of Aran were old Miss Digby of Landenstown and her niece's offspring: the Hon. Thomas Kenelm Digby St Lawrence, Henrietta Eliza of Sloane St, London, who married Captain Lee Guinness and became Lady Guinness, and the unmarried Lady Geraldine Digby St Lawrence; down to the end of the century different combinations of these resounding names and titles appear on the ejectment notices served on those Aran tenants who for one reason or another failed to contribute their mite to the upkeep of the noble family. By 1911 the surviving proprietors, the two last-named ladies, had agreed to sell out the estate, but it was not until 1922 that the Land Commission finally took possession of the islands, for the sum of £13,721 paid in land stock, and began to distribute the land among those who had worked it and in many cases created it out of rock. It seems entirely appropriate to the Digbys' role in the island story that not a stone remains identifiable of Digby House.

Walking on from this obscure corner associated with unknown saint and absentee landlord – two figures reduced to abstractions and invested with essential goodness and badness respectively, perhaps only by our ignorance of their humanity – one comes into a quietly pleasant quarter of the island, in which one might imagine nothing had ever happened, but which has in fact been disturbed by two events, rather alike in their murderous futility, bearing dates 1584 and 1920. (Perhaps, all the same, one should not complain about just two such incidents over the last four hundred years; these fields are less blood-soaked than many!) Where the road running north-westwards through Baile an Dúin emerges from the last of the village, it opens up a view on the right hand, of low-lying sandy pasturage divided into small plots, stretching to the seashore half a mile away. This area is Log na Marbh, the hollow of the dead, and in a field a couple of hundred yards below the road, by a modern water-tank, is a squarish mound with traces of stone kerbing and a small upright stone, in which, I was told, nine murdered Connemara men lie. The invaluable Fr Killeen noted down the more detailed tradition still current in the 1940s, identifying the event with a battle recorded by no lesser authorities than the Four Masters. I give their account of it in all its antique tangledness, so expressive of the nature of this, the last outbreak of clan warfare in Iar-Chonnacht:

A.D. 1584: A contention arose in Iarchonnacht between the descendants of Owen O'Flaherty and the descendants of Murchadh, the son of Brian na nOinseach O'Flaherty. The cause was this: The head of the race of Owen O'Flaherty (Tadhg the son of Tadhg na Buile, i.e. the Mad, son of Murchadh, who was son of Owen), and the race of Dónal an Chogaidh (of the Battle), son of Gilduff, took the island of Ballynahinch from Tadhg the son of Murchadh na dTua, who was the son of Tadhg O'Flaherty, for the race of Owen were saying that the island was theirs by right, and that Tadhg took and kept possession of it by unjust violence. But be this as it may, as to the taking of the island Tadhg prevailed over them, and he left not a single head of cattle in any part of their country to which he came that he did not kill or carry off. And the others though unequal in power did great injury to Tadhg.

On one occasion this Tadhg, the son of Murchadh, went with the crew of a boat in the month of June on a nocturnal expedition in pursuit of the race of Owen O'Flaherty to Aran, and overtook them at break of day when they were unprepared between sleep and vigilance on both sides of the prow of the ship. And unfriendly was the salutation he made them on that shore, and indeed the island [Ballynahinch] was not worth all that was done about it on that one day, for Murchadh, the son of Edmond Óg, son of Edmond, son of Hugh, the proprietor of Leitir Mealláin, who joined the race of Owen O'Flaherty, was killed, as were also the sons of the seneschal of Clann Maurice, who was along with them on the same predatory excursion, and also Tadhg Salach [dirty] the son of the O'Flaherty

[Tadhg] himself, and a great party of the race of Owen O'Flaherty besides these nobles. Thus they continued at war with each other, until the English made peace between them in the succeeding Autumn, when the island was given to the race of Owen O'Flaherty.

To make what passes for sense in a murderous world out of this, one should remember that the divisions between the two branches of the O'Flahertys were fomented by Queen Elizabeth's statesmen-soldiers, the better to control the rebellious clan. The chief of the eastern branch, Murchadh na dTua (of the battleaxes), had been recognized by the English as head of the clan, whereas under the old Brehon Law the rightful head was a member of the western branch. The latter had five castles around the coast of Connemara and a central one on the lake-island of Ballynahinch. Murchadh na dTua (who was now Sir Murrough O'Flaherty, having traded in his Gaelic identity for feudal rights and title) seized Ballynahinch and installed his son, Tadhg; this Tadhg was then ousted by the sons of two famous chieftains of the western branch with the intimidatory names of Tadhg na Buile (of the rage) and Dónal an Chogaidh (of the war). Some of the western party then went to Aran, where they were set upon and slaughtered by the Tadhg of the eastern branch. In the end it seems the English re-established the westerners in Ballynahinch, but it was Sir Murrough who in the year 1587 received a grant of all the lands and castles of Iar-Chonnacht 'to hold to him and his heirs for ever by the twentieth part of a knight's fee, as of the manor of Arkin in the Great Isle of Aran'. This scheming was a tiny part of Elizabeth's European strategy, in itself a part of the vast upheaval of the Reformation. A fraction of the dire energy of that centuries-long storm broke up the old world of Connemara; a vicious little eddy from that wreck span itself to death in this backwater of Aran.

The quiet little road goes ambling on from 'the hollow of the dead' towards the bay at Mainistir, a summer's day stroll margined with wildflowers and tall grasses, with a reminder of winter rain storms in its torn-up surface. After a quarter of a mile it passes a small stone plaque set among the stones of the field-wall on the left, which the stroller may well not notice:

PRAY FOR THE SOUL OF LAWRENCE MC DONOGH
SHOT BY CROWN FORCES DECR 19 1920
DIED 23 R.I.P.

The 'Crown Forces' were the Black and Tans, a body of licensed ruffians scratched together and put into heterogeneous uniform by the British government earlier in that year, to throw into the campaign of murder and retaliation the RIC was losing against Sinn Féin. Fifty of them came to Aran, in search of three armed members of the Volunteers who had fled from Galway to hide out with friends and relatives in the island. An old man early awake in Cill Rónáin saw in the dim winter dawn a man-of-war in the bay and soldiers landing from rowing-boats, and ran to warn his neighbour, Pádraig Ó hIarnáin, who had been sheltering one of the fugitives. I am told that a woman in another household heard the Black and Tans coming into the town and thought at first it was Connemara men bringing in cattle to winter. She looked out of the window and saw armed men, and just had time to hide her money-box under her petticoats before they burst into the house. They turned the place upside-down in search of drink, and went roaring off again, one of them wearing the veil he had torn from a large statue of the Virgin. (The Black and Tans seem to have had an urge to add feminine touches to their motley – in their drunken night of murder and arson in Clifden three months later they broke into a haberdashery, and went dancing through the streets wearing corsets over their uniforms!) Ó hIarnáin had run off to hide in a crevice of the Creig Mhór, taking his gun with him, but the Black and Tans arrested his brother, who was in bed with flu, and left him tied up on the quay all day. Later they found a horse they mistakenly thought was Pádraig's, and shot it between the eyes. Detachments of soldiers, obviously acting on information, hurried east and west along the main road to certain other houses. Pádraig Mac Giolla Phádraig of Cill Éinne, who had sheltered another of the Galway men, was arrested, and in Eochaill, where a Pádraig Ó Domhnaill was the target, his next-door neighbour was taken by mistake, but managed to escape from his captors. Máire Gill tells me that two uncles of hers were seized and dragged behind the Minister's gate in Cill Rónáin, and her grandmother was brought out to see them shot; one of the islandmen had connections with the Irish Republican Brotherhood, the other did not, and it is indicative of the complexity of conflicting loyalties that it was a third uncle, home on leave from the British armed forces, who came by in his uniform and got them off.

Later that morning some of the Mainistir people were on their way to chapel in Cill Rónáin, when they were turned back by two of the Tans. One lad, Larry Beag, determined not to miss the Mass, went down to the coast road and tried to creep along to Cill Rónáin in the shelter of the wall; one of the Tans saw him from the main road, aimed with the telescopic sight of his rifle at a gap in the wall, and shot him. Larry died a few days later, on the 23rd of December.

Another warship came into Port Mhuirbhigh that dawn, and soldiers visited houses in the west of the island. One man arrested in Fearann an Choirce was Máirtín Breathnach, who had been training the island Volunteers. (There were about seventy of them, I have been told; they had no arms, but they drilled on the roads and in Johnston's big fields in front of Kilmurvey House, no doubt to the annoyance of Johnston himself, who was by no means a supporter.) In Gort na gCapall the Black and Tans were looking for the chief of the Aran Volunteers, Thomas Fleming. Thomas's father had come to Aran as a young mason, building the teachers' residences, and had married a sister of Liam O'Flaherty, and it was in the O'Flaherty house that Thomas and his wife were living. It was four in the morning, and he would have been caught but that his mother-in-law was heating milk for the baby when the soldiers arrived; she opened the door with the baby in her arms, and delayed them for a couple of seconds while Thomas ran upstairs and squeezed out of the gable window. He had to hang from the window ledge by his fingertips for a moment until a soldier with a flashlamp went inside, then he dropped to the ground and took off for the crags. (We used to hear the details of this adventure from Thomas himself, whom we knew as a spry old man who would hop off his bicycle to sit on a wall with us and chat. He told us whom he suspected of having informed on him: a *poitín*-drinking Fearann an Choirce man who often visited Galway and seemed to have mysterious access to ten-pound notes, and who once showed him a poem in praise of a brave Black and Tan fallen in battle; this man soon afterwards left the island, and was followed to Tipperary, and shot.)

The three Galway Volunteers, who had been spending most of their time hiding in a store on the Hill Farm, were not betrayed and the Black and Tans did not find them, which perhaps spared the island a gun battle and further retribution. But they were saddened by the trouble they had brought down on their protectors, and soon decided to move on. Early one morning, after receiving communion from the curate Fr Mártan Ó Domhnaill, a supporter of the cause, they were smuggled aboard the *Dun Aengus* and sailed back to Galway. That ended Aran's direct involvement in the War of Independence, which was terminated by the Truce of July 1921.

Lawrence McDonogh, I have heard an islander say, should be canonized, as he died for his faith just as much as St Laurence O'Toole. But this philosophical island is also surprisingly understanding of the Black and Tans. According to one of our neighbours, 'Some of them were decent men; they were just soldiers, doing their duty.' The same man was told by Mícheál Breathnach that, as he was being marched down to be shipped off to Galway gaol, he overheard one of the Black and Tans saying to another, 'It's a dirty business, punishing the innocent for other people's doings.' Indeed: a dirty business, and an unfinished one. Looking at Larry Beag's little memorial one could speculate as to how many of the seeds of hatred scattered in a December dawn of this quiet corner of Ireland will have found ample blood-rich ground to sprout in since.

From that uneasy thought I now turn back to the sleepy village. There are two short-cuts linking the north end of Baile an Dúin with the main road. The one nearest town, ancient, twisty and haunted, is called Róidín an Phúca, the little road of the pooka. The brow of the scarp it climbs up is the site of three successive notable monuments: the demolished *dún* from which the hamlet is perhaps named; the chapel or Mass house, which had gone by the time of the 1839 OS; and, still proudly extant, the pioneer of Aran bungalows, built in the 'sixties by the first island trawler-owner to become a millionaire. The other road, a little farther north, is straight, apart from an initial ramp up the scarp, and comparatively modern, with two pairs of semi-detached cottages symmetrically arranged on either side; they were built by the Congested Districts Board to replace some hovels nearby in 1915, and the only name I have heard for the road is Bóithrín na gCottageachaí, which I suppose one could call CDB-Irish. Either route will bring me back into the mainstream of Aran life.

CLIMBING THE HILL

Now and then, if M and I happened to be in Cill Rónáin on dole day, we would get a lift home in a pony-trap driven by an acquaintance from the west. Beartla was a proud man who did not like his neighbours to see him drinking in the Oatquarter pub, and so for him Joe Watty's pub represented the last chance, not only before the dry miles ahead, but before a whole dry week. Nowadays the pub is fashionable among the summer visitors; it has its name up in holiday colours, and a few benches and tables under the tree in its front garden give it an almost continental air. But in the seventies it was as obscure as a public house could well be, no sign betrayed its vocation, and few outsiders ever troubled its stagnancy. Joe Watty himself had passed on at a great age in 1975. I am told that he used to go down the *carcair* opposite his pub to stand in prayer before St Rónán's bed for twenty minutes every day. Perhaps he was so pious because of an early miraculous delivery, for he had been sleeping in one of the fishing-boats anchored in Cill Éinne bay that night in the winter of 1899 when the storm struck and three men were drowned, and he not only survived but slept undisturbed through it all. He died on the same day as de Valera, a fact I remember because when the news spread through the island a neighbour said to me,

'They're both in the same canoe now!' It was his son Pádraic Joe Watty who had the pub thereafter. He was himself elderly by then, and shy – he hung out no inn-sign because he felt he couldn't handle the tourists – and as he was also more interested in looking after his few cattle than in manning the bar, it frequently happened that the pub was shut when we passed.

. Our first visit to Joe Watty's was for a wake in honour of an old horse called the General, which we had just seen hoisted onto the steamer for Galway. The General had been born on Beartla's farm in Cill Mhuirbhigh. A big horse by Aran standards, he had harrowed the oatfield and dragged the seaweed cart up the hill year in year out, until he became too unsteady for the stony slopes and was replaced by a neat Connemara pony. On our evening strolls we often stopped to lean over a wall and watch him in one of the little pastures of his retirement; he would stand motionless for hours, it seemed, then turn himself upside-down and wriggle like a baby, his huge hooves going in all directions as if he were slithering on an icy patch of sky. His owner had told us that this was called *an luí mór*, the big lie-down; when a horse had been carting seaweed all day from four in the morning, it would be let loose to do that now and again, and then it would be as fresh as it was at the start. No doubt, at hurried times of the year in the bad old days, both horses and humans had to work till they dropped, to provide food for themselves and dowries for the Digby girls, and the idea of keeping an unproductive horse in grass did not arise. Ways of thought that linger past their time are not so easily disposed of, though, and when Horan the Galway butcher, who used to come out on the steamer each Saturday with big wicker hampers of meat and set up shop in Cill Rónáin for a couple of hours, and do a bit of horse-dealing on the side, offered our friend a few pounds for the General, a bargaining was initiated which after many weekly rounds ended in them spitting in their palms and shaking hands on a price. Then we were called upon to see the horse off and (an unspoken understanding) to get our friend out of Cill Rónáin again without too much drink taken. However, as we walked by Joe Watty's, Beartla's thirsty eye detected some sign of life in it, and he went up the weed-grown path to listen at the front door, which was locked. He turned to crook a finger at us, saying, 'We'll have but one!', and we had to follow him round the back, pushing past bushes, and through a derelict porch and the corner of a dark kitchen to the space behind the counter, where Pádraic lifted the flap for us to pass into the public part of the bar. The room was a dingy cell, in which two or three jarvies sat as silent as bottom-fish in a dark pool. It was lit, if not warmed, by a torn-up cardboard carton smouldering in the hearth; the vivid greenery pressing in at the tiny window-pane made it even chillier. M caused some wonderment by asking for a sherry, and Pádraic Joe

Watty had to search among piles of this and that in a back room to find a bottle with a bit of sherry left in it, and to grope along a high shelf for an encrusted sherry glass. Then we had to hear Beartla tell and retell the horse's whole Aran life, down to the last moment in the hold of the steamer, when the General had turned and looked at him climbing back up the iron ladder, and had made a little movement with his head (which Beartla demonstrated for us as a quick salute at the temple with two fingers together), 'just as if it was my brother emigrating to America.' It became more and more obvious that the horse should have been left to stand and roll and kick in its familiar fields, instead of being sold on, as Beartla now explained, to some east Galway farmer who would 'knock another year or two out of him.' By the time we had drunk our various fills – M's noxious-looking sip, my two reluctant halves, Beartla's four pints of porter effortlessly engulfed – we were all wordless, and we turned our heads to the long climb homewards in a stupor of regret.

The once populous but now derelict area behind this pub is called An Suicín, a name that also occurs in Galway city; the derivation is obscure, but it is probably from something that sucks, like a marshy patch or a swallow-hole. This used to be the poorest quarter of the village, in which a hundred or more people lived in a few long terraces of thatched cottages. Only two of these one-room cottages still stood, the decayed ends of rows which had otherwise been pulled down, when we came to the island, and I believe they too are levelled now. A woman whom we never saw, living in one of those two last fragments, used to shout all day long in passionate disagreement with nobody; we would hear her as we went by, the whole teeming unquiet past of An Suicín condensed into one disembodied voice. Or, if hers was the voice of the accumulated pangs of just the female part of life, then the generations of male voices, their endless sublimation of cramped circumstances into stories and jokes and boasts, are dismissively recorded only by the name of the narrow turning into An Suicín south of the pub, where the menfolk used to lounge about and talk: Coirnéal na mBréag, the corner of lies.

From Joe Watty's the road out of the village rises in *carcair* after *carcair*. The first is Carcair an Jabaire or Jobber's Hill, and is named from Pat Mullen's uncle, An Jabaire Beag, the little jobber or cattle-dealer, whose cottage, on its west side, was 'a meeting-place for the man from the east and the man from the west', as I am told. The hill seems to have been the place for faction fights, and people would say of any great fighter, 'A better man never walked down Jobber's Hill.' The little Jobber himself appears in Pat Mullen's novel *Hero Breed*, and shows us how to prepare for a stickfight. One can imagine him leaping out into the road here:

The little Jobber was a small man, about five feet in height and ten stone in weight, but he was finely built for all that and he carried a blackthorn stick in his left hand. ... His face became as white as chalk as he hurriedly tore off his bauneen and wrapped it round his right arm. ... He whirled on the gathering crowd and bounded to where he had a clear space for his stick arm. 'Is there any bully among you men that would take a chance of drinking his own blood this day by saying anything to the Morans? If there is, let him get his stick and stand opposite me!' Holding his stick part-way from one end, as a good stickman should, so that the forearm and elbow were protected from the glancing blow of an opponent, he waited eagerly, hopefully, with his eyes darting fire. His fury seemed to have penetrated to the stick quivering in his hand. ... The Jobber and his brother, in the meantime, had taken up their positions so that if attacked they would be more or less back to back, with plenty of stick room between them. 'It's not their first fight,' said Shawn in admiration, 'See the way they have placed themselves, back to back almost, with that high stone post on one side and that old shed a few steps away on the other. It is hard to rush them. Yes, they have been through a good many fights before.'

Leaving these anachronistic shades to settle their differences, and skirting round a sudden joyous outrush of youngsters from the gates of today's Technical School a little farther on, I press on up the hill, which brings to my mind now (writing far away from it) so many things seen and tales heard, that the time-dimension itself in that backwards perspective looks no longer string-like, but wide, a road on which creatures of different eras could pass and greet each other. Memories of another Aran faction fighter give a life to the last house of the village, long untenanted now, staring gloomily back down the hill with one gable-end to the road. Breandán Ó hEithir, the writer, broadcaster and despairing but indomitable battler for the Irish language, was born here in 1930; his father was a teacher from Co. Clare, who married Liam O'Flaherty's sister from Gort na gCapall, and the house is identifiable by its two little upstairs windows huddled under a central peak as one of the teachers' residences built to a standard design in the 1880s. It was of Breandán I was thinking when I wrote in 'Timescape with Signpost' that it is an awesome choice for a writer to entrust a life's work to an endangered language. I believe the anguish of that decision weighed more heavily on him as he grew older, and may have added some personal bitterness to the last, posthumous, polemics of his career. Shortly before his unexpected death in 1990, he had drawn up an internal report on the state of the Irish language for Bord na Gaeilge, the government body set to watch over its well-being. The controversy was provoked by the leaking of that report in the following year, and especially by its denunciation of the various organizations concerned with Irish as 'infested with elderly people who have not let a new idea into their heads for many years in case they might have to change their way of life, which is something they would now be unable to do', and its deeply pessimistic assessment of the Gaeltachts:

The 10,000 native speakers that are left in the country would only make up the normal attendance at the county final of a small county. ... Worse still, many of those speakers live in isolated pockets that are on their last legs and that are with difficulty described as Irish-speaking communities ...

Conradh na Gaeilge (the Gaelic League) did not appreciate Breandán's 'typically cynical view of Irish language organizations', and called his estimate of the number of native speakers 'a gross understatement', claiming that statistics of the £10 grants being paid to Irish speakers in the Gaeltachts suggested a figure more like 30,000. Had he been in a position to flourish his blackthorn stick Breandán would have quoted his own previously published opinion on those grants:

At first you had Irish and you got the grants and after a bit you saw no reason why you should speak Irish to get them or bring up your family through Irish at all. After all you could see that the wind and the tide and the heart of the State were with English; apart from the grants, no doubt, whose purpose was to buy your votes.

M and I first met Breandán at a course he was running for Bord na Gaeilge in An Cheathrú Rua in the autumn of 1978. The purpose of the course was to familiarize journalists with the economic life and institutions of the Gaeltachts. We could hardly claim to be journalists on the strength of the photocopied nature bulletins I occasionally produced for the Oatquarter schoolchildren, but the course sounded as if it might be an opportunity to learn something of this culture into which we had thrown ourselves so arbitrarily, so we put ourselves forward, and to our surprise were accepted without question. We took the boat to Galway, hitch-hiked out to An Cheathrú Rua, rented ourselves a thatched cottage, and reported to the hotel where the participants were to foregather. In the bar was a small and almost inanimate huddle of people, from which Breandán broke like a snipe on seeing us, and hurtled over to thrust an envelope into our hands – the grant cheque – as if it were of desperate urgency. It was clear why we had been so readily accredited; only four journalists had been tempted by the grant away from their metropolitan perspectives to spend a month visiting fish-processing plants and plastic-components production units in rain-sodden Connemara, and our participation made the course a little less of a numerical flop.

The month was not pleasant. M's determinedly positive attitudes alienated the world-weary, flu-prone Dubliners, who did as much of their research as they could in the numerous bars of the town. It soon transpired that none of us had enough Irish to benefit from the projected programme, and we bowed our heads to a crash-course in the twelve irregular verbs. The mock newsletter we produced for presentation to the Board was so abysmal that Breandán quashed it. Some Dublin ad-men came down to privilege us with a preview of a series of TV advertisements for Irish – 'It's part of what we are ...' – which so incensed me I became abusive and told them that the language movement should at least be able to recognize its enemy, *i.e.* the homogenizing materialism of which TV ads were the epitome. The only good times were those spent listening to Breandán holding forth at full throttle; we could not always quite identify his topics, nevertheless, it was exciting to hear an Irish that did not stoop to its half-competent recipients. (Both then and later we sometimes wondered if his unceasing flow of witty reminiscence was a way of holding intimacy at bay.) But he was often morose and *distrait*; he had just published an English version, *Lead Us into Temptation*, of his first novel *Lig Sinn i gCathú*, and reviewers were saying that if this was a sample of the literary riches being produced in Irish, it would have been better for the good name of the language to leave it untranslated. At the end of the month we were each to write a personal response to the course. None of us managed this in Irish, but M and I put together a few thoughts in English on journalism and its own curious sort of opportunistic integrity. Finally there was a formal dinner in the hotel, at which we graduates were much outnumbered by Bord na Gaeilge executives. Breandán, slightly the better for wine, made a speech, which suddenly became emotional, and to our surprise M and I learned that we had written something that was *'chomh fíor – chomh tábhachtach – tá sé thíos i mo phóca agam ag an nóiméad seo ...'* ('so true – so important – I have it in my pocket at this moment ...'). But what followed was not comprehensible, and as Breandán did not produce our writing from his pocket and we have forgotten what we had written, I fear this illumination is lost to the world.

Thereafter we met Breandán only at long intervals. When The Lilliput Press launched my *Pilgrimage* in the Peacock Theatre in Dublin, he spoke magniloquently. And when the *Times Literary Supplement* sent the book to Ireland's poet laureate for review he forwarded it as a matter of course to Breandán, the representative of island literature. Breandán's affectionate notice is probably the only one the severe TLS has ever published in which the author of the book under review is referred to by his first name. Then, in 1990, on my return to Ireland after a month abroad, I fell into conversation with a stranger on a train, who mentioned casually that she had recently attended Breandán Ó hEithir's funeral. I am lazy about friendships, and have lived to regret it.

Just beyond the old teachers' residence the road sidles up to the next scarp it has to climb, which steepens into a vertical rock-face called An Aill Bhriste, the broken cliff, along the left-hand side for a short distance. Here a 'grotto' has been made out of a nook of the cliff, with a conventional blue and white Madonna casting her eyes upwards. Once, as I approached, a donkey came to the edge of the cliff and appeared in that visionary space above her, twiddling its huge furry ears in benediction. Another time I glimpsed a minute goldcrest – a rare bird in Aran – flitting in the tapestry of rambling roses and old man's beard around her niche, the bright streak of its crown appearing and disappearing like stitches of gold thread among the cream and pink blossoms and shadowy greenery, all momentarily rendered as precious as a Crivelli. The last wedge of ground between the road and the scarp here is called Buaile na gCopóg, the pasture of the plantains, as I happen to know, because if I'm climbing the hill in company with some other shopper from the west and I run out of conversation, I fall back on place-name studies. Next, the road bends westwards, makes an effort and gets itself onto the next level by a steep ascent called Carcair na Ceártan, from a *ceárta* or forge that used to stand on the right of the road, run by a Micil Riabhach Ó Niaidh, a Connemara *poitín* smuggler of a hundred and fifty years ago. At this point one enters the next townland, Eochaill, which is supposed to mean 'yew-wood'. If ever there was a wood in it, nothing could be stonier than one's first view of it today. An Chreig Dhubh, the black crag, is the name of the great terrace of limestone pavement that comes into view stretching away to the south from the road here, and I have seen consternation in the faces of newcomers who have climbed so far, to find only this desert, and further bare hills rising before them. Old Beartla thinks that it is a disgrace to the island that the Cill Rónáin men didn't reclaim all this wasteland, instead of spending their days lying in the shelter of a wall and talking. In fact there is something lugubrious about this crag, and although I have often botanized across it and found as much fascination in its crevices as on other great crags to the west, it leaves me drained, as if by some localized side-effect of gravity. But it has a comic aspect too, which I owe to Beartla's voluminous commentary on every step of our way, on the many occasions I walked with him up this hill, sparing the pony of his side-car. He thinks that this crag, or a part of it, has another name, which sounded like Creig Arry. And what is the meaning of *arry*? I asked; he didn't know, but he thought it was somebody's name, as in Harry Stattle. And who was he? Again Beartla didn't know – but whoever he was he must have had great brains, because if a man did something very clever you would say '*Sáraigh sé Haraí Steatail* – He beats Harry Stattle!' It took me a moment to recognize Aristotle, the father of cleverness himself, in this

Aran dress. Of course the name of the crag, Creig Earraigh, whatever it means, has nothing to do with the philosopher, but I always think of him as I pass, and think too how Joyce, 'bringing to tavern and to brothel / The mind of witty Aristotle', would have relished Harry Stattle.

Curiously, Aristotle is a well-known figure in Irish folklore, and the tale of his marriage used to be told in Aran. It seems that Aristotle 'was very wise, very brainy, but he didn't like women at all', and he had a man to cook and keep house for him. This housekeeper often discussed his master's peculiarity with a woman who used to hang around the house, and they decided to trick him into marrying her. Aristotle always had breakfast in bed, and one morning the woman dressed herself in the housekeeper's clothes and carried in the breakfast to him. As soon as she was at the bed-side the housekeeper locked the bedroom door and ran for a lawyer, while she started to shriek that she was being kept in against her will. The judge-ment of the lawyer was that Aristotle would have to marry the woman or face a court case, and so he consented to marry her, on condition that he could put her from him if ever he found fault with her. She in her turn agreed to this, on condition that if he put her out she could take with her three loads of whatever she wanted from the house. So they married, and had a boy-child of whom Aristotle became very fond. But later he began to hate the woman, and to suspect she was too friendly with the housekeeper, and eventually he ordered her out. 'Very well,' she said, 'but remember our agreement, that if you put me from you I can take three loads of whatever I choose with me.' 'In with you and get your three loads,' he said, 'and get out of my sight for ever!' So she carried off the child as her first load, and left him in a safe place. Then she came back for the second load, and took away all the silver and gold and clothes she could carry. When she came back for the third time, she looked around the house for a while, pretend-ing she was searching for something. Aristotle was standing in the middle of the floor, and she walked up to him and said, 'I don't see anything else I'd rather have than you, so up with you on my back!' 'If that's how it is,' said the great thinker, 'wouldn't it be as well for you to bring back the other two loads? We'd be better off staying here than anywhere else, and perhaps we'll be more peaceful together in the future.'

Climbing the hill, especially on steamer-days when everyone was on the road, used to be a social occasion for us; at home we led such a private, hermetic life that sometimes when I answered a knock at the door I must have appeared blear-eyed from sleep, love, sorrow or the written word. But on the open road we were more convivial; only rarely did we hurry or lag in order to avoid sharing the long ascent with someone dull or cantanker-ous. Beartla was always a good companion on the road, but others could be tiresome, and whenever I was cycling up the hill and nearing the point where I would have to stagger to a halt and start walking, having no gears on my old black Raleigh, I used to look ahead and see what company offered, for once one had fallen in with a person it was difficult to part from him or her before the top of the last *carcair*. Conversely, if one wanted to impose oneself on a reluctant companion, to make some point at length, for example, the hill allowed one to do so as if by chance. M used this enforced pairing very effectively with a neighbour who we suspected was avoiding us. The ground of the difficulty was this. Strolling by Port Mhuirbhigh one day I had met him filling a donkey-cart with sand from the grassy bank between the path and the beach; I stopped and chatted, and brought the conversation round, very subtly as I thought, to coastal erosion. If the bank was damaged, I hinted, the winter storms would break through to the path behind it; if the path went, then the wall of the sandy field called the Vinegar would be undermined, and if the Vinegar was blown away, all Kilmurvey House's fine pastures would follow, and so on to Apocalypse. The man disagreed; the sea was always washing sand in and out of the bay, and there would be sand here after we were all dead. I returned the conversation to the fine weather and so on, and left him, as I thought, in perfect amity. Unfortunately a few days later official notice-boards appeared by the beach specifying the penalties for unauthorized removal of sand. The notices were soon thrown down, and it seems there was some muttering in the pubs that I with my privileged access to the ear of government had been responsible for them. However, because we rarely met him on the road and he was not very forthcoming at the best of times, it was some months before we began to wonder if our neighbour Wasn't Talking to Us. So when M one day saw him ahead of her pushing his bike up the hill, she strained every muscle to catch up, pretended to be overcome by gravity just as she was about to pass him, and then chatted with him on every topic but sand, remorselessly, all the way up the hill and two further miles back to the west, leaving him not merely mollified but cordial, confiding, entranced. (As to the beach, the sandbank is in tatters and the path has collapsed, but the Vinegar wall still stands. My certainties have suffered some erosion too, though; the storms of 1991 would have smashed the path with or without our neighbour's help, and I am inclined to agree that there will be sand there after we are all dead.)

The flat stretch of the road on a level with the black crag is only a couple of hundred yards long, and then begins another climb, Carcair Ghanly, past the opening of the side-road leading down to the village of Mainistir. Thomas Ganly, who came to Aran in the 1850s to oversee the building of the pier in Cill Rónáin and the lighthouse on An tOileán

Iarthach, married a Mainistir widow; a year later she died, leaving him her *cartúr* of land, and he very quickly married the young daughter· of the blacksmith Micil Riabhach, which caused a lot of talk. Thomas was from Antrim; his father was an Orangeman who married a Catholic and let his wife bring up the children in her own religion, but (as Breandán Ó hEithir puts it), some of the Ulster bigotry seems to have stuck to Thomas, for it is said he had to leave home after a row in which he broke a few Protestant skulls. He was no great farmer, according to family legend; once he saw some sheep grazing in one of his fields, and drove them down to the pound in Cill Rónáin, and then discovered they were his own and had to pay twopence a head to redeem them. Thomas's offspring gave Aran plenty to gossip about. On the night a mainland suitor came looking for her hand, his sixteen-year-old daughter Maggie eloped with a penniless Fenian from Gort na gCapall, Mícheál Ó Flaithearta. One of Thomas's sons, also called Thomas, was secretary of the Aran branch of the Land League. This Thomas and his brother-in-law Mícheál were arrested on suspicion of cliffing the Kilmurvey O'Flahertys' cattle, but were released for lack of evidence. He also ambushed Ó hIarnáin the bailiff near the old quay in Cill Rónáin once, and fired a shot which grazed the man's head and stunned him. When the bailiff came round, he saw a man called Kilmartin standing over him. The police searched Kilmartin's cottage, which was close by, and planted a revolver and bullets under the newborn baby in the cradle, and arrested him. Thomas got away to Boston, but very soon fell ill with galloping consumption; on his deathbed he confessed that he had fired the shot at the bailiff, the priest sent word to Galway and Kilmartin was released. All this caused so much *rírá* that Thomas's brother, the Rev. William Ganly, had to leave his curacy in Mayo and emigrate to Australia. A third brother, Pat, inherited the farm, was evicted, and reinstated in half of it, as I have told in 'An Ear to the Coffin'.

We know so much about the Ganlys because of the word-spinning, word-hoarding children and grandchildren of Maggie Ganly and Mícheál Ó Flaithearta, who include Liam and Tom O'Flaherty, Breandán Ó hEithir, and some of the Aran people I most enjoy talking to, and who have given me many of these details of the family history. Tom O'Flaherty wrote that he preferred his mother's side of the family, 'the emotional, witty, story-telling Ganlys', to the 'harsh, quarrelsome, haughty, 'ferocious O'Flahertys'', and his favorite relative was his uncle Pat, 'carefree and irresponsible... a great rebel, the best story-teller in Aran'. Anecdotes of Pat's high-spirited antics are many. He was a hero of the skirmishing with the land-agent Thompson. Once when eviction cases were pending against some Cill Éinne tenants he made the doctor drunk, took the dispensary key, climbed into its roof-space and from there into the agent's office next door, stole the iron box containing the eviction notices, rowed out and drowned it in the sea off Straw Island, so that the cases had to be dismissed. He was a 'playboy' in the Aran or Syngean sense, always ready for fun, for running races and jumping, even when he was old, and it is from him that the *carcair* has its name, for he used to sit on a boulder beside it, on sunny days a hundred years ago, exchanging badinage with the passers-by.

In fact Carcair Ghanly is one of the most joyous places in Aran. As one climbs, at whatever the cost in breath, the whole eastern end of the island falls away into a vast perspective with the other two Aran Islands and the hills of Clare beyond – but I will devote a chapter to this view when we reach the top of the hill – and if, having come from the western villages in the lee of the island's central ridge, one is swooping down it on a bicycle, here for the first time ocean appears to the south as well as to the north, and one is suddenly balanced on two immense blue wings. The most mundane errands are uplifted by this hill, even the week-in week-out delivery of goods from the steamer visible in the harbour below. Séamas complains about the *sclábhaíocht*, the slavery, of his coal business, but when grinding up the hill on his tractor towing a trailer heaped with sacks, he radiates power, and noise, and grimy nods. Stiofán with his vanful of Calorgas bottles salutes the other Stiofán with his vanful of Kosangas bottles, unprescient of the merger of Calorgas and Kosangas even then being planned out in the big world, and the slight *contretemps* which will ensue when it turns out that those Robinsons, with that British sense of fair play so much admired at least by the British, have been dealing with both of them. And here comes Robinson himself, sailing down the hill with a squeak of his old bike, a packet of fifty maps of Aran (1982 price £1.58 + 15% VAT, wholesale terms 33% off) bouncing around in a sally-rod basket on his handlebars, for delivery to the steward of the *Galway Bay* – 'I'm telling you, that fellow has his fortune made with them maps!' Yes, we all have our ad-hucksterish ways of living off the stones of Aran, and it is a good thing we have the daily bread of nature's beauty to supplement them, for they all involve a bit of *sclábhaíocht*; but they give us identities too, they validate our going up and down the hill in the eyes of society. Before I produced the map, it was a mystery to our neighbours what we were living on; one man said to me, 'We thought you must have money in rubber-mines or something.' But now I have an island nickname as definitive as those of the buyer from the seaweed factory in Connemara, who is Fear na Slata Mara, the searodman, and the representative of the Department of Agriculture, Fear na bhFataí, the potato-man: I am Fear na Mapaí, the man of the maps, and that is why I am on this hill.

Just one more steep bit, and we are there – Carcair Chlaí Chox, the slope of Cox's wall. Who Cox was nobody remembers, nor which wall is his. The only notable wall here marks the boundary between Mainistir and Eochaill villages; a little more robust and ivy-clad than the other field-walls, it threads its way between the handful of houses that have been built here in recent years, each one trying to steal the view from the last. The *carcair* becomes rather abrupt in its last few yards, as old Beartla points out every time we climb it. He was employed in building this stretch of the road many years ago – he remembers sitting with the gang of men by the road-side breaking stones with a hammer all day – and he told the young engineer in charge of the works that the slope should be graded a bit more, 'But he had a college education and *holive oil* on his hair, and he wouldn't listen to me!' So, even if we have made a mighty effort and cycled all the way up to this point, we are defeated at the last moment and wobble to a stop within sight of level going.

If we have forgotten anything from the shops in Cill Rónáin, this is where we will think of it. If there is a stylistic trick to round off this hill of anecdotes, this is when I must invent it. But what is style, compared to all that substance? Merely the complacent wave of the downhill cyclist to those pushing up.

BREATHING SPACE

Pausing to draw breath at the top of the road from Cill Rónáin, one looks round, and sees the earth drawing its breath too. From here the liquid Atlantic is hidden by the long ridge rising behind Eochaill village, but the Atlantic of vapour it continuously exhales rolls around and over the island to fill a vast bowl of vision in all other directions, and suspended moisture in the distances between the eye and its objects makes the distances themselves visible. In the deepest south of this aerial ocean there are often the ghosts of blue whales: Mount Brandon in Kerry, and sometimes a lower profile beyond it I used to name confidently as the Great Blasket, but which, checking with a map, I realize is Mount Eagle near the head of the Dingle peninsula. We wonder at these appearances, faded and reduced to two dimensions, not for what they are but for how far away they are, thinking of the precarious journeying and near-drowning of the light that reaches us from them, the dilution almost to extinction of the warm tones issued from those heathery Old Red Sandstone hills, in the scattered blue of sunlight astray among infinitudes of floating water-molecules.

The island chain itself – the eastern part of Árainn falling away from this height, the long grey back of Inis Meáin with that of Inis Oírr appearing above it, a paler parallel – is shown by this vaporous perspective to be rooted in the mainland beyond, the greater parallel of the Burren. Close at hand the stones of the walls and the wayside weeds are presented in detail by the high light-levels; in broader terms one can follow the complex argumentation of the middle-distant land with the sea – the broad tract of the bay ceded right up to the thresholds of Cill Rónáin, the varied points asserted beyond Cill Éinne – but then the progressive indefinition of the other islands reunites them with a background that looks as if it has been laid down by the rain itself in layer upon layer and frequently merges upwards into stratified mists. On occasion, though, when a general smother of cloud is driving over the islands and the wind tears a hole in it behind us to the west, a shaft of sunlight picks out some fragment of the mainland and holds it up for close examination; the Burren is a blue-black mystery, but suddenly the dome of Black Head terminating it to the north is spotlit – X-rayed, one might think, its rock-structure is so clarified – or the Cliffs of Moher appear above the south of Inis Oírr as a long line of stiff-folded gold-brocade curtains drawn against the darkness.

The rest of the ever-changing panorama this high point of the road offers swings into place as one turns to walk on westwards. Across the North Sound a vista of Connemara hangs before Aran eyes, a perpetual seductive dream of elsewhere. (In my first volume I expressed the wish for another decade in which to explore that 'as-yet hardly described land of marvels' as quittance for my decade of work on Aran; and in gratitude to life I hereby acknowledge that the wish has been granted.) Meteorology has ten miles of water on which to inscribe itself between the island and the mainland. Half-way across are two reefs, An Bhrachlainn Mhór and An Bhrachlainn Bheag, the big and little breakers, which remember a storm for days after it has died, throwing up great hills of smooth water that swell, blaze into foam, and sink back into calm again as they process to the east. Even in settled high-summer stillness the idle air stirs a little of the milky sky into the waters; a currach picking its way across the pallid meanders stands out like an insect on a pond. As full of ungraspable forms as the transitions between deep sleep and wakefulness, this wide separation of the two heartlands of my life does not look as if it could be crossed by any means of reality, and even the regularity of the high-speed ferries that now shuttle in and out from Ros a' Mhíl does not abridge its visionary potential. Sometimes dolphins briefly accompany these boats as if in empathy with our linear lives, before turning away into their own fluid dimensions. I remember, on one of these crossings, looking back along the white road of the wake, and an image forcing itself upon me of a dark shape on it, following and steadily overhauling the boat; as it came nearer I saw that it was a man on horseback, galloping. He swerved to overtake us, and, leaning from the saddle, threw a packet to me – a bird with bound wings, which broke loose as it fell into my hands and flew away, to Aran or to Connemara.

Having walked the intricate southern coastline of Connemara when mapping it some years ago, it is curiously fascinating now to retrace that walk in the edgeways-on view of it from Aran, as I can after rain has freshly washed the air. When raked by a westering sun, every roof-top glitters on the peninsulas and archipelagos that stretch out towards me, terminating in the little copper stud of the old watch-tower on Golam Head; I can identify the houses of people I met, name the granitic hillocks in the bogs and even some of the offshore rocks marked by patches of surf that look from here like white butterflies alighted on the sea. Behind these low-lying forelands stands the long precipice wall of Cnoc Mordáin, on which the afternoon sun hangs cloud-shadows, and to the west a distant obliquity makes a range out of scattered hills, from the ragged, arched back of Errisbeg near Roundstone, to a tiny knob almost isolated on the beginning of the Atlantic horizon, Doon Hill, which is the stub of an ancient volcano. The deepest recesses of Connemara float above Cnoc Mordáin as a third step into absolute distance, the long turf-brown plateaus of the Joyce Country to the east, and to the west the Twelve Bens' closely grouped cones of glinting quartzite. When we in Aran see the valley between these two mountain ranges seething like a cauldron with dark cloud and pallid streaks of hail, we bless the fact that the islands are not high enough to trip the heavy skies hurrying over them to spill the ocean they carry onto the streaming hillsides of Connemara, swelling its bogs and brimming its hidden lakes.

Tracking the passage of bad weather across the sound and away to the mainland is one of Aran's pleasures. During stormy winter days when the low sun, hidden behind the island, is being switched on and off by a succession of thunder-clouds coming in on the gale, the abysmal darkness of the northern sky is background to an intermittent rainbow of wonderful brilliance, forming and reforming in the same position. The perfect circle is so rare in our natural experience that, apart from the disc of the sun seen through mist, the iris of the human eye, and the ripples spreading from a disturbance in still water, it is difficult to think of other examples. The rainbow – not a complete circle, though sometimes from a height like the top of the climb here, a vague sketch of most of the lower arc of it is discernible in the mist drifting through the fields below – is so accurately drawn, as if by cosmic compasses, that it impresses upon some temperaments a certainty of its spiritual significance, and on others the question of its material mechanism. A ray of sunlight enters a raindrop, is reflected off the inside of its surface, and exits again, at some angle to its original direction. There is a particular angle at which the reflection is at its most intense, easily found by simple calculus to be about 42 degrees; I did it at school and have long forgotten how. The exact answer depends on the colour of the light, since rays of different wavelengths, corresponding to different colours, are bent by slightly different amounts in entering and leaving the medium of water. The sun's rays contain all colours, mixed together into white; they are reflected back to the eye from falling rain at haphazard angles, but at those certain calculable angles the various individual colours will be predominant. Thus the rainbow forms an arc at about 42 degrees to the continuation of a line from the sun through the eye of the observer. This arc, given the position of the sun and the eye, is fixed in the sky, a perpetually present geometrical abstraction, the Platonic idea of a rainbow, waiting only for the presence of raindrops to bring it forth in all the colours of the visible. Hence arises a lovely phenomenon I have often seen from Aran when an isolated squall is travelling along the North Sound. As the narrow column of rain passes across the arc of the potential rainbow, it makes each point of it manifest in succession. The effect is that a short sector of rainbow comes into existence apparently down near the waters of the Sound or out in the Connemara hinterland, and rises smoothly along its predestined curve, passing across the northern sky and descending again to extinction as the squall moves on. An iridescent dolphin, or perhaps a salmon, leaping in some solemn mystic time-scale up out of nothingness through our world of vapours and down again into nothingness. The mechanism of the apparition is clear; its meaning is open to our determination.

Above and around all the vast circus of the elements one commands from the top of this climb is the protective envelope of sky, the delicate, translucent skin of the globe. Its depths are of many intersuffusing layers, visible and invisible; the tenderness of its bending down to and wrapping over the horizon is often clear to the feeling eye. Sometimes dull, bruised by departed gales, sometimes glowingly reminiscent of kind weather, it embodies Aran's short-term memory, as opposed to the ancient lore condensed in the stones. Also it is an arcanum of high predictive signs: storm-dogs, mares' tails, rings round the sun, cirrus-cloud brush-drawings of tomorrow's winds. Sometimes it is all contradictory; urgent and vociferous here, sullen and opaque there; one doesn't know whether they refer to the past or the future, these clouds out of which one might expect hot snow or black lightning, these mist-banks full of mermaid ova and the dandruff of drowned sailors ...

But what have we done to this hilltop, this calm and attentive brow with which the island gazes upon the weather of the world? From where I stand in the road I can count no fewer than fifty poles carrying electricity or telephone wires. The delicate continuities are splintered. The mountain ranges are scratched, as if a vandal had scrawled on a painting with a nail. Even the sky is shoddy, defaced with graffiti. We must be blind, to let such things be done! Our blindness is that of grubs in the Apple of Knowledge.

MAINISTIR

Eochaill townland has four villages: Mainistir, Eochaill itself, Baile na Creige and Corrúch. The last three of these and the newer houses of the first lie ahead to the west, but to visit the old part of Mainistir one leaves the main road at Carcair Ghanly and follows a boreen that drops north-wards towards the sea. After crossing a quarter of a mile of rough fields and patches of crag, it zigzags down two lines of low cliffs separated by a narrow terrace, the rim of a bowl of greener pastures around the bay and shingle beach of Port na Mainistreach. The lichen-grey ruins of St Ciarán's church are under the second scarp-line, to the east, and the almost depopulated settlement stretches along a path to the west on the terrace. The two inhab-ited cottages, well cared-for and freshly whitened, separated by dark, roof-less ruins, stick out like the last teeth in an old jawbone.

Once upon a time people here used to complain of the fairies – Pat Ganly's house was badly infested, I am told – but now they grumble if one mentions such foolishness, and I once overheard a priest who was living on the island being scolded for referring to the steep, overgrown path that shortcuts the bends of the road down the scarps as Róidín na Sióg, the little road of the fairies, instead of Bóithrín an Teampaill, the boreen of the church. Those electricity poles have denatured night as well as day; nowa-days light is cheap and convenient, and spills plentifully from windows and torches and headlamps, whereas before it was used very sparingly. On moonless nights perfect blackness pressed close around the houses, and immediately outside the door was a realm of stumblings and strayings and mis-identifications, of pranks and mischief and spying too. Or were moon-lit nights more frightening – the luminous rock-sheets riven with abysses, the birds and animals restlessly astir? Sometimes in the dark all things reveal the secret we keep from ourselves by daylight and lamplight, that below the skin of what we see of them they are fathomless pools of potential appearances; it is as if other creatures' deeper vision of them takes priority and forces itself on our own eyes. And we too are objects of those alien visions; our self-recognitions are shaken. On Hallowe'en, the eve of the ancient Celtic feast of Samhain at the beginning of November, the children put on masks and go from door to door; one plays at pretending not to know them and trying to guess who they are; but in those last real Hallowe'ens we experienced before electricity came to the island, the children from a few hundred yards up the unlit road would arrive at our gate in such a panic of doubt about their own identities that they would be shrieking out as they rushed up the garden path, 'It's Gráinne! It's Clodagh!' The older boys, two by two, used to hobble in, dressed and masked as very old couples, and sit by the fire in silence, occasionally rapping on the floor with their sticks in a slow, solemn, almost unnerving rhythm; we understood that they represented the recently departed dead, who on that evening, which was like an imperfectly sealed gap between two seasons, have leave to revisit the earth. There was a faint threat of mischief, which never came to anything, though I remember reading of some lads who didn't get the welcome and the drinks they were expecting from an old man in Bun Gabhla, and stuffed a billygoat down his chimney so that its head appeared upside down in his hearth, the Devil himself, horned, hairy, hell-blackened – but that was in the Dark Ages fifty years ago.

The other creaking hinge of the year is May Eve, Oíche Bhealtaine, which together with Hallowe'en defined the two seasons, winter and summer, of the ancient Celtic year. On these nights, it was believed (and is still, to a degree), the fairies change quarters from one side of the island to the other, and it was not good to be out because they resented being seen. And just as the beginning of winter is threatening on this little island naked to the forces of nature, with the sudden encroachment of night on day and the first storms closing the seaways, so the beginning of summer is disturbingly full of challenge, especially for the young, with the scents and sounds of passion in every bush, and anguishing in another way to those who no longer feel that the challenge is meant for them. Night and lonely places fill with the shadows of these uncomprehended fears and longings; ghosts, fairies, the *púca*, the *mada mór* or big dog that has been seen at Carcair Chlaí Chox, the unidentified dark thing in the shadow of the thornbush, are born of the coupling of chthonic and psychic unknowns.

Mainistir, hidden under the hill, off the track to and out of sight of all the other villages, was particularly haunted by such creatures, and in some islanders' minds still is. An Oatquarter man told me he wouldn't live down there for a thousand pounds a month; he remembers that an old man coming home from a wake saw fairies making a coffin; one of them looked like the Devil, and the long glowing nails were flying into the wood from all directions. The hauntings of the Ganly house were inconsequential vague shoutings at night, harmless poltergeists' practical jokes. When the Ó hEithir family left the teachers' residence in Cill Rónáin and built themselves a new house by Carcair Chlaí Chox, the nine-year-old Breandán was told by a local woman that they had chosen a bad site, for everyone knew that the fairy host who lived up on the crags at Carcair na gCat used a path close by when they wanted to go west. And a neighbour, Máirtín Breathnach, walking into Cill Rónáin at dawn, had seen a man come out of Róidín Chlaí Chox and turn down the hill ahead of him; Máirtín tried to catch up with him, but although he walked fast, and then trotted, and then ran as fast as he could, the figure remained the same distance ahead. Going down Carcair an Aill Bhriste, Máirtín, who had not been afraid of the Black and Tans, was in a cold sweat of fear. The man turned the corner at a leisurely walk, and when Máirtín ran round after him there was nobody to be seen. That wasn't the end of the woman's stories, according to Brendán; she still had a trump to play:

She lowered her voice and put me under the seven warnings not to tell it to any living creature, but – my aunt had been seen near that place more than once, soon after her death. That put a new complexion on the story. This aunt had died in childbed when she was only a young girl. It was clear from old photographs and also from village tradition that she had been beautiful, and the tragedy had added to her beauty.

Oddly enough I kept these horror-stories to myself for a while, but they slipped out one evening when we had music in the house and I said that that should drive away the ghosts and the fairies. Unluckily my mother was present, and since she had not the least belief in fairies or superstitions I thought I would get a couple of 'salamanders'. But she only burst out laughing when I told the woman's first two tales. I had made up my mind to keep my aunt's ghost to myself, but after this success I decided to spill the lot. My mother listened quietly, and when I had finished all she said was 'Poor Julia!' and left it at that. The story was never seriously mentioned again, but I often remembered it, especially when I had to go to the well under the cliff and it was necessary to pass the spot where people thought she had been seen.

Whether poor Julia's child was born alive or not I do not know, but if not, it is likely that it was buried with many other tragedies in the mysterious hillock by the seashore, a little east of the foot of the Mainistir road, called An Atharla, the burial ground. The top of this is a roughly rectangular plot about forty yards long by ten wide, enclosed by a slightly-built field-wall, which appears to be standing on the decayed remains of an earlier wall and from a distance looks like a little ring-fort. It is difficult to make out if the unusually steep-sided mound is all natural or if it has been built up to some extent; there is talk of a buried doorway in its southern flank, but that seems structurally unlikely. Within the enclosure is a set stone just over two feet high on which is carved a Latin cross. Almost hidden in long grass are three even smaller stones on which one can just make out shallow grooves forming simple crosses, and a few uninscribed boulders. The crosses look like Early Christian work, and connect the site with the monastic settlement from which Mainistir has its name. The Ordnance Survey map of 1898 marks it as an 'Infants' Burial Ground', which implies that it was used for the burial of unbaptized babies. Up until two or three generations ago it was thought that the souls of stillborn children or those who died before baptism would go to Limbo and continue a nebulous existence, neither enjoying Heaven nor suffering Hell. The sorts of places they were buried in – often surreptitiously and by night – share the same ambiguous status, and in Aran it was usually under a 'mearing' wall between one person's land and another's, as if to avoid or dilute responsibility for their resting-places. In the Burren, children's burial grounds are often in a *lios* or 'fairy fort' which probably originated as a cashel wall around an early chapel, and which, while not consecrated ground, still has some lingering association with sanctity. Most Connemara villages have a small plot with a clutch of unmarked stones tucked away somewhere obscure, often on a townland boundary or on the no-man's-land of the seashore, unvisited, overgrown, and forgotten by all except the very old, some of whom still have bitter reason to remember them. Nowadays neither pope nor peasant would deny what comfort the proper graveyard can offer such failed scraps of life or their grieving parents, and the children's burial grounds with their evasive theology are abandoned to the grass and briars and whitethorn bushes of reconsecrating nature. They are, though, 'sheeogy places' still; the *sióga* or fairies make themselves felt there, brushing the hair on the back of the passer-by's neck. At twilight the Mainistir burial ground, rearing up gaunt and angular right next to the unfrequented road, nudges one with a thought of all the tormented circumstances buried in the phrase 'unbaptized infants'.

The name 'Mainistir' itself is a ghost. Among the churches listed by Archbishop O'Cadhla in the 1640s is

The church called Mainistir Connachtach, that is, the Connaught monastery, in the place of which being afterwards demolished was built a chapel dedicated to Saint Ciarán.

According to an inquisition of 1581, the territory of the islands then was comprised in three divisions, anglicized as Treumoynagh, Trueconnaght and Trueenagh, which obscurities one can puzzle out as follows: Trian Muimhneach, the Munster third, would have belonged to the O'Briens and presumably included Cill Éinne where their castle was. Trian Connachtach or the Connaught third, perhaps dominated by the O'Cadhlas and later the O'Flahertys from Iar-Chonnacht, included the Mainistir area. Trian Eoghanachta belonged to the Eoghanachta Ninussa and later the Corcu Modruad of what is now County Clare, and included the westernmost townland of Árainn, still called Eoghanacht. Mainistir Chiaráin must have ceased to exist by Elizabeth's time, for its land was among the properties of the monastery of Annaghdown (north of Galway city) which came into the Crown's possession on its dissolution, and even before Elizabeth took the islands out of the hands of the rivalrous O'Briens and O'Flahertys she was making grants of 'a ruined chapel and land in the island of Aryne'. This titbit was dispensed in 1566 to a Florence Lylly, chaplain; in 1570 to the Earl of Clanricarde, who built up a huge estate out of former monastic lands; and finally in 1578 to the Wardens of Galway.

Under the cliff that wraps this anciently-chosen spot away from the Atlantic winds, there are several springs, which keep its meadows green. Around the ruined chapel walls tall pillar-stones inscribed with crosses stand watch, the most patient of herdsmen, over ruminating cattle; they probably used to mark the 'termon' limits, within which there was a right of sanctuary. Some of the field-boundaries are underlain by the mounded remains of a cashel wall, not easy to trace in the ranker grass and briars. The chapel itself, one of the loveliest of the island's antiquities, is rather later than the Cill Éinne oratories. Its undivided interior is about thirteen gravelly paces long, half that in width, and open to the heavens. The oldest-looking part is the flat-topped doorway in the west gable, about three feet wide, the jambs slightly inclined so that it is a little narrower at the top. Having entered, stooping a little under the lintel made of a single five-foot-long stone, one confronts the east gable-wall, which is of a wonderfully simple and uplifting design. Its slim round-headed light, nearly ten feet high and only five inches wide on the outside, has an internal splay of finely fitted masonry, smoothly finished, lighter in tone than the rough stonework of the rest of the wall, opening out to a width of five feet. A moulding outlining the round head of the splay is borne on little corbels decorated with plant forms (the books say these are grotesque carved heads, but if so I cannot make them out). Another moulding embraces the bottom of the splay, passing under it like a sill and up either side of it to a third of its height, and then steps away from it on either side towards the upper corners of the gable wall, so that it seems to hold the whole window aloft with a priestly gesture above the simple stone altar. This is late Romanesque work, as is a smaller window in the south wall. A late medieval doorway in the north wall has a simple Gothic arch of two curved pieces of stone, and in the same wall, nearer the altar, is a square window with a low opening below it. Knee-high remains of walls outside the chapel at this point give the impression of a small building, perhaps a vestry, built very close to it, which has a flag like a grave marker or part of a pillar-stone lying in it. There are also traces of larger rectangular foundations, presumably of monastic buildings, immediately to the north, and also to the south-east, under the sheltering cliff-face.

A few yards outside the east gable is a pillar-stone, a limestone slab a few inches thick, about four feet high and fifteen inches wide, with an enigmatic combination of forms incised in the face turned towards the chapel. A cross is shown in outline, its shaft and arms linked by a double circle about its centre. The top of the shaft opens out into two little spiral curls, above which floats a double circle filling the width of the pillar, with a not-quite-vertical bar dividing its interior in two. The outer circumference of this circle is broken below and opens outwards into a pair of small curls that answer to and are poised between the pair on the top of the cross. Finally, above the double circle and just infringing its outer edge is a round hole piercing the slab, about two inches across. Westropp, who studied these ruins in 1878, was told by a fisherman that cloths drawn through this hole were used for curing sore limbs; and I have heard that people still come here, especially on August the 15th, the Feast of the Assumption, and make a wish by passing a handkerchief through the hole and walking round the stone nine times, sunwise. M and I usually improvise some such ritual whenever we visit. But these superstitious usages are minor mysteries compared to the lightly held balance, the sleep-walking sure-footedness, of the whole design. This is to my mind Aran's quintessential stone; elsewhere, stone exuberates into rose windows; here, into this diagram of ascesis. But the archaeologists say that the hole probably held the gnomon of a sundial, in which case the circle would have had painted marks on it, and the appearance of the whole must have been very different. Its present timeless beauty was not part of its time-telling purpose.

Another pillar, twenty yards west of the chapel, is just as beautiful – a single stone over nine feet tall and only nine or ten inches wide, with a rounded top. A cross is inscribed in outline on the face towards the chapel, with a small circle inside the crossing of the shaft and arms, and a semicircular cup-shape superimposed on the upper part of the shaft; the top of the shaft is finished off with an X, on which is balanced another cross made up of lines radiating from a small central circle, with cup-shaped terminals. Farther away in fields to the east and north-east of the chapel there are two smaller and rather rougher pillars, inscribed with crosses, and with slight bulges on either side as if the pillars themselves were thinking of assuming the form of crosses; in fact pillars of this sort are a link between the Early Christian cross-inscribed slabs and the medieval high crosses. Near one of these, a few fields north of the chapel, is a little graveyard called Reilig na nGasúr, the burial-ground of the children, which was mainly for infants, and has not been used since about the 1930s. Most of the graves are marked only with boulders, but there are a few gravestones, including one of a John Burke who kept a school in Eochaill and died in 1828, and two or three fragments of early cross-slabs.

The two main wells of the monastic settlement are fifty or sixty yards west of the chapel, in an open thickety patch of ground by the roadside, and in a minute field just above that. The roadside one is Tobar an Bhradáin, the well of the salmon, and its legend seems to have been quite forgotten by the villagers, who explain its name by means of the occasional exceptional runs of salmon which bring fish up into the most unlikely places. But in the *Life of St Enda* we may read:

And so, taking with him his holy followers, the man from heaven came to the island granted him, named Aran, and put into the harbour which is called Leamh-choill. For three days they were without food in that place, then God sent them a fish of amazing size, into the spring which is called the spring of Leamhchoill. From this fish the Almighty fed the one hundred and fifty who were with Saint Enda.

'Leamhchoill' being an error for Eochaill, O'Donovan in his OS letters was surely correct in identifying this miraculous spring with St Ciarán's well, which is only a few yards above Tobar an Bhradáin. In fact since Tobar an Bhradáin has changed its position by a dozen yards or so within living memory – these limestone wells are flighty things, disappearing from one place and reappearing close by as the rock-fissures open or get blocked up – one could say that they are virtually the same well. Certainly only a miracle could have brought a huge salmon so far up this streamless hillside; I picture it leaping from the sea like the rainbow fragments I have described, following the arc of the ideal across the sky and plunging down into this well.

Another remarkable fact about Tobar an Bhradáin I mention with reluctance, as it interrupts my mood – but such interruptions are part of the fabric of the island now, which this book must enact. After the drought of 1977 a concrete tank was built by the well to store its water, as was necessary for farmers with cattle nearby, and more recently a great circular storage tank of riveted metal sheets has been sited in a little hollow just below, to help cope with the hugely increased demand for tap-water throughout the island. These are the only ugly structures in this corner of the island, where natural and man-made beauty have had sanctuary for over a thousand years. Is it because we do not believe in miracles that we could not rise to stonework for the water of the miraculous salmon?

Tobar Chiaráin, the saint's well, is a little moss-lined hollow adorned by a splendour of *Chrysosplenium* or golden saxifrage, within a low U-shaped enclosure of huge limestone blocks, one of which is at least seven feet long and two-and-a-half feet square. It is still visited on the saint's day, the ninth of September, and a small pile of pebbles for counting the 'rounds' stands on a projecting stone at the open end of the enclosure; the pilgrim takes seven pebbles, walks around the outside of the enclosure saying the appropriate prayers, replaces one pebble, and so on till all are back in place.

St Ciarán mac an tSaor (*i.e.* son of the craftsman) is of course the founder of Clonmacnois, the great monastery set by a meander of the Shannon. His own biography, which dates from the ninth century, recounts many wonders concerning him, but it is only in the *Life of St Enda* that we read of his novitiate in Aran:

To this man of God came St Ciarán, the son of a woodworker. He stayed for seven years, faithfully serving in the monastery threshing house. In those seven years, so diligently did he perform his duty as thresher that in the chaff-loft no stalk could be found which had its head. The walls of his threshing house on Aran remain to this day.

Through miscopyings by Colgan, and misreadings compounded by forced interpretation by O'Donovan, this straightforward indication of the saint's character has been contorted into a story of him threshing so vigorously that even the straw was left unfit for thatching, whence the island's houses have had stone roofs ever since. Several other tales connect Ciarán with grain, including this, from the Lismore *Lives of the Saints*:

This was the work that was entrusted to him, to grind at a quern. Then mighty marvels came to pass. When he went to grind at the quern it turned of itself, and did so continually; and they were the angels of the Lord who ground for his sake. ... Once when he was in Aran drying corn in the kiln, Lonán the Left-handed was along with him, and he was always in opposition to Ciarán. And they saw a ship foundering before them. 'It seems to me,' said Lonán, 'that that ship will be drowned today, and that this kiln will be burnt by the strength of the wind.' 'No,' said Ciarán, 'that ship will be burned, and this kiln will be drowned with its corn.' And that saying was fulfilled, for the ship's crew escaped, and the ship was cast ashore beside the kiln. The kiln caught fire and the ship was burned. But the wind blasted the kiln and its corn into the sea where it was drowned, in accordance with Ciarán's words.

When Ciarán was to make his profession of monastic vows, he wanted to remain under the protection of Enda in Aran. But Heaven signalled other intentions for him:

After this St Ciarán saw a vision which he took care to tell his master. One night he dreamed that he was near the bank of the great river which is called Shannon and that he saw a great tree bearing leaves and fruit, and the tree cast its shade over the whole island of Ireland. He recounted his dream to St Enda, who said, 'You are that fruitful tree, because you will be great before God and men. You will furnish the sweet fruit of your good work, and you will be held in honour throughout the whole of Ireland.' And St Enda added, 'Now go, then, and fulfilling the word of God, build a monastery there.'

In another version, also given in the *Life of St Enda*, the great tree grows in the middle of Aran, and Enda sees many men digging it up and carrying it through the air to the banks of the Shannon, where it takes root and becomes immensely high, its branches extending to the sea. Clearly, Aran was not to be the place of Ciarán's resurrection; he was to go forth and found a monastery from which many other monasteries would sprout like the branches of a fruitful tree. On hearing this, all the monks, and Ciarán himself, wept bitterly. When his boat was ready for the journey, they all went down to the harbour to see him on his way, and returned to their monasteries in sadness.

When, with the permission of the holy abbot, Enda, Ciarán had left the island, Enda saw, in spirit, all the angels who used to serve the food of the spiritual life to the saints of Aran leaving with St Ciarán. This vision caused St Enda to become sorrowful, thinking that the holy spirits would not return again. He gave himself to fasting and prayer beyond his strength, and the angel of the Lord appeared to him, saying, 'Why are you sad, man of God, and why do you torment yourself so excessively?' Enda said, 'The reason for my sadness is that all the angels have left us and gone with Ciarán.' The angel replied, 'Since St Ciarán is very dear to God, He has sent His angels to accompany him. So do not torment yourself any more, for they will return to you again. Therefore cancel your fast in the name of the Lord.'

According to the Annals, Ciarán died in 545 at the age of thirty-three, only seven months after founding his church by the Shannon. That first humble building was probably of wood, for the tomb-shrine there now called St Ciarán's Church dates from some centuries later. His foundation prospered as Enda had foreseen, because it was sited at the natural crossroads of Ireland. The Shannon, the biggest river in Britain or Ireland, was an important route in itself, and near this point it was forded by the ancient east-west thoroughfare that followed the long glacial ridge of the Eiscir Riada across the central boglands. From its beginnings Clonmacnois had royal patronage. The prince who helped Ciarán set the posts of his church later became High King of Ireland; its famous Cross of the Scriptures may have been erected by another High King around 879, its cathedral contains the grave of the last High King, Roderick O'Connor, who died in 1198. For seven centuries, until it was sacked by the English in 1552, Clonmacnois was one of the most important pilgrimage centres of Ireland, celebrated throughout Europe. Its artwork – the hundreds of early cross-slabs, the richly carved high crosses, the illuminated manuscripts and the fantastically decorated 'Crozier of the Abbots of Clonmacnois', are still among Ireland's cultural treasures. Such was the tree that we can imagine towering up from the rustling bushes and quiet meadows of Mainistir.

AMONG THE THORNS

Certain areas of Aran are so heavy with the presence of the past that to linger in them leaves one as enriched and as drained as can the contemplation of a work of art. The fields that tumble down the hillside west of Mainistir village have this quality, and also a faintly disquieting atmosphere of their own I have often tried to characterize more exactly than by the words that first present themselves: *siógach, unheimlich,* spooky. These fields are small, crooked, interlinked by gaps in odd sequences, full of little stone-ricks and the thicketed mounds of collapsed stone huts. The thresholds of the gaps are worn into hollows, the gullies are bridged here and there by stones thrown down so casually or so long ago that it is difficult to be sure they are not accidental assemblages. The age of such places is more palpable than are the many centuries archaeology attaches to certain identifiable combinations of stones – the chapels and beehive huts and ring-forts – for in fact all the stones here look not only as if they have been disposed and redisposed many times but as if their present order is very old. And since the land is less used than it was a couple of generations ago, it is true that these stones have not been disturbed for a long time; the one or two men I see making their familiar twice-daily way to the cow at milking-time have been doing so for fifty or seventy years, and their sons and grandsons will not be following them. Briars invade from neglected corners; the hazel bushes, in which one occasionally notices obliquely truncated stems where rods were cut years ago, are spreading out of the dells, for nobody comes for hazel-rods now. In fact no one apart from those old men visits these out-of-the-way corners at all. The stiles and stepping-stones that help them over the walls and clefts are so clearly intended only for the toe and heel of the men who made them that, when I use them in scrambling from field to field looking for clocháns or wild-flowers, I feel as if I had crept into someone's house and am trying the armchairs, peeping into the books. This sense of intruding on a privacy makes one move quietly, furtively. On a silent summer afternoon, when one parts the bracken closing some tiny pathway, and suddenly a thousand bluebottles go up, one starts guiltily. Here one is in intimate contact with a world withdrawn into the past. Seeing it revealed thus in its obsessional, finicky, obsolete ways is touching, and at the same time illicitly exciting. If there is haunting here, it is not that some returned frequenter of these fields is peering into our time, but that I myself am trespassing back through gaps in walls of the past.

This world protects itself with prickles, spikes, barbs. The Eochaill people's land on the terraces running westwards from the old village of Mainistir is called An Sceach Mhór, the big thorn, probably from an old hawthorn under which a holy woman lies, a sleeping spiritual beauty. The brambles around St Asurnaí's grave and holy well, the inner sanctum of this thorny locality, are almost impenetrable, but the ruin of her little oratory nearby is welcoming, though few come there, as it is eremitically with-drawn from notice. A finger-post by the coast-road directs one to it along a path that absolves one from insensitive intrusion. It leads first across a few fields, or more accurately *creagáin*, patches of rock patched with grass, patches of grass patched with rock, and in spring splashed with primroses, celandines and daisies. Low blackthorn bushes lie along the walls, their dark, glossy twigs foaming with creamy blossom in April when they are still leafless. The hawthorns rooted in fissures of the pavement have been dwarfed by the prevailing wind into hummocks with their eastward rims spreading out on the ground; these limestone-warmed fringes flower earlier than the rest, so that the hunchbacked bushes trail lace-trimmed robes. Sharp eyes might notice that these grotesque, perfumed exquisites some-times wear tiny rings on their crooked fingers. Looking closely one sees that these are bands of minute brownish granules, the eggs of the lackey moth. When they hatch out the caterpillars spin themselves a communal web of silk that gradually envelopes several twigs. They take the sun on this web, twenty or thirty of them lying curved together in a velvet mat. After a shower, with a few raindrops glistening among their delicate blue-grey and orange stripes, the colony looks like a piece of barbaric jewelry, but when one bends to look at the gorgeous thing it stirs, breaks up, and creeps piece-meal into its foul tent.

Farther up the hillside the bushes are higher, and in late summer are hung with heavy festoons of honeysuckle, each blossom a seduction of claret and oyster-satin. The path becomes almost a tunnel through the scented foliage where it climbs the first scarp. Look at the ground here: thousands of limpet- and winkle-shells are spilling out of it, detritus of long-gone generations' ascetic and monotonous feasts. Such shell-middens are found all along the spring-line here. The narrow terrace above is what the islanders call *sean-talamh*, old land; fertile and well-watered, it never had to be reclaimed from the rock, or at least not in any period known to oral lore. The little oratory stands here, in the shelter of an ivy-covered cliff-face, above which are stonier reaches of the hillside.

Teampall Asurnaí is tiny – just sixteen feet by twelve – craggily built, dumpy. Its side-walls are three feet thick and bulge like the sides of a boat. The gables stand to just above head-height; in the east one, above the altar, is the base of a narrow window-light, and at the south-east corner a projecting stone which would have supported the barge of the roof. The Office of Public Works, statutorily charged with the disenchantment of Ireland, has treated this chapel with a lighter hand than usual, and wild flowers still flourish within and without. A plot of ground over a field-wall a few yards to the east, which used to be impregnably briary, has recently been cleared, revealing two prone cross-slabs and a broken quern-stone. To the west, in the next field, are the low remains of three-foot-thick walls outlining a rectangular building. The topmost stone of a window-light lies on one of these walls, which if it is from Teampall Asurnaí shows that it had a narrow slit window with an ogival point – fifteenth-century work, much later than the rest of the church. Under the cliff behind the church is a good spring. The cliff itself is full of interest. The gleaming, shadowy face of the clay band from which the water oozes at the foot of the scarp is covered with golden saxifrage, as if with layer upon layer of burnished thumb-prints; this, and Tobar Chiaráin further east and under the same scarp, are virtually the only places in Aran I have seen the plant. A flight of small rough steps has been cut into the rock-face for bringing water up to the pastures above. Just to the west a natural recess in a bulge of the cliff has been closed up with stones to make a little sheep-fold; it is called Scailp Pháidín Uí Uiginn, Paddy Wiggins' cleft, from a man who lived in it once after being thrown out of home by his wife. The wrinkled crag over it looks like a face, or an Archimboldo painting of a cliff that looks like a face, a likeness of the disconsolate Wiggins himself perhaps.

When O'Donovan saw this chapel in 1839, there was 'a small apartment adjoining the east gable called St Soorney's Bed, in which people sleep expecting to be cured of diseases, and about 20 paces to the east ... a holy

well called Bullaun na Surnaighe'. However, there is little trace of the apartment now, and whatever rites took place here have long been neglected. The
bullán, presumably one of those stones with a hollow originally used as mortars, often found near monastic sites and regarded as holy wells, must have
been in the little grave plot. But the Bullán Asurnaí and Leaba Asurnaí
known to the villagers of today are on the terrace below the chapel, about a
hundred yards away to the north-west. From above it is easy to see a
hawthorn tree taller than the rest which marks the spot, but it is still not
easy to get there, for the obsessively detailed subdivision of the land makes
every traverse into a succession of moves on a Lewis Carroll chess-board,
and rampant growth turns every fence into a quandary. A faint path runs
down the hill on the further side of the next field-wall west of the sheep-
pen, crossing the low, mounded remains of walls much more ancient even
than the ivy-knotted antiquities that serve today, and ends in a field where
a large glacial boulder sits on a little hummock. The well and the 'bed' or
grave are within a few yards of this landmark, and yet one may fail to find
either, for the place has nodded off in a torpor of neglect. Massive moss-cov-
ered walls and heaps of stone, the remains of another wall long-removed,
have been welded together by the overgrowth into a little oval precinct
around the grave, the entrance to which, disguised by nettles, is in the
south-east corner of the next field to the west. The grave is obliterated by
thorns (as de Sade wanted his to be), and is indicated only by a slim finger
of stone sticking up through the brambles, about three feet high, with the
faintest suggestion of a cross rubbed into one face. Although it has not been
the object of a *turas* or pilgrimage for generations now, with imagination
one can make out the trodden path of the 'rounds' about the knot of briars.
Another gap in the circle of mouldering stone opens westwards into a small
pasture, and the 'well', a granite bullaun-stone usually holding a bit of rainwater, lies half hidden by leafage on the left of this entrance. Above it is the
big thorn-tree, bent like an old woman; perhaps this is not the original holy
bush, which the 1898 map marks a little farther west, but simply the oldest
surviving tree in the vicinity, and therefore inheritor of the title.

The stories I have collected about this fane are various, odd, and tanta-
lizing. The bullaun, of course, never goes dry even in the droughtiest
weather. People from Connemara used to come here to be baptized – 'but
that was back in the pagan times'. The field by the bullaun has good soil –
it is under a scarp with a clay-band at its foot – but it has never been dug;
its owner once decided to set potatoes in it, and came with a load of seaweed on his horse, but the horse refused to carry it into the field. Finally
(and this is true; I heard it in Evelyn's shop in Eochaill village), somewhere
the cult of St Asurnaí still lives, for in 1978 a young Australian came

enquiring for the place, spent a day trying to find it and got terribly scratched, but failed to obtain what he had been told to bring home, two pounds of thorns from St Asurnaí's bush.

What recluse lies here, though, after what purifying or stultifying life? St Asurnaí is supposed to be the nun to whom a church is dedicated at Drumacoo in south Galway, but according to Fr Killeen the latter's right name was Sarnait. O'Donovan suggests the church is actually called Teampall na Surnaighe, the church of the vigils. In Archbishop O'Cadhla's list of Aran churches we have:

The church called *Tempull-Assurnuidhe*, which is said to be dedicated to St. Assurnidhe (or, perhaps, Esserninus), and this church is held in the greatest veneration among the islanders.

Esserninus was one of St Patrick's bishops sent to Ireland in 438, long before the foundation of Cill Éinne, and nothing connects him with Aran. If the matter was obscure when the archbishop wrote three hundred and fifty years ago, it seems likely to remain so. I will scratch myself no longer on the thorny question.

Turning away from the saint's grave, my eyes adjusted to shadows, I look deeper into the bushes, searching under them for the modest heaven of flowers to be found on the dark earth: the damp lilac silk tags of woodsorrel in summer, or sanicle with its little spherical clouds of minute flowers like puffs of hoar-frost; in the very early days of spring often nothing but celandines. In such a place I once saw a single yellow celandine blossom, its eight glossy petals sharply separate and spread as if it were straining to grasp as much definition for itself as possible out of its penumbral bower. It hypnotized my memory, so that I had to return the next day with a camera. But then I saw that the dim perspective of twigs I was looking through was as precise in its enmeshed tonalities and interpenetrating articulations as the star of hermetic knowledge shining in its depths. No camera could encompass this microcosm, and I came away with renewed respect for the eye, leaving the flower to the perverse purity of self-perfection.

LIGHTS IN THE DARKNESS

In the days when the only chapel in the island was at Eochaill, it would have been natural for funeral processions coming up the long rise from Cill Rónáin to pause at the top while the men carrying the coffin got their breath back, and no doubt mourners used these moments of rest to pile up little memorial cairns on the crags by the road. That, I imagine, is the reason why there are four of the well-built and lettered cenotaphs I have described, which probably developed out of the humble analphabet cairns, spaced out along the roadside on the right just beyond the brow of the hill. Because the ground slopes away behind them to the north shore, these tall square pillars, rigidly formal and surmounted by crosses, stand dramatically against the vast vague gulf of air rimmed on the far side by the Connemara skyline. Their inscriptions suggest that all four were built between 1863 and 1876, but on one of them is a plaque commemorating a Bridget Dirrane who died in 1811, the earliest date to occur on any of the roadside cenotaphs. Since the workmanship of this plaque is much more skilled and sophisticated than that of any other, I think it must have been imported, and perhaps it was exhibited elsewhere before being incorporated in this monument erected to commemorate a Dirrane of a later generation. On another of these four pillars, an immeasurably more ancient creature has been accidentally memorialized: a brachiopod, whose fossil shell, embedded in one of the plaques, gleams like a crescent moon in the grey limestone. This ghostly sign, positioned like a footnote-mark at the end of the inscription, refers one to the superstitious tremors these monuments used to cause in passers-by on the deserted road at night, aftershocks of which one or two islanders tell me they still feel, even though there are now a few houses nearby, and electric light showing in windows.

A little farther west, there was worse to fear than ghosts. Where the road slants up a little scarp, there is a spring among the hawthorn bushes in the hollow by it, called Tobar na nAdhairc, the well of the horns. A lady of Eochaill whom I met on the road by the well told me, euphemistically, that 'His Excellency' once put up his head there. Funnily enough, while she was speaking, a brimstone butterfly arose from the bushes hiding the mouth of the pit, distracting me and indeed tempting me into a little sin of egotism, for it was, I believe, the first of this species to be recorded from Aran.

The inextinguishable desire to see and be seen has assembled miscellaneous structures, now all in ruins, around the highest point of the island (a modest 406 feet above sea-level), south of Eochaill village. From the main road just beyond the well a boreen follows the line of sight up towards three of them that show on the skyline: the drab, flat-topped cylinder of a lighthouse, next to it a square signal-tower, and to the east the slouching coil of a great stone cashel. A fourth is hidden from below and in fact can hardly be seen until one is standing on it. When I first came across this last, obscured by low heathy growth in a field on the left of the boreen, I became excited, and started footing out what appeared to be the foundations of a rectangular building with labyrinthine corridors and cells, and traces of a small oval enclosure and a crooked wall just outside it to the south. Then the incomprehensible interior suddenly spelled out the word EIRE, and the curves outside it formed the numerals 50 below it, as if the level ground had swung up to present itself like a placard before my eyes. Later I learned that this sky-sign was built during what is known (in the bit of Ireland labelled Éire) as 'The Emergency', to proclaim the neutral territory to stray aircraft. Since then I have come across a similar sign with the number 51, on the island of Leitir Mealláin in south Connemara. The naval reservists of the Coastwatching Service who kept up the whitewash on this peaceable message had 'a little houseen' nearby, I am told; I could find no trace of it, but no doubt it was like the lookout post partially surviving on Leitir Mealláin: a concrete box consisting of a small three-windowed bay with just enough of a room attached to accommodate a fireplace and a door – a snug, with Atlantic view. There are in fact about a hundred of these lookout posts, each identified by its number; the first is at Dublin and the sequence runs clockwise round the coast to Donegal. Apparently when the existence of these signs was first reported by British aircrews it was thought that the mysterious numbers indicated radio frequencies, and Winston Churchill spoke angrily of Mr de Valera's treacherous communications with the Hun.

The dead lighthouse, together with its roofless single-storey living quarters and the old signal-tower, is surrounded by a high wall in which a rusty iron gate opens onto the boreen. It was built in 1818, by a man called Yorke, who it seems married the daughter of the family, Wiggins, whom he lodged with in Aran, later set up in business on the Long Walk in Galway, and owned two or three ships trading to Boston, which in their day carried a number of Aran emigrants to America. Yorke himself is now forgotten in Aran (those details of his life were noted in a copy of the census of 1821 by an amateur historian of Cill Rónáin, Colie Folan, two generations ago), but the gigantic stallion he brought in to cart blocks of limestone up to the site – they say it could drag a load of one ton – so impressed the islanders and their little Connemara ponies that 'Stail Yorke' is still a byword for strength here.

The other workers on this project have their memorial in the writings of Petrie:

The introduction, a few years since, of a number of persons into Aranmore for the purpose of erecting a lighthouse, has had an injurious effect on the character of the native inhabitants of the island. Their unsuspicious confidence and ready hospitality were frequently taken advantage of and abused, and their interesting qualities have consequently been in some degree diminished. Till that time robbery of any kind was wholly unknown in the island. ... Several petty thefts have occurred, and though they have uniformly been attributed by the islanders to the strangers lately settled among them, it would perhaps be rash to conclude that they themselves have hitherto wholly escaped the vicious contagion.

And since Inis Oírr had long lost its innocence through proximity to the Clare coast, according to Petrie, only Inis Meáin still preserved its 'delightful pristine purity'. J.M. Synge would have read this passage in his youth, and it probably helped to determine his preference for Inis Meáin – and so perhaps we owe the most luminous of Aran books to the darkening of Aran by its lighthouse eighty years earlier.

It was not only mainland viciousness but the mainland language that was brought in by the lighthouse builders. An absurd little anecdote from this period of immixture of English is still current. Once when the lighthouse roof was being repaired, the overseer set an islander called Conneely to melting the tar in a big cauldron over a fire. Conneely soon wandered off, leaving another man to keep an eye on the tar, and when he came back the cauldron was ablaze. As the two islanders were considering this phenomenon the overseer ran up, yelling 'Quench it, Conneely!' Conneely's reply was, 'Whoever *las* it, let he *múch* it!' (whoever lit it, let he quench it) – a formula that has the status of a classical tag on the island to this day.

In its time, according to Lewis's *Topographical Dictionary* of 1837, the lighthouse exhibited 'a bright revolving light from twenty-one reflectors, which attains its greatest magnitude every three minutes and may be seen from all points at a distance of twenty-eight nautical miles, in clear weather.' O'Donovan in his Ordnance Survey letters of 1839 ran amok over it: 'The Aran lighthouse shed such a stream of light as astonished me. It is a revolving light, and while it remains in view it looks like a meteor. It sheds such a flood of radiant light upon the welkin, the sea, and the eyes of the spectators, as apparently to put out the nocturnal lamps blazing in the firmament (as a tasteless poet would say).' But as a lighthouse rather than as a spectacle it was never satisfactory; it gave no indication of the length of the island chain, and being a mile inland it was invisible to boats near the tall cliffs to the south. In 1857 it was superceded by the present North and South Aran lights. Delapidation soon followed, no doubt. At the height of the Land War controversies in 1880 Thompson accused the villagers of Eochaill and Oatquarter of taking stones from the lighthouse, and fined them five shillings in the pound on the rateable values of their holdings. The curate, the Rev. Daniel McLoughlin, denounced the agent for this as 'a public, infamous and scandalous liar'. On the other hand, in Pat Mullen's *Hero Breed* we are told that the windows of the hero's cottage had been stolen from the buildings around the lighthouse. My judgment is that, while the curate had right on his side, the agent had the facts on his. Nevertheless, William Thompson will find no forgiveness in my book, for if he acted according to his lights, like Matthew Arnold's philistines he did not take sufficient care that his lights were not of darkness.

Nowadays all has long been derelict on the hilltop. The staircase leading up through the lower three levels of the lighthouse has been ripped out, and the octagonal light-chamber stares blindly around the island. But one memento of its history, which I was told about when I lived on Aran but could never locate, has since come to light; on a recent visit I saw that someone has picked out in whitewash the inscription on a stone in the west wall of the boreen, just twenty yards up from the road: Lt RW – and below that a date of which only the last numeral, a '9', is legible, and which must be 1819. In *Pilgrimage* I looked into the life of Robert Wilson, half-pay Lieutenant of Marines and lighthouse keeper, and, having then projected this man onto the field of my imagination, it was now almost disconcerting to find he had impressed himself so definitely upon reality; I felt an interior rotation, like that of the plan of the sky-sign turning itself into a word, as Wilson's plane of existence turned to accommodate this material trace.

Wilson and his wife and daughters, and the Under Lightkeeper Richard Kelly, lived in the old signal-tower next to the lighthouse, according to the census of 1821, so perhaps the single-storey living-quarters had not yet been built. Despite its medieval appearance this tower dates only from the invasion scares of the Napoleonic wars; it had been completed in 1805, the year of the Battle of Trafalgar. During the earlier war with the French Republic, the appearance of their fleet off Bantry Bay in 1796 and General Humbert's landing at Killala in 1798 had shown the government that the west of Ireland was the Kingdom's naked back, and when war was renewed in 1803, it was realized that the advance guard of any French force landing in Galway Bay could be bombarding Dublin within six days. So a grand scheme of signal-towers, martello towers and gun batteries was drawn up, and in 1804/5 fifty or so signal-towers were in construction, lining the coast from the Pigeon House at Dublin south and west and north again, to Malin Head in Donegal. Paul Kerrigan, a historian of military architecture, succinctly describes the operation of these towers:

At each station the signal mast was set up close to the tower; it consisted of a ship's topmast of fifty feet, with a cap and crosstrees to secure the thirty foot flagstaff above, while below the crosstrees was a thirty foot long gaff or inclined spar. A similar arrangement can be seen at naval establishments and yacht clubs today. Signals were made by showing the Union Flag, a blue pendant or long triangular flag, and four black balls (hoops covered with canvas) in various combinations on the flagstaff and gaff; communication was with ships of the Royal Navy offshore and between adjacent signal stations along the coast.

When Wellington made a tour of inspection of coastal defences in the south and west in 1806, he noted that one of the Kerry towers was superfluous as its neighbours on either side could see each other's lights; so it seems that lights were used for signalling by night. The Aran tower too would have been able to exchange signals with quite a number of others: one at Hag's Head in Clare, another on the highest point of Inis Oírr, and three more spaced out along the south Connemara coast, at Ceann Gúlaim or Golam Head, Cnoc an Choillín near Carna, and Slyne Head. The towers were all of a standard pattern, thirteen or fifteen feet square inside, about thirty-four feet high, with two stories, the walls sometimes slated against the weather. Their defensive features give them an antique look: the door, in the upper storey, was reached by a small ladder that could be quickly hauled up (as in the monastic round towers), with a bartizan – a balcony supported on corbels with an open floor through which assailants could be shot at – above it, and other bartizans at the rear corners to protect the side and back walls. Such a tower could defy any attack short of bombardment with cannon. Defence of the towers seems to have been in the hands of a body called the Sea Fencibles, a naval reserve of fishermen and merchant seamen set up in 1803, who manned hired vessels fitted out with 18-pounder guns and carronades and were stationed at such likely invasion sites as Killala, Galway Bay and the Shannon estuary. The Lord Lieutenant's reports to London show some anxieties about the loyalty of these volunteers, who might well have sided with any French expeditionary force and turned their guns against the English authorities. One imagines that the signal crews – perhaps just a midshipman and a couple of signalmen – had uneasy nights in such towers as this in isolated and disaffected Aran, listening to the wind battering at the door and shrieking around the parapets. After only a few years most of the towers were left unmanned, and in 1809 the government announced that those from Eochaill to Horn Head in Donegal were to be abandoned. After its second brief life as housing for the lightkeepers, the Eochaill tower followed the lighthouse into dereliction, and now it is a mere shell, its floors and ceilings gone. Patches of blueish weather-slating cling to its walls like fish-scales here and there.

A few little fields and gullies separate the lighthouse enclosure from the outer rampart of Dún Eochla. The great cashel has been looking out from this north-eastern corner of the island's central plateau for perhaps fifteen hundred years, perhaps much longer; nobody knows its date and it has not been investigated since the Board of Works shored it up during the drastic 'restoration' carried out in the 1880s. The inner rampart encloses a rather squarish oval area measuring ninety-one by seventy-five feet, and it is over sixteen feet high in places; with age it had grown potbellied, and the Board of Works' buttresses take the strain at the south-east and south-west. According to O'Donovan this wall is made up of three layers one outside the other, totalling thirteen feet in thickness, and raised to different heights to form two terraces around the inside; at present there is only one terrace, the outer two layers having been levelled off into a broad stable, walkway. Numerous little flights of stairs – more than the three O'Donovan recorded – lead up from the terrace to this outer parapet. In his day the north-eastern sector of the wall, where the doorway is, was nearly destroyed, but now it stands eight feet high on either side of the entrance. The doorway is just four feet three inches wide, and its jambs are made up of huge stones – over nine feet long and fifteen inches square – lying horizontally. Two stone huts inside the cashel were in ruins at the time of O'Donovan's visit; one has been tidied into an oval heap, but the other has totally vanished. The interior in general has a neatness and openness about it, which covers like thick make-up the face of the dishevelled ruin that so excited the romantics who rediscovered it. The outer rampart, up to twelve feet high in parts, consists of two layers totalling five and a half feet thick, forming a terrace and a parapet. It surrounds a roughly circular area about a hundred yards across, now divided by stone fences into several fields; the inner enclosure is off-centred towards the southern and higher-lying part of this area. The ground falls steeply to the north and east, giving the *dún* a commanding site over the Cill Rónáin valley, and wide views across to the promontory fort of Dúchathair that is darkly outlined against the Atlantic to the south-east, also to the smaller Aran Islands each crowned by a similar fort, and to the Burren's long western flank, on which there are eight or ten comparable forts as well as many minor ring-forts. What the network of political and economic relationships between these foci of settlement was, is unrecorded and perhaps irrecoverable, while their daily life, in the margins of the godlike deeds of Cú Chulainn, the wizardry of Fionn Mac Cumhaill or even of the Lives of the Saints, is hard to imagine.

Projecting my mind back into that dusk, I light upon a moment from the time when Oengus son of Nad Froích ruled at Cashel. A man is resting his back against the knobbly masonry of the great wall, enjoying a moment's rest from dragging yew logs from the wood in the valley below up to the highest point of the island, where the great midsummer fire is about to be lit. He is a crooked-legged, underfed, wheezing thing whom his master has humorously nicknamed Stail Yorke; both of them sometimes wonder where in the cycles of time that fabulous beast had its stabling. Distant corresponding fires are beginning to show in the twilight, from the Dún of Irghus on Black Head, the Dún of Conchúr on Inis Meáin, the lake dwellings of the Conmaicne Mara to the north. But the slave's eyes are following a small boat paddling into the bay of Port Chorrúch. It is too far away for him to make out that there are nine cloaked and cowled men on it, and that the boat itself is a stone – the annunciatory miracle, the impossible unsupported pivot upon which the island will soon be swung out of its ancient, familiar, horizontal web of mutual fires, and turned like a sky-sign towards Eternity. Staring, yawning, flexing his knees slightly to scratch his shoulder-blades against the old fort of Eochaill, Stail Yorke lets his mind go blank.

EVELYN'S SHOP

The only shop between Cill Rónáin and Cill Mhuirbhigh is in Eochaill, and gives that long, strung-out village what focus it has. The visitor unused to rural Ireland and unable to interpret the two or three tins and packets discreetly displayed in the window of the first house west of Bóithrín an Lighthouse would not know that it was a shop at all. This is Tigh Eibhlín, the house of Evelyn, and in it transactions are conducted according to the ways of an earlier, slower, more mannerly Aran. The space before the counter in the front room of the house is small, and it is the custom for only one person to go in at a time, while the other shoppers wait in the narrow hallway, leaning against the wall or sitting on the lower steps of the staircase. The analogy with the confessional is inescapable. The whispered exchanges in the shop itself seem to go on interminably while the rest of us, waiting patiently to reveal our mild desires for bacon, aspirin or woollen socks, stare out of the front door at the robin and the pied wagtail that share rights to the crumbs on the steps after bread has been delivered, or at the breakers twinkling on the shore half a mile below, or at the rain slanting across a thousand little grey fields. If anyone speaks it is about the weather, but usually the silence is unbroken, merely being underlined by the unintelligible monotone from within, which sinks to an intriguing hiss whenever some more personal information is being passed on – passed *in*, I should say, for I have never known any gossip to be passed *out* from Evelyn's sanctum. On the rare occasions when something is said in the hallway the prevailing silence puts it in quotation marks and gives it the status of a *bon mot*. I remember a young man who came bounding up the path to join me there in peering out at the drifting mist-globules, saying with deliberation, 'It's a fine – soft – damp – warm – *flexible* – kind of a day!' – producing the last adjective with the flourish of a magician finding yet another rabbit in his hat.

Sometimes in summer a tourist looking for icecream or a Coke discovers the shop. Evelyn, glancing out of her window, spots the unfamiliar face approaching up the path and calls out to us, *'Tá stráinséar ag teacht!'* ('A stranger is coming!'), and we all freeze into impenetrable silence. The stranger steps into the hall, looks blankly at the mutes on the staircase, just as I did on my first visit, walks straight into the shop behind whoever is occupying it, is served instantly, comes out again and goes off with another puzzled look, perhaps wondering if a wake is in progress. When this happens, I too sit unprotesting, immobile and expressionless like the natives, which gives me an exquisite sense of sharing one of the island's secret jokes.

Evelyn's can be less amusing in the winter, when the steamer is often gale-bound in Galway for a week or two and there is nothing in the shop but a tediously familiar selection of plastic buckets and the like. Even if the steamer does come, the goods unloaded onto the quay may be caught by a downpour, and then when the tractor with its trailer piled high with sacks and boxes at last arrives at the shop, and the patiently waiting customers pull their coats over their heads and run down to help unload it, the bottoms burst out of sodden cartons and children go chasing after rolling tins of beans, loaves have to be hastily grabbed together in damp armfuls, and dribbling flourbags and sticky packets of sugar lugged hastily up the steps and dumped into the back room, where the lady of the shop struggles with a mounting chaos of things spilt and spoiled, eventually to emerge, white in the face, and serve us with unruffled sweetness of manner.

On such wild days we shoppers from farther west, with the week's provisions hung about our bicycles, have to force our way home against the staggering blows of the wind. If the rain is not blinding us it is an exciting ride. For the first mile, the road takes the outside edge of one of the great steps of the island's northern flank, and the ground falls away so sharply on the right that it feels as if one were riding the crest of a huge breaker. Often a winter sunset exploded by the last of the gale into ragged purples and oranges comes flying to meet us from the western skyline; we know that our chimney draws well in such winds and a glowing fire will greet us with the proposal of long hours of reading. Only the densest fog can quite deprive us of the immense aerial amenities of this journey from Evelyn's. Even if the grey and green weave of the little fields is lost within fifty yards to either side, there are vaguely exhilarating pulses of light in the air, hints of clearances hovering above, vaporous nods and winks that make the deserted road unlonely. Do the elderly folk, though, who shop a little every day, plodding along with their canvas shopping bags, heads down whether it be sunny or drizzly, share any of our delight in the immeasurable annexe to Tigh Eibhlín that is opened up to the north by fair weather, in which Connemara is displayed as if on a shelf, supplementing the limited fare of Evelyn's shop with a paradisal trifle of sherry-soaked plumcake topped by a dollop of whipped cream bigger than the whole of Aran?

I wrote the above in 1982, and no sooner had I finished it than news came that Evelyn had retired and her house, the last traditional shop of the island, was closed. Too often, in writing of Aran, I am writing elegies un-awares.

LOCUS TERRIBILIS

An old saw gives this advice: 'If in Ireland, be in Aran; if in Aran, be in Eochaill.' ('*Má bhíonn tú in Éirinn, bí in Árainn; má bhíonn tú in Árainn, bí in Eochaill*'). The good sense of the first part is beyond argument; the second perhaps relies on the elevation and centrality of this village among the island's fourteen villages, the only one from which the outlooks to east and west confirm a sense of the wholeness of the island settlement. Some such thought must have helped to determine the siting of Eochaill chapel, which stands above the road a little west of the shop. It is a plain, white-washed, slated building, with no spire but a little bell-turret, and its best features are its airy situation and the broad flight of steps, flanked by veronica bushes and sloping lawns, running up to it from the gate. A plaque set in the gable of the porch states that:

> This house
> was erected for the greater Honor &
> Glory of GOD thro: the unwearied
> Exertions of our Beloved & much
> Esteemed Pastor the Revd. Michl.
> Gibbons AD 1833

From the extinction of the monasteries and the ruination of their churches, down to this date of 1833, the islanders worshipped in secrecy, and then as the Penal Laws were gradually relaxed, in mere obscurity, in buildings hardly different from their cottages, that also served as schools. About a hundred yards downhill from the present chapel a few stones of such a building can be seen, by a side-road called from it Bóithrín an tSéipéil. A Randall McDonnell is recorded as the teacher here in 1821, with 46 boys and 25 girls in his charge; oral history says he was a refugee from the suppression of the rebellion of 1798 in Mayo. The building of the comparatively grand chapel on its more prominent site above followed close on Daniel O'Connell's great victory, the Catholic Emancipation Act of 1829, by which nearly all the remaining restrictions on Catholic participation in political and social life were removed; his national campaign, funded by the 'Catholic Rent' of pennies contributed by an enthused populace, re-energized the Church in Ireland, and here we see Aran's response, erected in a time of cholera and want. Even the Protestant landlord, the Rev. John Digby, was moved to contribute £21 to Fr Gibbon's fund-raising appeal. 'Pobal Árann', the new chapel was called (*pobal* meaning literally 'congregation'), until St Brigid's in Cill Rónáin supplanted it as parish church in 1905.

Such is the message of renewal preached by this commanding height of the island community. But before entering, hear also the intimidatory peal of thunder with which the inscription on the porch prefaces its historical note:

Terribilis est locus iste
hic domus Dei est & Porta
Coeli & vocabitur aula
Dei Gen 28 C 17 V.

This is Jacob's exclamation upon waking from the dream of the ladder on which angels pass between heaven and earth: 'How dreadful is this place! This is none other than the house of God, and this is the gate of heaven.'

Can it be so? To step inside here chills my spirit. The air is dank with repetitious pieties. The walls are plain white plaster; nothing relieves the visual tedium. There is a gallery at the back, favoured by those who want to conceal their inattention and by the younger males in general, though many of these, I observe, prefer to lounge and lurk outside, taking an occasional peep in through the door at the progress of the service. The pews are kicked and scuffed. In the porch a foxed pamphlet, offering theology to girls in trouble, curls on a rusty drawing-pin.

Perhaps I imagined that last detail. Also, the place has now been refurbished; I have described it as I saw it when I first came to Aran, with a full set of anti-ecclesiastical prejudices. Now, although I understand that the Church's view of itself is that as an institution it is divine, and that its failings are due to the human weaknesses of its members, my (fallible) opinion is that the truth is the other way around: if the thing has any spark of worth, it is only because of the human nature of its members, many of whom do exceedingly well, considering they belong to a body mired in ontological error. At first we had no contact with the Aran clergy. Occasionally on our rambles we would see the dark-clad, portly figure of the parish priest in the distance; we had the impression that he was avoiding us, by turning aside down a boreen if necessary. Then during one period when I was alone in Aran, he called on me, under cover of some query about a bird or a plant. We found we had interests in common, and when M came back from London she was amazed to find that Fr Moran's visits had become an institution. Thereafter when he called she would show him into the little parlour where I did my writing, and serve us with two mugs of tea and a plate of biscuits, on a tray with a tray-cloth, and then retire on satiric tiptoe to the servants' quarters, as it were, pointedly leaving us to such patriarchal concerns as the classification of Aran's saxifrage species and the use of the filter in photographing clouds. But by degrees even she softened, and when Fr Moran was finishing off his great work of renovating the Cill Rónáin chapel, he was able to call on both of us for moral and aesthetic support. To our bemusement we found ourselves on our knees on the church floor helping to stretch hangings of holy emblems. The altar had been turned about to face the congregation in line with the edicts of Vatican II, the chilly plastering of the interior had been removed and the stonework pointed, the scaffold-like gallery and its staircase swept away, and the floor carpeted in pale grey; in fact a humanizing breath had blown through the entire building. A set of Stations of the Cross by a well-known woodcarver, Fr Benedict Tutty of Glenstal Abbey, had replaced the rows of morbid, blackish oleographs in pinnacled, gothic-horror frames. The general result, with its light tones and tasteful textures, seemed to me, an outsider, to bear some reassuring and unexacting relationship to heaven, more that of a departure lounge than a ladder. But the gallery-birds regretted their eyrie, and others of the faithful were not pleased; they resented sermons on the importance of wiping their feet, they did not appreciate Fr Benedict's post-cubist medievalism and thought his figures looked like monkeys. Our role then was to drop reconciling words into influential minds here and there about the island: wait and see, look again, perhaps with time ...

An attractive feature of the Christian year in rural western parishes is the celebration of the Mass in private houses. In each village, the honour of hosting the annual Stations, as the ceremony is called, passes from household to household in rotation. The form is that, after the hearing of confessions and the service, breakfast is provided for the priest and the curate, and to some this is the most stressful part of the obligation, even though nowadays it is understood that only the simplest repast is called for. Soon after our noted alliance with the priest, the Stations fell to the turn of an elderly bachelor in Cill Mhuirbhigh, a retiring and solitary man whom we had become fond of. He was very reluctant to take on the obligation, as his house was neglected to the point of sordidity, he had no *bean a' tí* or house-wife to play hostess at breakfast, and he feared that if he asked any of the neighbouring gossips to step in they would be ferreting through his pri-vacy. However Fr Moran was insistent – he probably saw it as a chance to reintegrate the old fellow into the community – and to our surprise old Beartla, as I will call him, came and asked M if she would be his 'woman of the house'. It was an invitation into a sanctuary; she accepted it at its full weight.

The day before the ceremony I was sent down to Cill Mhuirbhigh to help Beartla freshen up the house. We swept and painted and laid linoleum; I condemned the rotting tea-chest on which his gas-ring stood, and fetched the similar but green vinyl-covered tea-chest from our own kitchen. Beartla exhumed from an outhouse a large, peculiarly long-legged table his father had made, to serve as an altar; he tied a rope around it and carried it to the house on his shoulders, struggling over the back wall rather than bringing it round by the gate in view of the neighbours. In the middle of all this the priest's big car drew up before the house; I had just time to swoosh the dust out of the back door and slap the green tea-chest into place before he was upon us. Everything passed muster; his only question to Beartla was as to who would be making the tea, and when he heard that it would be M, he looked taken aback for a moment, but raised no objection.

When the rough work was done, M appeared at the door with a sen-tence that had caught her fancy in one of Séamus Ó Grianna's Donegal-Irish novels; *'An bhfuil rud ar bith le déanamh annseo ar fearr fhoireas lámh mná dó ná lámh fir?'* ('Is there anything to be done here better suited to a woman's hand than a man's?') She prepared the breakfast table in 'the room', decked the altar, which was in the kitchen, with the stiff embroi-dered linen Beartla produced out of an ancestral coffer, polished up the two brass candlesticks, and laid out the ritual items according to Beartla's direc-tions – water to be blessed, in a plastic milk-can, a saucer of salt, two towels. The next day we were down there early in the morning, wrestling with the worn-out wicks of Beartla's kerosene stoves, trying to take the chill off the house without filling it with fumes. Then the people started to arrive, M withdrew to the room, and I hopped over the back wall and wan-dered the crags with the dogs until it was all over. About twenty people attended, and one of the rascal lads whom Beartla often chased off his property materialized in spotless white as altar boy. After Fr Moran had given a brief homily in Irish he came into the room (flushing out M) to hear confessions; people went in and out at a great rate, she reported. Then he celebrated Mass with the close-packed congregation standing in the kitchen; there was only one chair, for an old lady from across the street. Everyone shook M's hand as they filed out.

Afterwards M served tea and the bread rolls she had made for the occasion to the priest and the curate, declining their invitation to sit down with them but standing with Beartla at the end of the table. The meal concluded the event with decent simple formality. Once the clergy had gone, Beartla and I fell on the remaining bread rolls. He was joyful and amazed; 'If Anyone had told Me!' he kept saying, 'that an English Woman! Would be serving breakfast to the Priest! In my House!' – and we were not less amazed and pleased.

Later that morning Dara the postman came up the path to our door with more than the usual impetus. 'Is it true that the missus was *bean a' tí* at the Stations?' he asked as he handed me the letters. 'It is!' I replied. 'Well, it's all over Cill Rónáin that you're "turning"!' he said.

No, we are not turning. But we are glad to feel that the Church's monopoly of ceremony does not exclude our participation. Indeed we assert by our presence on such occasions, that Catholicism, that Christianity in general, is a dialect of a universal language. This is Aran's view too. (One inquirer into our religious affiliation, when I told him we were atheists, looked troubled for a moment, and then said as if to comfort himself and us, 'Ah well, it's all the same God really.') Of course there are difficulties in it, passages of the rites during which we just have to keep a low profile, not kneeling but not defiantly sitting back. I know that their religion has an eternity in pickle for such as us, but no islander has ever expressed disapproval of our stance. In fact the Aran woman who notes out of the corner of her eye how we slip into the back pew or stand just within the porch for the baptisms, weddings and funerals of those whose comings, pairings and goings concern us, probably murmurs a prayer that at the last we may be found, similarly discreetly, in heaven. And I thank her for her orisons.

A FOOL AND HIS GOLD

A hundred yards or so west of the chapel one leaves Eochaill village for Baile na Creige, the village of the crag – but only a native of one of the two villages, or an obsessed topophile, would know that fact, for the irregular scattering of dwellings along the roadside gives no indication of a boundary. Among the cottages of Baile na Creige is one, long reduced to the status of outhouse or 'store', which was formerly that palace of fantasy, the home of Micilín Sarah. The window at the back of it, through which the fairies used to come and go, is blocked with stones. Stains visible on its gable-wall are the remains of inscriptions daubed by the lads who used to play handball there: one in Irish, *'Go mbeannaí Dia de Valera agus a gComrádaithe'*, meaning 'God bless de Valera and his comrades', and one in English, 'Come and consult the famous alchemist'. Micilín the cliffman, crippled with cramps from nights on the spray-soused ledges, who swore to widow the raven, and was brought to court on the evidence of the beaks and legs of eleven score cliff-birds found around his cottage, has been met with in *Pilgrimage*, and I now turn to his inland activities, which were very various. He was not only republican patriot and alchemist, but packman, selling needles and threads around the villages, and ragman, collecting big sacks of rags to ship to Galway, and medicine man, having learned about herbs, it was said, from Red Indians during a spell in the States; also cobbler, dog-fancier and archaeologist, and in virtue of this multiplicity of minor roles, 'a sort of a king in Baile na Creige'. His mother's maiden name was Gillan; she and her brother came from Leitrim and she married a Mullen. She must have been a more remarkable person than her husband since it is her Christian name rather than his that is preserved in the familiar name of their son, but I have only heard one odd little tale about her. The blacksmith of Oatquarter was digging in a little field one day, when he overheard someone saying *'Forus, forus'* (the word used for calling pigs). Looking over the wall, he found Sarah in the act of luring his pigs out onto the road. He jumped over the wall and sent her on her way with his spade, for it seems she was addicted to denouncing people to the police for letting their animals stray on the King's highroad.

Micilín himself is profusely remembered, and his house was the gathering-place of talkers and listeners. He had 'a sort of imagination on him' that the sparkling bits in granite boulders were diamonds, and used to try to chip them out. He would show visitors gold and fossils and radium in the stones he had brought back to his cottage; 'I suppose there's but half an ounce of radium in the world,' said my Baile na Creige historian (who himself dated from the age of that dated metal), 'but Micilín Sarah thought he had some radium.' He also treasured old coins worn faceless; 'That's Queen Elizabeth's coin, *a bhuachaill!*' he would say, a blackish disc in his palm. (He used to say '*a bhuachaill*', my boy, to everyone; he would have said it to the King of England, I am told.) Once he showed such a coin to a group of Dublin girls who had come to giggle at the famous alchemist; one of them turned and picked an old shoe off the dunghill, saying, 'I wonder now, is this Queen Elizabeth's shoe?', and then fled from under his curses.

Royalty was much on his republican mind. Having eaten a peculiar fish he'd caught one day – perhaps it was a young porpoise – he pushed back his chair and said to the children who used to gather in his cottage, 'Well, I have my dinner eaten, and a nourishing dinner it was. But if it was known of, it would cost me dear, for the sturgeon is the property of the Royal Family and every one that's caught must be sent over to them!' Adults gathered around him too, expecting to be amazed. Once he drank off a half-pint mug of seal-oil, just to amaze old Dr O'Brien. The fairies were his regular visitors, coming in through the back window to eat their meals at his table while he sat by the fire – and beautiful women among them, according to Micilín himself. And if he saw them going out leaving the dishes in a mess, he would swear at them and tell them to come back and clear up, which they would do, for it seems fairies are frightened by big oaths.

Over my years in Aran I noted down much hearsay of the famous alchemist, and often wondered why I was hoarding it. Even now, having chipped these few glinting facets out of the inert lumps, I catch the cryptic mica scraps exchanging winks over my own alchemical delusions – that the old shoe on the dunghill can be turned by the furnace-breath of my assertion into the shoe of the crazy queen-mother of the craggy village, and that those crooked pennies can be brightened, dated and rendered unto the bent and salt-blackened little king whose image they bear. Sometimes I fear that all the stones of Aran do not equal one flower-carved finial of Venice, or an uneven paving-stone in San Marco. Perhaps there is nothing here but dull limestone and lumpy granite, foolish reminiscences of ridiculous old men, faded writings, blocked-up windows, a marginal and ineffectual history that does not feed the present, drossy stuff that chokes my flame.

IN SEARCH OF WASTED TIME

On the plateau above the villages west of the chapel, hidden from them by the skyline as if thrust to the back of their collective mind, is an area of many obscure ruins called Baile na mBocht or Baile na Sean, the settlement of the poor, or of the old. The latter name reflects or perhaps suggested an idea I heard from an Eochaill lady, that people too old to be of use around the house were packed off up there to live in stone huts and eat shellfish, in the hard old times. The other name is old; in the form 'Balleneboght' it occurs in an inquisition of 1581, in which it seems to denote a much larger portion of the island than it does today, and to include 'Monastercon-naght', *i.e.* Mainistir. Unfortunately there is a logical contradiction in the specification of these lands, making it impossible to equate some of them with today's territorial divisions. Consider these three propositions:

The land of Balleneboght and Monasterconnaght meares the sea on the South and North, on the East the land of Balleconnell and on the West Creagherie.

Balleconnell adjoins Creaghcappell on the South, Ballemegan on the East, Cloghan-eprior on the West and Killenan on the North.

Ochill adjoins Killenan on the South, the sea on the North, Monaster-con-naght on the East and Onaght on the West.

The proof of their mutual inconsistency is left to the reader, as the text-books say. This is not the only cul-de-sac one gets into, in exploring Baile na mBocht.

In fact this central plateau must have been populous and productive, at some unknown but probably pre-medieval period (the ruins, mainly collapsed *clocháin* or beehive huts, are not of types that can be dated by inspection, and have not been examined in this era of radio-carbon dating), but its remains are so decrepit, overthrown and half-buried as to accord with the suggestion in its names of callous rejection and neglect. Like the other stretches of Na Craga, it is a peculiar and disconcerting terrain, unfrequented for most of the year, monotonous and sometimes depressing especially on a dull day, silent except for the rattling alarm of the stonechats or the occasional melancholy '*weep-weep*' of a lapwing. The dolomitized limestone of these higher strata supports a dry, grudging, heathy pasture used as winterage, meanly subdivided by walls, quite unlike the open acres of bare pavement on the lower terraces. The plateau tilts slightly southwards to the cliff-tops, beyond which the sea-horizon stands paradoxically tall; nothing is to be seen in any other direction but vistas of walls, terminated by bare rigid skylines. Because the Ice Age has gouged channels across the plateau along the jointing of the rock, many of the little fields are narrow rectangular gullies, hard to climb in and out of over the walls perched unstably along their steep flanks. Everywhere are old structures reduced to stone-heaps by the gravity of centuries.

The ruins of Baile na Sean were first recorded by Aran's antiquarian rector the Rev. William Kilbride, who showed some of them to a visiting geologist, George Henry Kinahan, in 1866; Kinahan was a man of many interests, including archaeology, and he read an account of Baile na Sean to the Royal Irish Academy in December of that year. As his diary shows that he only spent one day or part of it 'out with Kilbride looking up

Cloughauns', and later corresponded with him on the topic, the detail of his account, which lists thirty-one monuments or groups of monuments, is clearly due to Kilbride's pertinacity. In Kinahan's paper the monuments are sorted into various categories, some of them familiar to archaeologists, such as 'doons', 'cahers' and 'cloghauns', and others tending from the ambiguous to the bizarre: 'cnocáns', 'fosleacs' and 'ointigh'. These latter are probably terms Kilbride acquired from local Irish-speakers. The literal meaning of *cnocán* is a hillock, but Kinahan explains that he is applying the term to 'beehive stone cells covered with clay'. The implied distinction between a cloghaun and a cnocán then is not obvious to the eye when the thing has lain in ruins with brambles growing through it for centuries. A 'fosleac' is, he says, a cell of flagstones set on edge and roofed with flags; the word obviously involves the Irish *leac*, flagstone, but I haven't found it in the dictionaries or in today's Aran Irish. One of his fosleacs he says could more accurately be called a 'ligaitreabh', which in a later paper he defined as a fosleac with its cover-stone supported on two or more pillars, the spaces between which are built up by small stones. The word clearly derives from *liag*, pillar-stone, and *áitreabh*, habitation, and Kinahan seems to have regarded all these structures as habitation-sites; in fact, though, his 'ligaitreabh' is a megalithic tomb. The most recalcitrant of these terms is 'ointigh', meaning, according to Kinahan, a stone hut not having an arched roof. No such word is known to the Irish language, but a later researcher of Baile na Sean, John Goulden, has solved the mystery: it is *áit-tigh*, house-site, pronounced in the nasal Corrúch accent. The whole terminology is as ruinacious as Baile na Sean itself, but it has its savour, for the amateur of ruins.

Goulden was a high-school teacher and occasional archaeologist with some experience of excavation. Under licence from the Commissioners of Public Works he investigated three sites in the summers of 1953-5, depositing minor finds with the National Museum, but never publishing the results of his excavations. His diaries, photographs and preliminary reports have recently been examined by Professor Waddell of University College Galway. Goulden's site 'Oghil I' was one of Kinahan's 'ruined cnocáns', an oval, grass-grown cairn with mounds of stone at either end and a pile of bigger blocks in the middle, about fifteen metres long and with a maximum height of 1.2 metres. Removal of heaps of broken stone mixed with chopped and broken bones and quantities of seashells revealed a roughly flagged floor bounded by a low wall, and some small cist-like structures of standing stones, all so ruinous that the site's function remained uncertain. The only artefacts were two limestone discs 62 and 45mm across, and a bit of deer-antler with perforations through it. Oghil II was more informative. This was another of Kinahan's ruined cnocáns, a mound with a depression in the middle like the last, crossed by a recent field-wall. Excavation revealed the lower levels of what Goulden interpreted as a circular stone hut about 6.4m across inside, its wall faced internally and externally with masonry and filled with rubble, and within it a smaller and more recent hut, with a lintelled door so low it would have had to be entered on all fours. Apart from the usual limpet-shells and animal bones he found a per-forated stone of the type used as spindle-whorls, a double 'bullaun' (a stone with hollows used as mortars), a stone axe and a stone hammer, and, according to a report in *The Irish Times*, 'the small shells which are always found attached to the *dileasc* and which convinced him that the islanders had been deriving comfort from the soothing weed for many centuries'.

Finally Goulden investigated what Kinahan had described as 'a group of three mounds, which appear to be the relics of a compound Cnocán.' By degrees a habitation-site appeared from under the piled debris, consisting of a circular room 7m across inside, with a narrow lintelled entrance only 60cm high to the west, and a larger east entrance, having two much smaller circular huts adjoining it on either side, from which a paved way ran east-wards for about 10m. A large triangular area had been removed from the rock floor of the big room, and reflagged; Goulden considered this to have been the basis of a tripod supporting a thatched roof. The smaller cham-bers, he thought, had had corbelled stone roofs, and in one of them were found two sandstone rotary quern-tops, which he thought might have been used to hold the pivots of a door. Other finds included some shards per-haps from a small tub-shaped pot, some fragments of iron, large pebbles used for pounding, half a small lignite or jet ring, part of a bone knife-handle, a fragment of polished stone axe-head, etc. Goulden concluded that these houses dated from the Iron Age, and nothing among the surviv-ing finds proves him wrong; however, techniques now available to researchers could give a different answer.

So much for old-fashioned archaeology, in its mode of rendering dust to dust. In search of other perspectives, I persuaded Seán Powell of Baile na Creige to show me round the area. Seán had been one of those employed by Goulden on his excavations; he is the old cliffman I quoted in *Pilgrim-age*. A short, thickset man with one sharp and one opaque eye, he was a meticulous guide, and would permit no divergences from his preplanned route and his sequence of anecdotes. We set off up Bóithrín Bhaile na mBocht, which starts in Seán's backyard and comes to a stop five hundred yards up the hillside. Two fields to the east of it was the first site he wanted to show me: Garraí Joe, Joe's garden. It was roughly circular, about thirty paces across, and with thick irregular masses of masonry here and there about its margins. Seán had shown this field to Goulden and told him that it was once a stony crag which Joe had been given, long ago, to make a potato-garden for himself; over three years he had picked so many stones off it, piling them up into huge walls around it, that the delighted owner took it back and gave him another stony field to start on. 'Nonsense!' Goulden had said; 'This is an old *dún*!' Indeed, whatever about the historicity of Joe – and one pictures him at his Sisyphean labours yet – Goulden was right; this is the remains of a substantial ring-fort, and it is surprising that neither the Ordnance Survey nor Kilbride and Kinahan had recorded it. One area of it, according to Seán, is 'thick with copper pins,' but he will permit no digging; it seems, like many such sites, this place is not quite canny. Seán's son Antoine tells me that Seán saw a rabbit there on the day of Antoine's birth, and again when the child was very ill. Of course rabbits are to be seen in most places in Aran on most days, but the fact that these rabbits were remembered shows that, if not exactly in the semantic field, they were hopping around its margins.

From Garraí Joe I could see some interesting-looking stone slabs sticking up in a field further up the hill, but Seán would not be diverted from the route; they marked a graveyard, he said, and we would return to them later on. So we crossed a few field-walls westwards and then turned up a narrow bramble-choked path to the crest of the plateau. Here we joined the main boreen of Baile na Creige, which runs from just west of Seán's house, right over the island to within a few hundred yards of the Atlantic cliffs. Originally the Powells had the land on one side of it, Seán explained, while the other side belonged to the Mullenses. It had been agreed between the two families that they would each give up a narrow strip of their territory for the purpose of building this boreen along their common boundary, and the Powells had carried out their side of the bargain by building half the width of the boreen plus its eastern wall, but the Mullens did not reciprocate, and so for a long time there was a half-boreen running up the hill. Later on the present wide track was built under some relief-work scheme, but it is still called Bóithrín na bPóil, not Bóithrín Bhaile na Creige. We went another hundred yards southwards along this track, and then eastward across half a dozen walls, ending up in a field largely occupied by two broad mounds: Goulden's Oghil III. In the eastern mound, aided by Seán's energetic indications, I could make out suggestions of the main enclosure, the two little corbelled chambers off it (which had collapsed when the material filling them had been pulled out, according to Seán – one of those little setbacks traditionally passed over in silence by excavators' reports), and the paved pathway going westwards to the other mound, which he said was made of nothing but periwinkle-shells. Everything had been put back after the dig, and the quern-stones had been left on the site.

Seán remembered vividly one incident from this dig. He had found a silver ring of wire – a bit thicker than this, he said, picking up a straw to show me – that was twisted like a corkscrew. Goulden was examining a stone with a hole through it at the time, but when Seán called out 'Attention!' and held up the ring, Goulden got so excited he threw away the stone, and afterwards searched for it in vain. Goulden then lectured the labourers for an hour and a half on the find, saying that as a piece of silver they would get maybe £5 for it from the bank or a jewellers', but that in fact it was worth £2000 and he was going to give it to the Museum, which Seán thinks he did. But it is not among the objects deposited with the National Museum, nor does it figure in Goulden's report. So, did the 'village of the poor' have more riches than it has been credited with, or has it somehow been put upon again? Truth-values scutter off like rabbits in the undergrowth from such anecdotes. The most likely solution of the puzzle is that the object was a cheap modern reproduction of a silver torc and had been planted by one of the more knowing participants in the dig. The 'salting' of digs is a well-established way of livening-up the science of archaeology. I have been told of one case in which the intended saltee was an eminent professor, but such was the quality of his excavation that he never found the hidden object. Of course this may just go to show that not only does the born archaeologist have a sixth sense guiding the trowel to the significant find, but a seventh to divert it from what should not be found.

On the way down the hill again Seán took me to the 'graveyard' – an irregular structure about seven feet long and two or three across, aligned east-west, of rough slab-like stones set on edge. Goulden had told them that it was a grave, said Seán, and they had not believed him because they thought that 'you couldn't have buried a fly on that *creig*!' But one day when Goulden was away in Inis Meáin a couple of the workers took their picks over to it for a private dig. To their surprise they were able to root stones out of its floor down to arm's-length; then they came to a cross-stone they couldn't shift, and piled everything back so that Goulden wouldn't know. In fact this monument – one of Kinahan's 'fosleacs' – might be some sort of cist grave.

Some time after this conducted tour I spent a few afternoons exploring Baile na Sean by myself. In an early draft for this chapter of my book I recorded the fruits of those September hours. As examples:

Three hundred yards farther along the boreen is a very short branch to the west, and in the third field counting west from the end of this are the remains of a rectangular and a circular clochán, very ruinous ...

and:

Two fields south of the above is a twelve-foot-high heap of stone topped by a tall growth of ivy, that looks from a distance like a bit of a ring-fort. However, it seems to be the result of energetic clearance of a little field and the piling up of stone from a ruined clochán, of which some corbelling can be made out to the north-west...

There are several pages of such diligent plod, arranged into two itiner-aries, the first taking one up Bóithrín Denny from the chapel in Eochaill to the boreen that runs along the spine of the island, and back by Bóithrín na bPóil, and the second following the boreen up the hill south of the medieval chapel in Corrúch and then by ramifying narrow paths west and north again, both with numerous excursions into the interiors of these loops. No coherent image of the place emerges from this dry stuff, nothing that explains what I thought I was at – playing the Schliemann of a dwarfish Troy, perhaps. Why did I spend so much time interrogating this amnesiac rubble? It may be of some help to future researchers that I have pinpointed all Kinahan's sites on the six-inch OS map, as his own article provides only a rather out-of-scale sketch-map by Kilbride; and I have added another dozen or so unidentifiable ruins to Kinahan's tally, which I am told were the despair of the field-workers on the Galway Archaeological Survey when they came to the islands a year or two later ('Oh no, not another of Tim Robin-son's cnocáns!'), because they had to go and find all these featureless hum-mocks among the hundreds of hummocky fields, and measure them up and write reports on them. A few of the sites of Baile na Sean are worth indi-vidual description, and I can thread those into the weave of this book some-where, but they are poor pickings from those hours of scrambling over tot-tering walls and thorny hollows. Again I follow my own footfalls:

... But usually, when one is nearly exhausted by the endless succession of obstacles and pitfalls, one is heartened by finding a rarity – such as a frog-orchid, or some more than usually odd conjunction of old stones, or a family of plate-sized horse-mushrooms to take home for dinner.

Crumbs of comfort, scraps brought by ravens to the hermit Paul in the desert! The wearisomeness of this chill *Thebaid* was not only due to its countless grey fields and proliferating walls and vacuous ruins, but also to the crushing weight of nothingness above it, the harsh, empty, birdless blue skies of those long afternoons. The light was nullifyingly even, reducing the mysteries of the past to tedious puzzles. An old, poor place, it seemed, all grappled down into meaninglessness by the briars. Nothing stands, from the life of the people who crept in and out of those little huts and com-forted themselves with a chew of sweet seaweed, and whose one silver trea-sure was a delusion. I wasted my time there.

Coming down disconsolate from Baile na Sean after the last of these explorations, I stopped to talk to one of the wilder-looking and more retiring islanders, a man I never met on the roads, who was cutting down brambles in a field that held more stone than grass. I leaned over the wall near where he was kneeling to drag at a tangle of briars with his great scythe, and asked him in Irish about a certain ruin that, Seán had told me, was once a chapel. He shuffled himself around on his knees to look in the direction I was pointing, and shook his head in silence; it seemed to take him a minute to collect the powers of speech that had wandered off into his solitude, and then it was as if he had never heard of the place. After a desultory conversation I left him, wondering if I had made myself comprehensible. From farther down I glanced back. Joe (it wasn't Joe, of course, but in the low perspectives of bramble-arches it might as well have been he) was still kneeling there, staring up the hillside in the direction I had indicated, a dark knot in a faded tapestry.

That evening I suddenly got sick – perhaps it was just eye-strain, from locating myself again and again in the lattice of field-walls on the map, as tenuous as a spider-web in that seething, unilluminating glare – and I spent the night trailing miserably between bedroom and bathroom, until I was absolutely empty from end to end.

THE FOUR BEAUTIES

A dozen cottages, most of them beside the road, a few reached by boreens running uphill or down from it, constitute Corrúch, the last of the villages of the central height and the townland of Eochaill. Looking down the hillside falling northwards from it one sees the shinglebank and seaweed-covered shores of Port Chorrúch half a mile away; it may be from the shape of this bay, or from one of the smaller inlets within it, that the area derives its name: *corr-fhuach*, bent or uneven cove. But if that is too humdrum an origin, one can discover a better one by mumbling the name of a saint, Caradoc Garbh. I will let myself briefly be drawn into the wild-goose chase for this saint.

In that intriguing list of churches drawn up by Archbishop O'Cadhla and published by Fr Colgan, we have:

Ecclesia Kill-namanach .i. Cella Monachorum, dicta, quae S. Cathradhocho, sive Caradoco, Monacho, cognomento Garbh .i. aspero, dicta est.

(The church called Cill na Manach, *i.e.* the church of the monks, which is named from the monk Cathradhoch or Caradoc, called Garbh, *i.e.* rough.) Roderic O'Flaherty adds to this the statement that Port Caradoc is in Eochaill; hence it is to be identified with Port Chorrúch. However, no such saint as Caradoc is known to even the most inventive of hagiographers, apart from these scholars who have taken O'Cadhla at his word.

O'Flaherty's mention of it seems to imply that the church was extant when he was writing in the 1670s, but in 1839 O'Donovan's most diligent enquiries could find no trace or tradition of it. Since then various investigators have tried their hand at identifying it. Fr Ó Domhnaill says it is a certain ruin near Bóthar na gCrag south of Baile na Sean; John Goulden suggests another one a quarter of a mile up the hill from Corrúch village; Fr Killeen almost convinces himself it is Cill Charna near Cill Rónáin, but ends his lucubrations with a sigh: '*In tenebris ambulo.*' I have no opinions on the matter, and am content to watch this ghostly church flit from place to place pursued by antiquaries lay and clerical, all 'walking in darkness'. Caradoc, or Cathradhoch as he first appears, is I suspect only a mishearing of the original form of the placename, Corr-fhuach.

If Caradoc is the mere wind of a word, it is not so with the four saints connected with the one known church in Corrúch; they shared a provocative, fragile and dangerous characteristic: beauty. The church is called Teampall an Cheathrair Álainn. The noun *ceathrar* (from *ceathar*, four, and *fear*, man) means 'a set of four persons' – 'a foursome' would be accurate but sounds too modern, since these special numerals are an ancient Indo-European feature of the language – and so the name means literally the 'church of the beautiful four', or less pedantically, 'the church of the four beauties'. Since the church itself has inherited that challenging quality of its dedicatees, I shall approach it cautiously, starting with these saints' legends.

The names of the saints are not familiar to the islanders, but according to O'Cadhla they were Fursey, Brendan of Birr, Conall and Berchan, and were said to be buried in the one tomb, in the cemetery of the church. Fursey or Fursu is famous; he was one of the great missioners of the seventh-century Celtic Church, and founded the monastery of Peronne in France, where, according to the *Annals of Tigearnach,* he died in 649. A member of his community wrote his biography within a quarter of a century of that date, and it is one of the two earliest surviving Lives of Irish Saints. This work states that after twelve years of missionary work in Ireland he withdrew with a few monks to an island in the sea, but it does not name Aran. Fursu himself wrote an account of Heaven and Hell, which he saw in a feverous vision once when he was ill, and so initiated a genre which culminated in Dante's *Divine Comedy.*

Brendan of Birr is also known to sacred history; he is said by the same annals to have died in 573, and is buried at Tallaght. His connection with islands has a note of the fabulous about it. In a work perhaps originally composed in the eighth century, *The Voyage of Maol Dúin*, the hero and his companions wander limitless oceans, visiting islands full of wonders, and in one of these they find a small church covered with ivy, and meet an aged cleric; he tells them that he is the sole survivor of fifteen disciples of Brendan of Birr, who went on a pilgrimage with their master, and found this hermitage. But, again, the island is left unidentified.

As to Bearchan, again there are several saints of that name, none with any known connection with Aran. The one O'Donovan opts for is supposed to have been a disciple of Kevin, the saint of Glendalough, and his beauty is the subject of this story:

A man named Cronan who was first a tanner but afterwards became a holy and pious man before God and men, and built a noble church for God, sent a message to St. Kevin requesting him to send a faithful and proper brother to him, through whom he might transmit his secrets to St. Kevin. St. Kevin without hesitation sent him Bearchan, a monk, alone, according to the custom of ancient times. That brother, commencing his journey through woods and desert mountains, met a woman alone on the way waiting for a guide to conduct her through the desert, and she, seeing Bearchan, said to him, 'Oh man of God, for the sake of the omnipotent Lord permit me to go with you through the wilderness.' The brother therefore for the sake of the Lord permitted her in her faith to go with him as far as her own village. On observing the beauty of Bearchan she was captivated in love of him, for he was truly beautiful and then in the flower of his youth. She tempted him frequently with alluring language. At length on their coming to a certain river she said to him, 'I request of you, Sir, in the name of Christ to wait for me till I take a drink of water and bathe myself in the river, for I am now wearied with travelling.' She did this wishing to show him the beauty of her person. On her stripping off her clothes St. Bearchan laid his head on the ground, not wishing to look at her, and he was overcome with sleep. The woman, coming out of the water and seeing him asleep, was very desirous of lying along with him, and lifting up his cloak began to lie down by his side, embracing him with her hands. But the soldier of Christ, being roused from his sleep, resisted her with fortitude, and, extricating himself from her grasp, began to strike her with his staff on the back and sides.

Now St. Kevin and St. Cronan, far off in their cells, saw all these proceedings by the divine power, and St. Cronan said, 'Act manly, oh good brother Bearchan, by scourging the immodest woman.' But the most holy Kevin said, 'Oh son, indulgent Bearchan, spare and do not beat the wretched woman.' By the will of God Bearchan, far off in the desert, heard these words expressed by the saints sitting in their own cells, and on hearing the command of his master St. Kevin he ceased from striking the woman. And she, doing penance, was conducted by St.

Bearchan through the wilderness as he had promised, and, magnifying the sanctity of the man of God, told her friends what had been done on the way.

The fourth saint's name, Conall, is a common one; Fr Killeen says we can be quite sure that St Conall mac Mainecaoil, a great traveller and a relative of Colm Cille's, spent a while in Aran, but the grounds of this surety must have been in the nature of a personal revelation, for he cites no evidence.

What is known of the saints named by O'Cadhla, then, varies from comparatively well-founded history, to myth, edifying anecdote, and mere guesswork, and it is hard to hold them together in the mind as the four beauties of Aran. But whoever they were, their reputation is spreading. Synge visited their church with his old half-blind guide, Martin Conneely, during his first visit to Aran, and noted the legend of the holy well there in his journal:

At the church of St. Carolan, which I have just visited with my old guide, there is still a holy well remarkable for many cures. While we visited in the neighbourhood an old man came to us from a near cottage and told us how it became famous. A woman of Sligo had one son who was blind. She dreamed of a well that held water potent to cure. So she took boat with her son following course of her dream and reached Aran. And when she landed she came to the house of my informant's father and told what had brought her but when those around offered to lead her to the well near by she declined all aid saying she saw still her way clear before. She led her son from the boat and going a little up the hill stopped at the well. Then kneeling with the blind child beside her she prayed to God and then bathed his eyes. In moments his face gleamed with joy as he said: 'Oh mother look at the beautiful flowers.' Twice since the same story has been told to me with unimportant variations yet ending always with the glad dramatic cry of the young child.

By the time he tidied up this passage for inclusion in *The Aran Islands* Synge had realized that 'Carolan' was '*an ceathrar álainn*', the four beauties. And in his play *The Well of the Saints*, there is a strange and disillusioned inversion of the story he was told in Aran: 'Did you ever hear tell of a place across a bit of the sea, where there is an island, and the grave of the four beautiful saints?... There's a green ferny well, I'm told, behind of that place, and if you put a drop of the water out of it on the eyes of a blind man, you'll make him see as well as any person is walking the world.' When Martin and Mary Doul, a weather-beaten pair of blind beggars, hear that a saint is going round the countryside curing people with water from this well, they look forward to seeing at last the beautiful couple they believe themselves to be; the play begins as an ache of longing for physical beauty. But when the miracle has been accomplished and they see their own decrepitude, they quarrel. Then their sight gradually fades away, and, refusing the saint's offer to cure them again, they withdraw into the world of sounds and their own imagination, which has proved less delusive than that of vision. The energy of the play is perhaps provided by the fusion, in Synge's creative mind, of the story of the well of the four beauties (many holy wells are supposed to be able to cure the blind, but here the idea of personal beauty is associated with the common theme) and of the experience of being shown the well by a half-blind man, his guide, another Martin.

So this well, at first known only in the islands and in neighbouring mainland areas, and then perhaps as far afield as Sligo if there is any truth in the story Synge was told, is now famous throughout the world, through his play, and through his book on Aran. It is necessary, for reasons that will become painfully clear, to describe with care what the literary pilgrim will find here.

The setting is precious in itself. This lap of land, with the sheltering hillside curving up from it, seems to attract the spring early; people come here to search for the tiny leaves of shamrock in mid-March, before St Patrick's Day. The green slope above is one of the best places to see the limestone bugle, a great rarity, hardly known in Ireland except from the Aran Islands and two points on the mainland opposite the ends of the island chain, in Connemara and the Burren. It is not well known even here, for it blossoms before the botanical tourists come, at the end of April, when it is a neat square pyramid two or three inches high, of copper-stained or even purplish leaves that hide the intensely blue flowers, as saints hood their heavenly radiance; later it goes slack and is lost among the seedy flush of summer grass.

The church is almost as neighbourly to the houses of Corrúch as they are to each other. A boreen dodges between the cottages on the south of the main road, and as soon as it clears their back-gardens and begins to climb towards Na Craga, one can see the gables of the ruin sticking up among the walls of little fields on the right, just a hundred yards away. A stile in the boreen wall admits one to the first field, which is partly of bare crag from which big blocks have been levered out at some period, and partly of bright green, closely grazed turf. Before crossing the next stile, one should diverge a few paces to the left, and look at a small slab of limestone built into the bottom of the field-wall; it has an oval hollow in its upper surface, half covered by the stones above, and usually there is a little water lodged in it. This is the first of the three holy wells that people 'doing the rounds' here used to visit, but whether this *bullán* is a natural formation or the work of hands I cannot tell. From the stile here the path lies along the top of a low, thick wall, the remaining fragment of a cashel that encircled the monks' little settlement long before all these other walls existed. Twenty steps further along the way is a small upright blackthorn bush, and at its foot among ferns is a round of sky sunk deep into the ground – another holy well, very obscure but not forgotten by at least some of those who perform the *turas* to the church on *Lá Mhuire*, the Feast of the Assumption, and other holy days. This is not *the* well of the four beauties, which is behind the church, but nevertheless, it is of this well that I hear the story, very much as Synge heard it a century ago, of the mother who brought her blind child here in hope of a cure; they both searched for this secretive well, and it was the child who found it first.

From the blackthorn another length of mossy wall, like a low walkway skimming the oddly-shaped, interlocking plots of meadow, leads southwards to a stile into an enclosure which, were it not distinguished by the ruined church within it, would be just another meadow full of wild-flowers. The roof of the church is gone, but the walls, built of large, rough blocks of grey limestone, stand raggedly to waist-height in places and over head-height in others, enclosing a space about nine paces long and four across. One stoops to enter, through the simplest possible Gothic doorway in the north wall, only two foot four inches wide, each side of the head of which is a single stone shaped to the curve. The window-opening in the east gable is a narrow lancet with an ogee'd head, in fifteenth-century style. Below it is a plain stone altar, and on its left a small projecting shelf or bracket carved from a single stone; window, altar and shelf relate as economically and consequentially as successive gestures in a familiar ceremony. In the north wall, near the altar, is a small, lintelled window. The west gable is badly gapped. Looking through it one sees a tall standing-stone about a hundred yards away, and almost (but not exactly) in line with it, another even taller pillar three hundred yards farther off; the horizon profile of Dún Aonghusa on the heights far beyond is again almost, but not quite, on the same significant-looking bearing.

Behind the church the land rises in two close-set steps of two or three feet each, so that the next meadow to the south is at head-height, and a considerable spring fills a rectangular basin at the foot of the little scarp. This is Tobar an Cheathrair Álainn, the Well of the Four Beauties, the official and renowned one, into which visitors throw coins; only the people of the nearest villages know of the other little wells. The rite of the *turas* here involves walking around this well and the church alternately, saying the rosary. The *leaba* or 'bed' of the four beauties adjoins the chapel; it is a low-walled compartment built against the east gable, floored with what look like five gravestones. The islanders regard this as the burial-place of the four saints, and up to a few decades ago men used to sleep in it to obtain a bless-ing before going on a journey or in thanks for recovery from illness; the blacksmith of Fearann an Choirce tells me that he and his brothers Patrick and Colman ('Tiger') King used to sleep here now and again, not for any particular reason but, as it were, as a general spiritual prophylactic. But when O'Donovan visited in 1839 he was told that four flat stones side by side in a field just east of the nearer pillar-stone mark the saints' graves. Those stones are still there, and they look like early Christian graves, but nowadays they are not associated with the four beauties. Micilín Sarah, alchemist and antiquary, did a bit of 'rooting' there once, and found, according to one account, nothing, and according to another, the bones of a seven-foot-tall German teacher from the monastery of the four beauties! The pillar stone itself is a single 'flag' of limestone, about nine feet high and two across. The farther one, which because of the number of intervening field-walls is more easily visited from a *róidín* in Fearann an Choirce than from the church, is even more impressive, being over eleven feet high. They are called Na Spéicí, the spikes, and there is a tradition that the mighty men of old who set them up used to play hurley between them; however, their near-alignment with the church makes it likely that they had some Christ-ian significance. O'Donovan, whose sense of humour was itself rather megalithic, wanted his assistant William Wakeman to inscribe one of them with a lengthy rigmarole in Old Irish and Latin exhorting one to pray for Seaghán Mac Emoind óig mic sen Emoind, Mic Uilliam, Mic Chonchob-hair, Mic Emoind Uí Donnabháin – that is, O'Donovan himself. Wake-man excused himself from the task because of the continuous rain during his visit, but in his sketch of the eastern pillar-stone accompanying the Ordnance Survey Letters, part of this phantom inscription can be seen.

In O'Donnell's *Life of St Colm Cille* an instance of miraculous knowl-edge is recounted:

On a time Colm Cille went to visit Ara of the Saints where dwelt Enda of Ara and many other holy men. And it happed that he and the other saints aforementioned were saying their hours and their prayers as they made the round of the church-yards of Ara. And they saw a very ancient tomb, and a passing great and unmove-able stone thereon. And the saints marvelled greatly at the age of the tomb and the size of the stone. And Saint Baithin that was with Colm Cille asked the saints of the place who it was that was buried in that tomb.

'That know we not,' say they, 'nor have we heard who is buried therein.'

But he to whom naught was concealed that had befallen or should befall, to wit, Colm Cille, did make an answer to them and say:

'I know who is buried here,' saith he. 'On a time there came an abbot of Jerusalem to sojourn with the saints of Erin, by reason of renown of their faith and their good works, and by reason of the rigor of their rule and of their lives. And he came by adventure to this island and he died here. And he it is that is buried under that flagstone.'

And to prove that Colm Cille spake truth, there came an angel of God to bear witness for him before Enda and the other saints. And then Colm Cille uttered this quatrain:

> Let us tarry now, O Baithin,
> Beside Talgaeth, versed in psalms.
> Let us tarry there till morn,
> With the abbot of Jerusalem.

The location of this tomb is not stated, but an island tradition puts it a few paces west of the church of the four beauties, where there are some stones that look like the foundations of a small building. Seán Gillan, the last of the story-tellers of Aran, gave me a very circumstantial account of its discovery, which perhaps owes something to the reports of Micilín Sarah's archaeology. If I understood his Fearann-an-Choirce Irish correctly, it seems that so many monks came to St Enda's monastery that they were starving, for whenever one of them celebrated Mass they all had to fast for twenty-four hours. So, to give them 'fair play', Enda set out with them to find a new site for a monastery, and they came to this spot at Corrúch. Enda's only reservation about the place was this grave close by, for he didn't know whether a pagan or a Catholic was buried in it. But Colm Cille told him that it was indeed a Catholic, in fact a priest, and that he was seven feet tall and had been there for 350 years, and that he was so-and-so the Abbot of Jerusalem. 'How would you know that?' asked Enda, 'I'm older than you and I don't know that!' 'Well if you don't believe me,' said Colm, 'write to the Pope and ask him the name of the Abbot of Jerusalem 350 years ago, and you'll see that I'm right.' So they wrote, and a year later they got a reply, and Colm Cille was proved right.

No angelic witness here, just common-sense second sight, and the sort of postal service you'd expect in an out-of-the-way corner of Christendom. In fact the legendary associations of this place, which in the Middle Ages were evidently widespread, have long folded in their wings and nestled down into homeliness. Fursu's feverish vision, in which the world appears below him as a dark valley between two fires, and Brendan's wanderings on fantastic oceans, both have come to earth in this mild hollow, landlocked away from too much sea or sky. Pilgrims no longer walk from Sligo for the water of the Well of the Four Beauties, nor is it carried by itinerant holy men through the glens of Wicklow as in Synge's play. Similarly the various sorts of beauty associated with this site have settled over the centuries into something native and villagey; instead of the beauty of the lustful female that the medieval misogynists feared as the snares of Hell, or the beauty of the saint that both reveals his purity to the world and provokes danger to his soul, we have old blind Martin, Synge's guide and creation, thinking more than he should about the young girls. Nowadays, the monks long gone, the world is as much at home in the church as is the church in the world; the sun and rain bring out the wild flowers within the shelter of its walls perhaps even earlier than those outside. The wrens creeping like mice in the crevices of the field-walls around it point out the domestic scale of the church and its surroundings; all that I have described, apart from the far-off pillar-stones, can be walked round in a few minutes. Beauty has gathered like moss, quietly subsuming the ruins of exorbitant spirituality and extravagant legend.

And yet the quietude of this beauty gives it an edge of poignancy; one holds one's breath for its life. I wrote that there are wild-flowers within the walls; that is no longer so, and the interior is floored in crunchy gravel. The Office of Public Works has taken the site into its well-meaning but clumsy hands, and placed a cattle-grid before the door, so that one can no longer enter without a clatter. Previously, I suppose, the cattle were kept out by a few twigs of thorn, or if they did get in they kept the grass from growing too rank, and nobody minded the mess. But that will not do, now that hundreds of visitors come to see what they have read of in Synge, in my own maps, in countless touristic handouts. Whenever I think of revisiting the church, I fear to find a tarmacadamed path driven through the little fields, and the stiles replaced by iron gates, for the rough little old ways I have described will not bear the traffic of today. We are too many; what is to be done? This quarter-acre of stones is as vulnerable as a porcelain cup left out on the road. Beauty flirts recklessly with destruction; even a book like this can only risk an attempt at beauty because it can be wrapped away like a cup in the ruggy stuff of fact and learned reference. But the book is perhaps the only sanctuary. All I can do is to point out what is there, and in so doing preserve, at least, an image of it.

THE BED OF DIARMAID AND GRÁINNE

Gráinne, the daughter of King Cormac Mac Art, was to marry Fionn Mac Cumhaill, chief of the king's warrior-band, the Fianna. But during the feast celebrating her arrival at Tara she set her eyes on one of Fionn's followers. 'Who is that sweet-voiced, freckled man with the berry-black curls and the glowing cheeks sitting next to Oisín?' she said to her neighbour at the table.

'That is Diarmaid ua Duibhne, the greatest lover of women in the whole world,' she was told. So Gráinne filled a drinking-cup and had her hand-maiden pass it to Fionn and others of the heroes, and a deep sleep fell on them. Then she went and sat between Oisín and Diarmaid, and said, 'I wonder that Fionn, old enough to be my father, should ask a woman like me to be his wife; it would be fitter for me to get a man of my own sort.' 'Don't say that, Gráinne,' said Oisín; 'If Fionn heard you he wouldn't have you, nor would he let anyone else have you.' 'Would you be my protector, Oisín?' asked Gráinne. Oisín answered, 'I would not. A woman who would lie with Fionn, I wouldn't bother with.' 'Would you be my protector, Diarmaid?' asked Grainne. 'I would not,' answered Diarmaid; 'I would have nothing to do with a woman who would lie with Fionn and Oisín.' 'Well,' said she, 'I put a *geis* (a magical obligation) on you, that unless you take me with you out of this house tonight before Fionn wakes, you will not be a true hero.' Then Gráinne went away, and Diarmaid said to Oisín, 'What shall I do about this *geis* that's put on me?' 'You are not responsible for the *geis*,' said Oisín, 'and I say you should follow Gráinne. But beware of Fionn's anger.'

So Diarmaid parted with his comrades, and many tears were shed. To Gráinne he said, 'Ours is a bad journey. It would be better for you to be with Fionn than with me, and I do not know where in Ireland I will take you.' 'I will not part from you until death parts me from you,' said she. 'Well, walk on then,' he answered.

They stole Gráinne's father's chariot and two horses, and fled to Athlone on the Shannon; there they left the chariot in the ford and a horse on either bank, and they walked a mile westwards in the current, and stepped ashore on the Connacht side. That night Diarmaid felled the heart of an oak-wood and built a rampart with seven doors out of the timber, and made a bed of reeds for Gráinne in the middle, and watched over her as she slept. But Fionn's trackers soon found them, and his warriors surrounded their fort. Diarmaid came out in sight of them and kissed Gráinne three times to make Fionn jealous. Then Diarmaid's foster-father, the god Aonghas, came with the speed of the wind from Newgrange, and carried Gráinne to safety in his cloak, but Diarmaid remained to face his destiny. He went from door to door of the fort, asking who was outside. At each door one of his old comrades named himself and promised that Diarmaid would not be harmed if he came out that way, but because Diarmaid did not wish to draw Fionn's anger on any of them he did not come out until he found the door at which Fionn was waiting to kill him. That door he opened, and pole-vaulted on his spear over the heads of Fionn and his men, and put his shield on his back and ran to where Gráinne was hidden. And

Gráinne's heart nearly leapt out of her mouth with joy when she saw him.

The next morning Aonghas advised Diarmaid how to avoid capture. 'Do not climb into any tree with a single trunk or go into any cave with a single entrance or land on any island with a single harbour. Wherever you cook, do not eat there. Wherever you eat, do not sleep there. And wherever you lie down at night, do not be there in the morning.' In that manner the lovers travelled all over Ireland, pursued by Fionn, and eventually they came to Aran. There, as at all their resting-places, they made a bed out of huge slabs of stone; Diarmaid carried the two side-stones under his oxters, and Gráinne brought up the cap-stone in her apron. And Gráinne watched over Diarmaid as he slept:

> *Cotail becán becán bec,*
> *úair ní hecail duit a bec,*
> *a gille día tardus seirc,*
> *a meic uí Duibne, a Díarmait...*

> Sleep a little little bit,
> A little sleep will do no harm,
> O youth to whom I give my love,
> Diarmaid son of Duibhne.

> Sleep a moment sweetly here,
> By the water of this well,
> While I guard my Diarmaid,
> Foam of the wind-blown lake.

> O playboy of the western world,
> I will watch for you tonight.
> For us to part would hurt as much
> As parting of soul and body.

> In the east the stag is wakeful,
> Bellowing through the night;
> Although he's in the blackbirds' wood
> He does not think of sleeping.

> The hornless doe is not asleep
> But leaping through the bushes;
> Leaving her unslept-in lair,
> She's bleating for her speckled fawn.

> Instead of sleeping in their trees
> The birds are noisy in the woods;
> Instead of sleeping on the bank
> The duck is swimming on the lake.

The curlews do not sleep tonight
On the stormy mountainside,
But their cries are sweet and clear
Wakeful between the torrents.

Before dawn they were on the move again, hunted on towards the rest of their story: long wanderings and many escapes, Fionn's eventual resignation to his loss, the birth of their children, Diarmaid's death when Fionn delayed in bringing him a healing drink of water, and Gráinne's eventual marriage with Fionn, at which the Fianna mocked them both and she hung her head in shame. The spirit of the warrior band was broken by this adventure. Oisín went off with his own love to the Land of Youth, and when he returned he found that the Fianna were extinct and a dwarfish race had inherited the earth. He met St Patrick and told him all the deeds of his lost companions. That is how we know of the Hunting of Diarmaid and Gráinne.

In fact the legend does not state that the runaways came to Aran, but on the shoulder of the plateau above Corrúch is an ancient compilation of stone called Leaba Dhiarmada 'is Ghráinne, the Bed of Diarmaid and Gráinne. There are hundreds of such 'beds' in Ireland; some are just curious formations of boulders thrown together by nature, but most, like this one, are the ruins of megalithic tombs. The story that seemed to account for these enigmatic structures is still well known, and some Araners have not relinquished belief in Diarmaid and Gráinne; one old man wanted me to tell him how they travelled to the island. (The folksy details of how the gigantic couple collected huge slabs of stone to make their beds, that I have inserted into the medieval tale, I heard from a farmer in the Burren who had such a tomb on his land.)

Fionn, Diarmaid, Gráinne and the rest were all Celtic deities once, until rawly Christianized monks fresh out of the woods of paganism recast their myths as hero-tales, and they acquired the ambiguous passions and distressed loyalties that make them not much more or less incomprehensible than ourselves. Compared to such storm-driven wraiths, the solid beings who built tombs like the one above Corrúch are difficult to grasp. But the flown chrysalis of Stone-Age humanity is here on the hilltop; we can at least look into it, and speculate.

The easiest ascent to the tomb is by the boreen running up past the Church of the Four Beauties. The slope of fields above the church is known as Na Clocháin from the ruined stone huts there; I had better glance at them in passing as I shall not return this way. On the west of the path is Clochán an Phúca, the hut of the púca, which used to be a mass of fallen stone, confused but with potential, until in the 'seventies the Office of Public Works set its local employees, unsupervised, to tidying it up, which they did with a will. The 'linders' or beam-like stones that had formed its roof were too heavy to lift out, so they sledge-hammered them; traces of a partition-wall dividing its interior into two rooms (a rather unusual feature recorded in a plan made for the Ordnance Survey in 1840) were swept away, and all the bits and pieces arranged neatly around the perimeter, making the exterior walls an impressive eight feet thick instead of about three. One field away to the north-west of this *clochán* is a roofless rectangular ruin which has also been eviscerated by its conservators. Two chunks of carved stone lying on one of its walls can be fitted together to make the top of a Gothic window with two small trefoil-headed lights, which suggested to John Goulden that this building was perhaps Cill na Manach, the 'lost church of Aran' so many antiquarians have tried to locate. On the other side of the track and above a further little scarp of the hillside is some utterly confounded structure; it looks as if a small roundish field has been filled wall-high with stones. A local man who did some 'rooting' here tells me he saw plastered masonry and windows with lintels down among the wreckage. Fr Killeen thought this was 'a dun destroyed in an act of war', but the Rev. Kilbride regarded it as 'a *coenobium* of a colony of monks'. Indeed these and a few other even obscurer ruins of the area may well have been associated with the ecclesiastical settlement below.

A few dozen yards beyond the point at which the boreen levels out onto the plateau of Na Craga there is a narrow turning to the west, a *róidín* running between high ivy-clad walls, of which those on the right are supposed to be part of 'a cashel of about sixty feet in diameter' recorded by Kilbride in the 1860s – but I cannot make out anything of it now. This tiny, twisty way is called Bóithrín an Dúin Bhig, the boreen of the little fort, not from this *dún* but from another quite substantial one on the north-west shoulder of the plateau, a few hundred yards farther on. But before one comes to that, the jutting uprights of the megalithic tomb appear against the sky, on a knoll in a field to the right. One's first impression is of something empty, skull-like, staring westwards.

On nearer approach, it looks like a small flat-roofed hut built out of rectangular slabs of limestone – the sort of slabs that are to be had in plenty here, as a glance around the half-barren field confirms. Four slabs set on edge make two side-walls three to four feet high, another slab closes the eastern end, the roof is of three slabs laid across, the western end is open. Along the south side and close to it, five pillar-like stones up to five feet high form an outer wall. I notice that nearly all the main slabs have a distinctive veneer of another mineral on one face – chert, perhaps; I forgot to bring home a sample – indicating that they were all levered out of the same stratum, which an exploration of the immediate neighbourhood would probably identify. The opening is three foot four inches high and four foot six wide; one could creep into it and lie down, for the compartment is about eight feet long. At the other end it is only two foot six high and two foot nine wide. Originally the entrance would have been closed with another flagstone and the whole thing buried in a cairn of stones and earth; in fact there are traces of a mound on the south of the tomb. One feels that the open, larger end is the front. Thus the tomb looks westwards across lowlands and three far-separated villages, to the opposite hillside and Dún Aonghasa.

There has never been an archaeological investigation of this tomb, though its structure was carefully recorded in the 1960s by Dr Ruaidhrí de Valera and Seán Ó Nualláin and it figures as no. 21 in Vol. III of their monumental *Survey of the Megalithic Tombs of Ireland.* Indeed it is possible that excavation would reveal little or nothing about the people who built it or their reasons for doing so. J.T. O'Flaherty in the 1830s would have identified this table-like construction as a Druidical altar; the Rev. Kilbride in the 1860s saw it as what he called a *ligaitreabh* or 'pillar-house'. In calling it a tomb I am already assimilating it to concepts that have been evolved out of generations of consideration of hundreds of similar structures elsewhere in Ireland and farther afield. To approach these particular stones with understanding one has first to step back, through generalization and classification.

In the first volume of their great work de Valera and Ó Nualláin proposed a division of Irish megalithic tombs into four categories, which have proved sturdy enough to withstand some recent battering. Passage Graves, of which the vast tumulus of Newgrange in the Boyne valley is the best-known example, consist of a passage leading into a burial chamber, the whole usually buried in a round mound. Portal Dolmens are the dolmens of romantic Ireland, with a single chamber formed of a cap-stone – sometimes a huge boulder – perched on three or more uprights, of which the front pair, the portals, are the tallest. Court Cairns have one or more suites or 'galleries' each of two or more chambers, covered by a long cairn and entered from one or more open courtyards defined by upright stones. And the Wedge-shaped Gallery Graves have one main chamber, sometimes with a small portico or antechamber and a small closed rear chamber, and usually decreasing in height and width from front to rear. Nowadays archaeologists refer to these classes as passage, portal, court, and wedge tombs.

So what we have in Corrúch is a simple type of wedge tomb. The act of classification immediately opens up questions of distribution, affinities, origins. All the identifiable mgalithic tombs in the Aran Islands are of this type: one in Inis Oírr, reduced to hardly more than a low outline; one collapsed but still impressive, and another so ruinous it is difficult to be sure about, in Inis Meáin; this one, the best-preserved, in Corrúch, and another halfway down the hillside north of Oatquarter. (This last is so obscurely tucked into an overgrown corner of a field, of whose walls its stones form part, that although O'Donovan saw or heard of it in 1839 it was not located until 1980, when I came across it, just too late to include it on my revised map, and right beside a path we had taken a hundred times before on our evening strolls.) Farther afield, there are about seventy wedge tombs in the Burren, some of them fifteen or more feet long and very simply constructed out of a few enormous slabs. Other notable concentrations of wedge tombs are in Sligo and north-east Mayo, east Clare and west Tipperary, and west Cork. In all there are about five hundred in Ireland, and their builders clearly preferred uplands of sandstone or limestone with thin, well-drained soil-cover, rather than the danker shale-lands and the lush river valleys. Such areas would have been only lightly wooded and were easily cleared by axe or fire to create grazing land; the wedge-tomb builders were primarily pastoralists rather than tillers of the soil.

Although some twenty-three wedge tombs have been excavated in recent years, in only three cases has material been found in them that could be radio-carbon dated and definitely associated with the primary period of use of the tomb. A small wedge tomb rather similar to the Corrúch one in the townland of Altar near Schull in Cork was excavated by a team from University College, Cork, in 1989; hardly enough human material to make a handful was found, but among the tiny scraps of cremated bone was one unburned tooth, and this proved to date from between 2316 and 1784 BC. The consensus is that wedge tombs were being built from about 2500 to 1700 or perhaps 1500 BC; this means that they span the last centuries of the neolithic period and the early Bronze Age – a time as progressive as that of the initiation of settlement and tillage in the early Neolithic around 4000 BC. It is known that copper was mined in Munster and traded throughout Ireland and to Britain; for instance there are primitive workings on Mount Gabriel in Cork dating from the end of the neolithic. Perhaps the tombs should be associated with a brief 'Copper Age' preceding the decisive technological advance to the use of bronze, a mixture of copper and tin. (Copper is easily mined and extracted from its ore but is rather soft unless mixed with tin; but tin is not to be found in Ireland, and in fact there was a trans-European trade in Cornish tin.) But if the wedge-builders were probably among the earliest metal-workers in Ireland, it seems that the occasional bronze axe-head or copper ingot that has been found in a tomb was placed there as part of a ritual deposit, a votive offering, perhaps long after the use of the tomb for burial had ceased, for the Bronze Age adopted a new rite of single burials in small stone-lined pits or cists, as opposed to the grand communal tombs of neolithic times. But long after the original function of the tombs had been forgotten they preserved something of the numinous, as they do to this day, which suggested other ritual uses for them. Thus the Altar tomb was used as late as AD 124-224, in the Iron Age, for the deposition of offerings of sea-food. In what we might call our own era some of them served as mass rocks in the seventeenth century, when Catholic priests had to minister to their flocks in secret and celebrate the sacraments in hidden places; hence the name of the townland, Altar, in which the tomb near Schull stands. A lady from the Burren told me that when she was a child the St John's Eve bonfire was lit on the top of a huge wedge tomb near her house, and she heard the great roof-flag crack; so one could say that this wedge was indeed a druidical fire-altar only fifty years ago. They have also had their secular uses. Several in the Burren were inhabited until late in the last century; I have read of a doctor visiting a woman in childbirth who was living with her family and their cow in a tomb near Kilnaboy. Another one in the Burren, that the Megalithic Survey missed, had a little door fitted and was in use as a goose-pen in the 1960s. All this usage and reusage means that the structures have been repeatedly robbed or refurbished or spring-cleaned, and that whatever happens to be found in them today probably has nothing to do with the original builders.

In the heyday of the Megalithic Survey an attractively clearcut picture of the origins of the wedge-tomb builders emerged. There are in Brittany fifty or so tombs rather similar to the wedge tombs of Ireland, called *allées couvertes*, and this fact, together with the predominantly western and in particular south-western distribution of the Irish wedge tombs suggested that their builders first entered the country from Brittany, occupying the peninsulas of Cork and Kerry, and from there spreading northwards and later eastwards, settling wherever they discovered pasturage to their liking. More recently it has been proposed that the wedge tombs evolved from the Irish court tombs, which are mainly found in the northern half of the country, and spread thence to the south and west. Few archaeologists would be dogmatic on the question nowadays.

One important difference between the *allées couvertes* and the wedge tombs is that the former generally face east and the latter almost invariably west to south-west. When I took Professor Rynne of UCG to see the wedge tomb in Fearann an Choirce, he climbed up on top of it and delivered an impromptu burlesque lecture, to myself and a stray dog who was accompanying us, on the abiding cultural differences between the laborious

Breton peasant, up every morning in time to pay his respects to the rising sun, and the convivial Irishman rolling home rejoicing in the glow of sunset. Undoubtedly the west had some significance for the wedge-tomb builders which it did not for those of the earlier types of megalithic tomb; Newgrange, with its long passage and burial-chamber briefly probed by the rising sun at the winter solstice, represents some belief perhaps of the identity of death and rebirth, but the west does not enter into it; court tombs, which were evidently the sites of funerary ceremonial, are often aligned to the north, and portal tombs to the east. But it is this people who, whether they came from Brittany or from Britain through northern Ireland, eventually colonized the west, turned their gaze to the horizon under which all the lights of the sky disappear, the threshold of a region into which no human can penetrate, in this life at least. Perhaps only those who move on until they live on the western edge of the world can feel this dire fascination of the forbidden compass-bearing. The Celts of the Iron Age, or at least those of them who, having wandered or been driven out of the depths of Eurasia, arrived at the ocean wall, situated their Tír na nÓg, their land of youth, beyond the Atlantic horizon. Aftercomers, even the most recent blow-ins like myself, even if we know nothing of the beliefs and rituals of the wedge-folk, feel the pull of magnetic west in our bones. America counts for nothing in this European mind-set; America is only what Columbus thought to find, the nether edge of the farthest East.

Westwardness entrains the drift of this book like a quiet but irresistable undertow. From the Bed of Diarmaid and Gráinne I can look ahead and scan the lowlands I will soon descend into, the waist between Port Mhuirbhigh on the north and the bay at Gort na gCapall on the south, which almost severs the farther, ultra-western, third of the island. Diarmaid and Gráinne themselves, sitting here of an evening in a time-dimension oblique to that of history, could see not only the valley but all that has happened and will happen in it. On the opposite skyline, files of men carry stones to build the ramparts of Dún Aonghasa, and flocks of tourists toil up the hill to admire their work. Lower down, a rain-soaked Dublin architect is directing the transformation of a thatched cottage into Kilmurvey House. On the main road coming up from Port Mhuirbhigh two saints quarrel over the division of the island; one of them is on horseback and the other has welded the horse's hooves to the ground. Near the southern shore a Beartlaiméid Ó Flaithbheartaigh is founding the village of Gort na gCapall, and his great-great-great-great-grandson, Liam O'Flaherty, is skipping across the crags to Oatquarter School while writing his first story in his head. Archaeologists are fossicking around their bed; the lovers rise with a sigh — they are bigger than anyone we have ever seen, but without the crude bulk and pitted skins of giants; they are immaculately beautiful – and begin to make their way towards their next resting-place. But they dare not enter the last third of the island, which is too near to being an island with only one harbour. At all costs they must avoid being trapped against the unclimbable wall of westernness.

MODALITIES OF ROUGHNESS

Very nearly all of the next townland, Cill Mhuirbhigh or Kilmurvy, is visible from the megalithic tomb that looks out across it like an empty eye-socket of the hillside; the nearer boundary is a narrow slot of a gully running across the slope below and about fifty yards west of the tomb, and the farther one, two miles away, is only just behind the skyline of the opposite rise. The three villages in the intervening lowlands are far apart; one can trace their interlinking roads by the lines of telegraph-poles, thin as insects' legs from here. Fearann an Choirce or Oatquarter – it is the only Aran village to have an English name that is not just the Irish one anglicized, *i.e.* misspelt – begins close by to the north-west, its nearest houses hidden by the last shoulder of the plateau and the further ones coming into view as they straggle down the main road towards the bay. Gort na gCapall is near the south coast in a slight hollow, a very inadequate-seeming shelter against the Atlantic, which in certain lights appears from here to rise steeply behind it or even lean over it menacingly. Cill Mhuirbhigh village itself is far off, near the north coast, with Kilmurvey House (which spells itself with an 'e') a little aloof from it, withdrawn into the greyness of the hillside beyond. The terrain embracing these three villages is arranged like a vast amphitheatre facing north and focused on the bay of Port Mhuirbhigh. A crescent of dunes rims the beach, then there comes a broad green arc of big fields belonging to Kilmurvey House, and around that a mosaic of tiny pastures and tillage plots belonging to the smallholders of the townland. A cliff of ten to twenty feet wraps itself with a rugged tenderness around all this good land, and the wide terrace of almost uninterrupted grey rock above it curves like an immense battered horseshoe from Cill Mhuirbhigh village, south to Gort na gCapall and then north again to Fearann an Choirce. Above that is another cliff and an even wider horseshoe terrace, this one of craggy land a little more hospitable than the one below and therefore criss-crossed by walls, with the Atlantic taking a bite out of it on the south. Finally a tumble of tip-tilted fields at one's feet here on the east, answering to a similar slope closing the vista to the west.

The end of the terrace below the tomb and overlooking the village of Oatquarter is called An Scairbh, the rough place. And since I was for a dozen years a besotted Oatquarterite, courting moods that echoed well off stone, I know the modalities of its roughness intimately. I used to browse from field to field here as if leafing through a well-loved anthology, or find myself caught wordless in the middle of a page by the disappearance of a question-mark, a lizard's tail, into the margin. If the text frequently held me up with obscurities, long practice gave me great fluency in its grammar, though perhaps memory flatters in showing me drifting across this terrain as little impeded by stones and thorns as a cloud-shadow. So now, although I could return to Corrúch by the boreens and follow the main road to the village, I prefer to work my way down to it across An Scairbh, from the point this itinerary has reached, despite the weird impracticability of the route.

Just a hundred yards west of the Bed of Diarmaid and Gráinne – a hundred yards that involves crossing five field-walls and the little ravine of the townland boundary – is An Dún Beag, the small fort. Its rampart is reduced to a knee-high bank with a more recent field-wall on top of it, enclosing an oval space about seventy yards long and half that across, divided into three fields full of rank grass and brambles. Given its strategic, even precarious, perch on the brink of the steep slope falling north and west from it, this was no mere cattle-yard. I am told that it had a *chevaux-de-frise* of stone spikes on this slope until the Dirranes, the principal family of the village below, took them to build walls; how long ago this is supposed to have happened I do not know, but none of the nineteenth-century antiquarians noted any such feature.

A few fields below the fort is a big stony, brambly mound that looks like a collapsed *clochán*, from the vicinity of which a narrow, many-elbowed path makes a relatively sensible north-westward descent to the village. But that is not the route I am taking; instead I scramble down south-westwards from the *dún* and drop into a steep-sided ravine full of chest-high hazel-scrub. When one of the villagers first told me that there was a wood a mile long on this hillside I was incredulous, but it is true, or nearly true; the area of scrub is only ten or fifteen feet wide, but it is half a mile long at least and was probably once longer. It fills the ravine, which runs southwards, with the jointing of the underlying rock, until interrupted by an embankment where Bóthar na gCrag descends from the uplands. This wood is called simply and uniquely An Choill, the wood. According to J.T. O'Flaherty, among the many reminders of druidism on Aran are 'evident vestiges of oak groves'. That was an antiquarian's fantasy even in his time. Even in the days of the magnificent oak-forests of Celtic Europe, where the dim, lofty, sacred grove, the *nemeton*, prefigured the Gothic cathedrals, in Aran the druids would have had to make do with the equivalent of a little provincial chapel, difficult to stand straight in and with not much oak in its composition; and for centuries even that much woodland has been reduced to a second childhood. I once inveigled M into this toy forest, to savour an Alice-in-Wonderland experience: crouching in it one can look along mossy glades lit with exquisite pale lilac flowers of wood sorrel, and then by straightening up, grow through the canopy to giant stature and see far over the treetops.

There was in fact a giant here once, whose gory legend I took down from old Seán Gillan. He was an O'Flaherty called Pádraic Mór (Big Patrick), who went on the run after the Cromwellian army took the castle of Aircín in 1651, and lived in a cave, or perhaps a cleft with a few flags laid across it, in this ravine, and became known as Fathach na Coille, the giant of the wood. One day his brother came to warn him that the English soldiers had discovered his whereabouts, and the two of them went to live in another cave in a little cliff above the turlough at Gort na gCapall village. Pádraic, although a peaceable man, was a great fighter, whereas his brother, in Seán's words, was only *réasúnta* (reasonable). One day the brother went out to milk the goat, and met an English soldier. 'I'm a soldier as well as you!' said the brother, and they began to fight. The Englishman had a sword of Swedish iron and an armoured vest against which the Irishman's sword bent like a snake, so that he had repeatedly to step back and put his foot on it to straighten it out. Finally he wounded the Englishman in the belly, but the dying soldier seized him by the head and thrust it into the wound, and stifled him in his bowels. A month later, at Christmas, the English soldiers came across Pádraic's footprints in the snow and followed them back to his lair. Pádraic heard the men's footsteps on the flag above his cave, and counted nine of them, and killed them as they appeared one by one in the mouth of the cave. Eventually, however, he was captured by a force of three hundred soldiers, taken as a prisoner to Caisleán Aircín, and there hanged – *'agus sin an deireadh a bhí aige!'* ('and that was the end of him!').

Have I got the horrible details right? Seán's Irish I found difficult to follow, so I took the precaution of writing the tale out in English as I had understood it, for him to read and check; later he told me that my version was correct, but I cannot find it now, and there are some obscurities in what notes I can unearth – a pike with a hook for pulling a man off a horse entered into it somehow, and whether it was the brother who smothered the soldier in his bowels or vice versa I am not sure. The two or three other islanders who had heard something of Pádraic Mór always referred me to Seán, the last of the storytellers; but Seán is now dead and I fear that what I have put down here is as much as survives of this legend. Is it only a legend? Very likely there were O'Flaherty fugitives on the island after the defeat of 1651, but the incident of the sword that bent like a snake (I remember Seán's vigorous mimicry in describing it) sounds like an echo from the Bronze Age, from that mysterious Copper Age of the wedge-tomb builders, even. The Giant of the Wood may have been an outlaw from history for three thousand years before Pádraic Mór joined him in the greenwood shade.

Extricating oneself from An Choill is a matter of working along the clifflet forming its western rim to find some combination of fallen stone and tree-roots and matted ferns by which one can clamber up, and then locating the beginning of a path, about five hundred yards south of the *dún*, that wriggles through the network of field-walls, first west and then south. Bóithrín na Coille, the boreen of the wood, is only about three feet wide, and in any particular year whether it is reasonably passable or arched over by briars that have to be negotiated one by one depends on whether or not Rónán Dan Phatch of Gort na gCapall has cattle in one of the fields it serves, for no one else comes this way. Instead of following it south until it escapes into the wider Bóthar na gCrag, I shall take a minute branch off it to the west, which curls down i..to a nook of the scarp below it. Perfectly named An Poll i' bhFolach, the hole in hiding, in a chill April this sheltery spot is always a week or two more optimistic about the coming of spring than its surroundings. A gleam of water catches the eye; look behind you halfway down the path, and you see the spring-well of Clochán an Airgid with all its attendant flowers that I described, pages back. No, that is impossible, even in a labyrinth; this well faces west, the other east. And indeed on a second look this one is more like the Well of the Four Beauties behind the ruined chapel at Corrúch. The scarp in which these wells are formed is the common factor; on a map it outlines each of the upland areas of the three Arans like a contour. Its profile varies little along its length: the land rises in distinct stages from the flat bare crag at its foot, first in two sharp steps, each of them a limestone stratum about four feet thick, then the clay-band that conducts water to this and to many other springs, and above that a rough hillside not so clearly stratified. This sequence – pavement, two steps, clay-band, hillslope – is instantly recognizable once it has been pointed out (as Conor MacDermot of the Geological Survey pointed it out to me when he was mapping the Aran and Burren limestones), and one meets it again and again, giving a family resemblance to places one would never otherwise have associated with each other, such as the hillside below the second rampart of Dún Aonghasa and that below Túr Mháirtín. The clay-band has the resounding name of the Asbian-Brigantian contact, from the two subdivisions of the Lower Carboniferous respectively below and above it, which can be identified by their fossil contents and rock-chemistry in other parts of Ireland and Britain, the Asbian being so called from Little Asby Scar in Cumbria where it is particularly well exposed, and the Brigantian from the ancient territory of the North British tribe, the Brigantes. The transition from one type of deposit to the other corresponds to a change in the Carboniferous ocean dated at 330 million years before the present, and the presence of clay at this level shows that at that time this was dry land, and for long enough for overlying rocks to be rendered down into soil. So, that glint, catching the attention in the obscurity of 'the hole in hiding', is the cutting edge of a vast discrimination in earth-history.

The path down to the well – hardly more than a sequence of steps worn into the scarp-face – exists for and because of people fetching water to cattle in the fields above; similarly a little path leads out of the walled oasis of green around the well, down the two limestone steps and out onto the open crag, for the convenience of people with cattle in some small fields under the scarp; these two paths then make a secretive short-cut from An Choill, in Brigantia as it were, to An Scairbh, in Asbia, which is no part of their purpose. One alights from this bramble-frought time-tumbling past the 330-million BP mark onto a superb limestone pavement, the best in the islands, so smooth and with such wide intervals between its grykes that a set could be danced on it without fear of broken ankles. Low walls, easily stepped over, divide it into a few areas which, after the poky topography one has fought through above, have the breadth of agoras, piazzas, civic spaces suitable for decorous and convivial rites – utterly deserted, though; one is far off any usual route to anywhere usual here. Often, wandering back home from a walk on the cliffs, M and I used to rest on the crag nearest the well, the level emptiness of which is enhanced by one single powerful presence, a roundish granite boulder four or five feet high. We would lie starwise on the pavement by it and close our eyes and let the sun or the breeze or even the first drops of a rain shower explore our faces. After a few minutes our shoulder-blades would have fused with the limestone and we would be whirled along by the earth's turning, the dynamo that generates all our little norths and souths and easts and wests.

But I soon tire of transcendental flight and start poking about again, questioning the ground I stand on. This remarkable boulder, for instance; it looks as if it were put there to make a point, for it stands like a sculpture on a little pedestal, a natural swelling of the limestone floor. Since there are no other such swellings on this exceptionally level and smooth pavement, this one must be due to the presence of the boulder; it must represent the thickness of limestone that has been dissolved off the rest of the pavement by rain since the boulder arrived to shelter this one spot. In fact the diverted rainwater spilling off the rim of the boulder has excavated a moat a few inches deep all around the pedestal, accentuating it and making it difficult to judge its exact height; however, the bottom of the boulder appears to be about eight inches above the general level of the pavement. There are quite a few 'perched boulders', as such glacial erratics are called, in Aran (but this one is the best), and several have pedestals of that order of height. Hence, in the fifteen thousand years since the melting away of the glaciers that brought them across from granite Connemara, eight inches has been lost off the limestone of Aran. That is an average rate of attrition smaller than the current rate for the Burren, where scientists deduce from the concentration of dissolved calcium carbonate in stream-water that the relief of the area is being lowered by half a millimeter per annum. Perhaps that high figure betrays the pollution of our contemporary world, spreading even into this ocean-washed desert. But the process is not a uniform planing-down of the surface; run-off is directed by unevennesses and irregularities, which themselves are exacerbated by these currents, so that channels grow and coalesce, fissures widen, solidity is sapped and rock is rendered down to rubble. The polish and perfection this crag has attained, a reflection of the petrology of a particular stratum, is a passing phase in its descent to obliteration.

If so much has been erased, do we know what sort of landscape this was, for instance when the first humans moved in, perhaps six thousand years ago? In Connemara, where bogs have been accumulating over much of the time since that period, researchers can reconstruct the history of the flora by identifying the types of pollen-grains preserved at various levels in the acidic peat. This is not so easy in areas without bogs and has not yet been attempted in Aran, but some similar studies have been carried out of pollen from the sediments of lakes in the south-east of the Burren, and most recently from a bog on an isolated patch of shale in the north-west of the Burren, which would include wind-blown pollen from limestone areas almost as exposed as the Aran Islands. In the south-east, Mullaghmore is a famously primeval-looking landscape, but its seemingly immemorial stoniness is a historical phenomenon and developed only after about AD 400. In the Stone Age that area was covered in hazel-woods, with much pine, elm and oak. The elm declined drastically in Ireland at about 3100 BC, just as it has done throughout Europe in our own time, and it may be that something like Dutch elm disease was spread by increased coming and going of humans. In any case the first settlers started thinning the forest about that time; the earliest activity at the great portal tomb of Poulnabrone in the central Burren has recently been dated to about 3000 BC. The large number of wedge tombs in the Burren show how attractive it was to the graziers of from five to fifteen hundred years later, around the end of the Stone Age and the early Bronze Age. The pollen-record from the north-western site does not go back quite so far, but it suggests that as early as 1250 BC the landscape was largely open grassland, and the sorts of weeds present indicate that it was heavily grazed and not much disturbed by tillage. There still were oaks and hazels (the oak is virtually unknown there now), and in the period from AD 200 to 580 the hazel-scrub won back a good deal of the land, owing to some unexplained remission of the pressure of humans and their animals on it, just as is happening now in many areas of the Burren drained by emigration over the last hundred years. Extrapolating all this to the Aran Islands, one can picture the Stone-Age voortreckers arriving here and finding forest, thinner and more dwarfed by exposure than that of the Burren, growing on a soil perfect for cattle-rearing; they probably knew as well as does the Aran man of today that 'limestone puts bone on a beast'. They would have returned to the mainland with the good news, and brought their animals and chattels and gods and diseases across by currach. Since then the battle has mainly gone against the wood; fire and axe and hoof and tooth have stripped the land; rain and wind have carried off the unbound soil. The Iron Age, the feeding of the seven great cashels, if they were contemporaneous, must have depleted the environment, and perhaps by the time the saints arrived the islands were already as Roderic O'Flaherty described them, 'almost paved over with stones, soe as, in some places, nothing is to be seen but large stones with wide openings between them, where cattle break their legs'. Only in this century, on some sheltered hillsides, does the Giant of the Wood increase his holding once more.

That story is at least an attempt to answer the first question posed by the perched boulder, but one is immediately led on to others. There is something of the classroom or examination-hall about the crag this boulder stands in; everything here is well lit, separated out, reduced to essentials, so that if we cannot understand, it is our fault. The boulder itself, pedagogical on its podium, demands clarity of thought: observe this, comment on that, deduce the other. A few long straight fissures draw elementary geometrical figures on the the blackboard-smooth pavement; I stump around and look at them this way up, that way up. What sort of surface was revealed by the removal of the post-glacial soil-cover? Was this pattern of grykes and clints seen by pre-Euclidian eyes?

One fissure at least demonstrates the answer with gratifying rigour. It runs right across the crag for dozens of yards, passing exactly under the boulder and bisecting its pedestal. It is a few inches wide all along its length, but if one lies down and peers under the boulder one can see that just at the top of the pedestal, where not even the gales can blow rain into it, it narrows to a hair's breadth. A textbook exemplar! The fissures have been opened up only since the ground was bared and rainwater began to work its way into the joints of the limestone. At least that is true of most of them; I can think of one, a very wide one on the next terrace below An Scairbh, that is stuffed with glacial till and so must have been open during or before the last Ice Age. Of course the warm spells between the Ice Ages – we may be living in one such – may also have seen erosion and fissuring of the limestone surface, but most traces of that would have been scoured away by the most recent glaciation. And to qualify the thesis further: not all the joints are open yet. Here by the boulder are some grykes that taper to a point and are continued by fine lines that look as if they had been drawn by a stonemason with scriber and steel rule. It is difficult to account for this: on a stratum that looks perfectly level and uniform, why is the joint closed here and open there? A freak of the irregular stripping away of the soil-cover? Or perhaps a joint can remain closed for some time after the baring of the surface, until some chance opens up a bit of its length, after which, because water-flow into the opening would be most concentrated at its advancing corner, the rest of the joint is comparatively rapidly unzipped. The fact that such effects are still legible on the present-day surface shows how tender and newborn it is, and how short will be its life. Once a fissure is open it will widen inexorably as the rainwater swills over its rim; erosion acts fastest on edges and corners, picking off the more exposed molecules, or so I have read in some textbook. But is that what is happening here? Looking around this crag again, I see a joint that is closed along most if its length apart from two or three short stretches, which are full of standing water; when I splash in one of them, the water in another slops and gurgles. So there is an open level of the joint, running underground like a drainpipe; in fact I can peer some way along it and see that only the upper inch or less of the joint is still tight. Solution is taking place from below; the agency is stagnant, not flowing, water. What does this imply about the closed joint running through the boulder pedestal? Science shrugs its shoulders like an Aran man, and looks off into the distance.

However they do it, grykes eat clints. Other things being equal, an area of crag with big clints will also have wide grykes. (Simple, at least on the flowing-water theory: for clints of similar shapes, the rainfall on them is proportional to their areas, *i.e.* to the squares of their perimeters; therefore the run-off per unit length of a perimeter is proportional to its length; therefore longer perimeters are more rapidly eroded.) But 'other things being equal' is not the normal state of affairs in this landscape of entropic dissolution, and in walking it one's footsteps have to learn a vast variety of fissurings, carpet-patterns of the void woven into the rock. Just north of An Poll i' bhFolach the two steps of the 'Asbian-Brigantian contact' form plat-forms running along the hillside, four and eight feet above the terrace on which the boulder perches. The lower platform is so closely divided by par-allel fissures that it consists of large slabs standing on edge, the outer ones leaning and about to fall over onto the terrace below, of a size and shape that the builders of the wedge tomb above would have found handy, while the upper platform is dissected into even thinner blades of stone. It seems that certain strata are predisposed to fissuring in particular patterns. A geol-ogist, David Langridge, explored this question for his M.Sc. dissertation in 1969. He roughly classified the types of pavement by the average width of the clints (measured between the north-south grykes, which are nearly everywhere the best developed). Pavements for which this measure was less than 45 cm are nearly all on the uppermost stratum of the island, where they cover most of its exposure; this is the regularity that underlies the monotonous terrain of Na Craga. At the other extreme, pavements with clints over 105 cm wide occur principally on the terrace below An Scairbh. Broken, rubbly surfaces in which clints and grykes are scarcely definable are found mainly on the lowest levels of the island. These patterns of jointing reflect the interplay of stresses in the earth's crust with the strengths of par-ticular strata, which in turn depend on their thicknesses and composition, and so the question is plunged back into the sea in which these strata were deposited, its depth, temperature, chemistry, fauna and flora – matters not beyond all conjecture, and which I quit with a certain sense of duty unful-filled.

Making my way northwards from the crag of the perched boulder towards Oatquarter, I pass over several strikingly different ground-patterns developed on the same terrace; those answers from the Carboniferous sea-depths, even if I had them, would not explain this. The most tremendous of these terrains – probably the most tremendous in Aran – is a three- or four-acre crag called Leacrachaí an Fháin, the flagstones of the slope. Here the surface is riven by gullies six or ten feet deep, full of grass and heather, into a number of ridges only a few yards wide and several hundred yards long, aligned with the usual north-south major set of joints and interrupted here and there by smaller crosswise gullies following the minor joints. These ridges have bevelled edges and smoothly undulating tops; they rise and fall by two or three feet in waves thirty to forty yards long from crest to crest. The gullies are explicable: the ice-flow, coinciding in direction with master joints, has plucked out blocks of stone one after another. But the whale-back ridges? I thought I had the explanation when I noticed that here, in addition to the usual north-south set of joints, there is another set crossing them at an angle of only a few degrees; if there is some regular variation in the lateral spacing of joints in each of these sets, their intersections would tend to be closer together in certain zones evenly spaced out along the ridges, and these zones would be more vulnerable to erosion than the intervals between them. However, I think my simplistic geometry is inadequate to the elemental mix of rule and randomness in this topography. It must have been the Ice Age that moulded these ridges. Passing across this part of the island, the glacier danced a little. Why? Science answers, 'You wouldn't know!'

From the next crag to the north, a little path, Bóithrín na Scairbhe, the boreen of the rough place, leads down to the village, between greener, more humanized, patches of land reclaimed from the rock. But before I leave the geo-illogical uplands, the typical north-south bent of this boreen prompts me to ask one more question of the ground. What caused the characteristic pattern of the jointing, from which that of the grykes derives, and thence that of the fields and paths? What is the origin of this direction I have called 'Aran North', this prevailing wind in the stone? The major jointing in the Burren is parallel to that in Aran, and what attempts at explanation of it I have read are in terms of compressive forces emanating from the south during the phase of earth-history known as the Hercynian, when the Harz mountains, in ancient Hercynia, were born, and here the Carboniferous sea-bed was being lifted. But such a force would not give rise to north-south jointing; also, I am told, the limestones of north Mayo are jointed with the same orientation, and that is near the limit of Hercynian influences. Paul Mohr, the professor of Geology at Galway, whom I pester with these questions, has wondered if this regional effect is connected with a major tectonic event more recent than the Carboniferous: the parting of Europe and North America and the opening-up of the Atlantic in Jurassic times, two hundred to a hundred and fifty million years ago. Such a gigantic rifting would have exerted huge tensions on the lands to either side. A mere speculation, he insists, he never dared to publish it. Well, there it is now, for daws to peck at. It appeals to me, for if it is true, then the Aran farmer in his boreen, and this book in its devious criss-crossing of the island, are walking arm-in-arm with the Atlantic and talking of the break-up of Pangaea.

THE BLOOD OF THE HEART

Long ago, as I have been told by one of the elders of the village, a man from
Fearann an Choirce travelled as far as Athenry looking for a calf with the
makings of a good cow. When he had been walking about that neighbourhood all day, he met a woman carrying a wooden firkin of water and asked
her if she would give him a drink of it. 'Gladly,' she replied, 'And I guarantee you never drank better, unless you ever tasted the water of Tobar
Ghrióir in Árainn.' 'Why!' said the islander, 'That's the water I've been
making my tea on all my life!'

Tobar Ghrióir, Gregory's well, the pride, the very source itself, of the
village, is under the scarp of An Scairbh where the road twists north to
climb down it. The villagers revert to its water when the piped supply fails
for some mechanical reason or tastes salty after a gale; I have filled many a
bucket there myself, when helping out at the nearby guest-house, Gilbert
Cottage. After long droughts the flow is a mere seepage, but if you pluck
one of the stiff fronds of hart's-tongue fern that grow by it, fold it length-
wise and jam it into a crack of the wet rock-face, water will come rolling
off its point like pearls off a broken thread. There are two stone-lined
troughs built against the foot of the scarp, a long one to which beasts wandering the road have access, and a small one reserved for humans, defended
by a little wall with a stile in it and tucked into the corner between the scarp
and the ramp of the road. A fool washed out an oil-barrel in it once, and
Bríd Gillan, an outspoken octogenarian living nearby, took a can of white
paint and wrote on the rock-face above it, 'God gave us this well – keep it
clean.' Twelve years later, I notice, just enough of this lettering shows
through the mosaic of mosses, lichens and ferns to give the rock an air of
cryptic significance.

Water, shelter, a little soil from the shale-band – the usual 'givens' of the
scarp-faces, the usual narrow dispensation of natural treasures – have been
repaid by generations of unstinted labour here, so that the village, starting
at the foot of the slope by the well and accompanying the road westwards
for a few hundred yards, is a green respite from the grey barrenness above
and below it. The cottages and houses and bungalows are interspersed with
hayfields, potato-plots and pastures, nearly all of them on what is called
'reclaimed land'. (The term 'reclamation' seems to imply the winning back
of something lost, but if anyone ever squandered aboriginal soil here it

must have been a thousand or two thousand years ago.) *Stócáil* ('to stoke' or 'to prepare', according to the dictionaries) is the local word for the process of making fertile land out of bare or nearly bare rock. The method is as follows. First the plot is cleared of loose blocks, which are piled into stacks or used to build walls. The grykes are filled in with small stones, and the smooth clint surfaces broken up with a sledge-hammer or by dropping a boulder on them. Then the ground is spread with basketsful of sand and seaweed carried up from the shore, supplemented sometimes by shale or clay scraped out from under the scarps and little winnings of soil and turf accumulated along walls or scooped up from fissures. A potato crop can be grown in the first year on such a mixture, and the depth of soil increases as more sand and seaweed is added year by year.

The earliest description of the process I have come across is in Samuel Ferguson's account of his visit to Aran in 1852, shortly after the Great Famine:

Re-entering among the rocks, we passed through another village, the pathway to which runs between enclosures apparently of a very unprofitable kind; for, in several cases, the only thing enclosed is the bare surface of limestone, no earth having yet been laid down; and, when earth does occur, it is wholly adventitious, having been carried from a great distance and spread upon the rock. Yet these patches of fictitious soil yield very good crops of oats and potatoes. ... This practice of forming artificial fields, recalls the Fir-Volgic origin of the early inhabitants of Arran. ... These Fir-Volg, according to their own account, were Thracians, who had been enslaved in Greece, and there employed in carrying earth in leathern bags, to form the artificial terrace-gardens of Boeotia.

This agreement of contemporary practice with ancient origin-legend appealed to the nationalist antiquarianism of Ferguson's time. However, it seems likely that land reclamation became important only as food demand outgrew the capacity of the indigenous soils under the scarps and on Na Craga, during the generations of rapid population growth leading up to the Famine. Most of the new land would have been for that fateful crop, the potato, the only filling available for the cavernous hunger of the labouring man. (Even today the main meal of the day is still sometimes referred to as *na fataí*, the potatoes.) According to information gathered in the course of the British Association's visit in 1857,

Of the entire area of the Aran Isles, amounting to 11,288 acres, only 742 were under crops, of which 692 were sown with potatoes in 1855.

It is interesting to compare these statistics with those of a 'base line' report drawn up in 1893 for the Congested Districts Board, according to which, on the 578 holdings of £4 valuation or less, potatoes took up on

average an acre and a quarter, and barley, rye, and small amounts of oats
and cabbages, only another quarter of an acre. Making some allowance for
the 117 larger holdings, this indicates that about 1200 acres were under
crops, nearly all of them potatoes. There were 562 families in the islands in
1893, and if these figures are anywhere near the truth, they imply that the
average family had reclaimed about an acre of land for crops over the two
preceding generations. No doubt some reclaimed land was under grass too.
This rate of activity was evidently enough to attract the attention of visitors, and the fact that he made his own land became part of the romantic
image of the Aran islander, along with the currach and the pampooty. It
was also an index of his exploitation, and as such first appears in the
unlikely context of *The Lives of the Irish Saints*, by Canon O'Hanlon. When
visiting St Brecan's church in Eoghanacht some time before 1873, the
Canon was shown a '*gort* or small garden' by a peasant, who told him that
his grandfather had made it by laying sand and seaweed on the naked rock,
and that the tenant had also built the house close by and the wall enclosing the holding:

For that poor homestead and plot – where not only were the improvements but
the very soil created by the peasant's unaided toil – one pound annually was
extracted as rent. No human ingenuity could procure much more than such a
return, from the culture of that gort; and yet this was only a solitary instance of
similar hard cases which fell under the writer's observation.

By the 1890s, when Ireland itself was the object of symbolic reclamation, the Aran man forced to pay rent on land he had created himself
became an icon of the oppressed nation. Mary Banim, writing for the
Weekly Freeman, placed this figure in a long perspective of wrong:

Naturally, there is not a spot of earth on any of these islands; but the law of their
owners, since the English gained possession of them, has been to exact from every
tenant that a certain portion of the rock shall be broken up, sea-sand and seaweed
carried up, load by load, by the men and women, and thus gradually accumulated
on the spot partially cleared of the upper crust of stone; but when this little patch
of land is made, it is appraised by him who says he owns the stones, and the maker
henceforth has the privilege of paying a smart rent for what the labour of his own
and his children's hands has made. ... With the exception of the landlord, and perhaps of his agent, all who see the place are of the same opinion as Mr Labouchère,
one of the cleverest of English journalists. Here are that gentleman's words, taken
from 'Truth':

'I give it as my deliberate opinion that the inhabitants of Arranmore ought, in
justice, to pay no rent whatever. ... The island is as much theirs as if they had made
it with their own hands. With their own hands thay have, most truly and literally,
made it, so far as it is a place capable of supporting human life. ... I declare, if I

were an Arran fisherman, I would sooner throw my rent into the Atlantic Ocean than pay it to any landlord whatever.'

The CDB report of 1893 noted that potatoes were sown year after year in the same plots as there was no tillage land to spare for the rotation of crops. However, in the 1920s the spread of a parasite known as eelworm made it necessary to leave potato-fields fallow for four or more years after cropping them, and despite the declining population there was a further investment of effort in 'making land'. Government grants for the work were introduced in the 'thirties. Pigs were also fed on potatoes, until the rising cost of fuel to cook the mash for them made pig-rearing uneconomical. An elderly man of Fearann an Choirce, looking back to the heroic days of his father, tells me, 'Each man planted as many potatoes then as a whole village does now.' That was the era of the most famous representation of land-making, in the film *Man of Aran*. Choosing a spectacularly primeval crag as the site of his new field, Tiger King shatters it with magnificent hammer-blows; the Siegfried rhythms of the sequence culminate in his lifting a mighty boulder above his head and dashing it down with giant strength. Meanwhile Maggy, his wife, delves a handful of soil out of a crevice and sprinkles it delicately on the ground, twiddling her fingers to get rid of the last grain ('You'ld think it was flour!' commented an Aran lady I watched the film with once). In the opinion of the anthropologist John Messenger, the use of the boulder is the film-maker's invention, part of the 'nativism' and 'primitivism' that distorts most accounts of the Aran Islands. However, the natives are not averse to a little nativism and primitivism themselves, and Tiger King's brother has shown me huge boulders that the Tiger and he shifted, or incorporated high up in walls, just to show that it could be done. Also, an Inis Meáin description of land-reclamation contemporary with Flaherty's film states that the ground-surface was broken up with a *ceann mionnáin*, a roundish granite boulder weighing about a hundredweight, lifted onto the shoulder and flung down. Peadar Ua Concheannain's is perhaps the first account by a practitioner; I quote part of it, in the rugged and vigorous Irish orthography of his day:

Is lom fuar sgéirdeamhail go deimhin fhéachas an t-oileán carraige seo i súilibh an strainséara agus bíonn iongantas an domhain air cia'n chaoi is féidir leis na daoinibh maireachtáil ann chor ar bith. Ní i nganfhios dá gcnámha é, creid mé ann, arae tá siad moch agus deireannach ag stócáil agus ag réidhteach, ag réabadh 's a' pléasgadh, agus ag maolú uláin agus carraigeacha cloch le ceann mionnáin, sin agus ag dúnadh sgalprachaí agus ag tarraingt fhód agus sgrathachaí le na gcliabh thiar ar a ndruim, agus dá sgaradh amach ar na breaclachaí garbha sin ag iarraidh bheith a' déanamh talmhan de.

[Indeed this craggy island looks a bare cold rugged place in the eyes of the stranger, who is amazed that the people can live on it at all. Not unknown to their bones is it, believe me, for early and late they are reclaiming and preparing land, shattering and blasting, and flattening ledges and stony crags with a crushing-stone, that and blocking up the crevices and hauling sods and clods in baskets on their backs, and spreading them on the rough stone-patches they are trying to make into fields.]

All the factors bearing on it – population, the potato-diet, pig-rearing, farming in general – having fallen away, the making of land is now at an end. I only once saw it being done, in 1973. In the course of a walk near Gort na gCapall, M and I stopped to pass the time of day with a man who was stirring a few sods of grass around with a spade, trying to make them cover a small area of crag, which showed through his incipient field as through a worn-out carpet. It was a grey cold day; he stood there as grey and cold as a monolith, and looked at us expressionlessly. 'Are ye enjoying your holidays?' he asked; it was clearly his mechanical response to the sight of strangers. We had been on the island for several months at that time, and hastened to tell him that we were not on our holidays, and for some reason M added, 'We're poor people!', as if that were a guarantee of our ground-edness. 'Oh, ye're poor people,' he echoed tonelessly. I wondered uneasily how my labour compared to his, mine at that stage being nothing more than vacant wandering about the island. Perhaps we were unnerved by an imagined implication of his task, that he had sculpted himself through timeless toil out of rock. Later on, though, a neighbour told me that the man had no need of another field and was making it with an eye to the grant rather than to any living crop.

Let none of these connections with irrealities that I have drawn be seen as making light of the work. The pleasant greenness of Fearann an Choirce was largely created, over a hundred years or more, by its inhabitants, through a process as sparing (in a profound sense) as that by which a snail secretes its shell. Helping Mícheál King in a field that, fifty years earlier, his father got the first crop off by laying out lines of seed-potatoes on a little crushed shale and seaweed, and covering them with upside-down sods of grass shaved off the crags here and there, I share his pride in the fact that its soil is now four inches deep, and as I carry a bucketful of stones off it to the great mossy cairn of them in the far corner, I feel I am lending a hand in a labour, not open-endedly timeless, but well found in history. A poem by Tomás Ó Direáin, brother of the more famous Máirtín, shows us an Aran man in prayer on the site of a field to be:

> Féach é ina sheasamh ar an leic,
> Atá liath agus lom ...

(See him standing on the flag, / Which is grey and bare ...)

It ends elementally:

> *Le allas a bhaithis,*
> *Le fuil a chroí,*
> *Déanfaidh sé talamh*
> *As na scalpachaí.*

(With the sweat of his brow, / With the blood of his heart, / He will make tilth / Out of clints and grykes.)

Having no better words to commemorate the blood of the heart, I will note the names and properties of some of the fields of Fearann an Choirce.

First, just west of Tobar Ghrióir and tucked under the scarp, Garraí an tSeanbhalla, the garden of the old wall, a hay-field with a mass of overgrown stone-work at the far end of it, origin unknown. Next to it, by the roadside, is a roofless cottage with empty doorway and window-openings, inhabited by nettles, from which the field behind it is called Garraí an tSeantí, the garden of the old house; the Kings, hereditary blacksmiths, lived here until they moved further down the road, a generation back. The first of them to settle here was Gregory, who – but no! Each of these houses has its story, which I will tell (with certain neighbourly omissions) later on, but for this chapter the fields alone can supply more of the third vital fluid of the village – talk, the others being water and blood – than I can deal with.

So, opposite the old King house, where the water that shows itself in the well resurfaces, having percolated under the ramp of the road, is Gairdín na Sailí, the sally-garden, a tiny quarter-circle nestled into the curving fall of the road, full of osiers, which used to be regularly coppiced and orderly but now are inextricably rampant. The only basket-maker we knew of lived a little way back east, in Baile na Creige: Joeen na gCloch, Joeen of the stones (he had been a mason as well), a big old man who used to sit like a grounded hulk on the rising ground before his cottage, and who answered our greetings with a surly roar – he was very deaf – that for a long time kept us from going up to watch him at work. To make one of the big potato-baskets used with a straddle on a horse or donkey, he would start by spiking sally-rods into the ground two inches or so apart, outlining a rectangle, and then weave rods horizontally through them, one after the other, knocking each one down against the last with the edge of his hand, so that the basket grew from the ground upwards, upside-down. When the walls were complete, the uprights would be bent over and woven together to make the base, and finally the whole thing was uprooted and the spikes shortened back to the rim with neat oblique penknife-cuts. I persuaded

Joeen to make me a smaller version of such a basket for the handlebars of my bicycle, and in later years this became the feature by which I was recognized all over Connemara; old boatmen in particular would flag me down to reminisce about the fine sally-rods, long enough to go round a turf-basket, that they used to bring back from Aran in return for turf itself.

Having irrigated the sally-garden, the water trickles through its wall and disappears underground in the next field, Gort an Bhiolair, the garden of the watercress. I watched a man rather crossly dealing with a newborn calf here, hoisting it to its feet, poking his fingers down its throat to make it swallow the crucial first milk from the cow, the thick yellowish 'beestings'. It was not his calf, and he came away from the slobbery job grumbling about its owner who had missed the critical hour, having gone into Cill Rónáin 'for a pound of butter', his invariant excuse for a session in Joe Watty's pub. South of that field and just outside Gilbert Cottage is Garraí na Ceártan, the field of the smithy. The King's old smithy is now an outhouse or 'store', next to the guest-house. From here the road straightens itself out again and runs west. Along its north side is an alternation of bungalows and cottages, and opposite them a sequence of rough meadows collectively known as Gort an Éadáin, the field of the face, referring to the cliff-face of the scarp, which closes them to the south. Once, perhaps fifty or sixty years ago, two men were digging shale out from under the scarp here; they broke off to go home for dinner, leaving their baskets in the field, and when they came back there was a white rabbit in each basket, which frightened them so much they abandoned the work and never took it up again. Or so I am told – with the same reluctance I have noticed in the telling of a few other Aran anecdotes which the teller believes to be both true and false and therefore unsuited to the Aristotelean ears of outsiders.

After Gort an Éadáin the scarp swings away to the south, leaving the road exposed to the breath of the Atlantic. Mícheál King's house – a large cottage with ample loft-rooms that make it almost two-storied – stands, a little defiantly, farther out than the original village cluster into this sudden spaciousness. The area around it is called An Mullán Mór, the big boulder, from a huge granite erratic which Mícheál tells me was 'the only landmark in Aran', until the Kings broke it up with 'block and feather' when reclaiming the land; a fraction of it lies by their front gate still. The lichen-grey house has the loneliness and wilful isolationism of ageing bachelorhood about it, and I know the wasteland underlies by a very few inches the greensward about it; nevertheless, for a few years An Mullán Mór was for me the dream-field of a childlike age.

One dark evening shortly after our arrival on the island I was walking by when Mícheál came stumbling down to the roadside wall with a gift:

five hen-eggs, luminous in the twilight, nested in his cupped hands. For good measure he also gave me a turn of speech useful for expressing a reservation: 'A decent man – but did you ever have to divide five eggs with him?' He soon took to calling on us for help with his residual farming, rather than be beholden to his neighbours, and this initiated us into many country ways and sights no longer to be found on the mainland. When Mícheál's hen, having hatched out her eggs in some secluded bramblebush, led a wobbly line of chicks to his doorstep, we helped him to herd them to the little sty or *póirín* attached to the barn behind the house. He was insistent that we imitate him exactly, advancing gently with arms slightly spread and palms towards them, murmuring '*Póirín, póirín*', and I realized that indirectly we were miming his mother spreading her skirts to herd chicks generations back from these. In the margins of Mícheál's scything and harrowing and potato-spraying I would search out the old-fashioned weeds that have been long rooted out from modern farmlands: vaporous greygreen fumitary, long-headed poppies, Lady's mantle, wild carrot, all the lovely little cranesbills – the long-stalked, the Pyrenean, the cut-leaved, the dove's foot, the shining-leaved – and precious rarities such as thale cress, and, best of all, penny-cress, with the heart-shaped translucent purses full of flat round seeds that must have delighted country children everywhere once. (But how did I miss the cornflower, rediscovered in Fearann an Choirce in 1987, having been thought extinct in Ireland for thirty years?)

Mícheál had only one milk cow, and wanted to teach me to milk it so that I could stand in for him when he went off to Galway for a few days. The agreed convention is that one squats by the cow's right flank to milk; if I forgot this and approached from her left she would look backwards at me out of the corner of her eye and turn herself right round in one jump. Often she would not 'stand' for me at all, but rambled off from field to field with me patiently stepping after her, holding out the plastic bucket like a begging bowl and repeating the charm that was supposed to lull her into a co-operative mood, '*Sonas ort!*' ('Fortune on you!'). Mícheál would knit his brows over this, and go up to where M was watching from the safety of a high flowery bank, and say, 'You would think with all his education he could milk a cow!' But I got the knack of it to some degree, and then there were many dawns in which the cow's overhang sheltered me from the drifting rain while I participated in the ancient insanitary magic of milking a cow in Aran, dipping my finger and thumb into the milk to lubricate her warty teats, cursing her when she suddenly let fall a splatter of dung, dipping into the milk again when I had finished to make the sign of the cross on her haunch. Sometimes I had to take some of the milk to a calf that had been weaned, that is, dolefully separated by walls from its mother, some weeks previously. Leaning over the built-up 'gap' and holding the bucket down to the calf, feeling the roughness of its newly de-horned skull thrust against my knuckles, seeing the long threads of milk and saliva curve away with the wind as I lifted up the bucket and spilt the last drops into its gaping mouth, I used to wonder if I would ever find exactly as much or as little strangeness in these actions as an Aran man does.

Also, I learned to ride Mícheál's Connemara pony in the meadows of An Mullán Mór – and 'not unknown to my bones was it!' She had just been unhitched from the harrow and loosed into a fine flat field. Mícheál, seeing me considering flinging myself onto her back with the virile abandon of an Aran lad, called out, 'Mind the hins!', but since all the hens were out of the way at the other end of the field I ignored him, and leaped up, and bruised my ribs on the 'hins', which, I learned too late, are the iron projections of the yoke to which the harrow is linked. My chest hurt for weeks. I never lived out my fantasy of galloping a bareback horse into the surf at Port Mhuirbhigh, leaning back with halter held high in the heroic and antique style I admired, for instance, in a ten-year-old known as Tom Tom Mhikey Tom, the butcher's son.

But there are deeper sources of misunderstanding than the lexicon of skills between people of different cultures. An anthropologist might have frowned over all this Edenic time in An Mullán Mór as the classic but unstable alliance between a slightly marginalized member of a traditional society, and a potentially transient incomer. I suppose it is a wonder that my part-time participation in the life of the Man of Aran, or at least of his younger brother, lasted as long as it did, and ended, I hope, without too much heartache on either side.

Mícheál's is almost the last of the reclaimed land on this level of the island; opposite it on the north of the road is Creig Chol Citte, of which a bit has been reduced to a lawn of suburban neatness in front of Máire Bhríd Rua's little b.&b., and the rest, left wild, occasionally supports a donkey in existence for a while. Col Citte (*i.e.* Colm the son of Cáit), the man who heard the fairies churning at Clochán an Airgid, is remembered by the older neighbours as a great worker who, by the time they were getting out of bed, would have already begun his second journey of the day with a load of seaweed from the shore to his potato-gardens south of the village. On his *creig* there are a few little heaps of stone, memorial cairns – though who they memorialize is unknown – built while funerals passing here took a rest after climbing the hill from the west. Just beyond them are high, half broken-down walls surrounding the overgrown yard and low ruins of the National School built in 1868. These walls used to have coloured glass windows in them, a whim of a schoolmaster called Moloney, whom middle-aged islanders remember as a curiosity for his plus-fours and his 'great liking for trees'. It was to protect his trees and shrubs that he had the walls built both around the school and the teacher's residence a little further on. In our time a tall gawky *Cordyline australis* – we supposed it was a palm-tree until a visiting botanist put us right – still grew by the ruins of the school, tattered by gales and hacked by children, as inappropriate, pathetic and evocative as a bit of stage scenery left behind by travelling players; even today its rotting broken-off stump sprouts a few green fronds. Creig na Scoile, the crag of the school, over the road from it, no longer exists as such, since the present school was built on it in 1945 and in the last few years has been joined by the Irish-language summer school, a rather ambitious piece of architecture which rears a tall prow against the great sea of rock behind it – An Chreig Mhór, the big crag, on which for years I nourished my solitude. Between the two schools is one of the square pillar-shaped cenotaphs, in a rather shaky state from generations of children climbing on it, whose weather-beaten plaques are illegible until the sun comes round to the west far enough to graze them with its rays, when suddenly one can read:

> Lord have me
> rcy on the soul of
> Ann Dirran who
> died in 16th yr. of
> her age 1846
>
> This Monunent
> was Erected by
> her Father
> Patrick Dirrane

There were also, I am told, a number of small memorial cairns on this crag which were swept away when the school was built. Despite these funereal reminders, a fine flat bit of pavement here was the village dance-floor. A little farther west there is a modern plaster Christ Crucified; occasionally I used to see old Uncle Colman from Gilbert Cottage kneeling in prayer before it, when he thought there was nobody on the road. Perhaps Creig na Scoile was a place associated with gatherings and ceremonies of various kinds, for the St John's Eve bonfire is still lit on a grassy margin of the road just east of it. Each village of Aran has its bonfire-stand, usually a neat round stone-built platform about a yard across and two or three feet high; visitors are puzzled by these sooty little altars, nowadays often draped in coils of fine wire from the worn-out tyres that contribute a large part of the blaze. Nearly all the Celtic magic of this midsummer festival is lost now – the throwing of embers into the fields to bring luck to the crops, the driving of cattle between two bonfires, the leaping over the flames – but if the night is fine the villages of Aran and those of Connemara still remind each other of it across a dozen miles of sea.

Another people held their revels just down the road. A green patch, thirty paces by twenty, three days grazing for Mícheál's cow, has been walled off from the few hundred yards of rough ground between the schools and the former teacher's residence. Its perimeter is thickly lined within by blackberry bushes which reduce its open area to that of a good-sized room – a ballroom, perhaps, for this is Móinín an Damhsa, the little meadow of the dancing. I used to wonder if it was the meadow itself which was supposed by this name to dance, for its surface is just two or three smoothly swelling waves of grass and daisies. When Mícheál's elder brother Patrick, who used to revisit the island occasionally, told me the meadow was so named because someone once saw fairies dancing in it, Mícheál looked displeased, and I half suspected Patrick of testing my credulity. But recently I came across the following, in *The Fairy Faith in Celtic Countries* by Evans Wentz, published in 1911:

Our next witness is an old man, familiarly called 'Old Patsy', who is a native of the Island of Aranmore, off the coast of Galway, and he lives on the island amid a little group of straw-thatched fishermen's homes called Oak quarter. As 'Old Patsy' stood beside a rude stone cross near Oak quarter, in one of those curious places on Aranmore, where each passing funeral stops long enough to erect a little memor-ial pile of stones on the smooth rocky surface of the roadside enclosure, he told me many anecdotes about the mysteries of his native island.

Twenty years or so ago round the *Bedd* of Dermot and Grania, just above us on the hill, there were seen many fairies, 'crowds of them,' said 'Old Patsy', and a single deer. They began to chase the deer, and followed it right over the island. ... When I asked Patsy where the fairies lived, he turned half round, and pointing in the direction of Dun Aengus, which was in full view on the sharp sky-line of Aran-more, said that there, in a large tumulus on the hillside below it, they had one of their favorite abodes. 'But', he added, 'the rocks are full of them, and they are small fellows.' Just over the road from where we were standing, another place was pointed out where the fairies are often seen dancing. The name of it is *Moneen an Damhsa*, 'the Little Bog of the Dance'.

Evans Wentz was a young American anthropologist studying under the Celticist Sir John Rhys at Oxford. He brought to bear on 'Old Patsy' and a hundred other 'witnesses' in Ireland, Scotland, Wales and Brittany, a theory synthesized out of William James's religious psychology, Yeats's occultism, and the investigations of the Society for Psychical Research. His conclusion was that, after Patsy's and his compeers' tales have been sifted of all 'ethnological, anthropomorphic, naturalistic, or sociological influences on the Celtic mind', there remains a residue of the veridical and unexplained, 'the x or unknown quantity in the Fairy-Faith'. Fairies, it seems, are discarnate consciousnesses, instances of the common 'protoplasmic background of all religions, philosophies, or systems of mystical thought yet evolved on this planet', and that the Celtic Otherworld, like the classical Hades, is but the lower arc of the soul's cyclical progress from birth to rebirth. All this is very wonderful, but to me not as wonderful as the fact that when, years after leaving Aran, I opened Evans Wentz's crabbed tome for the first time, out jumped Móinín an Damhsa, my favourite blackberry spot, as from a pop-up book, complete with a pair of small tortoiseshell butterflies, the smell of a cow-pat, and the ringing of stone as Mícheál 'knocks the gap' to let his pony in to graze.

Immediately beyond Móinín an Damhsa is the Residence, as it is still called. The little house is almost hidden by the walls of its garden, which have empty window-frames in them here and there. These are thick, double walls, eight to ten feet high in most places, and on the south-western, windward, side of the house, eighteen feet high; it is said that Moloney paid Joeen na gCloch thirty shillings for building them. A rusty old farmyard gate of tubular iron lets one look into the garden from the road. All around it, Moloney's shrubs – laburnums and lilacs, a richly scented *Escallonia*, some evergreens I looked up once, *Griselinia littoralis*, *Pittosporum crassifolium* and *Pittosporum tenuifolium* – have grown up to the tops of the walls and been bevelled off by the wind. The rest is a little hayfield now, with a few Jerusalem anemones and montbretias, relics from the former tenants' gardening. At the farther end of the grass-invaded garden path a cypress, a contorted mass of thunder-dark green, leans across the faded primrose-yellow façade as if to tap on the door. There is a sash window on either side of the door and two small ones above it, drawn together under a central gable. The house is one of those with a distinct face, in this case a simple and affectionate one like that of a domestic pet. I pause at the gate, my hand on the bolt. Residence. Domicile. Sanctuary. Termon. Temenos. Nemeton. ...

This is the last of the village proper; from here the road drops steeply down a scarp that marks an ancient mythological boundary between east and west, and the scatter of houses beyond are distinguished (by those who like distinctions) as the hamlet of Creig na Córach, the crag of the just division. But first there is more to be said about the fields of Fearann an Choirce, and then I must call in on some of the other houses, those inhabited by rain and nettles as well as those with people in them, before entering this Residence, that seems to stand like a *dún* against, or in advance of, a further degree of westernness.

SPUDS

Potatoes left uneaten in dark outhouses over winter open their eyes towards the spring, and put forth pallid tubes of growth. If these sprouting potatoes are then put into the earth they give rise to new plants, or rather clones of the old ones. But if this is repeated over two or three years the stock becomes less productive, as if an accumulating tiredness blurs the genetic message. So it is best to start afresh each year with seed-potatoes provided by the Department of Agriculture and obtained by them *ex nihilo* in some way we in Aran have not thought of enquiring into. The first I knew of this yearly distribution of seed-potatoes was from printed notices that appeared overnight pinned to the doors of ruins by the roadside and other prominent places; one was tied to the orange-brown sphere of a big iron buoy rusting in the grass near the beach. I puzzled out the unfamiliar Irish of bureaucracy: each holding of not more than £15 rateable value is entitled to a hundredweight of oats or two hundredweight of seed-potatoes at a reduced price, preference being given to the smaller holdings. The January wind soon tore down these annunciations, but the process of the year had been initiated.

Potato-planting in Aran is supposed to be completed before the cuckoo calls, and the man who doesn't get his spuds in early enough is derided as a cuckoo-farmer. There is a logic in timing things thus, as a cold spring should delay both the start of vegetable growth and the migrations of birds, but it is a back-to-front logic since the bird gives its timekeeping cry after the event. People do not take the cuckoo as seriously nowadays as they used to. A story is told in Inis Oírr of a joker who saw his neighbour cutting up seed-potatoes in preparation for planting, climbed onto the walls of the cashel overlooking the village and imitated the cuckoo; the man thus convicted of laziness was so disgusted he abandoned his work and fed the potatoes to his hens. I determined that, before the cuckoo called, I would learn how to set a potato-garden, a skill as definitive of a true islandman as the rowing of a currach. Meeting an elderly man I knew having his horse shod at the forge, the first step in the process, I arranged to learn from him.

Towards the end of March, when the oriental carpets of redweed that had lain under the winter rains in the fields selected to be this year's potato-gardens had bleached and ravelled and almost melted into the ground, word came that the potatoes would be arriving on Saturday's steamer. Séamaisín and I jolted along the three hilly miles to Cill Rónáin on his 'common cart' to collect his quota. It was a mild, hazy day; columns of smoke were rising from bramble-patches being burned out of the corners of fields. The sophisticates of Cill Rónáin used to call people from the west of the island *'asailíní an Chinn Thiar'*, little donkeys of the west end; Séamaisín was old enough to remember the gibe, and shy enough to be glad of my support on the crowded pier. But on his cart he was at ease and talkative, and as bent on self-improvement as I was. He was an odd-looking little fellow; all his features seemed to have been tucked into a cleft in the middle of his face, from which they peered out at me questioningly. What was the right English for the *gráinneog*? (Hedgehogs are unknown in Aran.) Does it have ears? Does it hop about? Had I ever seen an animal like Dara Kenny said he'd found in a store last winter, with no legs, and two wings like parasols, and ears it could make bigger and smaller? He had heard I had a book with pictures of all the birds in it; did it have a picture of the peacock? I suddenly felt the silliness of a bird-book that didn't illustrate the finest bird of all. Neither did it mention the saying he gave me, that the peacock would die of pride but for the two skinny legs under him. Nor could my plant-book have told me that there were male and female briars, the females being those that bend over like an arch and grow into the ground again, while my fish-book was ignorant of the fact that a horsehair that falls into a well will grow a little head and turn into an eel. Séamaisín would not hear of objections to this theory; tiny eels were found in springs up on the crags that no big eel could find its way to, and horsehairs were living things, so it 'stood to reason'. It was clear that the potato season was going to be an induction into a medieval logic.

Down on the pier we joined the semicircular herd of men, each clutching a scrap of paper, around the pile of knobbly sacks which the agent was dispensing 'on production of the documentation'. Vans, tractors, common carts and small donkey-carts were jumbled together trying to get as close by as possible. 'Look at the great sack I carried!' gasped a plump fellow collapsed in the tail of a van. When Séamaisín got his two sacks he spelled out the brandname UP-TO-DATE printed on them, tapping each letter with his finger, as if he suspected he was being fobbed off with old potatoes. I pushed forward to help him carry them. He showed me how to hold the sack by grasping a potato inside each of its ears, and he was most particular about our style in heaving it up onto the cart: 'Don't swing now! Don't swing now! Now – swing!' We sat on the sacks for the drive home. Passing Powell's shop on our way out of town, he stopped to buy a pound of butter, leaving me holding the reins. He was a long time gone, but fortunately the horse's natural inertia kept it where it stood. Shopping was difficult for a

bashful man, he explained; he'd been standing back from the counter waiting for a heap of women to finish gossiping. On the cart again he recovered
his standing. Plodding up the hill we overtook a donkey-cart that was
making little progress; 'The shafts are too low!' he shouted at its owner,
who leaned against a wall and nodded wearily, speechless with drink. As we
rattled down from Baile na Creige, he pointed out the little field by the
roadside, Buaile Phatsa, Patsy's milking-pasture, in which he intended to
plant the potatoes. Although it had been a pasture for some years it was, he
explained, a *garraí loirg*, a garden in which potatoes had been grown before,
as opposed to a *garraí bán*, fallow grassland never broken up for crops. The
blackweed he had spread over the grass a few weeks earlier was satisfactorily 'stuck to the ground', he said, and we were to start the next fine day. I
went home to consult Estyn Evans's *Irish Folk Ways* on spade-ridges or
'lazy-beds'.

It seems that there is a boundless variety of ways to make a ridge, but
in its simplest form,

... the strip of grass that is to become the furrow is notched centrally down its
length and the sods on either side are each undercut by two spade-thrusts and levered over on to the beds, where they lie flat, grass to grass, like closed hinges.

And there is a multiple rationale to the process:

Not only does this method make full use of the humus and decaying grass but it
prevents the sets from becoming waterlogged and rotting, for the whole bed is
raised above the water-table. And the unbroken sod checks the down-wash of
plant nutrients. The trenches or furrows between the ridges provide open drains,
and the lazy-beds are always carefully aligned with the slope of the land. Moreover
when the trenches are dug a second time for earthing the potatoes, they often go
deep enough to penetrate the hard layer of iron pan which tends to form under
heavily leached soils by the washing down of iron salts. Breaking the impermeable
pan not only improves the drainage but provides minerals which are returned to
the topsoil when the potatoes are earthed.

Clearly this was not all applicable to Aran's few inches of droughty, stony
earth, which surely would have a logic all its own.

On the twenty-seventh of March Séamaisín and I started to set Buaile
Phatsa. When I arrived he was stamping and peering about, bending down
to interrogate the ground obliquely for the tracks of the old ridges. I gathered that although the field had been roughly flattened after the previous
potato crop, it was important to have the new trenches where the old ridges
had been, so that one was digging out the deeper and more compacted
earth. Then he snapped a couple of hazel twigs off a bit of scrub in a corner,
and pegged out a length of string where the first edge of the first ridge was

to run. He inspected the withered scraps of blackweed littering the grass; since not all the salt had been washed out of it, he decided not to lay the potatoes on it straight away lest they get burned. I was set to find pebbles, which Séamaisín arranged in a row a couple of inches inside the string, as stand-ins for the potatoes, which would be stabbed into the ridges later on. When there were no more pebbles to hand he ran into the next field and came back crumbling a bit of dry cow-dung to complete the row. 'Wasn't that a good idea I had!' he said. He removed the string, took up his long-handled spade, and, guided by the row of pebbles, started to open the ground with the speed and ease of a chef filleting fish. The sods were not square as in Estyn Evans's diagram, but triangular; as a sod was hinged by one of its sides over onto the row of pebbles, it left behind it a comple-mentary triangle of grass with its point towards the ridge, which was then scooped up and dropped upside-down onto the ridge beside its mate; the first sort, I learned, was the *scraith bhoird* (edge-scraw), and the second the *scraith láir* (middle-scraw). Every now and then a stone came up, and was flicked off the spade to the margin of the field. Séamaisín backed steadily the width of the field, a neat rectangular trench about ten inches wide obe-diently coming into existence under his stabbing and twisting blade, flanked by the first side of the ridge. Then he pegged out the string for the next trench, using a notch on his spade-handle that marked off a distance of about four feet, to ensure that it would be parallel to the first. The notch was old; for many, many seasons it had kept new trenches in step with old ridges. The handle itself was grey, its varnish worn off long ago, and smooth, fed by the copious spittle with which Séamaisín lubricated his hands. The left-hand bottom corner of the blade was worn into a large quarter-circle, and before tackling the second trench he took the spade over to a granite boulder that sparkled in the wall, and sharpened it until its edge gleamed like a scimitar. A discussion of granite – had these useful boulders always been here? How long ago did they come? Were there people here then? – led us into the theme of earth-changes in general. Séamaisín had a theory that the ground moved up and down with the tides, causing the cracks in houses to widen. He had also heard that the earth itself moved, but he said that it was difficult to see how that could be. 'If I come and make a mark on the ground there, and I come and look at it, it might be in the same place for twenty years!' The homophony of earth (*talamh*) and Earth (*An Domhan*) does not obtain in Irish, and before I could decon-struct its false logic, Séamaisín was at work opening the second furrow, turning the sods back to complete the first ridge. The size of the sods was judged to a nicety so that each one fell pat into its place, butting up against one from the first trench to close in the grass like a neatly carpentered box-lid. Soon the whole ridge was complete. It stretched for twelve yards across the bright grass, as grand as the shadow of the campanile on the Piazza San Marco.

It was then my turn to sharpen my spade. I was to work back along the furrow Séamaisín had just finished, doubling its width by turning in sods for the first edge of the next ridge, while he constructed that ridge's farther edge by opening up a third furrow. This task of 'turning in' is junior to that of 'opening up', the line of the trench having already been established, and is traditionally the part of the learner. I played my role as beginner satisfactorily; the earth or Earth met my spade at the wrong angles, my edge-scraws broke at the hinges, my middle-scraws were not congruent with the triangular spaces they were to be inverted into, stones stubbed bluntly against my keen blade. Séamaisín came round to look along the bit of ridge I had put together, and remarked consolingly that potatoes would probably grow just as well in a ridge as crooked as a ram's horn; nevertheless, 'If any stranger came by, now, I wouldn't like them to see that!' Why then, I wondered, had we set to work in this roadside field, since it was a commonplace of our village that the men of certain other villages had nothing better to do than to stroll around criticizing other people's potato ridges? I sucked the blister in the cleft between my thumb and first finger, and absorbed Séamaisín's remarks on the importance of not letting the levered-over sod break, for if it does, weeds will grow out of the side of the ridge, and of making the central sods cover the space they are intended for, so that the blackbirds wouldn't see bits of rotting seaweed poking out and destroy the ridge by pulling at them to get the maggots. When he had slapped the ridge into shape with the back of his spade we continued. On the next ridge I ran into a shallow place where the spade could not find its way between the stones; I felt like saying, 'It can't be done here; let's skip this bit,' but I persevered, remembering a young teacher at the technical school who had left a hummock that was hardly more than a rock-outcrop in his garden unridged, and had been called upon by a deputation of villagers who insisted he finish the job and promised that the impossible bit would give the best of the crop. Gladly I watched the clouds gathering that would bring down a curtain of rain on the scene of toil.

A few days later the sun appeared again. I strolled up to see if Séamaisín was at work, and saw that he had completed the garden. Thirty-two ridges stood, proud, parallel, level-topped, above the knobbly rock of the trenches. I found Séamaisín in his bare kitchen, seated on a wooden chair with a bucket on another chair facing him, cutting up seed-potatoes. The concrete-floored room was chill and the cracked cast-iron kitchen range full of dead ashes, while the back door was left open, in the Aran bachelor's fashion, to let the wind keep him warm. He showed me how to cut the potatoes into bits each with one eye, to make them go further, and told me that when rats eat a potato in a ridge they leave the eye so that they will have potatoes in the future: 'See! The Nature!' he exclaimed, with a wink at its roguery. He was in high spirits, looking forward to ridging a lea garden he owned down on the sandy land near the beach, exulting in his strength and skill: 'When I've no drink taken for a fortnight,' he cried, 'I could drive a spade through that floor!' As he worked he repeated a garbled scrap of verse, that never got beyond lines I came to know by heart:

> They could've let the poor man live
> And yet as lordly be
> For ruined cabins were no stuff
> To build a lordly hall ...

When the bucket was full, we walked down with it to the Plains, as he oddly named the arena of slanting fields around the bay, and surveyed with relish the smoothly swelling hillocks of rabbit-nibbled sward and rain-washed blackweed in his lea garden. A few primroses showed among the briars along the foot of its south-facing wall, over which a suddenly sun-intensified vision of the white-pocked, blue-black sea and the snow-dusted peaks of Connemara glared at us. Having pegged out his line, Séamaisín put down the bits of seed-potato in three staggered rows to adumbrate the ridge to be, and spat on his hands, evidently with as much expectation of pleasurable hours as I would have felt (reminded of it by the arrangement of the seeds, at the four corners and central points of a succession of squares) in settling down to read Sir Thomas Browne's *The Quincunx, or the Garden of Cyrus.*

I learned some refinements of the art that day: how to pierce the scraw with a little stab of the spade before folding it over, exactly at the right point for the potato to grow up through the slit, 'to give it a chance, like!', and how to bevel the edge of the ridge with quick pats and rubs of the back of the spade so that the rain would run off it. In a nearby field a man was ridging a field for mangolds to feed his cow next winter. His technique was quite different; the bare sandy soil, in which some crop had been grown the previous year, had already been shaped into long thin banks about four feet apart – Séamaisín said they were called *uaille*, but I cannot identify the word in the dictionaries – and seaweed had been laid in the spaces between them. Now he was crouched like a sprinter, using the full length of the spade-handle at a shallow angle, rapidly scooping soil out of the middle of a bank to build up a ridge on the seaweed beside it; the sharp crests of soil he left on either side of the bank became the firm sides of the ridges to right and left of it. However, Séamaisín did not encourage my observation of this rival, and recalled me to our own ridges. 'Keep your eye on the seed!' he cried, whenever my furrow strayed from the rectilinear. The ground was extremely shallow – in fact it was clear that the principal reason for ridging in Aran is to double up the depth – and I became scrupulous about prizing the last spoonful of soil off the bedrock exposed in the trench. Two pied wagtails flew into the field and fought furiously on the ridges. One by one Séamaisín and I forged the great brown ingots of earth.

The early days of April were blustery and spiteful; *Laetheanta na Bó Riabhaí*, the days of the brindled cow, Séamaisín called them. (The old cow was congratulating herself on having survived the winter, but cruel April overheard her and borrowed a few days from March to finish her off.) I joined Séamaisín for intermittent spells on the ridges, but it was the middle of the month by the time we completed the garden in the Plains and returned to Buaile Phatsa. And there, one late afternoon hour that had unexpectedly been wafted up from the south while we were quincunxing the ridges with spuds, the cuckoo called, two notes as exotic in grey Aran as sugared almonds: pink, blue. Old Nora Fleming, passing down the road, tall and slim in her long black shawl, paused on hearing the first cuckoo for the eighty-third time in her life, lifted her beautiful grey face and murmured to us, 'I suppose it's the same one comes every year.' Séamaisín glanced sideways at me to see if I appreciated the antiquated unreason of this, and turned the peak of his cap to the rear to shield his neck from the sun. M came up the road and took a photograph of us at work, overruling his protests at being recorded looking 'two hundred years behind the times'. Cuckoo-farmers, but disdainful of her obsolete cuckoo-calendrical jokes, we went on jabbing up-to-dates into the earth.

The final act of the planting season is the 'trenching' of the potatoes when they begin to show above the ground, that is, throwing the soil that has washed down into the trenches up onto the ridges again. This also gives an opportunity of perfecting the ridges for perfection's sake. My part in the task was to work along each trench, prizing out stones and loosening the soil around and under them. Séamaisín followed me, shooting spadefuls of my scanty winnings in broad fans evenly across the ridge or in soft packets to plump out slight hollows, and now and again with a quick to-and-fro movement, flicking a dab onto the rim and licking it into the bevel with the back of his blade. Reading between the lines of the ridges I discovered again the precious contradictions of rock and earth. And during that long sunny day with the cuckoo calling, Séamaisín passed on lots of life-wisdom, some of which made my heart pale: for instance, how to clean a deep gash by pouring milk on it and letting the dog lick it; and how to cut a short length of elderberry-twig, make a notch round it near either end, split it lengthways, take out the pith and fill each half with a mixture of 'bluestone' or copper sulphate and olive oil, fix them together again by a bit of twine round the notch at one end, like a clothes-peg, then peg it round the bull calf's scrotum above the stone and tie the other ends together, so that the 'strings' are burned through and the animal castrated by gentle degrees. This useful tip led us into a discussion of breeding and heredity. Did I think ducks ever bred with seagulls? He had two peculiarly thin white ducks – they had waddled in and out of the field we were working in several times during the day – and recently some tourists had asked him what sort they were; he had said there was a bit of the seagull in them, and they had believed him! 'That was good enough for them!' he cried, weak with laughter, pillowing his face in his arms on the wall. Then, following an obscure chain of associations, 'Do you think will they ever get rid of the Royal Family?' When I answered that I hoped so, he laughed again, but uneasily; he seemed to feel that this was rather daring. We started to hack out the briars that were already stretching towards the ridges from the rough margins of the garden. As he wielded his spade he asked me if monkeys ever bred with apes, because he had heard that 'the man' came from a monkey and an ape. He speared his spade vertically into the earth and leant on it to hear my exposé of Darwinism. He had once seen a monkey, he told me; the Guinnesses' yacht had moored in Port Mhuirbhigh when he was a lad, and he was climbing out of his currach onto the jetty when he heard a noise, 'mmm, mmm', and saw this thing in the yacht, holding its little paws up; he had thought it looked like a person. But if that was true about the monkey and the ape, what about Adam and Eve and the Earthly Paradise? As I fumbled among different orders of truth, scientific and mythic, his attention wandered and he began to recite scraps of school-learning and folklore: 'Palestine is a small country on the eastern shore of the Mediterranean', and something about the dog's nose being cold because it was stuck out of a window of the Ark for forty days and forty nights; until we both came to a baffled halt and stood looking at each other in absolute mutual incomprehension. Then he seized his spade and said, 'Well, whatever about religion, we've got to get out the briars!' – which Voltairean flash reignited our energies and set us slicing through the knotted roots again. We worked away, caps reversed, while the cuckoo called and called and called, dinning its prehistoric, bang up-to-date, binary logic into our brains.

BLACK HARVEST

The logic of the cuckoo is, of course, 'As ye sow, so shall ye reap.' But even in the best of times this is simplistic, and since the cuckoo sang as blithely as ever during those years of 'distress' that disfigured almost every decade of the last century, it can also be heard as a black joke. The potato is vulnerable to drought and to blight; it needs care in cultivation and in storage. 'Cleaning', *i.e.* weeding, the gardens is a task that bows the back and cramps the mind into vegetable hatreds: scutch grass, that breaks at the nodes when you pull it and regenerates from the smallest remainder ('I *hate* scutch grass!' I hear Mícheál cry); shepherd's purse that flowers and seeds itself a thousandfold during a few days' inattention; docks with great taproots that cannot be dragged out without cracking the ridges. Water is a problem on Aran; it used to be said that the potatoes would be good if they got rain on St John's Day and St Macdara's Day, that is June the 24th and July the 16th; but frequently they did not. Potatoes are often stored in the field where they have been harvested; they are heaped into a low mound, a layer of bracken or withered potato stalks over them, and covered in soil to make a *maolán* or 'clamp'. This protects them from rain and frost, but one can still be disappointed on opening it up, for, as Mícheál explained to me, the rats are 'cute' enough to leave no sign on the outside of the clamp to say that they are inside it, building nests and with lots to eat. Also, potatoes that looked healthy enough on being clamped might turn out to have been infected with the blight, and to be melting away.

Potato blight threatens on muggy days in July and August, when the spore of *Phytophthora infestans*, the fungus that causes it, spreads rapidly. Nowadays official blight warnings and insistent radio advertisements for proprietary fungicides remind us to spray the crop several times in the summer months. Until recently the Aran farmer would make up a solution of copper sulphate, and spatter it onto the leaves with an old paintbrush or, in earlier days, a bundle of heather. Neglect such precautions, and the spore may wash down from the leaves into the ground and affect the tubers, tingeing them with an inward-speading darkness. The effect of a severe infestation is vile. I remember the face of an Inis Meáin farmer who had just discovered that there was nothing in his ridges but sacs of black slime. One's instinctive repulsion is doubled by a historically transmitted shudder. The potato famine of 1845-9 left a soft blackness of despair at the heart of rural Ireland, which I think will not be dispelled by all the grants in Europe.

The blight organism followed the potato itself from the Americas, with a delay of two-and-a-half centuries. During that period the potato had become a staple of the poor throughout much of northern Europe, but nowhere else had they been forced into such a dependence on the one food-stuff as in Ireland. A vast population growth and an unprecedented degree of exploitation had been made possible by the fact that a family could feed themselves almost totally by cultivation of a small potato-patch, liberating all the rest of their time, energy and land for the production of rent. The amount of potato the farm labourer forced down himself, when he could get it, was formidable; one reads of a father's advice to his son on ensuring his share of the midday meal: have a potato in each cheek, one in each fist, two more at the back of your two fists, and your two eyes stuck into two others in the basket. 'We'll have the potatoes again at seven,' said the old lady who looked after me in Inis Meáin on my first visit, having served me with bacon and cabbage at midday; to her, *na fataí*, the potatoes, were still synonymous with food. The variety of potato most widely planted in Ire-land in the years before the Famine, the 'Lumper', was very productive but watery and disease-prone; again one reads of landlords' agents who would raise the rent of a tenant seen growing a better quality of potato. Thus the two million or more acres of potatoes planted in Ireland in the spring of 1845 constituted, in the words of one authority, 'a vast congested potato slum, ripe for devastation by epidemic disease'.

Cruelly, the immediate cause of the disaster was a well-meaning attempt to remedy the instability of the situation. The Belgian government was conducting field-trials of various newly imported strains of potato to find one resistant to another disease, dry rot; the blight spores seem to have come in with these, either from Mexico or the central Andes region. In June the disease was noted in Flanders, by August growers in south-east England were prophesying a calamity for the poor, and by September the plague had reached Ireland. Over the next few years a million people died of starvation or fever, and more than a million fled the ruined country.

In Connemara, any enquiry into local lore will bring you to the famine-grave in the bushes behind the ruined cabin or among the rocks of the seashore. Such a thing has never happened to me in Aran. Official reports and oral tradition both indicate that there was perhaps only one death from starvation in the islands, that of a woman in Cill Rónáin. The blight was less severe here, and although the fishing was limited by the lack of suitable boats and nets, there was always shore-food — winkles, sea-urchins, a few sorts of edible seaweed — for those who conserved the stren-gth to gather it. Nevertheless, there was undoubtedly severe want; in the spring of 1846 Indian meal was distributed from the coastguard station, and the local relief committee reported that three hundred and forty people lacked food and fuel and were too weak to undertake cultivation. But island memory hardly distinguishes between this period and the other spells of recurrent tribulation of that century, so far as concerns its own suffering. The sufferings of Connemara were made vivid to Aran, however, by the number of refugees who came across the channel, lived in little hollows of the inland cliffs and worked unpaid for anyone who could afford to feed them, and most of whom were eventually forced by the bailiffs to return to their own deathly shores, lest they become an expense to the middleman or the landlord. Some Aran tenants were persuaded to let their Connemara labourers go, by the threat of having their potato-patches taken from them (but Mícheál tells me that the bailiffs did not trouble the blacksmith of Oatquarter about the people he was harbouring, because they got a better service from him than from his rival in Cill Rónáin). Also there was forceful resistance to this sentence of repatriation; one bailiff came riding home on his donkey, dead, apparently throttled by some fiddlers and other musicians from Connemara.

But even in those lowest years, the insufficient and undependable crop of human kindness sometimes reached fruition, as the following scene from oral history shows. I leave the word to the teller, old Seán Gillan of Oatquarter:

When the Great Hunger was ravaging the country – it must have been in about 1846 – things weren't too bad in Árainn. Of course the odd stranger came in and lots of stories with them about the bad state of people outside. But not a single person died here, of hunger at any rate. Plenty of other things killed them. But the blight didn't come here. And isn't it an odd thing that the gardens nearest the sea were the soundest. Dónall Mhicil noticed this, and that year he sowed potatoes in bits of land he had all the way from Corrúch shore west to An Duirling Bhán. Patches here and there, only four or five ridges in each, perhaps, but all the same he had the most potatoes in this village or in the island if it comes to that. There wasn't so much as one rotten potato among them. Fine healthy potatoes. You could say everyone in the village had good enough potatoes that year.

Did you ever hear tell of the Bideachaí? An amazing pair, always outside, slaving from morning to night, cutting seaweed, picking winkles, manuring the ground, fishing, reaping, sowing, reclaiming land. The Bideachaí had a mare, a big black mare. But the two of them were no size at all. Little men, stumpy, you'd say. They were strong, wiry, healthy, but they were short. And the mare was big. They used to have problems with her on the shore and in the garden. They had a lump of stone to stand on when they were topping a load of seaweed or throwing the rope over the load. You wouldn't know for the life of you why they bought such a big horse. But that's what they had when they were bringing the potatoes home from the garden out in the end of October. They were down there in the garden,

with a straddle on the horse and two heaped-up baskets on the ground by the
potato-clamps. There's great weight in a basket of potatoes, as anyone knows who's
handled one, and they couldn't work out how they were going to hang them on
the straddle. They would have been able to put one of them up between them of
course, but then one man would have to stay and take the weight of it while the
other basket was being put up on the other side, and neither of them was strong
enough to lift a basket by himself. It would be awkward to empty out the baskets
and then fill them on the straddle. But while they were discussing the question this
stranger came by from the west. He'd come in at Port Mhuirbhigh. He said, 'God
bless the work!' and stopped to look in over the wall. One of the men inside asked
him if he'd mind coming and taking the weight of a basket while they lifted the
other one. In through the gap with him – the gap was knocked. 'Let you two lift
that one while I stay on this side,' he said. The two men thought he meant that
he would lift the basket on his side with one of them when they had got the other
one up. 'What peg shall I put it on?' he asked. 'The one nearest you,' said they.
They hung their basket on the pegs of the straddle. One of them stayed under it.
The other ran round the back of the horse to lift the other basket with the stranger.
My God! Hadn't my man got the basket up! A grip on the rim of the basket
between finger and thumb of each hand, one heft and up it was! You know yourself what a feat that was. The little man just stood there with his mouth open,
gulping with amazement. 'Do you think I could get a couple of week's work
around here?' asked the stranger. Perhaps he thought that some help was what the
two men needed. They told him that Dónall had sowed a lot of potatoes and that
it was almost certain he'd need help. Everyone in the area heard about that basket.

My man was picking potatoes for Dónall for three weeks. I don't know what
agreement they came to between them, but no doubt they made some agreement.
It was the Hunger that had driven him in, and it was well-deserved luck for
Dónall. He was well fed at Dónall's and he recovered well. He was strong, powerful, with a great capacity for work. Ribs like a boat, and two shoulders on him like
a rowingboat. Later on they found out he was a brother of Big Seán Thaidhg who
was famous around Camas and such places. There's a big stone down there in the
ravine by that boreen at Diarmaid and Gráinne's bed. It's still to be seen. Two hundredweight in it if there's a pound. Well, that stone was well out on the path at
that time. It was awkward if you had a load to bring up on a horse or a donkey.
You had to take your hand off the load or the creel, and it's many a load went
under a horse's belly there. My man noticed this stone, and he said to Dónall that
it would be as well to throw it out of the way. He was on horseback and Dónall
was riding pillion. Dónall said he wouldn't mind lifting it out of the way with him.
'Don't you bother getting down,' said my man, and he grabbed the stone between
his two hands and lifted it clean off the ground and dropped it four feet from the
path. It's there in the ravine still, with a bit out of it that flew into the air when it
fell. There was force in that lad!

When the potatoes had been picked and brought in, the big fellow was waiting for a boat to take him home. Out in November a boat came into Port Mhuirb-

high for the night, and it was to go out the next morning. Dónall said goodbye when he went out that morning, thinking that my man would have taken himself off by the time he got home. Probably Dónall hurried with whatever he was doing outside, for he was on his way home quite early. He was coming up across Creig na Córach when he noticed someone up by the well looking under a thornbush. That was a queer thing! Up he went. Who was it but my man from outside! He was only wearing one pair of trousers. The men used to wear two pairs of trousers, white homespun and grey tweed, at that time. He'd taken one pair off and he was filling them with potatoes. He'd tied each leg with a bit of straw rope. He'd been hiding the potatoes there, at night probably, so that he could take them home. No doubt he got a shock when Dónall came on him – but really Dónall got a worse one. 'My poor fellow,' said he, 'It's funny you didn't ask me for them! They would have been yours and welcome. Throw those away now, and come with me.' Well, the end of the story was that they filled two big baskets with potatoes in Dónall's little house. Then they filled two more baskets, and each of them overflowing. The Bideachaí gave them their own horse and they took the load west to Port Mhuirbhigh.

The poor man had lost his courage because of what he'd been through, and his fear had stopped him from asking Dónall for the potatoes.

A MOUTHFUL OF ECHOES

I begin my house-visiting at the top of the village, with the foundation-legend of Gilbert Cottage, as I have often heard it told.

At Grand Central Station a man stepped out of the crowd saying, 'Carry your bag, sir?' and took the suitcase out of Stephen Dirrane's hand. Stephen and his uncle Colman trotted after him through the crowd with increasing anxiety as he got farther and farther ahead of them, because all the money they had saved through their years of work in America was in that suitcase. Just as he was about to disappear from sight, two other men leaped out of nowhere and knocked him down. They were plain-clothes detectives who had been watching the thief, and thanks to them Stephen and Colman came back to Aran with their savings intact. So they were able to buy the cottage by Gort an Bhiolair, the watercress field, in Fearann an Choirce, that had once belonged to a distant forbear, Gilbert Dirrane. Stephen, who felt the cold after those malnourished years, lit a huge fire in the grate, and set about realizing his dream of offering visitors comfort and good food, on the island that had treated his youth with such harshness and thrown him out into the world at the age of sixteen.

First a kitchen was added to the back of Gilbert Cottage, and then a little garden of marigolds was wrested from the crag by the front door. At intervals of a year or two the cottage sprouted further additions: another storey, extra rooms behind the kitchen, a long loft above those. The original interior was all knocked into one sitting-room, which was still quite small, and a dining-room built in front of it; then two snug little alcoves for candle-lit *tête-à-têtes* were built out from the dining-room, replacing the plot of marigolds, with terraces on top reached by a very narrow outside staircase. The building has the look of a provisional arrangement that has lasted long enough to weather into endearing familiarity; cube is balanced on cube as in photographs one has seen of sub-Saharan towns. The interior is dark, an old curiosity shop. Every bit of wall-space is filled with antique clocks, painted plates, the text of the Declaration of the Irish Republic, a poster-reproduction of Frederic Burton's Victorian weepy 'The Aran Fisherman's Drowned Child', mirrors, old lamps, and, since his death a few years ago, photographs of Uncle Colman. The fire, a glowing quarter-sackful of coal, is appreciated even in summer by visitors mortified by the unaccustomed damp of Aran. Colman, who used to be a boilerman, would tend it, and spent his winters by it, sitting up, tall and rigid, always clean-shaven and wearing a neat lumberjack shirt. Occasionally, we heard, he would go into Galway and get drunk, but that was as hard to imagine as a grandfather clock getting drunk. Starved of speech sometimes, when M was in London for long autumn months and there were no visitors on the island, I would come up to Gilbert Cottage to phone her, which was a comfort even though the telephone, one of the first in the island, was in a cubby-hole under the stairs in which I had to lean sideways like a wind-blown thorntree, and often I could hardly hear her over the sighing of the waves and the crackling of the stars. Then I would sit for a while opposite Colman by the fire, and Stephen would come and go with large and frequent glasses of red wine, and sometimes recite sad folksongs, making his eyes very round and pathetic:

> *Cé hé sin amuigh a bhfuil faobhar ar a ghuth*
> *ag réabadh mo dhorais dhúnta?*
> *Mise Éamon an Chnoic atá báite fuar fliuch*
> *ó shíorshiúl sléibhte is gleannta ...*

> Who's that outside with hoarseness in his voice
> beating down my closed door?
> I am Éamon of the Hill, who is drowned wet and cold
> from endless walking in mountains and valleys ...

– which would make us huddle round the fire even closer. Or Colman would intone a reminiscence of the America of innocent frontiers:

THERE WAS AN OLD INDIAN MAN. HE HAD A FINE HEAD OF HAIR. 'BY GOD,' I SAYS
TO HIM, 'YOU'VE GOT A FINE HEAD OF HAIR FOR YOUR AGE!' 'I HAVE,' HE SAYS, 'AND
DO YOU KNOW NOW, WHEN I WAS A YOUNG MAN ALL MY HAIR FELL OUT,' SAYS HE,
'AND I WAS ASHAMED AND I NEVER TOOK MY CAP OFF. WELL,' SAYS HE, 'I WENT TO
BUFFALO ONE TIME, AND I MET AN INDIAN, AND SAYS HE, 'YOU GIVE ME FIVE DOL-
LARS, AND I'LL GIVE YOU A BOTTLE WITH SOMETHING IN IT,' SAYS HE, 'AND IF IT
DOESN'T GIVE YOU SOME OF YOUR HAIR BACK – I WON'T SAY ALL OF IT – YOU CAN
WRITE TO ME AND I'LL SEND HALF YOUR MONEY BACK – I WON'T SEND ALL OF IT –
OR I'LL SEND YOU ANOTHER BOTTLE.' 'WELL BY GOD,' SAYS HE, 'I'D GIVE ANYTHING
TO HAVE A FINE HEAD OF HAIR, AND I'LL GIVE YOU TEN DOLLARS, AND IF IT WORKS,'
SAYS HE, 'I'LL SEND YOU ANOTHER FIVE.'' WELL, I DON'T KNOW WHAT WAS IN THE
BOTTLE, BUT HE RUBBED IT IN EVERY DAY, AND HE PUT A WARM CLOTH ON HIS
HEAD AT NIGHT, AND BY GOD IT COME UP! THEM INDIANS, YOU KNOW, THEY HAVE
A LOT OF REMEDIES, OUT OF THE GROUND.

The famous used to come to Gilbert Cottage to escape from fame; once
M had to calm Stephen's nerves in the kitchen and serve lunch on his behalf
to the wife of an American of inconceivable power and riches, and shoo the
security men out to sit on the garden wall because their gigantic shoulders
were blocking the light of the little windows, while the poor woman lingered at table and let hour after hour of the afternoon dissolve in her wine-
glass. Gilbert Cottage was the choice of all official and important visitors
to the island. Nowadays there are other guest-houses offering more spacious comforts, many visitors prefer to be nearer the nightlife of Cill
Rónáin, and Gilbert Cottage is left to settle into the past. The joins of its
structure are no longer so regularly plastered over, and the snug corners are
not fussed over with dusters. Stephen talks of religion, to which he gave no
heed in the frenetic years of construction and cooking, and tells one that
material things do not last, that what is built up falls down again. House
and master grieve for Uncle Colman.

Nevertheless, this is still the place to find those who come to Aran for
talk, and who prefer the fireside to the television lounge or the voice-
quenching din of the pub. Recently I found there a linguist, Dr James
Duran of California, whose grandfather, an Ó Direáin, was related to
Stephen's forebears. Dr Duran was completing a study of the Irish of Aran,
and in particular that of Árainn itself, which was relatively neglected in
favour of the smaller islands by previous researchers. Our conversation
ranged from the regrettable decay of the Indo-European case system over
the last two thousand years, to the use of the word *blackin* for shoe polish
by Gort na gCapall children – the Cill Rónáin children laugh at them for
talking of putting *blackin bán* (white blacking) on their trainers. I had
sometimes heard Cill Rónáin people complaining of the difficulty of

understanding people from Fearann an Choirce, and was interested to learn that there are two sub-dialects in Árainn, the linguistic boundary lying between Corrúch and Fearann an Choirce. However, the significant differences between local speech patterns are not to be looked for in such oddities of vocabulary as '*blackin*', which can crop up anywhere by historical accident, but in the pronunciation of the most ordinary and common words. Thus in western Árainn the word *siar*, westward, is pronounced as in standard Irish, whereas in eastern Árainn it tends to be pronounced as *séar*. A form peculiar to eastern Árainn is the pronoun *muinn*, we/us, which is *sinn* in Standard Irish; western Árainn uses the Connemara form *muid*. There are similarly subtle differences between the Irish of the three islands, and there is a distinct tinge of Clare (*i.e.* Munster) in that of Inis Oírr, though all of them are very close to Connemara Irish. As to the future of the language in Aran, Dr. Duran is much more optimistic than the late Breandán Ó hEithir or the geographer Reg Hindley, on whose work Breandán relied. In Cill Rónáin, for example, where Professor Hindley thought Irish was in a state of collapse, there has in fact been a resurgence of the language. To quote from a draft paper on the subject Dr Duran showed me:

Kilronan has always been an English-speaking town, but Irish independence and the small government grants of money awarded to Irish-speaking families (now the '£10 grants') stimulated the interest of families in Kilronan in the language. Nevertheless, only thirty years ago, it was common for people from western Inis Mór to be shamed into speaking English by the shopkeepers when they went into Kilronan to do their shopping. Something happened in the mid-1970's, however, which totally reversed the situation, as the following incident illustrates. A young woman from western Inis Mór went overseas in 1972 and returned in 1977. When she went into a Kilronan shop to make a purchase, and spoke English to the shopkeeper, as she was used to doing, she was greeted with, 'Well, aren't we posh now that we've been overseas and have learned a bit of English!' The enraged customer then responded with, 'Well isn't it nice that we've learned enough Gaelic to do business with the customers!'

Professor Hindley, it seems, was struck by the fall in the number of '£10 grants' awarded in recent years, but in fact Cill Rónáin families often do not even apply for them, because they are no longer a significant addition to the family income, and the monolingualism they presuppose is not seen as necessary to the preservation of the language. As Dr Duran writes:

If I, as a stranger, go in to have my bicycle fixed at the Kilronan pier, and drift into English while discussing the virtues of bicycle parts, it will be the teenagers that insist on continuing in Gaelic while we handle the technological problems of the modern world. Teenagers are proud of being bilingual. They are catching up educationally rapidly with the rest of Ireland, and in fact the large floods of foreign visitors to the Aran Islands every summer can help foster a sense of being 'European', that is, multilingual and multicultural in a world where knowing the English language is an advantage, but not the sole measure of a person's intellectual capacity or of his/her cultural refinement.

As to Aran's English, it is so vigorous and savoury that much of what talk my memory brings back from the houses of Fearann an Choirce is in English. I used to call in on Stephen's stepmother, Bríd Gillan, in her cottage just behind the guest-house. In both Irish and English she has an incisive tongue greatly feared by her neighbours and relatives. In her youth she went to Tipperary as a priest's housekeeper, and joined Cumann na mBan, the women's nationalist organization founded by Countess Markievicz. Both there and later in Dublin, where she became nurse to the children of General Mulcahy, she carried food and messages for the IRA men in their guerrilla war against the British. I heard her describing her arrest by the Black and Tans once on Raidió na Gaeltachta. Her captors told her they had done dreadful things to the Countess and threatened to do the same to Bríd. The lapidary English sentence with which she quelled the ignoble brutes stood out for me among the vaguer details of her Irish narrative:

> WHATEVER
> was Done
> to the
> COUNTESS MARKIEVICZ
> I will count it an
> HONOUR
> if it is Done
> to ME.

In her eighties Bríd still had the vigorous stride of her revolutionary youth – a standard military pace, a fraction too long to be exactly 'the walk of a queen' – and a way of discharging her words individually like rounds from a heavy revolver. 'When you're past eighty-two,' she told me once, 'you're not so Spry – or not so Bright – or not so Nice – as you were when you were young (I don't know how nice I was when I was young) – and it's Time – to take a little Trip – to the Other Side.' But Bríd has no marching orders for the Other Side as yet; she has received the congratulations of the Presidents of Ireland and the United States on her hundredth birthday, and still tends the roses round the door of her home, Cliff Top Cottage. But the republic she had fought for was a disappointment to her; in fact she once told me that it was a dictatorship, that had (vainly) tried to limit the size of an extension to her cottage. However, God had evidently approved this work, for while it was in progress and half the house was roofless it had survived a terrible storm, the events of which Bríd recounted to me with great emphasis. The joists and floorboards of the attic kept lifting up and settling down again; she scattered holy water around as much of the extension as she could reach, then lit a sacred candle to watch over it while she and her husband retired to the old part of the cottage, which was under the protection of the Sacred Heart. Even if, as she told me, we are just grains of sand, she was not afraid, for, 'Why should God let the roof be blown off just to please the Devil or a few evil spirits that might be around, when He had only to blink an eyelash to keep it on?' And indeed no harm was done. 'Now,' she concluded, 'I don't know Who Believes, or Who Believes in What, or ...' (the impetus of her delivery driving her inexorably onwards) '... What Believes in Who – BUT THAT WAS A MIRACLE!'

The Gillans came to Aran from Leitrim some time before 1821, when the census lists Peter Gillan, forty-eight, a weaver, his wife Rose and their six children. Róisí Mhór, as she was called, was the midwife I have mentioned who was drowned off Inis Meáin one stormy night. Perhaps her skills were inherited by Bríd, who also served the island as a midwife. Certainly Peter's craft was passed down through subsequent generations, and I believe the old loom is still in existence, in one of the little thatched barns behind the Gillan family home, a small neat house just east of Gilbert Cottage, on the boreen running down to the shore. I sometimes used to find Bríd's brother Seán, the story-teller whom I have quoted extensively, poking about in the 'street', the space inhabited by chickens and dogs and clumps of comfrey between his cottage and the barns. The plot in front of the cottage was always scrupulously orderly, whether it was ridged for potatoes, a golden sea of rye, or a constellation of little haycocks. Seán himself was exemplary, as neat and bright-eyed as a wren in his eighties (he died at the age of ninety-eight; a brother of his in Connemara lived to be a hundred), but the family situation was decayed within and I rarely penetrated the house. Seán's reminiscences were for me the gateway to the old, vanished, Fearann an Choirce which clustered around the bends in the boreen where it wound down the scarp below Cliff Top Cottage:

There were seven houses down there on the east side of the road. I only remember the last of them. In fact it was I who knocked it down about twenty years ago, long after the two old women died, the Nancies, as they were called. You wouldn't believe how small it was! From here to there, about eight feet long and six feet wide. You wouldn't know how in the world they lived inside in it. The two of them were always quarrelling with each other, and then nobody would go near the house. They used to be throwing things at each other. My grandfather told me it was a right hullaballoo. But the last of them died a good while back now. A good while, three score years perhaps, or more.

But when the house was knocked, you wouldn't believe the rafters that were in it! The thickness of them! And it was here in Fearann an Choirce those trees were felled! There was a wood back there on the left-hand side, along the bottom of the cliff. Water flows out there. Soft ground, a sort of turlough. That is where they cut the trees those rafters were made from. I tell you no lie! I took them myself and put them in that little cabin north of my own house. They're still there. Not a bit of woodworm in them, just as they were. That was the last of the seven houses. The house of the Nancies.

Seán's grandfather would have been the weaver described in Tom O'Flaherty's account of the making of his first suit of clothes:

In Aran the boys wore woollen petticoats until they reached what I then considered an advanced age. We had one old black sheep [whose] wool was enough to supply my father's requirements; but now that I was growing out of the red petticoat stage another black sheep was necessary. Unluckily all the black lambs this sheep produced were males! If I had to wait until she had a female I might be in petticoats for the rest of my life. Then the weaver decided to do something about it. He decreed that my mother and I pray for a black female lamb. Our prayers were answered. Now I wouldn't have to go through life dressed like a woman!

I always helped my mother prepare the wool for the weaver. After it was washed we spread it out on the flags to dry and I stood guard over it. After it was thoroughly dried we teased it into a soft fluffiness. Then it was carded into rolls ready for the spinning-wheel. When mother had a number of spindle-fuls spun I held the spindle while she wound the thread onto a ball. Then the great day arrived when we took the balls of thread, *ceirtlíní* we called them, to the weaver. ... The weaver's loom had a great fascination for me. I sat for hours at a time watching our craftsman throw the shuttle, operate the crude machinery with his legs and now and then sprinkle the thread with a home-made lubricant. The odour of this lubricant was not as incense to the nostrils.

(Another villager let me into the secret that this 'home-made lubricant' was urine, and the weaver had to put up with catcalls of *fiodóir fuail*, pissweaver, because of it.)

In Thomas Mason's *The Islands of Ireland*, published in 1936, is a splendid photograph of the Gillan's old loom at work. It is still kept in one of their little outhouses, but only spiders weave on it. Behind every house in the village there are similar stores, barns, sheds, most of them adapted from abandoned ancestral cabins, clinging like a temporal shadow to the village of today, and stuffed with things that might come in useful if ever history repeats or reverses itself. Accidental resurrection of this material can be touching, painful, or sometimes comic; sometimes one would not know how to react to it. An elderly neighbour called Colm Mór used occasionally to greet me with a sentence from Pádraig Ó Conaire's essay, 'M'asal Beag Dubh', which for many children is their first taste of literature, and for Colm had remained the summit and epitome of the written word: '*I gCinn Mhara bhíos nuair chuireas aithne ar m'asal beag dubh i dtosach.* (In Kinvara it was that I first made acquaintance with my little black donkey).' Ó Conaire was brought up in the respectable shopkeeping family of that name (anglicized as Connery) of Ros Muc in Connemara, lived a wandering Bohemian life, contributed notably to the rebirth of Irish prose writing, and died drunk and neglected in Galway, where there is now a statue of him. Our neighbour, having declaimed that unforgettable inaugural sentence of 'My Little Black Donkey', would sometimes break into a paean to artistic glory: 'And now they're gone, the Connerys of Ros Muc! Judge Connery with all his law and all his education, and Canon Connery, they're all dead, and it's not them the ladies come round to see and look at his statue!' Since we ourselves had just reached the Little Black Donkey stage of Irish literature I asked him if he still had his copy, and he promised to look for it. A few days later he came to the door with a tattered school text of the Ó Conaire essay, which he said he had found with a lot of other old books in the pigsty. I was eager to inspect this hoard, and went back to his house with him and round behind it to the disused pigsty, which was full of dust and decay. The literature was under some old sacks in a stone trough. In semi-darkness we picked layer after layer off the pile of mouldering copybooks and calendars from the days of his youth, and suddenly under our noses was a dingy photograph of half a dozen naked girls, standing side by side almost at attention, with permed waves in their hair and rosebud lips. We stood there gaping at them wordlessly; they looked as surprised to see us as we were to see them. Colm was the first to recover powers of speech. 'Them are people!' he said, and turned them aside.

The Kings were another family that settled in Aran around the beginning of the last century and passed down their trade almost to the present day. Gregory King, thirty-six, smith and farmer, figures in the 1821 census, with his wife Kate and a son aged three, his mother-in-law Mary Joyce, and two stepchildren from Kate's previous marriage to a Dirrane; in the same household are an elderly weaver, James McDonnell and his wife, and a house servant, Tom Lee. They have a quarter-acre of land. Mícheál King tells me that Gregory came from Renvyle in the north-west of Connemara; he was a member of the Whiteboys, one of the secret societies behind what the newspapers called 'agrarian unrest', and had to flee the locality after threatening a landlord. Tobar Ghríóir, also called Tobar an Ghabha, the well of the smith, at the head of the village, is named from him, and the roofless house close by it was his. The old smithy, now an outhouse, is next to Gilbert Dirrane's cottage; Mícheál has pointed out to me among the nettles by its door the stone trough in which the red-hot iron was quenched, and from which pregnant women used to drink because of the magic properties of iron. By an odd chance I have a record of some of the conversations that took place at Gregory's forge. George Warren, a Protestant bible-reader from the Irish Island Society, was at work in Aran in the winter of 1854/5, and a single volume of his journal which was somehow acquired by the archaeologist John Goulden has passed through my hands. Unfortunately it does not cover his arrival or his leaving the island, but it shows his persistence in calling on five or six families each day and trying to redirect them from reliance on the priest, the Blessed Virgin and the saints, to repentance and the unmediated word of God. 'Be ye instant in season and out of season,' says St Paul, and Mr Warren evidently ordered his life by that word. I select the following from many similar entries:

Tuesday 19th December Visited the forge at Farnachurke where I met five men & after some time, I turned the Discourse on the shortnefs of time & the length of eternity, & the love & all sufficiancy of our Lords sufferings, throgh repentance and faith, but repentance sounded very strange in some of thier ears, & some seemd to take some notice of what I said – Visited Griggory Kings, George Gailliams [*i.e.* Gillans] Dannial Dirrans, and Patrick Dirrans, Farnachurcke, & all seemd very civil, & liftened all I said, & made no reply, but at Guilliams, where we had some reasoning, & he admitted that my reasoning was very plain present in all thirteen—

Wednesday 27th December Visited the forge at Farnachurcke, & met some men there, & after some time I turned the discourse of the Means of grace, but was paid but little attention to as they were all young lads, present five.

Friday 29th December Visited the forge at Farnachurcke, & after some time, I turned the discourse from the war, to eternity as I met some old men there I shewed them that was what should trouble us, & one man said that I was right, but that they never thought untell they were laid on a sick bed & I reasoned with them on the danger of living in such a way & on the 6 of the 14 of John, & some began to pray present eight—

Thursday 11th January Visited the forge at Farnachurcke, & done no good, as all was noise & bustle with sledge & hammer—

After a couple of months of this, Mr Warren turned his attention to Cill Rónáin and Cill Éinne, but found the people there immured in fear of the priest, love of drink, and belief in Purgatory. His journal makes sad reading; the only living note in it is the echo of that 'noise and bustle with sledge & hammer' from Gregory King's forge.

In the time of Gregory's grandson, early in this century, the Kings built the new house a couple of hundred yards further down the road, and reclaimed the crags around it. It is a large cottage with ample lofts lit by windows in the gable-ends, that make it almost two-storied. All around it are evidences of the vigour and enterprise of the family: the huge concrete tank built against the back of the house to collect rainwater for gutting fish, the kiln in which limestone was burned with turf to make lime for white-wash and fertilizer, the sties and *póiríní* and barns full of tools such as a great two-man saw in a frame with a handle at either end, with which the rafters of the house were cut from baulks of timber washed up on the shore, the spinning wheel, the kelp rakes made in their own forge, the tram-nets, the eighteen-foot pitchfork for gathering seaweed. When increasing traffic made it difficult to work with horses at the old roadside forge they built another behind the house, in which their great leather bellows has not yet breathed its last. The field-walls around the forge are draped with rusty chains salvaged from wrecks, out of the links of which horseshoes were beaten before the mass-produced shoes of Swedish iron became available. All this vigour, still tangible in the stout double walls of the green fields won from the rock, only began to slacken in recent times. Mícheál's broth-ers left the island, Patrick to become a garda and Tiger (after his brief celebrity as the Man of Aran) to work in the Woolwich Arsenal as a smith; he later organized teams of Irish labourers, and a survivor of one of these has told me that Tiger used to pay for their keep in a hostel where they had to burn the bugs out of cracks in the walls with candles. (We met the Tiger once in his latter years, at a reunion of Aran Islanders in the Irish Club in Camden Town; I remember how, when the Archbishop of Tuam was brought over to where he was sitting, the Tiger began to rise like a surfac-ing whale, and the table rocked and the big pints of Guinness went tum-bling, and he grew and grew until we all looked like the runts Oisín found in Ireland on his return from Tír na nÓg.) Then Mícheál's father died – some years after but because of having been 'tackled' by a bull, according to Mícheál – but his mother lived on for years, and in the end only Mícheál was left to run the farm and the smithy. The momentum of the year, like a great flywheel, keeps him going, the horse has to harrow the field to grow the hay to feed the horse, but time has outgrown the necessary tasks, and sometimes when a summer Sunday evening was still bright at nine o'clock I used to find him roving his land in an agony of boredom, and he would groan from the depths of his being, 'Oh, that was a long day!'

Nevertheless, even in the 1970s the smithy often relived old times. In spring when the jaunting-cars were being readied for the tourist season, smoke rose quite frequently from the forge chimney; the horse stood patiently, tethered to the wall, while Mícheál reproved the inadequacies of the modern shoe with a few taps of the hammer, Oscar the dog would hang around ready to dart in between the horse's legs and snap up the hoof-parings, and I would hang around too, and carry juicy morsels of talk back to M in the evening. One day I listened to men discussing a Turkish weightlifter who could lift half a ton, and one of them explained how this could be achieved by training; for instance, he said, if you had a cow in calf, and you went out to the field on the day the calf was born and lifted it up, that would be easy; and if you did the same thing every day you would always be able to lift it, so that when it grew into a fine bull and the day came for shipping it to Galway there would be no need of the winch and you could hand it up onto the steamer yourself. Another time when Mícheál and myself were repainting his sidecar, M brought us out mugs of tea, and we squatted down to drink them. Mícheál put his mug on his knee, and said, '*Tá mé i mo shuí anois ag bord nárbh fhéidir leat a cheannacht ar ór ná ar airgead.*' ('I'm sitting now at a table you couldn't buy for gold or silver.') 'Is that from a story?' I asked, and bit by bit he recovered from the depths of memory a story his father had heard from a cobbler in Cill Mhuirbhigh. It concerned a schooner that sailed into Westport with a cargo of wheat. The hatches were left open for a few days before unloading began, to let the vapours clear from the hold. But when the captain inspected the cargo he found that salt water had seeped in around the edges of the hatches, and the grain was damp and ready to sprout. The merchants refused to take it, and the captain was in a fix. However, another man turned up and offered to buy it cheap, and he and the captain agreed on a price. But since they knew nothing of this man the captain asked the mate to find out what style of life he led. The mate followed the man and found him in a thatched cottage with as many holes in the roof as there are stars in heaven, sitting on a stool with his mug on his knee. The man welcomed the mate and fetched out the whiskey bottle, and by the time the mate got back to the ship he was quite merry. 'What sort of a place does he have?' asked the captain. 'It has more windows than any mansion,' said the mate, 'and the table he sat at you couldn't buy for gold or silver.' 'Say no more!' cried the captain, 'He's our man!' So the deal went ahead, and the man bought the wheat and paid for it. Then he spread it out on sheets, and the weather was fine and it soon dried out, and the next year the Famine came, and his fortune was made. His name, Mícheál thought, was Vanderbildt or Levenstein or something like that.

A smith has an affinity for iron; he can sense its presence by smell or magic; Mícheál has told me that he can always find a cast shoe or a link or hook lost off a harness and kicked into the grass of the roadside. Similarly iron tends to find its way to the forge, whose dark shelves and dusty win-

dowsill are littered with odd bolts and nuts that sometimes after long separation achieve a new conjugation in use, twisted hinges that might live to
squeak again, rusty cleats, stanchions, toggles and pulleys discharged from
the sea but still fit for odd jobs on the waterfront. And among all this
lumber I have found an accumulation of generations of anvil-talk. The son
of the smith watches and listens as the raw matter of reality is heated, ham-
mered out, quenched, shaped into useful and durable items, which in his
turn he will be called upon to reshape and improve and adapt to other days.
Mícheál is generally admitted in Fearann an Choirce to be the best man for
genealogies, which in this densely interwoven community are much discussed, sometimes with pride or anxiety, but often with a disinterested fascination, like a puzzle. If a particular field is mentioned in an anecdote, we
have to diverge into the question of its ownership before the story can proceed, and thence into genealogies, which either ramify uncontrollably and
have to be summarized with an exclamation of 'Oh, there's a crowd of them
in it!' (*e.g.* the Ó Direáin clan, so numerous in this village), or successfully
pursued down to a personal acquaintance ('Oh, I knew him as well as an
old penny!'). Thus everything is worked over again and again, every place,
personality or event is traversed from every angle, everything is shown to
be connected with everything else, every story contains all stories. And now
by some quirk of elective affinity I have fallen heir to four generations of
these anvil-words. Difficult as I find its country elisions and density of local
reference, after years of repetitious neighbourliness and companionship a
portion of this matter has lodged itself in my head – only a fraction of the
whole, but more than I know what to do with. The fact that I could, for
example, recount the course taken by the last hare to be hunted in Aran, or
imitate Fr Farragher's domineering way of taking the hammer from the
hands of Mícheál's father and forging a horseshoe himself, sometimes feels
like a burden, a responsibility it might take more than a lifetime to discharge.

The next buildings down the road from the forge are the national
school and the summer school, with the ruins of the earlier national school
opposite them, and a little farther away, the former teacher's residence.
Whatever joyful rumpus or dull rumour of rote-learning emerges from the
living schools, I hear the echo of a thunderous silence from the dead one.
The original of this silence lasted for six months, from January to May, in
1911; it is part of the island's history.

David O'Callaghan, of Broadford in Limerick, came to Inis Meáin as
national school-teacher in 1880, and married the schoolmistress. He took
over the Oatquarter National School in 1885, and was driven from the
island in 1914. A go-ahead cleric dominated most of this period: Fr Far-

ragher, who was a curate under Fr O'Donoghue and returned to the island as parish priest in 1897, was the driving force behind the buying-out of the Hill Farm and its division between the Cill Éinne tenants, and later in the foundation of the Aran Fisheries Co-operative Society. At first O'Callaghan was not opposed to the priestly drive to material improvements. He became the secretary of a little agricultural bank under the chairmanship of Fr Farragher, which he ran from the Residence; it was known popularly as Banc na mBanbh, the piglet bank, because it lent money for the buying of piglets, repayment being due on sale of the fattened pigs. (Unfortunately some who could have benefited from it did not do so because they tasted the copper spoon of charity in it; Mícheál remembers hearing old men boast that, poor as they were, they 'never went to Banc na mBanbh'.) O'Callaghan was also concerned in the fisheries; in 1895 he had two currachs let out to islanders and was among the founders of a fishing co-operative. But he soon became deeply interested in the islanders' culture. He learned Irish and spoke it with his neighbours, as appears from this account of the 'evil eye' he gave the ethnographer A.C. Haddon in 1890 or '91:

Numberless are the tales told of the Evil Eye and of those who have succumbed to it, and of those who have been cured. Among the latter is one which was related to me lately as having happened to the narrator himself:—

'Well, master,' he says, 'and you don't think there is such a thing as the Evil Eye?' 'No, Pat,' said I; 'I don't think there is.' 'You don't think there is? Well! I tell you there is, and I am the man who can tell it to you. You see me now,' he says; 'I suppose you don't think much of me today; yet, thirty or forty years ago, I was one of the best men in Aran. I was one night at a dance, and although you would not believe me now, I was then a fine dancer. I was praised by all in the house while I was dancing, but just in the middle of the dance I fell down dead on the floor.' 'Dead, Pat?' 'Yes, dead,' said he; 'for I had not a kick in me then, nor for two days after. Well, my friends, knowing what was the matter with me, got every person in the house to throw a spit on me, saying at the same time, "God bless you", but to no purpose. I remained dead, thrown in a bed in the corner near the fire, for two days, when a young woman comes in and spits on me, saying "God bless you, Patrick, you are very ill;" when I went of one jump from the corner to the middle of the floor, and began to dance; and I was well from that out.' 'Of course, Pat,' I said, 'You married that girl?' 'God bless you,' said Pat, 'I thought you had sense till now. I did not, nor would I, if there was not another girl in Aran.' This is as close a translation, as possible, of Pat's story as told to me in Irish.

O'Callaghan also contributed lists of Aran words to Fr Dinneen's famous dictionary, and an Aran folksong to a pioneering collection published in 1892 by Dómhnall O'Fotharta of Callow in the west of Connemara, a fellow schoolmaster and enthusiast for what he called '*an teanga bhinn bhríoghmhar, teanga treun tuilteach, teanga uasal ard ársa ár sinnsear féin*' ('the sweet lively tongue, the strong overflowing tongue, the noble, high, ancient tongue of our own ancestors'). Such teachers were at that time totally reversing the ethos of the national schools; whereas it had been the policy to beat the Irish language out of the pupils and to turn them into loyal subjects of Her Majesty, it was now the schoolmasters and mistresses who were insisting on the importance of Irish, even in the face of parental opposition, and who were revealing to native speakers that their language had an existence in books. Liam and Tom O'Flaherty were among those taught to read and write Irish in Oatquarter National School. Returning to Aran from America thirty years later Tom O'Flaherty remembered O'Callaghan with the greatest respect:

Mr. O'Callaghan did great work. He was no cheap Jingo nationalist of the type who froths at the mouth at the mention of an Englishman; but he hated British imperialism with all its works and pomps. He was the first *Sinn Feiner* in the island, and had no difficulty in making one of me. ... I wondered where my old schoolmaster was, if he were still alive, and if he recollected the many tricks I played him on him for which he thrashed me with violence and with demoniacal fury. He was a fine man. How many workers like O'Callaghan are forgotten when the ideals for which they struggled are realized in whole or in part, while the blatant politicians and the gentlemen who always managed to pick the winning side are honoured?

O'Callaghan was a member of the Gaelic League from soon after its foundation in 1893, and when Patrick Pearse was thinking of starting an Aran branch in 1898 it was natural for him to canvas the opinion of 'Dáithí Ó Ceallacháin'. At the inaugural meeting of the Aran branch, chaired by Fr Farragher, O'Callaghan delivered 'a scathing indictment of the National School system as worked in the Irish-speaking districts, maintaining that where Irish is the home language of the people it should be taught simultaneously with English from the time the child first enters the school'.

Over the next few years relationships between the two rival leaders of the island community deteriorated. In 1905 O'Callaghan resigned from the secretaryship of the bank, and in 1907 Fr Farragher resigned from the position of school manager for a time in an attempt to get rid of the teacher. Then came 'the time of the Saucepans', the bomb-attack on the Presbytery arising out of a feud over the distribution of the Hill Farm lands, and the sentence of boycott pronounced from the altar by Fr Farragher on those responsible and anyone who had dealings with them. O'Callaghan, deeply involved in the web of island relationships, refused to ban certain pupils from his school as directed by the priest. Farragher tried to have him dismissed, but O'Callaghan had the respect and support of the Inspectors of the Board of National Education and was able to hold out against him. Just before the beginning of the January term in 1911 the priest spoke from the altar about O'Callaghan's school:

[I] would not recommend parents to send their children to that school if they had any other; not telling you not to send them there, but if you take my advice you won't. As you know I have not visited that school for some time, and when the Priest does not visit the school there is something out of place, and I believe the fault is not mine.

As a result O'Callaghan found the school deserted when he came to open it. He remained facing empty benches to the end of the school day; he came the next day at the appointed time and did the same, and maintained this dignified and lonely vigil throughout the winter and spring, until the school closed at the end of May. In the following year he took Fr Farragher to court for the words he had spoken from the altar, but the jury found that the priest had spoken in good faith and without malice, and the slander action failed. Fr Farragher was awarded costs, and as O'Callaghan refused to pay, eventually had him evicted from the Residence. O'Callaghan wrote a last plaintive letter to a Galway paper before leaving the island, in February 1914:

Dear Mr. Editor, – I was evicted from my residence on yesterday, 16th inst. at the suit of Rev. M. Farragher, P.P., Aran Islands, for the recovery of his legal expenses in the case of Callaghan v. Farragher. ... The late Mr. Gladstone styled an eviction 'a sentence of death'. These sentences were carried out in the past by a few evicting landlords, but it is rather a novel incident for a priest professing national sentiments to play the role of evictor.

Of course it was not a sentence of death; O'Callaghan went on to teach elsewhere, and even, I am told, revisited the island in about 1931, at which time Liam O'Flaherty was writing up his old schoolmaster as the eponymous hero of *Skerrett*. O'Flaherty, who as pupil to the teacher and altar boy to the priest had seen them both as towering figures, made of their conflict a titanic struggle for the island's soul. He ends his version of their story with these words:

Thirty years have passed since Skerrett's death and already his name has become a glorious legend on that island, where his bones were not allowed bleach and moulder into the substance of the rock, which was so like his spirit. His enemy ... has also become a legend, but his legend grows less with the years, while that of the schoolmaster grows greater. ... He aimed at being a man who owns no master. And such men, though doomed to destruction by the timid herd, grow after death to the full proportion of their greatness.

However, O'Callaghan inhabited a more complex and less teleological world than does his literary counterpart. A few Dublin Gaeilgeoirí are aware of his role in the preservation of the Irish language in Aran, but on the island itself his spirit is locked up with that of the priest in the puppet-booth of folk memory. The Residence is now Mícheál's, for the educational authorities eventually sold it off to his father, and together with its other dilapidated fixtures and fittings he has inherited something of its history, from which he has acted out a few scenes for me. The first shows me the villagers and the curate assembling in the Residence for the annual Stations. It was customary on such an occasion for the householder to send a horse for the parish priest, but the teacher has omitted to do this, and after hearing the confessions in the living-room the curate has to emerge into the kitchen and tell the people that as the priest has not arrived they will have to wait until the next Sunday to receive the Sacraments. The next scene takes place on that Sunday: the priest paces up and down outside the chapel wondering if the teacher will apologize, but when he arrives the teacher comes bounding up the steps and pushes past with an off-hand greeting. Sorrowfully the priest speaks from the altar, saying how glad he is that it was no islander who has done this thing. Finally, I see the teacher swaggering back to the Residence with his cronies and crying, 'I wouldn't send a *cat* for that old devil!'

The Residence stands almost on the brink of the scarp marking an ancient boundary which I will use to fractionate off a further essence of Aran, and so it provides a convenient full stop for the eastern portion of this book. It is a neat little house, perfectly symmetrical, of the standard 1880s design of such residences; an architect has described it for me as follows:

This two-storey house has an unusual front elevation. The traditional straight-ridged slated roof, with gable-ends, has a feature central gable with a decorative scalloped fascia. The two small square windows of the upper storey are gathered together within the gable directly under the fascia. At the intersection of the gable with the main roof ridge is a central chimney-stack. The entrance porch is plain and small, with a lean-to roof having a sprocket-supported fascia; there is a glazed lunette fanlight above the single solid entrance door. On each side of the entrance porch is a rectangular window, which is four-paned, as are the windows at first-floor level.

The history of the Residence after the eviction of O'Callaghan, and the tenure of his successor, Moloney, whom I have already dealt with, is soon told. For many years it was rented out by the Kings to summer visitors, and stood gathering damp into its bones through the winter; then in 1972 it was taken for a longer period by a couple from London. I have not been in a good position to hear much talk of these people, and the following is put together out of the blurbs of a few books and maps they have subsequently published, one or two rather cagey newspaper interviews, and a C.V. concocted as part of an unsuccessful grant-application to Galway County Council.

Tim Robinson was born in England in 1935, attended the grammar school in Ilkley, a small country town in the Yorkshire Dales, and did his National Service as an RAF radar-fitter in Malaya. He went to Cambridge to study physics, switched to mathematics, obtained a second-class degree, and has not maintained any links with his college or his contemporaries. He married in London (little information is available about his partner), and took up a teaching post in Istanbul preparing Turkish students for entry to Robert College, an American foundation now known as the University of the Bosphorus. After three years he relinquished the academic life and moved to Vienna, where he embarked on a career as a painter under the name Timothy Drever (his mother's maiden name was Drever; she was Scottish). His first exhibitions were at the Galerie Fuchs and Galerie Nansen-Haus; the former was the focus of a belated surrealist group known as the Wiener Schule, and the latter had some obscure connection with the Cold-War propaganda instrument, Radio Free Europe, but it does not appear that 'Drever' was associated with either ideological tendency. He returned to London in the 1960s, exhibited abstract works in such bastions of the avant-garde as Signals Gallery and the Lisson, and in 1970 had some critical success with a large 'installation' entitled 'Moonfield', in the Camden Art Gallery. However, he shortly thereafter disappeared from the London art scene and resurfaced in Aran, reverting to the name of Robinson. A projected novel never materialized, but in 1975 he published a rudimentary map of the islands. This was followed by more detailed maps of the Burren in 1977 and of the Aran Islands in 1980. In 1982 the Robinsons left the island for no known reason and were next heard of in Roundstone, a small fishing village in the west of Connemara. There 'M' (as she is designated, in her brief appearances in one of Robinson's books) established a small concern called Folding Landscapes to publish the Aran and Burren maps and a map and 'gazetteer' of Connemara that appeared after long delays in 1990, together with some related prose works. In 1989 the collected output of Folding Landscapes won the Ford European Conservation Award as Ireland's offical entry. This seems to have suggested to Robinson that it was incumbent upon him to participate in local environmental controversies, but little has been heard from him on such topics in more recent years. A TV film entitled *Folding Landscapes* by Michael Viney and

David Cabot hinted at a metaphysical or perhaps merely mathematical background to Robinson's mapping procedures. The first volume of his book on the Aran Islands, or rather on one of them, *Stones of Aran*, was published by The Lilliput Press as long ago as 1986; a second volume is promised, but has been so long in gestation that by the time it appears the first will have been forgotten.

This 'career' can best be described, I think, as inconclusive. The Residence has stood empty for many years now, and gives an impression of internal collapse; its garden is occasional grazing for the blacksmith's horse. If one asks Mícheál about its former resident, he says merely, 'Tim Robinson? Oh, I knew him as well as an old penny!'

II
RESIDENCE

RESIDENCE

The weed-grown path, north-south, bisects the rectangle of our garden. The house is symmetrical about the same axis, and at times the solar system nods to this fact. At six o'clock of an equinoctial evening the half-moon, seen from the gate, stands just above the chimney-pot, its diameter exactly vertical. A long braid of starlight and dark matter divides the glamorous night of Aran above the garden: the Milky Way, the home-galaxy seen from within. As the earth rotates, this vast pointer swings across the dial of the sky at half the rate of an hour-hand; twice a day, therefore once a night, it is aligned with the garden path. Life is repetitious enough for us to rehearse tomorrow's words, it provides respites in which one can try to make sense of unrepeatable acts like our coming to Aran; it suggests that a book is a compilation of sentences. I think much about these things, thinking nothing of them. Once, chatting with a passing islander at the gate on a summer evening, I aired my knowledge of the constellations (which in fact does not extend much beyond the two Bears and the Seven Sisters), and he said, 'I suppose now, if you were put down in the middle of the Mediterranean' – that being the most impressive-sounding sea he had to hand – 'you could find your way to shore, on the strength of your education!' But education assumes that yesterday's lesson is valid today, and as a might-have-been mathematician whose thumbs ache from milking a cow, I know that nothing happens twice, that if today you find the right words to greet your beloved or the passer-by, it does not mean you will do so tomorrow; nor does a surplus of meaning in one sentence stand to the credit of the next. At six o'clock of a midwinter evening the half-moon is high in the sky above the chimney, and tilted; the slant of its flat side, according to a little diagram I have drawn in the margin of my manuscript, represents the inclination of the earth's axis to the plane of its orbit about the sun. So the midwinter moon says Here we go, spinning through space like a stone skipped on water; if we slow, we sink – but we will never slow. And why should I accept even that assurance from the backslider of the heavens, every evening a little later, a little older? However, I do not envy those with a southern hemisphere to their minds, whose night skies are certified with the Cross. Mine are queried constantly by those three constellations, the Greater, Lesser and Least Question Marks, and I like it so.

The garden wraps around the house like an old coat, out at elbows, suitable only for gardening in, pockets full of seeds and string. Moloney built high walls to temper the wind to his shrubs, and put windows in the walls to sun them; the glass is long gone and blackbirds hurtle through their panes of air. The garden is neither battlefield nor neutral ground between nature and the domestic, but a bazaar of exchanges and thefts. As I tug out yards of goosegrass and bindweed, the guardian robin watches me from the bushes, its eye glinting through first one triangle of twigs and then another. Donkeys wandering the road make a note of what they see, and come back by night to nose the gate open and rip the young carrots out of my neat ridges. The white stonecrop does not grow in our garden, but it must have done so once and been thrown out of one of the windows with garden rubbish, for it flowers on a heap of stones outside and has crept along the grykes to the east and to the south for a hundred yards or more. When I wanted a rockery (a curious wish, on Aran!) and brought in stones from the crag with interesting saxifrages and cranesbills, various grasses came too, and soon all I had was a grassy mound.

To the left of the house, where the cypress lifts its derelict limbs into the windy spaces above the walls, there is a gateway which once had a high wooden gate in it, leading to the back yard and a stone outhouse, its doors, windows and corrugated iron roof half wrecked by storms. Gusts funnelling through the gap between this store and the house are to be respected; in squally weather when we have to run out for a bucket of coal or to disentangle the sheets on the clothes-line strumming across the yard, we find ourselves adopting the crouched, hen-like scuttle we have noted in certain village housewives on their rare sallies into the open. The floor of the yard is a single huge flag of the limestone bedrock, the two or three fissures across it filled in with concrete. We often dine there, moving cushions around to catch the last of the sun. In high summer we sunbathe with our backs to the back of the house, naked as the rock, melting into a drowse but keeping an eye awake for the horsefly that materializes out of a tiny crescendo whine into sudden immobility beside us on the baking stone, and an ear for the click of the front gate or the tactful whistling with which the postman always announces his approach. Sometimes the small stone enclosure is too intense with life for comfort. One spring there was an exceptional emergence of six-spot ladybirds; the split husks of their larvae were everywhere on the whitewashed rear wall of the house, with the adult beetles oozing out as glossy as fresh drops of blood. Every summer there comes a humid day on which the ants take their mating flight, and by sunset the yard is littered with fallen wings and spent bodies.

The thick, solid, chin-high wall closing the yard off from An Chreig Mhór, the great crag, is of big blockish stones mortared together, with alternate stones of the topmost course set on end as a rough castellation. It is inhabited by little ferns – wall-rue, common spleenwort, the rusty-back, which is rather an Aran speciality – and is knobbly enough to be climbed with ease; I once scrambled over it from the other side holding a butterfly in my cupped hands, an unfamiliar moth-like one I'd caught on the crag and was bringing home to identify (a dingy skipper, it turned out to be). It is a good wall to lean against with one's morning coffee and look over at the level acres of rock stretching southwards to the Atlantic. If the ocean is still and grey it is hard to make out in this low perspective where stone ends and water begins, somewhere beyond the rooftops of Gort na gCapall half a mile away. But farther to the right of the view the edge of the land rises, and Dún Aonghasa is profiled against the sky. I had not realized how much the daily sight of that fold of mysteries, in uninterrupted co-presence with my own home, meant to me, until we returned from a brief absence to find that an electricity pole had been erected exactly on that line of vision. I have no belief in the flow of Celtic energies and the psychic virtues of ancient stone, no respect for the theory of ley-lines, based as it is on the fusty paradigms of Victorian physics – but some communication was broken by that damned pole. On seeing it for the first time I felt that my presence in Aran was unsettled, that the idea of leaving Aran could be explored, as one's tongue worries at a tooth that has been loosened by a blow.

The front door of the Residence is difficult to open; it has sagged on its hinges and drags on the tiled floor within. Now and then I rasp a bit of rotten wood off the lower edge with whatever tools I can find, but it soon lapses a bit farther and jams again. The hallway is just space enough to turn around in and hang up a coat. And there is sometimes another obstacle to getting through it, an image that fills it completely with horror. A very old lady I met on the road one day told me about the death of David O'Callaghan's wife, whom she could remember. Mrs O'Callaghan, she said, was very fat and heavy, and she liked a drop of drink. One day she staggered against the kitchen range and set herself on fire. She tried to run out of the house to scream for help from anyone passing the gate, and she died in that little box of a hall – perhaps the door jammed even then. But we pass through the hall so often that the idea of Mrs O'Callaghan's death there is fading, like linoleum due for renewal.

Two doors open off the hall, the living-room to the left and the kitchen to the right. The living-room has a little hearth, and a sash window at either end. When we moved in, it was papered in a curious pattern of sea-weed-coloured bricks which undulated subliminally because the wallpaper was half detached from the damp plaster, and the yellowish net curtains had tattered hems because, as Mícheál explained, his dog Oscar had once been locked in here accidentally and had clawed at them in jumping up to the windows. But once we had scraped down and whitened the walls and filled an alcove with bookshelves, it became a charming room. Its front window faces into the lower boughs of the cypress; once during a sudden battering downpour I looked out to see a sparrowhawk perched within a few feet of me, as impatiently self-contained as a clenched fist. The back window faces onto the yard and the great crag beyond. I used to write up my diary at a table before this window. Some days rave on for pages, others expire in a phrase. One entry, I see, reads in its entirety:

September 24th, the Light Arches, dullest of moths, dead on the windowledge this morning.

I have no memory of this unmemorable September 24th, on which I must have alleviated my boredom by leafing through the pictures of dozens of species of dull, ochreous, brindled moths in my childhood copy of Richard South's *The Moths of the British Isles*, and savouring the names of the Light Arches, the Reddish Light Arches, the Dark Arches, the Cloud-Bordered Brindle, the Clouded Brindle, the Brindled Ochre – a nomenclature which I take it was the great achievement of rural Anglicanism in its early nineteenth-century torpor, a state I thoroughly understand. Too many days I have sat at this table, staring vacantly at the view over the back wall of the dozen roofs of Gort na gCapall, which looked smaller than the cauliflowers of spray slowly burgeoning from the rim of the land behind them and apparently hanging above them for moments before subsiding. I was supposed to be writing, or researching, or thinking. Oscar would come rattling in and hop up to lie in the sunlight on the table-top; sometimes it hardly seemed worth disturbing him by lifting his paw aside to put another word on my paper. Or the chorus-line of M's slips and nighties belly-dancing in the breeze on the rope outside would lure me from my withered plant specimens into erotic reveries. Later I made myself a study out of a room with only a tiny window, upstairs.

The kitchen, with its concrete floor, its ceiling of mahogany-painted board that Mícheál thought was real mahogany and would not let us repaint, its rudimentary furnishings that had suffered many a summer letting and winter mouldering, and the scullery and bathroom in the dank little back-extension opening off it, were the most intractable parts of the Residence. During our first brief summer visit to Aran, lodging at Gilbert Cottage, we had noted the engaging expression of the frontage of the house, but had not seen the interior. Mícheál, whom we happened to meet at its gate, had mentioned that he sometimes let the place to visitors 'for seven pounds a week; that's a hundred and forty shillings'; and later on in

London, faced with a sudden bifurcation of life's paths, we had recalled that modest and comfortable-sounding arithmetic, and wrote to book the house for an indefinite period from the middle of November. My diary of our arrival:

Mr. King was at home, by chance, as he hadn't got our last card, so I collected the key and ran down from his gate to ours because I was too excited to get into the taxi again. The house was just what I had hoped for, bare and a little bleak inside, with potato ridges in the garden, and the wind blowing through the empty window-frames in the high walls round it. We were soon alone in it, and began making it liveable. I tried to make a fire in the living-room but it wouldn't go. The kitchen stove, a little Jubilee range, burned well enough though. Mr. King ran down with a craggy lump of home-made soda bread and a whiskey bottle full of milk, though milk is scarce on the island at this time, he says. We had nothing to make tea with so we walked a mile back to the shop at Eochaill, which was shut, and then another couple of miles to Kilronan. A vicious hail driven into our faces by the wind forced us to hide behind a gatepost. I enquired at the post office about our trunk, but it hadn't arrived. In the shop M learned that the hens weren't laying in this weather, that no meat was to be had, that we could order bacon after tomorrow's boat from Galway had delivered it, and that yesterday's storm had cut the telephone link. When she said, 'I hope we survive the winter!', the lady of the shop looked amazed, and said, 'With the help of God and His Blessed Mother, you'll survive!' She gave her some salted rockfish. The shopkeeper's van brought us back with our load, a few cans of stew and spaghetti etc. We had tea and arrow-root biscuits, and rearranged the furniture. We put the settee in front of the range, with a little form as a table. Through the kitchen is a scullery with a sink and a back door and a window giving onto the yard, a level area of shiny wet rock between the outhouses and their spouting gutters, and to the right out of that the bathroom, both damp and draughty, but Mr. King has pointed out the big key-holes we can stuff up in the back door, and the lump of stone for holding the sacking in place under the door, so no doubt we will get used to it. A short walk later; the sun had a halo round it, and we had to shelter from a couple of showers. We ate fried cornbeef on toast and bread and marmalade, read by the range, then up the narrow staircase in procession with candlestick and chamberpot. Once the candle was out the darkness was perfect. I woke once or twice, almost terrified by the roaring of the wind and the rattling of hail in the fireplace, and this solid alien presence of darkness. 'Tiefe schauervolle Nacht' – I don't know where I got the phrase but it was in my mind all night. M had a bad night too, and was chilled at first, and apparently had a little cry later on.

But M is courageous and resourceful, and soon took the place in hand, gradually bearing down my feeling that every ridiculous derelict detail of it, such as the lump of stone holding the wet sacks in position against the gale under the back door (which Mícheál had pointed out with the air of a landlord showing a prospective tenant the controls of the central heating) was more respectable than all the comforts we had abandoned in London and should not be changed. We scraped the fungus from under the leaky stone sink in the scullery, we got tea-chests and covered them with plastic table-cloths from Evelyn's shop to make working surfaces and storage places. We survived the winter. One morning I found that the sun, striking obliquely through a knot-hole in the back door, had left a golden guinea on the floor; I put my hand down to it, and called M to admire it glowing in my palm. As I lifted it towards the knot-hole it fluttered and dwindled, until I had it dancing like an angel on the tip of my finger. When I poked it back into the hole and took away my hand, it flitted instantly back to the same spot on the floor. Despite all our improvements the Residence, a jackdaw nest among the stars, never ceased to be subject to drips, draughts, cosmic con-jurings, elemental percolations.

The stairs begin in the back right-hand corner of the kitchen, where a fan of three wedge-shaped, hollow-trodden steps leads up to what looks like a cupboard door; inside, they turn left and climb the narrow stairwell unsteadily, creaking like an old man going off to bed. At the top is a small landing with three low doors of flimsy tongue-and-groove, an old wooden chest full of bedclothes and the smell of mothballs, and a knee-high window looking out to the rear of the house. With the door of my writing-room open I can look across the landing and out of this window at the great crag beyond the back wall of the yard; in fact An Chreig Mhór is for me an adjunct to that cramped little study and in some ways the most familiar room of the house. I have botanized so intensively on it that most of Aran's extremest rarities have turned up there, and I watch over their wel-fare as if they were part of the family circle: for example, *Calamagrostis* (Praeger: '... that very rare Irish grass, the Wood Rush'), waving a fine foxy whisk out of a deep crevice; the unobtrusive *Neotinea* or dense-flowered orchid, rare in the Burren and practically unknown elsewhere (Praeger: 'It is strange that it does not occur on the Aran Islands'); the common butter-wort that catches flies on its sticky leaves and is so well adapted to life on the unnourishing bogs of Connemara that it is an ecological scandal here, where it clings to the bare sides of two or three tussocks of black bog rush in a watery little gully. Plant-hunting is a relief and distraction from writ-ing, but that too happens on the crag. If I cannot lay my hand on the phrase I am searching for in my room, I stroll out, scramble over the back wall and go rooting for words among the crevices of the rock. The crag is my testing-ground for the aerodynamics of sentences, a rebounding-place to prance upon when a chapter comes to its own conclusions and sets me free. Since we look down into it every time we go up or down stairs, the crag, even in its most unhomely aspects – by moonlight for example, astir with rabbits like splatters of ink on a silver tray – is not impossibly remote from domesticity. I have even gone down there for reassurance when time seemed to have got lost in the darkness of the night. I remember one starless, three-o'clock vigil, crouched in the lea of a granite boulder under steadily drifting drizzle, unable to make out anything of the world but a wavering layer of dim ellipses floating a foot above the ground, the flowers of hundreds of moon-daisies, forming a false bottom to all appearances.

Of the landing's three doors the first, on the left, with a dented brass knob like an unripe fig, is the bedroom door. The room is small, an attic with sloping ceiling. The high ends of the black wrought-iron bedsteads we found there on our arrival seemed almost to bar entry; later we tackled the rusty bolts and dismantled the bedframes, and replaced them with floor-hugging bed-ends made out of planks from an old crate. M dispelled the morosity of the damp-stained walls and impending ceiling with avocado-green, flower-sprigged wallpaper and billowing lace curtains that trawled the skies from the tiny dormer window and came back full of light and fragrance; there seemed no reason why we should not enjoy a Laura Ashley fantasy of nineteenth-century country living just because we were living in the country and indeed in the nineteenth century. The small tortoiseshell butterflies that besiege the house on hot days, looking for a dark corner that will become their winter quarters, come in at this window and congregate on the opposite corner of the ceiling, where they hang like the faded standards of their glorious summer campaigns. The bedroom has become our secret retreat too, from both nature and society. With the wooden shutters on the inside of the window closed and a blanket stuffed into the crack between them, our Tilly-lamp can tell no one we are at home, and even when the wind gets one fist down the chimney and the other somehow into the wall-cupboard, it cannot buffet us here, while the oil-heater toasts the dampness into a cosy fug and we lie on the floor examining with voluptuous lingerings a newly arrived parcel of books. Concerned friends now and then post us a few cassettes of music, which fall into our hands like messages whirled up by storms raging very far away, and which become through repeated hearings as spent as old pennies or else so overcharged with meaning as to be unbearable. Monteverdi's Tancred and Clorinda mutually unrecognized in their armour, hacking at each other in the dark with the intimacy of lovers quarrelling in bed – but I close the door on this. So much has happened in that room, of which I shall never write.

The next room, straight ahead at the top of the stairs, about eight feet square, with a hard chair by a postage-stamp of a window dedicated to bare rock, was at first a common boxroom and sulking-room. Then one day the ceiling collapsed because of the unstaunchable leaks in the roof, and some plaster fell off its interior walls, revealing that they were built of ancient sods of turf, grey and twisted like senile bricks, which came tumbling round our ankles when we tried to patch the holes. We had to get a local workman to help me wrestle bulging sheets of hardboard into position and nail them to the joists, and then, having the hammer in my hand, I went on to build a desk-like construction under the window out of plastic-coated chipboard delivered from Galway by the cargo boat, and proudly presented the room to M as her study or boudoir. Occasionally My Lady of Silent Reservations withdraws herself into it, leaving me nervously dislocated. What is she doing in there, hour after hour? – weeping herself to death? – writing that feminist thesis we used to joke about, entitled 'Derrida, I married him'? – or is she savouring her solitude like a cat grooming its fur?

My own room, apart from its little window looking onto the front garden, was initially a void, the interior of some lopsidedly truncated Platonic polyhedron. I installed a peculiarly tall table made by Mícheál's father, and a chair that to match it had to be supplemented by several cushions. The room is so small that from my perch I can reach almost all the shelves I have contrived around the walls. Over the years these have filled up with specimens of rocks and fossils, files of correspondence with the botanists, geologists and archaeologists from whom I extort knowledge, drafts of stories, volumes of diary, record-cards of placenames, and parcels of copies of my first map of Aran. One of the functions of a publisher is to protect the author from the physical reality of the book, its weight and volume multiplied by the print-run. Only the self-published know the sudden condensation of the ideal into inert mass, upon the printers' delivering. By the time I had lugged the boxes of the Burren map upstairs, the joists of the ceiling below were sagging under the product of that initially empty room.

Stones of Aran was begun here too; the lumpy stuff of fact and feeling was excogitated through a machinery of emptiness and silence into something that would lie on a page. The pain of that process! How can it be, that a contrivance of 'negative capability' is sometimes blocked for days or weeks at a time, jammed, seized up? Research is easy; however severely it taxes the eyes in libraries or the body in the field, it is a distraction and a relief. Remembering, noting, filing, identifying, querying, confirming – one has resources that can be squandered on such preliminaries. But for the finding of a form of words, there are no resources. Education, vocabulary, information, even wit, imagination, sensibility – these are teeth tensed to snap together, pressing out too-ready formulations; the mind aches with the stress of holding them apart, preserving the space in which words can think themselves into shape. Somehow this is not so bad on winter days, with the rain splattering on the window and the oil-heater singeing my shins, but on a still, hot afternoon it is sometimes unbearable. The intensely alert silence of the garden, the white emptiness of the road going by the gate, the wide amnesia of the world towards me – and then the sudden fidget of a blackbird in the shadow under a bush, exactly 'the sound of the clapping of one hand'. Turns of words cunningly composed to disorientate the mind reveal their banality. A linguistic philosopher, I forget who, put together as a specimen of a meaningless sentence, 'Colourless green ideas sleep furiously.' Seeing the invisible flickering of the air above the hot stone of the garden path, I know exactly what he did not mean to mean. Hopelessly sensible nonsense! I give up. I go downstairs.

The house is empty; M must be sunbathing. I make two mugs of coffee, carry them through the silent inferno of Mrs O'Callaghan in the hall and round to the back of the house. 'Did you write a sentence?' asks M who really believes that I can write sentences. 'Bits of one,' I reply, eyes and voice uncertain, dazzled, after the deep shift in the word-mine. I strip off and lie beside her. The light is enprismed between the whitewashed south-facing wall of the house, the grey limestone so hot we have to lie on rugs, and the black shadow-side of Moloney's back wall. Butterflies are dithering between the stone-hard sky and the chinks in the masonry of the outhouse, entering crouched like pot-holers, backing out, unfurling themselves again. The hour ripens for another heat of the undecidable beauty competition between left breast and right breast. There is no more than a grain of salt between them, but it soon becomes the centre of gravity of the cosmos. The garden sleeps furiously, the road passes by, the world is unmindful, as we mould each other's bodies into their brief perfections.

Afterwards, lapsing back into ourselves, we drift into half-imagined conversations. 'Did you notice how at that moment the Milky Way swung into alignment with my spine?' 'In broad daylight? It was merely that we happened to be lying north-south, as recommended by Marie Stopes.' 'Well, did you hear the sun pounding the stone on either side of us with the flats of its hands?' 'I did not. And you didn't notice that the postman called, and left a parcel of books on your rump.'

Remembering such times, I am moved to a declaration: that making love with Máiréad has been the sustaining joy of my life. There's a certainty! And where else but in the secret heart of my book could I dare such simplicity? From where, proclaim it to so wide a world?

III

WEST

But writing has no rights of residence; it is driven onwards from any achieved moment of symmetry. Unbalancing forces energize the westward progress of this book, for instance. I cannot name them, but for a few months of my first year in Aran they took on a form that, looking back on it, seems like a literary contrivance, and at the time was distressingly imme-diate, literally next door.

The school, as I have mentioned, is just east of the Residence. The first time I passed it when the children were out in the schoolyard, they all flocked to the roadside wall to look at me, with the sudden dense whirring rush of starlings; I found their faces unreadable, gnarled, dark, fist-like. They were too shy to say much, and when they did muster a few words – 'Where ye from?' – they could not understand my answer, and repeated unnervingly, 'Where ye from?' Finding it increasingly difficult to pass the school, I began to know the times at which they would be playing in the yard or inside at their lessons or spilling out onto the road and scattering homewards. Time, in such places as London, is a disease of the wristbone; one sees sufferers glance anxiously at the glittering lump. I had come to Aran to escape the infection, and bitterly resented its outbreak here. The school became an obstacle dividing the island in two, a constant nagging presence like an aching tooth.

What alarmed me in this situation was that I was unable to wrench my mind away from the problem. I am familiar enough with my tendency to obsessions and panics to be able to distinguish subjective from objective threats. Nothing about the kids themselves troubled me; they were not aggressive or even unmannerly, and the worst I could have said about them was that they showed directly what the adults were too polite to hint at, that we were strangers, oddities, curiosities. (At that period there were no other non-island households in Árainn, and no visitors stayed through the winters.) I found myself roving the crags behind the house or the fields below the scarp to the west with a constant directional consciousness of the school, like a numb and wary side to my face, a film over one eye. The search for plants – this was my first season of botanizing and the beauty of each species struck me as with lightning when it made its entrance into the year – became a counter-obsession, deliberately cultivated to offset the other. But I would come home from an afternoon's apparently idle and carefree strolling with rings of anxiety deposited round my eyes. What was this about? My mind went spiralling back through my own childhood, my schooldays, my three years of teaching, the stresses of our own decision not to have children: nothing there that recognizably prefigured my present experience. There were other possible sources of unease too. Vietnam was approaching its crisis; Nixon announced 'the biggest bombing raid in history'. In our previous life we had participated in the great anti-war demonstrations in Trafalgar Square, raged at the American Embassy in Grosvenor Square, donated art-works to 'Medical Aid for Vietnam'; now here I was on the bomb-crazed pavements of Aran, picking flowers. Art is a guilty business, a desperate search for self-justification outside the sphere of justice, and I was not even producing art. I had a nightmare about a radio announcer saying, 'Tonight we bring you the worst news ever. Over to our special reporter ...' – but the special reporter was so horror-struck by whatever it was that he could only babble incoherently.

When, eventually admitting to myself that I could not solve this problem, I told M about it, she took thought, and began to cultivate our relations with the children. We soon became the most interesting features of their daily lives; those whose homeward way passed our gate started calling in on us, to marvel at such unfamiliar items as our ranks of books, the typewriter, my binoculars and magnifying glass. The girls would arrive in a rush and fling themselves into the house crying, 'Don't let the boys in!', and the boys would hang around the gate disconsolately until we promised to see them on the next day. They brought their schoolbooks and taught us Irish; I drew pictures of the birds of Aran for them. Mícheál disapproved strongly; they would only take advantage of us, he said. One day when he was working on the potato-ridges in the garden, a lad larking about on the crag outside threw a stone at a sheet of corrugated iron that filled in a disused doorway in Moloney's walls, and Mícheál leapt out through one of the empty window-frames with a bull-like bellow and chased a scattering of them off in the direction of Gort na gCapall. Every bit of devilment in the island starts in Gort na gCapall, he told us. All this frequentation was at first alarming, then became a routine, sometimes troublesome, often vitalizing. The children revealed their individualities, and some became friends; 'Ye were the only people who ever took any notice of us', they told us when they and we were some years older. Even today, having long left the island, we are occasionally hailed in the streets of Galway by a strapping seaman or punk-clad art-student, and I am puzzled to identify him or her with one or other of the small darting creatures that once caused me such distress.

What this episode might mean I do not know, but, clearly, in coming to this place I had stepped into some unfamiliar westernness of the psyche.

Other newcomers have had a conviction of their alienage in Aran forced upon them by the barren rocks, the aggressive weather or the incomprehensible language, and have fled. For me, such a recognition would crack the foundation-stone of this book. If Aran is to become a microcosm of the island-universe to which, I believe, I belong without residue, how can I bear even a trace of immanent xenophobia in it? But perhaps 'belonging' is something to be earned, or learned. If so, the only escape from the unease of the threshold is, paradoxically, to go on farther, to explore to the end. By coincidence, our house turned out to be perched on the edge of a boundary, instituted by the saints of old, that I can turn to advantage in my westward progress. But I did not know that, at the time; the boundary I knew I had reached was drawn by interior demons.

The saints' boundary arose in this way. St Enda and St Breacán proposed to divide the island between them. They agreed that, on an appointed morning and after celebrating the Mass in their respective monasteries in Cill Éinne and Eoghanacht, they would walk towards each other, the boundary to be established where they should meet. But St Breacán and his followers got up at an unholy hour, gabbled through the Mass, and set off on horseback. As they were climbing the hill towards Fearann an Choirce, one of Enda's monks saw them, and ran to wake his master, who beseeched God not to let them approach any nearer. Instantly Breacán and his monks found that their horses' hooves were fixed to the rock, and they had to wait there until Enda came and released them. The hoof-marks were visible in the rock at Creig na Córach, the crag of the just division, for many centuries, until the wicked agent Thompson made the people build the road over them, to spite their ancient traditions. Later on the pious Fr Killeen had a plaque set in the roadside wall to mark the spot, at the foot of the steep slope immediately west of the Residence.

While the *Life of St Enda* tells of the division of the island between him and the abbots of eight other monasteries, neither it nor any of the old sources on St Breacán give the above legend; however it is well known in island lore, and there is a version of it in Ó Domhnaill's *Oileáin Árann*, including the postscript about Thompson. (Fr Mártan Ó Domhnaill was curate here from 1920 to 1934. His book, the first Irish-language one on Aran, is the most prolix work I have ever come across, but it is the only source for certain pennyworths of information, and is full of charm; a song in it, 'Árainn i bhfad i gcéin', 'Aran far away', which appears to be his own composition, is still sung.) A middle-aged Gort-na-gCapall man told me that the boundary was defined not just on the road, but right across the island from Poll Uí Néadáin on the south coast to Poll na Loinge on the north; he remembered that when he was young there was an old man who knew exactly where it ran through the village. From Gort na gCapall it followed a pronounced scarp, a sharp cliff in fact, to the main road just below the Residence, but nobody can now tell me how it found its way down the northern flank of the island to the shore. It may be that this faded tradition is a memory-trace of an actual boundary existent at some distant period, though it fits in neither with the division of the island into four townlands, consolidated by but anterior to the Ordnance Survey of 1839, nor with the tripartite schema recorded in Elizabethan inquisitions. If, as seems likely, Dún Dúchathair and Dún Aonghasa antedate the other big cashels, it is even possible that this was the point of balance between those two primitive powers.

Certain other fragments of lore shore up the significance of this point of just division. The steep slant of the road down the scarp used to be called Carcair an Phobaill, the slope of the congregation, because there was a little chapel beside it. Mícheál points out a few stones of this building in the bracken of a field tucked under the scarp immediately north of the road, and says he heard it was a ruin even in his great-grandfather's time; Dara the postman adds that it was so small the priest could scatter holy water on the whole congregation in one go. A couple of hundred yards further west, an area consisting of a few fields on the other side of the road used to be called Muirbheach na Croise, the sandy plain of the cross, and there is a slender pillar-stone about eight feet high, perhaps not ancient, incorporated in a field-wall there, which may or may not have something to do with the name – but when I enquired about it locally the most I could elicit was the cryptic observation, 'There was no harm in the man that put that there.' Island memory of these things has decayed. The 'hill of the congregation' has lost its old name; for a generation or two it was Carcair Uí Cheallacháin from O'Callaghan the teacher, and nowadays it is just An Charcair Mhór, the big slope. Only Fr Killeen's plaque checks the amnesia of the landscape here, the ruination of its meanings. But ruins have their own capacity for housing the imagination; this romantically half-effaced boundary means more to me than the mapped and historically situated ones, and not just because I lived upon it for so long. If there is a privileged site from which to view the quality of westernness, it must be this: a house on the border between east and west in the westernmost of three islands off the west of Ireland. The very western tip of Árainn itself, or for practicality's sake a cottage in the farthest village, where empty horizons and undiluted sunsets could impose too terminal an interpretation, might not be so conducive to this meditation as my liminal perch, with that never quite cured sore point of no return just the other side of it.

The scarp itself, the rough seam along which east and west are cobbled together, was exalted by my feverish botanical displacement activity into splendorous Gothic complexity; imagine a cathedral peeled like an apple in one long spiral strip, and the peeling thrown down across the island and passing so close to the house that a few steps could take me from my morning coffee-mug to breathless adorations before plants niched like saints in the unwound façade. In that first Aran spring each new flower opened another eye in me, piercing the gloom of winter. I will never see flowers like that again, each one suddenly shining not only out of the wet rock or decayed undergrowth around it but out of the time in which that space had been dark, as if a beam had arrived at last, rejoicing, from a star formed long ago, light-years away. It was not the famous rarities or even the one or two new discoveries I made that most enthralled me, but the underfoot beneath-notice nearly-nothings; the field madder, for instance, its mauve four-petalled blossoms each only a tenth of an inch across, in clusters of a dozen or so arranged as if it were crucial to show off each one to best advantage. Some plants I took home and examined with a magnifying glass, awed by the scale and finish of their architecture. Two great milky-white trunks curving up and smoothly swelling into egg-shaped terminals each with a faint blue stripe across it – the stamens of the bird's eye speedwell, which is merely so many dots of prettiness to the rambler, and sheds its little yellow-centred rings of blue petals like enamelled earrings on the mantlepiece if you bring it home. The hairy bittercress is a negligible weedy thing on the scale of a passing pace, but its four white petals under the glass are voluptuously curved flanks of satin-smooth angel-flesh, making the paper they lie on look unwholesomely yellowish and pitted. In the earliest days of the year these revelations were sparse; in January just one or two left-over blossoms of herb robert, asterisks footnoting the previous season; in February the little rice-grains of whitlow-grass scattered in the grazed-down margins of the paths, and then the common scurvy-grass on the coastal rocks (these lovely things named like so many diseases of the earth!); in March the lessons in yellow – *this* is primrose yellow, *this* is buttercup yellow, *this*, subtly different, is celandine yellow. By April spring was pressing ahead faster than I could see or write about it; I could hardly bear to be in the house in case something else was coming into being. The first bloody cranesbill, the first early purple orchid, the first spring gentian, each an explosion of sense-data, each beaming its existence into the world, carrying no message, quite independent of my observation or interpretation. I admired the heraldic simplicity of tormentil, a little yellow Tudor rose of four petals set edge to edge; behind the ring of petals is another of eight narrow green sepals, four of them pressed against and backing the petal edges, the alternate four slightly reflexed, one below each petal. The wild strawberry has exactly the same arrangement with five petals and ten sepals, with an extra stylish detail: the petals are slightly separated so that the pale green of the sepals shows between them. Drawing the tormentil plant, following out the logic of its stem and leaves and flowers, and then finding exactly the same structure in the much larger and superficially quite dissimilar herb bennet, I entered deeply into the reasons for classifying them both, together with the wild strawberry, in the rose family. These miracles of singularity, I found, had their places in the schemes of reason and the causality of evolution, beyond my comprehension, but in principal comprehensible. That there are miracles, is explicable; that there are explanations, is miraculous.

In the midst of this almost hysterical collecting and classifying of shapes and colours, I was sometimes aware that I was playing off the wild-flowers against the school-children, whose shrill cries at playtime flew through the air to me – *at* me, it felt, though I knew it was not so – like thrown knives. Their tiny silhouettes appearing and disappearing on the horizon as they scrambled about on the walls of the playground threatened my eyes like thorns. The sky-parallel crags became arenas of phobia as well as entrancement, the cupped fields flowing with buttercups and daisies were poisoned by anxiety, the fraught intricacies of the ivied scarps netted me in compulsions.

Even after the children had became individualized persons and lost this edge of menace, I found that my botanical browsings never quite ensured peace of mind. Under any leaf there could be a splinter off a ragged edge of my fragmented past. Some uneasy thought, such as a doubt about the value of my writings, could be working its way towards me along the fissures of the crag, like the cockerel that the wicked old wise women used to set wandering at random to carry off disease. Imagine it: the corner of the eye catches an incomprehensible knot of colours appearing and disappearing, scratching its way along the other side of a wall; it finds a gap and comes out into the open, a beribboned cockerel, its eye a dew-drop of malice tilted towards you. There is a paper tied to it, which might be – well, no matter what, you have to read it, caught out in the open here. For me, it might be, for instance:

STONES OF ARAN: PILGRIMAGE – A BAD REVIEW
Ancient Celtic tradition associates the northern province of Ireland with battle, the east with prosperity, the south with music, the centre with kingship, and the west with knowledge. Tim Robinson's book on Aran conforms to this schema in asserting the knowability of that western island. His method is the patient accumulation of detailed fact, with the occasional excursus into the wider conceptual

structures within which alone those facts have significance. The difficulty in this approach is, on the one hand, that an adequate provision of background information would overweight the book or bring its progress to an awkward halt, and on the other that without such background the facts are mere curiosities or momentary distractions. Thus even the rather rudimentary potted history of the Land League is too long for its position in the book, on the brink of an exciting cliff-top adventure story as it were, whereas the brief mention of *Saccamenopsis* is a stumbling-block to readers not familiar with the general principles and findings of stratigraphy and the fossil record. Worse still, even the suitably informed reader cannot take the facts adduced here at face value. Minor mistakes abound (E.P. Wright was Professor of Botany in UCD, not of Zoology in TCD, for instance) and there are some lamentable misinterpretations. The rendering of the headland west of Port Mhuirbhigh as Cora Scaití Ciúin, the sometimes calm point, is DIY etymology at its most inept; as the late Éamonn Ó Tuathail has pointed out, the name is Cora Scath Tí Chuinn, from a house of the Quinn family which provided a mark for boatmen skirting the reef. As for the cross on the sill of Arkin Castle, which Robinson takes as the very seal of truth of the Cill Éinne legend, it probably dates from 1818 like similar ones carved here and there around Galway by a man called Healy. In other fields professional research has already made Robinson's account obsolete (*cf.* C. Cotter, 1993, 1994, on Dún Aonghasa, for example). Such failings are only to be expected; a multidisciplinary study demands the modesty of teamwork, and the best that can be said of Robinson's attempts is that he manages to fall between more professorial chairs than most amateurs.

A more fundamental flaw is the work's uncertainty and equivocation about its own purpose. Striding roughshod over the bounds of specialisms and genres, it seems to imply that some overarching meaning of it all is going to be revealed through the juxtaposition or pile-up of viewpoints, but alas this higher truth never quite emerges, and in trying to be 'not just' a historian or geologist or botanist or even a poet, Robinson ends up being nothing in particular. If some philosophical question had been formulated in the volume under review, one might look forward to an attempt to answer it in the forthcoming volume, but since no such level of generality is attained in *Pilgrimage*, one fears that *Labyrinth* will be no more than a further tangle of observations and anecdotes united only by a high-flown style – for Robinson would clearly have us know he is no mere polymath of the natural sciences but a literary adept too; hence the prevalence of unsignalled quotations and half-buried references, particularly to such touchstones of the English littérateur as Proust, Ruskin, and *The Wind in the Willows*.

Although Robinson disclaims aspirations to transcendency he seems drawn to the brink of it, perhaps by some dim afterglow of belief as is betrayed by the title *Pilgrimage* itself. But what is the point of a pilgrimage to an empty shrine? He sets off bravely enough with the concept of the 'adequate step' which is mysteriously to totalize all modes of comprehension, but by the time he gets back to his starting-point it has been tested to destruction and he discards it like a worn-out boot.

Having completed this null circuit, which leaves him and us no more than 'marginally better-informed' about some of the stones of Aran, our hero turns inward, to the labyrinth. Clearly his temperament is not one to go bull-headed for minotaurs, but seeing him wander off clueless one does fear that he will blunder into factual booby-traps or be ambushed by the irrational.

Perhaps all that is so. However, my hard hour on the crags has lasted too long now for reconsiderations. Whatever wrong turnings have brought me to this point, there is only one way out, and it lies westward. Only by reporting these cliff-edge experiences (which I am as likely to find on a petal's rim as on the lip of the ocean) can I get in step with the world again, and I find that to approach them and then crawl back to safety I must cling onto as much factuality as I can grasp at a time. Perhaps such dizzy penultimates are, strictly speaking, indescribable. But dreams are notoriously untellable (if in reality not more so than reality itself), and yet we succeed in telling our dreams; this is because we all dream, we each fail to describe our dream and therefore recognize the ways in which others fail, and so their failures to describe their dreams direct us unerringly to those dreams in our own experience. And if there is no community of experience to appeal to, it has to be created. The drug addict addicts others to the drug out of a craving to communicate the drug-state; the writer instils into the reader the words induced in the writer by experience. Mad faith that the same words will induce the same experience in others! – so that one can say, '*That* is what I would say, if it were possible to say it!', and trust that the other will recognize that unsayable.

THE VILLAGE OF CONTENTED WOMEN

As a poem of Máirtín Ó Direáin's whisperingly reminds us, at Christmas-time Aran puts candles in its windows to welcome the Holy Family.

> *An eol duit, a Mhuire,*
> *Cá rachair i mbliana*
> *Ag iarraidh foscaidh*
> *Do do Leanbh Naofa,*
> *Tráth a bhfuil gach doras*
> *Dúnta Ina éadán*
> *Ag fuath is uabhar*
> *An chine dhaonna?*

Deonaigh glacadh
Le cuireadh uaimse
Go hoileán mara
San Iarthar cianda;
Beidh coinnle geala
I ngach fuineog lasta
Is tine mhóna
Ar theallach adhainte

Oh Mary do you know
Where to go this year
Begging shelter
For your Holy Child
When every door
Is slammed in His face
By the hate and pride
Of humankind?

Graciously accept
My invitation
To an isle of the sea
In the antique West;
Bright candles will shine
In every window
And a fire of turf
Will glow on the hearth.

A candle is added for each day of Christmas, and so on a windy Twelfth Night if we stoop to peer past the candle flame gasping in the drafts of our scullery window, Gort na gCapall, a mile away, looks like the dots of a row of dominoes, a child's game the vast turbulent blackness takes care to step over as it races towards us across the crags.

Liam O'Flaherty was born in Gort na gCapall, and in the after-swell of his stormy prose many wild words have been written about the situation of this tiny hamlet, giving one to understand that it is menaced by waves that mount two-hundred-foot-high cliffs. In fact it is a quarter of a mile from the sea, and is wrapped around to the south by a low scarp that gives some shelter from the wind and must have protected it much more effectively when the dwellings were all single-storied and had the blunted ridge-lines of thatch. Of the eleven houses all but two comparatively recent ones stand close together on a cliffed terrace above a green hollow of marshy fields, where in winter there is standing water and in summer a three-layered haze of red, lilac and pink formed by ragged robin, lady's smock and bogbean, flowering at different heights above the damp greensward. All the houses face north. Six are of the two-storied slate-roofed design introduced by the Land Commission in the 'fifties, with plain flat façades, a window on either side of the front door, the straight line of the eaves drawn close above the three upstairs windows, and a chimney topping each of the high end-gable walls. The rest are cottages; we saw the last of their thatched roofs replaced by concrete tiles in the 'seventies. Then there are the huddled old stores and barns and odd empty-windowed wall-corners and bereft gable-ends tucked in here and there, relics of ancestral cabins. A rough continuation of the side-road and a branching boreen link all this present and past habitation into a relaxed neighbourliness. The form of the village is, as it were, the story of the village; only the very newest houses, spilt out onto the crag below it to the north, betray a modern disinterest in old tales.

Perhaps the mutually unintrusive but companionable spatial relation-ships of Gort na gCapall gave me fond preconceptions of the community, but my years of visiting there have not proved them delusive. On the other hand, the layout itself of Aran's more linear 'street-villages' suggests the side-long glance of envy and malicious supposition, and in one or two of them I sense a rural claustrophobia compounded by the anomie of suburbia. The dull stress bears hardest on the women, who either escape early to the main-land, or live out lives even more straitened in spatial terms than do the males. I remember one or two girls who looked as if they had been born to dance, but folded away their silken youth with their wedding-dresses and set themselves like jugs on the shelf of their marriages, becoming matronly overnight in expectation of expectation. Later on, bored by their monosyl-labic husbands, they might find consolation in fantasy. Making a sequence of visits in one of these villages after a winter's absence from the island, M found one young wife in a state of exhilaration. 'I suppose you've been hear-ing all about me!' she cried. 'No!' said M, and instantly regretted her hon-esty. 'You haven't?' The woman was disappointed; the thought of the scarlet doings the neighbours might be crediting her with had been warming her through the dull months. Or, if their own lives were irremediably prosaic, they thought that perhaps ours were not. For several years we wintered in London, and I used to return in March to air the house and set the vegetable garden. My preparations and M's reappearance a month or two later were always noticed, in this island so grateful for assurance that the winter was over, and in fact she often coincided with the first bright weather, or came flushed with triumph over the last of the storms or fogs that might have delayed her. Adding to her bridal glow in my eyes were the stylish garments she came in, Courrège, Laura Ashley, Kenzo, each in their turn and only a season or two past their peak of fashion, rescued from the dowdy piles in Kilburn charity shops. It had not occurred to me that anyone saw all this as anything but a tribute to myself, to the respringing of our love. But after a few years one of M's street-village Bovarys took her aside and said, 'Can I ask you something? Every time you come back from London, we notice that you look great. Tell me – do you have lovers in London?'

Some women, though, were gone beyond the mild stimulant of vicarious romance. Worn down by a coercive biology, their skirts hemmed by ever-more clutching hands and mouths and eyes, they had fallen into embittered exhaustion. In our earlier years in Aran the District Nurse, a nun, was instructing wives in the Billings Method, a way of charting their ovulatory cycles by inspection of vaginal secretions. Approved by the Church as a means of determining the right time to conceive, the method also could not help but indicate the right time not to conceive, and, it being better to fudge than to burn, use of this knowledge was acceptable too. However, as a method of birth control it was not the best; among the factors it took no account of were the ache of moonlight, and a husband's indifference to 'safety' after a few pints in the pub. As the first crop of 'Billings Babies' ripened, one victim of these delusive haruspications said to me, 'The Nun is the only one it seems to work for!' A few years later, two children later, that same woman's despair had taken on an edge of viciousness. It was at the time of the vet's annual visit to castrate the bull-calfs; 'That's all there is for it,' she said, 'the men will have to go to the vet.' Eventually the Nun retired gratefully to her cloisters, weary of the conflict between her own good sense and the eternal verities.

Could all those children get their sufficiency of love, I wondered? Some of them had the dark petals of sadness under their eyes. And even if love is as shareable as loaves and fishes, time is not, speech is not. The imaginations of some of these children were word-starved. I once took a six-year-old for a stroll from his house, down a boreen, across a field, up another boreen. As we reached home I said, 'Let's tell them we've been to Dublin!' but he struck me down with 'That's all lies!' It was also part of the 'natural' way of things that the woman of the house would have sole care of the elderly and infirm. The string of children might therefore be competing for attention with a bed-ridden ancient, such as the grandfather-in-law of whom I heard one exasperated mother complaining: 'If he was younger he'd have died long ago, but *him*!' – laughing in bitter recognition of the old fellow's staying-power. While many women seemed to win through to serene grandmotherhood after all those years in which their own identities could only appeal for consideration through their varicose veins, angina or depression, others did not, and I saw them carrying their lives like heavy sacks.

But it was not like that in Gort na gCapall (though of course my knowledge is limited, and perhaps my memory is selective, tending to group similars together, to organize my book). In that magic round of nests, children however numerous were bright with love, aged grandmothers smiled by the hearth, husbands were welcomed home from the pub even when they were, as one wife expressed it, 'a little hilarious'. Once, walking home from a funeral, I fell in with a cosy widow from this contented village, and we chatted about the departed. 'It must be hard, going,' she said. 'Why can't we just live in Aran for ever!' For herself, I knew, she would have specified Gort na gCapall as being neither west nor east nor south nor north of anywhere better, and well located even in regard to Paradise.

My approach to Gort na gCapall from the Residence was most often goatwise: I would lever myself over the back garden wall, hop across a corner of the great crag to the ragged edge of cliffs marking the saints' boundary, clamber along it, swarming around the ends of walls that stopped on the brink, squeeze down a little crevasse where the cliffs loop around the marshy pocket below the village, browse there on its beautifully indiscriminable subspecies of Irish marsh orchids, and pop up the scarp again by steps trodden into it by long-ago water-fetchers, directly into the heart of the village. If M was with me we would take a less acrobatic but equally picturesque route (it was linguistically picturesque too), down the main road a little and then south by a narrow *róidín* between the houses of Creig na Córach that leads to a chaming spring at the foot of the cliff-line, Tobar an Bhuaile Bhródúil, the well of the proud milking pasture (proud, pleased, or something in between, as in the phrase *chomh bródúil le cat a bhfuil póca air*, as proud as a cat with a pocket); thence by stiles and grassy zigzag ways through a child's paradise (in spring) of buttercups and lambs and rabbits, called An Chrangaire, *crangaire* being old-Aran for *cnagaire*, a sixteen-acre holding; finally joining the Gort na gCapall road where it begins its gentle climb by Aill an Tine Chnáimh, the cliff of the bone-fire (the Irish preserves the etymology lost in English), site of the village bon-fire on midsummer's eve. Or if M was dressed for (a favourite word of hers) *bothántaíocht*, going from *bothán* (cottage) to *bothán* for gossip and amusement, we would avoid the prickly vegetation one had to push through in the *róidín* by taking our bicycles, purring down the main road to the T-junction and pedalling along the quiet side-road between green pastures, riding tall between the low walls, regally regarding the ruminants.

On weekday afternoons Gort na gCapall gave the impression of being discreetly at home to itself. With the children at school and the menfolk on the sea, in the fields or pony-trapping tourists to and from Dún Aonghasa, the women would have the place to themselves. Dogs drowsed on the garden walls, hens scratched under the veronica bushes. Turning left, the road passes Bridgie Fitzpatrick's and Maggie Conneely's, and then, increas-

ingly stony and grassy, becomes Bóthar na gCrag. Bridgie, her capacious
motherly face, her alert, amused eyes, became my reference-point when I
was first mapping that quarter; she stayed me with sandwiches, and, read-
ier with the pen than her menfolk, noted down placenames for me from
their talk:

Near Port Bhéal an Dúin there is Poll Uí Aodáin can't say if this spelling is correct,
its a great cliff for fishing & young fellows go down there to the shore by rope, not
a very safe way but they do it. I hope this little helps you in your good work, it is
something well worth doing for the Island.

Maggie I used to meet when collecting fishing-history from her husband Gregory, who having lost a leg and a trawler in his early days had come
back from that disaster to become the father of the contemporary fleet. I
remember how her two daughters throughout their early teens seemed to
reflect between them a single handsome and cryptic look intercepted from
their mother, as if their faces were hand-glasses held up to each other.
Turning the other way at the entrance to the village, Maeve's was on the
right. A sensible Dublin woman with a good job in Guinness's, she had
fallen in love with the island, married a lively young farmer, had her family
quite quickly, inherited a sweet-natured fireside granny for them, and now
combined capable domesticity with part-time secretarial work for the little
factory in Eoghanacht. Beyond her house was Winnie's cottage; it was
Winnie who would have chosen to live on in Aran for ever. Her husband
had been drowned long ago, but then she shared in the winning of the
sweepstake with a lady in Cill Mhuirbhigh; she remembers the money
being brought in and piled on the table, and the village children calling to
lay their hands on the pile for luck. A quietly smiling presence in Winnie's
background when I called (to map her potato-plot for a planning application for a septic tank, and to drink a glass of whiskey in return) was her
sister, who apart from going to Mass lived a retired and sheltered life.
Finally the boreen, bordered with mauve-blossomed common mallows and
tall yellow mulleins, turns up west between Winnie's cottage and another I
didn't know so well, and ambles off towards the storm-beach and the rock-
torn maelstrom behind it, as if the sea were just a crotchety old neighbour
who should be called in on now and again.
The feminine world of Gort na gCapall was not, however, totally open
to me, a man. If I nodded into a kitchen here on my way home from the
cliff-tops, the ladies would make a hospitable but unexcited move to the
kettle. But if M appeared in the doorway behind me, all eyes would light
up, arms would be flung open, sweeping me aside as of no consequence.
Then if any relict village male was hunkered down by the range in the hope

of a cup of tea he would get up wordlessly, sidle out of the back door, and cover his superfluousness by picking through a heap of old nets in an out-house. I might soon join him there to talk of fishing, potatoes and history, while M would be examining Aran sweaters and learning new stitches, and nosing out the secret history of the craft – which, it turns out, is not what it is supposed to be.

As the world has read in a thousand glossy magazines, each family in Aran has its own repertoire of stitches passed down from mother to daughter since time immemorial, rich in Celtic significances and useful in the identification of the corpses of its drowned menfolk; Synge wrote a play on this morbidly intriguing aspect of daily life in the islands. Through the Tree of Life, the Honeycomb, the Carraigín Moss, the Bobailín, the Castle, the Anchor, the Little Fields and Crooked Roads and dozens of other stitches brought by St Enda from Coptic Egypt, dolorous mother-love and man's ineluctable fate are entwined into garments of universal sales appeal.

Understandably, the Aran women who knit sweaters, socks and bob-bled caps for sale either from their own houses or through marketing orga-nizations that supply them with the wool, prefer not to disturb the tourists' belief in this contemporary folklore. To begin unpicking it, one could refresh one's memory of the Synge play, *Riders to the Sea*. A fisherman has not returned; a body is washed ashore far away, and a bit of a flannel shirt and a stocking from it are sent to his sisters for identification:

NORA, *who has taken up the stocking and counted the stitches, crying out.* It's Michael, Cathleen, it's Michael...
CATHLEEN, *taking the stocking.* It's a plain stocking.
NORA, It's the second one of the third pair I knitted, and I put up three-score stitches, and I dropped four of them.

In fact stockings were almost the only item knitted on the islands at the period of Synge's visit, and as he observed himself, the younger men were just beginning to adopt 'the usual fisherman's jersey', that is, the plain blue jerseys on sale in Galway as in all towns of the Atlantic seaboard. Maeve's mother-in-law Katie, who was shortly to take to her bed for her latter years, told M that only stockings were knitted in her youth, and that she never knitted a sweater until she married. She vividly remembered the first time she used a cable pattern, having memorized it off the back of a visitor sit-ting in front of her in the chapel. Bridgie had been taught to knit at school in the late 'twenties by Mrs Ó hEithir, who had learned from English and American magazines, and was the only teacher to teach knitting in the island. The sweaters they knitted had plain bodies and patterned yokes of cables, shadow diamonds and moss stitch, and were dyed navy or black;

Bridget taught her own mother how to make them. The 'bawneen' sweaters of unwashed and undyed wool, with narrow panels of various patterns running from hem to shoulder, now synonymous with Aran, were a later development. By the early 'thirties a fashion had evolved in Aran of dressing little boys in white sweaters involving some patterned stitches for their first Communion; visitors drawn to the islands by Robert Flaherty's presence noticed these, and their demand for adult-sized versions initiated a new employment – one of the many ways in which Flaherty unwittingly intervened in island history. The stitches used were those common to many areas of western Europe (the local word for a sweater being *geansaí* or gansy, pointing to an influence from Guernsey). Some had probably been introduced by Scottish and Donegal fish-wives brought in by the Congested Districts Board, others arrived in knitting patterns sent home from America by 'Yanks', the Araners' emigrant relatives. Certain stitches were local inventions – there is one known as *Praiseach Pheige Cuaig*, Peggy Cooke's mess, though no one would dare use the name in her hearing (this Peige Cuaig was Máirtín Ó Direáin's mother and has long gone beyond taking umbrage, which is why I can mention it). Soon a craft of amazing complexity was in rapid evolution; the sweater became a broad field for the display of taste both good and bad. Most of it is done by memory, and it is astonishing to see, as I have, an old lady knitting as she trots down a boreen to the cow. In about 1935 the artist Elizabeth Rivers introduced her friend Muriel Gahan, founder of the famous Country Shop in Dublin and the dedicated champion of Irish crafts, to some of the best knitters, and for the first time Aran knitwear went on sale outside the islands. Soon after that Pádraig Ó Máille's, the famous old dress shop in Galway, began to sell Aran knits, and Pádraic Ó Síocháin of Galway Bay Products in Dublin began exporting them in large numbers to America, which necessitated regularizing the sizing; before that, as he says, 'If the Aran knitter had a small husband, you got a short jumper. If she had a long husband, you got a long jumper.' (Ó Síocháin's book, *Aran – Islands of Legend*, has done its bit for the propagation of the romantic mythology of Aran knitting.) The cash income was of great importance in those pinched times, and M's friends could remember exactly what had been bought with their first earnings. In the late 'fifties the typical price paid to a knitter for a garment was £2.10s, the wool being supplied by the dealer, and twenty-five years later it was around £12. Today most Aran sweaters are made in Donegal, and by machine. The professionally designed machine-made products in alpaca and other luxury yarns from the Inishmaan Knitwear Company penetrate the most sought-after markets, and its founder, Tarlach de Blácam, paces the crags with his mind on the lira, the yen, and the politics of Peru. (Fortunately his company also still fosters the hand-knitting tradition of Inis Meáin, which seems to be even richer than that of Árainn.) Perhaps the Aran bawneen reached its apogee in 1985 when one of Jean Paul Gaultier's male models paraded in tight-knit trousers, sweater and cap in snow-white wool, an outfit that certainly would have identified him had he been washed ashore drowned.

It is very difficult to persuade an Aran hand-knitter to calculate or even guess what her hourly rate is at the price she gets for her output; M in 1986 thought it was about 50p for a fast worker. The mistress of an Aran household does not think of knitting in these terms, or evades the question by saying, 'It passes the time; I might as well be doing something while I'm waiting for the potatoes to boil.' Pride in craft, mental and manual activity however limited, solace the long hours, especially in winter. But when I was making my map and lodging in cottages throughout the three islands, I sometimes heard the sigh with which the 'woman of the house' took up her knitting having served my breakfast, and I smelt exploitation, resignation to an ancient wrong, something indeed passed down from mother to daughter. Nowadays fewer and fewer women are finding it worth their while to knit for sale. M found that among the mothers of younger school-children few could knit with the speed and skill of their elders, and most preferred to earn proper wages of £60 or £100 a week in the little factory in Eoghanacht. The only young wife who knitted professionally was our neighbour Máire Uí Fhlatharta in Fearann an Choirce, whose husband was away on the South Aran Light for half the time and who had a toddler to care for; she could knit a sweater in one long day, and she relished the independence of her income, small though it was compared with the factory wages, but she had failed to persuade her friends to join her and felt isolated in her craft. Sadly, at all age levels, nobody actually enjoyed knitting. Only the rudiments of the skill were taught in the primary schools, and one never saw a young girl take up the needles.

So it seems that as the myth of Aran hand-knitting spreads worldwide, at its origin the reality is fading. What radiated from those knitting-courts where M gloried and drank tea, was a comfortable sense of the pastness of the past, a mutual congratulation of retired heroines. All were happy to reminisce and to show M their stitches, all were happy not to have to bend their fingers to it for hour after hour. The click of needles was no longer as close to them through the waking hours as the pulse; they had time for their own hearts. True, one of Bridgie's sons had laid it down, in a school essay he showed me on the theme 'Woman's Place', that 'A woman's place is in the home, because when a man comes in he wants his tea.' But even men and their irrefutable arguments could be accommodated in these women's lives. For whole afternoons at a time, Gort na gCapall, like Cranford, was 'in the hands of the Amazons'.

Meanwhile, talking to 'himself' in the outhouse, I was learning that history, even in Gort na gCapall, is a matter of men. ...

STORM-DRIVEN MALE

Maidhc Mhicil Phádraic Bheartlaiméid Bhriain Bheartlaiméid was the name by which Liam O'Flaherty's father thought of himself, when he wanted to rehearse his descent from Beartlaiméad Ó Flaithbheartaigh, the first inhabitant of Gort na gCapall. According to Liam's elder brother Tom, this Beartlaiméad or Bartholomew 'built his house upon a rock, not for reasons of security or because he considered the rock symbolical of continuity, but because he did not want to waste a piece of good pasture or tillage land under a house'. Four generations later, when such communal undertakings as the basking-shark hunt were being planned, it was an O'Flaherty that convened assemblies on the *carcair*, the rise leading into the village. An old man recalled the scene for Tom:

Your grandfather took the lead of all the men in the village, since it was his great, great grandfather who first settled in the village and everybody was related to him. ... [He] told the men to get the full of their mouths of food and return to the carcair. Indeed they were not long eating for they were as excited as if they were going to a wedding, and the young girls of the village put on their brightest shawls and came to the carcair to watch the young men who were putting airs on themselves in front of the girls. ... Your grandfather was a hard stern man, and my skin to the Devil if he could get three words out of him without one of them being a curse, and that day he cursed plenty because he was excited. ...

In the next generation it was Maidhc Mhicil (Mike son of Michael) who led the village. He had run off with Maggie Ganly from Mainistir, the sixteen-year-old daughter of Thomas Ganly the lighthouse-builder. Liam's earliest memory of his mother was the romantic story of her marriage, told while she was combing his hair:

She told it as one tells a fairy-tale to amuse a child, how her handsome young lover came by night on horseback to her father's house and abducted her, at the very moment when another suitor from the mainland was there asking for her hand; how she was married at dawn in the chapel and went to live in an old deserted house in our village, penniless and unforgiven by her parents. Her fairy-tale ended with her marriage. After that, her life was a tale of hardship and misery, an endless struggle to find food for her many children.

It was the time of the Land League, of the cliffing of the Kilmurvey House cattle, the shooting of the bailiff; Maidhc was imprisoned a couple of times on suspicion of his part in these crimes. The household narrowly escaped eviction when her first son, Tom, was just old enough to remember the event:

She stood at the window which gave a view of the road that led to our village. She held me in her arms and she moaned unceasingly. I cried out loud. We were going to be evicted. Presently we saw helmeted policemen coming around the bend. 'Tá na cneámhaire a' tíocht – the villains are coming, little white son,' my mother said. 'Soon we will have no house to shelter us.' There they came, up out of the hollow, a great muster of them, led by a sergeant. They were accompanied by three disreputable fellows from the mainland, whose business it was to throw out our furniture, lock and nail the doors after the tenants were evicted. I was still weeping when the sergeant entered. I do not recollect what he said. I know he was a kindly man. I suppose he told my mother that he was sorry to perform this painful duty. Maybe he was too. I remember the 'rogees' with hammer and nails fastening the door that opened to the north. Then they quenched the fire on the hearth and when this was being done my mother moaned as if her heart was being torn out. It had a searing effect on my infant mind. I never got over it. The bitterness born within me by the act only grew stronger with the passing of the years. Gently the police sergeant told my mother she would have to go out into the yard. Before she left she whispered a few words in my ear that made me cry for all my lungs were worth. The sergeant turned away his head for a moment. Then he placed a coin in my hand.

I had not noticed my father at all until then. He had lived a rather eventful life and an eviction was only another incident. He was a Fenian and a Land Leaguer, and most of the time he forgot he was the father of a large young family. He was used to police attentions and accustomed to jails. I don't know how it happened and I never enquired in later years, the subject was too painful, but suddenly the 'rogees' were drawing the nails out of the door. We entered our home. Soon the kettle was singing merrily on the fire.

My mother always expressed the belief that if my father thought of his own affairs a little more and about those of the community a little less, the world would be a much better place to live in. She did not understand that she had fallen in love with and married an incurable rebel, and not an ordinary husband. And rebels are easier to fall in love with than to live with.

Both Tom and Liam attended Oatquarter National School under David O'Callaghan, the Sinn Féiner and Gaelic Leaguer, who taught them to read and write their native tongue. When Sir Roger Casement visited the school and asked if any pupil could 'grind his way through' an Irish column from a newspaper, O'Callaghan proudly called forth Tom, who performed so well that Sir Roger gave him half a crown, and later sent him books, including Fr O'Leary's *Séadna,* which, though little read nowadays, was then regarded as the foundation-stone of modern literature in Irish. Although Casement planned to send him to college, 'fate intervened' (as Tom's unrevealing account has it), and he emigrated to Boston in 1912, where he became active in social-revolutionary circles. He began his journalistic career by writing for the *Daily Worker* and the *Labor Defender,* and after he had been expelled from the Communist Party in 1928 as a Trotskyist, for the *Militant.* A sick man, he returned to Ireland in 1934, and helped to found a remarkably radical (and remarkably thoroughly forgotten) Irish-language weekly called *An t-Éireannach.* Written for the working classes and for the Gaeltacht in particular, anti-fascist, internationalist, out of sympathy with the self-absorbed and religiose tone of the language movement of that time, the newspaper lasted just three years. Some pieces Thomas wrote for it later appeared in English versions in his two books, *Aranmen All* (1934) and *Cliffmen of the West* (1935). These collections of Aran stories and reminiscences are full of tenderness and irony – but in the world of writing it is his brother who is O'Flaherty. Thomas died in 1936.

Liam O'Flaherty was born in 1896. He too attracted attention at school. His earliest literary composition horrified O'Callaghan, he tells us, and he was thrashed for it. This was a story of a murder in an Aran potato-garden: a woman brings his tea out to her man working in the garden, and because the tea is cold he kills her with his spade and buries her between two potato-ridges. 'The point of the story', according to O'Flaherty, 'was the man's difficulty in getting the woman, who was very large, to fit into the fosse.' O'Callaghan may well have been shocked by this melodramatic assault on the Gaelic League's idealization of the Irish peasant, but he recognized his pupil's abilities and drew him to the attention of a visiting priest, who arranged for him to train for the priesthood. When Liam, aged thirteen, left the island for Rockwell College in Tipperary, it was the first step in a career that zigzagged wildly away from Gort na gCapall and would eventually lurch across the stage of fame. He went on to study at Blackrock (where he organized a corp of Republican Volunteers) and then at Clonliffe seminary in Dublin, although he later claimed that he never felt any vocation and indeed 'despised the priesthood and thought it was more noble to do the ordinary chores of our society as a lusty male, to till the earth, to be strong and brave at sea, to marry and beget children, to raise one's voice with authority in the council of one's fellows' – nor did he want 'to suffer the humiliation of wearing a priest's womanly rig'. However, after only a few weeks at Clonliffe, 'I danced on my soutane, kicked my silk hat to pieces, spat on my religious books, made a fig at the whole rigmarole of Christianity and left that crazy den of superstition.' A brief period at University College Dublin gave him Catullus, Connolly and Marx instead, but then in 1915 he flung himself into the nightmare of history by joining the Irish Guards, and underwent an experience which, he says, saved him from becoming just another narrow-minded Irish patriot. For this step, which, even more than his baulking at the priesthood, was responsible for the outcast position he later rejoiced in, he adopted his mother's family name of Ganly, probably because of its Ulster Protestant resonance.

One night in 1917 a lost and bewildered Private Ganly and two others were hiding in a hole near Langemarck in Belgium, drinking whiskey from the broken neck of a bottle and watching shells bursting among a platoon of advancing guardsmen, when there was an annihilating flash and roar. He awoke to blood and hysteria; he was dragged to a dressing-station where someone picked a scrap of mangled flesh off his tunic saying, 'What's the matter with you, mate? This part of you?' It became impossible for him to speak, although he felt he had something important to communicate. Later he attacked a doctor who seemed inimical, and was held and doused with cold water, and his voice came back to him. *'Melancholia acuta'* was the citation with which the war rewarded him. He felt he would go through life with that shell bursting in his head.

Liam's wanderings after his discharge, recounted with the immediacy and terror of hallucination in a fragment of autobiography called *Two Years*, read as if he were searching for bits of his psyche splattered worldwide. Deciding, as he says, to cut himself adrift from everyone he knew, he goes off to London on his winnings at a race-meeting, and spends the lot in a forty-eight-hour debauch in that city whose 'majestic size satisfies the human craving for something that is eternal because it is too vast for comprehension'. After being thrown off various jobs for his insubordinate attitudes, he ships as a stoker on a tramp-steamer, across the sea which is for him the masculine half of beauty, 'the more beautiful because it was more strong', and feeling himself 'young, carefree, plunging towards a romantic and tropic land'. He approaches Rio with the same sense of awe and romance as he did Galway on his first trip with his mother on the steamer *Duras*, but his experiences of the brothel-quarter and the beach where he lives rough with hobos leave him with the knowledge that 'each country is as dull and commonplace as the next, each person intrinsically as disappointing as the previous one I have met'. He sees a headline about the declaration of the Irish Republic, and ships for Liverpool: 'So ended my first expedition to the Tropics, in disillusion and without any credit to myself, unless I could count among my gains the renewal of my faith in the superiority of European man.'

By the time he reaches Europe, though, he has lost interest in Irish revolution, and signs on for a Mediterranean voyage. The inhabitants of the Balkans, he finds, are 'a bad smell', and as barbarous today as the Romans found them two thousand years ago. But an epic drinking-bout in Smyrna culminates in his being lugged off by two blacks to the divan of a Circassian woman, who justifies everything he has heard of her breed ('How can a woman of your beauty and refinement be content to live in a house like this?' 'C'est la guerre.'). He sails on, he is cured of *delirium tremens* by a storm at sea, he arrives at Montreal. Despairing of living up to his concept of man's destiny, which is 'to struggle towards the perfection of his species to a state of godliness', he walks off into the night and the waste places. He takes odd jobs on farms, but 'it is almost impossible to believe how uncivilized these French-Canadian peasants are', and it is in a condensed-milk factory that he finds a god he can worship, 'this god of machinery, more powerful than any god man has yet created'. After a wall of piled-up boxes of condensed-milk tins collapses on him, he wanders off, and after some months finds himself in the lumber-woods of northern Ontario. There he meets an agitator from the International Workers of the World, 'the type of a new aristocracy that was to spring from the machine'. Expelled from the lumber-camp as Wobblies, the two of them have to walk fifty-five miles and flee a forest fire; then they jump trains to Port Arthur on Lake Superior. In a labour-camp near there he falls in love for the first time, with an Irish settler's daughter, and realizes 'the tragedy of my sex, which lies in the impossibility ever to completely conquer that shadowy phantom which is the soul of woman'. Leaving her, he sneaks across the American border, and goes to join his brother in Boston. In the James Connolly Club there his sceptical spirit is aroused, by opposites, to comprehension of the power and beauty of American capitalism. His wild two-year excursus peters out in unsuccessful attempts to write, and a succession of lost jobs. He feels a growing inner madness 'forcing me to retire within the walls of my mind. – Where? What place could be more remote than the rock of my nativity?' And so, by debauch from port to port, he makes his way home, and arrives 'like a ghoul, speechless, gloomy, a companion of the rough winds and of the breakers'.

Aran was only tolerable for a few months. It was noticed that he 'ducked and went to pieces' whenever a ship's hooter sounded in the bay. Soon he was in Dublin working as a journalist, and helping to found the first Irish Communist Party. At that time a socialist revolution in Ireland did not seem an impossibility, and trade unionists were occupying mills and factories in various towns. When O'Flaherty failed to persuade his comrades in the Party that the hour was ripe, he undertook his own adventure. In January 1922, shortly after the Provisional Government had taken over from the British authorities under the Anglo-Irish Treaty, he led the 'Dublin Council of the Unemployed' in a peaceful but militarily disciplined occupation of the Rotunda Concert Rooms, as a protest against the high rate of unemployment in the city, and hung the Red Flag out of a window. A large and hostile crowd rallied outside and was only restrained from attacking the occupiers by detachments of the IRA and the police. After two days Commander-in-Chief O'Flaherty and his two hundred or more supporters came out quietly. O'Flaherty went to ground in Cork for a while, before briefly rallying to the IRA occupation of the Four Courts. Disbanded from that lost cause, he and a companion joined the crowds watching the Free State Army extirpating the IRA from some hotels they were still holding out in, and he overheard one old woman telling another that Liam O'Flaherty, 'that tried to sell Dublin to the Bolsheviks', had been shot dead, 'thanks be to God!' His companion wanted him to join the Flying Columns the IRA would soon be setting up in the countryside, but O'Flaherty felt that he agreed with the old woman: politically and militarily he was dead. Leaving Ireland to its Civil War he went to London, bought a typewriter and began another life.

Wandering in the fog and mud of the London streets, depressed by his initial failure to write anything of worth, he suddenly thought of Aran, and joyfully determined to make himself the spokesman of its harmonious simplicities. The novel that came out of this inspiration, *Thy Neighbour's Wife*, was accepted by the publishers, Jonathan Cape, on the advice of Edward Garnett, literary godfather to a generation that included Galsworthy, D.H. Lawrence and Conrad. The background is the Aran of the 1900s, the social comedy of its emergent middle class detailed in a facetious and satirical Victorian style which is progressively over-ridden by a deeply felt account of the protagonist's spiritual predicament. The island curate loves his neighbour's wife, who could have been his had not a mistaken sense of vocation blinded him to his true nature at the crucial moment. Now, seeing her turn away from her evil husband to the love of a handsome, rebellious O'Flaherty figure, he takes to drink, and in an agony of doubt and despair remembers the saints of old who tested their faith by going to sea in the bare framework of a currach. He sets himself adrift from the island's westernmost point – that inescapable locus of ultimate truths – but, out on the darkening ocean with the storm rising, he undergoes 'a transformation':

The curate died. The intellectual died. The visionary died. The drunkard died.

The lover died. The pious, shrinking conscientious priest, fearful of himself, torturing himself with doubts and temptations, they all died. There remained but Hugh McMahon the man, the human atom, the weak, trembling being, with the savage desire to live.

The instinct of self-preservation awoken in him, he gloriously masters the waves until he is rescued. Then, in a disappointing last paragraph, he takes himself off to the foreign missions in fulfilment of a vow made to a God one had thought he had just outgrown. Nevertheless, in these concluding pages O'Flaherty's cardinal theme has triumphantly announced itself: Life, its sacred greed for yet more life, its solidarity with Death.

In his next novel, *The Black Soul*, the magnificent amorality of the island itself drums home the moral. A dark, tormented, shell-shocked Stranger comes to recuperate in the westernmost village; his hosts are a splendid specimen of womanhood called Little Mary because she is so tall – she is not quite a peasant, being the illegitimate daughter of a landlord – and Red John, her feeble, despised and rejected husband. The narrative of the Stranger's growth towards wholeness is scanned by evocations of the successive seasons from winter to autumn, four rhapsodic passages seemingly flung together with the careless profusion of nature itself. The Stranger's 'Black Soul' is his hyperactive intellect, locked in futile debate with itself, which has to be silenced before his life can meet Little Mary's at that summit of love which 'only a god could describe'. Also, just as Red John's miserable person has been spurned by Little Mary, so the Stranger has to disregard the passion of another woman, whose cultivated, idealistic mind exacerbates his morose self-questionings. Finally Red John runs mad (and O'Flaherty conveys the despair of the losers in life's game just as feelingly as he does the triumph of the winners), and the Stranger, for no reason that his Black Soul can provide or counter, braves a perilous cliff-ledge on 'The Hill of Fate' at the end of the island to rescue him. Red John expires at that moment, but the Stranger, having faced the reality of death, is rewarded with the will to life, and he carries Mary off to the mainland. 'The most elemental thing in Irish literature', the poet AE called it, and indeed if one can put up with the novel's windy longueurs it is bracing to let its welter of imagery smite one's face like sea-spray.

Spring Sowing, a collection of short stories, followed *The Black Soul* in the same year, 1924. The title-piece is as well formed an expression of the beauty and sadness of O'Flaherty's Gort na gCapall as one could hope for. Martin and Mary rise very early one February morning:

They ate in silence, sleepy and bad-humoured and yet on fire with excitement, for it was the first day of their first spring sowing as man and wife. And each felt the glamour of that day on which they were to open the earth together and plant seeds in it. ... Mary, with her shrewd woman's mind, munched her bread and butter and thought of ... Oh, what didn't she think of? Of as many things as there are in life does a woman think of in the first joy and anxiety of her mating. But Martin's mind was fixed on one thought. Would he be able to prove himself a man worthy of being the head of a family by doing his spring sowing well?...

Still, as they walked silently in their rawhide shoes, through the little hamlet, there was not a soul about. Lights were glimmering in the windows of a few cabins. The sky had a big grey crack in it in the east, as if it were going to burst in order to give birth to the sun. Birds were singing somewhere at a distance. Martin and Mary rested their baskets of seeds on a fence outside the village and Martin whispered to Mary proudly: 'We are first, Mary.' And they both looked back at the little cluster of cabins, that was the centre of their world, with throbbing hearts. For the joy of spring had now taken complete hold of them.

Martin sets to work on their first potato-ridge 'as if some primeval impulse were burning within his brain and driving out every other desire but that of asserting his manhood and of subjugating the earth', and Mary has a moment of terror in the face of 'that pitiless, cruel earth, the peasant's slave master, that would keep her chained to hard work and poverty all her life until she would sink again into its bosom'. For the moment her love is gone: 'Henceforth she was only her husband's helper to till the earth.' But at the end of the long day they are rejoiced by the five ridges they have created:

All her dissatisfaction and weariness vanished from Mary's mind with the delicious feeling of comfort that overcame her at the thought of having done this work with her husband. They had done it together. They had planted seed in the earth. The next day and the next and all their lives, when spring came they would have to bend their backs and do it until their hands and bones got twisted with rheumatism. But night would bring sleep and forgetfulness.

As they walked home slowly Martin walked in front with another peasant talking about the sowing, and Mary walked behind, with her eyes on the ground, thinking.

Despite the 'thundering good review' O'Flaherty boasted he had got out of AE for *The Black Soul*, the book was not a success in England, and Garnett told him the critics had killed it for ten years. According to O'Flaherty's highly self-dramatizing memoirs, *Shame the Devil*, this rejection made him vow to return to Aran and never leave it again. But when he arrived, the mute fear he detected in the islanders told him that they thought he had been infected with the madness of prophecy, 'the greatest sin in the eyes of the herd'. (In fact Aran merely regarded him as a writer of dirty books. Fr Killeen's manuscript history of Aran states that the O'Flahertys of Gort na gCapall took the side of the 'saucepans' in the famous dispute over the Hill

Farm lands, and 'as a result developed a bitterly anticlerical attitude. Liam's filthy novels illustrate the fact.') His mother had died soon after his notorious escapade in the Rotunda – because of it, he half-believed – and now he found that his father was in his dotage. He realized for the first time how his sister, now a teacher and lodging in Cill Rónáin, must have suffered, coming to look after the old man each evening after school:

With horror I saw the house where I was born, falling rapidly into ruins. ... But more desolate than the house and its surroundings was my father himself, that doddering old man who shook hands with me and mumbled half-articulate words without knowing me. ... Could this shapeless man be the handsome young lover about whom I had heard at my mother's knee in childhood?... When he tried to bow, he curtsied like a woman.

Three days later O'Flaherty fled back to Dublin.

O'Flaherty claims that he wrote his next and most successful novel, *The Informer*, with a cynical determination to make money and with an eye on Hollywood. Indeed John Ford made a famous film out of it, but O'Flaherty's work in itself, a nightmarish condensation of his experience of revolutionary intrigue and the Dublin slums, is so convincingly visualized that it unreels like a black-and-white film in the skull. There followed a wide variety of writings: other novels with a background in Dublin and revolution, more short stories, a disabused account of a trip to Stalin's Russia, a remarkably (for him) even-toned satire on this island of 'priests, politicians and prostitutes' called *A Tourist's Guide to Ireland*, the historical novel *Famine*, and a projection of his highly sexualized vitalist philosophy onto the Celtic otherworld called *The Ecstasy of Angus*.

The best of his Aran novels, *Skerrett*, appeared in 1932. It opens with the energy of a wave rushing ashore: the arrival of the new schoolmaster, his meeting with the parish priest who is at first his ally in a civilizing mission, and later his rival for dominion, his seizing control of the undisciplined school by indiscriminate beatings, the death of his adored son and the lapsing of his pitiful wife into alcoholism and insanity – but then it falters and fidgets as a wave does at the top of its reach, too many events are included for the quite insufficient reason that they really happened, and the narrative only partially recovers itself for the mournful backwash, Skerrett's defeat, his withdrawal to the book's equivalent of Gort na gCapall, his final humiliation, and his posthumous triumph in the island's memory. Skerrett is O'Flaherty's old schoolmaster O'Callaghan, and the priest Moclair (an opulent psychological portrait, with the subtlety and sensuality of one of Titian's cardinals) is Fr Farragher, whom the young Liam would have had opportunity to study from below, as it were, while serving him at Mass.

The topography of Aran is reproduced with an exile's passionate fidelity, almost every step taken can be located in reality, every exclamation, groan and sigh uttered in the five little rooms of that 'paltry cottage, one storey and a half in height' still echoes through the Residence in Oatquarter.

During this highly creative decade O'Flaherty suffered recurrent bouts of depression and nervous collapse. He had 'married and reproduced his kind', as he puts it, but in 1932, unable to write more, he left his wife and baby daughter and undertook the journey into himself described in *Shame the Devil* (1934). This is a troubling and perplexing document, a vividly dramatized account of a period of mental anguish, in which his former personalities split away and stand before him in accusation. These sub-selves and the various interlocutors met in his wanderings furiously debate civilization and barbarism, communism and fascism, nihilism and transcendence, Ghenghis Khan and Pythagoras, suicide and drink; they have in common only the absolutism of their convictions. It is difficult to attribute any particular opinion in the book to O'Flaherty 'himself' precisely because of this proliferation of fragmentary selves, and sometimes one is glad of this; for instance when he is well embarked on something very unpleasant about the Jewish refugees he sees in Paris, he meets someone who praises the Hitlerites for driving them out of Germany, and he leaps to the defence of the Jewish race on the grounds that it produced Marx. The book resounds with Zarathustrian chest-thumping, and ends with the trumpet-call of 'overcoming': Man, through his intellect and creativity, is clawing his way up a wall or cliff towards the achievement of Godhead. As to Woman, the following 'strange thought', as he calls it, is at least left uncontradicted:

But then, what is that creative urge other than a form of insanity, an overbalancing of the physical organism; more likely due to some 'lack' in the organism than to the presence of some quality not possessed by the ordinary male. To females I deny this creative urge, except in so far as they feel the urge to create children. And that urge in itself is the outcome of a 'lack' in their construction.

Some homespun, pre-Freudian version of this must have been what was occupying Mary's mind on that walk home from her spring sowing. Woman is, by biological predestination, cyclical, subordinate, earthbound, a metaphysical peasant.

Incorporated at the end of *Shame the Devil* is the short story with which he burst out of this spell of introspective sterility, 'The Caress'. A party of Aran men mockingly accompany a dried-up bachelor in a drunken match-making expedition, breaking off to amuse themselves by galloping a mare up and down the beach. (The equation of a desirable woman with a mare, explicit in several of O'Flaherty's works, is diffused into the structure of this one.) In the chaotic upshot, lusty youth and beauty find their way to each other in the purity of desire, the old snatch what ignominious pleasures they can, the ridiculous bachelor is dragged home like a sack.

After the 'fifties O'Flaherty published nothing more and disappeared from the Dublin literary scene. Several of his novels had been banned by the so-called Free State's Censorship Board on publication and were hard to obtain, and it was not until 1976 that Wolfhound Press began to republish them, a slow process which is still not complete. Nowadays, however, there is a tatty and much underlined copy of *Dúil*, his collection of short stories in Irish, in every school satchel, and the Aran clergy smile a sophisticated smile over *The Tourist's Guide*.

O'Flaherty's returns to Aran were rare, but in 1980 he was persuaded to take a day-trip attended by an RTÉ film crew and an *Irish Times* photographer. At Gort na gCapall he was presented with an indefinite number of little relatives, all female as it happened, until he protested, 'Show me the boys! I'm not interested in the girls!' Outside the house he was born in, he stopped to apostrophize a rock: *'Bail ó Dhia ort, a chloch mhór; tá aithne agam ortsa!'* ('The blessings of God on you, big stone; you I know!'). Portraits of O'Flaherty from all periods of his life show a virile, sombre and romantic personage; now the photographer had him pose against the grey waters of Port Mhuirbhigh, a craggy pyramid of accumulated experience. Long before this, he had written:

I was born on a storm-swept rock and hate the soft growth of sun-baked land where there is no frost in men's bones. Swift thought and the swift flight of ravenous birds, and the squeal of terror of hunted animals are to me reality. I have seen the sated buck horn his mate, and the wanderer leave his wife, in search of fresh bosoms, with the fire of joy in his eye.

When the cameras had had their fill, he turned to the companion of his latter years and said, 'Come on, Kitty, let's get the hell out of here!' It was his last time in Aran. He died four years later, at the age of eighty-eight.

THE SHINING WAYS

I have mentioned three ways of getting from Fearann an Choirce to Gort na gCapall; a passage in O'Flaherty's *Skerrett* points out another. A villager called Ferris is walking home from the chapel with the schoolmaster:

He left Skerrett a little to the east of the school and turned up towards his village of Cappatagle along a footpath over the crags. In his rawhide shoes he hardly made any sound moving over the flat rocks, that had been polished as smooth as glass by the impress of human feet for hundreds upon hundreds of years. He moved rapidly, tall, lean, erect, with sudden jerks of his shoulders as he lengthened his stride now and again to cross a fissure between the rocks. His walk was like a dance, a movement perfect in rhythm and significant of some mystic bond between this beautiful human energy and the wild earth over which it passed.

Skerret, so heavy and solid compared to this lithe and deer-like islander, struck the road with regular thuds as he went west.

Note the echo of Synge's celebration of the sacrament of walking, in *The Aran Islands*, after the shoes he arrived in have been cut to pieces by the sharp fossils in the rock, and the natives make him a pair of rawhide shoes:

At first I threw my weight upon my heels, as one does naturally in a boot, and was a good deal bruised, but after a few hours I learned the natural walk of man, and could follow my guide in any portion of the island. ... The absence of the heavy boot of Europe has preserved to these people the agile walk of the wild animal ...

Two markers of Skerrett's progressive alienation from the forces of modernity emanating from the island capital are his adoption of rawhide shoes and his building himself a cottage in Cappatagle as a potential retreat from the national school and the teacher's residence. Cappatagle is Gort na gCapall (and Ferris, the islander still in communion with the wild earth and the hundreds upon hundreds of years, is Liam O'Flaherty's father). Thus Gort na gCapall is represented as the home of natural good feeling in contradistinction from Cill Rónáin, while Fearann an Choirce is the field of conflict between the rival value-systems. When I first read the novel I was happy with this ideological situating of Gort na gCapall, which agreed what I myself felt about the place, but the geographical relationship between the villages puzzled me, for I thought I knew that there is no such footpath across the crags as O'Flaherty describes.

Certainly a track leads southwards from immediately east of the school; it shortly peters out, but one can persist in the same direction by climbing field-walls until one reaches the near end of a *róidín* coming to meet it from Bóthar na gCrag; we often went that way to the cliffs, and because it was a favourite route I marked it on my first map of Aran by a string of dashes, as something aspiring to be a path. However, soon after its publication I received a copy of my map through the post, on which that dashed line had been energetically crossed out and replaced by another string of dashes veering south-west to Gort na gCapall, defying the rule my explorations had determined, that paths tend to work along the natural grid of directions given by the north-south and east-west sets of fissures. The sender was a Pádraic Ó Flaithbheartaigh, formerly of Gort na gCapall and now living in Enniscorthy, or as he insisted on spelling it, Inis Corthaigh. On his next visit to his native island he called on me, and led me across the crags to Gort na gCapall pointing out the amenities of the way: a few blocks thrown down to help one across a gully, a narrow clearance through an area cluttered with loose stone, a tread cut in a rock-face, a slit in a wall just wide enough to step through one shin at a time. The ordinary Aran stile, I learned, consisting of two or three long through-stones sticking out on either side of the wall, is called the *staighre* (stairs) and is used between two fields within the one person's holding. The other sort, marking a right-of-way, is the *céimín* (little step); it is an opening, usually not quite coming down to ground-level, between two uprights set so close together a sheep could not squeeze through. Since such a gap is virtually invisible until one is opposite it, and the other little orderings of stone making up the foot-path are indistinguishable from the rest of the stony chaos until they are almost underfoot, our effortless oblique traverse felt to me like a run of good luck. I trotted after Pádraic Dan Phatch across this familiar terrain with a new and disorientating freedom, such as one would find on being shown how to pass through the walls of one's own house.

This footpath is Gort na gCapall's right-of-way across Fearann an Choirce territory, its shortcut to the school and the main road leading on to the chapel and Cill Rónáin. 'There used to be a shine on the rocks so many people went across there,' an old man of Gort na gCapall told me later on, 'but since the bicycles came out no one goes that way'. There is a similar right-of-way going south-west from Cill Rónáin to Bóthar na gCrag, of which Dara the postman says, 'There used to be a white line worn by the nailed boots all the way across the crags; you could even see it at night.' So in fact it was 'the heavy boot of Europe' that for a while paved these ancient paths with a new magic, until the advance of technology left them to the slow recarpeting of lichen. What O'Flaherty calls a 'mystic bond between this beautiful human energy and the wild earth over which it passed' was actually something less ineffable and more interesting, a temporary concatenation of compromises between nature's immortal symmetries and the ordinary mortal's will to cut corners.

Over the years I have been shown several others of these formerly shining ways. A particularly attractive one, which was much used at night by seaweed-gatherers and kelp-burners, runs from the upper end of Fearann an Choirce down to An Duirling Bhán, the village's kelp-shore, dropping from terrace to terrace by little steps nested in ferny clefts of the scarps. It would be reasonable to suppose that there was one cutting north-south across the great crags behind Cill Rónáin, and the tradition that the saints used to go that way between Mainistir and Cill Éinne probably represents the memory of such a path. If Nell of the Tower knew that short-cut and could follow it by night, something of her mystery might be explained; if there was a 'shining way' from Gort na gCapall right across the back of the island along the line of the present Bóthar na gCrag, then Nell might well have been able to make her famous journey from Gort na gCapall to Cill Éinne faster than the man on horseback going round by the road through six hospitable villages. Few people would have known any of these intimately local routes other than the ones linked with their own village; the exceptions would be such anomalous characters as wise women and cartographers, who are not above cultivating a reputation for paranormal powers of way-finding.

Today's schoolchildren seem not to know of the short-cut to Gort na gCapall, or they prefer the chance of a lift along the roads. The sides of one or two of the little stiles have leaned together, quietly closing the way; grey forgetfulness has wiped away the footmarks that mapped out Aran for the moon. I spoke about this way once to a lady of another village who was born in Gort na gCapall, and it was as if I had reopened the gates of Eden. Raptly she recalled the adventures of that daily to-and-fro with her school-friends. The spots they rested their hands on in clambering up and down ledges were polished smooth, she said. Once she dropped the silvery cap of her new fountain-pen down a fissure; they could see it glinting, but 'You might as well have been looking down into Hell, that *scailp* was so deep!' They marked the spot with a pile of stones, and that evening her brothers came with a crowbar, levered out a great slab, and reached out the pen-top. She could show me the very slab today, she remembered every stone of the way. And as she talked, her eyes reflected the gleam of silver gifts un-wrapped after years unseen.

MOONGRAZING

The finest limestone pavements of the island lie like a fallen sickle moon, some days old, some days new, along the curve of the land beyond Gort na gCapall; one can walk over great open tracts of rock, west and then north-westwards, all the way to the village of Cill Mhuirbhigh. On one's left are, at first, the jagged ridge of the storm-beach around Port Bhéal an Dúin, and then the slightly higher ground, sparsely grassed and salted by spray, rising to the cliffs of An Sunda Caoch. A few hundred yards inland on one's right, the terrace-edge is a sharp drop of fifteen or twenty feet, rimming a busily subdivided lowland of milking-pastures and potato-gardens. The walk from village to village could be made as little as a brisk mile, with only a few awkward walls and ravines to be negotiated, but the best route is indefinitely more complicated.

Pádraic Dan Phatch first showed me the bee-line right-of-way across the crags from Gort na gCapall to the villagers' favourite fishing perches on the cliffs. This used to be another of the silvery ways I have described, but its moonshine had long evaporated; I remember that at one point when I was walking a couple of paces to one side of him he gestured me back onto the correct path, which he could see or perhaps feel through his feet, although to me its humps and cracks were as illegible as the rest. Pádraic, that day, was an exile home on holiday, his long strides and declamatory reminiscences were an exultant reappropriation of the land of his youth, and the jottings I made on my map in his turbulent wake were far from clear to me afterwards. So I returned several times to go over the ground at my own pace, and gradually accommodated my eyes to catch the residual luminosity of the past even in the brightest present-daylight; and then I found that, apart from the fishermens' short-cut, I could make out yet another and finer web of human investment in these crags.

Some of the stiles of the right-of-way have collapsed or been filled with stones, but the first is clear to see, a substantial *staighre* in the wall of the boreen from the village where it turns south to the shore, and the second, a *céimín*, is straight opposite it, across a hundred yards of pavement which the glaciers have moulded into long smooth billows. After that the route is crossed by more recent walls, and the next clear *céimín* is three hundred yards farther west. My wanderings over the intervening crags in search of traces of the true way revealed so many intriguing little adjustments of the ground to the foot that I ended up by mapping it in detail; any islander seeing me nosing out these rocky hints and nudges might have wondered if I had trodden on the *fóidín mearbhaill* or 'stray sod', for one who steps on such a spot loses all sense of direction and has to wander till moonrise, the only remedy being to take off one's coat and put it on again inside out.

I am tempted to write a guide to this crooked acre, to push further into absurdity the pretensions of this book to comprehensiveness. But such a guide would have to be addressed to the cow's hoof rather than the human foot, and would fall into a browsing, straying gait, petering out in ruminative stillness, for the expanse of stone is interrupted by oases of grass, and the purpose of all this micro-engineering is to link these into a maze of grazing, that the desert may yield meat and milk. Thus:

To begin at the beginning (Oh Cow!), you should wait patiently while Rónán Dan

Phatch or Oisín Rónáin Dan or whoever is conducting you throws down the 'gap' in the boreen wall twenty yards south of the first stile mentioned above. An unusual oblique gully in which some knee-deep and more than worthwhile grass is growing guides a narrow track to the next gap, beside the second stile; this track looks comparatively recent, and where it crosses rock the fissures have been filled with small stones and the way edged with larger blocks and surfaced with clay for your comfort. Beyond the second gap there is a deeply fissured outcrop on the right; roll your eye at this and remember Tom O'Flaherty's essay 'Bó i Sgailp'. (Easily translated: *bó*, a cow, is one of the noble ancient words of Irish, and indeed as the late Professor Vendryes puts it in his indispensable and most regrettably uncompleted *Lexique étymologique de l'Irlandais ancien*, 'C'est le nom indo-européen de l'animal bovin, conservé dans la plupart des langues' – and he instances among others Sanskrit *gầuḥ*, Greek βοῦς, and of course the Latin *bos*; from *bó* derive such foundational terms of Irish culture as *bóthar*, a road, originally a way that could accommodate two cows, *buachall*, a boy, originally a cow-boy, and, to butter you up no further, Boand, the cow-goddess who gave her name to the River Boyne. The word *sgailp*, nowadays spelled *scailp*, plural *scalpachaí* or [my preference] *scailpreachaí*, a cleft, fissure, cave, etc., is in Aran of almost equal weight, being with *creig* the most important term of topography in this island composed almost entirely of *creigeanna* and *scailpreachaí*. Hence: *bó i sgailp*, a cow in a cleft.) Picture, then, young Tom's alarm when:

...the most weird and feared cry that ever smote the ear of Aran islander fell on the village like the crack of doom.

'Bó I Sgailp! Bó I Sgailp! Bó I Sgailp!'

The meaning of this was that somebody's cow had caught in a cleft among the rocks, and that it was almost certain the animal was lost.

In that case the precious beast had broken its leg and had to be 'put down'; here though there is no danger of such a disaster, because Dan Phatch himself long ago built a little rim of stones around the patch of *scailpreachaí*, to guide you leftwards. Better still, the stones he used were fished out of a saucer-like depression of broken ground in which the grass therefore grows unimpeded; room to swish one's tail here! A trodden path winds south-westwards across the grass to another gap, giving onto a crag that is deeply scored across by long depressions a couple of yards wide made by the glaciers that grazed the island fifteen or twenty thousand years ago. Each of these *gleainníní* or little glens has a thin carpet of heather and some mouth-fuls of grass to be snatched while following the first of them to the north for a few paces. Now cross the intervening rib of limestone to the next *gleainnín* – the fissures at the crossing-point have been packed with stones and a row of small blocks placed on either side to stop you straying onto rock which might be slippery after rain. The second hollow offers thirty or forty paces of grazing flavoured with tormentil, milkwort, fairy flax and a dozen other herbs too minute to be savoured individually but all said to be good for you. This brings you to the wall separating this enclosure from the one north of it, which is even less interpretable as a field than this enclosure. A bit of smoothening and infilling of the *creig* has made a pass-able route along the wall – mind your flanks, especially if pregnant, on the pro-jecting angles of its stones – to a gap in the western wall of the enclosure, opening into another grassy hollow going south again. A cutting hacked through the next long finger of rock – rather narrow and sharp-edged at hock-level, please note – opens up one more dip the glacier bulldozed out for grass to grow in. The *staighre* in the wall immediately west of it is of course not good enough for cows, but the wall makes this a sheltered corner in which to chew the cud.

The point to which I have brought the cow is only two hundred yards from the gap in the boreen wall, and after so many closely considered paces it is exhilarating to rove more widely over the crag of almost uninterrupted bare rock to the north, which forms a salient of the terrace-rim, sticking out like the nose of the Man in the Moon over the lower land beyond. The tip of it is called Aill na Sagart, the cliff of the priests, and there is a vague tra-dition that the Mass used to be celebrated here, perhaps during the time of the Penal Laws against the Catholic religion some three hundred years ago. It is a lofty-feeling spot, though I suppose it is not more than twenty feet above the little fields that congregate around its foot. A green and flowery boreen, a favourite walk of ours when the primroses are in bloom, passes immediately below on its many-angled way from Gort na gCapall, of which the nearest houses are not far away on the right, to Cill Mhuirbhigh beach, half a mile ahead to the left. This fertile area is called An Caiseal, for no clear reason; a *caiseal* can be many stony things from a great stone fort like Dún Aonghasa (which overlooks the entire scene of this chapter from the western skyline), to a little pile of stones left over from a children's game, but this is Gort na gCapall's most stone-free land, of good *dur-amhán*, sandy loam, and well watered from springs under the terrace-rim. Seen from above like this, the fields in their low walls look up with the innocency of rooms in a doll's house when one lifts the roof and peeps in. This would be the setting of 'Spring Sowing' – in fact there they are, Martin and Mary, at their midday bread and butter and tea. Should one look?

Martin ate heartily, revelling in his great thirst and his great hunger, with every pore of his body open to the pure air. And he looked around at his neighbours' fields boastfully, comparing them with his own. Then he looked at his wife's little round black head and felt very proud of having her as his own. He leaned back on his elbow and took her hand in his. Shyly and in silence, not knowing what to say and ashamed of their gentle feelings, for peasants are always ashamed of feeling refined, they finished eating and still sat hand in hand looking away into the dis-tance. Everywhere the sowers were resting on little knolls, men, women and chil-dren sitting in silence. ...

From Aill na Sagart I look away, into the distance. Poking my nose into the island's tender moments, when there is work to be done, sense to be harrowed out of the rock! Back to my moonscape!

In that distance beyond Cill Mhuirbhigh bay, a crisp pleating of grey-blue and fawn along the horizon represents the highlands of Connemara. According to most accounts of the last Ice Age it was from an ice-cap on the mountains to the right in this vista, the Maumturks, that our local glaciers emanated. Listening to one's footsteps ringing on the pristine pavement above Aill na Sagart one could imagine that the ice had only just retired from its polishing. The name of this particularly fine tract of crag is Creig na Leacht, and it seems that here *leacht* means, not a monument or cairn, but simply the same as *leac*, a 'flag' or rock-sheet. When a low sun plays obliquely across this wide-open expanse it adumbrates every inequality of the surface, overlaying the rock with transparencies, dim maps of all the dimly understood processes that have worked on it. Among these diagrammatic apparitions are a number of approximately parallel channels, a few feet wide and a few inches deep, their shelving flanks delicately carved into scarps of half an inch or so, traceable in places for thirty yards or more; they look like gentle rivers of space or fossilized breezes. They have not been created by erosion along particularly close-set joints of the limestone, like the much deeper *gleainníní* with their bottoms of broken, fissured stone and heathery sward, for these channels have floors as bare and smooth as the surrounding pavement. I have noted them in many parts of the island, but these on Creig na Leacht are the most striking examples. They seem to occur mainly, or at least to be more apparent, on rock-exposures with very few joints, that is, on the hardest, purest limestone, and they tend roughly north-north-east, just a few degrees more easterly than does the principal set of joints. (Here their bearing is about 21 degrees east of true north, whereas the main joints, the field-walls and the *gleainníní* run at about 12 degrees east, *i.e.* in the direction I have been calling Aran North.) That they pre-date the opening-up of the joints by weathering is demonstrated by the fact that they run on from clint to clint; where the rainwater swills off them between two clints their lips have been worn down into wide funnels, but otherwise their beds are continuous across the grykes. This seems to suggest that although they have been modified by weathering since the crags were left bare, basically they are the work of glaciation – and, looking out along them, their perspective converges very convincingly on the Maumturks. However, if they were excavated by loose rock being dragged across the land surface by ice, one would expect them to be very varied, whereas throughout the islands they are rather similar in their dimensions. My sources of geological understanding are unwilling to commit themselves to

an opinion on the origins of these tracings, so I leave them among the enig-
mas of Aran.

'Solution-hollows' are common features on smooth pavements like
this, and they too pose their questions. They are usually rather flat-bot-
tomed, a few inches deep, with sharply defined, near-vertical sides, and as
varied in shape as puddles on roads. Many hold rainwater long enough for
algae to flourish in them, not only the free-swimming single-celled sorts
that under the microscope look like bizarre clockwork toys, but grape-sized
blobs of a blue-green alga called *Nostoc*, sometimes enough of it to cover
the floor of the hollow. In a dry spell this squashy stuff is reduced to a black
soil and generally blows away, but if some of it remains and accumulates,
mosses and herbs will seize their chance and eventually the hollow may be
plugged with a grassy 'scraw' or sod; thus *Nostoc* is in the front line of the
vegetable world's unremitting struggle to take over the crags in the teeth of
the wind and the herbivore. But this primitive life-form may be an agent
of creation and destruction at an even deeper level; for it secretes a weak
acid which attacks limestone. The solution-hollows themselves are the
work of *Nostoc*, slowly eating out nests for itself from whatever little toe-
holds its spore wash into. The cratering of clint-surfaces by this almost
amorphous slime is one of the forces rendering Aran down to oceanic
solutes once again. On the way to this end, *Nostoc* helps make the place
liveable, fit for grass, cows, humans, books. It may also explain those fissures closed on the surface and open below, that I puzzled over in 'Modalities of Roughness'. But it leaves another puzzle in its wake, that often
makes me halt and kneel to examine it when I am mooning about the
crags. The curiosity is that many of the solution-hollows have rims standing a quarter or half an inch proud of the pavement and fretted into little
crests and thorn-like points. One might wonder if these have been built up
by deposition of calcium carbonate, as a side-effect of the chemical activity
of *Nostoc*, but so far as I can see they are composed of exactly the same limestone as they arise from, and have been carved out of it. Why would such
delicate structures not be abolished in their incipiency by erosion? Why
have they been excepted from the general polishing-down of the surface?
Again, I search the land and the literature of limestone in vain for an
answer.

To see the unarguable signature of the last Ice Age, one should make
for a prominent cluster of perched boulders on another little headland of
this terrace, a third of a mile to the west. Most of them are of limestone and
so must have been ripped out by the ice not much farther to the north, for
the limestone strata feather out (to borrow a neat term from the geologists)
somewhere under the North Sound, exposing the underlying Galway gran-

ite. The biggest of the limestone boulders – it has a prostrate juniper bush growing on top – has toppled off its pedestal, revealing a small sample of what the pavement surface looked like before it was rubbed down by ten thousand years of rain. On this unweathered patch are a few 'glacial striae', scratches made by stones embedded in the ice. The limestone specialist Conor MacDermot pointed them out to me one day when we were roving these crags, exclaiming and hypothesizing over every step. Somehow these tentative, almost childish markings which have only escaped erasure by a fluke give the glaciers more presence in my mind than all their titanic works displayed around us. Also I am pleased to note that their orientation is the same as that of the mysterious channels of Creig na Leacht (but I could get no confirmation from Conor the Hammer of the glacial origin of the latter).

We agreed that day that, if ever it became necessary to select a suite of crags for preservation, it should be these, from Gort na gCapall to Cill Mhuirbhigh. (Fifteen years later, having seen the casual wrecking of other superb areas of pavement by quarrying and building, I think some such measure is urgently necessary.) Towards the north-western end of this crescent an oblique set of grykes, bearing about 128 degrees east, replaces the normal east-west set. This feature seems to correlate with very broad clints and correspondingly wide grykes. Many of these grykes are eighteen inches or more across, six or ten feet deep, and are enlarged at their intersections into cavernous funnels which the rain gargles down. As for the clints, one of them even figures in a census return; Patrick O'Flaherty of what was later to be called Kilmurvey House, after enumerating his own household for the census of 1821 adds, 'There is a little to the south of Patrick O'Flaherty's house a large sheet of flag 130 steps long.' This would be on Creig an Tobair, the last crag of this sequence, named from the well below its scarp, that delivers the water from those capacious grykes to the village of Cill Mhuirbhigh. These magnificent flags are so smooth, and sound so well underfoot, that they invite one to dance, and in fact it is said that when Lady Digby visited the island in 1888 a *céilí* was held in her honour here. The former O'Flaherty estate begins with the better land just west of Creig an Tobar, across the boreen leading up towards Dún Aonghasa, but the crag itself, like the others east of it, was Gort na gCapall territory. It was Gort na gCapall men who paid rent on those 130 steps of flag, and who with Nostocian persistence have stitched together a ragged cloak of pasturage over all the barren mile from here back to their village by countless interventions with the rock that the stroller might well not notice. There must have been some bitterness to drown when they made the rock ring to their steps, at the entertainment the O'Flaherty offered to their landlady.

A living has been made out of these crags in another way too; they have been cropped for tombstones. The main site of this bygone craft was just south of the clutch of glacial boulders, where large areas of the smooth upper layer of the pavement have been levered up, leaving ragged stone, but one can find half-finished tombstones, lying like table-tops propped on small boulders, here and there on most of Aran's larger-clinted crags. One or two have a little wall beside them thrown together out of loose blocks, to shelter the mason from the weather as he worked. It seems strange that it was the custom to finish the slab out on the exposed crag, but no doubt it was not possible to assemble the team of eight or ten men needed to shift such a stone, typically six foot by three, and eight inches thick, to the graveyard, with the necessary logs and planks and the quart of *poitín* to lubricate its progress, before the carving and lettering had been successfully completed. The use of these massive, horizontal, grave-slabs died out some decades ago, regretted by none because of the labour and indeed the danger involved in their transport, but leaving the field to sliced-bread religiosity supplied from Galway in glossy black or white marble. These nobly pro-portioned flags with their classic decorations of compass-drawn sun-bursts in the corners, diamond-patterned margins, formalized palm-fronds and the like, and their laconic 'Pray for the soul of ...', are a dignified collective memorial to those generations whose very ground was of equal nobility, and it is fitting that some of them still lie on the crags themselves. Mortal-ity echoes underfoot at such sites, though, and when it is particularized and named, even the monumental discretion of these crags can be tactless. Colman Dirrane, old Uncle Colman of Gilbert Cottage, mooching about on Creig an Tobair one Sunday afternoon of his retirement, found himself reading a tombstone that said, 'Pray for the soul of Coleman Dirrane', and it left him depressed for a fortnight. Why are there so many abandoned tombstones lying about to trip up one's mood? Some of them obviously have cracked during the rough-shaping process, and one can almost hear the curse that rang out across the crags when that happened. But several are virtually finished. One that hardly needs another tap of the chisel is still perched on its little props near the perched boulders of the glacier's own rough carving:

PRAY FOR THE SOUL
OF VALENTINE CONNOLLY
WHO DIED MAY THE 19 1894
AGED 29 YEARS
ERECTED BY HIS WIFE
SARAH

Why in fact did Sarah never erect it? I am told that this was one of the slabs carved for a Connemara grave – the Connemara people called them 'slates' – and that it would have been taken out in a turf-boat if some accident or disagreement had not intervened. I have since noticed many such Aran slabs in those evocatively jumbled, hummocky, cemeteries around roofless medieval chapels on the south Connemara coast. This export trade, now of course extinct, as is the importation of turf, seems to me like the last word in the grim comedy of relationships between the two neighbouring poverties of Aran limestone and Connemara granite. While the Connemara man was stripping the ground from under his own feet to sell it as turf to Aran, so that much of south Connemara was reduced to bare rock by the end of the last century, the Araner found a way of repaying him in bare rock itself, with his tombstone; thus Connemara lies under Aran at the last. But in the case of Valentine Connolly, was the last laugh, the last tear, with his wife Sarah, or with some Joeen na gCloch, little Joe of the stones, stonemason of Aran?

THE CLOCK

Not far from one corner of one of the crags traversed by the previous chapter – *I interrupt myself to apologize for this topographical vagueness, which, uncharacteristic as it is of this book, so dense with a superfluity of distances, bearings and dimensions specified more accurately than needful for a travellers' guide or a literary evocation of the Aran of my memories as to suffuse with space – and space of the most everyday sort, the mere objective underlay of more subjective measures, even if slightly humanized by my preference for inches and feet (body-bits, fossilized, but not quite cold), yards and miles and the human pace that guarantees them, rather than the metric arbitrarily hinged on the meridian of Paris and the false start of the Year One – to the point of intoxication the consciousness that is being built up, coral-wise, by this writing towards a sense, crystallized from oceanic solutes, of the coherence of mind with all that stems from and is still in a connection that can be symbolized as spatial with that universal origin, the dot, the full stop to nothingness in relation to which I stand at this moment like a fingerless finger-post at ground-zero, is an exception forced upon me by the existence, obliging me to break the continuity of my progress from east to west with this locational obfuscation, and inducing an irruption of indignation that makes me try to say everything at once, of people – my curse on them: may they wander moon-cold crags for eternity! – for whom, because they would use me as a guide to something they could break out of the continuity of Aran to steal, being so lost to a sense of where things should be that one has to deny them the knowledge of where things are, apology should be addressed to Aran itself, that stone-deaf land from which all our apostrophes re-echo, readdressed as, in this instance, the apology of the human mind to itself—* is a mark on the pavement, a dark spiral that draws the eye in like a vortex, reproving one's bovine ramblings and calling for concentrated presence, persistence in looking. It is a fossil; Conor MacDermot identified it for me as that of a nautiloid, a cephalopod mollusc related to the modern octopuses and squids, and to the extinct belemnites whose conical shells are to be found here and there in the Aran rocks. Many species of nautiloids, some with straight or curved shells, others with coiled shells like this specimen, inhabited the waters from which the limestone was deposited. Their shells were divided by thin partitions into a number of compartments, the outer of which was occupied by the animal itself while those farther back were full of gas and functioned as buoyancy-chambers. All the nautiloids are now extinct except the pearly nautilus of the Indian and Pacific Oceans. Like the Aran nautiloid, the pearly nautilus has a shell coiled into a flat spiral, and it swims (in a style at once dreamy and sedate, as I recall from some TV nature film) with its coil in a vertical plane and its round eyes and wavering tentacles appearing in the aperture below.

My description of this fossil will perhaps give an exaggerated sense of its physical presence, because of the weight it assumes in my mind as I write about it. Of course in fossilization all the soft parts are lost and only the shell or part of it survives. The Aran specimen is unusually large, but it is only a foot across, and not much more than the two outer turns of the spiral is preserved, showing up as a slight ridge of rough, dark material in the smooth light-grey pavement. Two partitions are visible, the one the animal sat into, forming a concave curve across the outer whorl a few inches in from the aperture, and close behind that the one it had most recently grown out of. The texture and colour are those of crusted ash, the spectrum of life collapsed.

Hoping to bring this nautiloid to its glorious resurrection, my mind goes back to an illustration in a book of my childhood days, *The Story of Living Things and their Evolution* by Eileen Mayo, showing a pearly nautilus wonderfully striped in carmine on rosy white. This magically named creature used to conduct my imagination through phosphorescent seas across which jungle-archipelagoes breathed cinnamon and a diffuse longing for some incomprehensible adventure. Now it is this rough charcoal sketch of the nautiloid on the stark northern rock that draws me down to the sumptuous waters of the Carboniferous Period. Pangaea was coming into existence then; South America, Africa, Antartica and Australia were already fused together into a mega-continent the geologists call Gondwanaland, while North America, Greenland and northern Europe, united into another called Laurasia, were drifting southwards to join it. Aran's nautiloid lived in a shallow continental-shelf sea near the centre of this all-embracing land-mass. The world had long lost its initial nakedness to the poisonous rays of the sun and was wrapped in its sphere of protective vapours, into which a three-billion-year growth of microbial action had already released enough oxygen to fuel every complexity of life. All, or nearly all, of the great inventions of biology had found themselves out in the evolutionary exuberance of the previous few hundred million years: sexual reproduction, the many-celled organism, the eye, the protective shell, even the backbone and the lung. The coal-swamps, the monstrous reptiles, the first mammals and the first flowers were in the immediate future, soon to be followed by the break-up of Pangaea. But even before that tearing apart of the New World and the Old, the age of the nautiloids was over. Almost every species of them, together with ninety per cent of the species of shallow-sea animals and most of the amphibians, reptiles and proto-mammals, were extinguished over a few million years, about two hundred and fifty million years ago. Like the famous extinction of the dinosaurs just seventy million years ago, this par-tial apocalypse was perhaps triggered by the collision of a large asteroid with the earth, an accident the statistics of solar-system orbits suggest will happen on average every forty or fifty million years. But in its own terms the life-world of the nautiloid lasted for ever. Each individual one of them slowly created its coil by adding onto the rim of its aperture, building forward over the curved back of the previous whorl, as its millions of ancestors had and its millions of descendants would do. Each one hunted small drifting and darting things through the fretted grottoes of – but perhaps I should not describe that iridescent feathery world other than as a fantasy waiting to be dreamed, for the neurone webs were not yet woven that could see its loveli-ness (unless, for the cephalopod brain and retina are richly interconnected, the nautiloid itself had some dawning sense of its own and its world's beauty). Our world too, if 'the great star from heaven' of the Apocalypse does not fall on it too soon, will no doubt be caught up retrospectively in thousands or millions of years' time by faculties unimaginably different from the feeble gifts of love, wonder and knowledge we can bring to it. In the meantime, one's patient attention to one of the best bits of ground that could be covered by a pace or two is demanded, in the sign of the spiral the nautiloid traced on Aran.

A few square feet of the rock-surface around the spiral carry numerous scars and blemishes, which on examination turn out to be the remains contributed by a variety of the nautiloid's contemporaries to the bone-yard that was to become Aran; what fluke of sea-bed dynamics preserved such an exhibition-caseful of them just here is not apparent. When Conor was giving me their names, I noted their positions by taking the spiral as a clock-face, with twelve o'clock marked by the first internal partition. At five o'clock, then, and within the spiral itself, lies something that looks like fragments of a whitish comb embedded in the rock, while at two o'clock and just outside the spiral is a shape like part of a rounded leaf with delicate radial veins. These are both fossils of an extinct coral called *Caninia*. Like today's corals *Caninia* secreted a limy skeleton around itself, which remained after the soft body of the animal itself had decayed. It was a 'solitary' coral, a single polyp like a sea-anenome living in a cupped hollow in the end of the tube it built up for itself, which was usually an inch or two across and up to two feet long. The comb-like fossil here is part of such a tube seen in a longitudinal section, the teeth of the comb representing the successive floors the polyp formed under itself across the tube as it grew. The leaf-like fossil is a rather oblique cross-section of a tube, exposing the dozens of fine radial plates that supported the polyp in its cup. The original material of the coral skeleton has been replaced by calcite in the process of fossilization, and if one takes a lens to it the fine detail is seen to be made up of glittering crystals; it is in itself a labyrinth one could get lost in for hours.

A foot or so away from the nautiloid, at about three o'clock, is a scattering of much smaller marks like dark fingerprints, with indistinct radial patterns made up of the same white crystals; the lens reveals about twenty-four radii in each print. This is *Lithostrotion*, a 'compound' coral in which a large number of polyps have built up a communal skeleton of many loosely bunched tubes. *Lithostrotion* is frequent in the Aran limestones; the white-spotted pebbles found on the shingle-banks are wave-polished fragments of it. Next to this colony and at four o'clock by the nautiloid is another, an eruption of much smaller, crooked, interlinking tubes in which no radial lines are to be seen: *Syringopora*, a common member of a simpler and more primitive order of corals in which the radial plates or septa are scarcely developed. The polyps of a compound coral are not completely individualized creatures but interconnect within the skeleton. *Syringopora* has many short cross-tubes linking the branches of the 'thicket' (the geologists' apt term), giving it a thorny, matted look. And like pale birds in this thicket are three oval fossils of another solitary coral, *Dibunophyllum*, with many septa and tiny concentric plates between them making a pattern in the centre, like a spider's web according to the textbooks, more accurately a closely packed set of nested diamond-shapes.

Close to the last and an hour farther round the clock is another *Lithostrotion* colony, of a form in which the branches are so bunched together that in cross-section they look like the cells of a honeycomb. Parts of this fossil have been replaced by silica rather than calcite, and as limestone wears away faster than silica they stand out of the surface of the rock as if a finely tooled bronze bracelet were being revealed. The point in common with the other, round-tubed *Lithostrotion*, and which serves to identify it, at least among the Aran fossils, as a member of the same genus, is the flattened, rod-like structure in the centre of each tube; in these cross-sections it looks as if each hexagon or roundel has a tiny compass needle in it.

The last of the corals here is another solitary, *Palaeosmilia*, a pale patch like the thumbprint of a giant frost on the rock, touching the nautiloid at six o'clock. Its structure is incredibly delicate, with perhaps fifty septa (more than I can count) and innumerable tiny curved plates between them forming a pattern like overlapping round tiles or fish-scales. There is another *Palaeosmilia* four paces away at half past four, showing a longitudinal section in which the septa appear as a bank of slightly curved lines. A rough band across them perhaps records an accident to the creature, from which it recovered and grew on.

Some fauna other than corals of the Carboniferous sea can be sampled along this same half-past-four line. First, right by the nautiloid, is a spiral a couple of inches across, showing slight traces of ornamentation but none of the partitions that distinguish the nautiloids; it is a gastropod, a mollusc like the modern snail or winkle. Eighteen inches further out is something that looks like a shard of bone china – one of the large lamp-shells or brachiopods, *Gigantoproductus*, that I described in my first volume in connection with the shell-beds on the coast nearby. Immediately beyond it are dozens of white bits and pieces, some like beads or short rows of beads stuck together, and some like a thick letter O, which are the remains of sea-lily stems. Sea-lilies or crinoids are animals related to the starfish, with five plume-like arms for trawling the water, and all the Carboniferous species of them, like many modern ones, were anchored by a flexible stalk, which falls apart into short cylindrical bits after death. In places the Aran limestone is almost entirely composed of minute crinoid fragments. Finally, beyond the beads, are traces of some mud-dwelling invertebrate species; their boneless bodies have left no fossils, but their burrows have been filled in with some material that now shows up in the surface of the limestone as intermittent ribbons and patches of a darker tint. And all over the surrounding crag are other dim or pallid shadows of once brilliantly coloured creatures. At any hour of the clock the ghosts of Aran's gorgeous natal sea are around one's feet.

Lithostrotion, Palaeosmilia, Dibunophyllum – to some, these polysylla-
bles may sound like dog-eared labels curling in the drought of a museum,
but to me they are as fresh and exotic as the names Adam gave the beasts
were to him. As I have presented them here, they are so many isolated bits
fallen out of a structure of which I know little, in which each has its place
and its significance, naming a link in an evolutionary chain, indicating a
distinction between strata, commemorating a discovery, insinuating a
hypothesis. The only question that arises as regards this book is whether
they serve to focus vision or stand opaque between the eye and its object,
for I call on the past only to cast its colours on the present. And I have
found in practice that the attempt to learn the names of things magnifies
their features; even when detached from the apparatus of science such
nouns are powerful lenses. With them I peer into this rock-surface as if it
were a glass case in a museum – and when I lift my tired eyes to the
museum clock, whose spring winds back through so many aeons, sometimes its face is a stony blank, and sometimes it indicates the present
moment with a scrupulous and hard-won exactitude.

GOING TO CILL MHUIRBHIGH

O'Donovan's Ordnance Survey letters, 1839:

In the same townland of Kilmurvy about half a mile east of Mr. O'Flaherty's house
are visible the indistinct foundations of a church which is said to have given name
to the townland of Kilmurvy, which means the church of the Muirbheach or Sea
plain. It is at present, however, called Eatharla, a name which seems to signify a
cemetery. Stations are performed here with great solemnity on Good Friday, on
which the pilgrims walk round the whole island keeping as near the strand or edge
of the cliffs as they can.

This is the only substantive reference we have to 'the church of the sea-
plain', of which nothing is remembered. 'Atharla, site of' is marked on the
old OS maps, about forty yards south of the main road where it makes a
little detour around the head of Port Mhuirbhigh. On several occasions I
have hopped across the low roadside wall into the big field to look for it,
never quite reconciled to the fact that not a trace of it is to be seen. I was
usually on my way to the Conneelys' shop, guest-house and post office in
the village, half a mile farther west, which was a focus of the island for us.
If, to the islanders of long ago, going to Cill Mhuirbhigh meant going to

the church of the sea-plain, in our time it meant going to Conneelys'. Now Conneelys' lies derelict, and on recent visits to the island I have stayed at Kilmurvey House, the former O'Flaherty residence O'Donovan refers to, which in its turn has become for me the centre of gravity of the village.

The sea-plain itself, Na Muirbhigh Móra, around the head of the bay, is the heart of the Kilmurvey House farm, a smooth tract of sandy grassland divided by straight walls into near-rectangles of two thousand square yards or so, in striking contrast to the Gort na gCapallites' crumpled pocket-handkerchiefs of land immediately to the south in An Caiseal. Each year one or two of the fields are in hay, and dry cattle roam the rest. Parts of this area used to be tilled, and the evening sun brings out the shadows of old potato-ridges that must have seemed eternally long to those who had to dig them. In a damp hollow there are traces of unusually broad ridges, about three yards across, in which I am told flax used to be cultivated. On a knoll by the roadside at the west end of the beach is a small, walled cemetery, from which the Celtic cross marking the O'Flaherty grave-plot overlooks the entire productive basin of land; seeing it, I imagine James O'Flaherty JP watching the scythes work across his fields from that vantage point and reading the self-gratulatory motto 'Fortuna favet fortibus', 'Fortune favours the brave', on his father's tomb.

The westernmost of these big fields below the cemetery is favoured by a fortune of wild-flowers. A honeyed breeze rolls across the road from it in high summer; it breathes out more riches in an afternoon than the O'Flahertys gathered in all their history. The usual meadow-herbs such as purple and white clovers and the yellow kidney vetch, bird's foot trefoil and lady's bedstraw are abundant; there is also the less common squinancywort, and clambering and twining through all these a rare curiosity, the common dodder. This parasite, a network of reddish, hair-fine filaments, virtually rootless and leafless, blossoming in tiny clusters of minute pinkish bells, taps the juices of other plants through tiny suckers penetrating their tissues. It seems to enjoy a superfluity of sweets here; I think that much of the aerial mead intoxicating the bees is distilled by its flowers.

This field falls away shallowly to the south-west, and under the wall of the boreen going by it to An Caiseal are three hollows where water wells out of the ground after rain. One December M and I decided to walk round that way, after having been kept in for days by thunderstorms charging across the island on great thick smoky stalks of rain, each one darkening the house for a few minutes and turning the garden shrubs inside out before rushing off eastwards. Having edged our way down the road between the hard lumps of wind, we found that Bóithrín an Chaisil had disappeared into a small angry lake. There were two or three whooper swans on the water, and some wild duck I could not identify in the winter twilight. I went down again after calm had had a few days to establish itself. This time, it was the hour accurately termed in Irish 'the ring of dawn'. Stepping out of the house into a stillness that was just beginning to be quartered by birdsong, I found my wellington boots so noisy on the road I had to go back and change into shoes, by which time the moment of perfection had been replaced by some mere gritty-eyed early-morning clock-hour. But down by the wintery lake I was rewarded by a glimpse of a bird I hadn't seen in Aran before, the water rail, like a little grey-brown hen, going off high-stepping and tip-tilted into the ranks of curled dock along the further shore.

Even in droughty weather one would guess that the lower half of the field is a turlough, from the ragged hanks of black-brown moss on the stones of its southern wall, and the striking distribution of plants that are particular about how much immersion they can take. In their respective seasons the small dandelion-like autumn hawkbit, *Leontodon autumnalis*, and the big white ox-eye daisy make vivid contour-maps of the slopes around the hollows. The hollow nearest to the main road – Poll an Chapaill, the pool of the horse – must go down nearly to sea-level, for the stones in its bottom are draped with livid green tresses of *Enteromorpha* seaweed; it probably connects with an outflow of fresh water on the shelving beach across the road and four hundred yards to the north, that shows up in the bright clean sand as a dark patch smelling of vegetable decay. Each of the three foci of the turlough has its own flora. In Poll an Chapaill, on the mud between the stones there is water speedwell, and around that a stratum of silverweed and marsh bedstraw, with creeping cinquefoil on the rough outcrop that makes a little mantle to the swallow-hole. The second swallow-hole, a hundred yards further inland, is shallower. A dark-toned area of spike rush surrounds it, mixed with common redleg and the rather rare marsh yellow cress, *Rorippa icelandica*, and in the muddy centre grows a white-flowered crowfoot, *Ranunculus trichophyllus*. The third is in a small triangular field over the boundary wall in Gort na gCapall territory. Most of the hollow is deeply carpeted with silverweed, round its rim is a zone of marsh ragwort, and on the bare mud in the middle squats the miserable-looking toad rush.

In summer the air over these mud-ponds is zipping with small brown dragonflies; the common *Sympetrum*, I think. They mate in flight, with Kamasutral contortions: in both sexes the genitalia are under the tail-end of the long abdomen, but the male also has claspers on his tail and accessory sex-organs under the front end of his abdomen; with the claspers he holds the female by the back of the neck, she secures the grip by flexing her head or neck, and then she bends her own abdomen forwards and applies the sex-organ near the end of it to the male's accessory organ; and off they go, looped together like some letter out of an erotic alphabet. When she is ready to lay her eggs, her mate helicopters over the pond with the female still hanging from his tail and lowers her until she can dab her abdomen into the mud or the water again and again, washing off the eggs one at a time. Admiring these antics one day, I saw a lone dragonfly pursuing a linked couple. She – it must have been a she – attached herself by the neck to the tail of the other female, which brought the whole train of them crashing to the ground. The male quickly disengaged himself and flew off, the female in possession got herself free and darted after him, and the interloper stayed there flicking her wings. It was impossible not to see the three of them respectively as exasperated, insatiate, and disconsolate.

One day in the summer of '75 I found this last part of the turlough covered with ragged sheets of something like a thick whitish paper, draped over the rampant tussocks of silverweed; there were perhaps a hundred square yards of it. I was baffled as to this nature of this substance, which seemed to have appeared overnight and was to shrivel away over the following few days. Later I learned from Máire Scannell of the National Botanic Gardens that it was 'algal paper'. It forms in turloughs when hot weather causes microscopic algae (*Oedogonium* and other species) to proliferate in a matted scum, which is left high and dry as the water-level drops away, and is baked and bleached to the consistency of paper. Since then I have seen acres of it around one of the big turloughs in the Burren, but outside the turlough areas of the west of Ireland it is an exceedingly rare occurrence. A German scientist told me it had only been reported about a dozen times in Germany, where it is known as 'meteor-paper' because it used to be thought to fall from the sky. It is curious that Praeger, who recorded the turlough flora very thoroughly, makes no mention of the phenomenon, which suggests that it has become more frequent since his time – but why that should be, I do not know.

Loch an Mhuirbhigh, the lake of the sea-plain, is the name of this turlough. I love the place. Its moods are less coercive than the hyperventilating lucidity of the crags or the hypnotic intricacies of the thickety little scarp-foot plots. In its relaxed openness and the grace of its distinctions, not to mention the cards it keeps up its sleeve, the quality it suggests is *intelligence*.

Going on towards the village, the road climbs past an odd detached length of cliff like a bun sandwich, a thin slice of shale between two fat layers of limestone. The tall umbellifers flourishing on the cliff-face, with dark glossy leaves and yellowish flower-heads, are alexanders. The cemetery lies along the south of the road at the top of the slope, and opposite it is a wide, rough field looking back to the bay, called Fearann na gCeann and said to be a battle-site. The earliest reference seems to be J.T. O'Flaherty's article of 1824, though it is likely he got the information from Hardiman, who was a friend of the Kilmurvey O'Flahertys:

At the north extremity of the larger Aran, not far from Port Murvey, the islanders show a field, where human bones and sculls are frequently dug up, and for which reason it is called *Faran-na-ccan*, 'the field of sculls'. Here the O'Briens are said to have, at some remote period, slaughtered each other almost to extermination. This sort of self-destruction is the largest and impurest blot of the page of Irish history: it always has been, and alas! continues to be Ireland's sad and inalienable inheritance.

The 'remote period' must have been some time before the expulsion of the O'Briens by the O'Flahertys in the 1560s. The little cliff by the road is called Cnocán na mBan, the hillock of the women, who are said to have stood on it to see their menfolk making history. I am told that the cemetery itself was called Cnocán an Chochaill, or Reilig an Chochaill, the hillock or graveyard of the cloak, a name that perhaps has a connection with the story of St Colm Cille's cloak told in my first volume. According to an old villager, some such name was written on a flag set in its wall, but when the wall was being rebuilt in the 1930s a woman who was not quite right in the head took it and carried it on her back all the way to Teaghlach Éinne, and it is now lost. The old recumbent gravestones here are hard to read except in certain lights; now and then, in necrological mood, I used to kick through the tousled grass and little sandpits to see what death-notices were being posted by the circling sun. Old limestone and new marble agree that Hernon is the predominant name in this cemetery's mortal catchment area, principally the village itself. There are also many small, blank boulders marking the graves of those too young, too numerous or too humble to have been granted even one parting line by the hard art of writing. A stray occupies a discreet corner: A. Tizzard, a Royal Air Force gunner, fished up in the nets in 1941. Another non-Aran name occurs on a well-carved and prominent slab near the O'Flaherty tomb: a Jane Gibson, died 1824 aged five. There is a place – a vertiginous brink in fact – on the west side of the peninsula of Dún Dúchathair called Binse Ghibson, Gibson's ledge; it is vaguely supposed that some Englishman must have fished from it long ago, and I had marked the spot on my map without much expectation of ever learning more of the man. Then, years after I had left Aran, my telephone rang late one night, and Gibson spoke to me, through the voice of his great-great-grandson who was following up the clue of his name on the map in search of his ancestry. Thus I know that James Gibson was from the Scilly Islands and came to Aran as a coastguard with his wife Catherine and four children, of whom Jane was the youngest, in about 1823. They had another child who died at birth in the same year as Jane, and three more who survived, over the next eight years. Later James was transferred to Casla Bay on the south Connemara coast, where he died of a heart attack while pulling a boat ashore. His widow and orphans crossed Ireland in an open cart and eventually returned to Scilly. One son, John, born in Aran, grew up to be a pilot. A passenger on a liner he was piloting once happened to leave an early model of camera on board, and when the captain and the crew had all failed to make anything of it, John took it, mastered it, became well known for his photographs of wrecks, and founded a photographic business, Gibson and Co.

The highest spot in the graveyard is occupied by the O'Flaherty tomb, with its tall Celtic cross patriarchally surveying the former estate. The cross is primarily

> Sacred to the memory of James O'Flaherty J.P.
> Kilmurvey House who departed
> this life Oc^r 24th A.D. 1881
> aged 64 years
> Fortified by the last rights
> of Holy Church

– but various other O'Flahertys, an O'Flaherty Johnston and a Johnston are named on it too, whom I shall sort out when I come to the history of the house. On the reverse is the motto, *Fortuna favet fortibus*, and a coat of arms, rather worn: two rampant beasts of some sort support an unidentifiable object; below is a boat with four oars protruding from ports in its hull, and above, a crest with a long four-legged creature. To restore the lost detail and colour of these bearings, I shall have to go back to sources more lasting than stone. As to recovering The O'Flaherty himself and his legendary misdeeds, Máirtín Ó Direáin offers an important admonition. James O'Flaherty is the original of Ó Mórna, anti-hero of his long poem of that name; I quote and translate the beginning, which addresses itself to an inquiring passer-by such as myself:

> *A ródaí fáin as tír isteach*
> *A dhearcann tuama thuas ar aill,*
> *A dhearcann armas is mana,*
> *A dhearcann scríbhinn is leac,*
> *Ná fág an reilig cois cuain*
> *Gan tuairisc an fhir a bheith leat.*

Cathal Mór Mac Rónáin an fear,
Mhic Choinn Mhic Chonáin Uí Mhórna,
Ná bí i dtaobh le comhrá cáich,
Ná le fíor na croise á ghearradh
Ar bhaithis chaillí mar theist an fhir
A chuaigh in uaigh sa gcill sin.

Ná daor an marbh d'éis cogar ban,
D'éis lide a thit idir uille
Is glúin ar theallach na sean,
Gan a phór is a chró do mheas,
A chéim, a réim, an t-am do mhair,
Is guais a shóirt ar an uaigneas.

Oh mainland tourist straying by,
Who looks at a tomb on a clifftop,
Looks at escutcheon and motto,
Looks at words inscribed on a flag,
Do not leave the cemetery by the sea
Without an account of the man himself.

Cathal Mór Ó Mórna was his name,
Son of Rónán son of Conn son of Conán,
Do not rely on what they all say,
Nor on the crone's crossing her brow,
As testimony of him who is buried
In the vault of that graveyard.

Condemn not the dead on women's gossip,
Or hints let fall between elbow and knee
At the old folks' fireside,
Without regard for his breed and blood,
His standing, his power, the times he lived in,
And the risks of loneliness to his sort.

When I tell the O'Flaherty story, I shall bear all this in mind.

Between the cemetery and the village coming into view now a few hundred yards ahead, there is just one more of the Kilmurvey House prairies. The island's registered bull, an appurtenance of the house, was sometimes pastured here. At the entrance to the village a boreen to the left leads past Kilmurvey House itself to its old stables on the far side of this field. Once I found the bull standing sideways across the track outside the stables, filling it from the fuschia hedge on one side to the gate on the other. A small cow and a few men with sticks stood around it as if at a party before conversation had become general, while the bull raised its head and funnelled its dreadful, pitiable roar to heaven, and the naked shaft of its penis flickered like a snake below its belly. Bringing our neighbour Mícheál's cow to the bull was another occasional reason for going to Cill Mhuirbhigh. She was more amenable to being driven if she was accompanied by her calf of the previous year and the calf of the year before that, so whenever Mícheál saw from the moist state of her rear end that the time was ripe, he would call on me to help him, and with shoutings and runnings and dogs and sticks we would marshal the little herd down the hill, past dozens of wrong turnings, to the bull's quarters. The bull was sometimes rather dilatory in his duties, and we used to leave the cow and the calves there and come back for them in the evening. On one occasion Mícheál suspected that nothing had occurred in the meantime, and he decided to intervene. I lurked in the laneway and peered round the gatepost as Mícheál tiptoed out into the open field and tried to back the cow up to the bull invitingly, while the bull manoeuvered to keep between him and the calves. Whenever Mícheál was out in the middle of the field, he would turn to me and say in a stage-whisper, 'It's a bad place I'm in now!' I was never allowed to forget that his father had been tackled by a bull and died of it. After some dangerous skirmishing in a tight corner of the field, he got a halter onto the cow so that when the bull mounted her he could stop her staggering away from its weight. Then, with the bull pushing from the rear and Mícheál pushing from the front and leaning to right and left to check that the seed did not fall upon the ground, and with interference from a bull-calf that pushed in between the bull and the cow and tried to mount her, scrambling up like one of Beardsley's impish cupids on a mountainous Venus, the connection was made. When Mícheál led the cow out, pleased with himself, he told me that in Aran there are two nightmares from which men wake up in a sweat: one about being on the cliff-face and the rope breaking, and one about being charged by a bull. We both felt relieved and happy, coming back from Cill Mhuirbhigh in the evening sunshine. As we processed triumphally up the hill, Bobby Gill swerved his mini-van close in beside me and shouted boisterously, 'Did you get the job done?' My activities as farmer's boy were often a source of fun for the neighbourhood.

Coming back from Cill Mhuirbhigh! – I could write a chapter on that too, but I will restrict myself to a note on a field I forgot on the way down, one of the big Kilmurvey House fields, to the north of the road just before one reaches the village. The white campion flowered in it very plentifully one summer, and then gradually declined from year to year; it must have been introduced in hay-seed, for I saw it nowhere else in the island. The last of the corncrakes was heard in this field too, in 1978; I believe some

kind soul from the village tried to find the nest to move it when the hay
was due to be cut. I only once caught a glimpse of a corncrake, a nonde-
script buff-coloured fowl scuttling along the margins of this field. They are
furtive creatures that rarely take to the wing once arrived in their breeding-
grounds, and their presence is only revealed by the nocturnal, rasping calls
with which the males advertise their territories to potential rivals and
mates. The Romans borrowed the sound to call the bird *crex*, and science
even more accurately calls it *Crex crex*. We used to hear this strange repeated
name, like the grieving of some rusty little machine, when we were late in
returning from Conneelys' or were wandering the boreens in the midsummer twilight. We did not know at the time that the western seaboard is one
of the last haunts of the corncrake, and that it is approaching extinction
even here, because so much grass is now cut green for silage when the birds
are still nesting, rather than left to ripen as hay; perhaps also because the
Sahara, which it has to cross in its migration, is widening southwards by
the year. To us the plaintive creaking of the corncrake, repeated as endlessly
as the distant whispered thunder of waves falling on the beach, was part of
the natural pulse of the night. Neither of us liked to be too long abroad in
those still evenings; their perfection felt so finely balanced that it made
one's own mood vulnerable to falling into melancholy. Perhaps we would
have dared to listen longer in them if we had realized that their most characteristic music was soon to fall silent, probably for ever. What was it like,
the sound of the corncrake? To a future generation that will not have heard
either, I would say that it was like a very old clock being wound up with
careful turns of the key. If I speculate that this clock was the nautiloid
coiled in its crag, and its key the one I was told of that people used to step
over in the boreen long ago, it might seem that I did indeed spend too
much time out in those bewitching nights, that wrapped the island in mystery like a whole gently fallen skyful of meteor-paper. Magic, enchantment
– I am reluctant to use such words, so full of meaning and empty of understanding, about Aran's lucent obscurities, but one must be realistic about
what is expressible. Mícheál used to say, with simple truth, that there is
something about the noise the waves make on the shore at night that is
'hard to discuss'. And there are things about those evenings, coming home
from Cill Mhuirbhigh between the blue-black waters of the bay and the
honey-scented meadows, that I could not write down if all the sky were
paper and all the sea were ink. The sound of the corncrake is among them.

ANCIENT HISTORIES

As one reaches the top of the little rise by the cemetery, the village of Cill Mhuirbhigh comes in view ahead, fronted by a long flat-faced single-storey building the road gets past by jinking to the left, and the gaunt hulk of Conneelys'. A muddle of small two-storey houses, one or two bungalows, old cottages, and still older cottages now degenerated into outhouses and barns lie behind these, while Kilmurvey House keeps itself to itself off to the left. The long house almost denying entry to the village originated as a Protestant bible school perhaps as early as 1826; in 1855 the (Protestant) Church Education Society was leasing it from (the Catholic) Patrick O'Flaherty, and it was open intermittently down to the 1870s. Locally of course it was known as Scoil na Jumpers. During the Land War of the 1880s, when the O'Flahertys needed protection close to hand, it became a barracks, and later inhabitants were all nicknamed from this memory; thus Mikey whose loss with his boat *Lively Lady* I have mentioned was known as Mikey an Bheairic. Just behind this house a grassy track makes a short loop to the right between broken-down cabins, some of them patched up as sheds and others reduced to knee-height and full of rampant nettles, past two or three cottages the thatches of which were sagging and weed-grown in our time, and which have since been re-roofed and whitewashed. The track is Róidín na Sligeach, the little road of the shell-heaps, indicating that the poor folk who lived here formerly subsisted largely on shore-food. It rejoins the road just beyond Conneelys'; after that there are only a few more dwellings increasingly spaced apart among fields, and an old ball-alley wall on a flat bit of crag, and one is already at the end of the village.

Of the ten households extant in the 1970s, six were surnamed Ó hIarnáin, anglicized as Hernon. The Uí Iarnáin were a sept of the Uí Fiachrach, a people prominent in the early history of Connacht, and one finds the name still in Connemara. According to a brief history of his family written by Colm P. Ó hIarnáin of Eoghanacht (known as Colie Mhicilín to distinguish him from two other Colie Hernons), the first Ó hIarnáin to settle in Aran was from An Cnoc in the south Connemara island of Garomna. Beartla (Bartly or Bartholomew) and his brother used to bring turf across in their *púcán*, a wooden sail-boat like a small hooker, some time before the Great Famine, and on one occasion they were invited to a wedding in the village:

Aran in those days was more prosperous than Connemara and a wedding was a great social occasion with plenty of food, drink and jollification. Whatever happened, whether it was the food, drink, or romance Bartly was reluctant to return home and his brother had to return without him. At the time Inishmore was mostly inhabited by O'Flahertys and Dirranes. Bartly was employed by one of the O'Flahertys in Kilmurvey who had two daughters and no male heir. He was reputed to be a very hard-working and likeable young man, and within a year he was married to one of the O'Flahertys and inherited the farm. In the meantime he invited his brother Michael to join him on Aran where the prospects of making a living were better than at home. Michael came to Aran and in due course married one of the Dirranes of Kilmurvey, he also inherited the holding.

In the census of 1821 I find Bartly Hernon, farmer and labourer, aged forty-seven, his wife Anne, a flax-spinner, and five children of whom the oldest is twenty-four; this indicates that Bartly came to Aran in the 1790s, earlier than Colie thought. His brother Michael was sixty-five in 1821, and his youngest son, another Bartly, was eight. One of the roadside cenotaphs down near the pier in Port Mhuirbhigh commemorates a 'Bartholomon Hernon' who died 'in the 50 yer of his age 1863', and 'also his Dather died in the 21 Yer of her age 1871'. Clearly this is Michael's son Bartly. Colie's history goes on to say that the Hernons were very clannish and also ambitious to educate their children; as a result, the first Bartly's youngest son Martin was able to take on the job of administrator for the landlord, and became known as 'the Colonel':

Times were hard in those rack rent days, poor people who could not afford to pay the rent were evicted and the land taken from them and sold, very cheap at times, there is a story told to this day that a fourth of land (16 acres) was sold for a spade. Martin Hernon as administrator was in a position to help his brothers and relations to buy land and as a result of this when the third generation of Hernons arrived they had established themselves all over the island and practically owned Kilmurvey.

I have been told that the Colonel died in most peculiar circumstances: he was found dead, still riding his donkey, and it was thought he had been strangled by some Connemara people he was turning out of the island. Colie glides over the history of the Hernons as bailiffs, but their name crops up repeatedly in Antoine Powell's detailed chapter on the period. In 1867, he tells us, the Poor Law Commissioners were complaining about Martin Hernon's having driven a household out of the island, and in revenge for this complaint he evicted thirteen families, though they were all let back into their homes bar two. A Beartla Ó hIarnáin was bailiff in 1879 (Colie lists a Bartly as the second of Martin's three sons). At that time the agent

Thompson was having the main road widened and repaired; all the tenants had to work on it, unpaid, except of course the main tenant and middleman, James O'Flaherty. Ó hIarnáin announced that everyone through whose land the road passed was to put clay on it at their own expense, but an anonymous notice appeared on the court-house door threatening with punishment anyone who complied, and even the priest advised his flock not to work on the road without pay. In the event the only tenants to put clay on the road were Charde the Protestant shopkeeper, and Ó hIarnáin. In 1880 Ó hIarnáin applied for the post of Relieving Officer (the assessor of people's eligibility for relief) with the support of Thompson and James O'Flaherty, and another notice appeared on the court-house door threatening anyone who backed his application. As a 'land-grabber' and a creature of the landowners, he was the enemy of the Land League, then becoming active in Aran. His woodpile was burned, his sheep and his mare were stolen, he was boycotted, and the only place he could drink was in his brother-in-law John O'Brien's pub in Cill Rónáin (O'Brien had got his licence in the teeth of opposition from the priest, but with the support of Thompson, Kilbride and James O'Flaherty, because the other pubs were refusing to serve non-members of the League). In the darkest days of the Land War, a few months after the O'Flaherty cattle had been cliffed and when James O'Flaherty was dying in Galway, someone fired a shot at Beartla (from the cover of the Mullán Mór in Fearann an Choirce, I am told); a Gort na gCapall man was arrested for it, and since Aran was so disturbed that no judge would come out to hear the case, was taken to Galway, where he was sentenced to a short prison term. In 1886 Beartla was defeated in an election to the post of Poor Law Guardian by the candidate of the Irish National League, which by then was in the ascendant in Aran. Beartla had also retired as rates collector by the time of the battle of An Charcair Mhór in 1887, when the islanders drove off the rates collector from Galway and his police escort.

Not all the Hernons were on the side of the land-grabbers, though. It had been discovered that the branch of the family who had the post office in Cill Rónáin were spying for the Land League by opening letters to Charde and others, but the police took no action against them for fear of retaliations against the Chardes. And in 1897 a Pádraic Ó hIarnáin was a leading opponent of Fr Farragher when the priest was urging the tenants to pay the fine laid on the island for the damages of the Land War.

But all that is ancient history. For seven generations the Hernons have shared the lot of other Aran families, farming and fishing and emigrating (one of them – irresistible facteen, this, from Colie's history of the family – became Ladies' Tennis Champion of Korea). There are today about twenty

Hernon households in the island. Colm Ó hIarnáin of Cill Rónáin is as much of a notable now as he was when I wrote about him in my first volume. Colm P. Ó hIarnáin, author of several short stories and the ms. history I have quoted, died in 1989; I shall write about him too when I come to the Seven Churches where he lived. And it is when I think of the various elderly Hernon men and women of Cill Mhuirbhigh whom I used to meet on the shore and in the boreens, and who, named or unnamed, figure here and there in this book, and are now in Reilig an Chochaill, that I realize how precarious the future of the village was at the period of our frequentation of it, throughout the 'seventies and early 'eighties. As the old folk died and young ones emigrated, few were born to take their places. There were untimely losses too: Mikey of the *Lively Lady*, another young fisherman who slipped into the dark between a trawler and the quay at Ros a' Mhíl, a bride struck down on her honeymoon by some rare ailment; these individual tragedies sapped a community already reduced below the threshold of statistical recovery. However, a couple of families back from England with their children have moved into the village in recent years, and brought some cheer into its forsaken old age.

Perhaps in our earlier years in Aran we were not fully aware of the decline of Cill Mhuirbhigh because Conneelys' was our Mecca, and Máire Conneely's daughters, sons, daughters-in-law and grandchildren were in and out of its big, welcoming kitchen all the time. It was Máire who taught M how to bake bread in our first days here when we were puzzled by basic problems of survival, and who a year or so later said to me, 'Tim, why don't you make a map of the island?', so diverting me into my present walk of life, or at least a twenty-year-long detour from it. Her own life had been turned aside from a path already decided upon, in 1932, when she was well on the way to becoming a nurse in England. She was asked to do some cooking for the household of Robert Flaherty the film-maker, in the house they had rented by Port Mhuirbhigh. Mrs Flaherty gave her a cookery book, the first she had ever seen, and taught her how to make waffles. Máire stayed on instead of returning to England, and so met and married Mícheál Ó Conghaile, who worked for James Johnston, the O'Flahertys' successor, on the Kilmurvey farm. With Máire's earnings they bought their first calf, the basis of their future independence. (Johnston allowed them to put it in one of his fields, but his bullocks bullied it, and the memory rankles to this day, as does that of Mr Johnston's gentlemanly habit of shouting for Mícheál and expecting him to drop whatever he was doing on his own bit of land and come running.) James Johnston's younger brother, Captain George, had built himself a cottage on the village street, on a site that backed onto the immediate grounds of Kilmurvey House, and then in an hour of need sold it to Mícheál for a bottle of whiskey. The growth of Conneelys' from that beginning – first the shop, then the post office, then the guest-house – coincided with the decline of Kilmurvey House, and the mushrooming extensions of the cottage were no doubt seen as eyesores and impertinences. When the big two-storey wing went up, with windows looking out over the boundary wall, Mr Johnston had a barn built in front of it, only a foot or so from the windows, and Máire's lads had to be restrained from going out by night to burn it down. This class warfare was over long before we came to the island, and the two houses were on neighbourly terms, though the Conneely windows still have to look out through the skeleton of the barn. But now Máire has retired to a bungalow in Sruthán, her daughter Mary, who took over much of the running of the place towards the end, is nursing in Saudi Arabia, Máirtín, who inherited the house, has a trawler and lives in Ros a' Mhíl where his wife is a teacher – and Conneelys' lies empty and boarded-up, until the younger generation see their way to redeveloping it. Kilmurvey House, on the other hand, has entered into its happiest phase, as will appear.

The lane going south from the village by Kilmurvey House is the way to Dún Aonghasa; it passes the gates of the house on the right, the old stables on the left, and ends in a little open space before the village well, which is enclosed by a half-cylinder of wall with only a narrow entrance, like a little round tower tucked in against the first scarp of the hillside. The well used to overflow into a few marshy square yards of fool's watercress, water forget-me-not, water mint, water speedwell, and bright inverted heights of sky and cloud below them, that lapped onto the end of the lane. Now the space has been tarmacked as parking for mini-buses bringing tourists as near as they can to the island's prime tourist attraction – there is a narrow stile on the right here, beyond which the rocky climb to Dún Aonghasa begins. I regret the loss of this left-over scrap of the earthly paradise as much as I would the *dún* itself if a cliff-fall were to dump it into the sea. Pony-traps and side-cars stop a little further back, near the gates of Kilmurvey House, and in the busy season there are often half a dozen jarvies sitting or crouching on the grass verge there, backs to the wall and caps pulled down over their noses, waiting while their 'loads' as they call them climb the hill, admire the *dún*, and descend again; some of the more energetic and ruthless jarvies even whip their horses back to Cill Rónáin hoping to capture another load in this interval. A notice is affixed to the wall here, stating that Dún Aonghasa is one of the finest ancient monuments of Celtic Europe and exhorting the visitor to assist in its conservation. It is hardly credible, but Bridgie Hernon, the lady of Kilmurvey House, tells me that some people take this to refer to the house itself, and wander in to explore it; a visiting priest enjoying a late morning in bed there once was awoken by a couple who opened his bedroom door, looked in at him, and retreated saying to each other, 'I told you it was inhabited!'

Kilmurvey is, on the Aran scale, a Big House. Square, plain, and stolidly Victorian, it has two storeys, a hipped, slated roof, and a small central porch, with a big sash-window to left and right of it and three similar windows above. The lichen-grey plastering is relieved only by shallow rusticated architraves around the windows; there is no fanlight over the door, no pediment or pillars or battlements or any other fancy features. A small front garden is separated by a low wall from the big flat meadow, in which the grass is often tall and rank, that surrounds the whole and is crossed by a curving concrete drive from the gates. The back of the house incorporates the long single-storey farmhouse that preceded it, and a workaday yard and outhouses are hidden to the rear. Behind these premises is a walled orchard gone wild. Over its low door a stone plaque reads 'Patrick O'Flaherty Esq. 1809'. One steps through into the heart of a huge *Escallonia* bush, and the harsh tang of nettles mixed with the syrupy perfume of Himalayan balsam arises as one pushes through the undergrowth in search of the mossy old apple trees. A narrow belt of trees extends to right and left of the orchard in the shelter of the steep fifteen- or twenty-foot scarp with which the land begins to step up to the bare plateau to the west. This crescent of woodland, scarcely taller than the scarp-face, domed and bevelled by the western gales, is still deep enough to cast a spell not to be felt elsewhere on the island. In August, when men are pitchforking the haycocks of the meadow onto a high-piled cart, there are tenuous shin-high groves of enchanter's nightshade on the damp ground under the alders and sycamores, and the dim, tangled canopy overhead flickers with the shade-favouring sorts of butterfly such as the ringlet and the speckled wood. A trace of nostalgia for the regime of the Big House, even, has stolen into this wood, and persists in its shelter when it is denied all rights to existence by the harsh crags above.

On the edge of the wood, behind and to the right of the house, is the roofless ruin of a curious old chapel, Teampall Mhic Duach. To reach it one has to cross the field under the formal gaze of the side of the house, and for many islanders this is difficult; when one of our elderly neighbours took the opportunity of our company to visit it for the first time, he had to assure himself aloud, as we passed the glacial windows, 'I have the right to walk here!' The church is picturesquely half withdrawn into the dappled shade of the wood. A few paces from it is a craggy limestone slab about seven feet tall and two feet wide, with the outlines of a ringed cross sharply cut into its west face and a simpler cross, almost effaced, of single, broad grooves on the other. It leans slightly, as if it were dawdling about, enjoying an uncanonical hour of birdsong before a bell summons it from the church. But this broad-shouldered brother could hardly enter, for the door, in the west gable-end, is a narrow slot just five foot five inches high, twenty-three inches wide at the bottom and only fifteen inches wide at the top. It looks as if it were compressed by the weight of its tremendous lintel, a block of granite over five feet long. According to O'Donovan this lintel was damaged when a Scotsman tried to pull it out to make a quern-stone of it, and was stopped just in time by Patrick O'Flaherty; Wakeman has a better version of the story, in which the church itself prevents the sacrilege by grabbing the thief's hand in a crevice of the masonry and holding him until he confessed his evil intentions.

The church consists of a nave and a chancel separated by a round-headed arch. The western part, the nave, represents the original building, and one would guess from the great size of the blocks in its walls, the massive antae prolonging the sides beyond the west gable-wall, and the lintelled doorway with its inclining jambs, that it is of comparatively early date. But it seems that none of the Aran churches are quite as ancient as their architecture suggests, and in this case a recent radio-carbon test of mortar from the nave places it in the eleventh century. On the outside of the north wall, near the west end, is a block with an animal carved into it, a rather long, sinuous horse, perhaps, significance unknown.

The arch dividing the nave from the chancel is Romanesque, as is the lovely, slim, round-headed lancet window-light in the east gable. The chancel is a little narrower than the nave at ground-level and has been fitted onto the east end of the older building between its antae, but it has projecting parapets along its eaves bringing it out to the full width of the rest, probably added in the fifteenth century. These ragged crenellations give the church a romantic air; one can imagine some aged cleric defying the robbers of the wood from them, or preaching to inattentive wood-pigeons that go clattering off through the treetops every time he appears on their level.

Whoever the embattled priest of these woods was, he was not St Colmán Mac Duach, the dedicatee, for the latter is supposed to have studied under Enda in the far-back days of Aran of the Saints. A seventeenth-century history of Ireland, Geoffrey Keating's *Foras Feasa ar Éirinn*, tells us of Mac Duach's lifestyle:

When Mochua or Mac Duach was a hermit in the desert the only cattle he had in the world were a cock and a mouse and a fly. The cock's service to him was to keep the matin time of midnight; and the mouse would let him sleep only five hours in the day-and-night, and when he desired to sleep longer, through being tired from making many crosses and genuflexions, the mouse would come and rub his ear, and thus waken him; and the service the fly did him was to keep walking on every line of the Psalter that he read, and when he rested from reciting his psalms the fly rested on the line he left off at till he resumed the reciting of his psalms. Soon after that these three precious persons died, and Mochua, after that event, wrote a letter to Columcille, who was in I [Iona] in Alba, and he complained of the death of his flock. Columcille wrote to him, and said thus: 'O brother,' said he, 'thou must not be surprised at the death of the flock that thou hast lost, for misfortune exists only where there is wealth.' From this banter of these real saints I gather that they set no store on worldly possessions, unlike many persons of the present time.

Mac Duach is usually identified with Mochua, brother to the seventh-century King Guaire of Connacht. Guaire dispensed his legendary hospitality from Durlus Guaire, by Kinvara near the head of Galway Bay, and Mac Duach's principal foundation was six miles to the south of that, where the round tower of Kilmacduagh still looks out across the grey limestone plains stretching eastwards from the Burren heights. A tiny, ruinous oratory, a spring well and a cave under the great inland cliff of Eagle's Rock in the Burren itself are also associated with him. In this savage and lonely 'desert', accompanied by one follower, he observed Lent, living on one meal a day of a little barley bread and watercress:

And when Easter day had come, and Mochua had said Mass a desire for meat seized the young cleric, and he said to St. Mochua that he would go to Durlus to visit Guaire in order to get enough of meat. 'Do not go,' said Mochua, 'stay with me, and let me pray to God for meat for thee.' And on this he knelt on the ground and prayed with fervour to God, asking for meat for the young cleric. At the same time while food was being served to the tables of Guaire's house, it came to pass through Mochua's prayer that the dishes and the meat they contained were snatched from the hands of those who were serving them and were carried away over the walls of the dwelling, and by direct route reached the desert where Mochua was; and Guaire went with his household on horseback in quest of the dishes; and when the dishes came into the presence of Mochua he set to praise and magnify the name of God, and told the young cleric to eat his fill of meat.

The latter thereupon looked up and saw the plain full of mounted men, and said that it was of no advantage to him to get the meat, seeing how many there were in pursuit of it. 'Thou needest not fear,' said Mochua, 'these are my brother and his household, and I beseech God to permit none of them to advance beyond that point until thou hast had thy fill.' And on this the horses' hooves clung to the ground and they could not go forward till the young cleric had had his fill. ... It is a proof of the truth of this story that the Road of the Dishes is the name given to the five mile's path that lies between Durlus and the well at which Mochua then was.

As further proof, a farmer of that locality pointed out to me the imprints of the hooves on the rock, as well as the marks left by the plates and even the salt and pepper pots. I have indicated the spot on my map of the Burren, together with the grave of the young cleric, who, the farmer's wife told me, died of overeating.

On the other side of the lane past Kilmurvey House, in the field behind the old stable-yard, are the remains of another little chapel, for which O'Donovan could collect no name from the islanders, but which has somehow come to be labelled as Teampall na Naomh, the church of the saints, on the OS maps. It is a featureless, broken-down rectangle about fifteen feet long, the little window in the east gable and the narrow door in the west both almost obliterated. An arc of low stony mounds in the field just north of it indicates the course of a vanished cashel wall, which perhaps surrounded the chapel and may relate to a great mossy bank of stone behind and on the south of the house itself, among the trees by the orchard wall. From these two disjunct scraps it is hard to envisage what George Petrie saw here, fifty years before Patrick O'Flaherty's cottage was magnified into Kilmurvey House. This was:

... the great fortress of Muirbheach Mil ... erected by a prince of the Firbolgs about the commencement of the Christian era, the interior of which is occupied by two churches, and the numerous round houses of the monks of St. Mac Duach. When I visited Aran, in the year 1821, nearly half of the fortress remained, and the wall was in some parts twenty feet high, and thirteen feet thick at its summit.

He also discovered, near the churches,

... the ruins of a building that would have been large enough to serve the purposes of a refectory ... an oval structure, without cement, of fifty by thirty-seven feet external measurement, with a wall of six feet in thickness.

In fact the ancient references to this Mil, brother of the legendary Aonghas, suggest that his *dún* was on some other *muirbheach* or sea-plain in Galway or Clare, but perhaps some Aran chieftain resigned a cashel here to a community of monks, as happened elsewhere according to several Lives of the early saints. Little of all this remained even when O'Donovan was here in 1839. Westropp, writing in 1895, noted that

Mr. O'Flaherty, in making his garden near this church, found nine or ten oblong cells in groups of three, connected by passages. Many brass pins were found, and monumental slabs, with inscriptions 'like arrow-heads,' unfortunately broken up and used for the wall.

Now the only witness to St Mac Duach's foundation, apart from the two chapels, is his holy well, tucked away to the back of the meadow south of the house. It used to be the object of a local pilgrimage, but this died out a few decades ago, and the well itself is dry. Its fern-lined basin, shadowed by the margin of the wood, has a low horseshoe-shaped wall around it, built into which is a stone seat suitable for meditation on the transience of material things.

Having trampled though the nettles and the rank wet grass and the deep sense of privacy all around the back of Kilmurvey House, I will now look into the little front garden, as I find it in my memory from a recent revisiting of the island. A small antique cannon, an O'Flaherty trophy, perhaps from a wreck, lies by the porch. Also, a limestone block carved with a heraldic device, which used to be set in the wall by another gateway into the grounds south of the main entrance, until someone tried to carry it off, after which it was brought here for safety. Nobody seemed to know what it was, so I made a sketch of it and had it identified: a rowel spur, winged, the crest of the Johnston family. Otherwise, everything here is modern and everyday: a rectangle of lawn on either side of the path, a few marigolds and wallflowers, a child's tricycle, a couple of tourists' bikes leaned against the wall under one of the windows. I feel I am bringing in too much ancient history like mud on my boots. The old wooden door, I see, has been replaced by a plastic one since I was here last. As I approach, a gong sounds from within. This is not the moment to call; Bridgie will be in the kitchen stirring gravy and minding her new grandson while Treasa carries a laden tray into the dining-room, obstructed by her little girl scampering up and down the hall. In any case, I do not want to call on these old friends with one hand as long as the other, as they say. Bridgie has often asked me who could write the history of the O'Flahertys. I could not – the material is not to hand – but I could go away and do some reading, and come back with a tapestry of O'Flaherty lore, extended to cover the house's more recent occupancy. Would the gift be welcome? It might serve for the children someday, a present from the past to the future.

THE FEROCIOUS O'FLAHERTYS

Argent, two lions counter-rampant, supporting a dexter hand, couped at the wrist, gules: in base, an antique galley, oars in action, sable. – Crest, on a helmet and wreath of its colours, a lizard, passant, vert. – Supporters, on the dexter, a lion, gules, argent, armed and langued, azure; on the sinister, a griffin, argent, armed and langued, gules. – Motto, 'Fortuna favet fortibus.'

Mere modern trumpery, these armorial bearings, picked up with the rank of knight when one of the O'Flahertys of Iar-Chonnacht was suborned into the feudal system by Queen Elizabeth's crafty statesmen little more than four hundred years ago. Six hundred years before that ignominious event the Flaithbheartach from whom they all descended – the name means 'bright in sovereignty' or 'lordly in action' – was lord of Maigh Seola, the rich limestone plains east of Lough Corrib and the Galway river. Another four hundred years back his ancestor Duach (called Teangumha, copper-tongued, 'from the sweetness of his voice; for the music of the harp was not sweeter than the sound of his words'), ruled the whole of Connacht. Duach himself was great-great-great-great-great-grandson of Eochu Mugmedon (lord of slaves), the High King of Tara, while behind Eochu, in the Celtic dawnlight of *Lebor Gabála*, the Book of the Taking of Ireland, looms the magic father-figure of Éremón, pre-eminent among the Sons of Míl who won the island from the Tuatha Dé Danann.

A magnificent descent – but descent is what it was, from those semi-divine beginnings. For according to the medieval genealogists who tried to make history out of these Iron-Age myths, Eochu had four sons by his wife and then another by a woman he had carried off during one of his raids on Britain. One day when they were thirsty from hunting, the five sons found an ugly hag guarding a well, who said she would only give water to the one who would kiss her cheek. Niall, the illegitimate son, embraced her, and she changed into a beautiful girl, a goddess in fact, the incarnation of sovereignty. So it was Niall who became High King of Ireland (he was the famous Niall of the Nine Hostages) – and his descendants the Uí Néill held the high kingship almost uninterruptedly for six centuries. But the O'Flaherty line comes down from Brión, one of the legitimate brothers. He had to content himself with the kingship of Connacht, which for generations was disputed between his descendants the Uí Briúin, and the Uí Fiachrach, who stemmed from another brother, Fiachra.

Duach Teangumha, the third or fourth Christian King of Connacht, was defeated and killed by one of the Uí Néill who was battling his way to the High Kingship, in about AD 500. Subsequent generations of his line must often had need of the magical assistance of their totemic lizard, that lives on in the O'Flaherty crest; tradition has it that when a chief of the Uí Briúin, weary from battle and flight, fell asleep, a lizard warned him of the near approach of his enemies by running up and down on his face and tickling him with its nails. The cognomen of Amhalgadh Earclasaigh (*earc sléibhe*, lizard) suggests that it was of him this tale was told. The genealogies put him at the end of the sixth century, and while his father had been King of Connacht, he was merely king of Iar-Chonnacht (West Connacht), which at that time probably meant Maigh Seola and did not include the lands west of Lough Corrib. Eight or ten generations after him comes the

Flaithbheartach or Flaherty from whom the clan took its name.

The stronghold of the early O'Flahertys was a fortified *crannóg* or lake-dwelling in Lough Hacket, near the present Headford. Two headlines are preserved of its troubled centuries: in 990 it was 'swallowed in an hour' by a great storm; in 1036 it was destroyed by the King of Connacht, and several O'Flaherty chiefs were slain. The O'Connors were the rising power in Connacht then, and the Annals recall a few grim deeds from their long struggles and treacherous accommodations with the O'Flahertys. In 1051 Maigh Seola was overrun by the King of Connacht, Hugh O'Connor 'of the Broken Spear', who put out the eyes of the O'Flaherty chief. To blind an enemy was the usual way, short of killing him, of unfitting him for kingship. In 1092 a period of peace was broken by the chief Flaherty O'Flaherty, when the O'Connor king, Roderick of the Yellow Hound, foster-father to Flaherty's sons, during a friendly visit to him, was seized and had his eyes put out, and was consequently dethroned.

This Flaherty O'Flaherty, having installed another O'Connor in Roderick's stead, received his own territories back in return. A description of Maigh Seola from this period lists the various clans subject to the O'Flahertys, including the O'Hallorans, O'Dalys, O'Duanes and O'Kennedys; it also names the hereditary officers to the O'Flahertys, such as the O'Canavans and O'Lees, medical 'ollaves' (masters or experts), also their masters of the horse, standard bearers, brehons or judges, ollaves of history and poetry, masters of the feast, stewards and bee-keepers. However, this great following did not bring security, and in 1098 Flaherty O'Flaherty was assassinated by the vengeful foster-father of the king he had blinded.

The early part of the next century was dominated by the campaigns of King Turlough O'Connor against his rivals for the High Kingship of Ireland. The O'Flahertys were subject to the O'Connors by then, and several O'Flaherty chieftains died in Turlough's ceaseless campaigns. The tide of battle swept to and fro, with now the Connachtmen laying waste north Munster and destroying the O'Briens' palace at Kincora, now the Munstermen bringing devastation even into Iar-Chonnacht. A castle newly built at the mouth of the Galway river (the town did not as yet exist) was repeatedly fought over, destroyed and rebuilt. Turlough, styled 'the Augustus of Western Europe' by the Annalists, had a long and intermittently triumphal reign as King of Connacht and High King of Ireland. His fleet was crucial to his successes, bringing his forces up the Shannon to burn down Limerick and devastate the surrounding parts of Munster, defeating the combined fleets of his Ulster enemies, the Scottish Isles and the Isle of Man in the greatest of ancient Irish sea-battles, off Inishowen. The O'Flahertys contributed their ships to this fleet, for as lords of the inner bay of Galway and of the huge expanse of Lough Corrib they were a naval power – a fact commemorated by the 'antique galley' of their coat of arms. A poem of this period refers to 'the warlike O'Flahertys':

To flee from their onslaught is meet;
To them belongs the watching of the fair harbours.

The O'Flahertys were not solely devoted to war, though. At Annaghdown on the eastern shore of Lough Corrib was an ancient ecclesiatical site attributed to St Brendan of Clonfert. Under the O'Flahertys a priory arose there soon after 1195, and Annaghdown became a bishopric roughly co-extensive with their territories, to which they supplied several bishops. The monastery was burned down in 1411, but some of its fine Romanesque stonework can be seen in the ruins of the later cathedral, together with the remains of cloisters with a distinctly military air; in the dangerous world of the O'Flahertys even their religious capital had to be fortified.

Turlough O'Connor died in 1156, and it was during his son Rory's High Kingship that one of his rivals, Dermot Mac Murrough, brought the first Anglo-Norman mercenaries into the island, in 1167. Chain-mail, the crossbow, the battle-steed, a new discipline and ideology of conquest, rapidly brought ancient Ireland to its end. By a treaty of 1175, Rory became a vassal of the King of England, holding Connacht directly from him and paying tribute. The treaty did not long delay the Anglo-Normans' advance. They first invaded Connacht in 1177, coming as far as Tuam and sending an expedition to burn Galway before being put to flight. In 1196 the O'Flahertys rose in revolt against the aged Rory O'Connor and were crushed by his rebellious younger brother Crobderg (red-hand), who captured the O'Flaherty chieftain and handed him over to the English to be put to death. Two years later, Rory, the last High King of Ireland, died as a pilgrim at Cong, the monastery his father had founded at the head of Lough Corrib.

Differences over the succession left Connacht open to the fateful advent of the Normans. William de Burgo had paid good money for a grant of Connacht to King John of England, and was looking for an opportunity of seizing the land to go with the parchment. In 1202, and after devious and treacherous combinations between Anglo-Norman and Irish forces, he was celebrating Easter with the recently crowned Crobderg in Cong, while conspiring with the O'Flahertys against his host. These plans failed, and within a few years he was dead, and for the first time the O'Flahertys were driven out of Maigh Seola by the O'Connors. Soon they had to hand over all their ships on Lough Corrib, were ousted from their fort at Galway, and retreated into the wild terrain of mountains and bogs to the west.

The de Burgos were a powerful family at court, however, and the paper grant of Connacht always threatened. When, in 1235, the Norman lords undertook the systematic reduction of Connacht, the de Burgos' share was to include Maigh Seola. The O'Flahertys, although confined behind Lough Corrib, were still seen as a danger, and the English attacked them and forced them to co-operate in pursuit of some of the O'Connors' troops. On this occasion the O'Flahertys dragged their ships from the head of Lough Corrib to Killary Harbour, a distance of seven miles, sailed from there to Clew Bay and joined with the English in committing slaughter and devastation in the islands of the bay. Perhaps because of this, when the O'Flahertys petitioned King Henry III of England to be restored to their ancient lands, the King was willing to concede that, although 'mere Irish', they and their ancestors had always showed fealty and service to him and his predecessors by assisting the English to reduce the Irish. But the lords in possession were not so amenable, and repeatedly invaded the O'Flaherty refuges beyond Lough Corrib. Meanwhile Norman tower-houses had risen all over Maigh Seola, just as in the Welsh borderlands a century earlier.

The name Iar-Chonnacht after this period refers only to the region almost severed from the rest of Ireland by Lough Corrib and the long fiord of Killary Harbour, the almost inviolable homeland of the O'Flahertys. The previous chieftains of these lands were subordinated, the English dared not penetrate so far west, the O'Malleys to the north were in alliance most of the time, and for three hundred years the O'Flahertys' main enemy was their own feuding selves. In Connemara, the remoter half of this territory, was a *crannóg* of some strategic importance, controlling the lowest ford on the main river flowing southwards out of the boglands. The history of Ballynahinch (Baile na hInse, the settlement of the island), as it was called, is almost synonymous with that of Connemara. Near it, during this relatively settled period, the O'Flahertys founded two modest religious houses, a Carmelite monastery on the lakeshore in about 1327, and a Dominican priory at the sea-mouth of the river about a century later.

For the Celts of old, wealth was measured in cattle, but after their retreat into this land of bogs and rainswept stony hillsides the O'Flahertys would have been more dependent on their flocks of sheep, and wool was the basis of their sea trade with the Atlantic fringe of southern Europe. But as the outside world changed, with the little walled town of Galway growing into an outpost of commercialism and civility, the unregulated, untaxable comings and goings of the O'Flaherty sails came to be regarded as mere smuggling. Although O'Flahertys now intermarried with the Burkes (*i.e.* the de Burgos, hibernicized), to the citizens of Galway, and especially to the merchant families of Norman origin who formed its oligarchy, Iar-

Chonnacht was still the abode of the alien, against whom their walls had to be manned, and it is said that over Galway's north gate was inscribed the prayer, 'From the Ferocious O'Flahertys good Lord deliver us.'

Towards the end of the fifteenth century the O'Flahertys began to build Norman-style keeps or tower-houses, near their borders with Norman Ireland and all around the western coastline. The finest of these still stands: Aughnanure (Achadh na nIúr, the field of yews), about four-teen miles up the west shore of the Corrib from Galway – a substantial castle consisting of a six-storey tower-house with an inner and an outer walled enclosure or bawn, and the remains of a sixteenth-century banquet-ing hall; its most famous appurtenance was a flagstone in the floor of this hall which revolved upon itself at the touch of a secret lever, dumping the unsuspecting victim into the river below. Most of the other castles were much simpler towers consisting of about three large vaulted rooms one above another, within a single enclosure. At the natural crossroads of Bal-lynahinch such a tower-house was built on the ancient *crannóg* itself, using stones from the nearby Dominican priory which it seems had fallen into disuse at that period. The folk memories that still haunt the ruined castles of the sixteenth-century O'Flahertys are not of worthy and heroic clan leaders but of petty local tyrants or fairy-tale ogres. From Renvyle on the north-westernmost peninsula of Connemara, one hears of two serving girls who saw the O'Flahertys hanging someone in the castle; they fled in terror, and rather than be taken alive, flung themselves over cliffs into two creeks that still bear their names, Fó Cháit and Fó Mhairéaid. People living oppo-site the ruins of Doon, the castle that dominated the long narrow bay of Streamstown, remember how a local man was peaceably smoking his pipe one evening, when a spark from it floated off downwind, and a shot rang out from the castle; this incident forewarned the man, so that when he was invited to dinner by the O'Flahertys, he left his hat outside the castle door as an excuse to step outside again, then flung himself into the sea, swam across the bay and ran off along the other shore. The O'Flahertys pursued him, and although they had to go round the head of the bay they eventu-ally caught up with him, and a patch of red rock on the seashore still marks where his blood was spilt.

Of all the O'Flahertys, Tadhg na Buile ('of the rage or frenzy') of Aird is the best and worst remembered. Tales of his oppression of the poor were recorded from old story-tellers in Carna in the 1930s. His castle at Aird was at the head of a little creek, and the only entrance was an arch through which a boat could be floated into a lock in the bawn; the well was outside the bawn, and a servant girl would come out in a little boat to fetch water:

This is how he was killed. There was a widow's son from Inis Leacan [an island a few miles to the north-west] who had been away at sea for a long time. Tadhg hadn't been at Aird when he left. He came home and his mother put some food before him. 'I don't have any sauce,' she said. 'I have a crock of butter for Tadhg na Buile and if I don't give him that he'll take the cow from me.' 'What sort of a person is Tadhg na Buile?' he asked. She told him. 'Give me the butter,' he said, 'and leave it between myself and Tadhg.'

The widow's son went east in the evening and got into talk with Tadhg's servant girl. She let him in. He went up to the place where Tadhg was asleep and he stabbed him in his bed. His wife Síle was in the bed. 'Throw him out', she said, 'before he soils my bed.'

And so Tadhg was thrown out of the window, and is buried where he fell.

A similar tale is told of a Marcus O'Flaherty of Aughnanure (whom I do not find in the genealogies). Two sheep belonging to a poor widow trespassed onto his land, and as recompense for the grass they ate, he sheared the wool off them. The widow's son then murdered him, and his ghost used to be seen in a wood near the castle. Once he appeared to a basket-maker there, who saw that the O'Flaherty's feet were thin and withered. The ghost explained his state:

> *Gach dlí géar dár cheap mé,*
> *Gach creach mhór dá ndearna mé,*
> *Chun tíghe Dé ní dheachaidh mé;*
> *Allus lucht an tsaothair*
> *Agus a bheith go géar ar na boicht,*
> *Ach sé féarach an dá chaorach*
> *A chaolaigh mó dhá chois.*
> *Bím oíche sa ngil,*
> *Oíche sa tsruth,*
> *Oíche ag fuaidreamh na gcnoc*
> *Fliuch fuar í mo leaba,*
> *Tá fearthainn innti is géar-ghaoith.*
> *Tá íoc na huaire ar m'aire-sa —*
> *Is t'aire ar do chléibhín.*

> For the hard laws I made,
> For the great lootings I took,
> I did not go to God's house;
> Sweat of the labourer
> And being hard on the poor,
> But it was the grass of the two sheep
> That thinned my feet.
> I am a night in the dew

A night in the stream,
A night wandering the hills.
Wet and cold my bed,
There is rain in it and sharp wind.
My business is penance by the hour –
And yours is your basket.

The man looked down at his basket, and when he looked up again the ghost was gone.

History hardly remarks the existence of the O'Flahertys for some generations after their withdrawal into Iar-Chonnacht, and it was not until the Tudor era that the little cogs of clan rivalry began to engage with the grander machinations of European politico-religious struggles. In 1538 Henry VIII's Deputy of Ireland visited Galway, and the nearest O'Flaherty chief, Hugh Óg, came in from his castle in Moycullen and formally submitted to the King's authority. Soon after that a period of intense feuding broke out among the O'Flahertys, which the English statesmen and the Anglo-Irish Burkes were able to exploit in order to bring them to heel. The Moycullen O'Flahertys were the first to be anglicized. When Hugh Óg was old and infirm he resigned his chieftainship to his son Murtagh, but Dónal Crón of Aughnanure, head of the senior branch of the O'Flahertys, seized the castle of Moycullen, murdered Murtagh, locked up Hugh in his own dungeon and starved him to death. Murtagh's infant son Rory was smuggled out of the castle by his people and later was taken to England to be educated. The Elizabethan policy of affecting young Irish chieftains to the court and to English values in this way had some failures notable in the history of the times, but with Rory it seems to have been successful, and on his return he was granted the castle of Moycullen again 'in respect of his good and civil upbringing in England'.

The western O'Flahertys remained intractable, however. The designated successor to Dónal Crón as chief of all the O'Flahertys at this period was his nephew Dónal an Chogaidh ('of the war'), whose castles were Ballynahinch and Bunowen in the farthest south-western corner of Connemara. (In the old Celtic way, the succession went to the most able and warlike among a small range of relatives, not necessarily to an eldest son.) Dónal's wife was as ferocious as himself; she was Gráinne Ní Mháille, of the sea-going O'Malley clan. Local tradition holds that Dónal was in dispute with the Joyces over a castle on an island in the north-western arm of Lough Corrib, from the fierce defence of which he was nicknamed An Coilleach, the cock; eventually the Joyces captured and killed him while he was hunting in the nearby mountains, and Gráinne continued to defend the stronghold with such spirit that it is still known as Caisleán na Circe, the Hen's Castle.

The doings of the remoter O'Flahertys were of less concern to the English than those closer to hand, and of these the most dangerous was the young Murchadh na dTua, Murrough of the Battleaxes, of Fuaidh (at the present Oughterard). His incursions into the territory of the Clanricardes (as the branch of the Burkes powerful in Galway now called themselves) were so vexatious that in 1564 the Earl of Clanricarde sent his troops into Iar-Chonnacht. Murchadh used his practised tactic of withdrawing into the western fastnesses, and then as the Earl's forces with their plunder of cattle were retiring towards the ford at Galway, he fell upon them; some got over the river, although 'such was their apprehension of death, that they knew not how', but most of them were drowned. After this disaster the English decided it would be easier to buy Murchadh's friendship than compel it, and he was issued with a pardon and appointed by the Queen to the chieftainship of Iar-Chonnacht. Since he was not the legitimate chief under Brehon law this instigated complex feuds among the O'Flahertys. In the 1560s the ascendant Murchadh spread his wings over the Aran Islands, driving out the O'Briens. Then, when the sons of the Earl of Clanricarde staged a rebellion against the Queen and planned to seize the castles of Iar-Chonnacht as their bases, Murchadh repaid his debts by betraying their plans; the Lord President of Connacht then besieged and took the castle of Aughnanure, held by descendants of Dónal Crón. As his reward Murchadh na dTua was given the castle, which was his family's seat thereafter. Next, Murchadh ousted Rory O'Flaherty from the castle of Moycullen, and in 1584 he tried to seize Ballynahinch from the western O'Flahertys – the aftermath of this was the killings at Log na Marbh I have already written about. He got his knighthood in about 1585 in connection with the 'Composition of Connaught', the comprehensive settlement under which the chiefs were to surrender the clan territories to the Queen and be regranted them as heritable property under feudal law. Murchadh signed, of course, and the anglicized Rory O'Flaherty whom he had expelled from Moycullen was probably reinstated at this time. In general the eastern O'Flahertys were docile thereafter, until the rebellion of 1641.

The western O'Flahertys, on the other hand, did not recognize the Composition, and neither did the Burkes of Mayo, who rebelled against the ruthless efforts of the new Lord President of Connacht, Sir Richard Bingham, to impose the settlement. But the Mayo rebels were soon suppressed, and Sir Richard Bingham sent his brother John into Iar-Chonnacht in pursuit of rebels there. Owen, the son of Gráinne and Dónal an Chogaidh, took no part in the rebellion but withdrew his men and cattle to the island of Omey, where a local chief Tibbot O'Toole kept a house of hospitality. (Omey is on the west coast a little south of Renvyle; it is accessible over the sands when the tide is out.) When Bingham could not find the rebels he came to Omey and was entertained there, and in the middle of the night his men seized Owen and eighteen of his followers, and took them, with four thousand cows, five hundred stud mares and horses and a thousand sheep (the figures are from a deposition made later on by the aggrieved Gráinne), to Ballynahinch. There Owen was stabbed to death and the others, including the nonagenarian O'Toole, hanged.

The Binghams' violent policies failed to make a reality out of the Composition, however, and Owen's younger brother, known as Murchadh na Maor, 'of the stewards', from his extensive domains, remained in control of the western coastline and the castle of Bunowen. When the rebellion led by Red Hugh O'Donnell broke out in the north, Murchadh was commanded to join with the O'Malley sea-lords to ship the English troops from Galway to Sligo. However, he chose to join the rebels, and brought his men to Munster with O'Donnell; but after the defeat of Kinsale he returned peaceably to Bunowen, where he died in 1626. His eldest son was Murchadh na Mart, 'of the beeves', so called from his custom of fortifying himself against the rigours of Lent by 'killing and devoureing in his one house, among his servants and followers everye Shrove Tuesday at night fifty beeves'. There is a tradition that the Earl of Strafford, Lord Deputy of Ireland, made the dangerous journey into the depths of this Murchadh's territory in 1637, but found on arrival at Bunowen that Murchadh was absent on some expedition against 'his enemies of Galway'; Strafford waited patiently for his return and was then 'received with all the rude profusions of Irish hospitality'. On this occasion Murchadh was knighted, but it is said that the true object of Strafford's journey was to spy out the land with the intention of robbing him of it.

However, it was not until the defeat of the rebellion of 1641 that the O'Flahertys, of both east and west, were finally thrown down. The longboats of Sir Murchadh na Mart had protected the western coast on behalf of the rebels, and he had joined his younger brother Colonel Edmund, in bringing their hundreds of 'rude kearns' against the fort at Galway. What befell Edmund after the Cromwellian victory I have already told; Sir Murchadh was luckier, in that he lost his lands but was allowed to retire to Aran, where he died in 1666 and was buried in Teaghlach Éinne. As to the opportunist eastern O'Flahertys who had so prospered in Elizabethan times, they also took the Catholic Confederate side in the rebellion of 1641, and lost all. The castle of Aughnanure, which had passed down in Murchadh na dTua's line, was confiscated, and both castle and land were granted, like so much else, to the Earl of Clanricarde.

The Moycullen O'Flahertys, although they regarded themselves as loyal to England, fared little better. Roderic O'Flaherty the historian was of this branch; he was only two years old when his father died, and by the time he reached his majority the patrimony had been confiscated. Even after the Restoration he received back only 500 acres, a tiny fraction of the territory, and by then he was so deep in debt they did him little good. 'I live a banished man within the bounds of my native soil,' he wrote, 'a spectator of others enriched by my birth-right; an object of condoling to my relations and friends, and a condoler of their miseries.' The unfortunate 'Ogygian' was yet to face further impoverishment. Fearing that he would lose even the rump of his estate through the oppressions that followed King William's defeat of King James, he signed it over to his friend the lawyer Richard Martin, who had wangled an exemption from confiscation. When the danger had passed and Roderic asked for his land back, Nimble Dick asserted that it had been a genuine sale, and the historian was left with just his cottage and his view of the Aran Islands. The great Celticist Edward Lhuyd visited him there in 1700, and later sent him a book and a letter, observing to another correspondent that 'Unless they come frank, [O'Flaherty] will, I fear, be unable to pay the postage.' Nine years later another antiquary, Sir Thomas Molyneux, wrote,

I went to vizit old Flaherty, who lives very old, in a miserable condition at Park, some three hours west of Gallway. I expected to have seen here some old Irish manuscripts, but his ill fortune has stripp'd him of these as well as his other goods, so that he has nothing now left but some pieces of his own writing, and a few old rummish books, printed.

Roderic O'Flaherty died in 1718. Hardiman records a tradition that his son Michael was a fool, and had him buried within the house, thinking that that would strengthen his own claims to the land. A humble scrap of oral lore I picked up in Connemara indicates that his unknown grave is at least very near the house, for the potatoes were put on to boil before the funeral left, and they were not yet cooked when the mourners returned.

By chance we have an Englishman's view into the lifestyle of the western O'Flahertys of the post-Cromwellian generation, for in 1698 a John Dunton took a 'ramble' around Ireland and was bold enough to visit Iar-Chonnacht, in which, he found, 'the old barbarities of the Irish are so many and so common, that until I came hither, I looked for Ireland in itself to no purpose'. A Galway gentleman gave him a recommendation to Murchadh na Mart's son Brian, 'the most considerable man in this territorye'. Brian O'Flaherty, he found, 'had converst among the English, had been at Dublin and was sensible enough of their one barbarous way in living, but sayd it was a thing soe habitual to them that it could not be suddenly removed'. The political upheavals had not upset the ancient pattern of the Celtic year, and O'Flaherty entertained Dunton in a temporary residence at a *buaile* or milking-pasture, to which he and his followers had removed with their cattle for the summer season; it must have been in north-east Connemara, because on the following day they took him to hunt the red deer in Gleann Glaise, a remote valley of the Maumturk Mountains.

This gentleman was among a greate company of his relations, as being the chiefe of the clan or family, when I arrived at his house, which was a long cabbin, the walls of hurdles plaister'd with cow dung and clay. They were a parcel of tall lusty fellows with long haire, straite and well made, only clumsy in their leggs, theire ankles thicker in proportion to their calves than the English, which is attributed to theire weareing broags without any heels; but this I leave to the learned. The men after the old Irish fashion as well as the weomen weore theire haire verie long, as an ornament, and to add to it the weomen commonly on a Saturday night, or the night before they make theire appearance at mass or any publick meeting doe wash it in a lee made with stale urine and ashes, and after in water to take away the smell, by which their locks are of a burnt yellow colour much in vogue among them.

There was a mutton killed for supper, half of which was boyled and the other half roasted, and all devour'd at the meale. After supper the priest, who as I suppose was as a sort of chaplaine to the family called for tables to play for an half-pennorth of tobacco, but was reprimanded by the lady of the house for doeing it before he had return'd thankes. I made the priest a present of my tobacco which was wellcome to them all; even the lady herself bore them company in smoakeing and excus'd it by urgeing the need they were in of some such thing in that moist country, which I could not contradict. ... One thing I saw in this hous perhaps the like not to be seen anywhere else in the world, and that was nine brace of wolfe doggs or the long Irish grey hounds, a paire of which kind has often been a present for a king. They were as quiet among us as lambs without any noys or disturbance. ...

The house was one entire long roome without any partition. In the middle of it was the fire place with a large wood fire which was in no way unpleaseing tho in summer time. It had no chimney but a vent hole for the smoake at the ridge, and I observ'd the people here much troubled with sore eyes; which I attributed to the sharpe smoak of the wood, and they also allowed it but sayd that they had newly put up this for a Booley or summer habitation, the proper dwelling or mansion house being some miles farther neare the sea, and such an one they commonly built everie yeare in some one place or other, and thatch'd it with rushes or coarse grass as this was; we all lay in the same roome upon greene rushes. ... I wonder'd mightily to heare people walking to the fire place in the middle of the house to piss there in the ashes, but I was soone after forced to doe soe too for want of a chambrepot, which they are not much used unto.

Other O'Flahertys of this generation abandoned the old Connemara life and went to England; among them a son of Colonel Edmund's, also called Edmund, who became an army captain. He returned after the Restoration and took a lease of some land at Renvyle, that had been con-fiscated from his father and was now held by absentee landlords, the Blakes of Lehinch in Mayo. His son used to be famous as Éamonn Láidir, Edmund the Strong; folklore celebrates his many horseback sword-fights with Richard Martin, then the principal landowner in Connemara, and his fol-lowers. One sees this 'Nimble Dick' as the epitome of those who had eeled their way to fortune under the new dispensation, and Éamonn Láidir, hack-ing his way out of the circle of Richard's men, as the doomed but obdurate O'Flaherty spirit. He died in poverty in about 1749, and later on his gigan-tic bones were exhumed and exhibited as objects of curiosity in the old chapel of Ballynakill near Renvyle.

Éamonn's descendants continued as middlemen to the Blakes until about 1811, when Henry Blake first made the arduous journey by horse through the mountain pass of Maumturk and by boat down the Killary to visit his estate. That the O'Flaherty way of life still preserved much of its antique flavour, after yet another century in the retracted Celtic margin of the kingdom, is shown by Blake's description of the state kept by Anthony O'Flaherty JP, 'a middle-man, possessing an income of 1500l per annum, arising from his good management of profit rents, utterly unconscious of any other claims on the land':

'The big house,' then, was a thatched cabin about sixty feet long by twenty wide, and to all appearance only one storey high. It ostensibly contained an eating par-lour and sitting-room, from each of which opened two small bed-rooms. We had oral evidence in the night, that there was other accommodation in the thatch, but those who had the benefit of it were placed far beyond our ken. Conceive then our surprise at being gradually introduced to at least two dozen individuals, all parlour boarders. There was mine host, a venerable old man of eighty-six, his young and blooming wife, a daughter with her husband, three or four gay young ladies from Galway, two young gentlemen, two priests, and several others, evidently clansmen and relations. ... A room full of company, the fumes of a large dinner, and the warmth of a bright turf fire, rendered the heat almost insupportable, and during the feast, amid the clatter of knives and forks, and the mingled voices of our party, we were indulged *ad libitum* with the dulcet notes of the bag-pipe, which contin-ued its incessant drone until the ladies retired from the table. I need not expatiate on the wine and spirits, though both had probably been imported duty free many years before, and were certainly good enough to tempt the whole party to pay a sufficient devotion to the jolly god.

But Mr Blake soon soured the jollity by announcing that he no longer intended to allow a middleman to stand between him and 'the immediate cultivators of the soil'. Within a few years he took over the O'Flaherty house and refurbished it as his family seat, demoting the former lords of Connemara even further towards the level of the common tenantry. That was the last substantial presence of the O'Flahertys in the west of Connemara.

Some of their eastern cousins, though, had been hanging onto the tatters of their former glory, largely conforming to the established Protestant church, and renewing their social standing in a more urbane mode. In 1687 the Earl of Clanricarde had leased the castle of Aughnanure and some land to a Brian O'Flaherty, the son of its previous owner, and later Brian bought out the freehold with £1600 of borrowed money. Unable to repay, he lost most of the estate and the castle, and retired to Lemonfield about two miles away. His grandson married the daughter of Sir Theobald Bourke, the sixth Viscount Mayo, and their son, Sir John, an army captain and deputy governer of the county of Galway, built a mansion at Lemonfield; he even had a descendant of the O'Canavans, the medical ollaves of the old Maigh Seola days, as his personal physician. The O'Flahertys of Lemonfield were considerable landlords down to the time of the Congested Districts Board, and held onto the mansion itself until the 1930s.

A notable member of the Moycullen line was Antony O'Flaherty, who died in about 1874. He was MP for Galway, and his house and demesne of Knockbane are admiringly mentioned in various accounts of the neighbourhood: 'Nothing that modern taste and capital could effect in rendering this one of the most charming residences in the country has been omitted.' But (according to E.V. Lynam, a chronicler of the O'Flahertys who himself had O'Flaherty blood in his veins) Knockbane was inherited by a Fitzpatrick descended from the Aran family, who then married his dairymaid, and 'the consequence was that the Congested Districts Board came in 1900 and swallowed him up, striped his land, pulled down Knockbane House, and left not a trace of Fitzpatrick or O'Flaherty at Moycullen'.

Such, then, was the dispersal of the seed of Éremón, into feuding warlords, politically unfortunate grandees, and bought-out gentry. Just one line preserved something of the O'Flahertys' quintessential westernness down to not much more than a hundred years ago. From what I hear in Kilmurvey House it must have been in the late eighteenth century, when the rest of the Aughnanure O'Flahertys were turning Protestant, that a branch of the family took itself off with priest, chalice, vestments and missal, to Aran. The heritage of ferocity in myth, history and folklore they imported into the Aran story – perhaps unwittingly, like a lizard that had crept into a corner of one of their linen-chests – is summarized above.

THE BIG HOUSE

I had hoped to present here a restoration of lapsed connections, an account of the Connemara origins of the Kilmurvey House O'Flahertys. On behalf of their memory I have run up an inordinate postage and phone bill and piled my desk with research notes and transcripts of old documents; yet, in a forest of criss-crossed branches, I cannot find the family tree. If the truth I seek were known, it would most probably be dull – Patrick O'Flaherty of Aran was the son of so-and-so, who was the cousin of so-and-so, of such-and-such an address in history. Unknown, it continues to preoccupy me, this absent fact, this handful of dust in an unopened chamber of my labyrinth.

O'Donovan, after summarizing the pedigree of the Lemonfield O'Flahertys in his letters to the Ordnance Survey, states that:

The other branches of this family now respectable are O'Flahertie of Knockbaun a very respectable gentleman; O'Flaherty of Kilkenny, the next heir to Lemonfield; P. O'Flaherty of Aran, who never married; Mr. O'Flahertie of Oughterard the Post Master and High Constable, is supposed to be the representative of the family of Moycullin.

Documents I have seen show that there were close if acrimonious relationships between the Aran O'Flahertys and those of Lemonfield, but none of the obvious sources (such as Patrick O'Flaherty's death notices in the newspapers) specify them or even mention who his father was. The reason for this null testimony may lie in the religious ill-feelings dividing the eighteenth-century generations, the conforming of most branches of the clan to the Established Church and the cleaving of the Aran branch to Catholicism.

The O'Flahertys are said to have brought their own priest with them from Aughnanure, and if so it seems likely that he was the Fr Francis O'Flaherty whose tomb, with the O'Flaherty crest and motto, in the graveyard at Cill Éinne I described in *Pilgrimage*. He was born in about 1757 in Aran, where his father, Beairtliméad, had a 'half-quarter' of land near Cill Rónáin, of which the name, Leath-cheathrú Bheairtliméid, is still known to one or two antiquarian-minded islanders. Francis was educated in Spain, like so many young men of family in those days when Catholicism was only just emerging from proscription, and served as a curate somewhere in Connacht before being appointed parish priest of the islands some time before 1800. The census of 1821 shows him, aged sixty-four, living in Cill Rónáin with his widowed sister Mary Broughton (the Broughtons were Catholic landowners of Inis Leacan, an island near Roundstone) and her three young children, his curate, a pilgrim called Mary Coen, a house servant and a seventy-eight-year-old beggar. In the porch of the chapel in Cill Rónáin is a medieval plaque of the crucifixion which Fr Francis is said to have brought from Rome; it was passed down in the Gill family – one of his sister's daughters married a Gill – until Fr Killeen carried it off for the church in a high-handed way that is still remembered with resentment. The Gills have a little shop in Cill Rónáin, two doors to the west of which, opposite the old rectory gates, is a long-empty two-storey cottage; this was Fr Francis's home, and his mounting-block used to be pointed out at its gable. George Petrie, visiting the Aran Islands for the first time in this same year of 1821, met the 'venerable pastor', and noted two traits strongly marked in his physiognomy: the courage requisite to his ministry in 'a cluster of islands washed by the waves of the Atlantic', and the purity of his mind, deriving from a total ignorance of the vices of humankind outside the innocency of Aran.

Father Frank is poor. The unglazed windows of his humble cottage, and the threadbare appearance of his antique garments, bespeak a poverty beyond even that of most of his flock. ... This is not the fault of his parishioners, by whom he is ardently beloved. They would gladly lessen their own comforts to increase his, and have frequently tried to force on him a better provision, which he has as often refused. 'What,' said he on a late occasion to Mr. O'Flaherty, who was remonstrating with him on this refusal – 'what does a priest want more than subsistence? and that I have. Could I take anything from these poor people to procure me comforts which they require so much more themselves? No, no, Pat, – say no more about it.'

The figure of the priest is unique in appearance, from the peculiarity of his costume. ... He wears a long coat of antique cut, and over that a similar one of larger size; both are of the same dark blue colour, and are, I should suppose, the only habiliments of the kind on the island. They are characteristic of their owner, old and almost worn out, but still uncommon and respectable.

I saw Father Frank frequently. Sometimes near his cabin, moving along slowly, supported by a stick that was once the handle of an umbrella, and attended by some of the islanders receiving his advice; at other times in the morning, on a rugged pony, similarly attended, descending some rocky path to his home, after passing the night with a sick, or perhaps dying, islander.

At the time of Petrie's departure for Inis Oírr, Fr Francis was suffering from a severe cough which was depriving him of sleep, and Petrie had exhorted him to keep to his house. Sailing past Cill Rónáin in Patrick

O'Flaherty's boat on a squally day, Petrie fondly pictured the priest repos-ing by his fire after his week's exertions, and little supposed that he would ever see him again. When the boat arrived off Inis Oírr the breakers were too high for them to venture near the shore, but they saw a number of men descending the cliffs towards the beach, among them Fr Francis O'Flaherty, come to attend to some sick person: 'Thus it was that he was nursing him-self.' Later in the day, when the weather abated, they brought the priest back to Cill Rónáin:

The old man, exhausted by the day's fatigue, and too feeble to bear the pitching of the boat, except in a lying posture, stretched himself on a small mattress in the cabin, where he lay for some time apparently slumbering – his limbs stretched, his eyes closed, and his hands locked in each other and resting on his bosom, remind-ing me forcibly of some of those dying saints which the Italian painters have so often imagined. But though his body was at rest, his mind was not so; for it was concerned with the welfare of his flock. He had received, on the preceding evening, for the poor of his parish, thirty pounds of that money which the noble benevolence of England had supplied to her suffering sister, and he was anxiously considering the best way of discharging the trust reposed in him. After some time I heard him call Mr. O'Flaherty in a low tone of voice, and on consulting with him, it was agreed that he should send, on the following day, to Galway for the worth of the donation in oatmeal.

When I parted from this venerable man, I did not think it probable that he could outlive the coming winter. It gives me pleasure, however, to add that he still exists, and is at present in tolerable health.

In fact Fr Francis died just a few years later, in 1825.

To frame Petrie's sanctimonious picture, here is a fascinating glimpse of the 'Ferocious O'Flaherty' background to Fr Francis's priesthood, preserved by Fr Killeen:

The constant tradition of the island is that Fr. Francis's predecessor whose name is related to have been Stanford was by force driven away in order to secure the parish for Fr. Francis. Those who were instrumental in this act of violence were a Killeany family of the same stock as Patrick O'Flaherty gent. of Kilmurvey and related also to the priest. It is handed down that there were 21 men concerned and that they were the finest lot of men one could wish to see, all six-footers and of commanding appearance. But their size and strength availed them nothing. Within a year after the expulsion of Fr. Stanford 20 of them were dead of whom some were drowned, some killed in various ways. An islander who happened to meet Fr. Stanford in Galway was asked by the priest how were the O'Flahertys faring. The Aran man replied that 20 of them were dead and one alive. The priest said that one too would soon meet his end. And he was right. The last of the gang died soon afterwards.

Apart from Fr Francis, the earliest of the 'respectable' O'Flahertys I can document in Aran are named on a big gravestone lying before the altar in the ruined church of St Brecan in Eoghanacht. The coat of arms heading it distinguishes these O'Flahertys from the commonalty of the name, but the prime site occupied by their memorial means that it has been much knelt on and walked over, so that it is hard to read. (There is a parable on *Fortuna* here.) With some difficulty I make out:

> The Almighty God have
> mercy on the Soul of Anth
> O Flaherty jun
> a youth who
> was Endowed with Filial
> piety and promys Accomp
> lishment. Departed this Life on
> the 27 day of Octr 1795
> Orderd to be Cut by his
> Unkle Anthy O Flaherty

Islanders tell me that the forbears of Patrick O'Flaherty lived in The Seven Churches or Creig an Chéirín, until they bought the lease of the land in Cill Mhuirbhigh from a Stephen King. The story is that Patrick's father was an Aran farmer just like any other except that he was married to an outsider, and when news came that a wealthy relative of his had died, it was the wife, the more capable one of the couple, who went off to secure the inheritance. When she returned with the money, 'O'Flaherty hit a bang of his spade off a big rock and said "I'm finished with you for ever!" The christian name of this O'Flaherty has not been preserved even in Kilmurvey House lore; filial piety lapsed when the genetic thread came to an end in the 1950s, and as Bridget often told me with regret, a new era was marked by a bonfire of old papers. So I was at a loss in trying to link Patrick O'Flaherty with the 'unkle Anthy' of the inscription. However, on revisiting the house recently, I found that a bundle of documents, carried off by a researcher into some other question of Galway history twenty years ago and long forgotten, had just been posted home from oblivion. The parcel was delivered into my arms, and I bore it off with mixed feelings, reminding myself of the man who carries a heavy packet of labyrinths on his back, in a poem by Tristan Tzara. Since then I have wormed out of these crabbed, yellowish screeds a few hints of Kilmurvey House history, which I incorporate in what follows.

Patrick O'Flaherty, one can deduce from his gravestone and the census returns, was born in 1781. The earliest of the documents concern a Catherine O'Flaherty, spinster, of Galway, who in 1796 obtained judgment against a Walter Lambert of Cregclare for £2200 on a bond of the previous year. The Lamberts were major Galway landowners, and of course at that time £2200 was great riches. Under Catherine's will, dated 1799, small sums go to her brothers John and Anthony O'Flaherty and her sister Mary. A letter of 1804 from William, Archbishop of Armagh and President of the Court of Prerogatives Ecclesiastical, appoints Patrick O'Flaherty as administrator of this will, and, reading between the lines, one gathers that the original administrator and residual legatee had been John, who, having 'intermeddled' with the matter for some time, died; also, that Patrick was Catherine's nephew. Hence, most likely, Patrick was John's son, nephew to Anthony, and brother to the youth of unfulfilled promise. Another clutch of old papers refers to a complex law-case which Patrick, as Anthony's heir and administrator, pursued for some years after 1813, against Sir John O'Flaherty's son, Thomas Henry ; it concerns money claimed to have been lent by an 'Alise' O'Flaherty to Sir John for the completion of the mansion of Lemonfield. Whether this money was ever recovered, and what became of the money owed to Catherine by the Lamberts, does not appear, but here is the substance of the Aran legend of the O'Flahertys' inherited fortune.

I cannot learn exactly when Patrick established himself in what was to become Kilmurvey House; the Digbys first leased him one and a half quarters of Kilmurvey, for twenty-one years at £140 per annum, in 1812, 'on surrender of his existing interest in the property'. In fact, according to the inscription over its door, his walled garden or orchard was made in 1809. Also, at the back of the orchard there is a natural recess in the cliff-face, to which a front wall and a little door has been added; perhaps originally this was a sweat-house as I have heard suggested, but it has served more recently as a potting-shed. Family legend says that a French officer, on the run after the invasion of Mayo in 1798, was given shelter, or was held to ransom, in it by the O'Flahertys, and that he married a young woman of the family, or at least had a child by her called Marcella, a (French-sounding, in Aran ears) name that has been handed down among her descendants. If this bit of romantic costume-drama is true – and to prove it, the Frenchman's rusty sword lay on the hall table in Kilmurvey House until a guest stole it some years ago – then it seems that the O'Flahertys were already established in Kilmurvey when Patrick was a child. However, some details cannot be correct, for the Kilmurvey House documents show that Marcella O'Flaherty married Francis Macnamara of Doolin in 1810.

The census of 1821, taken by Patrick himself, states that he had five cartrons of land (most holdings in the village were of a half cartron). His household consisted of:

Patrick O Flaherty 40 Gentleman Farmer
Mary O Flaherty sister 37
John McDonough 34 house-servant
Owen Rieley 23 do.
Tom Kane orphan 4
Biddy Tool 50 Cook
Pegy McDonough 17 Kitchen Maid
John Boyle 78 Piper

The descendants of the aged piper, who sounds a note from the days when music had a place at the chieftain's table, were known by such nicknames as Mícheál an 'Pipe' down to the end of the century at least. A more up-to-date feature of the house is indicated by 'Bryan Flaherty, 55, gardener to Mr O Flaherty', living in the village. (This man would have been just as much a descendant of the original Flaithbheartach as his master, of course, and so an Ó Flaitheartaigh like any other, but Patrick O'Flaherty makes the distinction between his own and the common sort by allowing the 'O' only to his immediate family and to Fr Francis.)

George Petrie stayed at Patrick O'Flaherty's in that year of 1821, and left an account of the house's good cheer. This fervent Celticist and romantic did not look at his host with the cold and calculating eye Mr Blake had cast on the O'Flaherty of Renvyle just a decade earlier:

Would that I could convey to the mind of my reader even a faint outline of the character of our never-to-be-forgotten host! ... Such is the unaffected grace of his politeness, the mild charm of his conversation, and the sincere warmth of his hospitality, that though uninvited strangers, we were but a few minutes in his house when we felt all the full freedom of enjoyment that could belong to our own firesides, with old and congenial friends to share it. ... His house, however, bespeaks the simplicity of the place, as well as the usages of remote times. It is an oblong, thatched cottage, without a second story, containing five or six apartments, with a long porch, forming a kind of hall, attached to the centre of the front. The parlour is not boarded, nor do the chairs present the luxury of a soft seat. In the parlour are a few pictures, two of which, the portraits of a fine gentleman and lady, the work of a court painter, excited my curiosity. "That," said Mr. O'Flaherty, "is the portrait of an uncle of mine, and the other that of his lady. He was one of six brothers, all men of fine and striking appearance. He went to England to seek his fortune, and that lady, who was daughter of Sir Henry Englefield (a respectable English Catholic), and who had a large fortune, fell in love with him and married him. He was much attached to my father, and had those pictures painted for him.

I interrupt Petrie to report my following-up of this clue to Patrick's ancestry, which I spent an afternoon pursuing through the shadowy book-stacks of the London Library. I found the Englefields in a seldom-disturbed tome, Burke's *Extinct and Dormant Baronetages of England, Scotland and Ireland.* The Englefields of Wotton Bassett were indeed 'respectable Catholics'. The title was created in 1612, and a Sir Francis Englefield obtained a letter from Charles I protecting him from the penalties of recusancy, that is of denying the authority of the Church of England. Sir Henry Englefield, who died in 1780, had three sons and two daughters; thus I know that the lady in the portrait Petrie saw is either Ethelinda-Catherine or Teresa-Anne, but unfortunately the name of her husband is not given. Sir Henry's heir and the last of the line was Henry-Charles, also known in his turn as Sir Henry. Eminent enough to have been written up in the *Dictionary of National Biography*, he was a Fellow of the Royal Society, Secretary of the Society of Dilettanti, and, until he was objected to as a Catholic, President of the Society of Antiquaries. He published papers on astronomy and geology and even on a dyestuff ('The Discovery of a Lake from Madder', for which he won a gold medal from the Society of Arts). He was a friend of Charles James Fox, was painted by Sir Thomas Lawrence, and had a hand in the drafting of the Catholic Relief Bill of 1791. I was intrigued to find in the *Catholic Encyclopedia* a reference to a *Life of Sir Henry Englefield* by William Sotheby, London 1819, which I felt sure would tell me the only fact about this man of parts that concerns me: what was the parentage of his brother-in-law? But not even the catalogue of the British Library will admit the existence of any such book...

To conclude Petrie's panegyric:

Mr. O'Flaherty is a native of Aran, and he has never been further from his native rocks than to the city of Galway and the adjacent coast of Thomond. ... He is deeply religious, but altogether free from narrow prejudice. His religion has something of a romantic character, and he feels his piety more excited in the little deserted, roofless temple, among the rocks, beside his own house, than it possibly could be in the most crowded and magnificent church. In this solitary ruin he offers up his morning and evening prayers; and his figure in the centre of the nave, looking towards the mouldering altar, in the act of adoration, as I saw it once by chance, will never be effaced from my recollection.

Mr. O'Flaherty may be justly denominated the *pater patriae* of the Araners. He is the reconciler in all differences, the judge in all disputes, the adviser in all enterprises, and the friend in all things. ... In 1822 a great number of the islanders had determined to emigrate to America. A ship lay at anchor in Galway to convey them, and they proceeded thither accompanied by Mr. O'Flaherty, to aid them to the last with friendship and advice. Several days elapsed before the vessel was ready to set sail, and Mr. O'Flaherty still continued with them; but at last the hour to bid an everlasting adieu arrived. ... Men and women all surrounded him – the former with cheeks streaming with tears, and the latter uttering the most piercing lamentations – some hung on his neck, some got his hands or arms to kiss, while others threw themselves on the deck and embraced his knees. It is no discredit that on such an occasion the object of so much affectionate regard was more than unmanned, and it was a long time before his health recovered the injury, or his face lost the sorrowful expression caused by the grief of that parting.

My viewing of this touching genre-picture is troubled as if by an intrusive reflection, in the light of the bitter conviction of several villagers I have spoken to that their ancestors were turned off that good land under the scarp at Cill Mhuirbhigh to make room for the O'Flaherty garden, and that many islanders were forced to emigrate when the whole of Ceathrú an Turlaigh to the west was emptied by the landlord's agent and leased to the O'Flahertys. (It seems that the latter event happened at some period before Thomas Thompson succeeded his father as agent in 1848.)

As to Patrick O'Flaherty, 'judge in all disputes', this position was made official in 1830 or '31 when he was appointed Justice of the Peace. A later magistrate for the district including Aran gives this account of Patrick's sittings, which he probably gathered from the oral lore of legal circles as well as from that of the islanders:

He was the only magistrate in the islands, but ruled as a king. He issued his summons for 'the first fine day', and presided at a table in the open air. If any case deserved punishment, he would say to the defendant, speaking in Irish, 'I must transport you to Galway gaol for a month.' The defendant would beg hard not to be transported to Galway, promising good behaviour in the future. If, however, his worship thought the case serious, he would draw his committal warrant, hand it to the defendant, who would, without the intervention of police or anyone else, take the warrant, travel at his own expense to Galway and deliver himself up, warrant in hand, at the county gaol.

This was published in 1887, and J.M. Synge would probably have read it before his visit in 1898. Synge's own version also draws on the reminiscences of the old islanders with whom he discussed ancient justice and injustice:

I have heard that at that time the ruling proprietor and magistrate of the north island used to give any man who had done wrong a letter to a jailer in Galway, and send him off by himself to serve a term of imprisonment. As there was no steamer, the ill-doer was given a passage in some chance hooker to the nearest point on the mainland. Then he walked for many a mile along a desolate shore till he reached the town. When his time had been put through, he crawled back along the same route, feeble and emaciated, and had often to wait many weeks before he could regain the island. Such at least is the story.

One must remember that between the visit of Petrie and that of Synge lay half a dozen famines and the Land War, by which patriarchal attitudes had been starved out and shouted down; the truth about that 'first fine day' of Patrick O'Flaherty's reign had long been left desolate on the shore, bare, unaccommodated, and perhaps forked.

Petrie was to have the opportunity of thanking O'Flaherty again for his hospitality, and of proposing a toast to that 'fine old Irish gentleman', in 1857, during the British Association's famous banquet in Dún Aonghasa. O'Flaherty would have been well known to several of the eminent banqueteers, and especially to the director of the excursion, William Wilde. Wilde had visited the islands in 1848, and perhaps on other occasions, and later he built a summer home about thirty miles from Galway, near Cong. He had an O'Flaherty connection through his grandmother, and it is part of the lore of Kilmurvey House that Patrick stood godfather to his son, Oscar Fingal O'Flahertie Wills Wilde, born in 1856. (The earlier biographies of Oscar Wilde state that his godfather was King Oscar of Sweden, who it is alleged was treated for an ear complaint by Sir William; more scholarly studies such as Richard Ellmann's show that this is not so, but leave open the question of who was Oscar's godfather. If this is a little literary mystery, here is its possible solution.)

There is certainly some mystery about Patrick's wife, who is not named in any of the documents I have seen or mentioned in any contemporary accounts. According to the tomb by Port Mhuirbhigh, Patrick's son James died in October 1881 aged sixty-four; therefore he was born in 1816 or 1817 – but neither he nor his mother figure, at least identifiably, in the 1821 census. Gossip has it that when James heard his father was dying he realized that there might be difficulties about his inheritance, came home from Galway in a hurry with a priest, and got the situation regularized.

By the time James succeeded his father as the island's chief middleman and JP in 1864, the Hill Farm at Killeany must have been added to the O'Flaherty holdings in Cill Mhuirbhigh and Ceathrú an Turlaigh. If Patrick had enjoyed and dispensed some residual organic warmth of feudal relationship with the islanders, none of it was passed on to his son, who is remembered solely as a scheming exploiter, in league with the proselytizing minister Kilbride and the extortionate agent Thompson. A local newspaper, the *Galway Vindicator*, alluded to this falling-off in a verse of the anti-souper 'Song of the Arranman' I have already quoted in writing about the involved hostilities of the 1860s:

> There was a time, people of Aran,
> When O'Flaherty's voice would oppose,
> In thunders as clear as clarion,
> The tyrants and tract strewing foes.

But now, o degenerate son, you
May lend the vile system a name,
While they fondle the hope that they've won you,
We'll think of your conduct with shame.

At that time O'Flaherty owned the *Arran Yacht* in partnership with
Thompson, and used it in their monopolistic transport trade in kelp, bread
and other supplies. He bought a forty-foot smack, the *Breeze*, in 1870 for
£105, and employed a local crew in fishing. In the 1870s many tons of
stone were drawn from Carraig an Bhanbháin near Cill Éinne, and Kilmurvey House arose to eclipse the old family home; it is said that James
called in a Dublin architect to provide the style requisite to a gentleman's
residence. The stables and high-walled cattle-yard on the other side of the
lane past his main gates completed the demesne. From a window in one of
the outhouses there James O'Flaherty JP handed down judgment to lesser
islanders standing in the laneway. The yard was the fort and stockade of the
bailiffs' Indian Wars. I hear of the exploit there of an Ó Direáin from
Sruthán: he had lent his horse to a neighbour to bring back a sack of meal
from Cill Rónáin, and this other man was stopped by the bailiff because he
owed rent, and the horse and the meal were seized and taken off to O'Flaherty's yard. When he heard of this, Ó Direáin, who was a big powerful
fellow, took his blackthorn stick and walked over to Cill Mhuirbhigh,
pushed his way past O'Flaherty's men into the yard, leaped on his horse,
and when they tried to stop him by shutting the gate, smashed it down and
rode off. Nothing was done about him at the time, but when next he came
to pay his rent it was refused, and he eventually had to leave the island.

James O'Flaherty's wife Julia, whom he married in 1848, was the
daughter of Thomas and Julia Irwin of Cottage in Roscommon. Julia bore
him five daughters: Julia, Mary, Jane, Delia and Lily. James Hardiman was
a friend and trustee of the Irwins, and his son married the eldest daughter,
Julia (in fact in Galway they say that a boat-load of O'Flahertys threatened
to come over and call on him if he did not marry her). O'Flaherty's mistress was a married woman of Gort na gCapall; he is supposed to have had
four illegitimate sons, and their descendants are known by a nickname that
nowadays is born with a touch of pride. In fact James's extramarital capers
won him a nickname too: An Pocaide Bán, the white billygoat.

Thus James is the original of the man whose reputation makes the old
woman cross herself, in Ó Direáin's 'Ó Mórna'. According to the poem, he
was first led astray by a fawning bailiff who persuaded him that the womenfolk would deny nothing to one of his rank and ancestry; then his lonely
eminence on the island and the coldness of his wife drove him into melancholy excesses. (Ó Direáin apparently shares the belief that unenthusiastic

couplings result in girl children.) Maddened by the wild spring-tide of desire he storms through the island:

Ag cartadh báin, ag cartadh loirg,
Ag treabhadh faoi dheabhadh le fórsa,
Ag réabadh comhlan na hóghachta,
Ag dul thar teorainn an phósta.

Rooting up the grassland, rooting up the fallow
Speeding his plough with force,
Breaking the door of virginity,
Crossing the bounds of marriage.

But he has a certain satanic dash even in his drunken follies:

Tháinig lá ar mhuin a chapaill
Ar meisce faoi ualach óil,
Stad in aice trá Chill Cholmáin
Gur scaip ladhar den ór le spórt,
Truáin ag sciobadh gach sabhrain
Dár scaoil an triath ina dtreo.

Do gháir Ó Mórna is do bhéic,
Mairbh a fhualais sa reilig thuas
Ní foláir nó chuala an bhéic;
Dhearbhaigh fós le draothadh aithise
Go gcuirfeadh sabhran gan mhairg
In aghaidh gach míol ina n-ascaill.

Labhair an sagart air Dé Domhnaigh,
Bhagair is d'agair na cumhachta,
D'agair réabadh na hóghachta air,
Scannal a thréada d'agair le fórsa,
Ach ghluais Ó Mórna ina chóiste
De shodar sotail thar cill.

He came one day on his horse,
Weighted down with drink,
Stopped at Port Mhuirbhigh for sport
And scattered a handful of gold,
Wretches went scrabbling for sovereigns
Flung at them by the chief.

O'Flaherty howled with laughter,
The dead of his sept in the graveyard
Must have heard that yell from the beach;
And he swore with a leer of contempt

> He'd match every louse in their oxters
> With a sovereign and not feel the loss.
>
> One Sunday he was named by the priest,
> Threatened with authority's vengeance,
> Accused of the rape of virginity,
> Blamed for scandal to the flock,
> But O'Flaherty rode by in his coach
> Arrogantly trotting past the chapel.

Eventually the pangs of desire give way to the pains of age, and after lying for a while in his house in the wood, a house in which laughter has been rare, he joins his ancestors in the graveyard, and is eaten by the worm that does not distinguish between high and low degree. 'May your sleep be tranquil in the tomb tonight', prays the poet of this memorial.

My translation has of course brought the poem into a more literal relationship with Aran history than Ó Direáin may have intended. Perhaps it is the irritation of a single line in it that makes me do so. While Ó Mórna was giving himself to debauch, his land was administered by four abusive and extortionate stewards, says Ó Direáin, and he names them for us:

> Wiggins, Robinson, Thomson agus Ede ...

This is very specific. The first three names are familiar in the island's history; the fourth is not, but it was probably suggested by that of Charde, the Protestant school-teacher and shopkeeper. Thom(p)son is of course the land-agent whose misdeeds I have catalogued – but he was agent to the landowners, the Digbys, rather than to O'Flaherty, who was only a middleman, leasing land from the owners and subletting much of it to lesser tenants. Henry Robinson succeeded Thompson in this post in the 1880s; he was agent for a number of estates and in particular for the former Martin estate in Connemara, and he lived in Roundstone, in a house rather grander than O'Flaherty's. (Since I too live in Roundstone it is sometimes assumed that I descend from him, but it is not so; nevertheless this mention of his name spurs me to redress if not a historical injustice – for Robinson was a great evictor in his day – then a historical over-simplification.) As for Wiggins, the family may or may not have inherited its name and an ever-reducing proportion of its genes from some seventeenth-century Anglo-Saxon trooper gone native, but for many generations they had been smallholders in Cill Éinne under the same conditions as other families. However, the reasons for Ó Direáin's use of their non-Aranite name for one of his gang of petty villains, rather than that of his kinsfolk and neighbours, Ó hIarnáin, are quite comprehensible.

The unmasking of these names reveals James O'Flaherty as an actor in the cross-fissured capitalistic society of nineteenth-century Aran, rather than as the survivor from some archaic, amoral and almost heroic age Ó Direáin half-admiringly depicts. He was in shifting alliances with the representatives of other social powers transcending his own jurisdiction, notably the Protestant minister, the police and the land-agent. His implication in the politics of the relief committees and the management of the dispensary, his commerce with fisheries, kelp, cattle-raising and the transport of goods to and from Galway, and above all his role as land-grabber and, finally, victim in the Land War, have brought his name into many chapters of this book. Ó Direáin's poem, after a splendid beginning that promises so much more than the old crone crossing her forehead could tell us, shirks this perplexed social setting, which leaves his blood-driven and nobly transgressive Ó Mórna both circumscribed and anaemic.

In the real Aran, James O'Flaherty in his heyday had enough supporters, employees and hangers-on at least to put on a show. The archaeologist Thomas Westropp, describing his own first visit to Aran in 1878, happened upon a scene that could not have been repeated a few years later:

Kilmurvey is a poor fishing village of little note, behind it is the house of Mr O'Fflaherty – he had been living on the mainland for some years & happened to return that day so the natives (who at this time did not consider a landlord an ex officio target) decorated all the avenue with paper flags & held races & games before the door.

Within three years of this celebration – which perhaps marked the completion of Kilmurvey House – O'Flaherty was living under the protection of the new police barracks in the village, and had received the terrible blow of his cattle being driven over the cliff. Less than a year after that nightmarish warning as to his own safety he died in a Galway hotel, at the age of sixty-four.

James O'Flaherty's successor at Kilmurvey was his daughter Lily's husband, who had added her surname to his own, calling himself Patrick O'Flaherty Johnston, and was appointed JP in 1882. The Johnstons are reputed to have been a hard-riding, high-living set who married into the junior branch of the Macnamaras, wealthy landowners in County Clare. The Johnston house near Doolin, 'Aran View', had been built by that Francis Macnamara who married Marcella, the sister[?] of Patrick O'Flaherty; Marcella's daughter Catherine had married Robert Johnston, and their son was Patrick Johnston. The Macnamaras numbered among their forbears the famous eighteenth-century duellist Fireball Macnamara, and the senior branch at Ennistymon House later gave rise to another Francis Macnamara, a bohemian aesthete friend of Yeats and Shaw, for whom the nickname Fireball was resurrected. This Francis used to visit his Kilmurvey relatives and indeed had an illegitimate daughter by one of them. When he abandoned his wife and children, they drifted into the protection of another of his friends, Augustus John, and one of the daughters, Caitlín, married Dylan Thomas – which is the closest connection between Aran and Llareggub I can contrive.

The Johnstons, as can be imagined, introduced a new tone to Kilmurvey House, which by chance was detected and recorded for us by Violet Martin and Edith Somerville, who passed by during their summer holiday of 1895, after they had surveyed and disapproved of the 'invertebrate walls' of Dún Aonghasa:

It is a pleasant descent to the village of Kilmurvey, down through the buoyant air of the hill side; the grass steals its way among the outposts of rock, till the foot travels with unfamiliar ease in level fields. Near Kilmurvey the Resident Magistrate's house shows a trim roof among young larch and spruce, a miracle of modernity and right angles after the strewn monstrosities of the ridge above; passing near it, a piano gave forth a Nocturne of Chopin's to the solitude, a patrician lament, a skilled passion, in a land where ear and voice have preserved the single threads of melody, and harmony is as yet unwoven.

But the world of the Irish R.M. was in decay, as the stories of 'Martin and Ross' exhaustively demonstrate. Aran memory is that Patrick Johnston 'scattered' the inheritance, shooting, fishing and drinking in Clare. When the Land Court sat in Cill Rónáin in 1886, he won a 40 per cent reduction in the rent of the Hill Farm, but by 1897 he was anxious to transfer the lease of it to the Congested Districts Board for the sum of £550. Nothing immediately came of this because Johnston could not get a renewal of the lease from the owners on terms that would have made it attractive to the Board, but he must have given up the Cill Éinne land soon afterwards. A rather desperate-sounding draft letter from him to a solicitor reveals that his wife had just heard that her sister (probably Delia) could not lend her the £500 she had hoped for, and was seeing Fr Farragher to arrange for the speedy sale of Ceathrú an Turlaigh; as for the Hill Farm, no one would purchase the lease under the present rent, and he could only surrender it to the agent. So both east and west wings of the estate were clipped, reducing the holding to the Kilmurvey House farm alone.

Patrick and Lily had three sons, one of whom died young, and three daughters. The family were in relatively poor circumstances by then; one son, George Irwin, had to go to the national school, and so grew up an excellent Irish speaker. He joined the Royal Irish Fusiliers and became a

Captain (and is remembered as the man who brought the first motorcar to the island; Máirtín Ó Direáin describes how the children of Sruthán marvelled at the beams of its headlamps when it was parked up on the hill at the chapel in Eochaill, and argued about whether it ran on oil or coal). Patrick died in 1927; his widow Lily, still remembered as a quiet little old lady – she had suffered a partial stroke – lived on until 1944, the last of the Ferocious O'Flahertys.

James Johnston, Patrick's elder son and heir, had gone to Africa, and returned to try and save the farm. He was one of the founders of the Aran branch of Fianna Fáil in 1927; the others were the former IRA leader Thomas Fleming and two school-teachers, Joe Flanagan (a friend of the candidate they wanted to canvas for, Dr Tubridy of Connemara) and Pádraic Ó hEithir (from whose reminiscences I have this); James's reason for joining, it seems, was that he was for anything the parish priest opposed! There is a disturbing portrait of James in Clara Vyvyan's reminiscences of her stay at the cottage Elizabeth Rivers rented from him in the late 1930s:

I find it difficult to write of James because I always feel that I never properly appreciated him. ... The other three of us all thought he was wonderful. I was just amazed and frightened as I listened to his starkly cynical stories that came out, one after the other, like puffs of smoke from a pipe. There was an unending succession of them, as if with each one he were trying to outdo himself in his own world of extravaganza, and always at the end he would utter a nasal 'Heigh!' on a rising note, as if he were calling us to attention or demanding applause. But perhaps he was merely saying; 'That's that, believe it or no.'... James had a larger house and more land than any of the others and he always seemed to have less work to do. In mainland life he would have been, no doubt, the squire of Kilmurvy, but here on Aran there were never any class distinctions, people were only old or young, men or women or children.

Typical of his stories was one he told her about Gort na gCapall:

'There was a famous wreck on that coast, a big vessel came ashore on the rocks near the village. No survivors of course. One corpse came ashore held up by its head and shoulders in a lifebelt but when they came to empty the pockets they saw it had no face. However, they took what they could find and then they cast it back into the sea. Two more came in together, they could hardly loosen them apart ...'

... and so it goes on in ever more ghoulish detail, ending with the whole village being rewarded with pensions because of their hospitality to the corpse of an American millionaire. Again and again during Clara's stay, James drifted into the kitchen and sat down by the fire in his long-belted raincoat that 'lent to him an air of seedy civilization', and began his stories of 'corpses, cruelty, and spells of witches'. Her last view of him is on the morning of her leaving:

Under the sea wall by Kilmurvey Harbour I found James sitting down and looking at the sea and smoking, occupied thus with three cronies. He had told us he
must be at work by eight o'clock and it was now well after nine. I never saw a man
who looked less like beginning a day's work.

That is James Johnston, caught in the perspective of Lady Vyvyan's holiday
snaps. From another social angle I pick up an auditory trace of him: a
merry clattering on the road in the small hours, as he rolls home from the
pubs of Cill Rónáin with a fellow roisterer, the painter Charles Lamb over
from his studio in Connemara for a spree – a sound that broke the sleep
and lodged in the memory of one of our Oatquarter neighbours when he
was a child sixty years or more ago.

Late in his life James married Bridget Coyne, the daughter of a substantial cattle-dealer from Ballybrit near Galway who often visited the
island. In 1947 Bridgie opened Kilmurvey House as a guest-house for the
first time. James died in 1953, leaving no offspring. Bridgie's second husband was Sonny Hernon, a Cill Mhuirbhigh neighbour. Their daughter,
Treasa, I first noticed as a skinny little girl with sparkling black eyes, taking
the lead in an Irish-language play in the school at Fearann an Choirce; she
soon became one of the little band who used to call in on us on their way
home. Sonny I remember as a small, neatly-built man, intent on his work
with the cattle, sparing with words. When the attics of Kilmurvey House
had to be emptied to make way for more guest-accommodation, the question arose of what to do with heaps of mouldering O'Flaherty papers:
'Burn them!' said Sonny, and a lot of stuff that might mortally have delayed
my progress to the end of this chapter drifted off in smoke over the crags.
Once, when I remarked to another villager how curious it was that the
O'Flaherty demesne had become a Cill Mhuirbhigh farm like any other, he
grumbled that at least in the old days one could rent a field from Johnston,
but now Sonny worked them all himself. Bridgie used to sigh, and say, 'He
comes in from his work; he has his tea; he goes out again!' But then Sonny
changed. 'The first I noticed of it', the neighbour told me later, 'was when
we were talking about the damage the rabbits do to the fields, and Sonny
said, 'Ah, the rabbits will be here after us!'' Stricken by premature senility,
Sonny vanished from the island into hospital, and lay there, null. Treasa
abandoned her studies and came home to work in the factory and help her
mother with the guest-house. It was a dark time: 'My husband is dead,' said
Bridgie, 'but we still have to visit him!' Sonny's death was not complete
until the end of January in 1980.

But now, returning to the island in 1993, I find the house full of laughter, the accommodation renewed – little bathrooms juggled into corners of the big old-fashioned bedrooms, decayed window-frames replaced, etc. – Treasa's amiable husband sitting in the kitchen when he is not off with his Cill Rónáin-based trawler, two grandchildren welcoming Bridget into a new phase of life, and the present moment vigorously reasserting itself. The parlour is still the same, with the TV set looking as if it had barged in among Lily O'Flaherty's Victorian knicknacks and James Johnston's worn-looking 'thirtyish travel books. The ancestral portraits that caught Petrie's attention in 1821 and mine a century and a half later still hang there, all the more impressive for the darkness of age: Patrick O'Flaherty's uncle Thady (that was his name, says Bridgie), a handsome, rubicund, portly personage, and Thady's wife, daughter to the 'respectable English Catholic' who had a large fortune, exhibiting a glacial expanse of bosom. Thinking about these reminders of the O'Flaherty past, I realize that this room is the setting of Ó Direáin's late, self-questioning poem, 'Neamhionraic gach Beo'. Máirtín the Sruthán village lad would of course never have been allowed into this sanctum of gentility, but when he was an established Dublin literary figure, Bridgie tells me, he used to call on the Johnstons. Evidently the well-upholstered hospitality of this room represented a seduction, and its antique fixity a reproach, which he had to address in obscure argument with himself:

Nuair a bhí tine is ól mar dhíon
Ar shíon na hoíche fuaire
Ba bhurla beag beadaí tú
I dteas na tine os do chomhair
Is ó mheidhir an fhíona taobh leat;
Ach d'aird fós ar do ghnó
In ainneoin tine, óil is teasa,
Ach ní rabhais ionraic ar oileán
Ná aon duine den bhuín a bhí i do theannta.

An seantriath ar an mballa
Gona mhéadal nósmhar,
Is a chaofach mná thall
Gona brollach nósmhar,
Atá ceaptha in dhá phortráid
Atá neamhbheo gan malairt
Le trí chéad bliain is breis –
Táid beirt ionraic ar oileán,
Mar tá cloch carraig is trá
I lár na hoíche fuaire.

When sheltered by fire and drink
From the cold of a stormy night
You luxuriated lumpishly
In the warmth of the fire before your face
And the cheer of the wine at your elbow;
Yet with your mind still at its business
Despite fire, drink and warmth,
But you were not faithful on an island
Nor were any of your companions.

The old chief on the wall
With his formal paunch,
And his lady wife there
With her formal bosom,
Who are captured in two portraits
Inanimate and unchanged
For three hundred years and more –
Both are faithful on an island
As are stone rock and strand
In the cold of midnight.

The idea of an inherent faithlessness between people and things leads the poet on into a troubled personal reflection, which I shall follow out when I come to write about Ó Direáin in his Sruthán setting. For the moment, I borrow from the poem only a sense of this room's four-square, thick-walled, heavy-curtained snugness, enhanced by the lament of the night wind in the trees outside.

There are many other relics of old times here, notably a portrait of Patrick O'Flaherty himself (perhaps it is only the naivety of provincial portraiture that gives him a nose like a bent knifeblade), a studio photograph of James O'Flaherty, solid-cheeked and bearded, as Eminent Victorian, a silhouette of James Hardiman. The unidentified subject of another portrait from Thady's era is familiarly known as Bob Hope from a rather striking resemblance. Well hidden away are the magnificent *Missale Romanum* (1732, from the famous printing-house of Plantin in Antwerp) and the vestments said to have been brought by the O'Flahertys' priest from Aughnanure. Hanging over the fireplace is an embroidery of the O'Flaherty shield and lizard crest. In a few years' time the new generation will begin to wonder about this lizard and its long tail of history, which they inherit no less inevitably for being biologically disjunct from it, since an old house is a habitable form of DNA; and then, I hope, the fireside entertainment I have made of it will not come amiss.

DÚN AONGHASA REVISITED

At the Second Battle of Moytura the Fomorians deployed a terrible weapon against the Tuatha Dé Danann, the single eye of their leader, Balor of the Poisonous Eye. Four men were needed to raise its lid by a polished ring, and its gaze could waste an army. But the god Lugh with a slingshot knocked it through to the back of his skull, so that it looked upon Balor's own supporters and turned twenty-seven of them to stone. Balor, whose name seems to mean 'the flashing one', is associated in mythology with Mizen Head in Cork, with Tory Island off Donegal, and perhaps with Land's End, the ancient Bolerion, in Cornwall; it has been suggested that he was the Celtic god of the setting sun. In the foggy timescape of myth this Second Battle is hard to distinguish from the First, the defeat of the Fir Bolg by the Tuatha Dé Danann. The outcome of this latter was (according to the pseudo-history of the *Lebor Gabála*), the retreat of the Fir Bolg to the western shores, and the building of Dún Aonghasa by their leader Aonghas.

If the south-west is bright, the plateau behind Cill Mhuirbhigh looks like a long dark curtain-wall, on which the central cashel of the *dún* is a turret at the farther, Atlantic end. I have often noticed that from a certain stretch of the main road a tiny rectangle of sky is visible through the gateway of the cashel, so that, as you walk or cycle down to the village from the east, it is as if an eye opens, fixes you for a minute or two, then closes. This look is not baleful, but it is both tremendous and ambiguous. After encountering it, to climb the half-mile hillside from the village to the cashel, and pass through that gateway, a slanting passage up through the thirteen-foot thickness of the rampart, is to submit to inspection by whatever lies within – which appears, rather intimidatingly, to be nothing.

Dún Aonghasa is so strangely and extremely situated, in immediate apposition to the precipice, as to suggest three possibilities: that it addresses itself to the rest of the island, as a last defensive toehold; or to the sea and the long vista of the Clare coast visible from it, as the citadel of some regional power; or to the beyond, as a temple. The first theory was the favourite of the Romantic era, but has long been abandoned as impracticable. The earliest full expression I have come across of the last theory is by W.Y. Evans Wentz, that Casaubon-with-attitude of the Celtic Twilight:

In Dun Aengus, the strange cyclopean circular structure, and hence most likely sun-temple, on Aranmore, we have another example of the localization of the Aengus myth. This fact leads us to believe, after due archaeological examination, that amid the stronghold of Dun Aengus, with its tiers of amphitheatre-like seats and the native rock at its centre, apparently squared to form a platform or stage, were anciently celebrated pagan mysteries comparable to those of the Greeks and less cultured peoples, and initiations into an Aengus cult such as seems once to have flourished at New Grange ...

Evans Wentz here is confusing Aonghas of the Fir Bolg with Aonghas of the Tuatha Dé Danann, who is associated with the Neolithic tumulus of Newgrange. Thence it is but a step for him to show that this same cult of 'the Celtic Zeus' was practised in the 'druidical temples' of Stonehenge and Carnac, and in one more hop we reach the Great Pyramid, whose main entrance, he tells us, is a passageway oriented to the south-east like that of Newgrange and having its opening under the Great Sphinx, but unfortunately not yet discovered.

Etienne Rynne, the professor of archaeology in University College, Galway, has long nursed the idea that not only Dún Aonghasa but the other six Aran forts and similar stone structures in the Burren and elsewhere in western Ireland were ceremonial sites. Unlike Evans Wentz, he advances arguments for thinking so:

There are four main reasons why monuments are built, namely, for living purposes, for burial purposes, for military purposes, or for ceremonial purposes. The first two alternatives can be eliminated without much trouble insofar as Dún Aengus is concerned. The place is in no way suitable for either living in or for burial: there is not enough earth there for even a shallow burial, and furthermore, it fits into no known funerary monument-type, while anyone who has ever been there in wet and windy weather conditions knows that living there would be out of the question – one does not try to rear a family on the edge of a high cliff, a permanent danger to children and even to adults, and where there are no adequate facilities for normal living, there being not enough soil to grow food for humans or pasture for cattle, not to mention the lack of fresh water on the site. ...

The third alternative, the military one, is less easy to dismiss. Should it have been built and used for military purposes then it could only have served as a place of refuge which, *ipso facto*, implies siege warfare. Quite apart from the fact that the ancient Irish did not normally engage in siege warfare, the site is quite unsuitable for such on many points. There is, for instance, no fresh water, no escape route, and the terraces of the inner citadel are not suitable for looking out over the ramparts for defensive or other such purposes (the top rampart is mainly a reconstruction carried out in the 1880s by the Board of Works and originally was at least 1m. higher). ...

By a process of elimination, therefore, one is left with the fourth and last alternative, that Dún Aengus was conceived, built and used for ceremonial purposes. ... By the same process of elimination all these related monuments can be interpreted as having been built for ceremonial purposes, purposes such as inauguration ceremonies, or for the annual or seasonal *aonach* (assembly/celebrations) of the *tuath* (tribe), where and when payment of tribute, making of treaties, arranging important marriage contracts, holding ritual games, promulgating laws, receiving honoured guests, etc., would have taken place. ... These ancient 'forts' are not only impressive in themselves but are sited in positions which immediately command attention and respect, generally in positions overlooking vast areas and thus eminently suitable as meeting-places for the people of the surrounding regions. Furthermore, their stepped and terraced walls are much more suitable for looking *inwards* than *outwards*, indicating that these monuments should more fittingly be regarded as amphitheatres rather than as forts. ...

When visiting Dún Aengus, therefore, ... the visitor should conjure up an image of druids, ollavs, bards, kings and nobles, all processing formally through the Dún's impressive entrance, some to perform rituals on the stage-like platform, some to assist in the innermost enclosed area, and others to stand on the surrounding terraced wall chanting incantations or singing sacred songs while viewing the solemn proceedings taking place against the dramatic backdrop of the wild Atlantic ocean whose waves sonorously thunder against the rock-face far out of sight below.

Recently an archaeologist of the rising generation, Michael Gibbons, undertook to correct his former professor on this question, pointing out that there were noticeable traces of habitation, including hut-foundations, in the western sector of the inner enclosure. The controversy caught the attention of journalists, who stepped forward to hold the combatants' coats. An article in *The Irish Times* quoted Michael Gibbons as follows:

In fact, Dún Aengus was probably built during a period of great maritime power by a people who held sway over all of Árainn and probably much of the Burren during the period 800 BC to AD 400.

While Michael Gibbons will allow that the platform of natural rock in the inner enclosure may well have been used for ceremonies — traces of rectangular temples have been found in other Iron-Age enclosures — ritual was not the *raison d'être* of the cashel.

In this same article I was as surprised as Professor Rynne must have been to read that he had 'suggested that Dún Aengus was built for ceremonial purposes, such as storm worship'. In hastily mugging up the background to the dispute, *The Irish Times* columnist had evidently noticed a passing thought of mine from *Pilgrimage*, quoted by Professor Rynne as a literary ornament to one of his articles on the *dún*: 'I would rather believe the place was built for the worship of storms, to which it is well adapted, ʃ to impress the neighbours.' Having escaped from literature through ʃence into journalism, this notion is now breeding in the wild; in Aran's newly opened Heritage Centre, under a picture of Dún Aonghasa the visitor can read that 'some believe it was built for the worship of storms'. Well, every idea has its day, and although I doubt if my little literary flourish would have impressed the Fir Bolg (though why not, if indeed Bolgios was a god of lightning, as O'Rahilly suggested fifty years ago?), it could come about that when religion returns to its roots Dún Aonghasa will be the official seat of communion with the sky's disinterested violence.

Meanwhile, and for the first time, a proper archaeological investigation of the *dún* has begun, and facts are being trowelled up and sieved out that may amount to evidence for one or other of the rival suppositions as to its purpose, or even bury the entire debate. This excavation is part of the Discovery Programme, a national – indeed a nationalistic – archaeological project initiated by the then Taoiseach Charles Haughey in 1991, the aims of which are '1. To work towards a coherent and comprehensive picture of human life on this island from earliest times', and '2. To formulate the results in ways that can be communicated both to experts and to the general public'. In pursuance of this programme the Late Bronze Age and Early Iron Age was selected as the 'core period' for intensive research (perhaps it was felt that 'life on this island' offered a more coherent picture then than it has done since), and a critical topic within that period was identified:

The Western Stone Forts Project was set up to address the questions posed by a group of large stone forts which occur along the western seaboard and on the western islands. Between twenty and thirty of these forts survive, mainly in counties Galway, Clare and Kerry. Dún Aonghasa on the Aran Islands, Grianán Aileach in Co. Donegal and Staigue in Co. Kerry are among the best known examples. ... At present we know little about the people who built these forts and the social or environmental conditions which prompted the construction of such large scale defensive monuments. ...

So, in 1992, Dún Aonghasa was invested by a team of eighteen or twenty young archaeologists – graduates, student volunteers, local recruits – under the director of the Western Stone Forts Project, Claire Cotter. During their third season I came out to the island to see what they were turning up. It was a foggy, almost rainy day, and the path that wanders up to the *dún* across one layer of crag after another was slippery. The decrepit outermost rampart, rambling across the hillside, has a stile in it like any field-wall. A hundred and fifty yards beyond it, the path climbs through the zone of thousands of stone spikes, towards a narrow opening in the second or middle rampart, which is tall enough – well over head-height – to impose a sense of enclosure on the quarter-acre of rising ground between it and the ponderous rain-blackened bulk of the central cashel. (This middle rampart has a terrace around its inner face – which shows, I think, that terraces are not necessarily connected with the viewing of spectacles, for which the rough slanting ground within is quite unsuitable.) I found some of the archaeological tribe in a little hut here, and asked them to take me to their leader. We went up through the low gateway into the half-oval of the inner enclosure. Beyond the cliff-edge nothing was visible except shifting dampness. A high wire fence cut off the western half of the enclosure and a few tourists were peering through the mesh at the work in progress behind it. 'How old is this place?' one of them called out in an Italian accent to a youth going by with a bucket of soil, who replied (in conformity with Article 2 of the aims of the Discovery Programme quoted above), 'We don't know.' I was admitted by a door marked 'Private' and presented to Claire (big Aran sweater and Viking ponytail), who laid down her trowel and showed me around the site.

I had always assumed that the interior of the cashel was so near to being a naked crag that it promised archaeology very little, but in fact there is a surface-layer a foot or so deep in the western sector, in the lea of the rampart. The turf had been peeled off an area about twenty yards wide all along the base of the western curve of the wall, except for two narrow strips at right angles to each other that crossed the bared rock like the axes of a graph. Anoraked forms were kneeling here and there, mapping small scatters of flat stones, brushing soil from crevices, picking out dozens of minute objects and putting them away in little screws of silver foil. Coordinate geometry reigned: regularly spaced parallel wires stretched across the site, the ground was sprigged with numbered dockets, people were treading cautiously to and fro with rulers, tape-measures and metre-square wooden frames. Beneath this rigorous network, Claire persuaded me to see certain configurations of stone as areas of paving and foundations of huts. The earliest of the huts is represented by an arc of low slabs set edge to edge, the basis of either a stone or a wooden building about sixteen feet in diameter. A small trough, floored and walled with flags, was a cooking place in which water would have been heated by dropping in hot stones. The blackish specks being laboriously collected out of the soil were bits of charcoal, which would all be sent away to be analyzed; the wood of hazel, oak, alder, Scots pine and willow or poplar had been identified. Much of the deposit around the hut-sites is of food debris: limpet and periwinkle shells, fishbones, seabird bones – the settlement must have been extremely smelly – and large amounts of cow and sheep bones, but very little pig, and, what is unusual for a habitation site, no remains of dogs.

Other finds – I saw some of them later on, in the house Claire and some colleagues were renting in Cill Mhuirbhigh – include fragments of coarse pottery, a pierced bead of blue glass about half an inch across and another a mere eighth of an inch across, a few quartz crystals, and a small round beach-pebble of limestone with white spots of fossil coral in it, such as can be picked up on the shore. Little items of bronze have been found too, such as small rings and a neat pair of tweezers, and some bone pins about three inches long, one of them with a decorative moulded head, probably for fastening a cloak. Also, a pebble with a groove worn in it for sharpening pins, and pieces of clay moulds used for the casting of axes, knives, a spearhead, a sword, a pin and a bracelet. While most of the dates determined so far cluster around 800 BC, the hut itself dates from about 1000 BC. What is being revealed here is clearly a Late Bronze Age settlement. Perhaps the Aran Islanders of this ancient village – much more ancient than anything that had been expected – were concerned, not so much with defence or empire or the ultimate mysteries, as with farming and fishing and the latest fashion in bone pins. A few disturbed remains of human burials were found south of the hut and elsewhere on the site, and just north of the hut in a natural hollow of the rock was the tiny skeleton of an infant, perhaps stillborn; had it lived, it would have lived some time between 800 and 400 BC. Below it, refuse such as animal bones and periwinkles yielded the earliest date of all, between 1500 and 1300 BC – back at the boundaries of the Middle and Late Bronze Age.

One of the lines of stones interpreted as hut foundations runs in under the cashel wall, which it seems was not itself built up from bedrock but rests on the layer of detritus. Does that mean that generations of people lived up here on the bald hilltop before the cashel was built? Perhaps there was an enclosing wall to this first settlement, but if anything of it remains, it is deeply buried within the cashel wall we see today. There is a low, lin-telled recess in the base of the north-western sector of the present wall, and when one crouches in this and looks to either side, about three feet in, a vertical joint in the masonry is visible which might indicate the face of the original wall. Also it is reasonable to suppose that there was at least a slight wall along the cliff-top; the archaeologists have built a dry-stone wall just a few feet high there, and it has greatly decreased their discomforts.

Remarkable as they are, the discoveries made so far say little about the dates and nothing about the purposes of the central cashel wall or the outer ramparts, and after three seasons of excavation the enigma of the *dún* has scarcely been broached. No houses or other structures of the same era as the cashel wall survive, and finds from later than the Bronze Age have been few. A finely carved comb of antler bone and a few other objects show that the *dún* was still in use in early Christian times, but what was going on there is still unknown. Since it overlays the Late Bronze Age deposits, the cashel wall, or at least its interior face, is of later date, presumably of the pagan or Early Christian Iron Age; a radio-carbon date of AD 600-800 has been obtained from material in the recess in the wall. But that wall itself was not built in a day; it is a complex structure made of several thicknesses, each with its face of carefully positioned and fitted blocks and its filling of loosely heaped-in stone. There are more such faces than correspond to the three levels of the wall – parapet and two terraces – for one of them can be made out in the stones composing the floor of the upper terrace. The recess was perhaps a doorway at one stage of the wall's development; it looks as if the stones closing it were pushed in from the other side when another layer was being added to the outside of the wall. Thus the wall we see today may have been built up over a great period of time by periodic thickening and raising of an ancient core.

The relationships of the two outer ramparts to the central cashel are still to be elucidated. Claire took me up the steps and terraces to the north sector of the cashel wall, which is about eighteen feet high here, and we leaned over the parapet and looked down at an area that had been excavated just outside it. The second or middle rampart, coming round from the east, turns southwards as if to approach the inner one at this point, but changes its mind and continues to the west. It is a massive construction in itself, eleven feet high and terraced on its inner face, but its present indecisive course looks like the result of changes of plan. Newly exposed foundations of a stretch of wall crossing the stripped ground from the kink in the middle rampart to the foot of the main cashel wall immediately below us showed clearly that at some period the middle rampart, or a predecessor of it, did indeed turn south here on a course that would have met that of the inner rampart. A deposit of kitchen-waste – bones and seashells – banked up along the east of these foundations continues under the inner rampart, which suggests that the foundations are earlier. Perhaps the middle rampart was partially demolished and re-aligned more than once. In fact all its eastern and northern length is underlain by an earlier wall, of which the newly discovered foundations mark a continuation. There is a recess in the north arc of this middle rampart as we see it today, which was evidently a gateway, and under it Claire's team have found the floor of an earlier, paved entrance with revetted sides, cut down into a shale-band of the hillside. It may be that this entrance and the wall later overlain by the middle rampart represent the first enclosure on this hilltop, a primitive Dún Aonghasa – but its date is not known. When the skeleton of an eleven- to thirteen-year-old was found buried in that early entrance close to its threshold, the archaeologists had high hopes of getting a radio-carbon date from it that would help fix that of the enclosure – but after some months the baffling answer that came back from the laboratory was: AD 910! What could this mean? Either it was a Viking burial, perhaps of a youth who died on board a passing long-boat, or there were at that late date natives of this famously Christian island who were not using Christian burial grounds. In either case, it shows that the gateway was still open then, and regarded as of some otherworldly significance. As to the farflung, eight-hundred-yards-long outer rampart, it is as yet uninvestigated. Thus the scale and longevity of the site seem more than ample to accommodate all the purposes imputed to it by rival theories.

After Claire had returned to her work I lingered on the ramparts and watched the strange scene for a while, never before having seen such purposive activity in the *dún*. Visitors to Dún Aonghasa usually look as if being here is a null state between coming up the hill and going down again; fuddled with space, they seem to float around as in an aquarium filled out of the vacancy beyond the cliff-edge. But now the concentration was palpable. Words were few and subdued; occasionally someone would scoop together a handful of dust – so it appeared – and take it across to another person, and they would put their heads together over it for a while, before returning each to their own square metre of ground. The mist welled up over the cliff, thickened, coiled a tentacle about a girl holding a surveyor's pole near the brink for a young man who was trying to petrify the flux with the theodolite's single eye. Claire stood motionless with a camera before a measuring-rod laid across a few stones as if on a makeshift altar; while I waited to hear the shutter fall, a fulmar came askance out of the grey, and was gone again. What was she recording, the measure of the stones, or the sacrament of measure itself? Everyone else was on their knees. Trowels rang on the rock like little bells. Dún Aonghasa, now, was a temple. The sacred rite of our times, the acquisition of fact, was being accomplished.

MALEDICTION

So the metric priests do not think Dún Aonghasa was meant for the worship of storms? Their colleagues in the Cultural Studies Departments must have told them that the storms of Aran are merely signifiers in the ideological construction of the West as Other by a post-colonialist discourse, scarcely worth packing a raincoat against. They shall learn otherwise, for while they were bent on their work I have called one up. At this moment a premonitory bolt hurtles along the

brink of the cliff: the peregrine falcon. Its stuttering scream says it has left a kit-
tywake exploded into guts and feathers on the rock of perdition. The air in the
dún twitches and wakes, crumples the sheet of mist into a ball and tosses it over
the cliff. The sea is momentarily in sparkling form, a trillion sine-waving heli-
ographs, but cumulus is raising fists along the southern horizon and darkness
wells from the west. A haze slides over the sun, capturing it in a pallid ring
decked to left and right with scraps of iridescence, the storm-dogs sailors fear.
Now the sun is thinned to a wafer, sinking through layers of wrack, dissolving.
A hollow thud rises through the rock-strata from a wave arching its back in the
cavern beneath. As the first big raindrops skim across the ground, the archae-
ologists hastily pin down flapping plastic sheets with stones. The tourists are
already scampering down the hillside, glancing over their shoulders at the
sudden boiling of the bay below the dún, where wave after wave of waves
assault the cliff, mad sappers ramming home short-fused charges, blowing
themselves up every time. I cling like a limpet to the parapet of the dún. The
loose stones chatter like cold teeth, the chinks are whining in the wind. Inis
Oírr, they say, would have been washed away once but for the limpet that held
onto it; now it is up to me whether this island stands. The sea groans, shifts like
the roof of a drunken cathedral, throws up staggering steeples, steeple-chasing
weather-cocks, gargoyles spewing molten lead. The sea is drunk on itself, a
welter of imagery. Space hurls itself at the island, block against block, cracking,
split into cuboid voids and mathematico-rhetorical grykes, riven by geologico-
ethical, Asbian-Brigantian disjunctions, every rift loaded with either/or. The
wind whips away the biblio-biota of the cliff-face, the scrappy choughs, grande-
dame gannets, ship-shape kittywakes, fulmars playing toy planes, the fox pen-
dulating on its fern, James O'Flaherty's ever-falling cattle. Shuffling of the sea-
index follows: thirty types of seaweed fly overhead, a sea-hare, a sea-stallion, the
middle cut of a basking shark with Tiger King trailing behind on a harpoon
rope, a currach full of holy water, a dolphin overstuffed with metaphor. Now
comes the rubbishing of the book of the interior, a tectonic revulsion against its
slow sedimentary style. Pages of limestone peel away, the nautiloid springs from
its rock screaming like an alarm clock, brachiopods whizz by like bullets. The
island's absurd fauna is scrapped, first the butterflies, the dingy skipper pursued
by the Californian man-eater, then the one-handed blackbird, the Connemara
cows with coughs, the Gort-na-gCapall cow with Sanskrit, a dog with some seal
in it, an armigerous lizard, rabbits hand-in-hand with cats, a stallion hauling
a lighthouse, all of them bundled away, knotted in rainbows and consigned to
the abyss. Suddenly a rival mage appears on the cliff-top, Seáinín Bhile's
Frenchman, pretending to conduct the Apocalypse with St Patrick's staff. I
humour him, let him wave on Bolgios armed with his lightning sword, then
blast him east to Ballinasloe. The entire cast is dismissed! The Caper and his

bride in their broken bed, Lhuyd wailing through the mist clutching his sprig of thrift, all the Victorian excursionists with coat-tails and sensible skirts reflexed, the French consul dancing a jig, the rector and the priest clutching each other's windpipes (I bang those two heads together with especial glee), Dr Stoney knocking in his coffin and his wife sucking poitín through the keyhole, Father Ferocious with his umbrella-stick, St Colman with his flying saucers, Nell-an-Tower polishing the rocks with her witches' broom, and her offspring gabbling the alphabet backwards, Micilín Sarah brandishing his otter-spear and thirteen-score razorbill legs at the raven's widow. Off with you, nothing but a pack of marked cards! This storm is flying right round the world, Aran is only a crumb of bread flung out on the doorstep of European culture, not worth snapping at in passing. That these invertebrate walls should set themselves up against the palazzi of Venice! I curse this ramified cul-de-sac of an island that has wasted half the footsteps of my life. Let the empty dúns be thumped like drums, let them be tilted on their rims and sent bowling down the hills, flattening Aran's fourteen ridiculous villages!

Patience, my hand. Patience, my mind. Patience, my heart. Your book will be finished yet.

AN UNFATHOMABLE PUDDLE

Patiently, one by one, the stories of Aran are to be heard out.

A boreen leads on westwards from the old ball-alley at the end of Cill Mhuirbhigh village, serving a row of small fields lined up like books on a shelf in the lea of the scarp on the left. After it has let one glance into about twenty of these plots, the track turns south, faces up to the cliff, and mounts it through a little pass. The land is very watery here, almost a turlough in fact, and there is a good spring at the foot of the way; hence the name of the track: Bóithrín Ghort Bheallach Uisce, the boreen of (the) way of water. This is ordinary water, limpid, plentiful, secular. There is holy water nearby too, but it is given sparingly and tastes of stagnancy. To find it one leaves the beaten track and climbs the knobbly shoulder on its right where it begins to rise up the scarp; a few stony angles and kicked-out toe-holds among the heather-tussocks can be used to scramble up to the stile in the field-wall rimming the crag above. This crag is superb: not much interrupted by walls, with smooth clints the size of variously sized rooms separated by the invisible, negative, step-through walls of the grykes, which here are deep and wide enough to demand individual attention from the walker. It lies along a terrace a few dozen paces wide, tending north-west-wards, between the sharp twenty-foot fall of the scarp now on the right, and the heathy hillside rising in smaller steps and steeps to the left. The holy well is about three hundred yards along the terrace, beyond the first field-wall to cross it. Bullán Mhaolodhair (anglicized on the OS map and pronounced more or less as Bullaunmalore) is its name, as recorded by John O'Donovan in 1839. He took Maolodhar to be a personal name, probably correctly, though nothing is known of such a person. A *bullán* is a hollow in a rock – it is the usual Aran word for a solution-hollow in a clint – and in fact this 'well' is not a spring but a puddle of rainwater that has, with the help of *Nostoc*, excavated a shallow bed for itself. Some blocks of limestone have been arranged around three sides of it, and a slab laid across, to form a small, low, rough canopy. A few old pennies lie in the ooze. The area is unfrequented, not on the way to anywhere, and what lore about the well survives is almost incomprehensibly garbled.

Yet when I first visited the *bullán*, one February day of unexpected spring sunshine, there was a bit of heather floating in it. Later, going down the boreen again, I met an elderly Hernon, Pat Mhicilín, with his horse and a cartload of feed-beet. A tall, winter-bitten man made out of a hank of sinews – he was the anonymous searod-gatherer in gloomy weather of my first volume, also the man who challenged me to match him with a spade when I found him digging potato-ridges one jubilating day by an efferves-cent tide – Pat Mhicilín was the village senior of old Cill Mhuirbhigh. But all he knew of the well was a vague story he had heard from King the black-smith about a saint who got lost on the crag; people went searching for him, calling, 'A Mhíl, labhair!' ('Michael, speak!'), and he thought that 'it stood to reason' therefore that the name of the well was Bullán Mhíl Lab-hair. As we discussed this unconvincing derivation, another elderly Pat Hernon, Pat Phaidí, came down the hill, wearing an old zinc washtub upside down on his head and hanging down his back like a huge cowl. The three of us had a long conversation; a few raindrops pinged off the tub now and again. Pat Phaidí looked very strange, his wizened face sunken to noth-ing in the tub except for his bright eyes intently addressing me. Behind his ears I could see twists of rag stuffed into the tub's leaks; it had obviously long served as a cow-trough in some field above. He had heard that a leper once lived by the well and used to warn people off by saying, 'Mé lobhar', 'I, a leper'; hence its name, Bullán Mé Lobhar. Katie, Bobby Gill's wife, would know the real story, he thought. Nobody visited the well now, he said, but in the old days people used to pray there. He had seen 'a fine scis-sor' left beside it once. But all that was in the past. Sometimes, long ago, he used to kneel down there himself and say a prayer. Gradually edging nearer to the heart of the matter, he asked if I had noticed a *thráinín* in it today. I had, of course – the heather stalk. He looked pleased, and embarrassed. 'Well, it was me that put that there, now!' he confessed. I was glad that I had registered the little sign, and that I had seen its significance emerge in this way, like a shy animal peering from its burrow. Looking back on that conversation, I think of *The Colloquy of the Ancients*, the medieval text that tells how St Patrick, the newcomer, meets the last of the followers of Fionn Mac Cumhall and takes down from their lips the place-lore of the Celtic Ireland his own culture will supersede. Both the Pat Hernons are gone now, as irrevocably as the last of the Fianna, and what I did not note down of their talk that day is irrecoverable.

This well saved a life a few months later. Happening by, I made my usual detour to it in response to its garbled stories, and in a little dip of the ground beyond it I saw a donkey standing very quietly. Its stillness made me look again as I turned to go; its fore-feet were caught in a cleft, and to judge by the pile of droppings, it had been there some days. I tried to pull its legs up but I could only release one of its hooves. It was Sunday evening, and I thought as I hurried down to the village that it would be hard to persuade anyone to leave the television or postpone the pub for a mere donkey. However the first household I called at – Katie Gill's – was thrown into commotion by the news, and I was closely questioned as to the colour, sex and size of this donkey, matters I had not well noted. Very soon no fewer than ten of us, with pickaxes and crowbars and a bucket of water, were converging on the scene. It did not take long for the men to prise off a layer of the crag and, carefully, so as not to panic it, lift the animal free without twisting its leg. It drank from the bucket, then wandered off. The evening was beautiful, very still, as unprotesting about what had been going on in it as the donkey itself.

On our way back to the village I gathered a few more homespun etymologies of Bullán Mhaolodhair. Katie's version was well worth hearing. A blind man from Connemara had heard tell of the well, and came to Aran to see if he might be cured. Somehow he was left to find his own way to it across the crag, and while he was groping and stumbling, he heard a voice calling his name, 'A Mhíl, a Mhíl!' He followed the sound, and found the well, and found he could see. But he saw nobody near; the well itself had called.

This to me sounds like truth – truth of the mythic sort, which is strictly pragmatic, truth one can use. For instance, since the tale substitutes hearing for seeing, it proposes this well as a point from which to listen to the landscape, hushing the garrulous faculty of vision and letting the island recompose itself as music. The terrace of the well, in fact, is not only an elevation of the island's inhabited northern aspect, but it swings back southwards around the hillside towards the heaped boulder-banks and hollow cliffs of the coast below Dún Aonghasa, and so is unusually open to both the human and the inhuman sides of Aran. If one waits by the well until the turbidity of the mind settles, then the scratching of a bramble stirred across the rock by the breeze gives one ground to stand on, and a raven tolling overhead rounds out a sky; the whine of a motor-scooter growing out of one distance and fading into the other traces the line of the road below, and draws with it the entire life history of the lee-side, while a southerly wind brings the muffled drumbeat of the ocean across from the caverns of Blind Sound. How appositely the name itself, Blind Sound, comes in! – as if to make the point that, to the making of a point, all other points are apposite. But my sense of this truth is both foundational and precarious. I have once or twice walked on this crag with my eyes closed, hoping that nobody was watching from the hillside above, which is invariably, apparently, deserted. (When I hinted to M that I had been walking Aran blind, she was rather alarmed and told me to keep my experiments for literature.) Aiming to get to the well from the field-wall fifty yards before it, I found that I could feel my way over the large crevices easily enough, but I always ended up on the sloping ground to the left, no doubt because of an unmasterable, visceral awareness of the cliff to the right. The experiment clarified the nature of a step, though. As the foot descends through space, a surface exactly the size and shape of the foot-sole receives it; this support is the top of a column of inconceivable height that goes down and down, narrower and narrower, until it rests upon a point, a nothing, at the centre of the earth, and from that point opens up again in the opposite direction like the cone of futurity opening out of a moment, into the unsoundable.

CLOCHÁN

The road that turns north from the end of Cill Mhuirbhigh meets the main road at a junction called Na Ceithre Ród, the Four Roads. The fourth of the four is just a boreen leading down to the shoreline from which the various Hernons bring up their seaweed, or used to, at any rate. Two hundred yards down this boreen a still narrower track leads off to the west, picking its way between low field-walls and hawthorn thickets until it comes in sight of the rounded back of an ancient stone hut, as lichen-grey and ferny as any other hump of the stony ground, which is kept like a bull on its own in a little field entered by a narrow stile.

This is the largest and best-preserved of Aran's 'beehive huts'. Its name is Clochán na Carraige, the *clochán* of the rock; but since An Charraig (the rock), in its anglicized form 'Carrig', is used in some nineteenth-century sources for Sruthán, the next village west from Cill Mhuirbhigh, I take it that the hut is named from the area it stands in. Its basis is rectangular, about nineteen feet long by seven and a half wide, but the corners are progressively rounded off, starting a couple of feet above ground-level, to give the body of the chamber an oval plan, from which both the ends and the sides converge inwards, the stones in each course over-sailing the ones below on the inside, until the space to be closed is reduced to a long two-foot wide slit and topped off with a row of eight flagstones. The outside height is about eight feet. This corbelled construction is very stable for a circular or short oval building, since each layer is self-wedging like the stones in an arch, but it leads to a design weakness in the sides of a longer building, and this *clochán* noticeably bulges inwards on the west. Its walls are very thick, however, and the stones were carefully laid with a slight slant towards the outside, so that it is still stable, and only a few drops of rain or coins of sunlight can slip into the interior.

The two doorways are opposite each other in the side-walls, as in a traditional cottage. One enters almost crawling, under long, heavy lintels, for the openings are only about three feet high; and then, straightening up inside, one feels tall, and one's head is in a shadow-zone of upside-down light. At the south end there is a little opening which probably served both as window and chimney. Looked at from outside, these dwarfish doorways and cyclops window, and the hunched masonry that seems to lift itself grudgingly and effortfully from the ground, give the hut a look of immeasurable agedness. How old in fact is it? Probably medieval rather than early Christian, but it is hard to say. The only archaeological find made in it was of some whale-vertebrae which had probably been embedded in the stonework, a mysterious but unilluminating detail. The building method is one that predates Christianity, and when, for churches and the better class of dwellings, it was replaced by vertical, mortared walls, it persisted in humbler circumstances, housing the poor, then sheltering domestic animals. In fact just two fields to the north of Clochán na Carraige is a little *poirín*, probably built for raising goat-kids in, oval, roughly corbelled, with a lintelled doorway, the whole just two feet high, and recognizably of the seed and breed of the old grey bull slumbering nearby.

Máirtín Ó Direáin, tutelary seer of Sruthán, asks on our behalf the question we know beforehand will not be answered:

Ceist do chuireamar ar an gcloch
Ach an chloch níor labhair má chuala,
An scraith ar an díon féin
Níor léir a lua ná a thuairisc
Ar an té a ghabh chuige an áit
Mar theampall, mar thearmann go suarach,
Mar dhuasionad, mar shuanlios,
Gan cuilce faoina cheann ach gruáin.

We put a question to the stone
But if it heard it did not reply,
Even the scraw on the roof
Reported obscurely its observations
Of him who took the place to himself
As church, as sanctuary in wretchedness,
As sorrowing-site and slumber-fort,
With lumpy pebbles for his bedding.

Ó Direáin imagines a penitent, an exile from the community, driven out by hot-tempered Enda, living here without even a pet bird on his shoulder. But,

Tá an chloch ina tost is ní scéithfidh a rún linn.

The stone is silent and will not spill us its secret.

In fact the building is rather too grand for a hermit's cell; it was obviously built by people of means. It does not smell of the rising damp of guilt or loneliness either. I see a good fire before the door, a row of razorbills on a spit, children playing 'I'm the King of the Castle' on the roof, and inside, a pile of nets and traps and otter-spears at one end and a glorious mating going on at the other, four bare legs in a maelstrom of dry bracken.

However, if this was, or could become, a seat of eremitic contemplation, then there is enough of mystery around to engage it for eternity. Leaving aside the perfect far-off dovetailing of Connemara and the sky, and the twinkling profundities of the sea just half a dozen fields away, there is, for instance, a stand of *Aquilegia* or columbine on the limestone-flagged field one crosses to reach the stile before the *clochán*. The only places I have seen this plant in Aran, apart from obvious garden-escapes, are here, on a crag by the roadside to the north, and in the little glen of the donkey near Bullán Mhaolodhair. The mystery (for me, at least) is not its odd distribution, or even the botanical puzzle of whether this plant of fens and woodland is native to Aran, but this: why does the sudden sight of it as one approaches across the rough mosaic of stone and short-cropped grass –

hardly even a sight, so little is there to stop the eye, only the slightest screening of what is beyond by half-a-dozen tall slender stems, the few unemphatic grey-green leaves and indeterminately blue-to-pinkish blossoms being lost at a distance – make my heart catch itself back, as from a brink? What do they look like, these stems? Like the edges of things, perhaps the edges of panes of glass set in the air; or the edges of shadows of things, shadows seen sideways on. What are these things, not recognizable from the edges of their shadows? I think the air will not spill its secrets any more readily than stone.

A POET AND HIS VILLAGE

People used not to like walking the empty half mile between the Four Roads and the village of Sruthán after dark. Old Mícheál of Cill Mhuirbhigh, Máire's husband, told me the story of a man coming home from shooting wild geese on Oileán Dá Bhranóg one night, whose horse baulked at a certain spot halfway along that stretch of road. The man thought he saw a dark shape near a well by the roadside, and he took out a piece of *airgead croise* ('cross-money', Mícheál explained, a two-shilling coin with the cross on the back), held it over the muzzle of his shotgun and fired at the thing, which vanished on the spot. Then he galloped home as fast as he could, dropping his geese on the road. He sent his sister back to pick up the geese, and she saw nothing out of the way, but the next morning when folk going to Mass passed the spot they found the road full of ashes, or of stuff like jelly. Curiously enough, although Mícheál said he knew the man to whom this adventure had happened, and remembered seeing the gun hanging on the wall of his cottage, the well is called Tobar na Cúig Scilleacha, the well of the five shillings, which suggests that the story goes back to the time of the five-shilling or crown piece, which also had a cross on it.

Nowadays there is a bungalow on Creig an Tobair, the crag opposite the well – it was built for Mícheál and Máire's retirement, though in the end Mícheál could not be persuaded to move in because of the area's 'sheeogy' reputation – but it is only used in summer, and so there is still an uninhabited gap between the house at the Four Roads, formerly a Hernon family's and now a youth hostel, and the beginning of the long settlement the knowledgeable can subdivide into Sruthán, Eoghanacht and Creig an Chéirín. While it is a perfectly pleasant and by Aran standards unremarkable length of road, one does feel that this is the beginning of An Ceann

Thiar, the western headland, which is quieter than the rest of the island and a little detached from it. The hostel virtually marks the limit of the tourist itinerary, which seems over recent years to have consolidated and standardized itself around the pubs of Cill Rónáin and the excursion to Dún Aonghasa. There was a little shop in Sruthán and a bigger one in Creig an Chéirín until the late 'seventies, but now there are none; indeed there are no shops west of Cill Rónáin. This change reflects the fact that more households have cars nowadays and that there is a regular mini-bus service along the island; but I wonder if it also means an ebbing of life from the west.

> Feadaíl san oíche
> Mar dhíon ar uaigneas,
> Már fhál idir croí is aigne
> Ar bhuairt seal,
> Ag giorrú an bhealaigh
> Abhaile ó chuartaíocht,
> An tráth seo thiar
>   Níor chualas.

> Whistling in the night
> As shelter from loneliness,
> As a wall for heart and mind
> Against a spell of gloom,
> Shortening the road
> Home from visiting,
> In the west this time
>   I did not hear.

Máirtín Ó Direáin's poem on returning to his birthplace names other sounds he did not hear in the west that time: the reveller's tipsy song, wild boasts about heroic ancestors, joyous shouts of the lads throwing the *cloch neart*, the fifty-six-pound weight, on a Sunday afternoon. And he concludes:

> Ní don óige feasta
> An sceirdoileán cúng úd.

> No longer for the young
> That narrow blasted reef.

But the title of the poem, 'Árainn 1947', one has to note, dates it. There has been much whistling, boasting and shouting heard since then in the west, and the villagers of Ó Direáin's own generation I used to know here as old folk were very lively. I remember a spry old lady I met on that road to Sruthán, carrying a heavy bag of rye; I gave her a hand with it, and when I thankfully set it down on her doorstep she blessed me, and added, 'It might have killed me – but what harm!' Not everyone is as sure of the necessity of their own life-world as the poet, whose mirror-lined skull brings the reflections of formative years to a focus of definitive brightness.

The *sruthán* or stream from which the village is named seeps out of the foot of a glen coming down the hillside from the south, forms a little turlough, disappears under the road, and reappears in other springs and turloughs here and there down the slope to Port Chonnla on the north shore. Ó Direáin's sister Máire, a friendly old lady I used to visit, told me that before the road was built up and surfaced the water used to flow across it; in fact, she said, a lot of little streams did so, with flowers growing along their banks, 'and it was very nice – at least we thought it was very nice.' Most of the remaining thatched roofs are along a boreen following the intermittent stream downhill from the road, between overgrown sally-gardens and tiny broken-walled potato-plots. A curious plant scarcely known outside of Aran and west Connemara, the wild leek, *Allium babingtonii*, grows here and there in the fringes of the village, and further down towards the shore there are little plots full of it. *Gáirleóg* is its local name, and its bulb tastes like a mild garlic. It often grows in what look like deliberate plantings; but Bríd Gillan is the only person I know of who uses it in cooking, and whether it is native, or a variety of the cultivated leek gone wild, is something botanists disagree on. It has a stem three or four feet high and as thin as a cigarette, topped in spring by a turban-shaped knob that later sheds its papery wrap to show a round mass of bulbils, from which little purplish flowers grow out on snaky stalks. Nodding out of neglected corners on its bowed or crooked stems, it accosts one like some irreducibly ascetic revenant from a monkish kitchen garden.

This original nucleus of the village straggling down from the main road is very decayed. I remember one family who called me in to witness their squalor; the old woman by the fireside had to put up with the *braon anuas*, the drip from the ceiling, because they did not want to mend the thatch lest the improvement spoil their chances of a council house. In another cottage I drank milk with goat-hairs in it, from a sticky cup, and queasily declined a slice from a fly-infested side of bacon (but then some of the best stories in this book came from that household). I once peered in at the window of a cottage left untouched since the occupant, an old bachelor, had been carried out dead. A huge thistle rooted in the rotten board of the sill inside filled the little window like a specimen in a display-case; behind it the shelves of the dresser faintly gleamed with dozens of the tall straight-sided cream-coloured jugs, often bearing nostalgic scenes of cottage life, that Araners used to buy from travelling salesmen, more for decoration than for use.

The village has stretched westwards along the road from this moribund cluster, as a few bungalows and council-built houses have been sited in the fields between the older cottages. The former teacher's residence is recognizable, being of the standard design with central gable. Here lived Máirtín Ó Direáin's old schoolmaster Joe Flanagan, who as Seosamh Ó Flannagáin used to collect Aran folklore (including the tale of Aristotle and his wife) for the journal *Béaloideas*, and was drowned with two others when returning by currach from Roundstone after a pilgrimage to Croagh Patrick. Ó Direáin's sister's cottage, a quarter of a mile along, is a little below the level of the road; one looks down into its tiny front garden bordered with the big round stones her brother Tom had brought up from the shore and which she used to whitewash every year. Her kitchen, all lime-bright walls and brown-painted woodwork, was of the traditional design, with a tall ceiling space and an open staircase going up to a loft over the two small rooms to the east. The *seomra* to the west was high too, with no loft over it; it was comfortable and easy-going, unlike the 'best room' apparently kept polished in gloomy anticipation of the next wake in so many cottages; it relaxed by a hearth, and kept its things on shelves made out of orange-boxes painted brown, with another box to hide the gas-cylinder because Máire did not like the look of it when gas first came to the island. Here, the traditional meant the full of life. I used to call in during my mapping of the village; she was fascinated by the progress of the work, and wished Tom could see it – though if he had a couple of drinks in him, she told me, he would be sure to say, 'Ara, you have it all wrong!' She was an ample, soft, welcoming person; remembering her, I think of well-risen bread. In between stuffing a chicken and boiling potatoes and making tea for me and eating biscuits, she would bring me out to the little area at the back of the house, half flagged, half grassy, with hens and kittens and the interesting weeds she wanted me to see, the pair of us bobbing over them like hens: calamint, which her mother used to put in a bowl, though they never used it as mint; petty spurge, which a doctor had told her is the thing for curing warts (it does have a caustic sap); mugwort, one of those old-fashioned herbs for rough-and-ready medicine or magic, rather rare nowadays outside Aran, and groundsel, which she called chickenweed because they used to feed it to young chicks, who she said 'craved for it'.

Máirtín, it seemed, used to return much less frequently to the island than Tom; in fact his poems and essays make it clear that the Aran he found on his visits did not match up to the one he had carried with him in his head from childhood. The original family home was a tiny cottage a hundred yards down a twisty path that links the western end of Sruthán (Sruthán Beag, little Sruthán, as it used to be called) to the foreshore at An Gleannachán. It had been empty for a long time, and Máire had the idea that M and I might move into it, but the thatch had caved in and the low walls looked as if they were digging themselves deeper into the earth and would shortly withdraw entirely from this world. This would have been Ó Direáin's *'teach caoch ar shúil bhóthair'*, hollow house at road's opening, in 'Dán an Tí', the poem of the house. (The word-play is simple but untranslatable: the literal meaning of the phrase is 'blind house by road's eye' – the house he left to begin his life's journey.) Each element of the house demands a hearing; for instance, the hearth:

> *Ba mise croí an tí*
> *Atá fuar is folamh*
> *Éistear liom feasta:*
> *Ar m'uchtsa tharla*
> *Leis na cianta fada*
> *Feistiú na bhfód*
> *Adhnadh is lasadh*
> *Spóirseach thine*
> *Laom is deatach,*
> *Thart orm coitianta*
> *Cuideachta is caidreamh*
> *Ó ghlúin go glúin*
> *Scéalaíocht is nathaíocht,*
> *Spíonadh is cardáil*
> *Sníomh is cniotáil*
> *An tae beag*
> *Tráthnóna an lae bheannaithe,*
> *An biadán, an chúlchaint,*
> *An sciolladh, an feannadh,*
> *An paidrín páirteach*
> *Thar dhoras á leathadh,*
> *Go domhain san oíche*
> *An t-airneán á leanacht,*
> *Is mar dhíon ar shuan*
> *An tae ar tarraingt.*

> I was the heart of the house
> That am cold and empty
> I am to be heard now:
> At my breast there was
> Through many long years
> Setting of turf-sods

Kindling and sparking
Blazing fire
Flame and smoke,
Around me habitually
Company and closeness
From generation to generation
Story-telling and joking,
Wool-combing and carding
Spinning and knitting
Afternoon tea
On the Blessed Day,
Gossiping, backbiting,
Scolding, flaying,
The family rosary
With the door wide open,
Until late in the evening
Visitors still talking,
And to ward off sleep
The teapot brewing.

In this nest Máirtín's mother brought up four children by herself. Her first husband was Labhras Phatch Sheáin, one of the currachmen whose drowning so perturbed the sea-caverns, as I recounted in 'Tides of the Other World' in my first volume. They had only been married a few months at the time. Then she spent three years in America, and returned to marry Seán Ó Direáin, who was a sick man for years and died when Mairtín, their eldest child, was only six or seven. As his reminiscences in *Feamainn Bhealtaine* reveal, a certain memory of this pitiful father was for Máirtín one of those wounds that weep life long:

I remember a peaceful, drowsy afternoon. The sort of afternoon that is reluctant to give way to evening. My father was walking down the 'street' [the space between the cottage and the boreen] on his way to the garden down by the shore. Not that he was able to do much at that time, but his peevishness would not let him stay indoors. I called him a couple of names and threw a couple of little pebbles at him. I think he burst into tears. 'Now do you see what you've done to your father?' said my mother. She would have been right to give me a thrashing, however severe it was. I took myself off behind the gable, choked with shame, heartbreak and disgust.

Since the sixteen-acre farm could not support them all, and Máirtín had no hand for farmwork anyway, he left the island for a job in the Galway post office before his eighteenth birthday. In the city he joined the Gaelic League and acted in the Taibhdhearc, the newly founded Irish-lan-

guage theatre. In 1937 he moved to Dublin, and worked in the Civil Service until his retirement. Many of his poems express the loneliness and frus-
tration of exile from his people and their language, and his disgust with the
Ireland that had succeeded to the vision of its founders. Thus, the poem
'Mothú Feirge' (feeling of anger) from his 1962 collection, *Ár Ré Dhearóil*
(our wretched era):

> *Feic a mhic mar a chreimid na lucha*
> *An abhlann a thit as lámha na dtréan*
> *Is feic fós gach coileán go dranntach*
> *I bhfeighil a chnáimh ina chró bréan*
> *Is coinnigh a mhic do sheile agat féin.*

> See, my lad, how the mice have gnawed
> The Host that fell from the hands of the great
> And see too each snarling whelp
> Hoarding its bone in its filthy kennel
> And, my lad, keep your spittle to yourself.

While his ancestors, he felt, had pitted themselves against the reality of
bare rock and won from it lasting testimony to their existence – *'Thóg an
fear seo teach / Is an fear úd / Claí nó fál ...'* (This man built a house / And
that man / A wall or a fence ...) – our rootless generation would have a
mean and unreal memorial:

> *Beidh carnán trodán*
> *Faoi ualach deannaigh*
> *Inár ndiaidh in Oifig Stáit.*

> A dusty heap of files
> Is what will last of us
> In a governmental office.

But Ó Direáin was not just the reproachful and embittered spokesman
of a discarded past, or the elegist of the elemental simplicities and ancient
pieties of Aran; he also represented a new growth, and one which has flourished since. As an Irish-language poet of the generation he inspired has
written, 'In place of the metres and rhythms of folksong, he set the free
verse of today dancing by the hearth of Irish – and it is a testimony to his
importance as pioneer and his poetical genius that he was the first major
poet to do so.' This was publicly recognized; in 1977 he received an hon-
orary degree from the National University of Ireland, and President Ó
Dálaigh presented him with the Ossian Prize, an international award
funded by the Freiherr von Stein Foundation of Hamburg for work in a

traditional or minority culture. Several other honours followed before his death in 1988. Even his own people had begun to be persuaded of his stature by then, though some of them still look on it with the same contemptuous incomprehension as their parents showed towards his earliest magical appropriations of their village. I translate literally:

I began making '*fearachaí cloch*' (tiny stone men). If the word *fearachaí* is strange to you, I heard it as many times as I have fingers from grown-ups talking to us children; yes, and *beannachaí* (tiny women) too. A sort of baby-talk, I suppose. I made a likeness of each man and each woman of the village. I had a likeness of each house too. A hole in the wall or a little hollow made in a cliff served for a house. Thin flat stones made young men for me; flat stones a bit wider for the fathers, ones a bit wider again for the women because of the shawls they wore. I never felt time passing in the company of these *fearachaí* and *beannachaí*. I had total power over them. I could put them to sleep and wake them as I wanted. I could set them drinking and revelling, scolding and tongue-lashing each other, fighting and quarrelling. With these creatures of stone in the palm of my hand I was a little god. I had a little world of my own in the field down below the house. A world I had shaped, creatures I had shaped. ...

People saw me from the road down there by myself, and soon they were wondering at me. They started to talk. I wasn't all right. My mother heard about it. She went soft and hard on me asking me to give up the stone habit and be the same as the rest, but I didn't like to. I became more guarded, more cunning. I moved my 'tiny families' to another little pasture where I thought no one would ever see me, but I was found out. 'Throw them away from now on,' my mother said. 'It's no wonder you're ashamed of yourself, and half the island laughing at you!'

No one forced me to give up the company of the stones. I grew out of it myself slowly and by degrees, as we all grow out of the ways of our childhood. In the city when I told the story they said it had been the 'creative urge' at work in me. But even if I had known that name for it at the time it would not have protected me. No notice would have been taken of me.

In one of his later poems Ó Direáin puzzles over the ontological status of his Aran. He recalls Bishop Berkeley's theory that 'to be' is nothing more than 'to be perceived' and that outside the contents of our minds nothing exists. Dean Swift once reproved the Bishop for his fantastic speculation by refusing to open the door to him – for why should he open an idea to an idea? Dr Johnson's plain-man's contempt for the theory was reported by Boswell: 'I shall never forget the alacrity with which Johnson answered, striking his foot with mighty force against a large stone, until he rebounded from it, "I refute it thus!"' Ó Direáin, born and bred on a rock, was predisposed to the common-sense view too:

Ní shéanaim go raibh mo pháirt
Leis na móir úd tamall,
Ach ó thosaigh na clocha glasa
Ag dul i gcruth bríonglóide i m'aigne
Níl a fhios agam a Easpaig chóir
Nach tú féin a chuaigh ar an domhain
Is nach iad na móir a d'fhan le cladach.

I don't deny I took the side
Of those eminent men for a while,
But since the grey stones started
To take the form of dream in my mind
I do not know, my dear Bishop,
If you were not the one who sailed the deep
And the eminent ones who hugged the shore.

This doubt, according to Mac Síomáin and Sealy, the editors of his *Selected Poems*, amounted to a weakening of Ó Direáin's governing myth (which, I take it, is the abiding integrity of the old Aran, as opposed to 'our wretched era'), and his subsequent work rarely matched the resonance of the earlier 'island poems'. These commentators interpret Ó Direáin's rather cryptic late poem, 'Neamhionraic Gach Beo' (faithless is every living thing), which I looked into in Kilmurvey House, as an expression of 'deep and growing dissatisfaction with his creative work'. If I understand it, the poem says that life is perpetually seduced by the present moment and is therefore a betrayal of the past, and that only lifeless objects, *'cloch, carraig is trá / I lár na hoíche fuaire'* (stone, rock and strand / in the cold midnight), stay true:

Sleamhnaíonn nithe neamhbheo
Siar ón mbeo go bhfágann é:
An amhlaidh sin a d'fhág
An t-oileán mo dhán,
Nó ar thugais faoi deara é?

Inanimate things slip back
From the living until they leave him:
Was that how the island
Left my poetry,
Or did you notice it?

How would I comfort his shade, if I met him haunting this changed island? All the old fellows he celebrated in his early poems, in their neat bawneens and trousers of homespun tweed, all the old ladies in their red petticoats and Galway shawls, are gone; so, even, are his sister Máire and the other dwellers under thatch of Sruthán I have mentioned. Stone and the cold of midnight will indeed outlast those and all other generations. But his own death has freed his poetry from the perspective in which he, and perhaps we, could see it as in decline. There are new generations of children in Sruthán, and they learn it at school. Even admitting the terrible possibility of the death of his language, Ó Direáin's version of Aran will be re-worded again and again throughout whatever future we have, which even if it lasts as long as stone is unlikely ever to forgo the solace of the western myth he so perfectly expressed. ...

And if he rejects all this as mere whistling in the dark, I would take him down the twisty lane to the field below the old house, and set him to search through the grass and the holes in the walls until he had reassembled those once-impassioned pebbles of his childhood games, which, it occurred to me once in passing the spot, must still be lying there; and together we would contemplate the mysterious essence of stones, which is not their constancy – they were his, they are mine, and will be another's – but their ability to absorb all the words we write on them into the darkness of their cores.

EOGHANACHT

The fourth and last of Aran's townlands is Eoghanacht; the anglicized form Onaght gives a good approximation to the pronunciation. Its boundary runs from Port Chonnla on the north coast, following the Aran-north line of the glen that holds the stream of Sruthán village and nicks each successive step of the scarp-slope of the island; then it continues the same line across the plateau to the cliff-coast not far west of Dún Aonghasa. The boreen that follows the boundary up from Sruthán, with zigzagging divergencies to help in mounting the scarps, must have been widened and improved around the end of the last century when Henry Robinson of Roundstone was the land-agent, for the steepest part of it is known as Carcair Robinson. Dún Eoghanachta, the last of Aran's great cashels, sits on the terrace of the hillside half a mile above the main road, and to visit it one climbs the *carcair* and then takes a smaller path rambling through the fields along the slope to the west for a few hundred yards. John O'Donovan laid it down that the ancient name of this *dún* has been lost, and that it is now merely named from the townland; but of course the opposite is likely to be the case, if this was the original hub of settlement in the western lobe of the island. In any case a wealth of time-lore is invested in the *dún* by the name of the Eoghanacht, as will appear, which compensates for its present bare and unengaging look of being some purely functional thing that has lost its function.

Before entering, however, I will diverge from the approach to the *dún*, and look at certain obscure remains almost in its shadow, one minor step of the slope down from it to the north-east. Among brambles and bracken and a spider-web of field-walls are some hummocks and ridges of half-buried stone, which an archaeological team under Dr John Waddell of University College Galway, in 1973, tentatively deciphered as collapsed clocháns, the foundations of a little chapel, and part of a surrounding cashel wall. The most interesting feature of this very decayed monastic settlement is a triangular flagstone standing up among other broken flags that lean and lie around it, the remains of a sort of reliquary. Such 'slab-shrines', tent-like shelters about a yard high made of two rectangular flags leaning together with triangular flags closing either end, were not uncommon in the west of Ireland, and two almost complete ones can be seen at Teampall Chrónáin in the Burren. The possible chapel wall is ten paces to the north of the shrine, and about nine paces long. The site is marked 'Kilcholan' on the OS maps, and O'Donovan took down its name as Cill Chomhla or Cill Chonan. He heard that it was regarded as the grave of a saint. I talked to the old lady who owned those fields, Grannie Hernon in Cill Mhuirbhigh, and her pronunciation of the name would agree with O'Donovan's first version. She also told me that there is a pot of gold buried there, guarded by a black cat which she often saw when milking the cow. And once, when some men were about to disturb the old stones in order to mend the wall between her land and Concannon's to the west of it, they stopped when a voice said to them, *'Éistigí! Éistigí!'* (Listen! Listen!). I could not have expressed the essential more succinctly myself.

Dún Eoghanachta seems to dominate the sky above these ground-hugging monkish remains, for its rampart comes close to the break of the slope and stands twenty feet high at that point. A little west of Cill Chomhla, near another boreen passing up the hill from Eoghanacht village, is a large grassy hummock in which, according to the owner of the land, the Fir Bolg are said to have buried their tools after completing the fort. (In fact this hummock seems to be a settlement site, or a *fulacht fia*, a cooking site, perhaps of the Bronze Age.) He had heard this from Micilín Ó hIarnáin, the father of Colie Mhicilín, whose short stories of Aran life I mentioned in my first volume. Colie himself was the nearest to a *seanchaí*, a custodian of traditional lore, that we had in Eoghanacht – at least, his Sruthán neighbour Máire Pheige Cuaig used to refer to him as 'him that has all the talk' – and he held that the settled belief of the old generations was that the forts were

built by the Danes. Colie told me about the Danes in the course of a long
walk up the boreen from Eoghanacht onto the high plateau to the south.
In a field a little beyond the point where the boreen gives up and leaves one
to clamber over wall after wall towards the Atlantic cliffs, we looked at the
traces of some very wide ridges. We agreed that flax had probably been
grown in them, but Colie said that such ridges used to be 'put down to' the
Danes, who it seems were secretive about their skills. They had some sort
of manure; what it was, nobody knew, but it was supposed to be *i gceann
an iomaire*, in the head of the ridge, and it saved them going down to the
beach for seaweed. He had a story about it, which after some pressing I got
out of him, though only as a deprecating aside about 'foolish beliefs'. When
the Danes were dying out and there was only one man and his son left of
them, the Aran people were anxious to learn the secret of this manure, so
they captured the man and the boy and threatened to put them to death if
they would not tell it. The Dane eventually promised to tell, on condition
that they first kill his son so that he would not hear him betraying the
secret. So they killed the boy, and then the Dane said, 'You may do what
you want with me now, for I will never tell the secret.'

   I had read of a similar folktale, widespread in Ireland, in which the
Danes' secret is the recipe for making beer from heather; evidently Aran's
preoccupations differed from those of the mainland. This Aran version was
new to me, however, and I asked Colie why he had never told it to me
before. 'I thought you wouldn't be interested in that old rubbish,' he
replied.

   Dún Eoghanachta has not been examined in detail since Westropp's
day, and the dating-methods of modern archaeology have not been applied
to it, but from its general appearance the cashel as we see it now is probably of the Early Christian centuries. It consists of a single massive ring-wall,
most of it over sixteen feet high, except to the east, where the entrance is
rather broken down. It would take about a hundred and twenty good paces
to walk round it. As it did not need to be buttressed like the other cashels
when the Board of Works restored it in 1884, it has retained its original
simplicity; it can even appear rather dull in its severity. The wall has a slight
'batter' or inward inclination, and vertical joints running up the entire
height of it show that it was constructed in a number of lengths, perhaps
each the work of a separate team. Many of the stones in it are three or four
feet long. The total thickness of the wall is about sixteen feet, and, like the
principal ramparts of the other cashels, it consists of three separately faced
layers; the innermost layer is only brought up to a height of four to six feet
and forms a terrace around the interior, but the outer two have been finished off (perhaps in the restoration) to a common height, and the distinc-

tion between them is obscured. O'Donovan in 1839 made out that the doorway originally had been only three foot four inches wide, but its height and other characteristics could no longer be determined; Westropp in 1910 noted that it had been rebuilt and was about six feet wide. The interior space or garth is a very nearly circular plot of nibbled-down grass about ninety feet across. Apart from the low foundations of three straight-walled huts against the inside of the rampart, the garth is bare and flat; it seems to lay itself out for pacing to and fro. At five points of the circumference, steep ladder-flights of steps lead up to the terrace, and three of them, according to Westropp, were continued to the top of the parapet by diverging pairs of smaller stairs set sideways into the wall. One of these pairs is still quite clear, but the others are very delapidated. Otherwise the general appearance of the interior is of Board-of-Works efficiency, tidy, disappointing.

If in average daylight the *dún* seems to regard the past with a bored and disabused eye, one should revisit when wisps of mist are blowing through it, as I saw them once, a cantering procession of the near-invisible. Or one should attend to its name, which is one of those that says '*Éistigí! Éistigí!*' Here is a thread of the Eoghanacht story, teased out of a tangle of myths.

Not long before history began, when Conn of the Hundred Battles, ancestor of the Connachtmen, was King of Ireland, a rival hero, Eoghan Mór, seized power in Munster. Eoghan means 'good conception', and he was to give rise to the dominant sept of early medieval Munster, named after him the Eoghanacht. He was also highly regarded in mythological retrospect by Leinster, which believed that during his fosterage by a Leinster king he had helped to build a fort, by throwing into position a great stone no one else could shift. The builder of the fort was Nuadhu, ancestor-god of the Leinstermen, and by this deed Eoghan earned another of his several magical names: Mugh Nuadhat, the servant of Nuadhu. Thus Eoghan represents the entire southern half of Ireland, immemorially embattled against the north.

When Conn brought his forces against Eoghan at the battle of Carn Buidhe (near the present Kenmare), Eoghan would have been killed but for the magic of Éadaoin, a famous beauty of the other world, who made rocks appear as soldiers in the eyes of Conn's army, spirited Eoghan and his men away to her seven ships, tended their wounds, and allowed them to sail off to Spain. The princess of Spain fell in love with Eoghan, and gave him a cloak of the skin of a wondrous salmon she had caught; hence his third magical name, Eoghan Taidhleach, from his bright (*taidhleach*) cloak. He married the princess, and when after nine years he became homesick, he brought her back to Ireland with a fleet and an army supplied by her father. There he united the southern provinces against Conn once again.

After many battles Conn had to agree to divide Ireland with Eoghan. The boundary ran from the head of Galway Bay to Dublin Bay, the north being Leath Choinn or Conn's half, and the south Leath Mhogha or Mugh's half, and the boundary itself being the glacial gravel-ridges of the Eiscir Riada, that provided a winding route across the central boglands. But they fell out again over the division of Dublin Bay; Conn attacked and routed Eoghan's army, Eoghan and Conn wounded each other, and finally Eoghan was speared to death by Conn's warriors. However, his son Ailill Ólom secured the territorial rights of the Eoghanacht, by mating with (raping, according to a hostile version circulated by the Connacht interest) the goddess Áine, tutelary deity of Cnoc Áine in the middle of the fertile plains of Munster.

The dawn-light of history shows an Eoghanacht dynasty ruling from the great rock fortress of Cashel, and establishing its collaterals and its subject-peoples throughout Munster. They expanded north-westwards to Galway Bay, ousting the Connachta from that region with the aid of their vassals the Dal gCais, suppressing the indigenes of Ninuss, which seems to have comprised Corcomroe, the Burren, and the Aran Islands, and establishing in their place a branch of the sept, the Eoghanacht Ninussa. This probably happened in the fifth century, for it is reflected in the legend of St Enda's being granted Aran by the king whom St Patrick himself had converted at Cashel, Oengus mac Nadfroích. Eventually the Eoghanacht lines were to be supplanted by the Dal gCais, from whom Brian Borumha, and so the O'Briens, descended; but in its prime the Munster of the Eoghanachta was probably the most advanced and peaceable part of Ireland, cultivating the beginnings of writing in Irish, trading goods and ideas with Aquitaine and Gaul.

Of the seven Eoghanacht septs, the least known to history is the Eoghanacht Ninussa. They had evidently lost their territory to the Corcu Modruad, the aboriginals of Corcomroe, by 1016, when the latter's king was killed by the Conmaicne (presumably those of Connemara) in the Battle of Aran, in the bay below Mainistir. References to the Eoghanacht Ninussa in the annals and genealogies for the intervening four hundred years are very sparse, and the name of Dún Eoghanachta is one of the few memorials of their reign. Another is *The Voyage of Maol Dúin*, one of the great *immrama* or voyage-tales, which after long oral evolution was written down in the ninth century by Aed Finn, chief sage of Ireland, 'for the elation of the mind and for the people of Ireland after him'.

Aran knowns nothing of Maol Dúin or indeed of the Eoghanacht, but this fantastic story may even be rooted in Aran, for the hero's father, Aillil Ochair Ágha, is described as a warrior of Árainn. I leap to the conclusion that he lived in Dún Eoghanachta. Maol Dúin's mother was a nun; again it is intuitively obvious to me that she lived in one of the huts of Cill Chomhla, in the shadow of Ailill's ramparts. Ailill had died before the child was born, and he was given to a queen of some other realm and reared in company with her three sons. Maol Dúin excelled them in all things, so that they became jealous and teased him with his ignorance of his parentage; this drove him to discover that his father had been killed by men of a Leinster sept. A druid in Corcomroe advised him to build a boat and go with a crew of exactly seventeen men to seek revenge. His three foster brothers insisted on joining the crew, and he accepted them reluctantly. They arrived off an island where they overheard a man boasting that he was the slayer of Ailill, but because the druid's council had been violated, a storm erupted just as they were about to land, and swept them out to sea.

The involuntary pilgrimage that follows perhaps represents an expiation of Ailill's sin against the Christian community, and the descriptions of some of its stations are allegories as crystalline as those of Bunyan. But mingled with these are dream-like episodes that read like the return of the suppressed matter of Celtic belief, and are both enigmatic and disquieting. It has been suggested that what we have here is the tattered remains of an oral, Celtic equivalent of the Tibetan or Egyptian Books of the Dead, a chart of the successive states the departed soul passes through. This guide-book to the adequate death touches upon thirty-three visionary sites, and only a full list can do justice to them:

An island of ants as large as foals; an island of great birds; an island of a horse with hound's claws; an island of giant horses running a race; an island in which salmon are hurled by the sea through a stone valve into a house; an island of trees, from which Maol Dúin cuts a rod that bears three apples, each of which sustains him for a fortnight; an island with a beast that can turn its body round inside its skin; an island red with the blood of carnivorous horses that rend each other; an island of fiery swine; an island with a treasure-house guarded by a little cat that leaps right through one of the foster brothers when he tries to take a necklace, and reduces him to ashes; an island with a palisade separating white sheep from black, and a guardian who sometimes moves a sheep from one part to the other, whereupon it changes colour; an island of giant cattle and swine separated by a river of fire; an island with a mill in which is ground 'all that men begrudge to one another'; an island of mourners in black, where one of the foster brothers becomes unrecognizable through grief, and is left behind; an island with fences of gold, silver, brass and crystal, segregating kings, queens, warriors and maidens; an island with a fortress approached by a glass bridge, where a beautiful maiden seems to have expected their coming, but when they try to woo her for Maol Dúin she puts them off, and they wake next day to find themselves far at sea again; an island of birds that shout; an island with many birds and an anchorite clothed only in his long hair, who had come there sailing on a sod of his native land, which by God's will had grown by one foot's breadth and put forth one tree every year since then, the birds being the souls of his kindred awaiting Doomsday; an island with a fountain that yields water and whey on Fridays and Wednesdays, milk on Sunday and certain feast-days, and ale and wine on other feast-days; an island with a forge worked by a giant; a sea of glass of great splendour and beauty; a sea like a transparent cloud, through which they look down on a land in which a monster preys on a herd of oxen; an island where the people shout 'It is they!' as if they had expected their coming and feared it; an island with an arch of water like a rainbow full of salmon over it; a silver column rising out of sight, with a silver net hanging from it, from which one of the voyagers brings home a piece to offer on the high altar at Armagh; an island on a pedestal with a door at its base; an island of women who try to seduce them into a life of perpetual youth and pleasure, which bores them, so that they leave after three months that seem like three years; an island with trees of intoxicating and soporific berries; an island with a hermit and an ancient verminous eagle, which renews itself in a lake; an island of mirth, where the last of the foster-brothers is overcome by laughter and has to be left; an island with a revolving rampart of fire, through the doorway of which, when it comes round to them, they glimpse a life of luxury and music; an island where a monk is doing penance for robbing the church, who advises Maol Dúin to forgive his father's slayers; an island where they see a falcon like the falcons of Ireland, which guides them homewards.

Finally, they come back to the island of the slayer of Ailill, where their arrival is being discussed at that moment, and are made welcome.

Separation of absolute essences seems to be a theme of this bizarre itinerary. Perhaps Maol Dúin's voyage takes us behind the scenery of this life, and shows how crudely and arbitrarily it is tacked together out of such opposites and abstractions as black and white, warriors and maidens, laughter and grief, solitude and company. If so, like all visions of the other world it is a reductive and delusory account of this one. The wonders Maol Dúin encountered are as nothing to those of his native island, if that was indeed Aran; our salmon-leaping rainbows match his. In fact with a little ingenuity I could show that each of the islands he saw was Aran, approached from a different direction.

Pilgrimage, the ritual of attending to things one by one as we come to them, enacts a necessity forced on us by our limitations, our lowly evolutionary stage of mind. In reality everything is co-present (or at least, and so as not once again to oversimplify, an uncountable number of stories struggle competitively through every event of space-time). Even a pilgrimage narrow-mindedly devoted to one end is endlessly ambushed and seduced by the labyrinth it winds through, while the most comprehensive course we can chart through the incomprehensible is an evasive shortcut. Here, standing in this boring dún of Eoghanacht, I am trampled down by all that I might have bethought myself to say of it, as by the phantom horses of the streaming mist. But I am the servant of finitude, and must press on.

SEVEN CHURCHES AND A FACTORY

Two jagged strips of land running from north coast to south correspond to two subdivisions of the village of Eoghanacht; each has its boreens running downhill to its share of seaweed in the bay of An Gleannachán, and uphill to a thousand fields of Na Craga. The eastern section is Ceathrú an Turlaigh, the quarter of the turlough; this was the land contentiously acquired by Patrick O'Flaherty and from which his son James's stock was driven over the cliffs. In the time of the Johnstons, the two-hundred or so acre holding was sold off for £400 to an islander from Inis Meáin who had returned from America with money. Máirtín Ó Concheanáinn was a brother of James Concannon, owner of the Concannon vineyards in California. The curious mansion he built for himself in 1903, like a flat-roofed version of Kilmurvey House, is set back from the road on the right, a little beyond the turning down to the old Ó Direáin cottage. As a child Máirtín Ó Direáin himself used to marvel at this big house next door, which his mother told him was like houses she had seen in America. He also saw with amazement the straw hat worn by a visitor to the house. Later he heard that some of the people staying there spoke Irish; in fact another of the Concannon brothers was Tomás Bán, the famous Gaelic Leaguer, and no doubt he often visited.

The smaller tenants of the village had their land in the western section, Ceathrú an Oicht, which used sometimes to be englished as Breastquarter, and is so called because it lies across the breast of the higher ground to the west. The boundary between the two quarters largely follows a slight notching of the stepped hillside, where erosion has found out a vulnerable major joint of the north-south set. This little glen cuts down through a line of low cliffs just above the village, and opens out into a flat space, now occupied by the factory, by the roadside. Immediately below the road, to the north, the same geological weakness has reproduced the same topography, a v-shaped recess in the rim of the next terrace, and here the naturally-provided sheltery site between the divergent cliffs is occupied by the group of monastic ruins from which the village gets its alternative name, Na Seacht dTeampaill or the Seven Churches.

When I first came to Aran, the factory was merely a large shed of cement-coloured cladding, with a surly generator growling in a kennel beside it, and I was shocked that anyone could have thought of siting such a construction just here, where the contrast between its deadly greyness and the living grey of old limestone masonry mottled with roundels of lichen was as painful as could be. How did it come about that the most comfortably off generation Aran had ever known was responsible for the first ugly building the valley of the Seven Churches had seen in the fourteen hundred years of its history? The obvious answers, that that generation was by no means prosperous in the perspective of twentieth-century Europe, and that the shed was merely the beginnings of a development that helped to keep the community together throughout the next two decades, are true, but evasive. A proper answer would be a full diagnosis of 'our wretched era'.

The number 'seven' is an invocation of the magical; there are in fact only two churches here, and the remains of probably eight other monastic buildings. They nest in the lee of the cliffs, casually clustered; all are ruins, roofless, some of them much reduced. But still, when one glances down into the site from the road it gives an impression of busyness, of concentration on its interior life; one hears the hum of these hives for the honey of the invisible. The many-cornered, uneven and overgrown spaces between them have been used as a graveyard for centuries; by the main church the ground is paved with obscurely lettered slabs, and everywhere it is lumpy with burials, so that the digging of a new grave is an anxious matter to the islanders, who hate to disturb old bones. The most recent head-stones of Italian marble, the sombre recumbent flags of the last century, and the dumb boulders marking infants' graves, are all in an elegiac huddle with Early Christian stones bearing cryptically abbreviated inscriptions, including the famous 'VII ROMANI', romantically supposed to mark the resting-place of seven pilgrims from the Holy City itself, drawn by the echo of Aran's prayers.

This quiet depository of time is almost in the heart of the village. Colie Mhicilín's cottage is set among the small plots and ragged bare rocky areas above its rim; I often called there in search of local guidance. Colie would edge me out of the kitchen, which was always billowing with daughters, into his stiff, chilly little 'room', hung with framed certificates for the five-pound and ten-pound prizes he had won at Irish-language festivals, and we would stand awkwardly at the table, looking at my maps or the lists of placenames he used to draw up for me. Then we would step out along the way he took to the cow every day: across a few yards of crag, down steps hardly more than toe-holds in a wrinkle of the scarp-face, along a path where elderbushes hiding a neglected holy well caught at one's sleeve, and so between the ruins, with a pause by his wife's recent grave, to the stile leading out onto the sideroad going down through a few big sandy fields to the bay. Sometimes he would stop, to give me one of his short stories *in extenso*, closing in on me with his watery eyes and spluttery breath. One of them was about a weasel looking through a hole in a wall at the goose it intended to kill; acting it out, Colie leaned forward, baring his yellow teeth and fixing his eyes on my throat. Paralyzed in my listening mode, I nearly despaired when he suddenly revised the story: 'No, there wasn't one goose, there were seven!', and I had to drag his attention back to the problem in hand, the correct identification of the various 'saints' beds' here and there around the monastery.

In the summer seasons of the 'seventies I used occasionally to find students at work in the Seven Churches, measuring up the old buildings and taking rubbings of the carved stones; they were from University College, Galway, and it is from the report published by their director, John Waddell, that I draw most of the archaeological facts I have stirred into the following account of the monastic site. Teampall Bhreacáin, St Brecan's church, is the hub of the settlement. This is the largest ancient church in Aran, with a nave and chancel both eighteen feet broad and totalling about forty-two feet in length, separated by a round-headed arch. The arch and the lancet window in the east gable, with its wide internal splay rising to a slightly pointed arched head, are thirteenth-century work, transitional in style between Romanesque and Gothic, formed of smoothly cut stone in silvery contrast to the harsher and darker masonry of the walls. The round-headed door in the south wall, and the window near it, were probably inserted two or three centuries later, and are contemporary with the altar under the east window and a partition wall dividing off the west end of the nave. Looking at the west gable from inside, one sees that it was made by enlarging an older gable, which, like the north wall, is made of much bigger blocks, including one a good six feet long. On the outside, one of the antae of the original building remains, like a pillar reinforcing the north corner of the gable wall. Clearly the south and east walls of this earlier church were removed, in order to enlarge it into the nave of the present church. There is an inscription on a raised band of stone on the old part of the gable: OR AR II CANOIN, 'a prayer for two canons' (the OR standing for ORÓIT). I wonder at the self-abnegation of this anonymous joint plea: dò these two individuals need the same prayer?

The other church is small and undivided, and probably dates from the sixteenth century, to judge by the slim, trefoil-headed window-light in its east gable and the doorway in the north wall, over which two undecorated curved bits of stone lean together to form the most basic Gothic arch. It is tucked into the corner of the site nearest the road, where the glen narrows into a cleft, and its name, Teampall an Phoill, the church of the hollow, simply reflects its situation; no doubt it had a more arcane name once, which is forgotten.

The domestic buildings of the monastery are of similar late medieval date. Five of them stand to a height of several feet, and the foundations of three more are traceable. They mainly have opposite doors in each of their long walls, like traditional cottages. One has two little windows with ogee'd heads cut out of single blocks, and another, a window of two trefoil-headed lights, quite simply constructed and chamfered, but richly decorative in its setting in the sober grey stonework. A curious toothy-topped wall zigzagging round the site is largely the creation of the Board of Works, who did some restoration-work here towards the end of the last century, but one stretch of it, near the stile by which one climbs down into the graveyard from the sideroad on the west, is also probably medieval. The blocked-up lintelled doorway in it, Colie tells me, was once tall enough for a horse and rider to pass through; over the years, what with burials and overgrowth, the ground-level has risen.

This, and another length of old wall with a pointed archway, between it and the big church, perhaps formed part of an enclosure around a number of 'penitential stations' or leabaí (literally, 'beds'), regarded as saints' graves, at which pilgrims used to perform their devotions. The nearest of these to the arched entrance is a roughly rectangular, double-bed-sized plot surrounded by a low dry-stone parapet. It is called Leaba an Spioraid Naoimh, the bed of the Holy Ghost, a dedication that puzzles people, as such 'beds' are usually named after their presumed makers or occupants. Colie Mhicilín told me he once heard an old man explaining to another islander that the Holy Ghost was buried in it. ('But that couldn't be,' added Colie, 'for the Holy Ghost is – God!' – with a slight hesitation, looking at me as if for confirmation of this theological conundrum.)

Within living memory both islanders and visitors from the mainland used to sleep in Leaba an Spioraid Naoimh in hope of or to give thanks for spiritual favours, and several cures – crutches thrown away, etc. – are attributed to the practice. An elderly Sruthán villager, Cáit Faherty, told me a story about a Connemara family who brought a loaf and a three-pound slab of butter with them, which they left to hand on the parapet overnight. A thief came while they slept, and was on the point of making off with the food, when it was miraculously turned to stone. The two stones are still there, she told me, but not many people know their story, so they are usually thrown aside or tidied away somewhere, and she used to go searching for them and put them back by the bed. The loaf was of the tall, round shape they used to make in pots, and the thief had broken one pound off the lump of butter, which Cáit always fitted together again with the rest. I have never seen these stones, which may well be lying around somewhere nearby, but they are visible in a photograph of the bed taken by T.H. Mason in the early 1930s. Mason had no Irish, and all he could gather about them, from an old man who had very little English, was that the cylindrical loaf-stone had some supernatural power or origin, and this led Mason to speculate, incorrectly, that it was a cursing-stone.

Part of the shaft of a high cross stands at one corner of this bed, and there are other chunks of it lying nearby. It is elaborately carved. On its west face, at the foot, is a square panel in which two serpents, arranged into four symmetrical whorls, bite each other's heads; above that is a panel of six abstract knots, and above that again, the lower part of a crucifixion, with the two thieves (it is supposed) shown as dangling manikins on either side of Christ's legs. Originally the cross would have been about seven feet high, with a ring around the intersection of the arms and the shaft, and deep cusps in the angles between them. Like two other crosses, now lying in fragments to the north and the south of the monastic site, it is similar in style to the Cill Éinne crosses attributed to a late eleventh- or early twelfth-century school of sculptors working both in Aran and Clare. Of the two fragmentary high crosses, one is on the bare craggy level above the monastery and near the main road, in a little enclosure Colie names as Leaba Bhreacáin, and which used to be regarded by the villagers as the saint's original chapel. Just a dozen paces east of it is St Breacán's holy well, Tobar Bhreacáin, a natural solution-hollow or bullán in the limestone, with a little canopy of rough limestone blocks over it that sometimes serves as a hearth for the village's St John's Eve bonfire. The bits and pieces of the cross were collected from around the ruins and put together by William Wilde in 1848, and unfortunately at some period they were cemented down. This cross was about twelve feet high, with a ringed head, and its visible face is decorated with panels of knots and fret-patterns. The third cross is in a low rectangular enclosure reached by crossing a field northwards from the graveyard. Only the stump is still standing, and eight substantial bits of the shaft lie beside it, having been gathered together by Samuel Ferguson in 1852. It was originally over thirteen feet high, with a small ring, and cusps in the intersections of shaft and arms. On what was its eastern face is a figure of Christ (crucified, presumably, but the arms and nub of the cross are missing), with a smaller figure on either side, too rudimentary to be definitely identifiable as the two thieves, or as the Virgin and St John, or as the usual occupants of this position, the sponge-bearer and the lance-bearer. The rest of the shaft-face and its reverse are carved with panels of plait-work, which here and there degenerates into tangles. These errors, made in the latter stages of what must have been months of chiseling, were no doubt severely criticized, but evidently they were not considered serious enough to lead to the stone's abandonment, so there they lie, for me to nod at, a monument to a labyrinthographer astray.

Next to Leaba an Spioraid Naoimh, on its south, is a low grassy platform with a stone surround, which archaeological reports refer to as Leaba Bhreacáin. By it there stands a large squarish slab with an incised cross in a double circle; one quadrant is missing, and the others are lettered thus: SCI BRE ... NI, which, when the contraction indicated by the line above the first group of letters is unriddled, and the missing letters plausibly supplied, is a dedication to St Breacan. This stone was found in 'St. Brecan's grave' in about 1825 when it was opened for the burial of some Galway ecclesiastic, but whether the grave, as opposed to the bed, of St Breacan is this present enclosure, or one in the south-east corner of the graveyard, is not clear, for archaeologists, Ordnance Survey and local tradition are at sixes and sevens over the names of these enclosures. Underneath the slab was found a little stone cresset lamp, now in the National Museum, with the inscription OR AR BRAN N AILITHIR, 'a prayer for Bran the Pilgrim', which I mentioned apropos of Oileán Dá Bhranóg in my first volume. A fragment of another inscribed cross-slab stands in this bed, reading OR AE MAINACH, ' a prayer for Mainach'.

There are fourteen more stones and slabs with inscriptions or crosses of various forms scattered around the graveyard. The 'Seven Romans' stone stands with two others by what Colie says is Breacán's grave, in the south-east angle of the cemetery wall. It is a slab about three feet high and one across, with a broadly grooved cross dividing its face into four cantons, inscribed VII RO MA NI. George Petrie, who first recorded it, took it to be the gravestone of seven pilgrims from Rome. However, it seems unlikely that a group of seven all died or were buried together. Macalister, writing in 1913, considered that the inscription was a dedication to 'the seven martyred sons of Symphorosa, who are named in the Irish martyrologies of Oengus and of Gorman, under date 27 June'. Recently Peter Harbison has pointed out that in early medieval Latin the word 'Romani' can mean those spiritually dependent on Rome, and quotes the 'Irish Litany of Pilgrim Saints', written around 800, which starts by invoking 'thrice fifty coracles of Roman pilgrims'. He suggests that the stone may have been commissioned by pilgrims from Rome or, more probably, by a group of Irish who had made the pilgrimage to Rome, to mark their stay in Aran. In either case he sees the stone as evidence for the thesis that Aran was an important station in an established pilgrim-route linking a rosary of the holy places of Atlantic Ireland – Mount Brandon and Skellig Michael in Kerry, St Macdara's Island off south-west Connemara, Inishmurray in Sligo, Glencolmcille in Donegal – all more easily reached by sea than by land. This pilgrimage would have been at its height in the twelfth century, but may have persisted until much later – it was in 1607 that the Pope granted a plenary indulgence to all who visited the churches of Aran on the Feast of Sts Philip and James, and on the Feast of St Peter's Chains. If so, we can picture the long (thatched?) buildings of the Seven Churches as the hostel offices, dormitories and refectories for an international coming and going of pious backpackers.

Another intriguing possibility, that does not preclude the above, is that the Seven Churches was an Augustinian monastery. I have come across two scraps of evidence. Firstly, a report sent to Rome in 1658 by the Archbishop of Tuam, John de Burgo, who had been expelled by the Cromwellians, stating that there was once a monastery of Canons Regular of St Augustine in Aran, 'whose name has slipped my memory in my exile in France.' Secondly, a note on Eoghanacht added to the census of 1821 by Patrick O'Flaherty: 'There are near this village ruins of 7 churches and a monastery of the Augustinian Order with a burial ground annexed.' These are the only mentions of an Augustinian foundation in Aran I know of; together they amount to – a speculation.

The Seven Churches is of course not the ancient name of this foundation; papal documents of 1302 and 1466, for instance, refer to it as 'Dísert Brecán', a *dísert* (literally, a desert) being a common term for the site of a hermitage. Brecán (Breacán in modern Irish) himself is one of the obscurer saints, and no early *Life* of him survives. Outside of Aran, he is associated with Kilbreckan in County Clare, and Cill Bhríocáin in Ros Muc, Connemara. A Brecán associated with King Guaire in Durlus near Kinvara, and another with Ardbraccan in County Meath, are perhaps not to be identified with 'our' Brecán, although the latter's coarbs or successors in Clare later asserted their rights to tribute from his namesakes' foundations. These claims are made in a poem purporting to have been composed by the saint himself, but probably dating from the fourteenth or fifteenth century, of which the sole surviving copy is written for some reason on a flyleaf of a manuscript on astronomy dating from 1443. Brecán, on his deathbed, addresses himself to his pupil and great-grand-nephew, on the essential matter of tributes due to him and his heirs:

> *Eridh suas, a Tolltanaigh,*
> *go ngabhmais tres dar salmaibh,*
> *a naoimh feta orrtanaigh,*
> *seal beg rem cur a talmain.*

> *Do deoin Mic Dhe dénasa*
> *an gabhail seo do ragha,*
> *scribhthar let mo scelasa*
> *& scribthar mo cana.*

> Arise, o Tolltanach,
> and let us recite our psalms,
> o quiet prayerful saint,
> for a while before my burial.

> God's Son willing,
> do you recite this canticle,
> write down my history
> and write down my dues.

The saint's continued protection of the ruling families in his territories, he makes clear, is provisional upon the payment of these dues to his successors: 'May their enemies not destroy them, provided they pay my taxes.' The king of Meath had given Brecán his harness and saddle, and his successor is entitled to the same, which as he points out, 'is not too onerous'. In Clare, Brecán had baptized the Maol Domhnaigh (Muldowny) clan, and for this his coarbs should have the right to a circuit (of free hospitality, I presume) every seven years, also a tunic from every maiden, a present from every ecclesiastical tenant, a large horn from every housewife, a lamb from every sheepfold; in return Brecán bequeaths good fortune and excellence of feasting to the handsome family and well-being to their cows. Various other clans are similarly assessed. In the Kinvara area of Doorus and Durlus he was in conflict with another saint, and had to curse the cows of the region so that 'they would feel the torment of thirst at the onset of bulling and lactation', but he got a screpall (threepence) from every household there. The contentious territoriality of this saint matches well with his role in the Aran story of his dividing the island with St Enda. The poem ends by stamping the seal of divine authority on his testimony:

> *Ag sin ní dom scelaibhsi*
> *Rí nime dam do reighid,*
> *a hucht Ísa admuim sin*
> *denasa, a daltain, eiridh.*

As me Brecan builideach,
mac rí Muman go treighaibh,
d'innsin scel na fuinidech,
a Toltanaigh, & eridh.

This is something of my story
revealed by heaven's King,
in Jesus's name I confirm it,
do it, o pupil, arise.

I am the prophetic Brecán,
accomplished son of Munster's king,
telling the tale of the western world,
o Toltanach, arise!

Thus the poem claims royal origins for Brecán, and the medieval genealogies do indeed situate him as the son of Eochaidh Bailldhearg of the Dál gCais, who himself had been baptized by St Patrick. The poem itself gives further details, no doubt drawn from earlier sources now lost. We learn that the saint's original name was Bresal, and that he was a cavalry soldier before his baptism. He was fostered and reformed by Pupu mac Birn, who some old sources identify with St Enda's successor Nem and with Enda's companion on the visit to Rome, Pupeus. Then he established his *dísert* at a place called Iubhar, where everyone was pleased when he expelled the devils. (Another medieval reference to Iubhar specifies that it was in Aran. The name means 'yew-tree', and the only Aran placename with such an element in it today is Eochaill, yew-wood, a few miles to the east of Dísert Brecán.)

The purpose of this confabulation is clearly to legitimize the claims of the foundations ascribed to St Brecán. The link with the royal line of the Dal gCais, which culminated in Brian Borumha, would have redounded to these foundations' prestige. But one detail of the poem, perhaps a chance survival from a more ancient tradition, seems to give the saint a pedigree from another dimension altogether. When he came to Aran, he tells us:

Brecan crodha clairingnech
do bí romam san Iubhar,
a cur as ro aemhasa
is do naemus a inadh.

Do rinnus fan Iubharsa
scel bec nach coir do leighadh,
do deoin De gan díchuinnus
do dicuiris an gégar.

Fierce Brecán clairingnech
was there in Iubhar before me,
I undertook to expel him
and sanctified his place.

I took action over Iubhar
(no harm to read the little tale)
by God's will and without violence
I expelled the fierce one.

This 'little tale' is read by the modern editor of St Brecán's poem as 'the account of his destruction of a reigning idol, Brecán, whose name he took, and of his conversion of the pagan sanctuary into a Christian *dísert*.' But that is to drag the episode out into the light of history, whereas surely we are on the cusp between history and mythology here, and what is happening under our eyes is the transformation of a local Celtic deity into a wonder-working Christian saint. This event took place in the realm of interpretations, not on the solid ground of Aran.

Some fourteen hundred years later an attempt was made to install the cult of the golden calf in the valley of the Seven Churches. Next to the grey shed I have mentioned, in which a few girls of the village made dolls for sale at Shannon Airport, an 'advance factory' arose in 1973, a factory, that is, built in advance of knowledge of any prospective lessee, in the hope that the grants and tax-breaks on offer from the government would tempt some company to locate part of its operations in this highly disadvantageous industrial *dísert*. Soon it was announced that a Birmingham jewellery firm would be taking over the premises, for the manufacture of keeper-earrings and other little items of gold. For some reason we, like many others, were dubious about this company, but an executive of Gaeltarra, the forerunner of today's Gaeltacht Development body, assured us that their *bona fides* had been checked out in Hatton Garden, which sounded impressive. An extraordinary number of public representatives and journalists were flown out to witness the opening of the new factory, and to hear the Minister say, 'The establishment of such an industry in a relatively isolated region is not only a major breakthrough in the development of our Gaeltacht islands, but, in this time of world economic depression, it can be regarded as a truly historic occasion.' Apart from the factory premises, Gaeltarra was investing £170,000 in training and equipment grants in the new enterprise, which was expected to provide over eighty full-time and some part-time jobs. However, Dara the postman with his usual sceptical delivery remarked to me, 'They're all here to see it open, but none of them will be here to see it closed!'

After the ceremony we met the works manager, who was still round-eyed from the experience of coming out from Galway in the *Naomh Éinne*, the old tub had stopped off Inis Meáin first, and the natives had rowed out to meet it in their currachs, 'like savages!' he said, obviously wondering if the values of Brum could be imparted to such anthropophagi. Relationships between the management and the indigenes were not good from the beginning. Soon an advert appeared in the papers; a foreman was required, who must be a disciplinarian. Clearly, the missioners of the Black Country suspected that certain theological concepts, such as '8.30 sharp every weekday morning', and especially '8.30 sharp even on the morning after a Sunday-night *céilí* dance', were not well developed here.

We also got to know a young worker sent across from the mother-factory, presumably as an example of what was required. Roy often called in at the Residence to reminisce about city life: the crunch of his Doc Marten boots as he walked down to the Bull Ring on a Saturday night; the roar of his motorbike when he was tormenting the bourgeoisie of the suburbs on a Sunday afternoon. We heard about his unrequited love for an island girl employed in the factory. She complained that the dance he performed in the Community Hall was too violent; but, as he tried to explain, it had to be violent because it was the Angel Dance. (Roy was a Hell's Angel, or had cherubic aspirations to be one.) One Friday afternoon when she was working a press that stamped out small components one by one, Roy offered to help her finish off a rush-job. The machine was controlled by two buttons, one on either side, which had to be pressed simultaneously, thus keeping the operator's hands out of harm's way. Roy kindly showed her a method of speeding up production: he would press one of the buttons for her, while she positioned the blanks and pressed the other. Inevitably, she nearly lost a finger, which blighted his chances for ever.

The proprietor of the business used to fly in occasionally with his teenage mistress and stay at a nearby guest-house. As it happened, we never met them, although Roy told me, man to man, that it would be worth while strolling up to have a look at the girl. Soon the guest-house owner was getting sick with anxiety as unpaid bills mounted up. We wrote letters on his behalf, to no avail. I remember the anguish in his voice, trying on the telephone with his limited English to get through the practised evasions of a receptionist in Birmingham, shouting at her, 'Tell him to tell him I told him to tell him!' Aer Árann were in a stronger position to get their dues; once when some factory executives were waiting in the plane for take-off, the pilot ordered them out, and left them stranded. It was about three years before the bubble burst. No more than about twenty-two had been employed, and suddenly they were told to take a week's holidays. Anxious renegotiations of terms took place between Gaeltarra and the management, but finally Gaeltarra had to move very quickly to prevent them shipping out machinery bought with the taxpayers' money. Dara's prophecy was fulfilled exactly. There was scarcely a word about the collapse in the papers. We wondered how much cultural damage had been done by the barbarian invasion brought down upon Aran by the official protectors of its well-being, but in the event, the island remained philosophical about its proven insufficiency to modern times.

A year later, in 1979, an Irish company, Telectron Ltd, took over the factory, with similar fanfares, for the assembly of telecommunications gear. I never knew much about the factory's internal dramas after that, but I believe it served the community well, to the tune of twenty to thirty reasonable jobs, until the interminable recession of the late 'eighties ground down the parent company and left only a tiny rump of it under local management in Aran. In its steady years it even enhanced the valley of the Seven Churches, for its gleaming paint and glasswork eclipsed the slovenly grey shed. Whenever I cycled by, hands were raised to wave behind the big plate-glass windows, and there were faces, difficult to put a name to among the reflections of old Aran's cloudy stones and lichenous skies, but smiling.

LOOKING OUT OF ARAN

Three hundred and fifty-four feet is no great height, but in attaining to it on the westernmost part of its tripartite plateau, Aran seems to gather itself up as if to crane over the horizon. Beyond the Seven Churches the road begins to negotiate the scarps obliquely, one by one, and at the top of each rise a boreen turns off to the left, to scale the hillside directly. The first little *carcair* is by the modern chapel of Sts Patrick and Enda, two hundred yards beyond the last old cottages of Eoghanacht village. The boreen that goes off round the west gable of the chapel and up the face of the hill is Ród na Creige Móire, the road of the big crag, and the big crag itself is the rim of the terrace that provided the site of the chapel. This was one of the customary places for erecting small funerary cairns, and there were also two, perhaps more, of the bigger, inscribed monuments on the crag, which were destroyed when the chapel was built in 1958. Two plaques from these have been set in the roadside walls; they are dated 1814 and 1811, and since the latter (together with the much more elaborate and probably imported Eochaill example already mentioned) is the earliest of them all, I transcribe it –

O Lord have mercy
on yᵉ Soul of Thoˢ.
Coneely died in
yᵉ 25 yʳ. of his
Age 1811

– not so much in honour of Thomas Coneely, but of his mourners, who perhaps initiated the custom, and whose creative act in so doing is, as mentioned in my earlier chapter on these monuments, one of the many aspects of Aran that surpass my understanding.

Tucked into the farther corner of the third field uphill from the chapel is another frustrated line of enquiry. Colie Mhicilín, conducting me up the boreen once, pointed out a spring well there, a seepage from between two layers of rock where the ground steps up a few feet at the back of the field, that collects in a water-worn channel and fills a beautiful natural basin. In a cleft beside it, and among the water-weeds of the pool, is a collection of small things left there by the clients of this well, which perhaps is not quite a holy one: a big whelk-shell for supping the water from, scallop-shells, a broken comb, rusty horseshoe nails, shards of pottery, a clay pipe-stem, buttons and coins (of which the most recent was dated 1974). It is called Bullán na Caillí, the rock-bowl of the old woman, a name which connects it with a *bean feasa* or woman of knowledge, a herbalist, a hag, a witch – the range of meanings of the word *cailleach* reflecting the perception that an old woman is always something more than just an old woman. In the middle of the last century there was a herb-woman living a quarter of a mile or so farther west; this is how an old man spoke of her to Ruairí Ó hEithir when he was researching Aran folk medicine in the 1970s:

In Creig a' Chéirín there was Máirín a' Chaiptín, who was married to Seán a' Dochtúra. She used to be going about the crags at night, gathering herbs probably. She was another one who would know beforehand about things that were to happen. She died about a hundred years ago.

One of her specialities was a cure for wind: she would inflate a sheep's or pig's bladder and let the air out slowly as she passed it over the sufferer's stomach, and the pain would disappear. She also had an inexhaustible supply of turf in her loft, until one day her father disobeyed her by going up to fetch turf from it himself, and found the room empty. (Perhaps it was not just herbs she brought home from her midnight prowlings.) Ruairí Ó hEithir suggests that she is likely to have been the practitioner of disease-transference Nathaniel Colgan heard about when he was botanizing in Aran in 1892. However, Colie could not, or perhaps did not want to, tell me anything about the well beyond its name, and could not confirm its connection with Máirín a' Chaiptín. Also, while he had heard of diseases being transferred to donkeys, and seemed to believe in that as a possibility, he would not allow that they might have been transferred to other human beings. I was left slightly irked by the refusal of all these hints to cohere into the story of this well.

In fact Colie was rather evasive on the topic of magic, which naturally arose as we walked on. A few fields further up the hill we saw a scrap of blue plastic material fluttering from a cranny in a wall. He said that some people would leave a rag like that in the corner of a field to ward off ill-luck. But I could not get it clear from him whether that particular rag was there to scare birds or fairies, or indeed whether or not such things were still done. I felt that if I had had some training in folklore research I would have heard – what I wanted to hear, that magic's writ still runs in Aran.

After climbing a scarp a quarter of a mile up from the road, and then another, Ród na Creige Móire suddenly sprouts four limbs, all elbows and knees, and then one or two more, with which it swarms over the brow of the hill and sprawls to its many ends, all a long way from anywhere; I remember how wearisome I found it, tramping out these rigmaroles one by one for my map. In a field full of brambles separated by another field full of brambles to the south-east of the first turn to the south of the first branch to the east of this aporia, are very indistinct remains of a stone hut called Clochán an Airgid, which houses the same vague tale of buried treasure as the Clochán an Airgid I described south of Mainistir. (I have to admit to myself that I sometimes found Aran boring and repetitious.) And half a mile up the second branch to the south off the westernmost branch, where the boreen stops for the space of a few fields and then starts again for no apparent reason, there are two *clocháin* with roofs and windows, the details of which I will not trouble to record as they are largely the result of an outburst of creativity on the part of the Office of Public Works' local employees in the 1960s.

And once again, beyond the nerve-ends of this boreen-system, now to be visited for the last time so far as this book is concerned, is the unnerving landscape of Na Craga, the familiar mesh of countless stony fields, all clenched and gnashed together like the cogs and ratchets of an antique clock long ticked to a stop, its key lost. Sometimes the tense stillness is more than stone itself can bear; as when a stone lying in the thin grass hears me coming, holds its breath hoping I won't see it, and at the very last moment as I am about to tread on it, snaps with anxiety and goes panicking off, a snipe, staggering up the sky, dodging imaginary gunshots, and flutters down as if exhausted into a distant field.

In retrospect now, I see these lonely quarters in high summer, with restless harebells reluctantly tethered against the breeze by their slim stalks, and all the other vegetation gone coarse and seedy: the knapweeds and hardheads, which after the purple thistle-like flowers have withered turn out their ruffs of silvery sepals that glint like mirrors; the scraggy devilsbit scabious and bartsia and yellow rattle. Down in the crevices, dewberry fruit, like blackberries but with just three or four big sachets of sweetness; the Araners call them *crúibíní*, trotters, from their shape. Aimlessly here and there about these light-scoured expanses goes the loosely fluttering grayling butterfly, that alights beside me as I sit on a rock, closes its wings to show the little eye-like roundels on the underside of the forewing for a moment, and then when no enemy has betrayed its presence by a move, covers them with the mottled grey hindwings and leans over, away from the sun, almost flat to the ground and looking so like a flake of lichen-covered limestone that it effectively disappears. Sometimes there are dozens of dark green fritillaries too: big, fast-flying butterflies, reddish-brown and black above, green and silver below, that dash from field to field with an impatient rattling of wings. On hot days these crags sizzle like frying-pans with insect life; grasshoppers spark to and fro, caterpillars ready to pupate have tantrums in their too-tight skins, the clover-heads are bowed under swooning clusters of six-spot burnet moths, rose chafer beetles like half-inch nuggets of green gold orbiting with the inertial fatalism of asteroids crash softly into purple beds of hemp agrimony. Everything is burning with particularities: *I* fly like this, *I* jump like this, *I* eat this, *my* wings have six red spots on black, nothing else is like *me*! And of each of these tiny egos, there are millions of replicas. They fly up from disturbed bushes like the contents of a jewellery-shop fleeing a blaze; they swarm and pluck at me in their paroxysms of individuation: am I not going to mention them, the small copper butterfly I saw at Clochán an Airgid, the unspotted form of the six-spot burnet, the cinnabar moths, the sapphire-bright common blues? And they will never understand, and if they could understand would never accept, that my book can only achieve its end by relinquishing its all-inclusive aspirations.

All these identical fields of shaggy grass and herbs struggling up through shattered rock are fiercely individualistic too, if one makes the mistake of paying attention to them. Thousands of names must have been given to them over the centuries, most of them forgotten; I have only recorded a few dozen. By the two restored *clocháin* is one called Creigeán na Banríona, the queen's crag-cum-field; Colie cannot tell me why. To the east of the end of the eastern branch of the boreen coming up south from Clochán an Airgid is Scrios Buaile na bhFeadóg, the open tract (this seems to be the local meaning of *scrios* in this context) of the pasture of the lapwings; and there are often lapwings on this plateau, or soaring above it, screeching and tumbling as if perpetually let down by the properties of air in their efforts to be free of the ground of Aran.

The one placename that best stands for these uplands in my mind, or for the tensions I associate with them, is Creigeán an 'Lookout'. This is the third field south of the final angle of the westernmost of the four branches of the boreen (I only specify this to convey the maddening intrication of place up here); it is close to the highest point of this end of the island, and is the first place one reaches, coming up from the village, from which the whole western sea-horizon is visible. Certain families used to keep a lookout posted here for sailing vessels inward bound for Galway, so that their menfolk could row out in their currachs to meet them and propose themselves as pilots through the rocks and shoals of Galway Bay. (Jokes were made about these Aran pilots. For example: the Araner assures the captain of the ship that he knows every rock in the bay, and is taken on as pilot. Soon afterwards the ship shudders to a halt against a rock. *Captain*: 'I thought you said you knew every rock in the bay?' *Araner*: 'I do – and that's one of them!')

I too often looked out of Aran from these heights, and sometimes, especially latterly, with a sense of longing. I learned the name of Creigeán an 'Lookout' not from Colie – it was almost outside his territory, being on the borders of Creig an Chéirín – but from an old man called Tomáisín Jamesie. Creig an Chéirin is divided into two quarters, Lios na dTrom ('the fort of the elder-bushes' is most probably the sense of this) and An Sliabh Mór, the big mountain, farther to the west. In broad terms the boundaries of these subdivisions run approximately Aran-north-south across the island, which is just under two miles wide here, but in detail they are extremely tortuous, and Tomáisín would trust nobody but himself to make sure I marked them down correctly on my map. I became obsessed with this problem, returning to the hunt for certainty again and again, struggling from field to field to field with Tomáisín, or by myself in accordance with notes taken down from his voluble directions, trying to identify a field-wall that was slightly thicker or more ivy-grown than the rest, or one that had no 'gaps' in it and therefore separated two holdings and probably two quarters. Sometimes I felt that I was caught in the knot of these obsolete and well-forgotten discriminations, so that, to lift my head from their tediously predictable and yet impenetrable dodges and tricks-of-the-loop, and look out at the distant great world, was almost an escape. Connemara in particular attracted me; at that period I was already mentally stretching a new, broader canvas for myself there. Aran felt too small, though I knew I would never get to the bottom of it. Sometimes, on returning to the island after a short absence, I would cycle to one end of it and look out, and the next day cycle to the other end and look out, and wonder how to get through the next few months. Also, there was something unsettling and illicit about the calm in which I lived here. Aran has had its famines and oppressions, even, on a small scale, its wars, but for a long time it has had only private troubles, and the great causes seem far away. I would read in the newspapers, several days late, about a world so full of horrors that my seclusion seemed to tempt fate; the sky when I looked out from Aran was rimmed with black, like blood under a bruised fingernail.

But if I had doubts about the worth of what I was doing, seeing myself against that horizon of deadly debate, Tomáisín did not, and was happy to accompany me on afternoons of rambling. Or did I delude myself? Was it merely that, as he told me once when I found him standing becalmed at the gate of his cottage, *'Níl tada le deanamh ag seanfhear'* (There's nothing for an old man to do)? In any case, my reading of the lines of his land gave him the gratification a palmist would have offered him: the tribute of attention, loading the worn traces of his everyday life with significance – and what that significance was, perhaps hardly mattered; it was in itself significant. So, when he could delight me by leading me through ever narrower *róidíní* to something worthy of being marked on a map, he was delighted with himself. Coming back from Bóithrín an tSléibhe Mhóir, the main path running south across An Sliabh Mór, we took a crooked little short-cut into Lios na dTrom territory called Bóithrín Thobar na hEochraí, the boreen of the well of the fish-spawn (that at least seems to be the sense of the name), and when he reached the well itself Tomáisín, who was ahead of me, turned round with the air of a showman, and pointed out a ruin hardly bigger than a dog-kennel hidden in the bushes. Unfortunately he saw that I had guessed what it was before he opened his mouth, and his face dropped; I regretted that. It was an old *poitín* still, like those I had been shown hidden away in similarly discreet corners of Connemara. In fact this one had been built by a distiller from the Maigh Cuilinn area who settled in Aran just after the Napoleonic wars, Pádraig Ó Tuathail. *Poitín* is still made in Connemara – in thousands of gallons, at least until the recent stiffening of the law against it – but not with the patient attention to quality of the old days. Ó Tuathail would have been a craftsman, selecting his barley-grain with care, steeping bagfuls of it in the well, then letting it sprout (perhaps burying the bags in a dunghill or a heap of turf-mould), drying it over a small kiln, grinding it with a hand-quern, soaking it in hot water and drawing off the 'ale', adding yeast and flour, and finally watch-

ing over the slow repeated distillation, the *singleáil* and the *dúbláil* – all this
to be done without attracting the attentions of the police or the coastguards. On one occasion he failed to keep a good look-out, and the smoke
of the still was seen from a naval vessel offshore; three or four men were put
ashore in a row-boat, crept up the hill and surprised him at work. He was
arrested and taken back to the ship. Fortunately one of the crew knew him,
and after walking past him once or twice took an opportunity of whispering to him in that language the foreigner does not know, *'A Phádraig, cá
bhfuil do chuid snámh?'* ('Patrick, where's your swimming?') Ó Tuathail
took the hint, leapt overboard and swam for it; a couple of bullets were
fired over his head, but he was let get away.

Tomáisín was pleasant to be with, lively in speech, agile over walls, a
neat and trim little man who despite his ordinary countryman's dress of flat
cap and tweed jacket reminded me of Máirtín Ó Direáin's old traditional-
ists:

> Maireann a gcuimhne fós i m'aigne:
> Báiníní bána is léinte geala,
> Léinte gorma is veistí glasa,
> Treabhsair is dráir de bhréidín baile
> Bhíodh ar fheara cásacha aosta
> Ag triall ar an Aifreann maidin Domhnaigh
> De shiúl cos ar aistear fhada,
> A mhusclaíodh i m'óige smaointe ionamsa
> Ar ghlaine, ar úire, is fós ar bheannaíocht.

> Their memory still lives in my mind:
> White bawneens and bright shirts
> Blue shirts and grey waistcoats,
> Trousers and drawers of homespun
> Worn by venerable old men
> Going to Mass on Sunday morning
> Walking all the long way,
> Who woke the thoughts of my youth
> To the clean, the fresh, and even the pious.

Unfortunately, despite his impeccable credentials as village ancient, I
came to the conclusion that Tomáisín's version of the boundaries was logically incoherent, and I had to search out an old bachelor I particularly disliked, and go over them again. Sometimes I suspect that folk memory owes
its reputation to the fact that there is nothing to check it against; the
guardians of oral lore got it wrong in the first generation, and every generation since has added its quantum of error.

Returning from such expeditions I sometimes came down to the village of Creig an Chéirín by a rather precipitous track called Ród na gCaiptíní, after the nickname of the family whose land it served. Na Caiptíní (the captains) were McDonaghs (as were sixty of the one hundred and twenty-one inhabitants of the village in Ó Tuathail's time, for example); the wise woman Máirín a' Chaiptín was one of them, as was her namesake and contemporary, Máirín an Chaiptín, the midwife, from whom the back road in Cill Rónáin is called Bóthar an Chaiptín. As I have mentioned, most Aran families have nicknames, which distinguish them better than the limited number of surnames can do, but since most of them originated in some anecdote that has been repeated for generations with a teasing or spiteful intent, they are not usually used in the presence of those named, and it is difficult for me to discuss them here. However, this particular nickname is not offensive. Mícheál the blacksmith told me how it was won. A party of little boys were chasing a wren; one lad outran the rest and caught the bird, and an old man looking over a wall at them cried out, 'Is tusa an caiptín!' ('You are the captain!').

Ród na gCaiptíní joins a more important one, Ród Charn Maoilín, which comes down from the highest point of the plateau, Carn Maoilín (meaning something like 'cairn of the flat-topped or bare summit'), and where this in its turn joins the main road at Carcair Chreig an Chéirín, there stands a rather faded-looking 'fifties single-storey house I often used to call in at. It was built by Éamonn Ó Tuathail, great-grandson of the poitín-maker, who used to teach in Eoghanacht school until he left the island as a consequence of some row with the priest. (I never met him, but in his last years we corresponded, and in the remissions of his terminal leukaemia we mentally revisited all these boreens, one of us in Dún Laoghaire and the other in Connemara, and he wrote out their names for me with voluminous and erudite elucidations. For several exiles, I am happy to hear that looking into Aran in this way, to help me improve the map from edition to edition, has been a passionate solace.) The present occupants of the house, who used to fortify me with tea for my cycle or walk home, are an Englishman, Arthur, and an Aran woman I think of as 'Arthur's Máiréad' to distinguish her from mine. For many years she was only intermittently at home, as she had to be taken into the huge Victorian psychiatric hospital of Ballinasloe for a month or two now and again. An excessive number of people used to have to make that eastwards journey by train or taxi, many of them for no better reason than that they were elderly and a little confused, or at odds with their relatives. It used to be regarded as natural that living in the west, and especially on an island, drove one crazy, and in Aran the commonest way of saying that something is maddening or aggravating is still 'Cuirfeadh sé sin soir thú!', 'That would send you east', that is, to Ballinasloe. So Arthur's Máiréad was lucky that she had someone to go and fetch her back from the hospital, which she feared; it was 'rough', she told us. She was born in Aran, and it seems she had fallen off a cliff in her childhood and had never been quite right since; nevertheless she had left the island as a young woman to stay with her brother Josie, who ran some boarding-houses in London, and skivvied for him as well as working in a Lyons' Corner House. There Arthur saw her, a slender, exotic beauty, and fell in love on the instant. He was a printer on a newspaper, separated from his wife. He took Máiréad under his wing; she was half-starved and he had difficulty persuading her to eat. Then they won a prize on the Irish Sweepstake, and suddenly had enough money to buy the Ó Tuathail house. Now, twenty years later, Máiréad was big and heavy, with the pale blondness of an evening cumulus cloud. Whenever I called in, Arthur would shout for her to come out of the bedroom she lurked in and make me a mug of tea. 'Ask him if he wants a biscuit!' he would add. She would take a packet of biscuits from the cupboard and say to me in a sudden, mechanical voice, 'Will you eat – *three*?' I would answer, 'I will!', and she would plank three biscuits on the kitchen table.

Arthur is short and square-faced, with a bristly sergeant-major's moustache and bright terrier eyes, and his head is stuffed with facts like a tin full of assorted nuts and bolts. He had a little car and used to drive with Máiréad into Cill Rónáin on steamer-days. Often he would collect our Sunday papers from Powell's shop – we used to save them to read on the following Sunday – and on the way home he would pull up at our gate and strut down the garden-path with them, crying out like a Cockney newsvendor, 'Star, News and Standard!' Then he would sit by our fire and bring us up to date with news from the west – drownings, thefts of cabbages, constipations of many weeks' standing. Máiréad would rarely come in with him, preferring to wait in the car, but sometimes we would hear her stumping round to the yard behind the house. A London friend visiting us during the winter, who was puzzled by the incongruity of Arthur's cheerful pragmatical presence in this darkly self-questioning island, once asked him why he stayed here. Arthur had no answer at the time, but a fortnight later he told me that he had been thinking about the question, and that the answer was: 'Love; Faith; Honour.'

When we first came to Aran, Arthur was the only non-islander living there permanantly. He was more active then, and used to go fishing for mackerel from An Grióir under the western end of the cliffs, so regularly in fact that I added a dot and a squiggle representing him to that point of my map, an almost microscopic memorial that delighted him. Nowadays he is too wobbly on his legs to clamber along the shingle-banks to An Grióir, and he has also had to abandon his vegetable patch. But he still holds out, long after I have left the island, and still holds his Máiréad back from that grey hole gaping in the east. That's Arthur: loving, faithful, honourable.

RUNNING OUT OF TIME

Followed from east to west, the topography of the island goes down to its end with the assurance of a queen. Having climbed in steeps and stops for breath for over a mile, the road swings around a cliffed cape of the plateau on its left, and discloses a landscape of grand finality, descending in four majestic steps to the tidal streams around the last low fragmentary islets and the lighthouse, beyond which is nothing but the sea's blue mantle, twitched by the desire of horizons.

From the bend at the highest point of the road one looks down into the village of Bun Gabhla, lodged in a shallow depression of the terrace below like a clutch of eggs on a plate. Behind the village this hollow gathers itself into a narrow valley running through slightly higher ground southwards as far as the Atlantic cliffs. It is this cut across the limestone strata that provides the village with the spring water accumulating in a marshy dell of sally-gardens among little rye-fields, and probably also with its name. In Connemara I find that placename elements deriving from *gabhal*, literally a fork or fork-shaped thing, often refer to a V-shaped valley or ravine, and so here it seems likely that the village name means 'foot of the valley'. But if this is so, it is not generally understood, and the name sounds a little odd even in the ears of the islanders, adding to their perception of Bun Gabhla as a place apart. Hidden from the rest of the island as it is by the corner of the plateau, exposed to all the frightful glories of the west the other villages cower away from, its very existence seems a little fabulous. For me too, it is remote and unfamiliar territory. Once or twice I called in on Maggie and Marcus there (Marcus was one of those I had in mind when describing the fishermen of Bun Gabhla in my first volume), and found their old uncle Tomáisín Jamesie lavishing the Irish language's treasury of comic endearments on their new baby, but theirs was the only cottage I knew. I remember that the first steps I made towards my first map of Aran were to walk up to that high corner of the road and sketch the relative positions of the ten houses laid out in an already map-like perspective below. As I worked, a mist rolled in from the sea and encircled the village. I saw a woman running out to fetch in the washing hanging behind her house, and a goose stretching its neck to hiss at her; then the mist obliterated the little scene, and a few drops of rain blurred my penmanship. I felt then that I would never know anything of the life of that place, and so it has turned out. I can only speculate, for instance, that the beam of the lighthouse sweeping over the rooftops gives night a pulse so familiar that its cessation in dense fog must wake the village, as one is woken by a ticking clock's falling silent. More clearly, I can feel how that cone of light, or as much of it as has failed to contact rock or ship or human eye, sails on over the horizon to drown itself in infinite space.

Below the village, the terraces of the island's north flank sweep round to the south-west, each broadening out into stark rock-floors several hundred yards wide, softened here and there by grassy hollows divided into fields. It is a sublime landscape – the adjective is inescapable – in its scale and clarity, and I often have it to myself; few tourists penetrate so far, and the villagers are usually off in their currachs or busy in the gardens near their homes. Salty gales scour across the wide-open surfaces; plants keep to the crevices. Rose-root, an arctic and montane succulent, is abundant, its sunset-coloured seed-heads ablaze in the late summer, almost down to sea-level. On a recent visit I was brought up short in my striding by a row of tiny greenish darts sticking up out of a fissure: the adder's tongue fern, a very rare plant on the islands, within a quarter of a mile of the western point. While I do not have the foot-by-foot knowledge of these crags that I do of the one over the back wall of the Residence, I have crossed them dozens of times and accumulated a stack of notes about their flora, and the Bun Gabhla people have given me much place-lore. Tomáisín has a tale of fairies seen dancing at midday down on An Scrios Mór, the terrace by the shore north of the village, and I have heard a few lines of an otherwise forgotten song about a strange mound, too big to be just a ruined *clochán* and said to be haunted, down Bóthar na gCrúibíní, the road of the 'crubeens' or dewberries, just south of the village. Also, Conor MacDermot has pointed out some geological features unusual in Aran: on Scrios na gCapall by the north-western shoreline, a long undulating channel cut into the limestone pavement by water flowing at pressure under a melting glacier; a small rift-valley enclosing Loch an Mhuirbhigh, the brackish lake at the western tip of the island, formed where the ground between two parallel faults has dropped a few yards ... But, at this point in my book, the tension between its sprawling content and its formal symmetries has to be contained; to cap this Neoclassical can of worms I need to reduce my ultimate steps on Aran to the elemental and emblematic.

Primarily, these crags are steeped in sunsets. The best of my memories of them are sunset coloured. Some years after leaving Aran I returned with two friends who were making a film and needed a sunset. I led them to the brink of a terrace on the north-west shoulder of the island. The sun, on a rococo stage of lavishly gilded cirrus, was retiring with the bravura of a diva well practised in farewell performances. But in the last minutes it dispensed with meretricious pomps, and reduced itself to a white-hot cutting-disc. As it poised itself to slice into the horizon, I remembered what I had read of the rare phenomenon called 'the green flash': When the sun's rays enter the atmosphere obliquely they are refracted earthwards, and so at sunset they are bent round the curve of the earth a little, making the sun visible for a few moments when, geometrically speaking it is already below the horizon; and since the longer wavelengths of the red end of the spectrum are refracted to a slightly lesser degree than the shorter ones, they are cut off first, and the very last glimpse of the sun is provided solely by yellow and blue light; thus, in ideal conditions, its disappearance is illuminated by an instant of emerald. This evening, conditions seemed to promise that ideal; the atmosphere was intently observant, the sky around the vanishing-point of day was as lucid as science. We 'inspectors of sunsets' held our breaths, and trained the camera on the sun as it shrank to a low dome, which appeared to spread a little way along the horizon to either side before gathering itself into a globule of fierce intensity, and vanishing. We saw no emerald; the sky shed its gold, the crags faded from copper to gun-metal, without spectral discontinuities. But, most unexpectedly, when we reviewed that day's work in the darkroom, there was the green moment in all its veridicity. Sadly, this epiphany like so many others ended on the cutting-room floor; in the final restructuring, the film's editor foreswore the clichéd closure of sunset.

However, it is a sunset that defines these crags for me still, and dresses them for this book. It dawned out of a dark evening in that summer, a wretched rainy season, when we were living temporarily above Creig an Chéirín while I made my first map of the island. Evening after evening I used to come back from the boreens, soaked and frustrated, to the damp cottage in which M had spent the day trying to dry out the clothes I had worn the day before. The cottage was lonely, surrounded by tall wet grass and puddles of cow-shit. By day the front windows looked down a grey slope to a grey sea, the back windows up a grey slope to a grey sky, by night we shuttered them up so as not to attract the attention of the only likely caller, a roaming bachelor half-crazed by lifelong fantasizing. We were befriended by an eight-year-old child whom we, still only half familiar with Aran's genealogical nicknames, knew as Mikey Mikey Tom Mikey. He used to cycle out from Cill Mhuirbhigh with a milk-pail before and after school, to see to cattle and sheep on the land his parents rented near the cottage.

He too was frequently wet and exhausted, and M would supplement the bit of bread his mother had, as he put it, 'thrown down in the pail' for him with cocoa and a boiled egg. He called in on her now and again, bringing an orphaned robin nestling, or to ask her to tell him if the cows started climbing up on each other, so that he would know when to take them to the bull. Once the school holidays began he was often labouring all day, milking the three cows morning and evening, weeding mangolds, saving hay or spraying potatoes, all by himself and with little to eat or drink. (He was probably one of the last of Aran's children to be worked in this way, which was only what their own experience had taught his parents to consider natural; we noted in later years that his younger brothers had an easier life, as modern values began to soften even this obdurately old-fashioned family.) Mikey offered to leave milk for us at the roadside below the cottage each morning in an old lemonade bottle; when we asked him the price he said, 'Fifteen or ten pence', but it was clear from the way he held them unseeingly in his palm that the coins meant nothing to him. We agreed on five pence, and arranged to return the empty bottle with the money in its cap to the same spot by the roadside. Sometimes he called on me to help him change the cattle from one field to another, which was difficult for him to do on his own, as the number of ways half a dozen beasts can go astray in the ramifying paths of Aran when driven from behind by one small boy is virtually infinite; also, although he was far quicker than I at 'knocking the gap' to let the cattle into the field and raising it up again after them, the big stones were a strain on him. On such occasions he would tell me not to leave any pennies in the milk-bottle cap the next day because I had done that work for him, and I would explain that since I wanted to learn that work from him there was no need to pay me. He was supposed to be saving the money for new shoes, but in the event he bought two goat-kids from one of his contemporaries, and built a little stone hutch for them on a nearby crag. Mikey Mikey Tom Mikey was the only entrepreneur in that lugubrious neighbourhood, whose few remaining inhabitants seemed to be either moribund or manic.

One evening, as I arrived home from a long day largely spent sheltering under inadequate bushes, the dripping sky suddenly cleared, and after dinner I sat on the doorstep with M to bask in the honeyed evening air. Then Mikey appeared, looking worried; his father was coming to ship some sheep out to An tOileán Iarthach the next morning, but in the meantime they had escaped from the crag they were supposed to be on. Reluctantly I got up to help him find them. We located a few on a crag towards Bun Gabhla, and chased after some others that showed briefly on a skyline, but they turned out not to be the right ones. It seemed absurd to be scampering about after sheep that would surely disappear again overnight if we did find them and put them back on their crag. We decided to split up; he went down towards the shore, I roved sunsetwards over the great shoulders of rock below Bun Gabhla. The golden eye of the lighthouse was opening and shutting. I became elated by the vast level tide-race of sunshine streaming around me, a light so palpable it might have been imagined by someone blind from birth, a warm liquid pressing in at the eyes, carrying sharp exciting crystals. I began to run, crossing the areas chopped up by shadow-filled grykes as easily as the great burnished rock-sheets, and leaping down the scarps from terrace to terrace as if the light were dissolving them and I could plunge through them like waves. If sheep were the goal of the quest, they hid themselves from my ecstasy and left me free to exult in the miraculous surety of my footfalls.

Looking back on it from this moment of writing, I believe I have transcribed this experience accurately. But, arising where it does in these last pages, it needs to be freed from a weight of significance. It took place early in my learning about Aran; it does not represent a summation, a reading, of the work I have done since, a hard-won adequation of step to stone. Only my favouring of spatial over temporal continuity, my childish filling-in of the island-shape with one long obsessive scribble of record and experience, brings it to occupy this privileged site. Unearned, promising nothing beyond the moment of itself, least of all was it a mystic flight above or from the ground of this book. What could be more natural than that space should reward me for my fidelity by providing this excursus from time, just where it would come in handy many years of writing later?

Meanwhile, Mikey had found a few more sheep. By the time I joined up with him again and we had driven them up to the crag and frightened them into jumping the wall into it, the sun had gone down. We spotted some more sheep on a higher crag, but decided to leave them there, and he set off homewards, dwindling down the hill on his bicycle. A full moon appeared between bars of cloud in the east as I climbed the path to the cottage, to find that M had been worried by my long absence, and, after her lonely day, disappointed of our evening together. So the episode ended sadly.

Indeed I have been gone far too long about this island (but see, my darling, the book I have found you among its stones!). And now, have I reached the end of it so soon? With so little seen, less understood, nothing possessed? Not quite, it seems, for at this last moment something comes into view to the west. Perhaps it is just a patch of mystic foam kicked up by dolphins, perhaps it is the material of a postscript to my Aran ...

IV
POSTSCRIPT

From the Isles of Aran and the west continent, often appears visible that inchanted island called O'Brasil, and in Irish Beg-ara, or the Lesser Aran, set down in cards of navigation. Whether it be reall and firm land, kept hidden by speciall ordinance of God, as the terrestriall paradise, or else some illusion of airy clouds appearing on the surface of the sea, or the craft of evill spirits, is more than our judgements can sound out.

What Roderic O'Flaherty writes as O'Brasil is more correctly Hy Brazil or Hy Breasail, *hy* being from the old Norse *ey*, island, and *breasail* an Irish word for reddish substances such as raddle, rouge and even blood, sharing an obscure etymology with 'brazil wood', the red dye-wood from which Brazil was named. 'Beg-Ara' is now Ára Beag or Árainn Bheag, Little Aran, in local tradition. From fourteenth-century Catalan maps down to a chart of 1865, Hy Breasail drifts about off the west coast of Ireland like flotsam from the wreck of Atlantis. According to a Dutch map of O'Flaherty's time it was at the Porcupine Bank, some hundred miles west of Aran, but locally it was thought to be nearer than that, as his account shows:

There is now living, Morogh O'Ley, who immagines he was himself personally in O'Brazil for two days, and saw out of it the iles of Aran, Golamhead, Irrosbeghill, and other places of the west continent he was acquainted with. The manner of it he relates, that being in Irrosainhagh [Iorras Aintheach, the Carna peninsula in south Connemara], in the month of Aprill, Anno Domini 1668, going alone from one village to another, in a melancholy humour, upon some discontent of his wife, he was encountered by two or three strangers, and forcibly carried by boat into O'Brazil, as such as were within it told him, and they could speak both English and Irish. He was ferried out hoodwink'd, in a boat, as he immagins, till he was left on the sea point by Galway; where he lay in a friend's house for some dayes after, being very desperately ill, and knowes not how he came to Galway then. But, by that means, about seaven or eight years after, he began to practise both chirurgery and phisick, and so continues ever since to practise, tho' he never studyed nor practised either in his life before, as all we that knew him since he was a boy can averr.

This story still exists in the oral realm, and surfaces in print now and again. In 1839 O'Donovan recorded a version with an additional detail that rounds out its sense. Lee, as he calls its hero, was among the crew of a fishing boat; they landed on an island they did not know, and were turned off it by a man who told them it was enchanted. As they were going away the islander gave Lee a book, with directions not to look into it for seven years. He complied, and having read the book seven years later, was able to practise surgery and medicine. The book, O'Donovan was told, had been passed down through Lee's descendants but had very recently been sold to a Dublin bookseller.

In fact this 'Book of O'Brasil' is a reality, and soon found its way into the library of the Royal Irish Academy. It is a fifteenth-century medical manuscript in Irish and Latin, with lists of diseases, symptoms, cures, etc., arranged in columns under such headings as *Prognostics, Causa, Signum* and *Evacuatio.* The Lees were hereditary physicians to the O'Flahertys in olden times, and Roderic O'Flaherty's editor, Hardiman, conjectures that the truth of the matter is that Lee, having lost his patrimony in the Cromwellian confiscations, dusted off his ancestors' old book, invented his O'Brasil adventure to advertise himself, and set up as a quack.

No such cynicism has been allowed to impede the development of the tale in its birthplace. In 1938 a collector for the Irish Folklore Commission took down an elaborate version of it from a well-known story-teller living near Carna. It begins with a customary rigmarole:

Long ago, and a long time it was. If I were there then, I wouldn't be there now. If I were there then and now, I would have a new story or an old story, or I would have no story at all.

Then we are told exactly where Lee lived, in Letterdeskert just west of Carna, and where he tied up his boat in nearby Cornarone. One day when he was sailing to Galway, the boat touched bottom in a place where he had never heard talk of there being a rock; he looked over the side and saw heather growing, but when he touched this land with the croisín he had for gathering seaweed, it vanished. Soon afterwards he was menaced by three huge waves, each of which he quelled by throwing a sod of turf at it. Then came an even bigger wave. He pulled out his pocketknife, opened it, and flung it at the wave; the sea fell calm again, and he completed his voyage.

A good while later, Lee was cutting heather for cattle-bedding on the hillside above his home, when he felt sleepy and faint, and was carried off through the air. He found himself in the house of an old man, the king of Little Aran. The old man took him upstairs and showed him the most beautiful woman he had ever seen, lying in bed, moaning and complaining about the knife plunged into her right breast. Lee was filled with remorse when he saw that it was his own knife; he pulled it out, and she rose up as well as she had ever been. 'Now', said the old man, 'you had better marry this woman and stay here with us.' But Lee explained that, being an only son, he had to stay at home until his sisters were settled. So they rewarded him with a book instead, which if he did not open it for seven years would make him the best doctor under the sun. Then he was magically returned to the hillside, walked down home, threw the basket of heather into the cowhouse, and put the book away.

For three years he resisted all suggestions that he open the book, but then a dear cousin of his fell ill, and he was persuaded to look out a cure for him. He found the remedy, but only three years' share of the knowledge in the book was readable; the rest of the pages had melted and turned as black as soot. However, that was enough to make him the best doctor in Ireland. Doctor Lee finally left Letterdeskert and travelled before him, curing both lowly and noble. He never returned, and it is supposed that he must have gone off to live with the beautiful woman of Little Aran.

This story is quite true. I know the townland of Cornarone. I was often there. I know where Lee had his house and where he used to moor his boat. It isn't many years since he lived there. 'Tis a true story, indeed, that happened in Carna in Conamara.

According to Aran islanders I have talked to, tradition holds that Árainn Bheag appears (or 'dries', like a shoal when the tide is very low) every seven years. Some Inis Meáin people, I am told, have seen the clothes laid out in the sun on its bleaching-green. If you could row out to it without taking your eyes off it, not even to blink, or if you could throw a spark of fire onto it, it would be yours. Alternatively, as the tales of it imply, it comes to the one who accepts its invitation graciously – and if Little Aran has fallen into the hands of a Connemara man, the Araners have only their own diffidence to blame. A currach crew from Iaráirne landed on it once, and were approached three times by a red-haired beauty who said each time, 'Am I not a fine woman?' The third time, one of the men, Tadhg Ó Neachtáin, was bold enough to reply, 'Arragh, how would we know that – fine or not fine?', whereupon she flung a handful of mud between his eyes, and he came home blind. A similar story was told to Lady Gregory in 1898 by a man from Inis Meáin:

There's said to be another island out there that's enchanted, and there are some that see it. And it's said that a fisherman landed on it one time, and he saw a little house, and he went in, and a very nice-looking young woman came out and said, 'What will you say to me?' and he said, 'You are a very nice lady.' And a second came and asked him the same thing and a third, and he made the same answer. And after that they said, 'You'd best run of your life', and he did, and his curragh was floating along and he had but just time to get into it, and the island was gone. But if he had said, 'God bless you,' the island would have been saved.

While I have not met any islander who claims to have seen Árainn Bheag, never mind landed on it, I have talked to one who has dreamed of seeing it, Dara Ó Conaola (but Dara is a writer, and therefore an unreliable dreamer). In his dream he was on the shore when it appeared, and he was glad that his brother came up behind him and saw it too, for otherwise nobody would have believed him. It was an island of two hills, with a tower at either end, and, he told me, it filled up that awful space out to the southwest, giving him a feeling of security.

But that was only a dream, and the dream of a mirage at that. In reality Pangaea is broken, and all the mysterious bits and pieces circulating in the slow vortices of Panthalassa – Atlantis, the Land of Youth, Maol Dúin's islands – have foundered, dragging down their rainbows. Now and again, perhaps once in seven years, some 'illusion of airy clouds' tricks us back into that sense of security. But the deep truths of myth act on me less than their deep falsities; recognitions of the latter are the cruel blades that facet the world like living crystal. That one's dwelling-place in the world can be possessed as by patriarchal marriage, that there is somewhere a book containing what one needs to know, that the wound can be cured by plucking out the knife – these are some of the illusions proposed by the Lesser Aran.

Supposing, though, that such comforting generalities were acceptable, what more particularly would I require from an otherwordly Aran? Cliffs against which the waves for ever lift their white hands, not in despair, not in joy. Paths lined with flowers that sing their identifications like birds, leading through an infinity of fields, in each of which is an old man remembering its name. A hermit's history nourished on the lashings and lavings of the sea. A Residence in a sunny corner between east and west ... But it seems I have already been been expelled, ferried out hoodwink'd and left back on the shores of the actual, for I am merely redescribing the Aran I have written up. And of that, the Greater Aran, all I demand now is some certification of its existence.

More accurately, I need to persuade myself that I am part of the same continuum of reality as Aran. My doubts do not arise in relation to its people, with whom I have the normal range of coexistences and whose loves and quarrels, committee-meetings and savage solitarinesses are as bone-familiar to me as those of any of my (human) race. It is true, on the other hand, that the transcendent perspectives of Aran sometimes give casual gestures the distancing charisma of blessing or prophecy. Once I was sitting on one of the western cliff-tops, half my sphere of vision dazzled by the sun-battered waves, when I saw a lobster-boat, that looked the size of a tea-chest, working in towards the base of the cliff three hundred feet below.

One of the argonauts looked up, saw me, and waved; it was Mikey from Cill Mhuirbhigh. This Mikey was later to be drowned, and a communication from him after that event would not have been more appalling than that cheerful greeting from the unworld gaping at my feet. But if Mikey, an acquaintance of every day, is part of this sea-contested land, then so am I. The real difficulty arises when it is untenanted except by myself. I walk along the cliffs, the sequence of lofty headlands behind me when I glance back at them already looking as remote as archaeological eras – Iron Age, Bronze Age, Stone Age – and fading into haze. If the promontory under my feet is the present, then those ahead are the nameless and unimaginable divisions of future time, the to-become-historical and the post-historical. I can walk around the bay from this peninsula to the next, bringing my sense of reality with me like the circle of visibility that accompanies one through a mist, but I cannot catch them all together into my presence. The foam that flashes and leaps in the sunlight below makes me think of Keatsean perilous seas; but the word that tolls me back to my sole self here is not 'forlorn', but 'casements'. Since I am not here just in fancy but in reality, why is it so difficult to abolish this window, to be outside, present, in this land which is not a fairyland, forlorn or otherwise, but a segment of my home-planet, a walkable extension of the ground I stand on at this moment? I suspect that my obsessive interest in the minutest particulars of Aran is a displacement-activity, a postponement of the unbuilding, or at least the de-charming, of those casements.

The either/or is this: to be simply present and not to know and remember it, or to be reflectively aware, which implies the mediation of imagery, of mirroring – and reflection multiplies mirrors as fast as mirrors multiply reflections. Writing is my way out of this labyrinth. But I am no abstract, deep-sea philosopher; if I raise a metaphor as a sail to catch the winds of thought, I am soon overturned by shoals, or fly to the horizon and lie becalmed there. Therefore I choose this Aran-building method, the slow deposition of facts and observations, coalescing and fusing under their own weight into tablets of stone; if these bear writing, it is thanks to certain alchemical fixatives concocted during those furiously sleeping afternoons in my little room in the Residence.

A writing (an utterance which has almost nothing in common with a true act of speech, as opposed to the glib self-quotation writers are prone to) may incorporate spontaneities, but it is not the work of a moment and does not issue from a single mental state; like the step, writing down a sentence holds open the possibility of returning, changed, to that point, to approaching it from the west rather than the east. Since rewriting is the essence of the sort of writing I am writing about, it might seem that the only exit from the endless walk is to leap over the cliff and leave it unfinished. In fact only the careful dispersal of its end throughout the whole book will render unnecessary a miracle of closure in the final sentence.

The virtue of reality is that no understanding is equal to it; no walk, however labyrinthine, wears out the stone. And so, the Aran I have written myself through is inevitably the Lesser one. But, whether it be the terrestrial paradise, an airy illusion of clouds on the sea, or the work of delusive spirits, I have brought back a book as proof that I was there. Perhaps when I open it in seven years' time it will tell me what I had hoped to learn by writing it, how to match one's step to the pitch and roll of this cracked stone boat of a cosmos; but for the time being I cannot read it.

SOURCES,
ACKNOWLEDGMENTS,
MAPS & INDEX

SOURCES

I EAST

SWORN TO THE TOWER

4   J.M. Synge, *The Aran Islands* (London and Dublin 1907; republished 1992, Penguin Books, London, with introduction and notes by Tim Robinson).
4   Taimín Ó Briain, *Amhrán an 'Chéipir'*, taken down for me by Caomhán Ó Goill from Taimín's brother, Antoine, in 1988.

MAIDENHAIR

7   E. Lhuyd, 'Some further observations relating to the antiquities and natural history of Ireland', *Philosophical Transactions of the Royal Society of London*, 27 (1712).
10   Synge, *op. cit.*

SERMONS IN STONES

12   H.C. Hart, *A List of Plants Found in The Islands of Aran, Galway Bay* (Dublin 1875).
13   N. Colgan, 'Notes on the Flora of the Aran Islands', *The Irish Naturalist*, Vol. II (1893).

DWELLING

23   (liverwort) Information from the late Tony Whilde, Corrib Conservation Centre.
24   Séamas Ó Murchú, 'An tAinm Áite *Inis Oírr'*, *Éigse* (1993).
25   Dara Ó Conaola, *Thatched Homes of the Aran Islands / An Teaichín Ceanntuí*, (Ceard Shiopa Inis Oírr Teo. 1988). (A dual-language text, but I have translated this and the succeeding extracts from the Irish version which is the fuller one.)
27   Information from a copy of the 1821 census made for and annotated by Colm Fólan of Cill Rónáin in the 1940s, in private possession.

THE FITZPATRICKS

33   Hardiman's appendices to Roderic O'Flaherty, *A Chorographical Description of West or H-Iar Connaught*, written 1684 (ed. James Hardiman, Dublin 1846; facsimile reprint Galway 1978).
35   (Earl of Thomond) Máire Mac Néill, *Máire Rua, Lady of Leamaneh*, (Whitegate 1990).
36   Hardiman's appendices to R. O'Flaherty, *op. cit.*
36   (ruination of Clare) From 'A petition of the inhabitants to Government, praying to be relieved from the monthly contribution'; quoted in Hardiman's appendices to R. O'Flaherty, *op. cit.*
37   I am grateful to Conleth Manning, Office of Public Works, for sorting out this little problem of Old Style dates, and so correcting an error in my monograph *Mementos of Mortality: The Cenotaphs and Funerary Cairns of Árainn (Inishmore, County Galway)* (Roundstone 1991).
38   (Rickard Fitzpatrick, sheriff) James Hardiman, *The History of the Town and County of the Town of Galway* (Dublin 1820; facsimile reprint Galway 1984).

38   Louis M. Cullen, 'Five Letters Relating to Galway Smuggling in 1737', *Journal of the Galway Archaeological and Historical Society (JGAHS)*, XXVII (1956-7).

38   Tomás Ó Cillín SP (Fr Thomas Killeen PP), Short Annals of Aran (1948) (typescript in the Archiepiscopal Library, Tuam, of which there are two or three copies in private ownership).

TALES FROM THE HILL

40   Seán Mac Giollarnáth, *Annála Beaga ó Iorrus Aithneach* (Dublin 1941).

40   Thomas Moore, 'Horace, Ode XXII Lib. I. Freely translated by Lord Eld-n', in *Poetical Works of Thomas Moore* (Paris 1827).

40   *Abhráin agus Dánta an Reachtabhraigh*, ed. Dubhglas de h-Íde (Dublin 1933).

40   (the Saucepans) Anecdotes from Dara Mullen, Cill Rónáin, Mícheál King, Fearann an Choirce, and others; historical details from Antoine Powell, *Oileáin Árann, Stair na n-oileán anuas go dtí 1922* (Dublin 1984).

43   (Richard Martin's smuggling) Shevawn Lynam, *Humanity Dick Martin, King of Connemara, 1754-1834* (London 1975; Dublin 1989).

44   William Stokes, *The Life and Labours in Art and Archaeology of George Petrie, L.L.D., M.R.I.A.* (1868).

44   Richard Griffiths, *Primary Valuation Book* (Dublin 1865).

44   Liam O'Flaherty, *Skerret* (London 1932; Dublin 1979).

44   Ó Cillín, *op. cit.*

45   See article on one of the founders of the Coláiste Gaeilge, Mícheál Ó Droighneáin, in *Beathaisnéis a Ceathair*, Diarmuid Breathnach and Máire Ní Mhurchú (Dublin 1994).

46   E. O. Somerville and Martin Ross, *Some Irish Yesterdays* (London 1906).

THE INVISIBLE TOWER

48   John Waddell, 'The Archaeology of Aran' in *The Book of Aran*, ed. John Waddell, J.W. O'Connor and Anne Korff (Kinvara 1994).

48   Peter Harbison, *Pilgrimage in Ireland: the Monuments and the People* (London 1991).

48   R. Berger, '14C Dating Mortar in Ireland', *Radiocarbon* 34 (1992).

48   R. O'Flaherty, *West or H-Iar Connaught*. For Murchadh na Mart see 'The Ferocious O'Flahertys' in this volume.

49   Conleth Manning, 'Archaeological excavations at two church sites on Inishmore, Aran Islands', *Journal of the Royal Society of Antiquaries in Ireland (JRSAI)*, Vol. 115 (1985).

49   (finding of stones) Ó Cillín, *op. cit.*

50   Liam de Paor, 'The Limestone Crosses of Clare and Aran', *JGAHS*, Vol. XXVI, Nos. 3 and 4 (1955-6).

50   Françoise Henry, *Irish Art in the Romanesque Period (1020-1170 AD)* (London 1970).

52   (Franciscans) J.R.W. Goulden, 'Kilnamanagh: The Lost Church of Aran', *JGAHS*, Vol. XXVI (1955); gives references to Wadding's *Annales Minorum*.

53   (Franciscan abbots) A. Powell, *op. cit.*

54   J. O'Donovan, Ordnance Survey Letters: Galway (typescript copies in various public libraries).

55   C. Manning (1985).

56   R. Berger, *op. cit.*

57   P. Harbison, *op. cit.*

58   *Annála Ríoghachta Éireann, Annals of the Kingdom of Ireland by the Four Masters*, ed. John O'Donovan (Dublin 1848, 1851, 1856). The spelling of these names varies wildly from source to source; I have given them as in the Annals; a dot over a consonant is equivalent to an 'h' after it.

ORCES 461

59 (Cormac mac Cuilennáin) ms. (RIA 23N II 178) quoted in Ó Cillín, *op. cit.*

ORIGIN AND VANISHING-POINT

61 The excerpts from the *Life of St Enda* are from a translation made for me by Ann Mohr of University College, Galway, of Plummer's edition of the manuscripts Colgan's version derives from (Charles Plummer, *Vitae Sanctorum Hiberniae*, Vol. II [Oxford 1910]).

65 Richard Sharpe, *Medieval Irish Saints' Lives* (Oxford 1991).

65 James F. Kenney, *The Sources for the Early History of Ireland* (Dublin 1979).

67 Sharpe, *op. cit.*

68 Hubert Butler, *Ten Thousand Saints: a Study in Irish & European Origins* (Kilkenny 1972).

68 Heinrich Zimmer, 'Keltische Beitrage II', *Zeitschrift für Deutsches Alterthum und Deutsche Litteratur* (Berlin 1889). (I am grateful to Dr Arndt Wigger for obtaining, and translating part of, this elusive source for me.)

68 *The Voyage of Saint Brendan*, translated from the Latin by John O'Meara (Dublin 1978).

69 Butler, *op. cit.*

70 'Influenza in Aran' in Hubert Butler, *Grandmother and Wolf Tone* (Dublin 1990).

71 Butler, *Ten Thousand Saints.*

DARK ANGEL

74 *First Report of the Commissioners of Inquiry into the State of the Irish Fisheries* (Dublin 1836).

75 Ruairí Ó hEithir, 'Folk Medical Beliefs and Practices in the Aran Islands, Co. Galway', unpublished M.A. thesis, University College Dublin 1983; my translations.

77 Nathanial Colgan, 'Witchcraft in the Aran Islands', *JRSAI* 25 (1925).

78 B.N. Hedderman, *Glimpses of My Life in Aran* (Bristol 1917).

80 Pat Mullen, *Hero Breed* (London 1936).

MEMENTOS OF MORTALITY

83 For detailed transcriptions of these monuments, see Tim Robinson, *Mementos of Mortality* (Roundstone 1991).

84 (shrines) Information from Jim Higgins, Galway.

86 Oliver J. Burke, *The South Isles of Aran (County Galway)* (London 1887).

87 J.M. Synge's 1898 notebook (ms. 4385, Manuscripts Room, Trinity College Dublin).

SOMETIME PLACES

92 R. Ll. Praeger, 'The Flora of the Turloughs: a preliminary note,' *Proc. R. Ir. Acad.*, 41B (1932).

94 *Peadar Chois Fhairrge: Scéalta Nua agus Seanscéalta d'innis Peadar Mac Thuathaláinn do Sheán Mac Giollarnáth* (Dublin 1934).

GOLD AND WATER

95 'Uisce Glan an Charna', Antoine Ó Briain, 1961, in *Nuacht Litir* (a cyclostyled local newsletter), Cill Rónáin, 19 May 1979.

97 (identification of church) Fr Mártan Ó Domhnaill, *Oileáin Árann* (Dublin 1930); also Ó Cillín, *op. cit.*

97 (cross) O'Donovan, Ordnance Survey Letters.

97 (local information on An Carna) Máirtín Ó Conghaile, Cill Rónáin.

100 (building of road) Seaton F. Milligan, *Excursion of the Royal Society of Antiquaries of Ireland*, reprinted from *Belfast News Letter* (July 9, 10, 11, 12, 1895).

DEVELOPMENT

105 Sir Henry Robinson, *Memories: Wise and Otherwise* (London 1924).

107 Sir Henry Robinson, *Further Memories of Irish Life* (London 1924).

107 W.L. Micks, *History of the Congested Districts Board* (Dublin1925).

107 Patrick Kane, 'Aran of the Fishermen', *The New Ireland Review* (April 1898).

108 (Land League) Powell, *op. cit.*

108 H. Robinson, *Further Memories of Irish Life.*

110 Powell, *op. cit.* The lines from the song were also given me by Antoine Powell.

113 J.M. Synge, 'In Connemara', originally published in the *Manchester Guardian,* (1905); also in *Collected Works II*, ed. Alan Price (Gerrard's Cross 1982).

STATISTIC AND SENTIMENTAL TOURISTS

115 Stokes, *Life ... of George Petrie* (1868).

118 Patricia Boyne, *John O'Donovan (1806-1861)* (Kilkenny 1987).

118 O'Donovan, *op. cit.*

119 W.F.Wakeman, 'Aran - Pagan and Christian', *Duffy's Hibernian Magazine*, I (1862).

120 I am grateful to Dr Máirín Ní Dhonnchadha of the Dublin Institute for Advanced Studies for translating these verses, from O'Donovan's *Ordnance Survey Letters: Galway.* For Colm Cille's poem, see *Pilgrimage*, p. 235.

121 For Roderic O'Flaherty see 'The Ferocious O'Flahertys' in this volume.

122 Put together from pp. 496 and 90 of 'Clonmacnoise, Clare, and Arran,' Parts 1 and 2, S.F. (Samuel Ferguson), *Dublin University Magazine*, XLI (1853). For the banquet in Dún Aonghasa see also *Pilgrimage*, p. 73.

123 Stokes, *op. cit.*

123 (Melville) *Galway Vindicator*, 28 May 1864. (I am grateful to Tim Collins, Centre for Landscape Studies, University College Galway, for this material.)

124 E. Percival Wright, 'Notes on the Flora of the Islands of Arran, West of Ireland', *Proc. Nat. Hist. Soc. Dublin*, Vol. V (1866). For references to other botanists' visits, see D.A. Webb, 'The Flora of the Aran Islands', *J. Life Sci. R. Dubl. Soc.*, 2 (1980).

124 John Beddoe, *The Races of Britain, A Contribution to the Anthropology of Western Europe* (1885).

124 Earle Hackett and M.E. Folan, 'The ABO and RH Blood Groups of the Aran Islanders', *Irish Journal of Medical Science* (June 1958).

125 (the cartoon) John C. Messenger, *Inis Beag, Isle of Ireland* (New York 1969).

125 James G. Barry, 'Aran of the Saints', *JRSAI* (1885-6).

125 Seaton F. Milligan, *Excursion of the Royal Society of Antiquaries of Ireland*, reprinted from *Belfast News Letter* (July 9, 10, 11, 12, 1895).

126 Thomas J. Westropp, 'The North Isle of Aran', *JRSAI*, 25 (1895); reprinted in *The Aran Islands and Galway City* (Dublin 1971).

126 Timothy Collins, *Floreat Hibernia: A bio-bibliography of Robert Lloyd Praeger 1865-1953* (Dublin 1985).

126 R. Lloyd Praeger, 'Irish Field Club Union: Report of the Conference and Excursion Held at Galway, July 11th to 17th, 1895', *The Irish Naturalist*, Vol. IV No. 9 (September 1895).

127 (steamer services) Powell, *op. cit.* See also Timothy Collins, 'The Galway Line in Context,' Part 2, *JGAHS* , Vol. 47 (1995).

127 Mary Banim, *Here and There Through Ireland*, reissued from *Weekly Freeman* (1896); reprinted in *An Aran Reader*, eds Breandán and Ruairí Ó hEithir (Dublin 1991).

128 Úna Ní Fhaircheallaigh, *Smuainte ar Árainn* (Dublin 1902). Brief biographies of these Gaeilgeoirí are given in *1882-1982 Beathaisnéis I-IV*, Diarmuid Breathnach and Máire Ní Mhurchú (Dublin 1986-95).

129 Seán Ó Ceallaigh, *Eoghan Ó Gramhnaigh* (Dublin 1968).

130 Patrick Pearse, 'A Visit to Inis Mór and Inis Meáin, August 1898', *Fáinne an Lae* (1898); translation by Breandán and Ruairí Ó hEithir in *An Aran Reader.*

130 (Pearse's speech) *Fáinne an Lae* (20 August 1898).

130 Letter to John O'Leary, from Paris, 1896, in *The Letters of W.B. Yeats*, ed. Allan Wade (London 1954).

130 Arthur Symons, *Cities and Sea-Coasts and Islands* (London 1897). Reprinted in *An Aran Reader.*

132 Lady Gregory, *Our Irish Theatre* (New York 1913); quoted in David H. Greene and Edward M. Stephens, *J.M. Synge 1871-1909* (revised edition, New York and London 1989).

132 (Synge on the cliffs) See my introduction to J.M. Synge, *The Aran Islands* (London 1992).

133 Synge's 1898 notebook.

134 A.C. Haddon and C.R. Browne, 'The Ethnography of the Aran Islands, County Galway', *Proc. RIA*, 18 (1893).

135 James Joyce, 'Il Miraggio del Pescatore di Aran. La Valvola dell'Inghilterra in Caso di Guerra,' *Il Piccolo della Sera* (Trieste 5 September 1912). Translated in *The Critical Writings of James Joyce* (London 1959): also in *An Aran Reader.*

136 ('Tiger, Tiger') Quoted from a *Dublin Opinion* of 1934 in Breandán Ó hEithir, 'Tiger King and *Man of Aran*', *Willie the Plain Pint – agus an Papa* (Dublin 1977). For the making of *Man of Aran* see also *Pilgrimage*, p. 161.

136 (Artaud in Aran) Information collected by Fr Connla Ó Dúláine, in *Nuacht Litir* (Cill Rónáin, 10 May 1880).

137 I have translated this and the following texts from *Oeuvres Complètes*, Antonin Artaud (Gallimard 1967), Vol. VII. See also: Stephen Barber, *Antonin Artaud; Blows and Bombs* (London 1993).

AN EAR TO THE COFFIN

142 Powell, *Oileáin Árann*, gives references to to Parliamentary Papers 1826-7, Vol. XII, Irish Education Enquiry, 2nd report, and 1835, Vol. XXXIII, First Report of Commissioners of Public Instruction.

142 Rev. Henry M'Manus, *Sketches of the Irish Highlands: Descriptive, Social and Religious. With special reference to Irish Missions in West Connaught since 1840* (London 1863).

143 Reports of the Island and Coast Society 1846, in *An Aran Reader.*

144 For Rev. Synge's letters see: Paul F. Botheroyd, 'The Rev. Alexander Hamilton Synge in the Aran Islands', *Cahiers Irlandais* (Rennes 1983); also *An Aran Reader.*

146 Rev. Dallas, quoted in D. Bowen, *The Protestant Crusade in Ireland, 1800-70* (Dublin 1978).

147 (jumpers rhyme) Information from Mícheál Báiréad, Roundstone.

147 (Dr Stoney) Information from Professor George Stoney, New York University.

148 These controversies are voluminously reported in many issues of the *Galway Vindicator* for the period.

150   'The Song of the Arranman', *Galway Vindicator* (30 December 1868); quoted in Powell, *op. cit.*; see also 'The Big House' in this volume.

151   (Ganly) See Powell, *op. cit.*

152   *The Irish Crisis of 1879-80; Proceedings of the Mansion House Committee* (Dublin 1881). This also includes Curran's report of his investigation.

156   (Ganly) Information from the late Mary Walshe, Cill Rónáin, and Alice Powell, Eochaill; see also Powell, *op. cit.* for the Land War events.

157   'Amhrán Shéamais Uí Chonchúir', from a version obtained in Aran by the late Éamonn Ó Tuathail, Dublin; a closely similar one was published in the local *Nuacht Litir* in May and June 1979; my translation

158   Rev. William Kilbride, *The Book of Psalms; a Metrical Version in the Irish language, of seventy of the psalms most commonly used in churches, to which are added some Hymns and Sacred Songs* (Dublin 1863).

BACKWATERS

159   Ó Cillín, *op. cit.*

160   J.M. Synge, *The Aran Islands* (London 1907; new edition 1992). (The name 'Digby' is replaced by a dash in Synge's text.)

160   Hardiman's notes to *West Connaught.*

161   (Digbys' removal to Aran) Ó Cillín, *op. cit.*

161   (Digby House) Admiralty chart (1844-8)

162   (1831 distress) *First Report of the Fishery Commissioners* (London 1836).

164   *Annals of the Four Masters,* quoted in Hardiman's notes to R. O'Flaherty, *op. cit.*

166   'Na Dubhchrónaigh', in *Nuacht Litir* (Cill Rónáin 6 and 14 April 1979); also reminiscences from Caomhán Ó Goill, Máire Bn. Uí Chonghaile, Mícheál King, Thomas Fleming and other islanders.

166   (Clifden episode) Information from John Barlow, Roundstone.

CLIMBING THE HILL

170   (An Suicín) Information from the late Professor T.S. Ó Máille, UCG.

171   (Bord na Gaeilge report) Liam Mac Con Iomaire, speaking on Raidió na Gaeltachta, 1 May 1991; also, *The Irish Times* (8 and 9 May 1991).

172   'An Teanga sa Ghaeltacht', in *Willie the Plain Pint - agus an Pápa,* B. Ó hEithir (Dublin 1977); my translation.

174   'Haraí Steatail' is also recorded from Carna in Connemara; see *Foirisiún Focal as Gaillimh,* Tomás de Bhaldraithe (Dublin 1985).

175   'Beart Sgéalta ó Árainn', in *Béaloideas,* Vol. 3 (1931-2) (three tales collected by Seosamh Ó Flannagáin, who was the schoolmaster in Eoghanacht).

177   Breandán Ó hEithir, 'Liam Ó Flatharta agus a Dhúchais', in *Willie the Plain Pint - agus an Pápa.* Also, information from Alice Powell, Eochaill.

177   Tom Ó Flaherty, *Aranmen All* (Dublin 1934).

MAINISTIR

185   B. Ó hEithir, 'Má Bhíonn Tu in Árainn Bí in Eochaill', *The Irish Times* (15 July 1977); my translation.

186   (1581 inquisition) Ó Cillín, *op. cit.* For these divisions see also F.J. Byrne, 'Eoghanacht Ninussa', *Eigse* (Earrach 1958).

187   (grants) Ó Cillín, *op.cit.*

188 T.J. Westropp, 'The Aran Islands', *JRSAI*, 25 (1895).
189 Charles Plummer, *Vitae Sanctorum Hiberniae*, Vol. II (Oxford 1910); translated for me by Ann Mohr.
189 O'Donovan, *op. cit.*
191 Plummer, trans. Ann Mohr.

AMONG THE THORNS

194 J. O'Donovan, *OS Letters*
196 Colgan, *Acta Sanctorum*, quoted in Hardiman's notes to R. O'Flaherty, *op. cit.*

LIGHTS IN THE DARKNESS

198 (Churchill) Information from Tim Collins.
199 W. Stokes, *Life ... of Petrie.*
199 ('Whoever *las* it...') Breandán Ó hEithir, 'Ciall Cheannaithe', *The Irish Times* (1977).
200 Paul Kerrigan, 'The Defence of Ireland 1793-1815,' *An Cosantóir* (February 1982).

LOCUS TERRIBILIS

205 B. Ó hEithir, 'Má Bhíonn Tu in Árainn Bí in Eochaill,' *The Irish Times* (15 July 1977).

IN SEARCH OF WASTED TIME

212 (1581 inquisition) Ó Cillín, *op. cit.*
212 G.H. Kinahan, 'Notes on some of the ancient villages in the Aran Islands, County Galway,' *Proc. RIA*, 10 (1867).
213 John Goulden's preliminary reports to the Royal Irish Academy, quoted in John Waddell, 'J.R.W. Goulden's excavations on Inishmore, Aran, 1953-1955', *JGAHS*, Vol. 41 (1987-8).
214 Waddell, 1987-8.

THE FOUR BEAUTIES

218 'Five Co. Galway Placenames', T.S Ó Máille, *JGAHS*, Vol. XXVIII.
218 J. Colgan, *Acta Sanctorum.*
219 An t-Ath. Mártan Ó Domhnaill, *Oileáin Árann* (Dublin 1930).
219 J.R.W. Goulden, 'Kilnamanagh: The Lost Church of Aran', *JGAHS*, Vol. XXVI (1955).
219 Ó Cillín, *op. cit.*
219 (Fursey) Richard Sharpe, *Medieval Irish Saints' Lives* (Oxford 1991).
220 (Brendan) Miles Dillon and Nora Chadwick, *The Celtic Realms* (London 1973). For Maol Dúin, see also 'Eoghanacht' in this volume.
220 I have slightly amended O'Donovan's translation, in his OS Letters (Galway 1839), of the 'Life of St Kevin' from the *Codex Kilkenniensis.*
221 J.M. Synge's 1898 notebook.
224 O'Donovan, *op. cit.*
224 A. O'Kelleher and G. Shoepperle (eds), *Betha Colaim Chille (Life of Columcille), compiled by Manus O'Donnell* (Chicago 1918). The phrase naming the abbot is unclear and varies between mss; O'Donovan makes him out to be called Santal. The name Talgaeth is given in James F. Kenney, *The Sources for the Early History of Ireland* (Dublin 1979), Section 219, 'Minor sources relating to Columba'.

THE BED OF DIARMAID AND GRÁINNE

226 I have based the opening of this version on a translation of the middle Irish original into modern Irish in *Seanchas na Féinne*, Niall Ó Domhnaill (Dublin 1943). The lullaby is a twelfth-century work; it is given in Gerard Murphy's *Early Irish Lyrics* (Oxford 1956) and I have used his prose translation as a crib. Gráinne calls Diarmaid *'cró gaile iarthair Gréc'* (battle-fence of western Greece), but given the hero's psychology my 'playboy of the western world' makes more sense today.

230 J.R.W. Goulden, 'Kilnamanagh: The Lost Church of Aran', *JGAHS*, Vol. XXVI (1955); includes a reproduction of the O.S. plan and elevation of Clochán an Phúca.

230 G.H. Kinahan, 'Notes on some of the ancient villages in the Aran Islands, County Galway', *Proc. RIA*, 10 (1867).

232 William O'Brien, 'Altar Tomb and the Prehistory of Mizen', *Mizen Journal*, No. 1 (1993).

233 (inhabited megalithic tombs) T.J. Westropp, 'Prehistoric Remains along the Borders of the Burren', *JRSAI*, Series 5, Vol. XV (1905).

233 (goose-pen) Information from Patrick Nolan, Gleninsheen, Ballyvaughan.

MODALITIES OF ROUGHNESS

239 Information from Conor MacDermot, Geological Survey, Dublin. For the terms Asbian and Brigantian, see 'A Correlation of Dinantian Rocks in the British Isles', T. N. George et al., *Geol. Soc. Lond.*, Special Report No. 7 (1976).

240 (solution of limestone) Frank Mitchell, *Shell Guide to Reading the Irish Landscape* (Dublin 1986).

240 Llubica Jelicic and Michael O'Connell, 'History of vegetation and land use from 3200 B.P. to the present day in the north-west Burren, a karstic region of western Ireland', *Vegetation History and Archaeobotany* (Springer-Verlag 1992).

243 David Langridge, 'Limestone Pavement Patterns on the Island of Inishmore, Co. Galway', *Irish Geography* Vol. 6 (3) (1971).

THE BLOOD OF THE HEART

245 (Tobar Ghrióir) Story from Mícheál King, Fearann an Choirce.

246 S.F. (Samuel Ferguson), 'Clonmacnoise, Clare, and Arran,' Parts 1 and 2, *Dublin University Magazine*, XLI (1853).

246 (British Association) *A Short Description of the Western Islands of Aran*, no author named (W.R. Wilde), quoted in Haddon and Browne (1892).

246 Congested Districts Board Report on the Aran Islands (1893), reprinted in *Island Life Series I, A World of Stone: The Aran Islands* (Curriculum Development Unit, Dublin 1977).

247 Canon John O'Hanlon, *Lives of the Irish Saints* (1875-97), quoted in Daphne Pochin Mould, *The Aran Islands* (Newton Abbot 1972).

247 Mary Banim, *op. cit.*, reprinted in *An Aran Reader*.

248 (grants, land reclamation) John C. Messenger, *Inis Beag* (New York 1969).

248 Peadar Ua Concheanáinn, *Innismeadhoin: Seanchas agus Sgéalta* (Dublin 1931).

249 Tomás Ó Direáin, 'An t-Árannach', in *Nuabhéarsaíocht 1939-1949*, ed. Seán Ó Tuama (Dublin 1950, republished 1974).

253 T.G.F. Curtis, H.N. McGough, E.D. Wymer, 'The Discovery ... of Arable Weeds ... in the Aran Islands,' *Ir. Nat. J.*, Vol. 22 No. 12 (1988).

255 W.Y. Evans Wentz, *The Fairy Faith in Celtic Countries* (Oxford 1911; reprinted Gerrard's Cross 1988).

SPUDS

257 (Cuckoo in Inis Oírr) Messenger, *Inis Beag*

259 E. Estyn Evans, *Irish Folk Ways* (London 1957).

BLACK HARVEST

266 Austin Bourke, 'Phytophthora and Famine', *Technology Ireland*, Vol. 22, No. 4 (July/August 1990).

267 Transcription of a tape recording, *Píosa seanchais bailithe ó Sheán Ó Giolláin*, Scoil Éigse Eoghanachta 1975-6; my translation.

A MOUTHFUL OF ECHOES

271 (*blackin'*) Information from Bertie Joyce, Cill Mhuirbhigh.

272 James Duran, 'The Irish Language in Aran', later published in *The Book of Aran*, ed. John Waddell, J.W. O'Connell and Anne Korff (Kinvara 1994).

273 (Bríd Gillan) Michael Finlan, 'Witness to a century of Irish history returns to her roots', *The Irish Times* (12 September 1994).

274 From the tape recording of Seán Ó Giolláin, Scoil Éigse Eoghanachta (1975-6); my translation.

275 Tom O'Flaherty, 'My First Suit', *Aranmen All* (Dublin 1934); slightly shortened and rearranged.

277 I am grateful to Professor John Waddell for showing me George Warren's journal, which is now in the possession of Patrick Gageby, Dublin.

281 Further details of O'Callaghan's life are given in *Beathaisnéis a Ceathair*.

281 A.C. Haddon and C.R. Browne, 'The Ethnography of the Aran Islands', *Proc. RIA* (1892).

281 *Siamsa an Gheimhridh*, Dómhnall O'Fotharta (Dublin 1892).

282 Tom O'Flaherty, *Aranmen All*.

282 (Gaelic League) *Fáinne an Lae* (20 August 1898).

283 The following account is based on Powell, *Oileáin Árann*, and Patrick F. Sheeran, *The Novels of Liam O'Flaherty* (Dublin 1976).

283 Liam O'Flaherty, *Skerrett* (London 1932, Dublin 1979).

284 I am obliged to Roddy McCaffrey of Robinson Keefe Devane, Dublin, for this description of the Residence.

WEST

ON THE BOUNDARY

303 An tAthair Mártan Ó Domhnaill, *Oileáin Árann* (Dublin 1930). His biography is given in *Beathaisnéis a Trí*.

304 I owe the idea that Creig an Córach may represent the boundary between the territories of Dún Dúchathair and Dún Aonghasa to Claire Cotter of the Discovery Programme (for which see 'Dún Aonghasa Revisited').

THE VILLAGE OF CONTENTED WOMEN

308 Máirtín Ó Direáin, 'Cuireadh do Mhuire', *Dánta Aniar*, Dublin 1943; my translation.

314 (jerseys) J.M. Synge, *The Aran Islands*.

315   This history of the Aran knitting is based on M.M.E. Robinson, 'The Four Dropped Stitches', unpublished essay (1982), and Deirdre McQuillan, *The Aran Sweater*, (Belfast 1993).

315   P.A. Ó Síocháin, *Aran, Islands of Legend* (Dublin 1962).

STORM-DRIVEN MALE

317   Tom O'Flaherty, *op. cit.*

317   Liam O'Flaherty, *Shame the Devil* (London 1934; Dublin 1981).

318   Tom O'Flaherty, *op. cit.*

319   Éamon Ó Ciosán, *An t-Éireannach, 1934-1937, Páipéar Sóisialach Gaeltachta* (Dublin 1993).

319   (Liam's first story) Quoted in Benedict Kiely, 'Liam O'Flaherty at Eighty', *The Irish Times* (27 August 1976); see also Liam O'Flaherty, *Shame the Devil.*

320   (shell) *Shame the Devil*

320   Liam O'Flaherty, *Two Years* (London 1930).

322   (Rotunda occupation) Breandán Ó hEithir, 'Biseach na hAoine', *The Irish Times* (18 November 1983).

322   Liam O'Flaherty, *Thy Neighbour's Wife* (London 1923; Dublin 1972).

323   Liam O'Flaherty, *The Black Soul* (London 1924; Dublin 1981).

323   Liam O'Flaherty, *Spring Sowing* (London 1924; Dublin 1976).

325   Liam O'Flaherty, *The Informer* (London 1924); *A Tourist's Guide to Ireland* (London 1929); *Famine* (London 1937; Dublin 1977), *The Ecstasy of Angus* (London 1931), *Skerrett* (London 1932; Dublin 1979).

327   Liam O'Flaherty, *Dúil* (Dublin 1953).

327   *The Irish Times* (17 June 1980), and personal information from O'Flaherty's niece, Mrs Alice Powell, Eochaill.

327   ('storm-swept rock') quoted in B. Kiely, *The Irish Times* (27 August 1976).

THE SHINING WAYS

328   (identification of Ferris) Breandán Ó hEithir, '*Skerrett*: Liam O'Flaherty' in *Islands and Authors*, ed. Proinsias Ó Conluain (Dublin 1983).

MOONGRAZING

332   Tom O'Flaherty, *Cliffmen of the West* (London 1935).

332   J. Vendryes, *Lexique Étymologique de l'Irlandais ancien* (Lettre B) (Dublin Institute for Advanced Studies, 1981).

333   Liam O'Flaherty, *Spring Sowing.*

335   (*Nostoc*) Information from Maura Scannell, National Botanic Gardens, Glasnevin.

THE CLOCK

340   Preston Cloud, *Oasis in Space: Earth History from the Beginning* (New York 1988).

GOING TO CILL MHUIRBHIGH

347   J.T. O'Flaherty, 'A Sketch of the History and Antiquities of the Southern Islands of Aran...', *RIA Trans.* Vol. XIV, Antiquities (1821-5).

348   Information from Michael Gibson, Burnham-on-Crouch, Essex.

348   Máirtín Ó Direáin, *Ó Mórna agus Dánta Eile* (Dublin 1957); my translation.

ANCIENT HISTORIES

352 (school) Griffiths' Valuation (1855), and Powell, *op. cit.*

352 Colm P. Ó hIarnáin, 'Hernon–Ó hIarnáin', unpublished typescript in my possession.

358 W.F. Wakeman, 'Aran – Pagan and Christian', *Duffy's Hibernian Magazine* Vol. I (1862).

358 (radio-carbon dating) R. Berger, *op. cit.*.

358 Seathrún Céitinn, *Foras Feasa ar Éirinn* (Geoffrey Keating, *The History of Ireland*), written *c.* 1633-6, translated and edited by D. Comyn and P.S. Dinneen, four vols (London 1902-14; reprinted1987).

360 George Petrie, *The Ecclesiastical Architecture of Ireland* (London 1845).

360 (Mil) T.J. Westropp, 'A Study of the Early Forts and Stone Huts in Inishmore, Aran Islands, Galway Bay', *Proc. RIA*, Vol. 28C (1910).

360 T.J. Westropp, 'Aran Islands', *JRSAI* 25 (1895), reprinted in P.J. Hartnett and B. Ó Ríordáin, *The Aran Islands and Galway City*, (Dublin 1969).

361 (Johnston crest) Information from Jim Higgins, Galway.

THE FEROCIOUS O'FLAHERTYS

361 (arms) Hardiman's appendices to R. O'Flaherty, *West or H-Iar Connaught*. This is also the source of most of the early O'Flaherty history in the following pages.

362 (Niall) Dr Dáithí Ó hÓgáin, *Myth, Legend and Romance, An Encyclopedia of the Irish Folk Tradition* (London 1990).

362 (Brión) Gearóid Mac Niocaill, *Ireland Before the Vikings* (Dublin 1972).

364 Shane Mór O'Dugán, quoted in Hardiman's appendices to R. O'Flaherty, *op. cit.*

364 (Turlough O'Connor) Michael Dolly, *Anglo-Norman Ireland* (Dublin 1972).

366 (Renvyle) *Hidden Connemara*, ed. Erin Gibbons (Connemara West Press 1991).

366 (Doon) Local folklore from Kill, Clifden.

367 (Aird and Aughnanure) Seán Mac Giollarnáth, *Annála Beaga ó Iorrus Aithneach* (Dublin 1941); my translations.

369 (Log na Marbh) See 'Backwaters' in this volume.

369 (Composition of Connaught) Hardiman's appendices to R. O'Flaherty, *op. cit.*

370 Anne Chambers, *Granuaile: The Life and Times of Grace O'Malley* (Dublin 1983).

371 (Roderic O'Flaherty) Hardiman's appendices, and Mícheál Bairéad, *Fadó Fadó*, in press.

371 Letters of John Dunton, in the Bodleian Library, Oxford, written 1698, published in Edward MacLysaght, *Irish Life in the Seventeenth Century* (2nd edition Cork, 1950).

373 Anon. (members of the Blake family), *Letters from the Irish Highlands* (London 1825; republished Clifden 1995).

374 (Sir John O'Flaherty) John Burke, *Landed Gentry of Great Britain and Ireland* (London 1848 and later editions).

374 (Antony O'Flaherty, MP) *Hand-book to Galway, Connemara, and the Irish Highlands* (London and Dublin 1854).

374 E.W. Lynam, 'The O'Flaherty Country', *Studies* (June 1914).

THE BIG HOUSE

376 George Petrie, 'The Islands of Aran' (1822), quoted in Willam Stokes, *The Life and Labours in Art and Archaeology of George Petrie, LL.D., M.R.I.A* (1868). (I have rearranged and trimmed Petrie's verbose text in this and the following excerpts.)

377 Ó Cillín, *op. cit.*

377 George Petrie (1822)

378 (Patrick O'Flaherty's father) Personal communication from Pádraic Ó hEithir.

382 (Thompsons) Letter in *Galway Vindicator* (1880)

382 Letter from Philip Lyster, quoted in Oliver Burke, *The South Islands of Aran* (Dublin 1887).

382 J.M. Synge, *The Aran Islands*.

383 For a mention of Wilde's 1848 visit see 'Seven Churches and a Factory' in this volume.

383 (Patrick's marriage) Information from Pádraic Ó hEithir, through Liam Mac Con Iomaire.

383 (song) See 'An Ear to the Coffin' in this volume, and Powell, *Oileáin Árann*.

384 (the *Breeze*) Kilmurvey House documents.

384 (An Pocaide Bán) Information from Treasa Joyce, Cill Mhuirbhigh.

385 Máirtín Ó Direáin, *Ó Mórna agus Dánta Eile* (Dublin 1957), also in *Dánta 1939-1979* (Dublin 1980); my translation.

387 T.J. Westropp, 'Notes on Connaught and Clare, especially Aran and Sligo' (1888), Trinity College Library ms 973, printed in *An Aran Reader*.

387 M. MacMahon, 'Macnamaras', *Dal gCais*, No. 11 (1993).

388 (Francis Macnamara) Nicolette Devas, *Two Flamboyant Fathers* (London 1966), and information from Michael MacMahon.

388 E. O. Somerville and Martin Ross, *Some Irish Yesterdays* (London 1906).

388 (George Irwin O'Flaherty, and Fianna Fáil in Aran) Liam Mac Con Iomaire, *Agallamh le Pádraic Ó hEithir*, unpublished interview (Ennis 1993).

389 Máirtín Ó Direáin, *Feamainn Bhealtaine* (Dublin 1961).

389 C.C. Vyvyan, *On Timeless Shores* (London 1957).

391 Máirtín Ó Direáin, 'Neamhionraic Gach Beo', in *Ceacht an Éin* (Dublin 1979). See also 'A Poet and His Village' in this volume.

DÚN AONGHASA REVISITED

393 (Balor) Dáithí Ó hÓgáin, *op. cit.*

393 W.Y. Evans Wentz, *The Fairy Faith in Celtic Countries* (Oxford 1911; Gerrard's Cross 1988).

394 Etienne Rynne, 'Dun Aengus and some similar ceremonial centres', *Decantations: a tribute to Maurice Craig*, ed. Agnes Bernelle (Dublin 1992).

395 *The Irish Times* (21 April 1992).

396 See *Pilgrimage* for discussion of this idea from Thomas O'Rahilly, *Early Irish History and Mythology* (Dublin 1946).

397 *The Discovery Programme: Strategies and Questions*, Dublin 1992. I am grateful to Claire Cotter of the Discovery Programme for much information and guidance on this topic.

UNFATHOMABLE PUDDLE

403 O'Donovan, OS Letters.

CLOCHÁN

406 H.G. Leask, 'Finding of Whales' Vertebrae in Clochan-na-Carraige, Inishmore, Aran, Co. Galway', *JRSAI*, Vol. 73 (1943).

407 Máirtín Ó Direáin, *Ó Mórna agus Dánta Eile* (Dublin 1957); my translation.

A POET AND HIS VILLAGE

409   Máirtín Ó Direáin, 'Árainn 1947' in *Dánta 1939-1979*; my translation, here and in the following poems.
410   D. Webb, 'The Flora of the Aran Islands', *J. Life Sciences* 2 (1965).
412   Máirtín Ó Direáin, 'Dán an Tí', *Ár Ré Dhearóil* (Dublin 1962), also in *Dánta 1939-1979*.
413   (drowning) Information from Éamonn Ó Tuathail.
413   Máirtín Ó Direáin, 'In Aois na hÓige,' *Feamainn Bhealtaine* (Dublin 1961); my translation.
414   'Mothú Feirge' in *Dánta 1939-1979*.
414   'Stoite' (uprooted) in *Dánta*.
414   Tomás Mac Síomóin, 'Bile a Thit' in *Anios* (27 March 1988); my translation. See also the introduction to *Máirtín Ó Direáin, Selected Poems/Tacar Dánta*, ed. Tomás Mac Síomóin and Douglas Sealy (Newbridge 1984).
415   Máirtín Ó Direáin, *Feamainn Bhealtaine*.
416   'Berkeley' in *Cloch Chornéil* (Dublin 1966), and in *Dánta*.
416   ('Neamhionraic Gach Beo') See also 'The Big House' in this volume.

EOGHANACHT

417   O'Donovan, OS Letters.
418   John Waddell, 'Kilcholan: an early ecclesiastical site on Inishmore, Aran', *JGAHS*, 35 (1976).
420   T.J. Westropp, 'A Study of the Early Forts and Stone Huts in Inishmore, Aran Isles, Galway Bay', *Proc. RIA*, Vol. 28C (1910).
420   (Eoghanacht myths) T.F. O'Rahilly, *Early Irish History and Mythology* (Dublin 1946; reprint 1984).
420   (Eoghan) D. Ó hÓgáin, *op. cit.*
421   Myles Dillon and Nora Chadwick, *The Celtic Realms* (London 1973).
421   F. J. Byrne, 'Eoghanacht Ninussa', *Eigse* (Spring 1958).
422   (Maol Dúin) Discussed and summarized in Alwyn and Brinley Rees, *Celtic Heritage* (London 1961). Text and translation by W. Stokes in *Revue Celtique* IX and X.

SEVEN CHURCHES AND A FACTORY

424   Information from Éamonn Ó Concheanáinn, Eoghanacht.
426   John Waddell, 'An Archaeological Survey of Temple Brecan, Aran', *JGAHS*, 33 (1972-3).
428   Thomas H. Mason, *The Islands of Ireland* (London 1936).
428   (high crosses) See 'The Invisible Tower' in this volume.
428   John Waddell, 'An Unpublished High Cross on Aran, County Galway,' *JRSAI*, Vol. III (1981). Also, Sir S. Ferguson, 'Clonmacnois, Clare and Arran,' Part II, *Dublin Univ. Mag.* (April 1853).
429   (burial in 'St. Brecan's grave') O'Donovan, OS Letters.
429   (VII ROMANI) George Petrie, *The Ecclesiastical Architecture of Ireland* (2nd edition Dublin 1845).
429   R.A.S. Macalister, 'The stone of the "Seven Romans" on Aran Mor', *JRSAI*, 43 (1913).
429   Peter Harbison, *Pilgrimage in Ireland* (London 1991).
431   The poem is published and discussed in: Anne O'Sullivan, 'Saint Brecán of Clare', *Celtica* 15 (1983). I have slightly rearranged her prose translation to make it look like verse.

431   (Division of the island) See 'On the Boundary' in this volume.

433   (factory) *Connacht Tribune* (11 July 1975).

LOOKING OUT OF ARAN

437   Ruairí Ó hEithir, *op.cit.*; my translation.

439   For the word *scrios* see *Pilgrimage*, p. 127.

430   (Pilot joke) Messenger, *op. cit.*

440   (Ó Tuathail) Information from Éamonn Ó Tuathail and Mícheál King.

441   Máirtín Ó Direáin, 'Cuimhní Cinn', *Dánta Aniar* (Dublin 1943); also in *Dánta 1939-1979*.

THE LESSER ARAN

451   R. O'Flaherty, *West or H-Iar Connaught*.

451   T. Mason, *The Islands of Ireland*, and T.H. Westropp, 'Brasil and the legendary islands of the north Atlantic: their history and fable. A contribution to the "Atlantis" problem', *Proc. RAI*, Vol. 30C (1912).

451   O'Donovan, OS Letters: Co. Galway.

452   R. O'Flaherty, *West or H-Iar Connaught*, Hardiman's footnote.

452   'Doctor Lee and Little Aran', in *Folktales of Ireland*, edited and translated by Sean O'Sullivan (London 1966).

453   (Tadhg Ó Neachtáin) *Ar Aghaidh* (1933); no author or source given.

453   Lady Gregory, *Visions and Beliefs in the West of Ireland* (1920).

ACKNOWLEDGMENTS

Leafing through my finished manuscript, I am reminded of many debts of gratitude, in roughly the following order:

Liam Mac Con Iomaire (UCD), Caomháin Ó Goill (Árainn), the late Tony Whilde (Corrib Conservation Centre), Pádraicín Ó Flaithearta (Árainn), Dara Ó Conaola (Inis Meáin), Conleth Manning (OPW), Ann Mohr (UCG), Dr Arndt Wigger (Wuppertal), Ruairí Ó hEithir (Dublin), Jim Higgins (Galway), Dara Mullen (Árainn), Antoine Powell (Árainn), Dr Máirín Ní Dhonnchadha (Institute of Advanced Studies, Dublin), Timothy Collins (UCG), Maura Scannell (formerly of the Botanic Gardens, Glasnevin), An tAth. Connla Ó Dúláine (Árainn), Professor George Stoney (NYU), Patrick Gageby (Dublin), Mícheál Bairéad (Roundstone), the late Éamonn Ó Tuathail (Dublin), Mícheál King (Árainn), Paul Kerrigan (Dublin), An tAth. Tadhg Ó Móráin (Louisburgh), Professor John Waddell (UCG), Seán Powell (Árainn), William O'Brien (UCG), Professor Etienne Rynne (UCG), Conor MacDermot (Geological Survey, Dublin), Professor Paul Mohr (UCG), Dr Michael O'Connell (UCG), Paul Gosling (UCG), Professor Jim White (UCD), the late Seán Gillan (Árainn), Stiofan Ó Direáin (Árainn), Professor James Duran (UCLA), Diarmuid Breathnach (Bray), Roddy McCaffrey (Dublin), Bridget Fitzpatrick (Árainn), Alice Powell (Árainn), Pádraic Ó Flaithbheartaigh (Balla), Professor Tomás de Bhaldraithe (RIA), Pádraic Ó hEithir (Ennis), Máire Bn. Uí Conghaile (Árainn), Bridget Hernon-Johnston (Árainn), Treasa Joyce (Árainn), the late Colm P. Ó hIarnáin (Árainn), Shevaun Lynam (Ashford, Wicklow), Michael MacMahon (Corofin), Ricca Edmondson (UCG), Michael Gibbons (Clifden), Claire Cotter (Discovery Programme, Dublin).

I would particularly like to thank Ann Mohr for translating the Latin Life of St Enda for me, and Liam Mac Con Iomaire for his help with translations from the Irish; mistakes in these are certainly not his.

I am grateful to the following for permission to quote copyrighted material: Dara Ó Conaola, Ruairí Ó hEithir and the Folklore Department of University College Dublin, An Clóchomhar Tta, The Lilliput Press, Wolfhound Press, the J.M.Synge Trust and the Board of Trinity College Dublin.

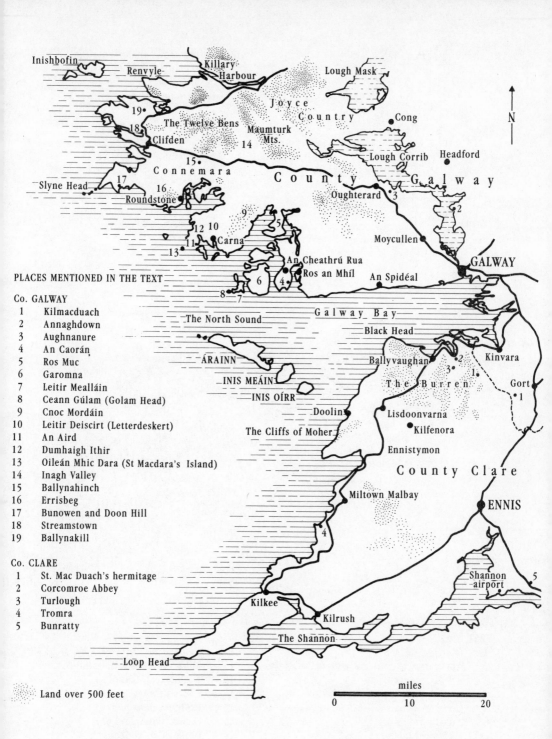

THE ARAN ISLANDS, GALWAY AND CLARE

ÁRAINN

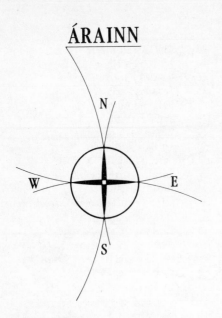

shading shows the orientation
of the principal set of fissures

high ground

low ground

sand, shingle

rocks exposed
at low water

T.= Teampall (church)

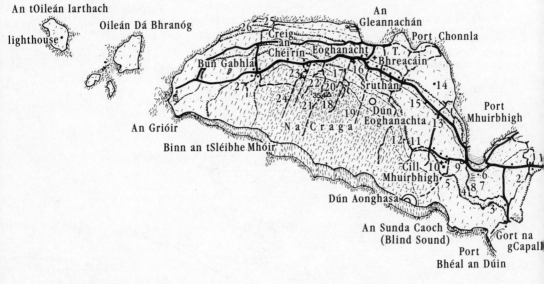

An tOileán Iarthach

Oileán Dá Bhranóg

lighthouse

An
Gleannachán

Port Chonnla

Creig
an
Chéirín

Eoghanacht

T.
Bhreacáin

Bun Gabhla

23

17

16

14

27

22

20

Sruthán

24

35

18

15

Port
Mhuirbhigh

21

19

Dún
Eoghanachta

13

An Gríóir

Na Craga

12

11

Binn an tSléibhe Mhóir

Cill
Mhuirbhigh

10

9

1

6

2

5

4

8

7

Dún Aonghasa

3

An Sunda Caoch
(Blind Sound)

Gort na
gCapal

Port
Bhéal an Dúin

EAST

1 An Teannaire
2 Poll an Ghamhna
3 Róidín Mháirtín
4 Na Muirbhigh Móra
5 Carn Buí
6 Fitzpatrick memorials
7 Killeany Lodge
8 stump of round tower
9 Róidín Docherty
10 Gleann Rúairí Óg
11 An Charcair Mhór
12 Bóthar an Screigín
13 Creig na bhFaoileán
14 Bóthar an Phump
15 An Turlach Mór
16 Poll Talún (site)
17 old reservoir
18 Cill Charna
19 Fán an Uisce
20 Creig an Chosáin
21 Carcair na gCat
22 An Coinleach
23 Clochán an Airgid
24 An Chreig Mhór
25 Catholic parish church
26 Technical school
27 Baile an Dúin
28 Log na Marbh
29 McDonough memorial
30 An Chreig Dhubh
31 Carcair Ghanly
32 Carcair Chlaí Chox
33 Tobar na nAdharc
34 ruined lighthouse and signal tower
35 Eochaill chapel
36 Bóithrín na bPóil
37 Teampall an Cheathrair Álainn
38 wedge tomb
39 An Dún Beag
40 An Choill
41 An Poll i' bhFolach
42 An Scairbh
43 An Chreig Mhór
44 The Residence

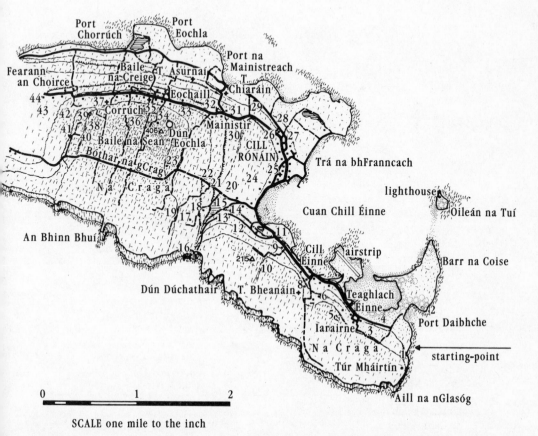

SCALE one mile to the inch

© Based on *Oileáin Árann, a map of the Aran Islands*, Tim Robinson, 1995

INDEX

All plant species are listed together under 'plants'; similarly for butterflies and birds. All names in Ó or O' are listed at the beginning of the 'O's.